Lecture Notes in Computer Science 4069

Commenced Publication in 1973
Founding and Former Series Editors:
Gerhard Goos, Juris Hartmanis, and Jan van Leeuwen

Francisco J. Perales
Robert B. Fisher (Eds.)

Articulated Motion and Deformable Objects

4th International Conference, AMDO 2006
Port d'Andratx, Mallorca, Spain, July 11-14, 2006
Proceedings

 Springer

Volume Editors

Francisco José Perales
Universitat de les Illes Balears
Department of Mathematics and Computer Science
C/Valldemossa km 7.5, PC 07122, Palma de Mallorca, Spain
E-mail: paco.perales@uib.es

Robert B. Fisher
University of Edinburgh
School of Informatics
James Clerk Maxwell Building, The King's Buildings, Mayfield Road, Edinburgh
EH9 3JZ, UK
E-mail: rbf@inf.ed.ac.uk

Library of Congress Control Number: 2006928839

CR Subject Classification (1998): I.4, I.5, I.2.10, I.3, I.2.10, I.6

LNCS Sublibrary: SL 6 – Image Processing, Computer Vision, Pattern Recognition,
and Graphics

ISSN   0302-9743
ISBN-10   3-540-36031-X Springer Berlin Heidelberg New York
ISBN-13   978-3-540-36031-5 Springer Berlin Heidelberg New York

Springer is a part of Springer Science+Business Media

springer.com

© Springer-Verlag Berlin Heidelberg 2006
Printed in Germany

Typesetting: Camera-ready by author, data conversion by Scientific Publishing Services, Chennai, India
Printed on acid-free paper   SPIN: 11789239   06/3142   5 4 3 2 1 0

Preface

The AMDO-e 2006 conference took place at the Hotel Mon Port, Port d'Andratx (Mallorca), on July 11-14, 2006, sponsored by the International Association for Pattern Recognition (IAPR), the MEC (Ministerio de Educación y Ciencia, Spanish Government), the Conselleria d'Economia, Hisenda i Innovació (Balearic Islands Government), the AERFAI (Spanish Association in Pattern Recognition and Artificial Intelligence), the EG (Eurographics Association) and the Mathematics and Computer Science Department of the UIB. Important commercial sponsors also collaborated with practical demonstrations; the main contributions were from: VICOM Tech, ANDROME Iberica, GroupVision, Ndigital (NDI), CESA and TAGrv.

The subject of the conference was ongoing research in articulated motion on a sequence of images and sophisticated models for deformable objects. The goals of these areas are to understand and interpret the motion of complex objects that can be found in sequences of images in the real world. The main topics considered as priority were: geometric and physical deformable models, motion analysis, articulated models and animation, modelling and visualization of deformable models, deformable models applications, motion analysis applications, single or multiple human motion analysis and synthesis, face modelling, tracking, recovering and recognition models, virtual and augmented reality, haptics devices, biometrics techniques. These topics were grouped into four tracks: **Track 1:** Computer Graphics (Human Modelling and Animation), **Track 2:** Human Motion (Analysis, Tracking, 3D Reconstruction and Recognition), **Track 3:** Multimodal User Interaction (VR and AR, Speech, Biometrics) and **Track 4:** Advanced Multimedia Systems (Standards, Indexed Video Contents).

This conference was the natural evolution of the AMDO2004 workshop (Springer LNCS 3179). The goal of this conference was to promote interaction and collaboration among researchers working in the areas covered by the four tracks. New perceptual user interfaces and linked emerging technologies strengthen the relation between the conference themes and human–computer interaction. The perspective of the AMDO-e 2006 conference was to strengthen the relationship between the many areas that have as key point the study of the human body using computer technologies as the main tool. The response to the call of papers for this conference was very good. From 81 full papers submitted, 53 were accepted. The review process was carried out by the Program Committee, each paper being assessed by at least two reviewers. The conference included several parallel sessions of orally presented papers, poster sessions and three tutorials. Moreover, the conference benefited from the collaboration of the invited speakers covering various aspects of the main topics. These invited speakers were: Thomas Vetter from Basel University (Switzerland), José Santos-Victor from IST (Portugal), and Petia Radeva from Computer Vision Center (UAB, Spain).

July 2006

F. J. Perales and B. Fisher
General Co-chairs
AMDO-e 2006

Organization

AMDO-e 2006 was organized by the Computer Graphics and Vision team of the Department of Mathematics and Computer Science, Universitat de les Illes Balears (UIB) in cooperation with IAPR (International Association for Pattern Recognition), AERFAI (Spanish Association for Pattern Recognition and Image Analysis) and EG (Eurographics Association).

Executive Committee

General Conference Co-chairs:	F. J. Perales, Mathematics and Computer Science Department, UIB (Spain)
	B. Fisher, University of Edinburgh (UK)
Organizing Chairs:	M. J. Abásolo, J. M. Buades, A. Delgado, G. Fiol, M. González, A. Igelmo, A. Jaume-Capó, C. Manresa-Yee, R. Mas, M. Mascaró P., M. Miró, P. Palmer, J. Varona
	Mathematics and Computer Science Department (UIB, Spain)
Tutorial Chairs:	M. González, J. Varona, F.J. Perales
	UIB (Spain)

Program Committee

Abásolo, M. J.	Universitat Illes Balears, Spain
Aloimonos, Y.	University of Maryland, USA
Aggarwal, J. K.	University of Texas, USA
Ayache, N.	INRIA, Sophia-Antipolis, France
Badler, N. I.	University of Pennsylvania, USA
Bibiloni, A.	Universitat Illes Balears, Spain
Blake, A.	Microsoft Rs, Cambridge
Boulic, R.	EPFL, Switzerland
Bowden, R.	University of Surrey, UK
Brunet, P.	UPC, Spain
Campilho, A.	University of Oporto, Portugal
Carlsson, S.	CVAP, Sweden
Cerezo, E.	Universidad de Zaragoza, Spain
Cipolla, R.	Univ. of Cambridge, UK
Cohen, I.	University of Southern California, USA
Costa-Orvalho, V.	UPC, Spain
Cristani, M.	University of Verona, Italy

Dalal, N.	INRIA, Alpes, France
Davis, L. S.	University of Maryland, USA
Del Bimbo, A.	Univ. di Firenze, Italy
Di Fiore, F.	Hasselt University, Belgium
Fengjun, Lv	University of Southern California, USA
Fernández-Caballero, A	Univ. Castilla-La Mancha, Spain
Fiol, G.	Universitat Illes Balears, Spain
Fleet, D.	University of Toronto, Canada
Flerackers, E.	Hasselt University, Belgium
Fua, P	EPFL, Switzerland
Gong, S.	QM Westfield College, UK
González, M.	Universitat Illes Balears, Spain
González, J.	CVC-UAB, Spain
Guerra-Filho, G.	University of Maryland, USA
Hilton, A.	University of Surrey, UK
Horaud, R.	INRIA, Alpes, France
Huang, T. S.	Univ. Urbana-Champaign, USA
Igelmo, A.	Universitat Illes Balears, Spain
Iñesta, J. M.	Universitat d'Alacant, Spain
Jain, A.	Michigan State University, USA
Kittler, J.	University of Surrey, UK
Kunii, T. L.	University of Hosei, Japan
Long, Q.	Hong Kong University of S& T, China
Marchand, E.	IRISA-INRIA Rennes, France
Mas, R.	Universitat Illes Balears, Spain
Mascaró-Portells, M.	Universitat Illes Balears, Spain
Medioni, G.	University of Southern California, USA
Mir, A.	Universitat Illes Balears, Spain
Miró, M.	Universitat Illes Balears, Spain
Moeslund, T.	University of Aalborg, Denmark
Moscini, D.	University of Verona, Italy
Murino, V.	University of Verona, Italy
Obrenovic, Z.	Univ. of Belgrade, Serbia
Oncina, J.	Universitat d'Alacant, Spain
Pentland, A.	Media Lab, MIT, USA
Perales, F.J.	Universitat Illes Balears, Spain
Pérez de la Blanca, N.	University of Granada, Spain
Pla, F.	University of Jaume I, Spain
Poggio, T.	MIT, USA
Qin, H.	Stony Brook University, New York, USA
Radeva, P	UAB-CVC, Spain
Raducanu, B.	CVC-UAB, Spain
Raymaekers, C.	Hasselt University, Belgium
Reid, I.	University of Oxford, UK

Serón, F.   University of Zaragoza, Spain
Shimada, N.   University of Osaka, Japan
Shirai, Y.   University of Osaka, Japan
Skala, V.   University of Plzen, Czech Republic
Susin, A.   UPC, Spain
Tavares, J.   Univ. do Porto, Portugal
Terzopoulos, D.   University of Toronto, Canada
Thalmann, D.   EPFL, Switzerland
Varona, J.   Universitat Illes Balears, Spain
Vetter, Th.   Univ. Basel, Switzerland
Villanueva, J.   UAB-CVC, Spain
Weinland, D.   INRIA, Alpes, France

Sponsoring Institutions

IAPR (International Association for Pattern Recognition)
AERFAI (Spanish Association for Pattern Recognition and Image Analysis)
EG (Eurographics Association)
MEC (Ministerio de Educación y Ciencia, Spanish Government)
Conselleria d'Economia, Hisenda i Innovació (Balearic Islands Government)
Mathematics and Computer Science Department, Universitat de les Illes Balears
(UIB)
Ajuntament d' Andratx, Sol de Ponent
Consell de Mallorca

Commercial Sponsoring Enterprises

VICOM-Tech S.A., www.vicomtech.es
ANDROME Iberica S.A, www.androme.es
GroupVision, www.groupvision.es
Ndigital (NDI), www.ndigital.com
CESA S.A, www.cesa.es
TAGrv S.L., www.tagrv.com

Table of Contents

Articulated Motion and Deformable Objects AMDO^{-e} 2006

A Study on Human Gaze Detection Based on 3D Eye Model
  Kang Ryoung Park 1

Robust Fake Iris Detection
  Kang Ryoung Park 10

A Study on Fast Iris Restoration Based on Focus Checking
  Byung Jun Kang, Kang Ryoung Park 19

A Spatio-temporal Metric for Dynamic Mesh Comparison
  Libor Vasa, Vaclav Skala 29

Facetoface: An Isometric Model for Facial Animation
  Alexander M. Bronstein, Michael M. Bronstein, Ron Kimmel 38

Matching Two-Dimensional Articulated Shapes Using Generalized
Multidimensional Scaling
  Alexander M. Bronstein, Michael M. Bronstein,
  Alfred M. Bruckstein, Ron Kimmel 48

Further Developments in Geometrical Algorithms for Ear Biometrics
  Michał Choraś 58

Composition of Complex Motion Models from Elementary Human
Motions
  Jörg Moldenhauer, Ingo Boesnach, Thorsten Stein,
  Andreas Fischer 68

Acquisition of Articulated Human Body Models Using Multiple Cameras
  Aravind Sundaresan, Rama Chellappa 78

Recovering Articulated Non-rigid Shapes, Motions and Kinematic
Chains from Video
  Jingyu Yan, Marc Pollefeys 90

3D Shape Reconstruction of Trunk Swaying Human Body Segments
  Takuya Funatomi, Masaaki Iiyama, Koh Kakusho,
  Michihiko Minoh 100

Combined Head, Lips, Eyebrows, and Eyelids Tracking Using Adaptive
Appearance Models
    Fadi Dornaika, Javier Orozco, Jordi Gonzàlez   110

Mobile Path and Spin 3D Tracking and Reconstruction
    *Federico Cristina, Sebastián H. Dapoto, Claudia Russo,
    Armando de Giusti, María José Abásolo*   120

Generalized SCODEF Deformations on Subdivision Surfaces
    Sandrine Lanquetin, Romain Raffin, Marc Neveu   132

Viewpoint Insensitive Posture Representation for Action Recognition
    Feiyue Huang, Huijun Di, Guangyou Xu   143

Ballistic Hand Movements
    Shiv Naga Prasad Vitaladevuni, Vili Kellokumpu, Larry S. Davis   153

Collision Detection Trough Deconstruction of Articulated Objects
    Roberto Therón, Vidal Moreno, Belén Curto, Francisco J. Blanco   165

Probabilistic Spatio-temporal 2D-Model for Pedestrian Motion Analysis
in Monocular Sequences
    Grégory Rogez, Carlos Orrite, Jesús Martínez, J. Elías Herrero   175

Predicting 3D People from 2D Pictures
    Leonid Sigal, Michael J. Black   185

Certain Object Segmentation Based on AdaBoost Learning and Nodes
Aggregation Iterative Graph-Cuts
    Dongfeng Han, Wenhui Li, Xiaosuo Lu, Yi Wang, Xiaoqiang Zou   196

Learning Deformations of Human Arm Movement to Adapt to
Environmental Constraints
    Stephan Al-Zubi, Gerald Sommer   203

Three-Dimensional Mapping from Stereo Images with Geometrical
Rectification
    A.J. Gallego Sánchez, R. Molina Carmona, C. Villagrá Arnedo   213

Transferring a Labeled Generic Rig to Animate Face Models
    Verónica Costa Teixeira Orvalho, Ernesto Zacur, Antonio Susin   223

Virtual Characters as Emotional Interaction Element in the User
Interfaces
    *Amalia Ortiz, David Oyarzun, María del Puy Carretero,
    Nestor Garay-Vitoria*   234

Face Modeling and Wrinkle Simulation Using Convolution Surface
Qing He, Minglei Tong, Yuncai Liu 244

Cascade of Fusion for Adaptive Classifier Combination Using
Context-Awareness
Mi Young Nam, Suman Sedai, Phill Kyu Rhee 252

Modeling Relaxed Hand Shape for Character Animation
Michael Neff, Hans-Peter Seidel 262

Boundary Fragment Matching and Articulated Pose Under Occlusion
Nicholas R. Howe 271

Object Tracking and Elimination Using Level-of-Detail Canny Edge
Maps
Jihun Park 281

Facial Expression Recognition in Various Internal States Using
Independent Component Analysis
Young-suk Shin 291

Gender Identification on the Teeth Based on Principal Component
Analysis Representation
Young-suk Shin 300

Grasp Motion Synthesis Based on Object Features
Yoshihiro Yasumuro, Masayuki Yamazaki, Masataka Imura,
Yoshitsugu Manabe, Kunihiro Chihara 305

Carrying Object Detection Using Pose Preserving Dynamic Shape
Models
Chan-Su Lee, Ahmed Elgammal 315

Person Recognition Using Human Head Motion Information
Federico Matta, Jean-Luc Dugelay 326

Matching Deformable Features Based on Oriented Multi-scale Filter
Banks
Manuel J. Marín-Jiménez, Nicolás Pérez de la Blanca 336

Principal Spine Shape Deformation Modes Using Riemannian Geometry
and Articulated Models
Jonathan Boisvert, Xavier Pennec, Hubert Labelle, Farida Cheriet,
Nicholas Ayache 346

Automatic Pose Correction for Local Feature-Based Face
Authentication
*Daniel González-Jiménez, Federico Sukno, José Luis Alba-Castro,
Alejandro Frangi*   356

An Adaptive 3D Surface Mesh Cutting Operation
Viet Quang Huy Huynh, Takahiro Kamada, Hiromi T. Tanaka   366

Action Recognition Using Motion Primitives and Probabilistic Edit
Distance
P. Fihl, M.B. Holte, T.B. Moeslund, L. Reng   375

Shape-Motion Based Athlete Tracking for Multilevel Action Recognition
*Costas Panagiotakis, Emmanuel Ramasso, Georgios Tziritas,
Michèle Rombaut, Denis Pellerin*   385

Finding Articulated Body in Time-Series Volume Data
*Tomoyuki Mukasa, Shohei Nobuhara, Atsuto Maki,
Takashi Matsuyama*   395

Emotional Facial Expression Classification for Multimodal User
Interfaces
Eva Cerezo, Isabelle Hupont   405

Posture Constraints for Bayesian Human Motion Tracking
Ignasi Rius, Javier Varona, Xavier Roca, Jordi Gonzàlez   414

Efficient Incorporation of Motionless Foreground Objects for Adaptive
Background Segmentation
I. Huerta, D. Rowe, J. Gonzàlez, J.J. Villanueva   424

Interactive Soft Object Simulation with Quadratic Finite Elements
Johannes Mezger, Wolfgang Straßer   434

An Alternative to Medial Axis for the 3D Reconstruction of
Unorganized Set of Points Using Implicit Surfaces
Vincent Bénédet, Dominique Faudot   444

Modeling Timing Structure in Multimedia Signals
Hiroaki Kawashima, Kimitaka Tsutsumi, Takashi Matsuyama   453

Human Motion Synthesis by Motion Manifold Learning and Motion
Primitive Segmentation
Chan-Su Lee, Ahmed Elgammal   464

Towards an Integrated Technological Framework for Modelling Shared
Virtual Spaces: Languages and Domotic Applications
Iosu Azkue, Alfredo Pina, Michalis Vazirgiannis 474

Agents with Personality for Videogames
Diana Arellano Távara, Andreas Meier 484

Monocular Tracking with a Mixture of View-Dependent Learned Models
Tobias Jaeggli, Esther Koller-Meier, Luc Van Gool 494

Towards Hands-Free Interfaces Based on Real-Time Robust Facial
Gesture Recognition
Cristina Manresa-Yee, Javier Varona, Francisco J. Perales 504

Upper Body Tracking for Interactive Applications
José María Buades Rubio, Francisco J. Perales,
Manuel González Hidalgo, Javier Varona 514

Author Index 525

A Study on Human Gaze Detection Based on 3D Eye Model

Kang Ryoung Park

Division of Media Technology, Sangmyung University,
7 Hongji-Dong, Jongro-ku, Seoul, Republic of Korea,
Biometrics Engineering Research Center
parkgr@smu.ac.kr

Abstract. Human gaze can give valuable tips for human computer interaction, but it is very difficult to detect human gaze position with one or two camera systems. Conventional method has the limitation of inaccurate gaze detection performance or not being able to track the fast motion of user's face and eye.

To overcome such problem, in this paper, we propose a new gaze detection method. Compared to previous works, our method has following three advantages. First, our method uses three camera systems, such as a wide and narrow view stereo cameras and allows user's natural head and eye movement. Second, to obtain gaze position on a monitor, we detect the 3D eye position and gaze vector of eyeball. Third, to enhance the eye detection performance, we use AdaBoost eye detector and PCA algorithm.

Experimental results showed that our method could be used for real-time gaze detection system.

Keywords: Gaze Detection, a Wide and Stereo Narrow View Cameras, 3D Eye Position and Gaze Vector of Eyeball.

1 Introduction

Human gaze can provide important tips for many applications such as view controlling in 3D simulation programs, virtual reality, video conferencing and special human-machine interface/controls. Most previous researches were focused on 2D/3D head motion estimation [2][11], the facial gaze detection (allowing for only head movement)[3-9][12][13][15] and the eye gaze detection (allowing for only eye movement)[10][14]. Wang et al.[1]'s method provides the advanced approaches that combines head pose and eye gaze estimation by a wide view camera and a panning/tilting narrow camera. However, in order to compute the gaze position, their method supposes that they know the 3D distances between two eyes, eye corners, both lip corners and the 3D diameter of eye ball. Also, they suppose that there is no individual variation for the 3D distances and diameter. However, our preliminary experiments show that there are much individual variations for the 3D distances/3D diameter and such cases can increase gaze errors. Moreover, the accuracy of their method rapidly drops down according as the distance between the camera and the user's face increases. More advanced method using narrow and wide view stereo cameras were shown [15]. However, in that method, user should gaze at 5 known

F.J. Perales and R.B. Fisher (Eds.): AMDO 2006, LNCS 4069, pp. 1–9, 2006.
© Springer-Verlag Berlin Heidelberg 2006

(pre-determined) positions on a monitor to obtain the 3D position information of facial and eye features in calibration stage. Also, it uses the method of mapping 2D feature information (in narrow view eye image) to the gaze position on a monitor, directly, without considering the 3D information of eye feature and it can be main factor to increase gaze error.

To overcome such problems of previous researches and systems, we propose the new method for detecting gaze position with three cameras composed of one wide and stereo narrow view cameras. To exclude the large specular reflection on glasses surface, we use dual (left and right) IR-LED illuminators for wide and narrow view camera.

In section II, we present the method of detecting facial and eye features. In section III, the method of computing 3D eye feature position is shown. In section IV, the method of calculating final gaze position on a monitor is explained. Experimental results and conclusion are included in section V and VI, respectively.

2   Detecting Eye Region in Wide View Image by AdaBoost Algorithm and PCA

In order to detect gaze position on a monitor, facial features in wide view images should be obtained. To detect facial features robustly, we implement a gaze detection system.

To detect the eye features in wide view camera image, we use AdaBoost eye detector and PCA (Principal Component Analysis). In previous work, AdaBoost algorithm is used for face detection and we adopt it for eye detection. Original AdaBoost classifier uses a boosted cascade of simple classifiers using Haar-like features capable of detecting faces in real-time with both high detection rate and very low false positive rates, which is considered to be one of the fastest systems [3][4]. For that, we trained 90 eye images and 90 non-eye images. Then, with trained AdaBoost eye detection classifier, we detect eye region from input test image.

However, some case of FAR (False Acceptance error which accept non-eye region as eye region) happen and to reduce it, we also use PCA eye detection to verify the

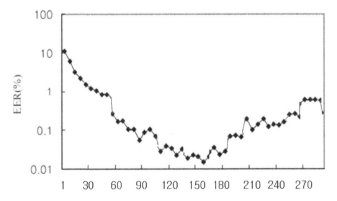

Fig. 1. The EER versus the number of the PCA eigenvector

detected eye region. For PCA training, we used 90 eye images with the size of 60*30 pixels. From that, we obtained total 1800 eigenvectors and found the optimal number of eigenvectors with which the EER (Equal Error Rate) for find eye region was minimized. Experimental results showed that the EER was smallest in case of 160 eigenvectors as shown in Fig. 1. Finally, experimental results showed that correct rate of eye detection was 99.8%.

In the detected eye region, we locate the accurate left and right eye (iris) center by the circular edge detection method [12]. Some examples of the detected eye regions are shown in Fig.2. Experimental results show that RMS error between the detected eye center positions and the actual ones are 1 pixel in 640×480 pixels image. Also, because the eye center detection is performed only in the detected eye region, it takes little time as 1ms in Pentium-IV 1.8 GHz PC.

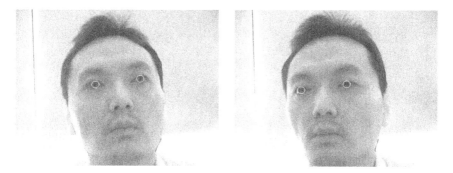

Fig. 2. The examples of detected eye region by wide view camera

3   Locating Eye Features in Narrow View Camera

Based on the detected 2D eye center positions in wide view camera, we try to pan and tilt the stereo narrow view cameras to capture the magnified eye image. However, with the detected 2D eye center positions in wide view camera, only the line of sight through the user's eye center point can be obtained by single wide view camera. To determine the accurate panning/tilting angles of stereo narrow view cameras, we should know the 3D Z distance between the user's eye and the wide view camera and it is infeasible with mono wide view camera. In addition, because we do not know the accurate panning/tilting angles, we cannot also determine the accurate viewing angle of narrow view cameras, with which they can capture the user's magnified eye image. However, we can preliminarily determine the initial viewing angle of narrow view camera based on following conditions without knowing the accurate panning & tilting angles by Z distance; 1) Most users tend to sit in the Z distance range of 50 ~ 70 cm in front of monitor. 2) The sitting heights (we define it as the Y distance between the origin in monitor coordinate ($\mathbf{X_m}$, $\mathbf{Y_m}$, $\mathbf{Z_m}$) and the facial center of most user) are about -20 ~ +30 cm on average (we measured them from 95 persons test data by Polhemus position tracker sensor [11]). 3) The stereo narrow view cameras capture the user's eye on the slant (on the wide view camera).

From the above conditions, we can restrict the initial viewing angle of narrow view camera as 4.3 degree (-2.15 ~ +2.15 degree, vertically) and obtain the magnified eye image by narrow view cameras (In this case, the diameter of iris is about 135 pixels at the Z distance of 50 cm) without knowing the accurate panning & tilting angle of narrow view camera. From the captured eye image, we can detect more accurate 2D pupil center and boundary points (we detect 6 boundary points with the angular interval of 60 degrees as shown in Fig. 3) by locating corneal specular reflection and circular pupil edge detection [12]. Experimental results show that RMS error between the detected feature positions and the actual ones are 1.2 pixels (of pupil center) and 1.1 pixels (of pupil boundary points) in 640×480 pixels image. Some examples of the detected features are shown in Fig.3.

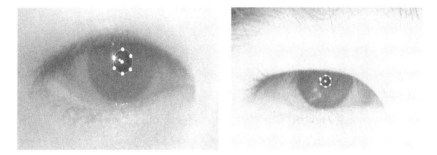

Fig. 3. The Examples of the detected eye features by narrow view camera

However, in some case of users with glasses, large specular reflection on the glasses surface happens by our illuminator. In such a case, our algorithm may detect the erroneous pupil center and boundary points and calculate inaccurate gaze position, consequently. To prevent such problems, our algorithm checks the average gray level of detected pupil region and if it exceeds in the predetermined threshold (we define it as 30), our algorithm commands to turn on the other illuminator in opposite side (from left to right, or from right to left) of narrow view camera and capture the clear eye image which does not include the occlusion of large specular reflection.

4   Computing 3D Eye Feature Positions

In this section, we explain the method of computing 3D eye positions by stereo narrow view cameras. Supposing that the point "M" (which is the pupil center of right eye) is observed by the left and right narrow view cameras, then we can obtain 3D positions of "M" by conventional stereo camera theory [8].

Considering the coordinate conversion between the left and right narrow view camera [8], we can obtain the relationship between two camera coordinates by affine transformation. Using them, we can obtain the Z distance (Z_l) of "M" point in the left narrow view camera coordinate. With the obtained Z distance (Z_l), we can obtain the 3D positions(X_l, Y_l, Z_l) of the feature point (M) in the left narrow view camera coordinate $(\mathbf{X_{N1}}, \mathbf{Y_{N1}}, \mathbf{Z_{N1}})$.

For that, we should know the camera (internal and external) parameters, whose parameters are not changed after initial camera setup. So, we perform the camera calibration procedures using calibration panel and parameter estimation method (Davidon-Fletcher-Powell method) [8][9]. In addition, we should know the remaining parameters of panning/tilting angles of left and right narrow view cameras in order to obtain the Z distance (Z_1). Those parameters are changed according to the panning/tilting operation of left and right narrow view cameras and we can obtain that information from camera micro-controller.

From above procedures, we can get the 3D position (X_1, Y_1, Z_1) of the feature point (M) in the left narrow view camera coordinate ($\mathbf{X_{N1}}$, $\mathbf{Y_{N1}}$, $\mathbf{Z_{N1}}$). In addition, the 3D position (X_2, Y_2, Z_2) of the feature point (M) in the right narrow view camera coordinate ($\mathbf{X_{N2}}$, $\mathbf{Y_{N2}}$, $\mathbf{Z_{N2}}$) can be obtained, consequently.

Then, we perform the additional coordinate conversion between the wide view camera coordinate ($\mathbf{X_W}$, $\mathbf{Y_W}$, $\mathbf{Z_W}$) and left narrow view camera coordinate ($\mathbf{X_{N1}}$, $\mathbf{Y_{N1}}$, $\mathbf{Z_{N1}}$). That is, we obtain the 3D positions of the point (M) (X_3, Y_3, Z_3) in the wide view camera coordinate [8].

For that, we should know the translation vector $\mathbf{T_{O1}}(T_{OX1}$, T_{OY1}, T_{OZ1}) between wide view camera and left narrow view camera coordinate and the tilting angle(α_1) and the panning angle (β_1) of left narrow view camera coordinate ($\mathbf{X_{N1}}$, $\mathbf{Y_{N1}}$, $\mathbf{Z_{N1}}$) about the wide view camera coordinate ($\mathbf{X_W}$, $\mathbf{Y_W}$, $\mathbf{Z_W}$). As mentioned before, we can obtain the information of (α_1, β_1) from camera micro-controller. To measure the translation vector $\mathbf{T_{O1}}$ (T_{OX1}, T_{OY1}, T_{OZ1}), we also perform the camera calibration procedures using calibration panel and parameter estimation method (Davidon-Fletcher-Powell method).

Finally, we perform the coordinate conversion between the wide view camera coordinate ($\mathbf{X_W}$, $\mathbf{Y_W}$, $\mathbf{Z_W}$) and the monitor coordinate ($\mathbf{X_m}$, $\mathbf{Y_m}$, $\mathbf{Z_m}$) and obtain the 3D positions of the point (M) (X_4, Y_4, Z_4) in the monitor coordinate. For that, we should know the translation vector $\mathbf{T_1}(T_{1X}$, T_{1Y}, T_{1Z}) (between wide view camera and monitor coordinate) and the tilting angle(Θ) and the panning angle (Φ) of wide view camera coordinate ($\mathbf{X_W}$, $\mathbf{Y_W}$, $\mathbf{Z_W}$) about the monitor coordinate ($\mathbf{X_m}$, $\mathbf{Y_m}$, $\mathbf{Z_m}$). Like above procedure, we also perform the camera calibration. Experimental results showed that the RMS error between the actual 3D position (X_4, Y_4, Z_4) (measured by Polhemus position sensor) in monitor coordinate and the calculated 3D positions was about 0.485 mm (0.27mm in X axis, 0.27mm in Y axis, 0.3mm in Z axis).

5   Computing Gaze Position on a Monitor

Consequently, we obtain the 3D position(X_4, Y_4, Z_4) of pupil center of right eye in monitor coordinate and apply the same methods for obtaining other pupil boundary points ($P_1 \sim P_3$, $Q_1 \sim Q_3$ as shown in Fig. 3). Experimental results showed that the average RMS error between the actual 3D position of pupil boundary points ($P_1 \sim P_3$, $Q_1 \sim Q_3$) in monitor coordinate and the calculated 3D positions was about 0.508 mm (0.28mm in X axis, 0.29mm in Y axis, 0.31mm in Z axis).

So, we can obtain the 3D positions of ($P_0 \sim P_3$, $Q_1 \sim Q_3$) in the monitor coordinate and final gaze vector of $\mathbf{S}$ by calculating the cross product of $\overrightarrow{P_0P_1}$ and $\overrightarrow{P_0P_2}$. Consequently, we can obtain the final gaze position on a monitor, which is the intersected position between the monitor coordinate (X_m, Y_m, Z_m) (in detail, the plane with Z_m = 0) and the gaze vector (S) (which has the origin of the 3D positions of P_0).

In case that user rotates his head to gaze at other positions on a monitor, the eye region may escape the image of narrow view camera. That is because the viewing angle of narrow view camera is very small (4.3 degree (-2.15 ~ +2.15 degree, vertically)). So, in case of user's head rotation and translation, we should pan and tilt the stereo narrow view cameras to track the eye image. When user's head is rotated and translated, the pupil center point (M') is moved. Then, the 2D projected positions in narrow view camera are also moved. From that, we can obtain the 3D position of M' in the left and right narrow view camera coordinate based on the method as mentioned in section 4. With the obtained 3D position information, we can calculate the panning and tilting angle of left and right narrow view camera and track the user's eye movement accurately. Experimental results showed that the processing time of tracking algorithm (including detecting the projected positions in image, calculating the panning & tilting angle and performing the panning & tilting of two narrow view cameras) was below 20ms (in Pentium-IV 1.8GHz PC) and our system can track the user's eye at fast speed of 50 Hz although the natural rotation and translation of user's head (, the speed of natural rotation is about 10 degrees/sec and that of natural translation is about 52mm/sec (which were measured by Polhemus position tracker sensor about 95 users)).

6   Experimental Results

The gaze detection error of our method is compared to those of previous methods [6][7][15]. The research [6] calculates the gaze position by mapping the 2D facial feature position into the monitor gaze position by linear interpolation or neural network without 3D computation and considering eye movements. The method [7] computes the gaze positions considering both head and eye movements, but uses only one wide view camera. More advanced method using narrow and wide view stereo cameras were shown [15]. However, in that method, user should gaze at 5 known (predetermined) positions on a monitor to obtain the 3D position information of facial and eye features. Also, it uses the method of mapping 2D feature information (in narrow view eye image) into the gaze position on a monitor, directly, without considering the 3D information of eye feature.

The test data were acquired when 95 users gaze at 23 gaze positions on a 19" monitor. Here, the gaze error is the RMS error between the reference gaze positions and the computed ones. 50% of 95 users do not wear glasses and 30% of them do glasses. The other 20% of them wear contact lens (10% wearing soft contact lens and 10% doing hard contact lens). At the 1st experiment, the gaze errors are calculated in two cases as shown in Table 1. The case I shows the gaze error about test data including only head movements and the case II does the gaze error about test data including head and eye movements.

Shown in Table 1, the gaze error and error variance of the proposed method is the smallest in any case. Also, we can know that our system performance is not affected by wearing glasses or contact lens. In our previous work [17], we obtained the gaze accuracy of 1.21 and 2.11 inches in case I and II, respectively. However, in that

Table 1. Gaze error and error variance about test data (unit: cm)

Method	[6] method			[7] method	[15] method	Proposed method	
	Linear Interpol.	Single neural Net	Combined neural Net			Without discrepancy compensation (section 6)	With discrepancy compensation (section 6)
Case I	5.1	4.23	4.48	3.40	2.24	0.87	0.64
Error Variance	1.2	1.13	1.17	0.91	0.84	0.15	0.13
Case II	11.8	11.32	8.87	4.8	2.89	0.89	0.67
Error Variance	1.48	1.45	1.41	0.98	0.87	0.14	0.15

research, we used only two cameras such as a wide and a narrow view cameras and the estimated 3D position is not so accurate as that by this paper. So, the gaze accuracy of the proposed method is better than our previous method.

At the 2nd experiment, the points of radius 5 pixels are spaced vertically and horizontally at 1.5" intervals on a 19" monitor with monitor resolution of 1280×1024 pixels as such Rikert's research [9]. The RMS error between the real and calculated gaze position is 0.622 cm (0.45cm in X axis, 0.43cm in Y axis and the error variance is 0.11 cm) and it is superior to Rikert's method (almost 5.08 cm and the error variance is 1.24 cm). Our gaze error is correspondent to the maximum angular error of 0.714 degrees (0.52 degrees on X axis and 0.49 degrees on Y axis) at the Z distance of 50 cm. The Shih's method [10] showed that an average gaze estimation error is under 1 degrees and our method is superior to the Shih's method. In addition, they use the one sided IR-LEDs to detect the gaze position. So, in case of user's with glasses, large specular reflections on glasses surface happen frequently and hide the whole pupil region in input image. In such a case, their method cannot detect the pupil region and calculate the user's gaze position, consequently.

At the 3rd experiment, we tested the gaze errors according to user's Z distance. The RMS errors are 0.61cm at 50cm (the error variance is 0.11 cm), 0.62cm at 60cm (the error variance is 0.12 cm), 0.62cm at 70cm (the error variance is 0.14 cm) and the performance of our method is not affected by the user's Z position change. At the 4th test, we measured the gaze error according to environmental lighting condition as shown in Table 2. (Case 1 : using fluorescent lamp, Case 2 : using halogen lamp)

According to table 2, we can know the gaze error is not affected by environmental lighting. That is because our gaze system uses IR-Pass filter in front of (narrow and

Table 2. Gaze error according to environmental lighting condition

Environmental Lighting Power		250 Lux.	500 Lux.	750 Lux.	1000 Lux.	1250 Lux.
RMS Gaze Error (cm)	Case 1	0.64	0.61	0.64	0.63	0.61
	Case 2	0.63	0.62	0.63	0.61	0.63

wide view) camera and IR illuminator to detect eye position. Especially, in case of lighting below 500 Lux. and over 1000 Lux., we can see that pupil region is dilated and extracted severely. It is spontaneous phenomenon for pupil to control the penetrated light to retina. However, in any case, the gaze error is not increased and we can know our method can be used irrespective of pupil's size.

Last experiment for processing time shows that our gaze detection process takes about 38ms in Pentium-IV 1.8 GHz and it is much smaller than Rikert's method (1 minute in alphastation of 333MHz). So, we can detect user's gaze position at realtime (per every image which is captured at the speed of 30 frames/sec). The research [1] also shows the angular error of below 1 degree, but their method supposes that they know the 3D distance between two eyes and that between both lip corners and there is no individual variation for the 3D distances. In addition, they suppose that they know the 3D diameter of eye ball and there is no individual variation for that. However, our preliminary experiments show that there are much individual variations for the 3D distances/3D diameter (from 95 users' test) and such cases can increase much gaze errors (the angular error of more than 5 degree).

7   Conclusions

This paper describes a new gaze detecting method. Experimental results show that the RMS error of gaze detection is 0.63 cm on 19 inches monitor. In future works, we plan to research the method of increasing the panning/tilting speed of narrow view camera by estimating the movement of user's head in order to decrease total processing time of gaze detection.

Acknowledgements

This work was supported by the Korea Science and Engineering Foundation (KOSEF) through the Biometrics Engineering Research Center (BERC) at Yonsei University.

References

[1] J. Wang et al., 2002. Study on Eye Gaze Estimation, IEEE Trans. on SMC, Vol.32, No.3, pp.332-350

[2] A. Azarbayejani., 1993, Visually Controlled Graphics. IEEE Trans. PAMI, Vol.15, No.6, pp.602-605

[3] P. Viola, et al., "Robust Real-time Face Detection", IJCV, Vol.57 no.2, pp.137-154, 2004

[4] Z. Ou, "Cascade AdaBoost Classifiers with Stage Optimization for Face Detection", LNCS, Vol. 3832, pp. 121-128

[5] K. OHMURA et al., 1989. Pointing Operation Using Detection of Face Direction from a Single View. IEICE Trans. Inf.\&Syst., Vol.J72-D-II, No.9, pp.1441-1447

[6] K. R. Park et al., 2002. Gaze Position Detection by Computing the 3 Dimensional Facial Positions and Motions. Pattern Recognition, Vol.35, No.11, pp.2559-2569

[7] K. R. Park, 2002, Facial and Eye Gaze detection. Lecture Notes in Computer Science, Vol. 2525, pp.368-376

[8] R. C. Gonzalez et al., 1995, Digital Image Processing, Addison-Wesley
[9] Steven C. Chapra et al., 1989, Numerical Methods for Engineers, McGraw-Hill
[10] Sheng-Wen Shih and J.Liu, "A Novel Approach to 3-D Gaze Tracking Using Stereo Cameras", IEEE Transactions on SMC, Vol. 34, No. 1, Feb. 2004
[11] http://www.polhemus.com (accessed on July 11, 2005)
[12] John G. Daugman, "How Iris Recognition Works, " IEEE Transactions on Circuits and Systems for Video Technology, Vol. 14, No. 1, pp. 21~30, 2004
[13] Jeong Jun Lee, 2004, "Eye Gaze Estimation in Wearable Monitor", Ph.D Thesis, the Graduate School of Yonsei University
[14] Y. L. Grand, "Light, Color and Vision", New York: Wiley, 1957
[15] Kang Ryoung Park, 2004, "Gaze Detection by Wide and Narrow View Stereo Camera", Lecture Notes in Computer Science (CIARP'2004), Vol. 3287, pp.140~147
[16] A. Gullstrand: The optical system of the eye. Appendices to part 1. In. Von Helmholtz H. Physiological Optics. 3^{rd}ed.
[17] Kang Ryoung Park, Min Cheol Whang and Joa Sang Lim "A Study on Non-intrusive Facial and Eye Gaze Detection", Lecture Notes in Computer Science (ACIVS'05), Vol. 3708, pp.52~59, Sept 20-23, 2005

Robust Fake Iris Detection

Kang Ryoung Park

Division of Media Technology, Sangmyung University,
7 Hongji-Dong, Jongro-ku, Seoul, Republic of Korea,
Biometrics Engineering Research Center
parkgr@smu.ac.kr

Abstract. Among biometrics such as face, fingerprint, iris and voice recognition, iris recognition system has been in the limelight for high security applications. Until now, most researches have been studied for iris identification algorithm and iris camera system, etc. But, there has been little researched for fake iris (such as printed, photographed or artificial iris, etc) detection and its importance has been much emphasized, recently. To overcome the problems of previous fake iris detection researches, we propose the new method of checking the hippus movement (the dilation/contraction of pupil size) and the change of iris code in local iris area by visible light in this paper.

Keywords: Iris Recognition, Fake Iris Detection.

1 Introduction

Among biometrics, iris recognition system has been in the limelight for high security biometric applications [1][2][4][7]. Iris is the region which exists between the sclera and the pupil [1]. Its main function is to contract or dilate the pupil in order to adjust the penetrated light volume into the retina. Iris patterns are highly detailed and unique textures that almost remain unchanged from 6 month of age to death. Fake iris detection is to detect and defeat a fake (forgery) iris image. In previous research, Daugman proposes the method of using FFT (Fast Fourier Transform) in order to check the high frequency spectral magnitude in the frequency domain, which can be shown distinctly and periodically from the print iris pattern because of the characteristics of the periodic dot printing [1][2][16]. However, such high frequency magnitude cannot be detected in case that input printed iris image is blurred purposely and the fake iris may be accepted as live one in such case. The advanced method of fake iris detection was introduced by iris camera manufacturer. They use the method of turning on/off illuminator and checking the specular reflection on a cornea. However, such method can be easily deceived by using the printed iris image with cutting off the printed pupil region and seeing through by attacker's eye, which can make corneal specular reflection [15]. Another approach using Purkinje image was shown [28], but it cannot detect the fake iris such as patterned contact lens. Another improvement of security can be the use of a multimodal biometric system. Multimodality means combining several biometric traits from possibly more than one sensor in an optimal way. Examples are the combinations of face and iris recognition [2]. This concept is reported to increase

F.J. Perales and R.B. Fisher (Eds.): AMDO 2006, LNCS 4069, pp. 10 – 18, 2006.

the accuracy of the system in terms of EER as well as the resistance to counterfeiting attempts, simply because all traits have to be counterfeited simultaneously. However, total cost and system complexity are inevitably much increased due to the combination of more than two biometric systems.

Another research [27] proposed the method of using hippus movement, which is the dilation/contraction of pupil according to environment light stimulus. However, such a method cannot detect the fake iris made by (semi-transparent) patterned contact lens. That is because the iris region of the contact lens is semi-transparent and dilation/contraction is also visible in such case though fake iris.

To overcome such problems, we propose the new method of detecting fake iris, which can discriminate the fake patterned contact lens by checking the iris code change near the pupil region based on Daubechies wavelet filtering and SVM (Support Vector Machine).

2   The Proposed Fake Iris Detection Method

2.1   Proposed Iris Camera and Controlling Illuminator

In this research, we use iris recognition camera with dual IR-LED and visible light illuminators. In case of the user with glasses, single IR_LED or visible illuminator can make large specular reflection (on glasses surface) which hides the whole iris region. In such cases, our system cannot recognize user and detect fake iris. So, we use dual illuminators. The IR (Infra-Red) pass filter is attached in front of iris camera in order to exclude the external visible light. The dual visible light illuminators are only used for making pupil's hippus movement and in such cases, the IR-LED illuminator of the same side is turned on also, because the iris image only by visible light cannot be seen due to the IR pass filter.

When the user approaches in the operating range of the iris camera, our iris system perceives it by Z distance sensing device and notifies it to the micro-controller of camera. Then, the micro-controller controls (On/Off control) the IR-LED and visible light illuminator selectively. In our system, the IR-LED illuminator is composed of two wavelength of 760 and 880 nm. Each wavelength illuminator (760 or 880 nm) can be turned on selectively. After the iris recognition system is started, our system turns on the left illuminator (760 + 880 nm) and performs the operation of capturing focused iris image. From that, focused and clear iris image can be captured and iris identification is performed. However, in case of users with glasses, the large specular reflection can happen on the glasses surface and in this case, the identification may be failed. Then, our system turns off the left IR-LED illuminator and turns on the right one and same procedure is iterated. Then, the specular reflection does not happen in iris region and iris identification is successful. After that, our system turns on the right visible light for about 1 sec and checks the change of pupil's size for detecting fake iris. Detain accounts are shown in following section.

2.2   Checking the Change of Pupil's Size (Hippus Movement) by Visible Light

By checking the simple change of pupil's size, we can detect the fake iris such as the 2D/3D printed/photograph iris, artificial eye and opaque contact lens. That is because such fake iris images do not show the change of pupil's size by the visible light. However, a live iris shows the distinctive change of pupil's size by visible light as shown in Fig. 1. Detail experimental results are shown in section 3.

To check the change of pupil size, we firstly detect the inner & outer boundary of iris by circular edge detection [1]. Then, we calculate the ratio of pupil radius to iris radius from iris images captured in case that visible light is off and on (Fig. 1 (a), (b)) respectively. If the variation of ratio does not exceed in the predetermined threshold, we regard the input iris image as fake one and vice versa.

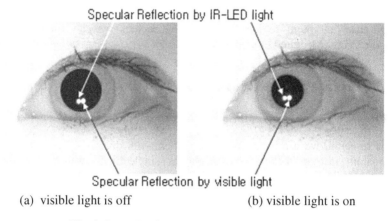

(a) visible light is off   (b) visible light is on

Fig. 1. Example of hippus movement of live iris

However, the semi-transparent lens as shown in Fig. 2 cannot be detected as the fake one by this method. That is due to the structure of semi-transparent lens. In detail, the lens has the structure of transparent iris region and semi-transparent iris pattern and lens wearer's pupil is live one. So, the hippus movement can be seen under transparent iris region, consequently.

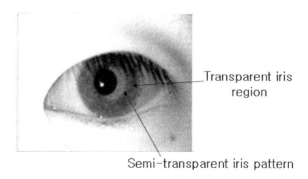

Fig. 2. The structure of semi-transparent patterned lens

So, to overcome such problems, we propose the enhanced method of checking the change of iris features in the local iris area (adjacent of pupil boundary as shown in Fig. 3 and 4). As shown in Fig. 3, the iris pattern of live iris is dilated and contracted in case of pupil's hippus movement and it is like rubber band model [1]. So, the iris pattern is not disappeared or appeared. However, the iris pattern of fake iris is not dilated and contracted like that of live iris. That is, the some iris pattern is hidden by the dilated pupil boundary as shown in Fig. 4 (b). So, we propose the enhanced method of checking the iris feature changing in the local iris area (adjacent of pupil boundary) and detecting the pattern contact lens.

In details, after localization of iris and pupil boundary by circular edge detection [1], we determine 8 iris tracks in the detected iris region. Then, we extract 4 iris track (adjacent to pupil boundary) images from that and convert it as rectangular image.

After that, we apply Daubechies wavelet filter in the rectangular image in case that visible light is on as shown in Fig. 3(a) and 4(a) and extract iris features. After that, the extracted iris feature values in the rectangular image are compared those extracted in case that visible light is off as shown in Fig. 3(b) and 4(b). If the difference of the iris feature values in the rectangular image do not exceed in the predetermined threshold, we regard the input iris image as live one and vice versa. Detail explanations about iris feature values by Daubechies wavelet filter are shown in next section.

The region for applying Daubechies wavelet

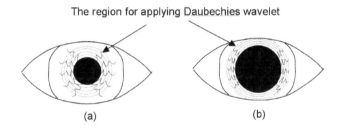

(a)   (b)

Fig. 3. The local iris region for applying Daubechies wavelet (Live Iris)

The region for applying Daubechies wavelet

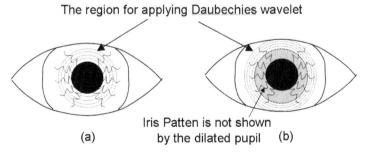

Iris Patten is not shown
(a)   by the dilated pupil   (b)

Fig. 4. The local iris region for applying Daubechies wavelet (Fake Iris by Patterned Lens)

2.3 Iris Feature Extraction by Daubechies Wavelet Filtering

As mentioned before, we use Daubechies wavelet filtering in order to extract the iris feature information [22]. Daubechies's wavelet is reported to have good localization trait and power of high texture classification compared to Gabor wavelet. In addition, Daubechies's wavelet has the characteristics of the orthogonality and factorization and provides compact support, but is not symmetric. Because we check the iris feature variations in local iris area, we use Daubechies's wavelet which shows better localization trait than Gabor filter. The iris region in 4 tracks as shown in Fig. 3 and 4 is passed through low-pass and high-pass filters to generate the low-low, low-high, high-low and high-high subbands, The decomposition process is recursively applied on the low frequency channel to obtain the lower resolution subbands. For iris features, we use two features i.e. standard deviation and energy from the grey-level histogram of the subbands [19]. In addition, we divide the subband images into local windows in order to get robust feature sets against shift, translation and noisy environment.

After extracting the mean and standard deviation by Daubechies wavelet packet, we performed the feature normalization, because features with large values have stronger influence in the classification process than that with small values. That is because we use the amplitude of wavelet filtering instead of the phase. In conventional wavelet filtering, we can use either amplitude or phase for feature. In iris recognition by Daugman [1], he used the phase component of Gabor wavelet filtering and the extracted iris feature is not affected by image contrast. However, the classification power of phase is reported to be inferior to that of amplitude. So, some research of iris recognition use the amplitude of wavelet filtering [30] and in such a case, the normalization of image contrast is required.

For normalization, we use the mean and variance of each feature value and normalize it by them. After normalization, all features have zero mean and unit variance. For the second feature, we calculate the energy (the energy from the grey-level histogram) of each subband images. For the better performance, we have to decide which subband has more discriminant power. If the decomposed image is $x\,(m\,,n)$ with $1 \leq m \leq$ M and $1 \leq n \leq$ N and in order to evaluate the energy of each subband, following equation is applied.

$$e \;=\; \frac{1}{MN} \sum_{m=1}^{M} \sum_{n=1}^{N} |x(m,n)| \tag{1}$$

In this step, we compare the energy with the largest value in the same scale.

2.4 Pattern Matching by SVM

With the transformed iris region in 4 tracks as shown in Fig. 3, 4 and detected features (standard deviation and the energy of each subband) by the Daubechies wavelet, we use SVM (Support Vector Machine) to determine live or fake iris.

SVMs been recently proposed as a new technique for solving pattern recognition problems [23][24]. SVMs perform pattern recognition between two point classes by finding a decision surface determined by certain points of the training set, termed as Support Vectors (SV) and SVs are regarded as data which are difficult to be classified among training. At the same time, the decision surface found tends to have the maximum distance between two classes. In general, it is reported that its classification performance is superior to that of MLP (Multi-Layered Perceptron). Especially, when plenty of positive and negative data are not obtained and input data is much noisy, the MLP cannot show the reliable classification results. In addition, MLP requires many initial parameter settings and it usually is performed by user heuristic experience.

In this paper, we use a polynomial kernel of degree 5 for SVM in order to solve non-linearly separable problem. That is why the dimension of input data is big, so we use the polynomials of high degree. In this case, the problem is defined as 2 class problem. The first class shows live iris and the second one does fake iris. It is reported that the other inner products such as RBF, MLP, Splines and B-Splines do not affect the generation of support vector [25].

Our experimental results comparing the polynomial kernel to MLP for SVM kernel show the same results. The C factor affects the generalization of SVM and we use 10,000 as C factor, which is selected by experimental results. We get 300 live iris image frames (10 frames * 30 persons) and 180 fake iris images (18 frames * 10 fake iris) for SVM training and testing.

3 Experimental Results

For experiments, live irises were acquired from 30 persons (15 persons without glasses and 15 persons with glasses). We make each person try to recognize 10 times and total 1500 iris images were acquired to test our algorithm. Our camera uses B/W (Black and White) CCD sensor and the color of fake iris does not affect our system performance. According to field test, we could know the normal approaching speed of general user to iris camera is about 10 cm/sec. Based on that, we collect the experimental data according to the approaching speed of user; 100 data at normal speed (10cm/sec ± 5), 100 data at fast speed (more than 15cm/sec), and 50 data at slow speed (below 5cm/sec). In addition, 50 data are collected in case that users approach to the camera not from the front but from the side.

In addition, we acquired total 10 fake iris samples for testing. They were composed of 6 samples for 2D printed/photographed iris image on planar or on/with convex surface. Also, 2 samples were acquired for 3D artificial eye. And 2 samples were for 3D patterned contact lens. With each sample, we tried to 18 times to spoof our counterfeit iris detection algorithm.

Experimental results showed the FAR was 0% (0/180) and the FRR was 0.33 % (1/300), but the FRR became 0 % allowing for the second trial. Here, the FAR means the error rate of accepting the fake iris as the live one. And the FRR means the error rate of rejecting the live iris as the fake one.

In case of using Gabor filtering for extracting iris features instead of Daubechies wavelet packet [1][2][16][29], the error rate was increased compared to that using Daubechies wavelet filtering. Because the optimal frequency and bandwidth of Gabor filtering are not known, we selected the optimal value by our experiments ($\pi/8$ for frequency and 12 pixels for bandwidth). The Gabor filtering showed the FAR of 1.1 % (2/180) and the FRR of 0.33 % (1/300). According to results, we can know that

Daubechies wavelet can show the better performance of extracting local iris features than Gabor filtering in case of using small region. Especially, we only extract the iris features in 4 tracks(as shown in Fig. 3 and 4) and the localization accuracy of iris / pupil boundary can affect the performance much more than using whole 8 tracks. Considering such condition, Daubechies wavelet shows the better performance than that by Gabor wavelet, because the mean value extracted by Daubechies wavelet can reduce the effect by inaccurate localization of iris and pupil boundary.

In case of using MLP for pattern matching instead of SVM, the error rate was increased. The MLP showed the FAR of 1.1 % (2/180) and the FRR of 1 % (3/300). In addition, the classification time using SVM was so small as 8 ms in Pentium-III 866Mhz.

Comparing to the fake iris detection method by Daugman [1][2][16] checking high frequency component in FFT domain, Daugman's method showed the FRR was 1 % (=3/300), but the FAR was over 52 % (94/180). That is because in case that input fake iris image is blurred, the high frequency component cannot be seen by Daugman's method.

Though we tested 300 and 180 data for live and fake iris respectively, it is difficult to assert that the data set can represent the general characteristics of whole live and fake iris. Also, the error may be increased in case of using more data set. So, it is required to evaluate the performance by theoretical and we distribute the extracted feature value of live and fake iris into feature space. Then, we take mapping the feature value distributions of live and fake iris into two 2D Gaussian functions. With the generated functions and the experimental decision surface by SVM, the FAR/FRR can be calculated by theoretical. Theoretical evaluation showed that the FAR and the FRR were 0.21 % and 0.38 %, respectively.

The total time for fake iris detection is taken 1,521 ms (on average), which includes 1,051 ms for turning on visible light and 470 ms for the processing.

In the next experiment, we measure the FAR (the error rate of accepting the fake iris as the live one) and FRR (the error rate of rejecting the live iris as the fake one) with distance between the input iris and camera. Table 1 shows the experimental results.

Table 1. Distance vs. the FAR and the FRR

Distance (mm)	80	100	120	140	160	180	200	220	240	250
FAR (%)	0.11	0.10	0.09	0.11	0.11	0.09	0.12	0.11	0.09	0.11
FRR (%)	0.34	0.31	0.33	0.30	0.32	0.33	0.33	0.34	0.30	0.34

As shown in Table 1, the FAR and FRR are almost same according to the distance between input iris and the iris camera. In the next experiment, we measure the FAR and FRR according to the change of environmental lighting condition with fluorescent lamp.

As shown in Table 2, the FAR and FRR are almost same according to the change of environmental lighting. That is because our iris camera has the IR pass filter and the functionality of AE (Auto Exposure).

Table 2. Environmental lighting condition vs. the FAR and the FRR

Environmental lighting condition (Lux.)	250	500	750	1000	1250
FAR (%)	0.11	0.10	0.11	0.11	0.10
FRR (%)	0.27	0.29	0.35	0.32	0.33

4   Conclusions

For higher security level of iris recognition, the importance for detecting fake iris is much highlighted recently. In this paper, we propose the new method of checking the hippus movement (the dilation/contraction of pupil size) and the change of iris code in local iris area by visible light. Experimental results show that the FRR (Error rate of rejecting live iris as forgery one) is 0.33% and the FAR (Error rate of accepting forgery iris as live one) is almost 0%.

To enhance the performance of our algorithm, we should have more field tests and consider more countermeasures against various situations and counterfeit samples in future. Also, the method for reducing processing time should be researched for user's convenience.

Acknowledgements

This work was supported by the Korea Science and Engineering Foundation (KOSEF) through the Biometrics Engineering Research Center (BERC) at Yonsei University.

References

[1] John G. Daugman, "High confidence visual recognition of personals by a test of statistical independence". IEEE Trans. Pattern Anal. Machine Intell., vol.15, no.11, pp.1148-1160, 1993
[2] http://www.iris-recognition.org
[3] Keith Jack, Video Demystified. Harris, 1996.
[4] Anil K. Jain, Biometrics: Personal Identification in Networked Society. kluwer academic publishers, 1998.
[5] Smart Cards and Biometrics in Privacy-Sensitve Secure Personal Identification Systems. A Smart Card Alliance White Paper, May 2002
[6] Ramesh Jain, Machine Vision, McGraw-Hill International Edition, 1995
[7] Tony Mansfield, etc, "Biometric Product Testing Final Report", Draft 0.6, National Physical Laboratory, March 2001
[8] Steven C. Chapra, Raymond P. Canale, Numerical Methods for Engineers, McGraw-Hill International Editions, 1989
[9] Rafael C. Gonzalez, etc, Digital Image Processing, Addison-Wesley, 1992
[10] D. Ioammou, W. Huda, A. F. Laine, "Circle Recognition through a 2D Hough transform and Radius Histogramming", Image and Vision Computing, vol.17, pp.15-26, 1999
[11] K. R. Park, 2002, Facial and Eye Gaze detection. LNCS, Vol.2525, pp.368-376

[12] K. R. Park et al., Apr 2000, Gaze Point Detection by Computing the 3D Positions and 3D Motions of Face, IEICE Trans. Inf.\&Syst.,Vol.E.83-D, No.4, pp.884-894

[13] K. R. Park, Oct 1999, Gaze Detection by Estimating the Depth and 3D Motions of Facial Features in Monocular Images, IEICE Trans. Fund., Vol.E.82-A, No.10, pp.2274-2284

[14] Steven C. Chapra et al., 1989, Numerical Methods for Engineers, McGraw-Hill

[15] http://www.heise.de/ct/english/02/11/114/

[16] Daugman J, "Demodulation by complex-valued wavelets for stochastic pattern recognition." Int'l Journal of Wavelets, Multi-resolution and Information Processing, vol. 1, no. 1, pp 1-17, 2003

[17] Vogel, et al. "Optical Properties of Human Sclera and Their Consequences for Transscleral Laser Applications", Lasers in Surgery and Medicine, 11(4), pp. 331-340, 1991

[18] J. Deng et al., "Region-based Template Deformation and Masking for Eye Feature Extraction and Description", Pattern Recognition, 30(3), pp.403-419, 1997

[19] G. Kee, Y. Byun, K. Lee and Y. Lee, "Improved Technique for an Iris Recognition System with High Performance", AI 2001: Advances in Artificial Intelligence, pp. 177-188, 2001

[20] S. G. Mallet., "A Theory for Multi-resolution Signal Decomposition: The Wavelet Representation", IEEE Trans. on Pattern Analysis and Machine Intelligence, 11(4), pp. 674-693, 1989

[21] R. E. Learned, W. C. Karl and A. S. Willsky, "Wavelet Packet based on Transient Signal Classification", Proc. of IEEE Conference on Time Scale and Time Frequency Analysis, pp. 109-112, 1992

[22] Jain Jang, Kang Ryoung Park, Jinho Son, Yillbyung Lee, "Multi-unit Iris Recognition by Image Checking Algorithm", Lecture Notes in Computer Science (ICBA 2004), July 2004

[23] Vapnik, The Nature of Statistical Learning Theory, New York: Springer Verlag, 1995

[24] Vapnik, Statistical Learning Theory, Wiley-Interscience publication, 1998

[25] Saunders, Support Vector Machine User Manual, RHUL, Technical Report, 1998

[26] J. Daugman, "Biometric Decision Landscape", Technical Report No. TR482, University of Cambridge Computer Laboratory, 2000

[27] Matsushita, "Iris Image Capturing Device and Iris Image Authentication Device", Japanese Patent (Issued Number : 2002-247529)

[28] Eui Chul Lee, Kang Ryoung Park, Jaihie Kim, "Fake Iris Detection By Using the Purkinje Image", Lecture Notes in Computer Science (ICB'06), Vol. 3832, pp.397~403, January 5-7, 2006

[29] Kang Ryoung Park, "New automated iris image acquisition method", Applied Optics, Vol. 44, No. 5, pp.713~734, Feb. 2005

[30] Li Ma et al., "Personal Identification Based on Iris Texture Analysis", IEEE Trans. on PAMI, Vol. 25, No. 12, pp. 1519~1533, December 2003

A Study on Fast Iris Restoration Based on Focus Checking

Byung Jun Kang[1] and Kang Ryoung Park[2]

[1] Dept. of Computer Science, Sangmyung University,
7 Hongji-Dong, Jongro-ku, Seoul, Republic of Korea,
Biometrics Engineering Research Center
9737001@smu.ac.kr
[2] Division of Media Technology, Sangmyung University,
7 Hongji-Dong, Jongro-ku, Seoul, Republic of Korea,
Biometrics Engineering Research Center
parkgr@smu.ac.kr

Abstract. For accurate iris recognition, it is essential to acquire focused iris images. If a blurred iris image is acquired, the performance of the iris recognition is degraded, because the iris pattern is transformed by blurring such as optical defocusing.

In previous researches, they use auto focusing lens for iris recognition camera, but it is too bulky and costly to be applied to mobile phone. So, we propose the new method to increase DOF region with new iris image restoration algorithm based on focus score without any additional hardware. Different from conventional image restoration algorithm, it can be operated at fast speed and used for real-time iris recognition camera.

Keywords: Iris Recognition, Iris Image Restoration.

1 Introduction

For accurate iris recognition, it is essential to acquire iris images with high quality. If a blurred iris image is acquired, the performance of the iris recognition is degraded, because the iris pattern is transformed by blurring such as optical defocusing [3][6]. The region which can capture good focused image by a camera is called as DOF (Depth of Field). To overcome the problems of fixed focusing and auto-focusing method, iris image restoration method was introduced by J. van der Gracht et al. [6]. They used a cubic phase modulation filter[6] with which MTF(Modulation Transfer Function) is changed according to degree of blurring, and then focused iris image can be obtained by restoring iris image with Wiener filter. However, because they have to compute both the normalized power spectrum of original image and noise, such procedure takes too much computation time to be used for real-time iris image restoration. In addition, they use additional hardware such as cubic phase modulation filter [6], but that has the problem that original iris pattern is transformed with it. To overcome such problems, we propose the method to increase the DOF region with new iris image restoration algorithm based on focus score without additional hardware.

F.J. Perales and R.B. Fisher (Eds.): AMDO 2006, LNCS 4069, pp. 19 – 28, 2006.

2 The Proposed Iris Image Restoration Method

2.1 The Overview of the Proposed Algorithm

Proposed iris image restoration algorithm is composed of two processing parts as shown in Fig. 1. In the first part of focus assessment, we measure the focus score for estimating the degree of blurring. In the next part of iris image restoration, the parameters of pre-defined PSF (Point Spread Function) are determined according to the measured focus score, and then we restore the blurred iris image with the PSF.

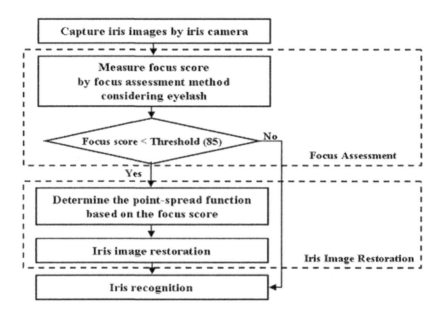

Fig. 1. Overview of proposed iris image restoration algorithm

In the focus assessment part, if the measured focus score is higher than the pre-defined threshold (we used 85 as threshold), it is determined that the captured iris image is focused. Therefore, the iris image is directly used for iris recognition, which can reduce the processing time of iris image restoration. On the other hand, if the measured focus score is lower than the pre-defined threshold, the iris image is regarded as blurred. Therefore, the iris image restoration is performed.

To determine the focusing threshold of 85, we use Bayesian rule. That is, the criterion for determining the good and bad focused images is whether the input iris image can be identified (authenticated) with his enrolled template or not. In case of bad focused image, because FRR (False Rejection Rate : the error rate of rejecting genuine as imposter) is increased, we regarded the false rejected iris image as bad focused one. If we try to restore the bad focused image and recognize with it, we can reduce the FRR. So, we applied the Bayesian rule to determine the threshold with which the equal error rate(the error rate in case that FAR is same to FRR) was minimized and we could obtain 85 as the threshold. For iris authentication engine, we used the Gabor based iris recognition algorithm [3]

In general, the nearer (or farther) the Z position of eye from DOF region become, the degree of blurring increases in iris image. So, the parameters of pre-defined PSF (Point Spread Function) which represents blurring have to be changed according to the degree of blurring for accurate iris image restoration. In our research, the degree of blurring is able to be estimated by measuring the focus score. Therefore, the parameters of pre-defined PSF in the iris image restoration step are determined by focus score, and then the blurred iris image is restored.

2.2 The Focus Assessment Method

The previous focus checking methods by *J. Daugman* [3] and Wei [17] do not well grasp high frequency bands caused by the fine textures of iris image, and especially the method by *J. Daugman* takes much processing time (15ms in 300 MHz RISC processor) due to the large sized kernel. In order to solve such problems, we propose new (5 x 5) pixels sized convolution kernel as shown in Fig. 2. As in *J. Daugman* method, the summated focus value by convolution kernel is passed through a compressive non-linearity of the form: $f(x) = 100 \cdot x^2/(x^2 + c^2)$, which can make a normalized focus score belong to the range of 0 to 100 [3]. Here, x is the total power spectrum measured by the (5 x 5) pixels convolution kernel as shown in Fig. 2.

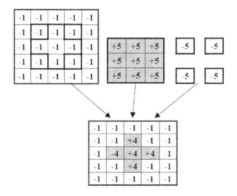

Fig. 2. The proposed (5×5) convolution kernel to measure focus score

In order to compare the performance of the Daugman's [3] and Wei's [17] convolution kernel to that of the proposed (5 x 5) pixels kernel, we inspected the 2-D power spectrum of each method. When the range of frequency is from 0 to |3.3| (in low frequency range), the cumulated amount by the Daugman's or Wei's convolution kernel is greater than that by the proposed (5 x 5) pixels kernel. However, this range represents low frequency components which are contained in an image. On the other hand, when the range of frequency is from |3.3| to |6.6| or from |6.6| to |10|, the cumulated amount by the proposed (5 x 5) pixels convolution kernel is greater than that Daugman's or Wei's convolution kernel. This range represents mid and high frequency components which are contained in an image. Therefore, the ability of passing the mid or high frequency component by the proposed (5 x 5) pixels convolution kernel is much better than that by Daugman's or Wei's convolution kernel. So, we can know our proposed convolution kernel can detect high frequency much better than previous convolution kernel. For the next performance comparison test, we have produced artificially blurred iris image from CASIA iris database [12] by Gaussian mask with various radius. In addition, we measured the focus score according to the degree of blurring. In general, if the curve of this graph has the shape that the slope near a focusing point and that in the blurred region are maintained to be steep, it is reported that the focusing algorithm shows good performance [7]. That is because in case that the slope is steep, the focus lens can reach the focused position fast and accurately. In addition, in case that the slope in the blurred region is also steep, the focus lens can determine its movement direction easily [7]. The proposed (5 x 5) pixels convolution kernel is more steep than the Daugman's or Wei's convolution kernel and we can know the focusing performance of our method is better than Daugman's or Wei's one.

For the third test, we compare the performance based on the convolved image in special domain by Daugman's, Wei's and proposed (5 x 5) pixels kernel. From that, we can know that the proposed kernel makes greater difference between the focused and defocused iris image than that by Daugman's and Wei's methods. That means that our focus checking method can discriminate the focused and defocused iris image much better than the previous ones.

For the last performance comparison test, we compared theoretically execution time by checking the total multiplication count. With the Daugman's (8 x 8) pixels convolution kernel, the convolution value is calculated per every fourth row and fourth column in the iris image [3]. Therefore the total multiplication count is 1,210,944(= 8x 8x 159(the number of kernel movement steps in the X direction) x 119(that in the Y direction)) in the image of size (640 x 480 pixels). With the Wei's and proposed (5 x 5) pixels convolution kernels, the convolution value is calculated per every third row and third column. Therefore the total multiplication count is 842,700(=5x 5x 212(the number of kernel movement steps in the X direction) x 159(that in the Y direction)) in the image of size (640 x 480 pixels). So we can know the Wei's and proposed (5 x 5) pixels convolution kernels take less processing time than the Daugman's (8 x 8) pixels kernel.

2.3 Enhanced Focus Assessment Method Considering Eyelash

As mentioned before, because we use (5 x 5) pixels convolution kernel for focus checking of iris image, we can reduce the effect of eyelash or eye wrinkle for calculating accurate focus score. However, there is still room for the performance of focus checking to be affected by eyelashes which are contained in the iris image. Because the eyelashes are high frequency components, the iris image containing many eyelashes has higher focus score than containing few eyelashes. Also, because there exists Z distance disparity between iris surface and eyelashes, it is possible to be wrongly determined that the iris image is focused due to eyelashes even though the iris region is defocused. In addition, it is possible to be wrongly determined that the iris image is defocused due to eyelashes even though the iris region is focused. To overcome those problems, we propose the enhanced focus assessment method excluding eyelashes detected by proposed eyelash detection algorithm.

In previous works, the eyelash detection algorithm was proposed by *Kong* [13]. This algorithm uses 1-D Gabor filter for detecting separable eyelash and the variance of intensity in the window of size (5 x 5) for detecting multiple eyelashes[13]. However, this algorithm does not use the characteristics of continuous connection of eyelash and does not show good performance of detecting eyelash. Therefore, we propose new eyelash detection algorithm using the characteristics of continuous connection of eyelash points. In our proposed eyelash detection algorithm, eyelashes are also classified into two types. One is a separable eyelash which is defined that an eyelash is easy to distinguish from other eyelashes. Another is multiple eyelashes which are defined that a lot of eyelashes are overlapped. Our proposed algorithm uses local window and adaptive threshold based on the measured focus value for detecting multiple eyelashes. And we also use convolution kernel such as eyelash detecting mask for detecting a separable eyelash. In order to detect eyelash, we firstly locate the iris region by circular edge detection algorithm From that, we can obtain the center position and radius of both pupil and iris region [3]. Because eyelid is the starting position of eyelashes in general, detecting eyelid is very significant for detecting accurate eyelash region. In previous works on eyelid detection, *Deng* proposed the method by region-based deformable template [14]. In this case, the deformable template is used for detecting entire eye, so it takes much processing time. To overcome such problem and detect only upper & lower eyelid, we extract the eyelid candidate position by local derivative mask and detect the eyelid region by curve fitting using two parabolic templates [3]. If iris region is overlapped by eyelid, the detected eyelid area becomes the starting position of eyelashes. However, if not, upper and outer boundary of the iris becomes the starting position of eyelashes.

From the detected iris, pupil and eyelid position, we can define the eyelash candidate region as shown in Fig. 3 and detect the eyelash by using above mentioned method. Then, the focus score is measured again (by proposed (5 x 5) pixels convolution kernel) in iris region excluding detected eyelashes. Because the size of the iris is different per persons, we use the normalized total power spectrum divided by the calculated count of (5 x 5) convolution kernels for focus score.

2.4   The Iris Image Restoration

In the frequency domain, conventional defocused image is represented as Eq. (1).

$$O(u,v) = I(u,v) \cdot H(u,v) + N(u,v) \tag{1}$$

where $O(u,v)$ is the Fourier transform of the blurred iris image by defocusing, $H(u,v)$ is that of the 2-D PSF which causes blurring, $I(u,v)$ is that of the original clear (focused) image, and $N(u,v)$ is that of noise [15]. From that, we can obtain the original clear (focused) image ($I(u,v)$) by Eq.(2) based on image restoration algorithm if we do not consider the noise term ($N(u,v)$). To consider the noise term in Eq.(2), we should use an conventional iterated method for iris image restoration, which takes much processing time and it cannot be used for real-time iris image restoration..

So, we do not include $N(u,v)$ by reducing it by (3 x 3) sized Gaussian filter, because $N(u,v)$ is very smaller than $H(u,v)$ or $I(u, v)$ as shown in Eq. (2).

$O(u, v) = I(u, v) \bullet H(u, v) + N(u, v)$ (by (3 x 3) sized Gaussian filtering $(G(u, v))$
$\rightarrow O(u, v) \bullet G(u, v) = I(u, v) \bullet H(u, v) \bullet G(u, v)$ $(\because N(u, v) \bullet G(u, v) \approx 0)$

$$\hat{I}(u,v) = \begin{cases} \dfrac{O(u,v)}{H(u,v)} & H \neq 0 \\ \dfrac{O(u,v)}{H(u,v)+c} & H = 0, c \neq 0 \end{cases} \qquad (2)$$

where $\hat{I}(u,v)$ is the Fourier transform of the restored image, $O(u,v)$ is that of the blurred image, and $H(u,v)$ is that of the 2-D PSF which causes blurring. c is constant. In our experiment, c is 0.05. Then, we restore defocused iris image with inverse filter using measured focus score as shown in Fig. 1. In order to perform the inverse filtering, we have to estimate the PSF. There are three conventional approaches to estimate the PSF for image restoration, which are the methods by observation, experiment and mathematical modeling [15]. It is reported that the iris pattern has the random shape and the mathematical modeling of the PSF for iris blurring is very difficult, consequently. So, we choose the method based on observation and experiment. From that, we can roughly estimate the point-spread function of iris pattern based on training of iris samples. As mentioned above, the degree of blurring is increased in proportion to the Z position farther from DOF region [3]. Because we can obtain the information about the degree of blurring by the measured focus score (as mentioned in 2.2 and 2.3), the variance value and filter size of the point-spread function are determined by the focus score which is measured by proposed focus checking method.

3 Experimental Results

We firstly tested the performance of proposed eyelash detection algorithm (as mentioned in section 2.3) with the CASIA database [12]. The CASIA database has 756 iris images with size of (340 x 280) pixels from 108 eyes of 80 subjects. Fig. 3 is some examples of our proposed eyelash detection result.

In order to know the accuracy of proposed eyelash detection algorithm, we calculated FAR (False Acceptance error Rate for accepting non-eyelash region as eyelash region) and FRR (False Rejection error Rate for rejecting eyelash region as non-eyelash region). We have calculated FAR and FRR with the CASIA database according to the percentage of eyelash as shown in Table. 1. False rejection cases frequently happen where eyelashes are across, and where a part of eyelashes are blurred.

Because our proposed eyelash detection algorithm uses adaptive criterion according to focus score, it is possible to detect eyelashes in blurred iris image. When we tested our proposed eyelash detection algorithm on an Intel Pentium-4 2.4 GHz processor, the execution time was 6ms on average.

In order to test the focus assessment method considering eyelash, we firstly classified CASIA iris images into that including eyelashes more than 10% or less and produced the blurred iris images by Gaussian mask with various radius.

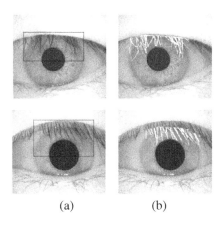

(a)   (b)

Fig. 3. The examples of our proposed eyelash detection result: (a) the searching region for eyelash detection (b) the detected eyelashes

Table 1. The FAR and FRR vs. percentages of eyelash included in eyelash searching box

Percentages of eyelash included in eyelash searching box (%)	Detection error rate	
	FRR (%)	FAR (%)
0 ~ 5	2.23	2.05
5 ~ 10	2.79	1.98
more than 10	2.71	2.34

We detected eyelashes with proposed eyelash detection algorithm and then we measured focus score by proposed (5 x 5) pixels convolution kernel in iris region excluding the eyelashes. So, we are able to obtain the result that the focusing slope of the iris image which contains much eyelashes (more than 10%) is similar to that which contains few eyelashes (less than 10%). From the experiment, we can know that the performance of our proposed focus assessment method is not affected by eyelashes which are contained in the iris image. We also tested the performance of our focusing algorithm based on FAR and FRR. FAR is the error rate of accepting bad focused iris image as good focused one and FRR is vice versa. Experimental results showed that FAR and FRR was 0.1%, respectively.

We have also tested our iris image restoration algorithm with iris images of the CASIA Database [12]. In the first experiment, we have produced the blurred iris images by Gaussian mask with radius of 2.5 pixels. Then we also restored iris images from blurred iris images by using the proposed iris image restoration as shown in Fig. 4.

In order to evaluate the performance of our restoration method, we measured the pixel RMS error. The RMS error between blurred images and focused original ones was 3.43 on average, and that between restored images and focused original ones was 3.12 on average. The performance is enhanced compared to that of previous work [18]. That is because the focus checking performance considering eyelash is enhanced compared to previous work and the PSF modeling becomes more accurate, consequently.

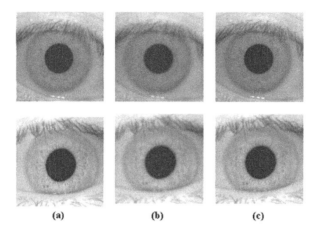

(a)   (b)   (c)

Fig. 4. The examples of iris image restoration results (a) original image (b) blurred image (c) restored image

The restored iris images showed lower RMS error than the blurred iris image. In the second experiment, we have tested the recognition performance of iris images with our iris image restoration algorithm. We had 648 authentic tests and 69,338 imposter tests from CASIA database. First, we enrolled the focused original iris image in the iris recognition system with the Gabor filter having the frequency of $\pi/16$ and $\pi/8$. After that, we computed the hamming distance between the enrolled iris image which is focused and the blurred one or the restored one. The hamming distance between the enrolled images which are focused and the blurred ones was 0.308 on average. In addition, the hamming distance between the enrolled images which are focused and the restored ones was 0.071 on average. The restored iris images show lower hamming distance than the blurred iris images. Also, some blurred iris images show the false rejection error (the error rate of rejecting the genuine iris as the imposter), whereas the restored iris images do not. From that, we can know that the restored iris images contain almost same iris pattern to that of the original iris images. The false acceptance error cases do not happen in any case.

In the third experiment, we have tested the total recognition time with the BM-ET100 made by Panasonic [5] according to user's initial Z distance. We measured the total recognition time of the total 50 persons (each person tries to recognize 5 times) according to initial Z distance. The depth of field is increased with the proposed iris image restoration algorithm. Consequently, the original operating range of the BM-ET100 is 48-53cm, but in case of using our iris image restoration algorithm it becomes 46-56cm. The normal approaching speed of users is 5cm/sec ± 2 in order to locate the eye in the operating range, which is measured by position sensing device [16]. The recognition time with our iris image restoration algorithm is 0.924 sec on average and it is reduced as much as 400 ms compared to that without restoration algorithm. In the fourth experiment, we have measured the execution time of our algorithm on an Intel Pentium-4 2.4 GHz processor. The execution time for checking focus score was 28ms, and that for iris image restoration was 90ms. Therefore, total execution time was 118ms. We have considered that our proposed algorithm would be used on mobile devices. So, we have measured the execution time of our algorithm on the PDA with Intel PXA270 624 MHz processor. Experimental results showed that the processing time was less than 2.3 second.

4 Conclusion

We have proposed iris image restoration which can overcome the limitation of the DOF of the optics. In the experimental result, the DOF could be extended from 48-53cm to 46-56cm with BM-ET100. Also, we could reduce total recognition time as much as about 400ms with proposed iris image restoration. In case that an iris image contains much eyelashes, focus assessment method has the problem that wrong focus score is measured. To overcome such problem, we measured focus score in iris region excluding eyelashes detected by proposed eyelash detection algorithm. As a result, the performance of proposed focus assessment method was not affected by eyelashes.

Our proposed algorithm took much execution time on the PDA with Intel PXA270 624 MHz processor, because the execution for both the FFT and IFFT took 2 seconds, respectively. To overcome such problem, we plan to research de-convolution in the spatial domain without the FFT/IFFT method in future works. In this paper, we suppose that the 2-D PSF is spatially invariant in an iris image. However, it is often the case that 2-D PSF is spatially variant even in an image. Therefore we need to study the method using variant 2-D PSF in future works.

Acknowledgements

This work was supported by the Korea Science and Engineering Foundation (KOSEF) through the Biometrics Engineering Research Center (BERC) at Yonsei University.

Reference

[1] John G. Daugman, "High confidence visual recognition of personals by a test of statistical independence," IEEE Trans. Pattern Anal. Machine Intell., vol.15, no.11, pp.1148-1160, 1993

[2] Ruud M. Bolle, Jonathan H. Connell, Sharath Pankanti, Nalini K. Ratha, Andrew W. Senior, "Guide To Biometrics," Springer, 2003

[3] John G. Daugman, "How Iris Recognition Works," IEEE Trans. on Circuits and Systems for Video Technology, vol. 14, no. 1, pp.21-30, 2004

[4] John G. Daugman, "Wavelet demodulation codes, statistical in- dependence and pattern recognition," Institute of Mathematics and its Applications, Proc. 2nd IMA-IP, London:Albion, pp.244-260, 1999

[5] http://www.panasonic.com/iris (accessed on 2006.2.2)

[6] J. van der Gracht, V. P. Pauca, H. Setty, R. Narayanswamy, R. J. Plemmons, S. Prasad, and T. Torgersen, "Iris recognition with enhanced depth-of-field image acquisition," Proceedings of SPIE, vol. 5438, pp.120-129, 2004

[7] Kang-Sun Choi, Jun-Suk Lee and Sung-Jae Ko, "New Auto-focusing Technique Using the Frequency Selective Weight Median Filter for Video Cameras," IEEE Trans. on Consumer Electronics, vol.45, no.3, pp.820-827, 1999

 [8] J. M. Tenenbaum, "Accommodation in computer vision," Ph. D. thesis, Stanford University (1970)
 [9] R. A. Javis, "Focus Optimization Criteria for Computer Image Processing," Microscope, vol. 24(2), pp.163-180
[10] S. K. Nayar and Y. Nakagawa, "Shape from Focus," IEEE Transactions on Pattern Analysis and Machine Intelligence, vol.16, no.8, pp.824-831, 1994
[11] Joseph W. Goodman, "Introduction to Fourier Optics 3/E," Roberts and Company Publishers, 2005
[12] http://www.sinobiometrics.com (accessed on 2006. 01. 11)
[13] W.K. Kong and D. Zhang, "Accurate Iris Segmentation Based on Novel Reflection and Eyelash Detection Model," Proceedings of 2001 International Symposium on Intelligent Multimedia, Video and Speech Processing, May 2 ~ 4 2001, Hong Kong.
[14] J. Deng and F. Lai., "Region-based Template Deformation and Masking for Eye Feature Extraction and Description," Pattern Recognition, 30(3), pp. 403-419, March 1997
[15] R. C. Gonzalez, R. E. Woods, "Digital Image Processing 2/E," Prentice Hall, 2002
[16] http://www.polhemus.com (accessed on 2006.2.2)
[17] Zhoushi Wei et al., "Robust and Fast Assessment of Iris Image Quality," Lecture Notes in Computer Science, Vol. 3832, pp. 464- 471, 2006
[18] Byung Joon Kang, Kang Ryoung Park, "'A Study on Iris Image Restoration'", Lecture Notes in Computer Science (AVBPA 2005), Vol. 3546, pp.31~40, July 2005

A Spatio-temporal Metric for Dynamic Mesh Comparison

Libor Vasa and Vaclav Skala

University of West Bohemia, Department of Computer Science and Engineering
Univerzitni 22, Pilsen, Czech Republic
{lvasa, skala}@kiv.zcu.cz

Abstract. A new approach to comparison of dynamic meshes based on Hausdorff distance is presented along with examples of application of such metric. The technique presented is based on representation of a 3D dynamic mesh by a 4D static tetrahedral mesh. Issues concerning space-time relations, mesh consistency and distance computation are addressed, yielding a fully applicable algorithm. Necessary speedup techniques are also discussed in detail and many possible applications of the proposed metric are outlined.

1 Introduction

Dynamic mesh extraction from multicamera recordings of real scenes has become a common task of computer graphics of these days. Algorithms running in real time are being developed and used in common practice, producing high quality dynamic meshes that can be used for all kinds of purposes, from 3D television to elaborate experimental techniques requiring exact measurement.

However, today's hardware is still far from being powerful enough to handle the produced data in the raw form. Limited bandwidth is usually the main bottleneck, but also processing power and memory requirements may become difficult to meet.

Various techniques of data rate reduction of dynamic meshes are already appearing, usually involving some kind of lossy value compression scheme combined with some elaborate prediction technique [3,7,5]. One can also expect that there will appear techniques of geometry decimation of the dynamic mesh, similar to algorithms used for static mesh simplification [8].

The purpose of this contribution is to provide an objective methodology of comparing dynamic meshes. Such technique will be needed in order to compare and evaluate the compression methods and we will show that it may be used for other purposes as well.

2 Problem definition

The problem we will solve is defined as follows: Let there be given a set $S = \{M_k\}_{k=1}^N$ of dynamic meshes. A dynamic mesh M is a sequence of triangle meshes of constant connectivity, which may be produced by some extraction technique [11,12]. We want

F.J. Perales and R.B. Fisher (Eds.): AMDO 2006, LNCS 4069, pp. 29–37, 2006.

to define a function $d(M_1, M_2)$ that will be a metric in the space of dynamic meshes. Namely, we expect the following properties:

$$d(M_1, M_2) = 0 \Leftrightarrow M_1 = M_2$$
$$d(M_1, M_2) = d(M_2, M_1)$$
$$d(M_1, M_2) < d(M_1, M_3) \Leftrightarrow \text{A human observer sees } M_2 \text{ as "more similar" to}$$
$$M_1 \text{ than to } M_3 \tag{1}$$

Of these conditions is of course the last one the hardest to achieve.

In the past, research was done in the field of comparing static triangle meshes [2,10], the basic idea is quite simple and is based on the definition of Hausdorff distance of two objects. The Hausdorff distance is defined as follows:

Let's have two static triangle meshes, m_1 and m_2. Distance of a point to a mesh is defined as a minimum of Euclidean distances of the given point p and all points p_m of the mesh m:

$$d_{p,m} = \min_{\forall p_m \in m} \left(\| p - p_m \| \right) \tag{2}$$

From this one can define a one-way (non-symmetric) distance of a mesh m_1 to a mesh m_2:

$$d'_{m_1,m_2} = \max_{\forall p_m \in m_1} \left(d_{p_m,m_2} \right) \tag{3}$$

A symmetric Hausdorff distance is then defined as

$$d_{m_1,m_2} = \max \left(d'_{m_1,m_2}, d'_{m_2,m_1} \right) = d_{m_2,m_1} \tag{4}$$

In the implementations of the Hausdorff distance evaluators both meshes are usually sampled in order to gain distance of a point to a mesh (usually some elaborate point to triangle distance test is used) and various acceleration techniques (space subdivisions etc.) are exploited in order to reduce the computational complexity that is quadratic in the raw form of the definition.

Our approach is to adopt the Hausdorff distance and use it for comparison of dynamic meshes that will be represented by static objects on 4D. In order to do so, we will have to address several problems that arise with the higher dimension of the problem.

3 Human Perception of Time Considerations

The Hausdorff distance measurement is based on the concept of the Euclidean distance. In 3D space there is no problem with units as long as the same units are used for all axes. However, in 4D we cannot use equal units, as one of the dimensions is time. Therefore we must answer the question which units should be used.

The key to the answer is the definition of the desired metric. It implies, that equal distance on each axis should cause equal disturbance in the mesh. It is important to realize that human perception of time is quite absolute and it is actually the spatial metric that causes problems. In computer graphics modeling it is quite usual to work with vaguely defined spatial units, while time is measured absolutely. Therefore, the question actually is "what spatial distance is equal to the given time span in the terms of human perception".

The problem is that distance of one unit may cause distance of half a screen in one model, as well as being barely distinguishable in some other model. One solution would be to consider the distance of point projections on human retina, but this distance also depends on the size of used screen.

Therefore we use a "relative distance", defined as distance in the model units divided by the size of the model's body diagonal. The task now is to find the coefficient alpha that will relate the relative distance to time units. In order to do so, we will have to perform subjective testing, but for the time of being we can do following considerations:

1. time span of 1/100s is almost unrecognizable for a human observer, while spatial shifts of 10% is on the limit of acceptability, therefore we expect alpha to be larger than $0.01/0.1 = 0.1$
2. time spans of units of seconds are on the limit of acceptability, while spatial shift of 0.1% is almost unrecognizable, therefore we expect alpha to be smaller than $1/0.001 = 1000$

Saying that, we can guess the value of the alpha coefficient to be about 10, i.e. time span of 100ms is equal to spatial shift of 1%.

4 Dynamic Mesh as a Static 4D Object

We have mentioned that in order to use the Hausdorff distance concept we have to represent the dynamic mesh as a static object in 4D. As static mesh in 3D consists of triangles, which are elements one-dimension lower than the dimension of the 3D space, in 4D we will represent the dynamic mesh by a static tetrahedral mesh. Note that tetrahedron is not a simplex in 4D.

We can extract one frame from such mesh by cutting it by a plane t=const, because a tetrahedron cut by a plane gives one or two triangles. The procedure that converts a dynamic triangle mesh into a 4D tetrahedral mesh is based on the idea, that a triangle in two consequent frames forms a prism in 4D (see figure 1). The process of conversion is therefore simply a process of breaking such prisms into tetrahedra. Each prism can be divided into three tetrahedra.

However, we must be very careful about the breaking. One can see that the sides of the prisms are not planar, and therefore we must explicitly make sure that the mesh we are creating will be continuous. Namely, we must make sure that a side diagonal in neighboring prisms is always equal. In order to do so, we propose the following subdivision procedure:

1. find a vertex on the base of the prism with lowest index. Create a tetrahedron that is formed by the whole top of the prism and this vertex.
2. find a vertex on the base of the prism with the largest index. Create a tetrahedron that is formed by the whole base of the prism and the vertex above the vertex with largest index.

3. create a tetrahedron formed by remaining two vertices on the base and two vertices on the top of the prism.

Because the relations of largest/lowest index are kept on each face, one can see that the created tetrahedral mesh is consistent.

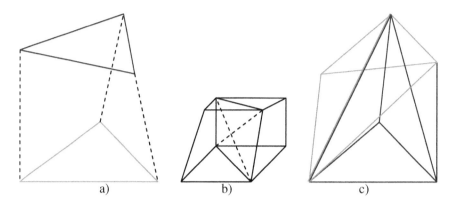

Fig. 1. Moving triangle as a 4D prism (green is the triangle in time t, blue is the triangle in time t+1), two possible diagonals on a common side, two tetrahedra used for consistent subdivision

5 Point to Tetrahedron Distance Test

Our distance algorithm is based on the point to tetrahedron distance test. A distance to a tetrahedron may be in fact distance to one of following entities:

1. distance to the body of the tetrahedron. Is only possible when the orthogonal projection of the point lies within the tetrahedron
2. distance to a face of the tetrahedron. Is only possible when the orthogonal projection of the point to the plane of the face lies on the face
3. distance to an edge of the tetrahedron. Is only possible when the orthogonal projection of the point to the line of the face lies on the edge
4. distance to a vertex of the tetrahedron

Of these distances we must choose the lowest that meets its projection conditions.

5.1 Distance to the Body of a Tetrahedron

A tetrahedron is defined by three 4D vectors of Euclidean coordinates, defined as follows:

$$v_0 = T_1 - T_0$$
$$v_1 = T_2 - T_0 \tag{5}$$
$$v_2 = T_3 - T_0$$

Therefore a tetrahedron in 4D has a normal vector n:

$$n = v_0 \times v_1 \times v_2 \tag{6}$$

Note that we are using cross product that is a ternary operator in 4D.

Any point P can now be expressed as follows:

$$P - T_0 = a\vec{v}_1 + b\vec{v}_2 + c\vec{v}_3 + d\vec{n} \tag{7}$$

We can find the combination coefficients by solving a 4x4 set of linear equations, for example using Sarus rule. The projection to the tetrahedron space lies within the tetrahedron if following conditions hold:

$$a \geq 0, b \geq 0, c \geq 0, (a+b+c) \leq 1 \tag{8}$$

In such case the distance can be expressed as $d*|n|$.

5.2 Distance to a Face of a Tetrahedron

The key feature one must consider is that a face in 4D (and a plane in general) has not a uniquely defined normal. Therefore, we must find a normal that is orthogonal to the face, and that passes through the evaluated point P. In order to do so, we can use the following procedure:

Let's have T_0, T_1 and T_2 vertices that define a face of the tetrahedron, and a point P.

$$v_0 = T_1 - T_0$$
$$v_1 = T_2 - T_0 \tag{9}$$
$$p = P - T_0$$

we can now find a vector **b** that is orthogonal to all three vectors by using cross product

$$\mathbf{B} = \mathbf{v_0} \times \mathbf{v_1} \times \mathbf{p} \tag{10}$$

A normal vector n that can be used for the projection can be found as

$$\mathbf{N} = \mathbf{v_0} \times \mathbf{v_1} \times \mathbf{b} \tag{11}$$

Now we can use a similar procedure to find where the projection lies. We can write

$$p = a*\mathbf{v_0} + b*\mathbf{v_1} + c*\mathbf{b} + d*\mathbf{n} \tag{12}$$

where we expect the c coefficient to be zero. If now $a \geq 0, b \geq 0$ and $(a+b) \leq 1$ then the projection lies on the face, and the distance is $d*|n|$.

5.3 Distance to an Edge of a Tetrahedron

For the distance of an edge one can use the properties of dot product that hold in 4D space. Let's define

$$v_1 = E_1 - E_0 \tag{13}$$
$$v_2 = P - E_0$$

It is well known that the line of the edge can be written as E_0+t*v_1.

In order to determine the distance, we would like to find the t parameter of an orthogonal projection of P to the line. One can derive that t can be determined as follows:

$$t = (v_1.v_2)/(v_1.v_1) \tag{14}$$

From the known value of t we can easily determine whether the projection lies on the edge (0<=t<=1) and eventually express the distance as

$$d = \sqrt{v_1.v_1 - t^2 v_2.v_2} \tag{15}$$

6   Acceleration Techniques

The distance tests shown above work for all kinds of tetrahedra (i.e. including obtuse tetrahedra), but may be very slow when each tested point is to be evaluated against each tetrahedron of the other mesh.

Our first acceleration technique is based on the following observation: A point can be projected to a face only if it is projected on at least two of the edges that define the face (for obtuse faces). Based on this idea we evaluate all edges before the faces. During the evaluation we increase a counter for each face if a point is projected to an edge that incides with the face (two counters representing two incident faces are increased whenever a point is found to be projected on an edge). A face is then only evaluated if its counter is larger or equal to two.

From the previous equations one can see, that evaluating an edge consists only of two dot products, one division and two comparisons, while evaluating the face includes solving a 4x4 set of linear equations (12). Moreover, the case when a point is projected to a face of a tetrahedron is a rare one. Therefore this simple technique provides a significant speedup of more than 50%. A further speedup can be achieved by postponing the square root operation that is part of each distance evaluation, to the latest possible moment, while keeping the square distances.

We are also utilizing spatial subdivision techniques in order to reduce the computational complexity. In a preprocessing stage we create a 4D grid of cells, where each cell holds a list of tetrahedra that intersect with the cell.

The usual approach determining which cells are intersected by some entity is to find a bounding box of the entity and mark all cells of the bounding box. Because the grid we are using is 4D, this would lead to unnecessary marking of many empty cells. Therefore, we have developed an improved technique based on the following observation: Each tetrahedron has its uniquely defined 3D space with a normal. This space is a hyperplane in 4D that divides the time-space into parts "above" and "below". We can evaluate each corner of a cell according to whether it is above or below the tetrahedron (each cell has 16 corners, it can be imagined as a hypercube). Only cells that are neither completely below nor completely above the tetrahedron can be intersected by the tetrahedron. In our experiments, including all the cells of a bounding box of a tetrahedron, have lead to an average of approximately 35 cells per tetrahedron (for given tetrahedral mesh and grid density), while keeping only the cells that satisfy our condition has reduced this number to cca. 8 cells per tetrahedron and led to a speedup of about 30% (including the preprocessing stage).

In the evaluation stage, a cell that contains the evaluated point is found and searched for possible closest tetrahedron. Further cells are subsequently evaluated only if they can provide a tetrahedron that is closer than the already found one, i.e. only if the closest point of the cell is closer than the current distance. This technique vastly improves the performance, depending on the density of the grid.

We have also included precomputation of reused values and some further improvements (usage tables that show which faces and edges were already evaluated for a given point etc.). Our implementation is capable of evaluating about 180 V-M distances per second, where the mesh consists of about 120 000 tetrahedra. This allows us to compute distances of moderately complex animations within minutes, larger animations still must be evaluated offline (hours of processing time are needed).

7 Applications

We have already shown the main application of the proposed metric, it is comparison of dynamic meshes decimated by various methods, but it is not the only field where comparison of animations can be used.

Another natural area where this technique can be used is artificial intelligence, where the metric can be used to recognize various actions and to respond to them. In our experiments we have compared two recordings of a human jump [11,12], and we have found that the distance of one jump sequence to the other is significantly smaller than the distance of a jump to the sequence that represents the human walking. Each frame of the human jump sequence consists of about 30 000 triangles, and we have compared 50 frame subsets of the sequence.

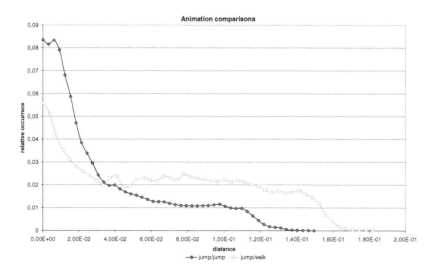

Fig. 2. Distance distribution experiments

The figure 2 shows the histogram of the measured distances for the above mentioned experiments. In order to compare longer time spans we have compared tetrahedral meshes that consist of only every other mesh of the animation, effectively reducing the frame-rate of the animation to one half of its original value.

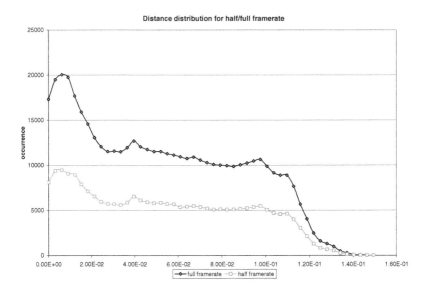

Fig. 3. Full/half frame-rate experiments

Our other experiment shows that such frame-rate reduction is possible, because it does not disturb the characteristics of the distribution of the error. Figure 3 shows the relative histogram of distance values for full frame-rate comparison and half frame-rate comparison of equal time span of an animation. The average difference is less than 4%, and the half-frame-rate curve keeps all the characteristics of the full frame rate. However, this is only possible when animation recognition is considered. The difference of 4% may be unacceptable when exact comparison for decimation evaluation is considered.

Another application is obvious from the previous one – the animation metric can be used to align animations in both time and space at the same time. This would require some slight changes in the software in order to look for average distance vector rather than maximum distance size but this can be done very easily.

One can also easily imagine applications like self-training, where the user would try to fit with her movements to some predefined pattern. Our method can then use rendering of the distance of the movements represented by surface colors that would tell the trainee where and when exactly she was following the pattern well or not. This technique can be used in wide range of areas from dance up to surgery training.

8 Future Work

The proposed algorithm is still computationally expensive; therefore we will put effort into acceleration techniques that would make its use easier and more comfortable.

We would also like to further develop the idea of representing a dynamic mesh by a static mesh in 4D and propose a decimation method based on this representation and some tetrahedral mesh decimation algorithm provided with appropriate criteria.

Acknowledgements

The authors would like to thank Mark Dobbs for proof reading. This project was supported by the 6FP NoE project 3DTV – Integrated Three-Dimensional Television – Capture, Transmission and Display No. 511568 and MŠMT ČR project 1P04LA240.

References

1. Chopra, P., Meyer, J.: Tetfusion: An algorithm for rapid tetrahedral mesh simplification. In Proc. IEEE Visualization, pages 133--140, 2002.
2. Cignoni, P., Rochini, C., Scopigno, R.: Metro: measuring error on simplified surfaces. Technical Report B4-01-01-96, Istituto I.E.I. - C.N.R., Pisa, Italy, January 1996.
3. Coors, V., Rossignac, J.: Delphi: Geometry-based Connectivity Prediction in Triange Mesh Compression. The Visual Computer 20(8-9): 507-520 May 2004.
4. Rossignac, J.: Edgebreaker: Connectivity compression for triangle meshes, IEEE Transactions on Visualization and Computer Graphics, Vol. 5, No. 1, January - March 1999.
5. Müller, K., Smolic, A., Kautzner, M., Eisert, P., Wiegand, T.: Predictive Compression of Dynamic 3D Meshes. Proc. International Conference on Image Processing (ICIP 2005), Genova, Italy, pp., September 2005.
6. Bayazit, U., Orcay, O., Gurgen, F.: Predictive Vector Quantization of 3D polygonal mesh geometry by representation of vertices in local coordinate system. Proc. of EUSIPCO 2005.
7. Ibarria, L., Rossignac, J.: Dynapack: Space-Time compression of the 3D animations of triangle meshes with fixed connectivity. Proceedings of the 2003 ACM SIGGRAPH/ Eurographics symposium on Computer animation, 2003.
8. Franc, M.: Methods for Polygonal Mesh Simplification. Internal technical report at University of West Bohemia, 2003.
9. Gumhold, S., Guthe, S., Straer, W.: Tetrahedral Mesh Compression with the CutBorder Machine. In Proceedings of the 10th Annual IEEE Visualization Conference, 1999.
10. Aspert, N., Santa-Cruz, D., Ebrahimi, T.: Mesh: Measuring errors between surfaces using the hausdorff distance. In Proceedings of the IEEE International Conference on Multimedia and Expo, volume I, pages 705--708, 2002.
11. Anuar, N., Guskov, I.: Extracting Animated Meshes with Adaptive Motion Estimation. Proc. of the 9th International Fall Worksop on Vision, Modeling, and Visualization, 2004.
12. Sand, P., McMillan, L., Popovic, J.: Continuous Capture of Skin Deformation. ACM Transactions on Graphics. 22(3), pp. 578-586, 2003.

Face2Face: An Isometric Model for Facial Animation

Alexander M. Bronstein, Michael M. Bronstein, and Ron Kimmel

Dept. of Computer Science, Technion – Israel Institute of Technology,
Haifa 32000, Israel
{alexbron, bronstein}@ieee.org, ron@cs.technion.ac.il

Abstract. A geometric framework for finding intrinsic correspondence between animated 3D faces is presented. We model facial expressions as isometries of the facial surface and find the correspondence between two faces as the minimum-distortion mapping. Generalized multidimensional scaling is used for this goal. We apply our approach to texture mapping onto 3D video, expression exaggeration and morphing between faces.

Keywords: isometric embedding, multidimensional scaling, correspondence problem, texture mapping, face animation, expression exaggeration, morphing.

1 Introduction

Finding correspondence between human faces is a key problem in numerous problems on the border between computer graphics and computer vision, including: facial animation [1] and modelling [2–4], caricaturization and expression exaggeration [5], cross-parametrization [6,7], texture mapping [6] and morphing [8,9]. In the motion pictures industry, one of the challenges is the creation of visually-realistic animated human faces. The rapid development of 3D real-time video acquisition techniques [10] opens a new way to create a synthetic character, by scanning an actor and replacing his or her facial texture with a virtual one, automatically mapping a single image onto a 3D video sequence. We call the effect achieved in this way the "virtual makeup".

The common denominator of the above applications is the *correspondence problem*, i.e. the need to identify the same points in two different instances of a single face (e.g. deformed by facial expressions) or on two different faces. Specifically, we consider the problem of correspondence between 3D facial surfaces, which appears to be significantly harder than its 2D counterpart. Unlike synthetic face animation [1], where the correspondence between meshes and textures is known, in our case the 3D sequence is acquired by a range sensor and therefore, the correspondence is not readily available.

In 3D morphing, the correspondence is usually established by finding a common parametrization domain for the surfaces. Such parametrizations can be constructed using a set of fiducial points, which, in most cases, must be selected manually [9]. A parametrization of faces that is common to all expressions has

F.J. Perales and R.B. Fisher (Eds.): AMDO 2006, LNCS 4069, pp. 38–47, 2006.

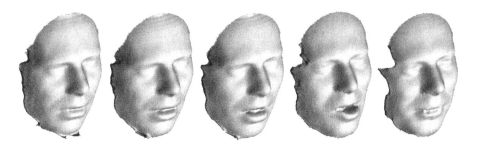

Fig. 1. Example of a 3D video sequence of an articulated face

been proposed in [11, 4]. A hybrid method based on fitting 2D facial images to a deformable 3D model of the face was proposed in [2, 3]. In [12], it was empirically shown that natural facial expressions can be considered as isometries of the facial surface. Multidimensional scaling (MDS) [13] was then used to construct an intrinsic geometric representation of the face for expression-invariant face recognition. Here, we adopt the isometric model to establish correspondence by finding the "most isometric" mapping between two facial surfaces. Our approach is based on a numerical procedure similar to MDS, allowing to embed one surface into another. We refer to this method as the *generalized* MDS, or GMDS for short [14].

This paper consists of five sections. In Section 2, we present the isometric model of facial expressions. Section 3 describes the GMDS problem for finding correspondence between facial surfaces and deals with its numerical implementation. In Section 4, we show some applications of GMDS to a number of problems related to face animation. Section 5 concludes the paper.

2   Isometric Model

Consider a 3D video sequence of an articulated face, acquired by real-time 3D scanner. We can think of the video as of a sequence of smooth compact connected two-dimensional Riemannian surfaces, denoted by $\{\mathcal{S}_0, \mathcal{S}_1, ...\}$. The *geodesic distances* (lengths of the shortest paths) $d_{\mathcal{S}_t} : \mathcal{S}_t \times \mathcal{S}_t \to \mathbb{R}$ on $\mathcal{S}_t$ are induced by the corresponding Riemannian metrics. These distances define the *intrinsic* geometry of the surface. The *extrinsic* geometry is captured by the vector field $\mathbf{s}_t : \mathcal{S}_t \mapsto \mathbb{R}^3$, representing the Euclidean coordinates of the surface points. We call $\mathcal{S}_0$ the *reference frame* or the *reference surface*.

Our goal is to find the *correspondence* between $\mathcal{S}_0$ and $\mathcal{S}_t$, represented by a bijective mapping $\varphi_t : \mathcal{S}_0 \to \mathcal{S}_t$. When only the geometry is available, this is a very challenging problem. Theoretically, the mappings $\{\varphi_1, \varphi_2, ...\}$ can be estimated by finding correspondence between some fiducial points or features [9]. Yet, the main limitation of feature-based approaches is the fact that they require a precise feature detector. Unfortunately, the number of features that can be robustly detected and tracked using facial surface geometry is usually small. The geometry of the facial surface contains mostly low-frequency information, while feature detection usually requires high-frequency information. A few points such as the eyes and the nose tip, can be detected sufficiently accurately based on the surface curvature. This implies that the correspondence is available only between a sparse set of points. Alternatively, dense correspondence can be found using optical flow applied to the texture, as done by Blanz *et al.* [4]. However, this approach requires the texture information, which is not always available.

In [12], we showed empirically in the context of 3D face recognition that the deformations of a face due to natural expressions can be approximated by *isometries* (distance preserving transformations). Under this assumption, called here the *isometric model*, all instances of the facial surface in our video are isometric, i.e. there exists a sequence of bijective mappings $\{\varphi_1, \varphi_2, ...\}$; $\varphi_t : S_0 \to S_t$ such that

$$d_{S_0}(s_1, s_2) = d_{S_t}(\varphi_t(s_1), \varphi_t(s_2)), \tag{1}$$

for all $s_1, s_2 \in S_0$. In practice, a genuine isometry between two surfaces does not exist, but can be approximated by finding a mapping that distorts the geodesic distances the least. Our claim is that such a near-isometric mapping establishes a correspondence between S_t and S_0. In the following, we will write φ_t, implying the correspondence found in this manner.

Practice shows that the surfaces need not to be necessarily isometric in order for the minimum-distortion mapping to be a good correspondence. This is due to the fact that in a broad sense, all human faces have similar geometry. Thinking of two faces as of flexible rubber masks, the correspondence problem is that of putting one mask onto the other, while trying to stretch it as less as possible. It is obvious that in most cases, the geometric features (like nose, forehead, mouth, etc.) of the two masks will coincide. A recent breakthrough in surgical face transplantation reinforces this claim. Consequently, given two faces of different subjects, we can still use the same principle to find correspondence between them. We exemplify this idea in Section 4.3.

3   Generalized Multidimensional Scaling

Let us be given the reference frame S_0 and another frame S_t. Our goal is to find φ_t as the *most isometric mapping* between S_0 and S_t, i.e., a mapping that minimizes the distortion of the geodesic distances. The isometric model guarantees that there exists φ_t with zero or at least near-zero distortion. Since we deal with discrete surfaces, we assume S_t to be sampled at the points $\{s_1, ..., s_{N_t}\}$ and represented as a triangular mesh. For notation convenience, we write S_t, intending its polyhedral approximation. We denote by $\Delta_t = (d_{S_t}(s_i, s_j))$ the matrix of all pairwise geodesic distances between the surface samples, computed numerically using, for example, the *fast marching method* (FMM) [15]. We are looking for a mapping $\varphi_t : \{s_1, ..., s_{N_0}\} \subset S_0 \to S_t$, such that $d_{S_0}(s_i, s_j)$ is as close as possible to $d_{S_t}(\varphi(s_i), \varphi(s_j))$ for all $(i, j) \in P \subseteq \{1, ..., N_0\} \times \{1, ..., N_0\}$ (some distances must be excluded; see Section 3.1). We refer to such φ_t as *partial embedding* of S_0 into S_t. Note that (S_t, d_{S_t}) is assumed continuous here, as $\varphi_t(s_i)$ can be any point on the polyhedron $\mathcal{S}_t$, i.e., can fall between the samples. In practice, we have to approximate the values of $d_{\mathcal{S}_t}$ from $(\{s_1, ..., s_{N_t}\} \subset \mathcal{S}_t, \mathbf{\Delta}_t)$.

The partial embedding φ_t can be computed by minimizing the *generalized stress* [16],

$$\sigma(s'_1, ..., s'_{N_0}) = \sum_{i=1}^{N_0} \sum_{j=i+1}^{N_0} w_{ij} \left(d_{\mathcal{S}_t}(s'_i, s'_j) - d_{\mathcal{S}_0}(s_i, s_j) \right)^2. \qquad (2)$$

Here, $w_{ij} = 1$ if $(i, j) \in P$ and 0 otherwise, and P denotes the set of pairs of points which are included into the stress computation. The optimization is performed directly on the images $s'_i = \varphi_t(s_i)$, in an MDS-like spirit. The optimal solution

$$\{s'_1, ..., s'_{N_0}\} = \operatorname*{argmin}_{s'_1, ..., s'_{N_0}} \sigma(s'_1, ..., s'_{N_0}), \qquad (3)$$

establishes a correspondence between the given N_0 points $\{s_1, ..., s_{N_0}\} \subset \mathcal{S}_0$ and N_0 points $\{\varphi_t(s_1), ..., \varphi_t(s_{N_0})\}$ on the polyhedron $\mathcal{S}_t$. In this way, we obtain a correspondence between a dense set of points, since N_0 can be as large as necessary. This is opposed to methods based on fiducial points, where the number of points is usually limited. Also note that the mapping we find is $\{s_1, ..., s_{N_0}\} \to \{s'_1, ..., s'_{N_0}\}$, and it will generally be bijective.

We refer to problem (3) as the GMDS (generalized MDS). It can be thought of as a generalization of MDS, in which the target Euclidean space is replaced with a general triangular mesh. Since s'_i may be arbitrary points between the samples of the polyhedron $\mathcal{S}_t$, the distances $d_{\mathcal{S}_t}$ between the vertices of $\mathcal{S}_t$ must be computed. We use the *three-point geodesic distance approximation*, a numerical procedure producing a computationally efficient $\mathcal{C}^1$-approximation for $d_{\mathcal{S}_t}$ and its derivatives, interpolating their values from the matrix $\mathbf{\Delta}_t$ of pairwise geodesic distances on $\mathcal{S}_t$ [16].

The numerical solution of the GMDS problem consists of bringing the stress (2) to a minimum over s'_i represented in some parameterization domain as vectors of coordinates $\mathbf{u}_i$. For example, if the surface $\mathcal{S}_t$ admits some global parameterization, say $[0, 1)^2 \mapsto \mathcal{S}_t$, every point on $\mathcal{S}_t$ can be represented by $\mathbf{u} \in [0, 1)^2$. Global parameterization is often readily available for objects acquired using many types of range scanners. Human faces usually fall into this category.[1] The minimization algorithm starts with some initial guess $\mathbf{u}_i^{(0)}$ of the points and proceeds by iteratively updating their locations, producing a decreasing sequence of stress values. In our implementation, we used a gradient descent algorithm safeguarded by inexact linesearch (Armijo rule) [18]. The complexity of the stress and its gradient computation is $\mathcal{O}(N_0^2)$. Since N_0 typically varies between tens to hundreds of points, GMDS is computationally efficient.

---

[1] For objects with more complicated topology, global parameterization may not exist; in this case, we represent a point on $\mathcal{S}_t$ by the triangle index m it and a vector $\mathbf{u}$ of *barycentric coordinates* [17] in the local coordinate system of that triangle.

Finally, we must note that GMDS is a non-convex optimization problem, like traditional MDS. Consequently, the use of convex optimization algorithms in this problem is liable to local converge [13]. Nevertheless, convex optimization is widely used in the MDS community if some precautions are taken in order to prevent convergence to local minima. Here, we use a multiscale optimization scheme that in practical applications shows good global convergence [16].

3.1   Selection of Weights

Expressions with open mouth do not fit into the isometric model, in which we tacitly assumed a fixed topology of the surface. Opening the mouth creates a "hole" in the facial surface. Resolving this problem is possible imposing a topological constraint on the facial surface, for example, assuming the mouth to be always open [19]. This is achieved by essentially cutting off the lip contour in the reference frame $\mathcal{S}_0$, either automatically or manually (in practice, the lip detector does not have to be very accurate).

An important issue arising after such a processing is the inconsistency of minimal geodesics. Let $\mathcal{S}_0'$ denote the reference frame after lip cropping. We assume that the geodesic distances on $\mathcal{S}_0'$ are given by the restricted metric, $d_{\mathcal{S}_0'}(s_1, s_2) = d_{\mathcal{S}_0}|_{\mathcal{S}_0'}(s_1, s_2)$ (this notation implies that $d_{\mathcal{S}_0'}(s_1, s_2) = d_{\mathcal{S}_0}(s_1, s_2)$ for all $s_1, s_2 \in \mathcal{S}_0'$). However, $d_{\mathcal{S}_0'}$ is computed numerically on $\mathcal{S}_0'$ and can be inconsistent with $d_{\mathcal{S}_0}|_{\mathcal{S}_0'}$. Potentially, the problem arises with minimal geodesics that are close to the boundary $\partial \mathcal{S}_0'$. Such geodesics can be substantially different on $\mathcal{S}_0$ and $\mathcal{S}_0'$, and the corresponding distances are therefore inconsistent. In order to resolve this problem, define the set P of consistent distances, excluding every pair of points (s_i, s_j), for which the minimal geodesic passes through the cropped region $\mathcal{S}_0 \setminus \mathcal{S}_0'$. Particularly, we exclude in this way the distances that would have been measured $\mathcal{S}_0$ across the lips on the original surface.

4   Applications

The knowledge of the intrinsic correspondence between two facial surfaces allows us to perform texture mapping onto all the frames of the video sequence. Moreover, we can also transform the extrinsic geometry of the faces, creating an interpolation or morphing effect between the 3D frames. Finally, the same approach can be applied to morphing between faces of different subjects.

4.1   Virtual Makeup

Our first application is the "virtual makeup" – expression-invariant mapping of a single texture image onto a 3D video of an animated face. We first draw the texture (represented as the field $\alpha_0 : \mathcal{S}_0 \mapsto \mathbb{R}^3$, consisting of the R, G and B channels) on the reference frame $\mathcal{S}_0$. Next, using the correspondences, we map the texture onto the rest of the frames in the 3D video.

A scheme of the procedure is depicted in Figure 2. The reference surface $\mathcal{S}_0$ first undergoes cropping that removes the lips and leaves only the facial contour.

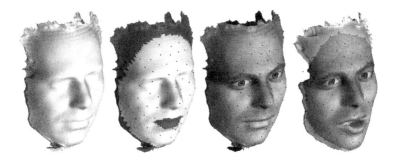

Fig. 2. Processing stages in the virtual makeup problem (left to right): reference surface; cropping and subsampling; texture mapping onto the reference surface; correspondence establishment using GMDS and texture mapping onto the target surface

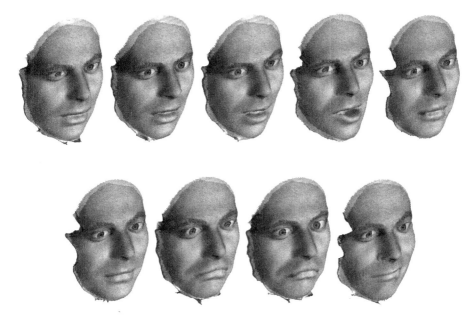

Fig. 3. Virtual makeup: a few frames from the video sequence shown in Figure 1, with a Shrek texture image mapped using the correspondence established by GMDS

The obtained region $\mathcal{S}_0'$ is subsampled using farthest point sampling, geodesic distance between the samples are computed using FMM [15]. The distances crossing the cropped lips region are assigned zero weights. Next, the texture α_0 is drawn on the reference surface. The points on $\mathcal{S}_0$ are then embedded into the target surface $\mathcal{S}_t$ using GMDS, which produces the correspondence φ_t. The mapping φ_t is used to interpolate the texture onto the surface $\mathcal{S}_t$, yielding a synthetic texture $\alpha_t = \alpha_0 \circ \varphi_t^{-1}$.

We tested our virtual makeup algorithm on a real 3D video sequence of a face, acquired by a structured light scanner at 640×480 spatial resolution, 3 frames per second (Figure 1). The lip contour in the reference frame was segmented manually. The cropped reference frame was sampled at 100 points; all the rest of the frames were sampled uniformly at about 3000 points. The surfaces were triangulated using Delaunay triangulation; then, the geodesic distances were computed using FMM [15]. The correspondence was found by embedding 100 points on $\mathcal{S}_0$ into $\mathcal{S}_t$ using a multiresolution optimization scheme, initialized with 8 points at the coarsest level. A MATLAB implementation of GMDS[2] was used. Figure 3 depicts a synthetic Shrek-like character, created from the video sequence by mapping a synthetic face texture image (drawn in Photoshop) using our algorithm. The faces produced in this way look real and the texture alignment is preserved even in case of strong facial expressions.

4.2   Expression Interpolation and Exaggeration

The correspondence found by means of GMDS can also be used to transform the extrinsic geometry of the surfaces. Let $\mathcal{S}_t$ and $\mathcal{S}_{t+1}$ be two adjacent frames in the 3D video, and let $\psi_t = \varphi_{t+1} \circ \varphi_t^{-1}$ be the correspondence between them. Let $\mathbf{s}_t : \mathcal{S}_t \mapsto \mathbb{R}^3$ and $\mathbf{s}_{t+1} : \mathcal{S}_{t+1} \mapsto \mathbb{R}^3$ denote the extrinsic Euclidean coordinates of $\mathcal{S}_t$ and $\mathcal{S}_{t+1}$, respectively. The extrinsic geometry of the surfaces is assumed to be at least roughly aligned by means of a rigid (Euclidean) transformation. Three points are enough for such an alignment. In our case, this is a simple task since the correspondence is known.

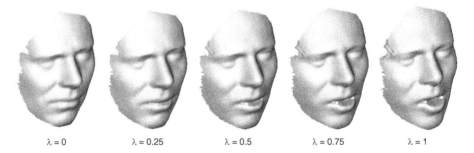

| $\lambda = 0$ | $\lambda = 0.25$ | $\lambda = 0.5$ | $\lambda = 0.75$ | $\lambda = 1$ |

Fig. 4. Expression interpolation between two frames in the video sequence (shown without texture to emphasize the natural look of the synthetic expressions)

We define a new surface $\mathcal{S}_{t+\lambda}$ with extrinsic coordinate given by the following convex combination:

$$\mathbf{s}_{t+\lambda}(s) = \lambda \mathbf{s}_t(s) + (1 - \lambda)\mathbf{s}_{t+1}(\psi_t(s)), \qquad (4)$$

for all $s \in \mathcal{S}_{t+\lambda}$ and $\lambda \in [0,1]$. The corresponding texture $\alpha_{t+\lambda}$ is defined in a similar manner. Varying the value of λ continuously from 0 to 1, we create a natural interpolation between the frames $\mathcal{S}_t$ and $\mathcal{S}_{t+1}$. The synthetic surfaces obtained this way have a realistic look (Figure 4). Such an interpolation is useful, for example, as a method of temporal super-resolution of a 3D video. Allowing for $\lambda < 0$ or $\lambda > 1$, we can create a new, exaggerated facial expression (Figure 5).

---

[2] Codes and demos will be published on http://tosca.cs.technion.ac.il

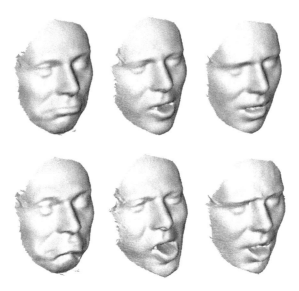

Fig. 5. Expression exaggeration. First row: original expressions. Second row: exaggerated expressions.

4.3   Texture Substitution and Morphing Between Different Faces

Relaxing the basic assumption of the isometric model, we can use GMDS in order to find the correspondence between two different faces. Though two different facial surfaces are not even approximately isometric, the minimum-distortion mapping appears to be a surprisingly good correspondence even in this case. In our example, as S_0 and S_1, we took a female and a male face from the Notre Dame database [20]. Each face was subsampled to approximately 3000 points and triangulated. The shapes were roughly aligned. Fifty points were taken on S_0 and embedded into S_1 using GMDS. The resulting correspondence φ_1 was then used to map the texture α_0 from S_0 to S_1. Figure 6 shows a synthetic face obtained by taking S_1 with the texture $\tilde{\alpha}_1 = \alpha_0 \circ \varphi_1^{-1}$ (male geometry with a

Fig. 6. Texture substitution: GMDS is used to find the minumum-distortion mapping between face S_0 and S_1 (by embedding S_0 into S_1). Using this mapping as a correspondence, the texture α_0 is mapped onto S_1.

Fig. 7. Morphing: the correspondence is used to transform the texture and the extrinsic geometry of S_0 into the corresponding texture and extrinsic geometry of S_1

female texture). Figure 7 shows a morphing effect between S_0 and S_1, obtained by interpolating the extrinsic geometry and the texture according to (4).

5   Conclusions

We presented an automatic geometric procedure for establishing dense correspondence between facial surfaces. Exploiting the empirical fact that facial expressions can be modelled as isometries, our approach is based on finding the minimum-distortion mapping between two surfaces. This mapping is computed by a procedure similar to multidimensional scaling (GMDS). The algorithm is computationally efficient, though currently not real-time. Our preliminary results show that near real-time performance can be achieved by exploiting multigrid optimization [21] and implementation on graphics processors (GPU).

Unlike feature-based methods, our approach does not require feature detection and tracking. We find correspondence between an arbitrarily dense set of points, as opposed to feature-based methods, which are usually limited to a small set of fiducial points that can be robustly detected and tracked. Moreover, our approach is applicable when 2D information (texture) is not available. The proposed method is generic and has a wide range of uses in computer graphics and computer vision. We demonstrated some applications, including the "virtual makeup" by expression-invariant texture mapping onto an animated face, texture substitution and morphing.

References

1. Y. Lee, D. Terzopoulos, and K. Waters. Realistic modeling for facial animation. In *Proc. SIGGRAPH*, volume 16, pages 55–62, 1995.
2. T. Vetter and V. Blanz. A morphable model for the synthesis of 3D faces. In *Proc. SIGGRAPH*, 1999.
3. F. Pighin, R. Szeliski, and D. H. Salesin. Modeling and animating realistic faces from images. *IJCV*, 50(2):143–169, November 2002.
4. V. Blanz, C. Basso, T. Poggio, and T. Vetter. Reanimating faces in images and video. *Computer Graphics Forum*, 22(3):641–650, 2003.
5. S. E. Brennan. The caricature generator. *Leonardo*, 18:170–178, 1985.

6. G. Zigelman, R. Kimmel, and N. Kiryati. Texture mapping using surface flattening via multi-dimensional scaling. *IEEE Trans. Visualization and computer graphics*, 9(2):198–207, 2002.

7. K. Zhou, J. Snyder, B. Guo, and H.-Y. Shum. Iso-charts: Stretch-driven mesh parameterization using spectral analysis. In *Proc. ACM SGP*, pages 45–54, 2004.

8. M. Alexa. Merging polyhedral shapes with scattered features. *The Visual Computer*, 16:26–37, 2000.

9. V. Kraevoy, A. Sheffer, and C. Gotsman. Matchmaker: Constructing constrained texture maps. In *Proc. SIGGRAPH*, 2003.

10. P. S. Huang, C. P. Zhang, and F. P. Chiang. High speed 3-D shape measurement based on digital fringe projection. *Optical Engineering*, 42(1):163–168, 2003.

11. G. J. Edwards, T. F. Cootes, and C. J. Taylor. Face recognition using active appearance models. In *Proc. ECCV*, 1998.

12. A. M. Bronstein, M. M. Bronstein, and R. Kimmel. Three-dimensional face recognition. *IJCV*, 64(1):5–30, August 2005.

13. I. Borg and P. Groenen. *Modern multidimensional scaling - theory and applications.* Springer-Verlag, Berlin Heidelberg New York, 1997.

14. A. M. Bronstein, M. M. Bronstein, and R. Kimmel. Generalized multidimensional scaling: a framework for isometry-invariant partial surface matching. *Proc. National Academy of Sciences*, 103(5):1168–1172, January 2006.

15. R. Kimmel and J. A. Sethian. Computing geodesic on manifolds. In *Proc. National Academy of Science*, volume 95, pages 8431–8435, 1998.

16. A. M. Bronstein, M. M. Bronstein, and R. Kimmel. Efficient computation of isometry-invariant distances between surfaces. Technical Report CIS-2006-02, Dept. of Computer Science, Technion, Israel, 2005.

17. M. S. Floater and K. Hormann. *Advances on Multiresolution in Geometric Modelling*, chapter Surface Parameterization: a Tutorial and Survey. Springer-Verlag, Heidelberg, 2004. To appear.

18. D. Bertsekas. *Nonlinear programming.* Atlanta Scientific, 2 edition, 1999.

19. A. M. Bronstein, M. M. Bronstein, and R. Kimmel. Expression-invariant representations for human faces. Technical Report CIS-2005-01, Dept. of Computer Science, Technion, Israel, 2005.

20. K. Chang, K. W. Bowyer, and P. J. Flynn. Face recognition using 2D and 3D facial data. In *ACM Workshop on Multimodal User Authentication*, pages 25–32, 2003.

21. M. M. Bronstein, A. M. Bronstein, R. Kimmel, and I. Yavneh. Multigrid multidimensional scaling. *Numerical Linear Algebra with Applications (NLAA)*, 13:149–171, March-April 2006.

Matching Two-Dimensional Articulated Shapes Using Generalized Multidimensional Scaling

Alexander M. Bronstein, Michael M. Bronstein,
Alfred M. Bruckstein, and Ron Kimmel

Department of Computer Science,
Technion - Israel Institute of Technology, 32000 Haifa, Israel
{alexbron, bronstein}@ieee.org, {freddy, ron}@cs.technion.ac.il

Abstract. We present a theoretical and computational framework for matching of two-dimensional articulated shapes. Assuming that articulations can be modeled as near-isometries, we show an axiomatic construction of an articulation-invariant distance between shapes, formulated as a generalized multidimensional scaling (GMDS) problem and solved efficiently. Some numerical results demonstrating the accuracy of our method are presented.

1 Introduction

Recognition of two-dimensional shapes (silhouettes) is an important problem with a wide range of applications, extensively addressed in computer vision literature (see e.g. [1,2,3]). One of the main difficulties in shape recognition arises from the fact that natural objects are non-rigid. A simplified model capturing to some degree this flexibility is the *articulated shape* model, assuming that the object is composed of rigid parts, each of which has a certain freedom to move. Such a model appears to be applicable to many objects in nature, for example, humans, animals, tools, etc [4].

Recently, Ling and Jacobs [5] proposed to use the inner (geodesic) distances for recognition of articulated shapes. The main claim is that the geodesic distances are insensitive to articulations and therefore can be used as robust descriptors of the shape. This approach is related to previous works of Elad and Kimmel on bending-invariant representations of 3D objects [6], in which multidimensional scaling (MDS) was applied to the geodesic distances measured on the shape in order to obtain its intrinsic-geometric representation.

Our current paper is strongly motivated by the study of Ling and Jacobs. Using the model presented in [5], we describe articulations as isometric (distance-preserving) transformations of the shape. The main contribution of this paper is an axiomatic construction of a distance that allows to discern between geometrically different articulated shapes while being articulation-invariant. Our distance is free of error introduced by approaches based on Euclidean MDS [6] and also allows matching of partially occluded shapes. The computation of our distance is formulated as a generalized MDS problem (GMDS) and can be solved efficiently.

F.J. Perales and R.B. Fisher (Eds.): AMDO 2006, LNCS 4069, pp. 48–57, 2006.

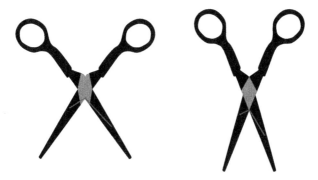

Fig. 1. Example of an articulated shape, consisting of four parts (black) and one joint (gray). The geodesic distance between two points is shown in red. Note that the geodesic distances change is bounded by the diameter of the joint.

This paper consists of five sections. In Section 2, we present the isometric model of articulated shapes and our articulation-invariant distance. Section 3 deals with numerical computation of the distance between articulated shapes using the GMDS. In Section 4, we present an experimental validation of our approach. Section 5 concludes the paper.

2   Isometric Model for Articulated Shapes

Let $\mathcal{S}$ be a shape, represented as a compact, connected, flat two-dimensional manifold with boundary. The metric on $\mathcal{S}$ is assumed to be Euclidean. Following Ling and Jacobs [5], we represent $\mathcal{S}$ as a union of K disjoint *parts* $\mathcal{S}_1, ..., \mathcal{S}_K$ and L *joints* $\mathcal{J}_1, ..., \mathcal{J}_L$ (Figure 1). We call such $\mathcal{S}$ an *articulated shape*. The minimal geodesics (shortest paths) on $\mathcal{S}$ consist of linear segments and portions of the boundary [5]. The geodesic distances between two points $s_1, s_2 \in \mathcal{S}$ are denoted by $d_{\mathcal{S}}(s_1, s_2)$. An articulated shape with $\sum_{i=1}^{L} \mathrm{diam}\mathcal{J}_i \leq \epsilon$ is called an ϵ-*articulated shape*. We denote by $\mathbb{M}_\epsilon$ the space of all ϵ-articulated shapes; $\mathbb{M}$ denotes $\mathbb{M}_\infty$.

An *articulation* is a mapping $f : \mathcal{S} \to \mathcal{S}' \subset \mathbb{R}^2$, which transforms each part $\mathcal{S}_i$ in a rigid manner and preserves the topology of the whole shape, such that different parts remain disjoint. For an ϵ-articulated shape, articulations are ϵ-*isometries*, i.e., have *distortion*

$$\mathrm{dis}\, f \equiv \sup_{s_1, s_2 \in \mathcal{S}} |d_{\mathcal{S}}(s_1, s_2) - d_{\mathcal{Q}}(f(s_1), f(s_2))| \leq \epsilon. \tag{1}$$

An ideal articulated shape has point joints ($\epsilon = 0$) and its articulations are true isometries. In practice, $\epsilon > 0$, yet, the joints can be often assumed significantly smaller compared to the parts [5]. We call this assumption the *isometric model* of articulated shapes.

The shape $\mathcal{S}' = \mathcal{S} \cap \mathcal{Q}$ produced by cutting $\mathcal{S}$ with a planar shape $\mathcal{Q}$, such that $\mathcal{S}'$ has the same topology of $\mathcal{S}$ is said to be a *cut* of $\mathcal{S}$; if $\mathcal{Q}$ is convex, $\mathcal{S}'$ is said to be a *convex cut*. Note that in general, any articulated shape can be cut of the plane, assuming the cutting shape is sufficiently complicated. The intrinsic geometries of $\mathcal{S}$ and $\mathcal{S}'$ may be different in this case. However, a convex cut appears to preserve the intrinsic geometry, in the sense that for every $s_1, s_2 \in \mathcal{S}'$, $d_{\mathcal{S}'}(s_1, s_2) = d_{\mathcal{S}}(s_1, s_2)$.

In practical applications, articulated shapes are usually represented as discrete binary images sampled at a finite number of points (pixels). A finite set $\mathcal{S}_r = \{s_1, ..., s_N\} \subset \mathcal{S}$ is said to be an *r-sampling* of $\mathcal{S}$, if $\cup_{i=1}^N B(s_i, r) = \mathcal{S}$, where $B(s_i, r)$ denotes the Euclidean ball of radius r centered at s_i. Since the shapes are assumed to be compact, every ϵ-articulated shape has a finite r-sampling for every $r > 0$.

2.1   Measuring Distance Between Articulated Shapes

Comparison of articulated shapes can be performed by defining a *distance* $d_{\mathbb{M}}$: $\mathbb{M} \times \mathbb{M} \mapsto [0, \infty)$. Here, we develop an axiomatic approach, requiring $d_{\mathbb{M}}(\mathcal{S}, \mathcal{Q})$ to obey the following set of axioms:

A1. *Articulation invariance*: $d_{\mathbb{M}}(\mathcal{S}, f(\mathcal{S})) \leq \epsilon$ for all $\mathcal{S} \in \mathbb{M}_\epsilon$ and all articulations f of $\mathcal{S}$.
A2. *Dissimilarity*: if $d_{\mathbb{M}}(\mathcal{S}_1, \mathcal{S}_2) > \epsilon$, then there does not exist $\mathcal{S} \in \mathbb{M}_\epsilon$ and two articulations f_1, f_2 of $\mathcal{S}$, such that $\mathcal{S}_1 = f_1(\mathcal{S})$ and $\mathcal{S}_2 = f_2(\mathcal{S})$.
A3. *Partial matching*: for every $\mathcal{S} \in \mathbb{M}_\epsilon$ and its convex cut $\mathcal{S}'$, $d_{\mathbb{M}}(\mathcal{S}, \mathcal{S}') = 0$.
A4. *Triangle inequality*: for every $\mathcal{S}_1, \mathcal{S}_2, \mathcal{S}_3 \in \mathbb{M}_\epsilon$, $d_{\mathbb{M}}(\mathcal{S}_1, \mathcal{S}_2) + d_{\mathbb{M}}(\mathcal{S}_2, \mathcal{S}_3) \geq d_{\mathbb{M}}(\mathcal{S}_1, \mathcal{S}_3)$.
A5. *Sampling consistency*: for every r-samplings $\mathcal{S}_r$ of $\mathcal{S}$ and $\mathcal{Q}_r$ of $\mathcal{Q}$, $|d_{\mathbb{M}}(\mathcal{S}, \mathcal{Q}) - d_{\mathbb{M}}(\mathcal{S}_r, \mathcal{Q}_r)| \leq 2r$.

In simple words, axioms A1–A2 guarantee that $d_{\mathbb{M}}(\mathcal{S}, \mathcal{Q})$ is a good similarity measure, assigning large distances for dissimilar shapes and small distances for similar shapes, while being insensitive to articulations. Note that we do not demand the converse of A1 to hold. In fact, two different ϵ-articulated shapes with intrinsic geometry differing by less than ϵ cannot be discerned in the framework of the isometric model. Axiom A3 allows us to match a portion of a shape to its whole. In order to make the partial matching well-defined, we restrict the cut to be convex. Axiom A4 provides basic metric properties. Note that demanding A3, $d_{\mathbb{M}}(\mathcal{S}, \mathcal{Q})$ cannot be made symmetric and thus the triangle inequality holds only in a non-symmetric manner. Finally, Axiom A5 enables a discretization and a numerical computation of $d_{\mathbb{M}}(\mathcal{S}, \mathcal{Q})$.

Here, we use the following distance between articulated shapes

$$d_{\mathbb{M}}(\mathcal{S}, \mathcal{Q}) = \inf_{\varphi : \mathcal{Q} \mapsto \mathcal{S}} \mathrm{dis}\, \varphi, , \tag{2}$$

which essentially measures the least possible distortion of embedding shape $\mathcal{Q}$ into shape $\mathcal{S}$. This distance is intimately related to the Gromov-Hausdorff distance [7,8,9]. A very similar distance has been proposed in [10] for bending-invariant matching of three-dimensional objects.

Theorem 1. $d_{\mathrm{M}}(\mathcal{S}, \mathcal{Q})$ *in (2) obeys axioms A1-5.*

Proof. A1: Let $\mathcal{S}$ be a planar shape and $f : \mathcal{S} \to \mathcal{Q}$ a surjective mapping with dis $f \leq \epsilon$. Define $\varphi : f(\mathcal{S}) \to \mathcal{S}$ by assigning to every $q \in Q$ an arbitrary point $s \in f^{-1}(q)$ in the pre-image of q. Since $f(\varphi(q)) = f(s) = q$, one has $|d_{\mathcal{Q}}(q, q') - d_{\mathcal{S}}(\varphi(q), \varphi(q'))| \leq \mathrm{dis}\, f \leq \epsilon$ for every $q, q' \in \mathcal{Q}$. Consequently, $d_{\mathrm{M}}(\mathcal{S}, \mathcal{Q}) \leq \epsilon$.

A2: Let there be two planar shapes $\mathcal{S}_1$ and $\mathcal{S}_2$ such that $d_{\mathrm{M}}(\mathcal{S}_1, \mathcal{S}_2) > \epsilon$. Assume that there exists a mapping $\varphi : \mathcal{S}_2 \to \mathcal{S}_3$ with dis $\varphi \leq \epsilon$. Then, $|d_{\mathcal{Q}}(q, q') - d_{\mathcal{S}}(\varphi(q), \varphi(q'))| \leq \mathrm{dis}\, f \leq \epsilon$ for every $q, q' \in \mathcal{Q}$ and, clearly, $d_{\mathrm{M}}(\mathcal{S}, \mathcal{Q}) \leq \epsilon$ in contradiction to the assumption. Hence, $\mathcal{S}_1$ and $\mathcal{S}_2$ are not ϵ-isometric.

A3: Let there be a planar shape $\mathcal{S}$ and $\mathcal{S}' \subset \mathcal{S}$ a convex cut of $\mathcal{S}$. Since for every $s, s' \in \mathcal{S}'$, $d_{\mathcal{S}'}(s, s') = d_{\mathcal{S}}(s, s')$, the identity mapping $\varphi : \mathcal{S}' \to \mathcal{S}$ yields $|d_{\mathcal{S}'}(s, s') - d_{\mathcal{S}}(\varphi(s), \varphi(s'))| = 0$. Hence, $d_{\mathrm{M}}(\mathcal{S}, \mathcal{Q}) \leq \mathrm{dis}\, \varphi = 0$.

A4: Let there be three planar shapes $\mathcal{S}_1, \mathcal{S}_2$ and $\mathcal{S}_3$ such that $d_{\mathrm{M}}(\mathcal{S}_1, \mathcal{S}_2) < \epsilon_1$ and $d_{\mathrm{M}}(\mathcal{S}_2, \mathcal{S}_3) < \epsilon_2$. Then, there exist two mappings $\varphi_1 : \mathcal{S}_2 \to \mathcal{S}_1$ and $\varphi_2 : \mathcal{S}_3 \to \mathcal{S}_2$ with dis $\varphi_1 < \epsilon_1$ and dis $\varphi_2 < \epsilon_2$. Denote by $\psi = \varphi_1 \circ \varphi_2 : \mathcal{S}_3 \to \mathcal{S}_1$. Invoking the triangle inequality for real numbers, one has

$$
\begin{aligned}
|d_{\mathcal{S}_3}(s, s') - d_{\mathcal{S}_1}(\psi(s), \psi(s'))| &\leq \\
\leq |d_{\mathcal{S}_3}(s, s') - d_{\mathcal{S}_2}(\varphi_2(s), \varphi_2(s'))| &+ |d_{\mathcal{S}_2}(\varphi_2(s), \varphi_2(s')) - d_{\mathcal{S}_1}(\psi(s), \psi(s'))| \\
&\leq \mathrm{dis}\, \varphi_2 + \mathrm{dis}\, \varphi_1 < \epsilon_1 + \epsilon_2
\end{aligned}
$$

for every $s, s' \in \mathcal{S}_3$. Hence, dis $\psi < \epsilon_1 + \epsilon_2$, implying $d_{\mathrm{M}}(\mathcal{S}_1, \mathcal{S}_3) \leq d_{\mathrm{M}}(\mathcal{S}_1, \mathcal{S}_2) + d_{\mathrm{M}}(\mathcal{S}_2, \mathcal{S}_3)$.

A5: Using the (non-symmetric) triangle inequality, one has $d_{\mathrm{M}}(\mathcal{S}, \mathcal{Q}) \leq d_{\mathrm{M}}(\mathcal{S}, \mathcal{Q}_r) + d_{\mathrm{M}}(\mathcal{Q}_r, \mathcal{Q}) \leq d_{\mathrm{M}}(\mathcal{S}_r, \mathcal{Q}_r) + d_{\mathrm{M}}(\mathcal{S}, \mathcal{S}_r) + d_{\mathrm{M}}(\mathcal{Q}_r, \mathcal{Q})$ and, similarly, $d_{\mathrm{M}}(\mathcal{S}_r, \mathcal{Q}_r) \leq d_{\mathrm{M}}(\mathcal{S}, \mathcal{Q}) + d_{\mathrm{M}}(\mathcal{S}, \mathcal{S}_r) + d_{\mathrm{M}}(\mathcal{Q}_r, \mathcal{Q})$, yielding $|d_{\mathrm{M}}(\mathcal{S}, \mathcal{Q}) - d_{\mathrm{M}}(\mathcal{S}_r, \mathcal{Q}_r)| \leq d_{\mathrm{M}}(\mathcal{S}, \mathcal{S}_r) + d_{\mathrm{M}}(\mathcal{Q}_r, \mathcal{Q})$. Since $\mathcal{S}_r \subset \mathcal{S}$ and $d_{\mathcal{S}_r} = d_{\mathcal{S}}|_{\mathcal{S}^r}$, according to (A3), $d_{\mathrm{M}}(\mathcal{S}, \mathcal{S}_r) = 0$. It is therefore sufficient to show that $d_{\mathrm{M}}(\mathcal{Q}_r, \mathcal{Q}) \leq 2r$. Let us define a mapping $\varphi : \mathcal{Q} \to \mathcal{Q}_r$ as $\varphi(q) = \arg \min_{q' \in \mathcal{Q}_r} d_{\mathcal{Q}}(q, q')$ (the mininmum exists, since $\mathcal{Q}_r$ can be replaced by a finite sub-covering). Since Q_r is an r-covering, $d_{\mathcal{Q}}(q, \varphi(q)) \leq r$ for every $q \in \mathcal{Q}$. If q, q' are both in $\mathcal{Q}_r$, then $|d_{\mathcal{Q}}(q, q') - d_{\mathcal{Q}}(\varphi(q), \varphi(q'))| = 0$. If $q \in \mathcal{Q}_r$ and $q' \in \mathcal{Q}$, then $|d_{\mathcal{Q}}(q, q') - d_{\mathcal{Q}}(\varphi(q), \varphi(q'))| = |d_{\mathcal{Q}}(q, q') - d_{\mathcal{Q}}(q, \varphi(q'))| \leq d_{\mathcal{Q}}(q', \varphi(q')) \leq r$. If both $q, q' \in \mathcal{Q}$, then $|d_{\mathcal{Q}}(q, q') - d_{\mathcal{Q}}(\varphi(q), \varphi(q'))| \leq d_{\mathcal{Q}}(q, \varphi(q)) + d_{\mathcal{Q}}(q', \varphi(q')) \leq 2r$. $\qquad \square$

In practice, it is useful to replace $d_{\mathrm{M}}(\mathcal{S}, \mathcal{Q})$ by an L_p-norm analog,

$$
d_{\mathrm{M}}^p(\mathcal{S}, \mathcal{Q}) = \left(\frac{1}{A_{\mathcal{Q}}^2} \inf_{\varphi : \mathcal{Q} \to \mathcal{S}} \int \int_{\mathcal{Q} \times \mathcal{Q}} (d_{\mathcal{Q}}(q, q') - d_{\mathcal{S}}(\varphi(q), \varphi(q')))^p \, dq dq' \right)^{1/p}, \quad (3)
$$

where dq is the standard area measure in $\mathbb{R}^2$ and $A_{\mathcal{Q}} = \int_{\mathcal{Q}} dq$. In the limit $p \to \infty$, d_{M}^p is just d_{M}.

Apart from giving a quantitative measure of similarity of two shapes, computation of $d_{\mathrm{M}}^p(\mathcal{S}, \mathcal{Q})$ also yields a *correspondence* φ between $\mathcal{S}$ and $\mathcal{Q}$. Such correspondence may be useful in many applications including tracking of silhouettes in video sequences and alignment of articulated shapes.

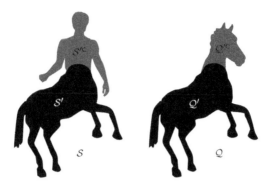

Fig. 2. A centaur (left) and a horse (right) share the bottom part of the body and differ in the upper part. This example is inspired by [11].

2.2   Comparison of Partially Overlapping Shapes

By virtue of axiom A3, $d_{\mathbb{M}}$ allows to compare between a shape and its portion. However, in a more general setting of partial matching, one shape does not necessarily has to be a portion of the other. As a motivating example, consider two planar shapes $\mathcal{S}$ and $\mathcal{Q}$ in Figure 2, which share some large similar portions $\mathcal{S}' \subset \mathcal{S}$ and $\mathcal{Q}' \subset \mathcal{Q}$, yet also have dissimilar portions $\mathcal{S}'^c = \mathcal{S} \setminus \mathcal{S}'$ and $\mathcal{Q}'^c = \mathcal{Q} \setminus \mathcal{Q}'$. We now outline a method to handle this setting as well.

Let us assume that the computation of $d_{\mathbb{M}}^p(\mathcal{S}, \mathcal{Q})$ gives us a minimum-distortion mapping $\varphi : \mathcal{Q} \mapsto \mathcal{S}$.[1] We define the *local distortion* at a point q as

$$\mathrm{dis}(q; \varphi) = \left(\frac{1}{A_{\mathcal{Q}}} \int_{\mathcal{Q}} (d_{\mathcal{Q}}(q, q') - d_{\mathcal{S}}(\varphi(q), \varphi(q')))^p \, dq \right)^{1/p}. \tag{4}$$

This allows to attribute each point in $q \in \mathcal{Q}$ a quantitative measure of metric distortion introduced by the mapping φ to the distances between all pairs of the form (q, q'), $q' \in \mathcal{Q}$. We can define a portion $\mathcal{Q}'(\rho) = \{q : \mathrm{dis}(q; \varphi) \le \rho\}$ consisting of all points with local distortion below some threshold ρ. This allows to segment $\mathcal{Q}$ to regions similar to $\mathcal{S}$ and those dissimilar to $\mathcal{S}$.

Omitting technical details, we can measure the relative area of the complement of $\mathcal{Q}'(\rho)$, $\mu(\rho) = 1 - \frac{1}{A_{\mathcal{Q}}} \int_{\mathcal{Q}'(\rho)} dq$, and construct a generalized distance function $d'_{\mathbb{M}}(\mathcal{S}, \mathcal{Q})$ assigning to each pair of shapes $(\mathcal{S}, \mathcal{Q})$ a monotonically decreasing function $\mu : [0, \mathrm{diam}\, \mathcal{Q}] \mapsto [0, 1]$. Such a function, essentially similar to a receiver operator characteristic (ROC) curve, allows many definitions of a partial order relation, which is necessary for measuring the similarity of the shapes. For example, given that the objects subject to comparison are ϵ-articulated shapes, we can set $\rho = \epsilon$ and use the relative area $\mu(\epsilon)$ of the dissimilar portions as the similarity measure. A dual approach is to fix some μ_0 (say, 80% of the shape area) and use ρ for which $\mu(\rho) = \mu_0$ as a measure similarity.

---

[1] We omit here some technical details: in reality, φ does not necessarily exist, yet $\mathrm{dis}(q; \varphi)$ can still be defined using a sequence of mappings φ_n with convergent distortion.

3   Generalized Multidimensional Scaling

We now address the issue of practical computation of d_M^p. Let $\mathcal{S}_r = \{s_1, ..., s_M\}$ and $\mathcal{Q}_r = \{q_1, ..., q_N\}$ be finite r-samplings of articulated shapes $\mathcal{S}$ and $\mathcal{Q}$ (for example, r can be the pixel size when the shapes are represented as binary images) and $\Delta_{\mathcal{S}} = (d_{\mathcal{S}}(s_i, s_j))$ and $\Delta_{\mathcal{Q}} = (d_{\mathcal{Q}}(q_i, q_j))$ be the $M \times M$ and $N \times N$ matrices of geodesic distances between the samples of $\mathcal{S}_r$ and $\mathcal{Q}_r$, respectively. The distances are computed numerically using the *fast marching method* (FMM) [12,13].

In this discrete setting, d_M^p can be formulated as

$$d_M^p(\mathcal{S}_r, \mathcal{Q}_r) = \left(\min_{s'_1, ..., s'_N} \sum_{i,j=1}^N a_i a_j \left| d_{\mathcal{Q}}(q_i, q_j) - d_{\mathcal{S}}(s'_i, s'_j) \right|^p \right)^{1/p}, \tag{5}$$

for $p < \infty$, and

$$d_M^\infty(\mathcal{S}_r, \mathcal{Q}_r) = \min_{\tau \geq 0, s'_1, ..., s'_N} \tau \text{ s.t } \left| d_{\mathcal{Q}}(q_i, q_j) - d_{\mathcal{S}}(s'_i, s'_j) \right| \leq \tau \tag{6}$$

for $p = \infty$, where $s'_i = \varphi(q_i)$ denote the image of q_i under the mapping φ. The weights a_i are selected as the normalized areas of the Voronoi cells of q_i. In practice, when the sampling is sufficiently regular, the simple choice $a_i = 1/N$ appears to be a more convenient alternative.

Problems (5) and (6) can be considered as a generalization of *multidimensional scaling* (MDS) [14] to general metric spaces. We call it the *generalized* MDS or GMDS for short. The optimization is performed directly on the images $s'_i = \varphi(q_i)$, in the spirit of MDS. Since s'_i may fall between the samples of $\mathcal{S}$, one has to compute the geodesic distances $d_{\mathcal{S}}$ between any two arbitrary points in $\mathcal{S}$. For this purpose, we use the *three-point geodesic distance approximation*, a numerical procedure is to produce a computationally efficient $\mathcal{C}^1$-approximation for $d_{\mathcal{S}}$ and its derivatives, interpolating their values from the matrix $\Delta_{\mathcal{S}}$ of pairwise geodesic distances in $\mathcal{S}$ [9].

The numerical solution of the GMDS problem consists of finding an unconstrained minimum of the following *generalized stress function*

$$\sigma(\mathbf{u}_1, ..., \mathbf{u}_N) = \sum_{i,j=1}^N w_{ij} \left| \delta_{ij} - d_{\mathcal{S}}(\mathbf{u}_i, \mathbf{u}_j) \right|^p, \tag{7}$$

where $\delta_{ij} = d_{\mathcal{Q}}(q_i, q_j)$ denote the elements of $\Delta_{\mathcal{Q}}$, $w_{ij} = a_i a_j$, and $\mathbf{u}_i \in \mathcal{S}$ are vectors of coordinates in $\mathbb{R}^2$ representing s'_i. When $p = \infty$, constrained minimization is used. In our implementation, we used a gradient descent algorithm safeguarded by inexact linesearch (Armijo rule) [15]. The complexity of the stress and its gradient computation is $\mathcal{O}(N^2)$. Typically, N varies between tens to hundreds of points, therefore GMDS is computationally efficient.

Like the traditional MDS, GMDS is a non-convex optimization problem, and therefore convergence to local minima rather than to the global one is possible[14]. Nevertheless, convex optimization is widely used in the MDS community if some precautions are taken in order to prevent convergence to local minima. Here, we use a multiscale optimization scheme that in practical applications shows good global convergence [9,16].

4   Results

In order to assess the proposed approach, three experiments were performed. In the first experiment, the Tools A dataset[2] consisting of 35 shapes of 7 different tools, was used (see Figure 3). The tools were classified into 4 groups: scissors, pliers, pincers, cutters and knife. All the tools excepting the knife have four parts and one joint. The knife has three parts and two joints. GMDS was used to compute d_M^p with $p = 2$ between the shapes. We used a multiresolution optimization scheme, initialized at 5 points at the coarsest resolution. A total of $N = 25$ points were used. Figure 4 visualizes these distances as Euclidean similarity pattern. One can observe that the shapes are clearly distinguishable and form groups corresponding to their classification (e.g. two different shapes of scissors and pliers are close to each other). Note that different articulations are also distinguishable, such that one (at least theoretically) can infer the articulation constant ϵ of each shape.

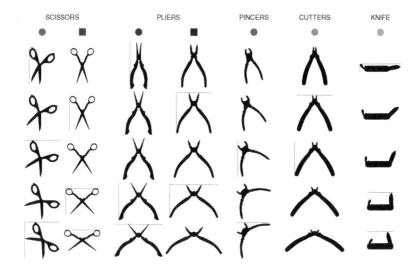

Fig. 3. Articulated shapes from the Tools A data set

In the second experiment, three partial probes for each of the seven tools from the Tools A dataset were used in matching against the set of 35 full shapes. Figure 5 presents the three first closest matches; due space limitations, only representative results are shown. In all cases, the first match was found correctly.

---

[2] All the data and codes will be available at http://tosca.cs.technion.ac.il

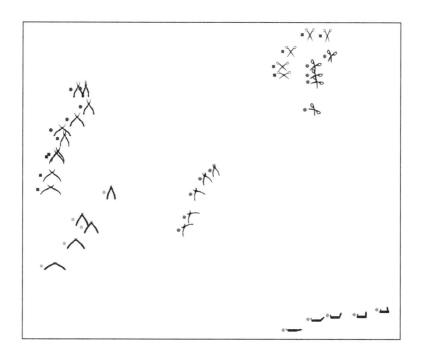

Fig. 4. Visualization of distances between the Tools A shapes

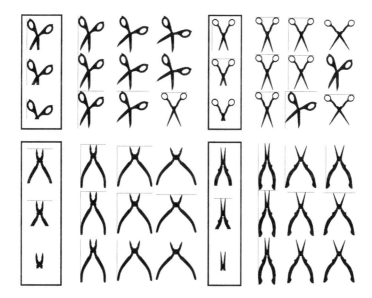

Fig. 5. Retrieval with partial probes: first three closest matches found for different partial probes (outlined)

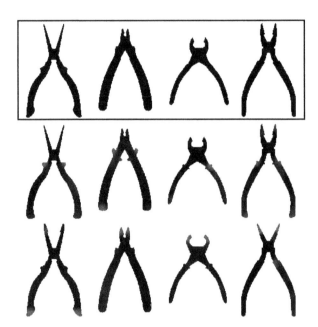

Fig. 6. Local distortion maps obtained by embedding two probes into model shapes from the Tools B dataset (top row). Distortion is represented in shades of red (high distortion) and black (low distortion).

In the third experiment, the Tools B dataset consisting of three instances with minute modifications of small details of four objects from the Tools A set were used. GMDS was used to compute the correspondence φ between the shapes; the embedded shapes were discretized at $N = 50$ points. Figure 6 depicts the local distortion maps, obtained by embedding various shapes to five references models from the Tools B dataset. Note that local distortion maps manifest high distortions in dissimilar regions, which allow to capture most of the local differences between the shapes; we attribute some misses to sampling errors.

5   Conclusions

We presented a generic framework for the recognition of articulated two-dimensional shapes based on the isometric model. According to this model, articulations arise from near-isometric transformations and therefore inflict small changes to the geodesic distances measured inside the shape. We showed a distance able to distinguish between shapes insensitively to their articulations. This distance is also capable of performing partial matching of shapes and finding local dissimilarities between them. The distance computation is formulated as an MDS-like problem, which is efficiently solved using smooth optimization techniques.

References

1. D. Geiger R. Basri, L. Costa and D. Jacobs. Determining the similarity of deformable shapes. *Vision Research*, 38:2365–2385, 1998.
2. Y. Gdalyahu and D. Weinshall. Flexible syntactic matching of curves and its application to automatic hierarchical classification of silhouettes. *IEEE Trans. PAMI*, 21:1312–1328, 1999.
3. S. Belongie, J. Malik, and J. Puzicha. Shape matching and object recognition using shape context. *IEEE Trans. PAMI*, 24:509–522, 2002.
4. J. Zhang, R. Collins, and Y. Liu. Representation and matching of articulated shapes. In *Proc. CVPR*, volume 2, pages 342 – 349, June 2004.
5. H. Ling and D. Jacobs. Using the inner-distance for classification of articulated shapes. In *Proc. CVPR*, 2005.
6. A. Elad and R. Kimmel. Bending invariant representations for surfaces. In *Proc. CVPR*, pages 168–174, 2001.
7. M. Gromov. *Structures métriques pour les variétés riemanniennes*. Number 1 in Textes Mathématiques. 1981.
8. F. Mémoli and G. Sapiro. A theoretical and computational framework for isometry invariant recognition of point cloud data. *Foundations of Computational Mathematics*, 2005. to appear.
9. A. M. Bronstein, M. M. Bronstein, and R. Kimmel. Efficient computation of isometry-invariant distances between surfaces. Technical report, Dept. of Computer Science, Technion, Israel, 2005. submitted.
10. A. M. Bronstein, M. M. Bronstein, and R. Kimmel. Generalized multidimensional scaling: a framework for isometry-invariant partial surface matching. *Proc. National Academy of Sciences*, 103(5):1168–1172, January 2006.
11. D. Jacobs, D. Weinshall, and Y. Gdalyahu. Class representation and image retrieval with non-metric distances. *IEEE Trans. PAMI*, 22:583–600, 2000.
12. J. A. Sethian. A review of the theory, algorithms, and applications of level set method for propagating surfaces. *Acta numerica*, pages 309–395, 1996.
13. R. Kimmel and J. A. Sethian. Computing geodesic on manifolds. In *Proc. US National Academy of Science*, volume 95, pages 8431–8435, 1998.
14. I. Borg and P. Groenen. *Modern multidimensional scaling - theory and applications*. Springer-Verlag, Berlin Heidelberg New York, 1997.
15. D. Bertsekas. *Nonlinear programming*. Atlanta Scientific, 2 edition, 1999.
16. M. M. Bronstein, A. M. Bronstein, R. Kimmel, and I. Yavneh. Multigrid multidimensional scaling. *Numerical Linear Algebra with Applications (NLAA)*, 13: 149–171, March-April 2006.

Further Developments in Geometrical Algorithms for Ear Biometrics

Michał Choraś

Image Processing Group, Institute of Telecommunications
University of Technology & Agriculture
S. Kaliskiego 7, 85-796 Bydgoszcz, Poland
`chorasm@atr.bydgoszcz.pl`

Abstract. The paper presents new geometrical methods of feature extraction from ear images in order to perform human identification. Geometrical approach is motivated by the actual procedures used by police and forensic experts. In the article novel algorithms of ear feature extraction from contour images are described in detail. Moreover, identification results obtained for each of the methods, based on the distance of feature vectors in the feature space, are presented.

1 Introduction and Previous Work

Ear biometrics seems to be a good solution for passive human identification systems. Ear images can be acquired from the distance even without the knowledge of the examined person. Ear biometrics is also highly accepted as single or hybrid (e.g. with face) biometrics by users in possible access control applications. According to users, ear biometrics is less stressful than fingerprinting. Moreover, our test users admitted that they would feel less comfortable while taking part in face images enrolment (people tend to care how they look on photographs). Furthermore, in ear biometrics there is no need to touch any devices and therefore there are no problems with hygiene.

Even though ear biometrics have not been implemented commercially so far, there are some known methods of feature extraction from ear images [1][2][3]. Those methods were discussed in our previous articles, in which we had also proposed our own new methods of feature extraction: concentric circles based method (CCM) and contour tracing method (CTM) [4][5]. Recently, various approaches towards 3D ear biometrics has been developed and published [6][7].

Hereby we introduce our further developments in feature extraction for human identification based on ear images. In Section 3 contour selection algorithm, geometrical parameters extraction method (GPM) consisting of the shape ratio ($GPM - SRM$) and the triangle ratio methods ($GPM - TRM$), as well as angle-based method (ABM) are presented in detail. In Section 4 identification results are presented and discussed. Conclusion and references are given next.

F.J. Perales and R.B. Fisher (Eds.): AMDO 2006, LNCS 4069, pp. 58–67, 2006.

2   Motivation for Geometrical Approach

Our methods based on geometrical feature extraction are motivated by actual procedures used in police and forensic evidence search applications. Nowadays, human ears and earprints are standard features of identity taken into account by forensic specialists and criminal policemen. In reality, well-established procedures of handling ear evidence (so called *ear otoscopy*) are based on geometrical features such as size, width, height and earlobe topology [8][9].

Therefore, by analogy to ear otoscopy, we decided to compute geometrical parameters of ear contours extracted from ear images. Such approach gives information about local parts of the image, which is more suitable for ear biometrics than global approach to image feature extraction. Moreover, geometrical features of extracted contours are more adequate for ear identification than color or texture information, which is not distinctive enough within various ear images [10].

3   Methods Based on Geometrical Parameters - *GPM*

In the proposed method of feature extraction from ear images in order to perform human identification, we use the geometrical parameters and properties of ear contour images. The first step of the method is the extraction of contours from ear images in such way, that the extracted contours contain distinctive information about shape and geometrical properties of given ear. Then for each of the extracted contours we construct the feature vector on the basis of the proposed geometrical parameters.

3.1   Contour Image Processing

We presented ear contour detection algorithm in our previous work [4][5]. Hereby it is enhanced by contour processing procedure. The aim of contour image processing is the selection of contours containing the most distinctive information characterizing human ear images. For each extracted contour c, we calculate its length:

$$L_c = \sum_{q=1}^{Q-1} \sqrt{(x_{q+1} - x_q)^2 + (y_{q+1} - y_q)^2}, \tag{1}$$

where:

- Q - number of contour points,
- c - number of contours, for $c = 1, \ldots, C$,
- (x, y) - coordinates of contour points,
- q - indexation of the current contour point.

After evaluation of ear images from our database we defined so called *short contours*, which are eliminated. We eliminate the contours for which:

$$L_c \le t \times L_c max, \tag{2}$$

where t is a sensitivity parameter (we use the value $t = 0.2$). In result of such processing we obtain images with the limited number of contours (Fig. 1).

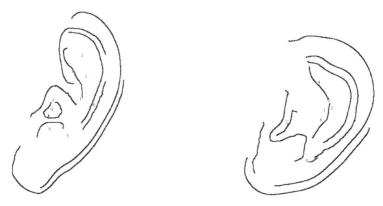

Fig. 1. Selected (longest) and numbered contours in test images 'macfir' (left) and 'szysob' (right), respectively

3.2 GPM - Triangle Ratio Method

The aim of the triangle ratio method is to extract invariant geometrical features which describe contours in ear image. Hereby we consider only the longest contour, but the method is applied to all the selected contours of the earlobe.

The method is based on finding the maximal chord of the contour and the intersection points of the contour with the longest line perpendicular to the maximal chord.

Maximal chord is denoted by $Chord_{\max}$ and is determined according to the following algorithm:

- we search for the first point of the longest contour l_{cmax} - let it be the point p_c with the coordinates (i_c, j_c). Let (i_b, j_b) be the coordinates of the current contour point p_b,
- we calculate the distances between the point p_c and the consecutive points p_b,
- the maximal chord is defined by:

$$Chord_{\max} = \max \left\{ \sqrt{(i_c - i_b)^2 + (j_c - j_b)^2} \right\} \qquad (3)$$

for: $b = 1 \ldots N$, where N is the number of contour points.

Then we extract ear contour features. In our case we use the properties of the triangle sidelines created in the following way:

1. extraction of the longest contour L_{cmax} within the ear image, contour length is calculated according to (1),
2. calculation of the maximal chord according to (3),
3. having computed the coordinates of the maximal chord and its length, for the current points of the contour we calculate:

$$A_b = i_c j_b - i_b j_c + i_b j_{bmax} - i_{bmax} j_b + i_{bmax} j_c - i_c j_{bmax} \qquad (4)$$

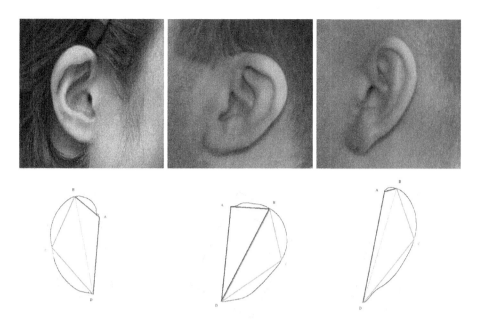

Fig. 2. Triangle ratio method for sample ear images 'prapod', 'szysob' and 'macfir', respectively. The images show the extracted longest ear contour with the triangles based on points $ABCD$.

and the maximal distance of the current point from the maximal chord:

$$r_b = \frac{A_b}{Chord_{\max}},\tag{5}$$

4. point for which $r_b = \max$ when $j_b \leq j_c$ determine the point B in the ear contour, while the current point for which $j_b \geq j_{bmax}$ determine the point C in the ear contour,
5. two triangles are created: the triangle ABD and BCD (the presented conditions (inequalities) are true for left images, for right ears inequalities are reverse),
6. we calculate the length of the line connecting the points A and C (those lines are heights of the triangles ABD and BCD respectively), those lengths are denoted as h_m and h_d,
7. we calculate the parameter b as the sum of the lengths of two lines connecting points A and C with the diameter under the angle of $90°$, that is $b = h_m + h_d$,
8. we calculate the lengths of the sides ab and ad of the triangle ABD and the lengths of the sides bc and cd of the triangle BCD,
9. we calculate the values of parameter $w1$ such as $w1 = ab + ad$ and, by analogy, $w2$ such as $w2 = bc + cd$,
10. we calculate the ratio $w = w1/w2$,
11. we calculate the triangles ratio according to (7).

Table 1. The parameters computed for the longest ear contours extracted from 3 test ear images 'prapod', 'szysob' and 'macfir' from Fig. 2

Parameter	$'prapod'$	$'szysob'$	$'macfir'$
$|AB|$	112.3	138.2	45.1
$|AD|$	267.0	329.6	387.1
$|BC|$	193.7	181.9	188.2
$|CD|$	218.8	256.0	280.2
$w1$	379.3	467.8	432.2
$w2$	418.5	437.9	468.4
w	0.906	1.068	0.923
$Chord_{max}$	343.0	362.4	411.3
b	186.4	245.8	151.4
db	1.840	1.474	2.730
h_m	72.2	125.7	39.6
h_d	114.0	119.9	111.7
tr	0.574	1.120	0.327

The parameter b is the sum of two lines connecting the points A and C with the maximal chord $Chord_{max}$ under the angle of 90°.
The parameter db is the length ratio calculated as:

$$db = \frac{Chord_{\max}}{b}. \tag{6}$$

On the basis of the previous calculations we can compute the triangles ratio tr, such as:

$$tr = \frac{h_m w_1}{h_d w_2}. \tag{7}$$

The results of the presented method for 3 test ear images are shown in Figure 2. The calculated values of the presented lines, parameters and ratios w and db for 3 ear images are shown in the Table 1.

3.3   GPM - Shape Ratio Method

Another proposed ear contours' feature is the shape ratio. We compute it for the meaningful contours in ear image selected by the method described in section 3.1. The shape ratio denoted as kk is computed according to (8):

$$kk = \frac{L_c}{d_{kp}}, \tag{8}$$

where:

- L_c is the contour length given by (1),
- d_{kp} is the length of the line connecting the ending points of each contour given by (11).

Table 2. Values of parameters computed for 9 selected contours in test image 'macfir'. L_c - contour length; d_{kp} - length of the line connecting the endpoints, kk - shape ratio; $Chord_{max}$ - the longest chord of the contour; b - length of perpendicular lines connecting most distant points with $Chord_{max}$; db - length ratio; cc - number of d_{kp} intersections with the contour; in some cases d_{kp} may be equal to $Chord_{max}$.

c	L_c	d_{kp}	kk	$Chord_{max}$	b	db	cc
1	572.6	387.1	1.479	411.3	151.4	2.730	0
2	280.8	103.4	2.019	126.5	109.1	1.159	0
3	282.6	207.0	1.365	207.0	68.9	3.004	0
4	138.2	118.3	1.168	118.3	19.6	6.036	1
5	509.3	285.9	1.781	339.7	121.3	2.801	0
6	132.8	121.6	1.092	121.6	7.8	15.590	0
7	175.8	110.9	1.585	110.9	54.9	2.020	0
8	128.8	10.4	12.385	43.9	36.6	1.120	0
9	97.4	64.2	1.517	68.0	28.7	2.369	0

Table 3. Values of parameters computed for 9 selected contours in test image 'szysob'. L_c - contour length; d_{kp} - length of the line connecting the endpoints, kk - shape ratio; $Chord_{max}$ - the longest chord of the contour; b - length of perpendicular lines connecting most distant points with $Chord_{max}$; db - length ratio; cc - number of d_{kp} intersections with the contour; in some cases d_{kp} may be equal to $Chord_{max}$.

c	L_c	d_{kp}	kk	$Chord_{max}$	b	db	cc
1	643.8	329.6	1.953	362.4	245.8	1.474	0
2	401.6	238.1	1.687	240.8	127.9	1.883	0
3	284.7	187.7	1.517	187.7	84.8	2.213	0
4	95.4	86.5	1.103	86.5	10.5	8.238	1
5	303.9	161.7	1.879	161.7	84.4	1.916	2
6	94.6	87.2	1.085	87.2	10.7	8.150	0
7	87.4	70.9	1.233	70.9	16.1	4.404	1
8	132.5	116.7	1.135	116.7	12.0	9.725	1
9	429.5	292.0	1.471	308.2	114.5	2.692	0

The shape ratio value is always $kk > 1$. Shape ratio allows contours classification into 2 classes:

1. linear contours for which $kk \cong 1$,
2. circular contours for which $kk \gg 1$.

The example of the circular contour is the contour number 8 extracted in the ear image in Fig. 1 (left). Its value in the Table 2 is $kk_8 = 12.385$.
The examples of the linear contours are:

− contour number 6 extracted in the ear image in Fig. 1 (left); its shape ratio is $kk_6 = 1.092$ (Table 2),

– contour number 6 extracted in the ear image in Fig. 1 (right), its shape ratio is $kk_6 = 1.085$ (Table 3).

The ratio cc is also proposed. It is computed as the number of intersections between the each maximal chord $Chord_{max}$ and corresponding contours c. It allows contour classification into 2 classes:

– simple contours, for which $cc = 0$,
– complex contours, for which $cc \geq 1$.

Most of the contours are classified as simple contours. The example of the complex contour is the contour number 5 extracted in the ear image in Fig. 1 (right). The combined feature vector containing the parameters computed by the proposed methods $GPM - TRM$ and $GPM - SRM$ for $c = 1, ..., C$ extracted contours is given by:

$$FV = \{(L_c, d_{kp}, kk, d, b, db, cc)_c\}. \tag{9}$$

3.4 Angle-Based Contour Representation Method - ABM

Each extracted contour is treated as an independent open curve. Each curve is represented by two sets of angles [11]:

$$\Phi = \Phi_w; 1 \leq w \leq \epsilon$$
$$\Psi = \Psi_w; 1 \leq w \leq \epsilon \tag{10}$$

corresponding to the angles between the vectors centered in the point p_0.
For each contour (curve) we search for the point p_0, which becomes the center of the concentric circles. The point p_0 is defined in the following way:

1. two ending points (i_p, j_p) and (i_k, j_k) of each curve are localized,
2. the equation of the line passing through those extracted points is $j = b_1 \times i + b_0$, where: $b_1 = \frac{j_k - j_p}{i_k - i_p}$ $b_0 = \frac{j_p \times i_k - j_k \times i_p}{i_k - i_p}$,

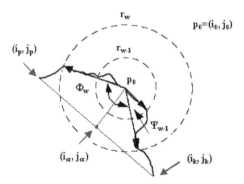

Fig. 3. Visualization of the ABM method for a chosen ear contour and 2 radii (concentric circles) with a centre in p_0

3. the distance between the ending points is computed:

$$d_{kp} = \sqrt{(i_k - i_p)^2 + (j_k - j_p)^2}, \tag{11}$$

4. the center point i_{sr}, j_{sr} of the line between (i_p, j_p) and (i_k, j_k) is computed in the following way. Let $\tan \gamma = \frac{j_k - j_p}{i_k - i_p}$ and $\triangle j = \frac{d_{kp}}{2} \cos \gamma$. Then $j_{sr} = j_k + \triangle j$,
5. knowing j_{sr} and the line equation we can determine i_{sr},
6. the line $j = \frac{1}{b_1}(i_{sr} - i) + j_{sr}$ perpendicular to the line between the contour ending points and passing through the computed center point (i_{sr}, j_{sr}) intersects the contour in the point p_0 with the coordinates (i_0, j_0).

The length of the maximal radius is determined by:

$$r_m = \sqrt{(i_k - i_0)^2 + (j_k - j_0)^2}. \tag{12}$$

For each contour we consider ϵ concentric circles with the radii $r_w = w \times \frac{r_m}{\epsilon}$ ($w = 1, \ldots, \epsilon$). For each contour the point p_0 becomes the center of the local polar coordinate system.
For each radius r_w we compute the angles:

$$\Phi_w = (\theta_{max} - \theta_{min})_w \tag{13}$$

$$\Psi_{w-1} = ((\theta_{max})_w) - ((\theta_{max})_{w-1}). \tag{14}$$

Having assumed that there are $c = 1, ..., C$ contours in the ear contour image, and that each contour is analyzed by w concentric circles, the feature vector is given by:

$$W = \{(\Phi_w, \Psi_{w-1})_1, \ldots, (\Phi_w, \Psi_{w-1})_c, \ldots, (\Phi_w, \Psi_{w-1})_C\}. \tag{15}$$

4   Experiments and Results

The experimental scenario involves the finite ear images database. One of the users, who took part in the enrollment process and his ear image is surely stored in the database, is chosen randomly. The acquisition of the user's test ear image is performed. Next, we compute the feature vectors for the test user and we search for the corresponding image from the database. In result of such scenario we obtain one ear image for which the computed feature vectors are the closest to test image feature vectors in terms of distance in the feature space.

Since there are no standard ear image databases, we performed all the tests on our own ear image database. We used images from 80 people so that we had an experimental database of 800 images (5 positions and 2 illumination values for a person). The input (query) images were taken for randomly chosen users in the conditions similar to those during the first enrollment. The feature vectors were calculated and the recognition decision was made based upon the proposed features. For each of the proposed method the classification formula was created on the basis of the distance in the feature space.

In the process of ear identification by Geometrical Parameters Method - GPM we calculate the distance between the feature vectors FV (9). The minimal distance difference between the test feature vector FV_{test} and the vectors from the database FV_{ref} is given by:

$$ans4 = \min \left\{ \sqrt{\left(FV_{test}^2 - FV_{ref_{c=1}}^2 \right)_{z=1} + \cdots + \left(FV_{test}^2 - FV_{ref_C}^2 \right)_Z} \right\}. \quad (16)$$

The image for which (16) is fulfilled is the obtained result for the test user. In 104 tests we obtained the correct identification result in all the tests.

In the process of identification by ABM method, the feature vectors W (15) are compared. The minimal distance difference between the test feature vector W_{test} and the vectors from the database W_{ref} is given by:

$$ans3 = \min \left\{ W_{test} - (W_{ref})_z \right\} = \min \left\{ dif2_1, \cdots, dif2_z, \cdots, dif2_Z \right\}, \quad (17)$$

for the value of the feature vectors difference in the feature space calculated as:

$$dif2_z = \sqrt{\sum_{c=1}^{C} \left\{ \sum_w [(\Phi_w)_{test} - (\Phi_w)_b] + \sum_w [(\Psi_{w-1})_{test} - (\Psi_{w-1})_Z] \right\}}. \quad (18)$$

for $z = 1, ..., Z$, where z denotes the consecutive feature vector in the ear image database and Z is the number of ear images.

The image for which (17) is fulfilled is the obtained result for the test user. In 104 tests we obtained the correct identification result in 94 cases.

The cumulative results for all the methods (methods CCM and CTM were introduced in our previous work [4][5]) are presented in the Table 4.

Table 4. The cumulative results of the presented identification methods (CCM and CTM were introduced in our previous articles [4][5]). The presented parameter is Rank-one-recognition.

method	number of tests	correct acceptances	false rejections	Rank-1
CCM	104	94	10	90.4
CTM	104	98	6	94.2
ABM	104	94	10	90.4
GPM	104	104	0	100.0

5   Conclusion

In the article we presented our further, novel developments in geometrical feature extraction methods for ear biometrics. The major contributions are the new methods: $GPM - TRM$, $GPM - SRM$ and ABM. Moreover, the method of ear contour image processing in order to select only the most meaningful contours was presented. The experiments and the achieved results were also discussed.

After experiments we came into conclusion that the proposed geometrical methods, which had been motivated by the manual process of feature extraction used in criminology, allow effective person identification on the basis of features extracted from ear images. The best results were achieved by the *GPM* method.

Further research is now being conducted in order to extract more geometrical and global (Gabor-based) features and weigh them properly in the multidimensional process of identification. Further experiments and evaluation of all the methods are also being performed. Furthermore, we examined user interaction in the enrolment step and we concluded that ear images acquisition is accepted by more users than other biometrics human identification methods, even face recognition.

References

1. M. Burge, W. Burger *Ear Biometrics*, in: *Biometrics: Personal Identification in Networked Society (Eds: A.K. Jain, R. Bolle, S. Pankanti)*, 273-286, 1998.
2. D.J. Hurley , M.S. Nixon, J.N. Carter, "Force Field Energy Functionals for Image Feature Extraction," Image and Vision Computing Journal, vol. 20, no. 5-6, pp. 311-318, 2002.
3. K. Chang, B. Victor B., K.W. Bowyer, S. Sarkar, "Comparison and Combination of Ear and Face Images in Appearance-Based Biometrics," IEEE Trans. on PAMI, vol. 25, no. 8, pp. 1160-1165, 2003.
4. M. Choraś, "Ear Biometrics Based on Geometrical Method of Feature Extraction", in: *F.J Perales and B.A. Draper (Eds.): Articulated Motion and Deformable Objects,* LNCS 3179, Springer-Verlag, pp. 51-61, 2004.
5. M. Choraś, "Ear Biometrics Based on Geometrical Feature Extraction," Journal ELCVIA (Computer Vision and Image Analysis), vol. 5, no. 3, pp. 84-95, 2005.
6. H. Chen, B. Bhanu, "Contour matching for 3D ear recognition," Proc. of Workshop on Applications of Computer Vision (WACV), 123-128, 2005.
7. P. Yan, K. W. Bowyer, "ICP-based approaches for 3D ear recognition," Proc. of SPIE Biometric Technology for Human Identification, 282291, 2005.
8. J. Kasprzak, *Forensic Otoscopy (in Polish)*, University of Warmia and Mazury Press, 2003.
9. J. Kasprzak, "Polish Methods of Earprint Identification", The Information Bulletin for Shoeprint/Toolmark Examiners, vol. 9, no. 3, 20-22, 2003.
10. M. Choraś, "Human Identification Based on Ear Image Analysis" (in Polish), Ph.D. Thesis, ATR Bydgoszcz, 2005.
11. F. Kamangar, M. Al-Khaiyat, "Planar Curve Representation and Matching," *Proc. British Machine Vision Conference,* pp. 174-184, 1998.

Composition of Complex Motion Models from Elementary Human Motions

Jörg Moldenhauer[1], Ingo Boesnach[1], Thorsten Stein[2], and Andreas Fischer[2]

[1] Institute for Algorithms and Cognitive Systems,
Universität Karlsruhe (TH),
D-76128 Karlsruhe, Germany
jomo@ira.uka.de, boesnach@ira.uka.de
[2] Institute for Sports and Sports Science,
Universität Karlsruhe (TH),
D-76128 Karlsruhe, Germany
stein@sport.uka.de, fischer@sport.uka.de

Abstract. An appraisal of human motions and particular motion phases is essential for a good interaction between a human and a humanoid robot. We present a new method for the analysis of human motions and the classification of motion phases. The method allows an automatic composition of a motion model for a complex motion from several elementary models. The elementary models can be retrieved from a motion catalogue according to the requirements of a current motion processing task. The method is based on the analysis of the hidden states in a complex HMM and considers the context of all elementary phases in an entire motion sequence. The analysis of motion phases with the new model is computationally more efficient and yields better recognition rates than conventional motion analysis with HMMs and winner-takes-all strategy.

1 Introduction

A practical interaction between a human and a humanoid robot requires a good understanding of human motions by the robot. On the one hand, the robot has to build up a model of its environment. The current motion state of the user is one substantial part of this model. On the other hand, the robot should accomplish its own motions in a human like manner. High acceptance of robots by humans can only be achieved if humans feel familiar with the behavior of the robots.

In the last years there has been a lot of work in generating purposeful motions for a humanoid robot. Only some examples for the various approaches are [1], [2], [3], [4], [5]. To fulfill a particular motion task, the motion must be planned, combined from elementary motion trajectories, and adapted to constraints [6]. A comparison of different methods for the determination of motion constraints and the identification of elementary motion phases can be found in [7]. The analysis of characteristics in motion phases has proved to be very important for the recognition of a human motion and the planning of robot motion trajectory [8].

F.J. Perales and R.B. Fisher (Eds.): AMDO 2006, LNCS 4069, pp. 68–77, 2006.

An expedient approach for the classification of phases in human motion trajectories is to use HMMs *(hidden Markov models)*. HMMs are well-known from speech recognition [9]. However, they have also become popular for the recognition of gestures [10] and sign language [11], [12]. A conventional HMM-based classification uses a winner-takes-all strategy for a set of HMMs. The strategy leads to the most probable model for an observation and thus to the class of the observation. The set of HMMs contains different HMMs that are specialized on a certain observation class. In [13], [14] it is shown how complex actions can be recognized by HMMs and a probabilistic grammar describing the adjacency of the HMMs on a higher level. In this work we present another classification method that uses the composition of the elementary HMMs from a motion catalogue to one complex HMM. The complex HMM can be used to analyze a long motion sequence. Hereby, we explicitly use the hidden states of the HMMs to get a mapping from model states to motion phases. In common HMM applications this state information is only implicitly used during model evaluation.

2   The Motion Catalogue and Elementary Models

The motion catalogue used for training and testing of the models in this work contains ordinary motions from everyday life. More information about this motion catalogue can be found in [7]. The subjects were asked to perform several tasks: setting the table with cup and saucer, pouring water from a coffeepot into the cup, and finally stirring the content of the cup. The motion data were acquired by a magnetic tracking system (by Ascension) with a long range transmitter and 6 sensors to track the entire right arm. A data glove (by Immersion) captured the angles of the finger joints of the right hand. The entire motion can be segmented in 13 elementary motion phases whereas the phases 6–8 can be further distinguished by the fill level of the coffeepot (full and nearly empty). In [7], additional phases 14–16 were introduced to distinguish the fill level of the coffeepot. After relabelling all phases the phases 6–8 only refer to the motions with the nearly empty coffeepot, while the additional phases 14–16 represent the same motion phases but with the full coffeepot.

Overall, 7 subjects performed the motions 10 times with the 2 constraints (fill level) resulting a total number of $7 \times 10 \times 2 = 140$ data sets in the motion catalogue. All data sets were manually segmented and labeled into the 16 motion phases. The features to describe each motion sequence are joint angles and angle velocities of the index, the thumb, the wrist, the elbow, and the shoulder with a feature vector $o \in \mathbb{R}^{2 \cdot 9}$ in each frame. The motions were recorded with a sampling rate of 86.5 fps and have a length of 17.2–23.0 s. To generate test and training data, every 10th motion was excluded from training data and tested against the remaining 9 motions. Doing this for all subjects, trials, and constraints we produced a set of 140 test/training configurations.

In [7], a set of 16 HMMs $\lambda_1, \ldots, \lambda_{16}$ was created from the training examples in the described motion catalogue. Each HMM is specialized in a certain motion

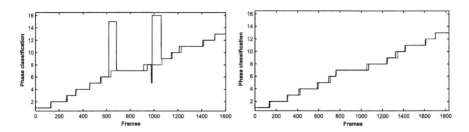

Fig. 1. Classification of phases with 16 HMMs ($N = 2$ states, window length $W = 30$). Left figure: data set with mean recognition rate compared to the results of all test data. Right figure: data set with one of the best recognition rates. (Solid line: classification result, dashed line: target classification from manual segmentation.)

Table 1. Recognition rates for the classification of motion phases by elementary HMMs with different parameters (window length W and number of states N) considering motion constraints and ignoring them

W	N	with constraints	w/o constraints
100	1	0.7464	–
30	1	0.8478	0.8796
30	2	0.8515	0.8875
30	5	0.8653	0.8673
30	10	0.8215	0.8403
1	1	0.8414	0.8721

phase. Using a winner-takes-all strategy the motion phases could be determined by shifting a window of length W over the testing sequences $O = o_1, \ldots, o_T$:

$$p_t = \arg\max_{n=1,\ldots,16} \left(P \left(o_{t-W} \ldots o_t | \lambda_n \right) \right). \tag{1}$$

The output probability $P(O|\lambda_n)$ for each HMM λ_n is calculated by the *forward algorithm* for HMMs (e.g., see [9]). Fig. 1 shows the classification result for two exemplary data sets in comparison to the manual phase classification. Recognition rates with different HMM configurations are given in Tab. 1.

3   The Concept of Model Composition

Considering the recognition rates achieved by the winner-takes-all strategy we can see that HMMs already allow a reliable classification of motion phases. Associating the states with phases, the models cannot be simplified any further by reduction of the state number. Thus, these models are *elementary*. It should be possible to analyze a very complex motion consisting of certain elementary motion phases in the motion catalogue by a complex HMM merged from elementary

HMMs. In the following, we show how the parameters of such a complex HMM can be automatically constructed from the parameters of selected elementary HMMs.

According to the conventional notation of HMM parameters we want to construct a complex continuous HMM λ with the parameters π, A, w, μ, U for initial state probabilities, state transitions, and mixture parameters. To tell the complex HMM from the elementary HMMs their parameters bear the indices for the motion phases they are trained for: $\lambda_{p=1,\dots,P} = (\pi_p, A_p, w_p, \mu_p, U_p)$. The parameters of these models are once determined by the methods in [7] and stay constant in the motion catalogue.

4   The Basic Composition Algorithm

To do the HMM composition of one HMM λ from the elementary HMMs λ_p we first combine the state transition matrices A_p to a big matrix A. W.l.o.g., we assume that all elementary HMMs have the same number of states N, i.e. $A_{p=1,\dots,P} \in \mathbb{R}^{N \times N}$. To gather all A_p as submatrices we initialize $A \in \mathbb{R}^{PN \times PN}$.

Previous works have shown that Bakis-models [9] produce proper HMMs for phase detection since the models have to run through a strict sequence of hidden states. A typical structure of an initial state transition matrix A_p without parameter adaptation by a training process, e.g. with *expectation maximization*, is given in (2). Following this design principle, the complex model is constructed to run through desired sequences of elementary motion phases. Thus, the matrix A has the structure of an upper triangular matrix. In contrast to elementary HMMs, the entries on the diagonal are not scalar values for transition probabilities between single states but the submatrices A_p. Analogously to the state transitions in the upper subdiogonal of the matrices A_p the Matrix A gets entries with the probabilities a_i for the transitions from the final states of $A_i, i = 1,\dots, P-1$ to the first state of $A_i + 1$ (see (3) for the detailed construction).

$$A_p = \begin{pmatrix} 0.5\ 0.5 & & \\ & \ddots\ \ddots & \\ & & 0.5\ 0.5 \\ & & 1 \end{pmatrix} \quad (2)$$

$$A = \begin{pmatrix} \ddots & & \\ & \boxed{A_P}\ \ 0 & \\ & & \ddots \end{pmatrix} \quad (4)$$

$$A = \begin{pmatrix} \ddots & & & \\ & \boxed{A_i} & & \\ & & a_i & \\ & & \boxed{A_{i+1}} & \\ & & & \ddots \end{pmatrix} \quad (3)$$

Since A has to be a semi-stochastic matrix (see [9]), the rows $a_{iN-1,1\dots PN}$ of A containing the transition probabilities have to be normalized. All other rows of A are already normalized since the matrices A_p are semi-stochastic themselves. To determine correct probabilities a_i the entries $a_{iN-1,(i-1)N+1\dots iN-1}$ are weighted

Table 2. Mean phase lengths T_p and transition probabilities $a_p = \frac{1}{T_p+1}$ for the phases $p = 1, \ldots, 16$. Phase 13 is the final phase. Therefore the transition probability is set to $a_{13} = 0$.

p	T_p	a_p	p	T_p	a_p	p	T_p	a_p	p	T_p	a_p
1	111.03	0.0089	5	96.64	0.0102	9	85.86	0.0115	13	111.88	0 (0.0089)
2	127.94	0.0078	6	24.45	0.0393	10	78.89	0.0125	14	36.09	0.0270
3	84.15	0.0117	7	145.99	0.0068	11	185.93	0.0053	15	88.99	0.0111
4	121.98	0.0081	8	75.49	0.0131	12	74.91	0.0132	16	77.34	0.0128

by the mean length T_i of the motion phase in the training sequences from the catalogue. Tab. 2 contains the phase lengths of our training examples. Afterwards the entire row is weighted by the factor $1/(T_i + 1)$. If the motion phase is final then the transition probability is set to $a_i = 0$ (see (4)). Hence, the following condition holds for rows $i = N, 2N, \ldots, PN$ of A:

$$\sum_{j=1}^{NP} a_{i,j} = \frac{1}{T_i + 1} \left(T_i \left(\sum_{j=1}^{N} a_{\lfloor i/N \rfloor+1;N,j} \right) + 1 \right) = 1 \tag{5}$$

and for all other rows

$$\sum_{j=1}^{NP} a_{i,j} = \sum_{j=1}^{N} a_{\lfloor i/N \rfloor+1;N,j} = 1. \tag{6}$$

Thus, matrix A fulfills the normalization criterion for a semi-stochastic matrix.

The initial state distribution $\pi \in \mathbb{R}^{PN}$ and the mixture parameters $U \in \mathbb{R}^{V \times V \times PN \times M}$, $\mu \in \mathbb{R}^{V \times PN \times M}$ und $w \in \mathbb{R}^{PN \times M}$ to calculate the output probabilities of λ are determined by simple composition of the parameters from the elementary models λ_p for all states $i = 1, \ldots, PN$:

$$\pi_i = \pi_{\lfloor (i-1)/N \rfloor+1;((i-1) \bmod N)}, \tag{7}$$

$$w_{i,1\ldots M} = w_{\lfloor (i-1)/N \rfloor+1;((i-1) \bmod N)+1,1\ldots M}, \tag{8}$$

$$\mu_{1\ldots O,i,1\ldots M} = \mu_{\lfloor (i-1)/N \rfloor+1;1\ldots O,((i-1) \bmod N)+1,1\ldots M}, \tag{9}$$

$$U_{1\ldots O,1\ldots O,i,1\ldots M} = U_{\lfloor (i-1)/N \rfloor+1;1\ldots O,1\ldots O,((i-1) \bmod N)+1,1\ldots M}. \tag{10}$$

5   Extension for Alternative State Sequences

The proposed construction can be extended to allow not only strict sequences of motion phases but branches in motion parts. These alternative motion parts are required, e.g., if the motion contains significant intra-individual differences during the performance of the motion and we want to detect these differences. A typical example in our motion catalogue are the differences in the motion phases during the manipulation of the coffeepot. Transitions to the additionally introduced artificial phases allow the distinction of the fill level of the coffeepot. Generally the sequence of motion phases can be specified by an adjacency matrix or a context-free grammar.

The consequence for the composition method is that additional probabilities for the transition in alternative phases have to be inserted in matrix A. Further on, it must be assured that the model reenters a consistent state at the end of the alternative phases. This can be realized by additional probability entries, too. The scheme in (11) shows the construction of the additional entries.

$$
A = \begin{pmatrix}
\ddots & & & & & & & \\
& \boxed{A_i} & a_i/C & a_i/C & & & & \\
& & \ddots & & & & & \\
& & & \boxed{A_{j_1}} & & a_{j_1} & & \\
& & & & \ddots & & & \\
& & & & & \boxed{A_{j_C}} & a_{j_C} & \\
& & & & & & \ddots & \\
& & & & & & & \boxed{A_k} \\
& & & & & & & & \ddots
\end{pmatrix}. \tag{11}
$$

Being in phase i, we want to reach the alternative phases $j_1, ..., j_C$ and return to a common phase k. The entries and positions of the submatrices $A_1, ..., A_P$ are determined as described in the previous section. The transition probabilities $a_{1,...,P}$ are also calculated in the same way. However, the probabilities are distributed over C alternative following phases by weighting with factor $1/C$. The probabilities for transitions back to the common phase remain unchanged. After an additional normalization of altered matrix rows as described in the previous section, the condition for the semi-stochastic matrix is still valid since for all rows i with new entries holds

$$
\sum_{j=1}^{NP} a_{i,j} = \frac{1}{T_i + 1} \left(T_i \left(\sum_{j=1}^{N} a_{\lfloor i/N \rfloor + 1; N, j} \right) + \sum_{c=1}^{C} \frac{1}{C} \right) = 1. \tag{12}
$$

The special cases of beginning or ending a motion in an alternative phase require no change in the construction method. However, no transitions from previous phases have to be generated in the first case and no transitions to a following phase in the second case. The complete composition algorithm can be summarized as follows:

```
// parameters:
//   λ₁,...,P: elementary HMMs with λ_p = (π_p, A_p, w_p, μ_p, U_p)
//   T₁,...,P: mean phase lengths
//   Ă ∈ {0,1}^{P×P}: pure adjacency matrix with entries ă_{p,q} = 1 if there is a
//        transition from phase p to Phase q and entries ă_{p,q} = 0 ohterwise
// result: the complex HMM λ
```

$P :=$ number of phases;

$D :=$ dimension of the feature vectors;

$N :=$ number of states in $\lambda_{1,...,p}$;

$M :=$ number of mixture components in $\lambda_{1,...,p}$;

$A := 0^{NP \times NP}$; // new transition matrix

for$(p := 1, \ldots, P)$ {

    // insert submatrix A_p in A:

    $h := (p-1)N$;

    for$(n_1 := 1, \ldots, N)$

        for$(n_2 := 1, \ldots, N)$

            $a_{h+n_1,h+n_2} := a_{n_1,n_2}$;

    // adaptation of transition matrix:

    $a_{h+N,h+N} := T_p/(T_p+1)$;

    $C := \sum_{q=1,...,P} ă_{p,q} - 1$;

    for$(q := 1, \ldots, P)$

        if$(ă_{p,q} = 1 \wedge p \neq q)$

            $a_{h+N,(q-1)N+1} := 1/(Cf)$; // $= a_p/C$

    // initial state distribution and mixture parameters:

    for$(n_1 := 1, \ldots N)$

        $i := h + n_1$;

        $\pi_i := \pi_{p;n_1}$;

        for$(m := 1, \ldots, M)$

            $w_{i,m} := w_{p;n_1,m}$;

            for$(d_1 := 1, \ldots, D)$

                $\mu_{d_1,i,m} := \mu_{p;d_1,n_1,m}$;

                for$(d_2 = 1, \ldots, D)$

                    $U_{d_1,d_2,i,m} := U_{p;d_1,d_2,n_1,m}$;

} // end for

return $\lambda = (\pi, A, w, \mu, U)$;

6   Results

The recognition of the motion phases in a motion sequence O is based on the state sequence Q calculated by the *Viterbi-algorithm* (see [9]) for the complex model λ:

$$Q = \underset{S=s_1 s_2 \ldots s_T, s_t \in \{1,\ldots,16\}}{\arg\max} (P(S, O | \lambda_n)). \tag{13}$$

The advantage of the proposed composition method is that the information about the states in the elementary HMMs does not get lost. The phases can be directly derived from the state indices:

$$p_t = \lfloor (s_t - 1)/N \rfloor + 1. \tag{14}$$

This property is important for an automatic implementation since no manual mapping from HMM states to motion phases is required.

Another advantage of the analysis of motion phases with a complex HMM is that no windowing of the motion sequences is required. An entire motion sequence can be applied to the HMM in one step. Considering the computational effort of the analysis this advantage is substantial. Given a motion sequence of length T, P phases, and P HMMs with N states, the effort for the classification with the winner-takes-all strategy is $\mathcal{O}(PTWN^2)$ where W is the window length. The effort for the analysis with a complex HMM is $\mathcal{O}(T(PN)^2)$. In this case the effort depends on P^2, however P can be restricted to a small number in many cases, e.g. $P = 16$ in our example. Further on, the transition matrix is sparse which allows an efficient model evaluation (see [9]). The size of P has much less influence on the runtime behavior than the window length W. Estimating a linear dependency between W and T leads to a much better efficiency of our new method compared to the conventional classification with HMMs.

Aside the computational efficiency, the analysis with complex HMMs leads to more reliable classification results than the old method. The middle columns of Tab. 3 contain the recognition rates for different HMM parameters. Fig. 2 shows the classification results in comparison to the manually segmented phases.

A significant improvement of the recognition rates can be achieved for the classification of motion constraints (see Tab. 3, right-most column). In comparison to

Table 3. Different HMM parameters (number of elemtary states N and mixtures M) and recognition results for the classification of motion phases (considering and ignoring constraints) and the pure classification of motion constraints.

N	M	phases with constraints	phases w/o constraints	constraints
10	1	0.28956	0.29685	0.67857
10	2	0.28957	0.29686	0.67857
1	1	0.82587	0.84346	0.82857
1	2	0.82587	0.84346	0.82857
20	1	0.82205	0.83420	0.94286
2	1	0.81772	0.82830	0.94286
2	2	0.81772	0.82830	0.94286
3	1	0.81164	0.82446	0.92857
3	2	0.80303	0.80860	0.96429
4	1	0.81487	0.82718	0.94286
4	2	0.80128	0.80575	0.96429
5	1	0.75685	0.76716	0.90000
5	2	0.75685	0.76716	0.90000

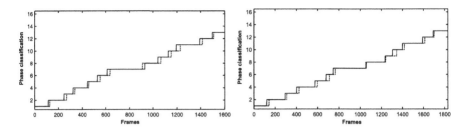

Fig. 2. Results of the phase classification with a complex HMM (16 × 2 states). The test data are the same as in Fig. 1. (Solid line: classification result, dashed line: target classification from manual segmentation.)

the conventional approach no isolated motion phases are analyzed by the complex HMM. However the complex HMM takes the entire motion sequence into account. Thus, the model is more robust towards strong variations during motion performance and only slight differences between phases in the same time. Erroneous transitions to the wrong alternative phase cannot appear (see Fig. 1 and Fig. 2). The best recognition rate achieved by the conventional HMM classification is 89.29 % whereas the complex HMMs yield rates up to 96.4 % (see Tab. 3).

7   Conclusion

The composition of complex HMMs from elementary HMMs of single motion phases leads to a new methods of motion analysis. The information about the sequence of hidden states calculated by the Viterbi algorithm is explicitly used to detect certain motion phases. Normally, this information is only used to calculate a better model probability in dependence of the Viterbi path. Usage of the full capacity of the state sequence leads to efficient and robust classification methods with heigh recognition rates. Even the difficult problem of constraint recognition can be solved with excellent recognition rates. The reason for this is that the model regards the entire motion and the motion phases in their context.

Furthermore, the composition of the complex HMMs is automated. The composition algorithm is generic and can be used to combine any elementary models to a complex one. Thus, it is possible to build up a model library with elementary HMMs and to combine them to the required model for a special classification task comparable to a construction kit. This is an important step towards an interactive extension of the robot's knowledge data-base which is one of the primary demands for a purposeful cooperation between the human and a learning humanoid robot.

Acknowledgment

This work is supported by the Deutsche Forschungsgemeinschaft within Collaborative Research Center 588 "Humanoid Robots – Learning and Cooperating Multimodal Robots."

References

1. N. Pollard, J. Hodgins, M. Riley, C. Atkeson, *Adapting Human Motion for the Control of a Humanoid Robot*, International Conference on Robotics and Automation, Washington, DC, May 2002.
2. A. Dasgupta, Y. Nakamura, *Making Feasible Walking Motion of Humanoid Robots from Human Motion Capture Data*, Proceedings of the International Conference on Robotics and Automation , May 1999, pp. 1044–1049.
3. M. Riley, A. Ude, C. Atkeson, *Methods for Motion Generation and Interaction with a Humanoid Robot: Case Studies of Dancing and Catching*, AAAI and CMU Workshop on Interactive Robotics and Entertainment 2000, Pittsburgh, Pennsylvania, April 2000.
4. R. Zöllner, T. Asfour, R. Dillmann, Programming by Demonstration: Dual-Arm Manipulation Tasks for Humanoid, IEEE/RSJ International Conference on Intelligent Robots and Systems (IROS 2004), Sendai, Japan, September 2004.
5. S. Schaal, A. Ijspeert, A. Billard, *Computational approaches to motor learning by imitation*, Philosophical transaction of the Royal Society of London, series B, volume 358, number 1431, 2003, pp. 537–547.
6. J. Kuffner, K. Nishiwaki, S. Kagami, M. Inaba, H. Inoue, *Motion Planning for Humanoid Robots*, Proceedings of the 11th International Symposium of Robotics Research (ISRR 2003), Siena, Italy, October 2003.
7. I. Boesnach, J. Moldenhauer, C. Burgmer, T. Beth, V. Wank, K. Bös, *Classification of Phases in Human Motions by Neural Networks and Hidden Markov Models*, in Proceedings of the IEEE Conf. on Cybernetics and Intelligent Systems CIS 2004, December 2004, Singapore.
8. V. Wank, A. Fischer, K. Bös, I. Boesnach, J. Moldenhauer, T. Beth, *Similarities and Varieties in Human Motion Trajectories of Predefined Grasping and Disposing Movements*, in Proceedings of the IEEE Int. Conf. on Humanoid Robots, Santa Monica, USA, 2004, pp. 311–321.
9. L. Rabiner, *A Tutorial on Hidden Markov Models and Selected Applications in Speech Recognition*, in Proceedings of the IEEE, vol. 77, no. 2, 1989, pp. 257–286.
10. J. Schlenzig, E. Hunter, R. Jain, *Recursive identification of gesture inputs using hidden Markov models*, Applications of Computer Vision, 1994, Proceedings of the second IEEE Workshop on, 5–7 Dec. 1994, pp. 187–194.
11. T. Starner, A. Pentland, *Real-Time American Sign Language Recognition Using Desk and Wearable Computer Based Video*, IEEE Transactions on Pattern Analysis and Machine Intelligence, vol. 20, no. 12, December 1998, pp. 1371–1375.
12. C. Vogler, D. Metaxas, *Parallel Hidden Markov Models for American Sign Language Recognition*, International Conference on Computer Vision, Kerkyra, Greece, September 22-25, 1999.
13. A. Bobick, Y. Ivanov, *Action Recognition Using Probabilistic Parsing*, Proceedings of the IEEE Conference on Computer Vision and Pattern Recognition, 23–25 June 1998, pp. 196–202.
14. A. Bobick, Y. Ivanov, *Recognition of Visual Activities and Interactions by Stochastic Parsing*, IEEE Transactions on Pattern Analysis and Machine Intelligence, vol. 22, no. 8, August 2000, pp. 852–872.

Acquisition of Articulated Human Body Models Using Multiple Cameras

Aravind Sundaresan and Rama Chellappa*

Center for Automation Research, Dept. of Electrical and Computer Engineering
University of Maryland, College Park, MD 20742-3275, USA
{aravinds, rama}@cfar.umd.edu

Abstract. Motion capture is an important application in different areas such as biomechanics, computer animation, and human-computer interaction. Current motion capture methods typically use human body models in order to guide pose estimation and tracking. We model the human body as a set of tapered super-quadrics connected in an articulated structure and propose an algorithm to automatically estimate the parameters of the model using video sequences obtained from multiple calibrated cameras. Our method is based on the fact that the human body is constructed of several articulated chains that can be visualised as essentially 1-D segments embedded in 3-D space and connected at specific joint locations. The proposed method first computes a voxel representation from the images and maps the voxels to a high dimensional space in order to extract the 1-D structure. A bottom-up approach is then suggested in order to build a parametric (spline-based) representation of a general articulated body in the high dimensional space followed by a top-down probabilistic approach that registers the segments to the known human body model. We then present an algorithm to estimate the parameters of our model using the segmented and registered voxels.

1 Introduction

The task of motion capture can be divided into a number of systematically distinct stages: initialisation, pose estimation and tracking. There exist a number of algorithms to estimate the pose using images captured from a single or multiple cameras [1]. Some of the problems encountered, especially in the monocular case, are the segmentation of the image into different, possibly self-occluding body parts and the complex articulated structure of the human body which results in wide range of body part configurations or poses. It is, therefore, often necessary to use a human body model to deal with the large number of body segments and to guide the tracking and pose estimation processes especially in bio-mechanical and clinical motion capture applications.

Krahnstoever and Sharma [2] address the issue of acquiring structure, shape and appearance of articulated models directly from monocular video using a

---

* This research was funded in part by NSF ITR 0325715.

F.J. Perales and R.B. Fisher (Eds.): AMDO 2006, LNCS 4069, pp. 78–89, 2006.

single camera and hence has has limited scope for complete human body model estimation. Mikic et al. [3] propose a model acquisition algorithm using voxels that starts with a simple body part localisation procedure based on template fitting and growing, and uses prior knowledge of average body part shapes and dimensions. Kakadiaris and Metaxas [4] present a Human Body Part Identification Strategy (HBPIS) that recovers all the body parts of a moving human based on the spatio-temporal analysis of its deforming silhouette using input from three mutually orthogonal views. The subject, however is required to follow a specified protocol of movements. Anguelov et al. [5] describe an algorithm that automatically decomposes simple objects into approximately rigid parts and obtains the underlying articulated structure given a set of meshes describing the objects in different poses. Cheung et al. [6] also describes a model acquisition algorithm where the kinematics is estimated using correspondence. Chu et al. [7] describe a method for estimating pose using isomaps [8] to transform the voxel body to its pose-invariant intrinsic space representation and obtain a skeleton representation.

We model the human body as comprising of several rigid body segments that are connected to each other at specific joints forming 1-D kinematic chains originating from the trunk as described in Section 2. These chains can be visualised as 1-D curves embedded in 3-D space. We exploit the 1-D nature of the chains and transform the voxel coordinates to a domain where we are able to extract the 1-D structure. We are thus able to register each voxel to its position along the chain for a set of frames that capture the subject in different poses. The model estimation algorithm involves locating the joint locations and estimating the shape parameters of the different body segments as well as the implicit estimation of the pose. We first estimate the joint locations and limb lengths from the skeletons and then compute the super-quadric parameters of the body segments from the voxels using the segmentation and registration results. While human dimensional variability is enormous across different demographics and sexes, it is not arbitrary. We can, therefore, use our prior knowledge of the approximate ratios between the stature and different long bones, as well as the joint location in our model acquisition algorithm. We describe the model estimation algorithm in Section 3, and the experiments in Section 4. Our algorithm is different from that of Chu et al. [7], in that we use Laplacian eigenmaps [9] in order to simultaneously segment and extract the one-dimensional structure of the human body. Belkin and Niyogi [9] describe the construction of a representation for data lying in a low dimensional manifold embedded in a high dimensional space. We obtain much better segmentation and explicitly compute the position of each voxel along the articulated chain that it belongs to. This step enables us to acquire the shape and joint model. Some other techniques for dimensionality reduction and reducing shape to pose invariant structure can be found in Elad and Kimmel [10], manifold charting [11] and Locally Linear Embedding [12]. However, we choose Laplacian eigenmaps as they best serves the purpose of extracting the 1-D nature of the curves. There is also a similarity to skeletal representation algorithms [13] that we expound on in Section 4.

2 Human Body Model

The human body model that we use is illustrated in Fig. 1 (a) with the different body segments as well as joints labelled. Each of these body segments has a coordinate frame attached to itself. The body segment can be described by an arbitrary shape in terms of the coordinates of this frame, and in our case is modelled using a tapered super-quadric. We choose tapered super-quadrics for their simplicity and versatility [14]. Some of the other shape models used to model human body segments are cylinders, CAD models and ellipsoids [3]. The tapered super-quadric (Fig. 10a) is described in equation (1), and is characterised by five scalar parameters x_0, y_0, z_0, d, and s. If sliced in a plane parallel to the xy plane, the cross section is an ellipse with parameters αx_0 and αy_0, where α is a scalar (Fig. 1 (c)). The length of the segment is z_0 as shown in Fig. 1 (d). The scale parameter, s, denotes the amount of taper, and the "power" parameter, d, denotes the curvature of the radial profile, $r(z)\sqrt{x_0 y_0}$, along the z-axis. For e.g., $d = 2, s = 0$, is an ellipsoid, $d = \infty, s = 0$ is a right-elliptical cylinder and $d = \infty, s = -1$ is a right-elliptical cone.

$$\left(\frac{x}{x_0}\right)^2 + \left(\frac{y}{y_0}\right)^2 = \left(1 + s\frac{z}{z_0}\right)\left(1 - \left(1 - 2\frac{z}{z_0}\right)^d\right) = r^2(z) \text{ for } 0 \leq z \leq z_0 \quad (1)$$

A joint between two body segments is described as a vector in the coordinate frame of the parent body segment connecting the origin of the parent segment coordinate frame to the origin of the child segment. The pose of the child segment is described in terms of the rotational parameters between the child coordinate frame and the parent coordinate frame. The pose of the model, φ, is a vector of the position and orientation of of the base-body (6 degrees of freedom) and the joint angles of the various articulated body segments (3 degrees of freedom for each joint). We observe that the joint locations cannot be easily obtained, even manually, from a single pose.

3 Model Acquisition Algorithm

We begin with grey-scaled images captured from multiple cameras. Simple background subtraction is performed on the images to obtain binary silhouettes (Fig. 2). We perform space carving using the binary silhouettes from the cameras and the calibration data to obtain a voxel representation where each voxel block is of size 30mm× 30mm× 30mm, which we find to be an acceptable compromise between complexity and accuracy. In the first part of the algorithm, we segment the voxels and obtain a parametric representation for the different articulated chains as well as register the chain to the body model. We then compute a skeletal representation of the subject for a set of key frames where the registration is successful. In the second part of our model acquisition algorithm, we estimate a simple stick model for the subject and progressively improve the model to finally obtain the parameters of the complete super-quadric-based model.

Fig. 1. Model   **Fig. 2.** Images and Silhouettes   **Fig. 3.** Voxels

3.1   Segmenting and Registering the Articulated Chains

Our key observation is that the human body can be visualised as consisting of 1-D continuous articulated chains embedded in 3-D space. We observe this in Fig. 3, in which we can identify the five articulated chains: the head and four limbs, attached to the trunk, the sixth segment. Our objective is to extract the 1-D structure and the position of each voxel along the chain using a parametric form, and thus segment the different articulated chains that have these 1-D structure. The articulated structure of these chains, however, make it difficult to segment them in normal 3-D space. We use Laplacian Eigenmaps to extract the structure of the underlying 1-D curve. Our objective is *not* to preserve geodesic distances between points [7] or reduce the dimensionality of the data [9], but to extract the one-dimensional manifold structure.

It is known that the Laplacian Eigenmap preserves local information optimally in a certain sense as described in Belkin and Niyogi [9]. Given a data set of k nodes (voxel coordinates), we construct a weighted graph $G = (V, E)$, with edges connecting two nodes if they are neighbours. We consider the problem of mapping the weighted graph to a $k \times m$ matrix $Y = [\mathbf{y}^{(1)}, \ldots, \mathbf{y}^{(m)}] = [\mathbf{y}_1, \ldots, \mathbf{y}_k]^\mathsf{T}$, where the ith row, $\mathbf{y}_i^\mathsf{T}$, provides the embedding for the ith node. A reasonable criterion for choosing a "good" map is to minimise, under appropriate conditions, the objective function given by $\sum_{i,j} \|\mathbf{y}_i - \mathbf{y}_j\|^2 W_{ij}$ (which imposes a penalty if vertices connected by an edge are not close to each other) subject to $Y^\mathsf{T}Y = I$ (which removes an arbitrary scaling factor). Standard methods show that the solution is provided by the matrix of eigenvectors corresponding to the k lowest non-zero eigenvalues of the generalised eigenvalue problem $L\mathbf{y} = \lambda \mathbf{y}$, where $W_i = \sum_j W_{ij} = \sum_j W_{ji}$, and $D = \text{diag}(W_1, W_2, \ldots, W_k)$, and $L = D - W$.

The concept of neighbours is natural because the voxels are positioned in a uniform spatial grid and constructing the adjacency graph is intuitive. We place an edge between two voxels if they are neighbours connected by a face, an edge

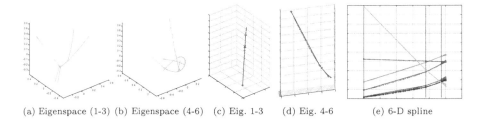

(a) Eigenspace (1-3) (b) Eigenspace (4-6)   (c) Eig. 1-3   (d) Eig. 4-6   (e) 6-D spline

Fig. 4. Extracting the 1-D curves in Eigenspace

or a corner. We thus obtain a sparse graph of size $k \times k$. We only consider voxels that belong to the biggest connected component in the graph. We compute $d = 6$ eigenvectors corresponding to the d smallest non-zero eigenvalues and thus embed the graph in a 6-D Euclidean space. We choose $d = 6$, because we wish to segment six different articulated chains. The graph embedding in the 6-D space is illustrated in Fig. 3.1(a-b). A close examination of the plot reveals six one-dimensional curves that we expect to correspond to the six articulated chains described earlier. We observe that the "bending" effect of articulation has been removed, as we would expect, because joint angles do not in general affect the computation of the adjacency matrix.

We observe that each articulated chain is an 1-D curve in 6-D space irrespective of the thickness of the body segment in normal 3-D space. This is a result of using the Laplacian eigenmap transformation and we observe that the 1-D nature of the curve is preserved even in higher dimensions (Fig. 3.1 (c)). This is an advantage over geodesic distance preserving algorithms [7] as we can easily fit 1-D splines to the data.

We describe a completely unsupervised algorithm to segment the voxels in eigenspace into 1-D curves. We represent the voxels in terms of an 1-D parameter in this eigenspace by fitting a cubic smoothing spline function to the data according to the following algorithm. All the computations are in the 6-D eigenspace. We begin each spline with a "pivot" node that is farthest from all existing spline segments. There are two kinds of curves, those that are connected at one end and those that are connected at both. The "pivot" node is at the free end or the middle in the first and second cases respectively. We create a cluster by adding nodes that are closest to the "pivot" node. We compute the principal axis for the cluster and the projection of each node on the principal axis (site value t). Thus, for each node, $\boldsymbol{y}_i$, in the cluster we obtain its site value t_i. We can compute a smoothing spline $\boldsymbol{f}(.)$ to minimise $\sum_i e_i$, where $e_i = \|\boldsymbol{f}(t_i) - \boldsymbol{y}_i\|^2$. We grow the curve by adding nodes that are close to each end. The principal axis used to compute the site value is recomputed locally using nodes at the growing end. The growth is terminated when the error of new nodes exceeds a fixed threshold, $CL\sqrt{d}$, where $C = 0.005$, L is the length of the average spline in eigenspace (set to 1 as we have normalised the eigenspace such that $\boldsymbol{y}_i \in [0,1]^6$) and d is the dimension of the space. We now have six spline segments as shown in Fig. 5(b-c). Fig. 5 (d) presents the segmentation results in the normal 3-D

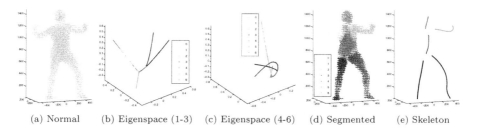

(a) Normal   (b) Eigenspace (1-3)   (c) Eigenspace (4-6)   (d) Segmented   (e) Skeleton

Fig. 5. The splines are colour coded according to their index. (d) and (e) denote the voxels colour-coded according to the index of the spline segments they belong to.

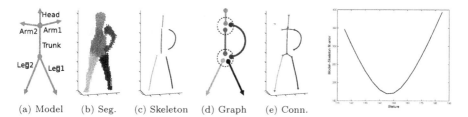

(a) Model   (b) Seg.   (c) Skeleton   (d) Graph   (e) Conn.

Fig. 6. Matching computed graph with body model   **Fig. 7.** Model fit error

space and we note that the segmentation is fairly accurate. Unclassified voxels are labelled 0. As noted earlier each node ($\boldsymbol{x}_i$ in normal 3-D space and $\boldsymbol{y}_i$ in eigenspace) has a site value t_i. This value denotes the position of the node along the 1-D curve and can be used to compute the skeleton in Fig. 5 (e) using a 3-D smoothing spline with the set of pairs $(t_i, \boldsymbol{x}_i)$.

Once we have the skeleton segments as in Fig. 5 (e), we would like to register them to the different segments presented in Fig. 6 (a). Each spline segment consists of a curve connecting two nodes. We can estimate the probability of a connection between nodes of different segments based on the distance between the nodes in eigenspace. We can also estimate the probabilities of a spline segment being an arm or a leg, for example, by examination of the properties of the spline in normal space such as its length and thickness. We choose that permutation of body segments that has the highest probability. In most cases, the registration is straightforward, but however, in poses like in Fig. 6 (b), there are ambiguities. We resolve these ambiguities by selecting that set of connections between segments that has the highest probability (Fig. 6 (e)). We can also identify cases where the number of segments is less than six due to segmentation errors.

3.2   Estimating Human Body Model

The human body model parameters cannot be reliably estimated from a single pose. We, therefore, select a set of $N(= 20)$ key frames from the sequence that

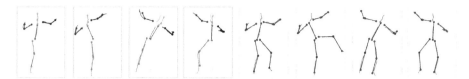

Fig. 8. Fit of initial skeleton model   **Fig. 9.** Optimised model

have been registered successfully. We estimate an initial skeleton-based model from the set of frames and progressively refine model parameters and increase model complexity. For e.g., we begin with a skeleton model and progress to super-quadric model. We use techniques that leverage our knowledge of the human body structure and use a top down approach. The stature (or height) of the subject is a key parameter that is strongly related to a number of human body model parameters, such as the lengths of long bones in the body [15]. Anthropometric studies have been performed on certain demographic groups to study the relationship between stature and the long bones in the body. These studies indicate that we can estimate the lengths of the large body segments for an "average" human subject (model skeleton) from the stature. For our initial model we construct the model skeleton (including joint locations and limb lengths) for an "average" human subject for a range of stature values. We fit line segments, corresponding to the trunk, neck, head, forearms, arms, thighs and leg segments to the voxel-skeleton in Fig. 6 (c), using the known lengths of the body segments. We also obtain an approximate estimate of the pose in the process. We identify the limbs on the left and the right by examination of their positions with respect to the trunk and also by examination of the joint angles between the limbs of the legs. We then compute the distance between the points on the voxel-skeleton and the line segments of the model skeleton obtained from the stature. The skeleton model fit error corresponding to the stature is computed and summed across key frames for each stature value in the range to determine the stature parameter that best fits the voxel skeletons. We note that there is a clear minimum in the error versus stature plot in Fig. 7 and we select the model skeleton corresponding to the minimum error stature value as our initial estimate. The computed skeleton of a few key frames with the model super-imposed on them are presented in Fig. 8. The two sets of parameters we are interested in estimating are the pose parameters (joint angles) and the body structure (joint locations). We can express the fit error as a function of the joint locations (X) and the joint angles (φ). We minimise the fit error by varying X while keeping φ fixed, and vice versa (varying φ while keeping X fixed), using optimisation techniques. X and φ are allowed to vary within a small region around X_0 and φ_0 respectively. The skeletons of a few key frames with the optimised model and pose super-imposed on them are presented in Fig. 9.

The next step is to obtain the super-quadric parameters given the joint locations and angles. We estimate the super-quadric parameters for the trunk, head, arm, forearm, thigh, and leg, as these body segments are large enough to be estimated using the resolution and quality of the voxels that we possess. On any

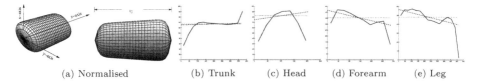

(a) Normalised   (b) Trunk   (c) Head   (d) Forearm   (e) Leg

Fig. 10. Radial profiles of different body segments: The solid line is the median radial profile. The dotted line is the super-quadric radius with scale parameter set to zero. The dashed line is the super-quadric radius with estimated scale parameter. The x-axis of the plots is the distance in mm along the z-axis of the body segment coordinate system. The y-axis of the plots is the radius value also in mm.

articulated chain, we know the position of each voxel along the chain. Using this knowledge and the estimated joint locations, we can segment each articulated chain into the different body segments that make up the chain. Using the estimated joint angles, we can also compute the position of the coordinate frame attached to the body. For a given body segment, we can thus normalise the pose using the body coordinate frame, so that the body segment is positioned at the origin and aligned with the z-axis as in Fig. 10 (a). We compute the area of the cross-section of the voxels, A_z, (plane parallel to the xy-plane) at different points along the z-axis. We assume that the cross-section is elliptical and find the parameters (x_0, y_0) (in (1)), from the area using the relation $A = \pi x_0 y_0$. A circle of equal area would have radius $r = \sqrt{x_0 y_0}$. We compute the radius of the equivalent circle, at different points along the z-axis, as $r_z = \sqrt{A_z/\pi}$, which we refer to as the radial profile (Fig. 10 (a)). We compute the radial profile in all the key frames for each body segment and use the median radial profile. The median radial profiles for some of the body segments are presented in Fig. 10 (b-e). We can compute the length, radius and the scale parameter of the body segment from the radial profile. If we wish to determine the parameters x_0 and y_0 of the super-quadric, we obtain the xy-histogram, $I(x, y)$, a function whose value at (x_i, y_i) is given by the number of voxels that have x and y coordinates given by x_i and y_i respectively. We find the values of x_0 and y_0 that maximise the function,

$$\sum_{(x,y) \in S_{x_0, y_0}} I(x, y), \text{ where } S_{x_0, y_0} = \left\{ (x, y) : (\frac{x}{x_0})^2 + (\frac{y}{y_0})^2 < 1 \right\},$$

and satisfy the constraint, $x_0 y_0 = r^2$. The model composed of super-quadric segments computed above is presented in Fig. 11(b).

We refine the pose using the super-quadric body segments and the voxels directly instead of the voxel-skeleton. The objective is to obtain the pose that maximises the overlap between the super-quadric model and the voxels. The pose is refined by bounded optimisation of the pose parameter to minimise the "distance" between the voxels and the super-quadric model. This "distance" measures the distance of each voxel from the centre of the body segment closest to it. The distance vector, $\boldsymbol{e} = [e_1, e_2, \cdots, e_N]^\mathsf{T}$, where $e_i = \min\left(e_i^{(1)}, e_i^{(2)}, \cdots, e_i^{(J)}\right)$

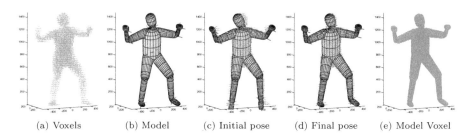

(a) Voxels   (b) Model   (c) Initial pose   (d) Final pose   (e) Model Voxel

Fig. 11. The model (b) constructed from initial estimate of the quadratic parameters compared with the voxels (a), and super-imposed with voxels before pose refinement (c) and after (d). (e) is the model in voxel representation.

and $e_i^{(j)}$ is the distance of the ith voxel with respect to the jth body segment and given as

$$e_i^{(j)} = \begin{cases} \exp\left(r_i^j - q_i^j\right), & \text{if } 0 \leq z_i^j \leq z_0^j \\ \exp\left(r_i^j + p_i^j\right), & \text{otherwise} \end{cases}, \text{ where } p_i^j = \min\left(\left|z_0^j - z_i^j\right|, \left|z_i^j\right|\right),$$

$$r_i^j = \sqrt{\left(\frac{x_i^j}{x_0^j}\right)^2 + \left(\frac{y_i^j}{y_0^j}\right)^2} \text{ and } q_i^j = \sqrt{\left(1 + s^j \frac{z_i^j}{z_0^j}\right)\left(1 - \left(1 - 2\frac{z_i^j}{z_0^j}\right)^d\right)}.$$

(x_i^j, y_i^j, z_i^j) are the voxel coordinates in the coordinate system of the jth body segment and $(x_0^j, y_0^j, z_0^j, s^j, d^j)$ are the super-quadric parameters of the jth body segment. Although the distance function appears complicated it is just a measure of how close the voxel is to the central axis of the super-quadric. The refined pose is the pose that minimises $\|e\|$. The pose of the subject before and after optimisation is presented in Fig. 11 (c) and (d) respectively.

4   Experiments and Conclusion

We use 15 calibrated cameras in our experiments positioned around the subject and pointing towards the centre of the capture volume. The images are 484×648 grey-level with 8-bit depth. The frequency of the capture is 3 frames per second. The units in the experiments are millimetres. The background subtraction algorithm does not perform very well on grey-scale images and as a result the voxel reconstruction is not of good quality at times. The algorithm is fairly robust to such errors and rejects frames where registration fails due to missing body segments or when the pose is not suitable.

We conducted experiments on four male subjects with different body mass, stature and BMI (body mass index). The same algorithm parameters were used in all the cases. Twenty key frames (where registration was successful) were used to estimate the model parameters as well as the pose at each time instant.

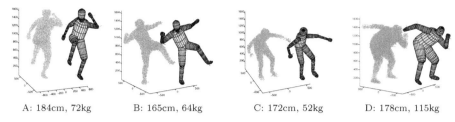

A: 184cm, 72kg   B: 165cm, 64kg   C: 172cm, 52kg   D: 178cm, 115kg

Fig. 12. Estimated models and corresponding voxels for different subjects

The results are illustrated in Fig. 12. We constructed a synthetic voxel image for each of the key frames using the estimated model and pose. We use the synthetic voxels (illustrated in Fig. 11 (e)) in order to evaluate the algorithm with respect to the data voxels (Fig. 11 (a)). We also estimate the model parameters using the synthetic voxels as *input*, so that we can compare the original pose and estimated pose. The pose errors were computed at 24 major joint locations as the absolute difference between the original and estimated joint angle values for all the key frames used in the model estimation algorithm. The results are tabulated in Table 1.

Table 1. Model and pose estimation error for real and synthetic data: Let N_D and N_M be the number of data voxels and voxels from the estimated models, and N_I is the number of intersecting voxels. Model Fill Ratio (FR) is N_I/N_M and Data FR is N_I/N_D. Note that each voxel is 1 cm^3. Volume is in m^3. Pose error is in degrees.

Experiment	Subject	Data		Model		Data/Model	Pose Error	
		Vol.	FR	Vol.	FR	Vol. Ratio	Mean	Median
Synthetic	A	0.083	0.909	0.081	0.935	1.030	5.7	2.2
	B	0.065	0.923	0.065	0.934	1.012	8.6	2.0
	C	0.057	0.858	0.054	0.902	1.052	7.0	2.2
	D	0.127	0.871	0.117	0.947	1.088	8.4	4.0
Real	A	0.088	0.766	0.083	0.812	1.059	–	–
	B	0.073	0.773	0.065	0.865	1.119	–	–
	C	0.063	0.690	0.057	0.765	1.111	–	–
	D	0.146	0.748	0.127	0.856	1.145	–	–

We have addressed the problem of model acquisition in great detail and provided the results of experiments conducted on different subjects. No prior measurements of the subjects were used. The only prior data used was a simple graph-based model of an "average" human subject and an approximate relation between the stature of an average human subject and the length of the long bones, as well as approximate locations of the shoulder, neck and pelvic joints with respect to the trunk. We have provided a systematic algorithm that aims to build a human body model in intuitive stages. We first perform segmentation and registration of the articulated chains that the human body is composed of. We have introduced a method to extract the different articulated chains that are part of the human body and also parameterise each voxel on the chain according to its distance from the joint. The latter is a key contribution and an important step in accurately estimating the skeleton and the body model parameters. In the next step, a skeleton is computed from the voxels and the parameters of the human body model are estimated and refined by computing the fit with the skeleton obtained from the voxels. We then compute the super-quadric parameters for each body segment and refine the pose and body model parameters using the super-quadric parameters and the voxels directly. We use distance measures between the model skeleton and the skeleton computed from the voxels to optimise the pose and joint locations and presented a method to obtain an initial estimate of the parameters of super-quadric segments.

Our method has advantages over other algorithms [7,13,3] in that we explicitly extract the 1-D nature of the structure using the Laplacian eigenmap transformation in high dimensional space. We also explicitly model the continuous 1-D structure using d-dimensional splines of a single parameter. We are thus able to segment the limbs at the joints using the spline-fit error as a natural indicator of when to stop growing the spline. We then use a probabilistic registration method in order to handle complex poses where the limbs may touch other body parts as in Fig. 6 (b-e) which are not considered in other methods such as [7]. The explicit modelling of the body segments as splines in the eigenspace domain also helps in creating the skeleton in the normal 3-D space. We then show that our segmentation and registration algorithm can be exploited to estimate the human body model parameters. We estimate the probability that the segmented body parts match our model, so that we can discard frames that have missing limbs due to possible errors in the voxel reconstruction.

References

1. Moeslund, T., Granum, E.: A survey of computer vision-based human motion capture. CVIU (2001) 231–268
2. Krahnstoever, N., Sharma, R.: Articulated models from video. In: Computer Vision and Pattern Recognition. (2004) 894–901
3. Mikic, I., Trivedi, M., Hunter, E., Cosman, P.: Human body model acquisition and tracking using voxel data. International Journal of Computer Vision **53** (2003)
4. Kakadiaris, I.A., Metaxas, D.: 3D human body model acquisition from multiple views. In: Fifth International Conference on Computer Vision. (1995) 618
5. Anguelov, D., Koller, D., Pang, H., Srinivasan, P., Thrun., S.: Recovering articulated object models from 3-D range data. In: Uncertainty in Artificial Intelligence Conference. (2004)
6. Cheung, K., Baker, S., Kanade, T.: Shape-from-silhouette of articulated objects and its use for human body kinematics estimation and motion capture. In: IEEE CVPR. (2003) 77–84
7. Chu, C.W., Jenkins, O.C., Mataric, M.J.: Markerless kinematic model and motion capture from volume sequences. In: CVPR (2). (2003) 475–482
8. Tenenbaum, J.B., de Silva, V., Langford, J.C.: A global geometric framework for nonlinear dimensionality reduction. Science **290** (2000) 2319–2323
9. Belkin, M., Niyogi, P.: Laplacian eigenmaps for dimensionality reduction and data representation. Neural Comput. **15** (2003) 1373–1396

10. Elad, A., Kimmel, R.: On bending invariant signatures for surfaces. IEEE Transactions on Pattern Analysis and Machine Intelligence **25** (2003) 1285–1295
11. Brand, M.: Charting a manifold. In: Neural Information Processing Systems. (2002)
12. Roweis, S.T., Saul, L.K.: Nonlinear dimensionality reduction by locally linear embedding. Science **290** (2000) 2323–2326
13. Brostow, G., Essa, I., Steedly, D., Kwatra, V.: Novel skeletal representation for articulated creatures. In: European Conference on Computer Vision. (2004)
14. Badler, N.I., Phillips, C.B., Webber, B.L.: Simulating Humans. Oxford University Press, Oxford, UK (1993)
15. Ozaslan, A., M. Yasar Iscan, Inci Oxaslan, H.T., Koc, S.: Estimation of stature from body parts. Forensic Science International **132** (2003) 40–45

Recovering Articulated Non-rigid Shapes, Motions and Kinematic Chains from Video

Jingyu Yan and Marc Pollefeys

Department of Computer Science,
The University of North Carolina at Chapel Hill,
Chapel Hill, NC 27599
{yan, marc}@cs.unc.edu

Abstract. We propose an approach to analyze and recover articulated motion with non-rigid parts, e.g. the human body motion with non-rigid facial motion, under affine projection from feature trajectories. We model the motion using a set of intersecting subspaces. Based on this model, we can analyze and recover the articulated motion using subspace methods. Our framework consists of motion segmentation, kinematic chain building, and shape recovery. We test our approach through experiments and demonstrate its potential to recover articulated structure with non-rigid parts via a single-view camera without prior knowledge of its kinematic structure.

Keywords: structure from motion, articulated, non-rigid, motion analysis.

1 Introduction

Articulated motion has been attracting research interests for decades. It is highly relevant to human motion, one of the most interesting motions in nature. Articulated motion with non-rigid parts is a good approximation to human motion. A system that can capture and recover that kind of motion has a wide range of applications in medical study, sport analysis and animation, etc. We propose an approach to analyze and recover articulated motion with non-rigid parts under affine projection from feature trajectories.

We model articulated motion with non-rigid parts as a set of intersecting subspaces. From this model, we derive our approach to segment the motion, build the kinematic chain and recover the structure. Compared to previous works on articulated motion, which assume that the parts are rigid [20][22][1] or use a kinematic model as a prior [2][3][4][5]. Our approach uses a unified framework to deal with rigid parts and non-rigid ones. Besides, it does not require prior knowledge of the kinematic structure, instead it can automatically builds the kinematic chain from analyzing the feature trajectories.

The following sections are organized as followed: Section 2, detailed discussion of our model of articulated motions; Section 3, our approach for motion segmentation, kinematic chain building and shape recovery; Section 4, experimental results; Section 5, conclusions and future work.

F.J. Perales and R.B. Fisher (Eds.): AMDO 2006, LNCS 4069, pp. 90–99, 2006.

2   Modeling Articulated Motion with Non-rigid Parts Using Subspaces

We are going to show that under affine projection the trajectories of rigid, non-rigid and articulated motions lie in some low-dimensional subspaces. Then we discuss the extension of the articulated case to non-rigid parts. The conclusion is that articulated motion with non-rigid parts can be modeled as a set of intersecting subspaces. The intersection between two motion subspaces may imply an articulated link of either a joint or an axis.

2.1   Articulated Motion Subspaces

The rigid, non-rigid and articulated motions are described as followed with respect to the subspaces they form.

- For rigid motions, the trajectories of a rigid object forms a linear subspace of dimensions no more than 4 ([16]).

$$M_{2f \times p} = [R_{2f \times 3}|T_{2f \times 1}] \begin{bmatrix} S_{3 \times p} \\ 1_{1 \times p} \end{bmatrix} \tag{1}$$

  f is the number of frames and p, the number of feature trajectories.
- The trajectories of a non-rigid object can be approximated by different weighings of a number of key shapes ([8][9]) and, as shown below, lie in a linear subspace of dimensions no more than $3k + 1$.

$$M = \begin{bmatrix} c_1^1 R_{2 \times 3}^1|...|c_k^1 R_{2 \times 3}^1|T_{2 \times 1}^1 \\ ... \\ c_1^f R_{2 \times 3}^f|...|c_k^f R_{2 \times 3}^f|T_{2 \times 1}^f \end{bmatrix} \begin{bmatrix} S_{3 \times 1}^1 \\ ... \\ S_{3 \times p}^k \\ 1_{1 \times p} \end{bmatrix} \tag{2}$$

  c_j^i $(1 \leq i \leq f, 1 \leq j \leq k)$.
- For articulated motions with rigid parts ([20][22]),
  - If the link is a joint, $[R_1|T_1]$ and $[R_2|T_2]$ must have $T_1 = T_2$ under the same coordinate system. So M_1 and M_2 lie in different linear subspaces but have one-dimensional intersection.
  - If the link is an axis, $[R_1|T_1]$ and $[R_2|T_2]$ must have $T_1 = T_2$ and exactly one column of R_1 and R_2 being the same under a proper coordinate system. So M_1 and M_2 lie in different linear subspaces but have two-dimensional intersection.

The articulated motion can be modeled as a set of intersecting subspaces. The intersections between two subspaces are the motion subspaces of a link, either a joint or a axis, with dimensions of 1 or 2.

2.2   Extension to Non-rigid Parts

In this section, we extend our discussion of articulated motion to non-rigid parts. A case in point is the human motion whose facial motion is non-rigid and whose head and body motions combined can be considered as articulated. We will focus on a typical non-rigid case and build some theorems; lastly, we discuss how this typical case can fit into the articulated motion subspace discussed above.

Let us consider a typical case of non-rigid motion: the non-rigid shape has rigid components. This includes human facial motion which deforms on top of rigid head motion. More formally, we are considering such a case that a non-rigid shape can be represented by linear combinations of a number of key shapes $S^1, ..., S^K$ that satisfy $S_i^1 = ... = S_i^K$ as long as its ith component is rigid.

We can prove then the following theorems.

Theorem 1. *If a non-rigid shape can be represented by linear combinations of $S^1, ..., S^K$ that satisfy $S_i^1 = ... = S_i^K$ for any rigid component i, the sum of the linear coefficients of any frame f is 1, i.e. $\sum_{i=1}^{K} c_i^f = 1$.*

Proof. Let S_i be a rigid component of the non-rigid shape. For any frame f, its 2D coordinates are:

$$M_i^f = [c_1^f R^f | ... | c_K^f R^f | T^f] \begin{bmatrix} S_i \\ ... \\ S_i \\ 1 \end{bmatrix} \tag{3}$$

Because S_i is rigid, M_i^f can also be written as the following.

$$M_i^f = [R^f | T^f] \begin{bmatrix} S_i \\ 1 \end{bmatrix} \tag{4}$$

By comparing Equation 3 and 4, we have $\sum_{i=1}^{K} c_i^f = 1$.

Theorem 2. *If a non-rigid shape can be represented by linear combinations of $S^1, ..., S^K$ that satisfy $S_i^1 = ... = S_i^K$ for any rigid component i, the rigid motion subspace formed by the rigid components is embedded in the non-rigid motion subspace.*

Proof. From Theorem 1, we know $\sum_{i=1}^{K} c_i^f = 1$ for any frame f. Let S_I be the set of all rigid components. We have the following.

$$\begin{bmatrix} c_1^1 R^1 | ... | c_K^1 R^1 | T^1 \\ ... \\ c_1^F R^F | ... | c_K^F R^F | T^F \end{bmatrix} \begin{bmatrix} S_I \\ ... \\ S_I \\ 1 \end{bmatrix} = \begin{bmatrix} R^1 | T^1 \\ ... \\ R^F | T^F \end{bmatrix} \begin{bmatrix} S_I \\ 1 \end{bmatrix} \tag{5}$$

Notice the left are trajectories in the non-rigid motion subspace; the right are trajectories in the rigid motion subspace formed by all rigid components. So the rigid motion subspace formed by those components must be embedded in the non-rigid motion subspace.

Now we can deal with articulated objects with non-rigid parts that satisfy the above specification. The result is similar to the rigid case because essentially it is the embedded rigid motion subspace that interacts with its linked part. This result remains valid if both linked parts are non-rigid[1].

- If the link is a joint, two subspaces have in general a one-dimensional intersection.
- If the link is an axis, two subspaces have in general a two-dimensional intersection.

Notice that for either case, we do not need to extract the embedded rigid motion subspace out of the non-rigid one in order to find the intersection. We can intersect the motion subspaces directly to find the joint or axis subspace.

3   The Algorithms

Based on the subspace model of articulated motion with non-rigid parts, we derive our algorithms for analyzing the motion and recovering it in the following. The motion segmentation is important to both learning the kinematic chain and recovering the articulated shape.

3.1   Motion Segmentation

Motion segmentation is the most important analysis of the articulated motion in our approach. Its result can be directly used by kinematic chain learning and shape recovery.

Previous works on motion segmentation has been mostly focusing on independent motions [7][11][12]. It is the independency between motions that is exploited in this group of works. In our articulated case, the intersection between motion subspaces violates this assumption and so they do not apply. As for more recent works of GPCA [17][18][19], though it can handle segmenting dependent motions, it requires a number of trajectories that is often too large to be satisfied in practice. For more details, please refer to [21].

We use the algorithm proposed in [21] which can segment rigid or non-rigid motion subspaces when they are either independent or dependent. The algorithm is described in the following.

- Trajectory Data Transformation
  Transform each trajectory of dimension $2F$ (F is the number of frames) onto a R^K unit sphere ($rank(W_{2F \times P}) = K$, $W_{2F \times P}$ is the trajectory matrix). This can be done by SVD, $W_{2F \times P} = U_{2F \times K} D_{K \times K} V_{P \times K}^T$, and normalizing each row of V. Each unit vector $v_i (i = 1...P)$ becomes the new representation of the corresponding trajectory.

---

[1] For cases where the non-rigid deformations between the articulated parts are dependent, it might be possible that higher dimensional intersections are obtained.

- Local Subspace Estimation
  Without knowing the underlying subspace each v_i belongs to, we estimate it from itself and its $n - 1$ closest neighbors, i.e. computing the subspace of $[v_i, v_{i1}, ..., v_{in}]_{K \times (n)}$ using SVD. n is normally chosen to be larger than the dimension of the underlying subspace.
- Spectral Clustering
  An affinity matrix can be built from the distance between every pair of the locally estimated subspaces for each v_i. Then we can perform spectral clustering and segment the trajectories. The distance between two equidimensional subspaces is typically represented by the sine of their largest principle angle[23].

  The principal angles [23] between two subspaces are defined recursively as a series of angles $0 \leq \theta_1 \leq, ..., \leq \theta_M \leq \pi/2$ (M is the minimum dimension of both subspaces):

$$\cos(\theta_m) = max_{u \in S^1, v \in S^2} u^T v = u_m^T v_m$$

where

$$\|u\| = \|v\| = 1$$
$$u^T u_i = 0 \quad i = 1, ..., m - 1$$
$$v^T v_i = 0 \quad i = 1, ..., m - 1$$

In our case, we define the affinity as below.

$$affinity(\alpha, \beta) = e^{-\sum_{i=1,...,M} sin^2(\theta_i)}$$

where $\theta_1, ..., \theta_M$ are the principal angles between two locally estimated subspaces α and β.

After segmenting the trajectories, we perform outlier rejection within each segment. This can be done using a RANSAC approach [6] that robustly fit the data into a subspace and reject outliers. The motion subspaces are formed by the remaining trajectories in each group.

3.2   Learning the Kinematic Chain

For two linked parts, either rigid or non-rigid, either for a joint link or an axis link, their motion subspaces are intersecting on at least one dimensional subspace (see Section 2.2), thus have at least one zero principle angle. In practice, the value will not be exact zero so a threshold is required. For parts that are not linked, the motion subspaces do not have this property and have a larger minimum principle angle. Depending on how independent the motion subspaces are, the minimum principle angles may vary.

Based on the above analysis, we will describe our kinematic chain building algorithm in the following.

– Build the proximity graph
  We use a graph to represent the proximity between every pair of motion
  subspaces.

$$G = (V, E)$$

  where $V = \{v_1, ..., v_S\}$ (v_i is the ith motion subspace; S is the number of
  motion subspaces) and $E(v_i, v_j) = \theta_{ij}$ (θ_{ij} is the minimum principle angle
  between subspace i and j).
– Find the minimum spanning tree(s)
  Based on the proximity graph we find a minimum spanning tree using Algorithm 1. The spanning tree corresponds to the kinematic chain that we
  compute.

Algorithm 1. Finding the minimum spanning tree

---

  let T be the graph of the smallest edge of G
  while T has fewer than $S - 1$ edges **do**
     find the smallest edge in G connecting T to $G - T$
     add it to T
  end while

3.3   Shape Recovery

After the segmentation, each part can be recovered individually from the segmented motion. For rigid parts, factorization method [16] can be applied directly.
For non-rigid parts, non-rigid shape recovery algorithms [8][9][10] can be used.

  The basic idea is to factorize the trajectory matrix into two matrix, one accounting for the rotation and translation of the camera and the other for the
object shape for the rigid case or key shapes for the non-rigid case.

4   Experiments

We test our approach in three real data sets.

  The first experiment is from a scene with non-degenerate data of an articulated
object with a rotating axis. The detected rank of the trajectories is 6. The
segmentation result is shown in Fig. 1. The ranks of the segmented trajectories
are both 4. Each articulated part can be recovered as a rigid shape using the
factorization method [16]. By putting all parts into the camera coordinates,
shape and motion of the articulated object gets recovered. Furthermore, with
the axis recovered in the camera coordinates, we can reanimate the articulated
motion by rotating a part around the axis and generate not only novel views but
also novel motions (Figure 2).

  The second example is an articulated puppet with 6 rigid parts: the head,
the upper body, the hip, 2 arms and 2 legs. A KLT tracker tracks a total of 114
features over 564 frames. The segmentation result is shown in Figure 3. After
outlier rejection within each segment, the remaining 97 features are shown in
Figure 3.

Fig. 1. (*left and middle*) A sequence of a truck moving with the shovel rotating around an axis. The color of a dot, red or green, shows the segmentation result. (*right*) The affinity matrix of local estimated subspaces is shown. The row and columns are re-arranged based on the segmentation.

Fig. 2. The shape and motion of the truck get recovered and reanimated. The black dots show the original position of the shovel. Not only novel views but also novel motions can be generated by rotating the shovel around the axis.

The minimum principle angles (the proximity graph) between 6 motion subspaces are shown in Table 1. The bold font indicates the edges of the minimum spanning tree of the graph. The kinematic chain are built from that and the links are recovered by intersecting linked subspaces[20][22] based on the kinematic chain (Figure 3). The recovered kinematic chain is correct. However, one can notice that the hip-body link is only marginally preferred to the lleg-body link. The reason for this is that the motion of the puppets leg is mostly restricted to a plane orthogonal to the image so that it is hard to differentiate between the legs and the hips.

Table 1. Proximity graph and its minimum spanning tree – Puppet

	larm	lleg	hip	rarm	body
rleg	0.0111	0.0007	**0.0002**	0.0126	0.0006
larm		0.0110	0.0060	0.0250	**0.0008**
lleg			**0.0002**	0.0170	0.0006
hip				0.0175	**0.0005**
rarm					**0.0003**

Table 2. Proximity graph and its minimum spanning tree – Person

	luarm	ruarm	body	rlarm	llarm
head	0.0015	0.0033	**0.0011**	0.0035	0.0065
luarm		0.0036	**0.0008**	0.0058	**0.0009**
ruarm			**0.0008**	**0.0003**	0.0145
body				0.0018	0.0033
rlarm					0.0103

Fig. 3. (*top left*) The segmentation of trajectories over 6 articulated parts of a puppet. (*top right*) Trajectories after rejecting outliers. (*bottom*) The kinematic chain built from trajectories and the links (white dots) recovered by intersecting the linked subspaces based on the kinematic chain. (This figure is in color. We invite the reviews to check out the video we supply as additional material).

Fig. 4. (*top left*) The segmentation of trajectories over 6 articulated parts of an upper-body human motion. (*top right*) Trajectories after rejecting outliers. (*bottom*) The kinematic chain built from trajectories and the links (white dots) recovered by intersecting the linked subspaces based on the kinematic chain.

The third example is an upper body motion of a person with 6 parts: the head, the upper body, 2 upper arms and 2 lower arms. The head has some non-rigid facial motion. A KLT tracker tracks the total of 268 features over 40 frames. The segmentation result is shown in the top left of Figure 4. After outlier rejection within each segment, the remaining 97 features are shown in the top right of Figure 4. The minimum principle angles (the proximity graph) between 6 motion subspaces are shown in Table 2. The bold font indicates the edges of the minimum spanning tree. The kinematic chain are built from the 6 motion subspaces and the links are recovered by intersecting subspaces[20][22] based on the kinematic chain, shown in the bottom of Figure 4.

The non-rigid part is the head which has a joint link with the upper body. The link can be recovered simply by finding the 1-dimensional intersection between both motion subspaces as discussed in Section 2.2.

5   Conclusions and Future Work

We describe an approach to analyze and recover articulated motion with non-rigid parts. The approach is based on the subspace model of articulated motion. The algorithms for motion segmentation and kinematic chain building are derived from this model. After segmentation, the shape of each part can be recovered by the factorization-based methods for rigid or non-rigid shapes.

Our approach can be further demonstrated. Due to tracking a complex articulated object is still an unsolved problem, the second and the third experiment do not provide shape recovery result. In the future, we plan to adopt or develop a tracking method that handles occlusion and reappearing features to generate tracks that cover the full shape of a complex articulated object. In the end, we plan to recover human motion using our approach.

Acknowledgments

The support of the NSF ITR grant IIS-0313047 is gratefully acknowledged.

References

1. H. Zhou, T. Huang, "Recovering Articulated Motion with a Hierarchical Factorization Method", Gesture Workshop 2003: 140-151
2. C.J. Taylor, "Reconstruction of Articulated Objects from Point Correspondences in a Single Image", CVPR, pp. 677, 2000.
3. C. Bregler, J. Malik, "Tracking people with twists and exponential maps", CVPR, pp. 8–15, 1998.
4. D. Hogg. "Model-based vision: A program to see a walking person", Image and Vision Computing, 1(1):5–20, 1983.
5. C. Sminchisescu and B. Triggs, "Covariance Scaled Sampling for Monocular 3D Body Tracking", Proc. CVPR, vol. I, pp. 447-454, 2001.
6. M. A. Fischler, R. C. Bolles. Random Sample Consensus: A Paradigm for Model Fitting with Applications to Image Analysis and Automated Cartography. Comm. of the ACM, Vol 24, pp 381-395, 1981.
7. J.P. Costeira, T. Kanade, "A Multibody Factorization Method for Independently Moving Objects", *IJCV*, Vol. 29, Issue 3 pp. 159-179, 1998.

8. C. Bregler, A. Hertzmann, H. Biermann, "Recovering Non-Rigid 3D Shape from Image Streams", Proceedings of the IEEE Conference on Computer Vision and Pattern Recognition (CVPR '00), June 2000.
9. M. Brand, "Morphable 3D models from video", CVPR, pp. II:456-463, 2001.
10. J. Xiao, J. Chai, and T. Kanade, "A closed-form solution to non-rigid shape and motion recovery", Proceedings of the European Conference on Computer Vision, 2004.
11. N. Ichimura. Motion segmentation based on factorization method and discriminant criterion. In Proc. IEEE Int. Conf. Computer Vision, pages 600605, 1999.
12. K. Kanatani. Motion segmentation by subspace separation and model selection:model selection and reliability evaluation. Intl. J. of Image and Graphics, 2(2):179197, 2002.
13. Y. Weiss. Segmentation using eigenvectors: A unifying view. In International Conference on Computer Vision, pages 975982, Corfu, Greece, September 1999.
14. A. Ng, M. Jordan, and Y. Weiss. On spectral clustering: analysis and an algorithm. In Advances in Neural Information Processing Systems 14. MIT Press, 2002.
15. J. Shi and J. Malik, Normalized Cuts and Image Segmentation, IEEE Transactions on Pattern Analysis and Machine Intelligence (PAMI), 2000.
16. C. Tomasi, T. Kanade, "Shape and motion from image streams under orthography: a factorization method", IJCV, Vol. 9, Issue 2 pp. 137-154, 1992.
17. R. Vidal and R. Hartley. Motion Segmentation with Missing Data using PowerFactorization and GPCA. IEEE Conference on Computer Vision and Pattern Recognition, 2004
18. R. Vidal, Y. Ma and S. Sastry, "Generalized Principal Component Analysis (GPCA) ", Proceedings of the IEEE Conference on Computer Vision and Pattern Recognition (CVPR'03), June 2003.
19. R. Vidal, Y. Ma and J. Piazzi, "A New GPCA Algorithm for Clustering Subspaces by Fitting, Differentiating and Dividing Polynomials", Proceedings of the IEEE Conference on Computer Vision and Pattern Recognition (CVPR'04), June 27 - July 02, 2004.
20. J. Yan, M. Pollefeys, A Factorization-based Approach to Articulated Motion Recovery, IEEE Conf. on Computer Vision and Pattern Recognition, 2005
21. J. Yan, M. Pollefeys, A General Framework for Motion Segmentation: Independent, Articulated, Rigid, Non-rigid, Degenerate and Non-degenerate, ECCV 2006
22. P. Tresadern and I. Reid, Articulated Structure From Motion by Factorization, Proc IEEE Conf on Computer Vision and Pattern Recognition, 2005
23. G. Golub and A. van Loan. Matrix Computations. Johns Hopkins U. Press, 1996

3D Shape Reconstruction of Trunk Swaying Human Body Segments

Takuya Funatomi, Masaaki Iiyama, Koh Kakusho, and Michihiko Minoh

Kyoto University, Yoshida-Honmachi, Kyoto, 606-8501, Japan

Abstract. We propose a method for acquiring a 3D shape of human body segments accurately. Using a light stripe triangulation range finder, we can acquire accurate the 3D shape of a motionless object in a dozen of seconds. If the object were to move during the scanning, the acquired shape would be distorted. Naturally, humans move slightly for making balance while standing even if the subject tries to stay still for avoiding the distortion of the shape. Our method corrects the distortion based on measured motion during the scanning.

Experimental results show the accuracy of our shape measurements. Trunk swaying degrades the accuracy of the light stripe triangulation from 1mm to 10mm. We can keep the accuracy of as good as 2mm by applying our method.

1 Introduction

For computer-aided design (CAD) of apparel, ergonomic and medical products, the 3D shape of each particular human body becomes more and more useful. In fact, several commercial products [1,2,3] based on the light stripe triangulation rangefinders have been developed to reconstruct the 3D shape of an individual.

Although the light stripe triangulation rangefinder can accurately (< 1mm) acquire the 3D shape of an object as a dense 3D point-cloud on the surface, it takes time to scan the whole object with a laser sheet. If the object moves during the scanning, the acquired shape becomes distorted and the accuracy is degraded. Naturally, humans move slightly for making balance while standing even if the subject tries to stay still and stop breathing for avoiding the distortion of the shape. Such movement is called *trunk sway*. Our goal is to maintain the accuracy of the light stripe triangulation for reconstructing the 3D human shape.

In order to cope with the distortion caused by the trunk sway for the measurement of human body by the light stripe triangulation, several methods [4,5,6,7] which reduce the time for measuring the shape by speeding up the measurement can reduce the distortion. On the other hand, we propose in this paper to measure the motion of human body due to the trunk sway so that we correct the distortion of the acquired shape based on the subject's motion. To obtain the motion, we estimate the rigid motion of each segment of the human body at each moment during the measurement by assuming that the human body consists of several rigid segments. For rigid motion estimation, we put markers on the skin and measure their 3D position with cameras.

F.J. Perales and R.B. Fisher (Eds.): AMDO 2006, LNCS 4069, pp. 100–109, 2006.

This paper is organized as follows. In section 2, we show how the 3D shape is reconstructed by the light stripe triangulation and discuss how the acquired shape is distorted by the subject's motion. We present our method in section 3. We show experimental evaluation of the accuracy of the measurements for all segments and the acquired shape of a right upper arm and breast in section 4. We conclude the paper with some discussion and future works in section 5.

2   Background

2.1   The Principle of Light Stripe Triangulation

The light stripe triangulation method reconstructs the 3D shape of an object as follows:

1. Project a laser sheet on the object.
2. Observe the projected laser sheet, which is observed as a thin stripe on the surface of the object, with calibrated camera(s).
3. Calculate the 3D position of the points that are on the observed stripe in the camera image from the position of the plane of the laser sheet and the pose of the camera using the triangulation.

From camera image at a moment, we can acquire only the partial shape of the whole object where is illuminated by the laser sheet. We call each of partial shapes as *stripe shape*. In order to acquire the full shape of the object, the laser scans the whole object and the cameras observe the scanning (see also Fig.1.) In comparison with other 3D shape capture methods, this method can acquire high resolutional and accurate shape but takes much time for scanning the whole object with the laser sheet.

2.2   Problem of Human Body Scanning

With the light stripe triangulation for a stationary object (see Fig.2-a), we can acquire an accurate shape. As for moving objects (see Fig.2-b), the acquired shape would be distorted by the object's motion during the scanning.

This distortion problem will often occur when scanning the human body. Some commercial products [1,2,3] take about a dozen of seconds to scan the whole body with accuracy of about 0.5mm. In order to acquire the undistorted 3D shape, the subject needs to stop moving during the scanning. However, the subject moves slightly for making balance while standing (trunk sway.)

The trunk sway is observed to assess postural stability in medical, physiological and biomechanical science. Generally, they observe the movement of body center-of-mass (COM) as the trunk sway and regard the trunk sway as the oscillation of an inverted pendulum. As has been reported in [8], the average absolute amplitude and the average frequency of the oscillation are about 5mm and 1Hz, respectively. Such oscillation will distort the shape acquired with the light stripe triangulation method.

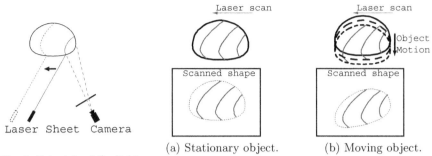

Fig. 1. Principle of the light stripe triangulation

(a) Stationary object.   (b) Moving object.

Fig. 2. Shape distortion due to object motion

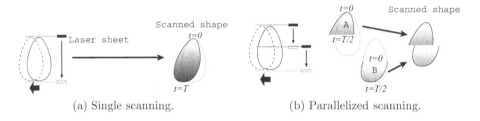

(a) Single scanning.   (b) Parallelized scanning.

Fig. 3. Mismatching problem in parallel scanning

We discuss two approaches for avoiding the distortion from trunk sway. One approach is speeding up the measurement for reducing the distortion. Speedy scanning will make the distortion small. The other, which we propose in section 3, is correcting the distortion based on the motion of the body due to trunk sway.

Speeding up the measurement. Several methods [5,6,7] have been proposed to speed up the measurement by parallelizing the scanning with multiple lasers. Although these methods are applicable to a stationary object, a problem will occur when they are applied to a moving object. Fig.3 illustrates vertical scanning of an object which moves horizontally. With a single laser (see Fig.3-a), the acquired shape is distorted due to the object's motion. In comparison with single scanning, parallel scanning can acquire less distorted shape (see Fig.3-b). However, the acquired shape is segmented, and each segment (A, B in Fig.3-b) will not match because the time of capture is different between borders (the bottom of A and the top of B). As mentioned above, speeding up the measurement can reduce the distortion, but cannot acquire the correct shape of the moving object.

3   Distortion Correction Process

In this paper, we propose an alternative approach to human body measurement that corrects the distortion of the acquired shape based on trunk sway.

Generally, the human body will change its shape with various postures due to muscle contractions. However, the shape will not change much locally when the subject tries to maintain the posture. We assume that the human body can be divided into some rigid segments, and the trunk sway of the subject is described as the set of rigid motions of each segment. Here, we divide the whole body into 11 rigid segments (s :=head, breast, waist and right and left upper arms, forearms, thighs and legs).

The acquired shape of a segment s using the light stripe triangulation consists of 3D points on the segment's surface as mentioned in section 2.1. The position of each point would be changed by the rigid motion of s due to trunk sway. This distorts the shape acquired with the light stripe triangulation. Acquiring the rigid motion during the scanning, we calculate the original position of each point and acquire the undistorted shape. Consequently, we have to measure shape and motion of the subject simultaneously.

3.1   Rigid Motion Acquisition

To acquire the trunk sway during the scanning ($t = 0, 1, \cdots, T$), we put N^s (at least three) markers on the surface of each segment s, and observe them with more than 2 synchronized and calibrated cameras to calculate 3D position using the triangulation method.

To calculate the 3D position of the markers, we need the 2D position of each marker on each camera's image plane and the correspondence of each 2D position among the cameras. The markers' positions on camera images are detected with pixel values. To observe the markers with cameras vividly, the observation should be performed in a bright place. On the contrary, the light stripe triangulation should be performed in a dark place to detect the light stripe clearly and measure the shape accurately. To solve this conflict, we use 4 synchronized and calibrated cameras as 1 unit: 2 are adjusted in exposure for observing markers and 2 are for observing the laser stripe. We employ Zhang's method [9] and the factorization method [10] for the camera calibration.

Let M_k^s ($k = 1, \cdots, N^s$) denote the k-th marker on a segment s. At time t, we express its 3D position as a 4x1 column vector in homogeneous coordinates, $\boldsymbol{M}_k^s(t)$. $\boldsymbol{M}_k^s(t)$ is calculated using triangulation with 2D positions of M_k^s on each camera image which acquired at time t. In our method, we track the markers on sequence of images $I(t)$ for each camera to get 2D marker positions $\boldsymbol{m}_k^s(t)$. We give the 2D position $\boldsymbol{m}_k^s(0)$ for all M_k^s of the initial frame $I(0)$ of each camera manually. For other frames $I(t)$, $\boldsymbol{m}_k^s(t)$ are estimated sequentially from their pixel value at $\boldsymbol{m}_k^s(t-1)$ on $I(t-1)$ and the pixel values around $\boldsymbol{m}_k^s(t-1)$ on $I(t)$. $\boldsymbol{m}_k^s(t)$ is estimated as the center of the area that has values similar to the pixel value of $\boldsymbol{m}_k^s(t-1)$ on $I(t-1)$.

We give the correspondences of the markers' 2D position among cameras manually. Then, we can calculate makers' 3D positions $\boldsymbol{M}_k^s(t)$.

Rigid transformation matrix estimation. From the obtained $\boldsymbol{M}_k^s(t)$, we estimate a rigid motion of segment s from time $t = i$ to j, $\boldsymbol{W}_{i,j}^s$ which is expressed as a 4x4 rigid transformation matrix. $\boldsymbol{M}_k^s(j)$ is given by $\boldsymbol{M}_k^s(i)$ and the rigid transformation matrix $\boldsymbol{W}_{i,j}^s$ as:

$$M_k^s(j) = W_{i,j}^s M_k^s(i). \tag{1}$$

We define an error function $E^s(W)$ as follows:

$$E^s(W) = \frac{1}{N^s} \sum_{k=1}^{N^s} \|M_k^s(j) - W M_k^s(i)\|. \tag{2}$$

Here, N^s is the number of markers and W is a rigid transformation matrix which is defined by 6 parameters. $W_{i,j}^s$ is estimated as the W that minimizes $E^s(W)$ using the Powell minimization algorithm[11].

3.2 Distortion Correction

With $W_{i,0}^s$ for all $t = i$ and all segments s, we can correct the distortion of the acquired shape. The distorted shape consists of $T+1$ stripe shapes which were acquired from the rangefinder at $t = 0, 1, \cdots, T$. To recover the undistorted shape, we transform each stripe shape which acquired at $t = i$ into that at $t = 0$ as using:

$$p^s(0) = W_{i,0}^s p^s(i). \tag{3}$$

Here, $p^s(i)$ denotes the point position which compose the stripe shape at $t = i$, and is expressed as a 4x1 column vector in homogeneous coordinates. With the above correction, we can acquire an undistorted shape as a set of $p^s(0)$.

To correct the distortion for each time t and each segment s, we segment the acquired full body shape into s segments manually, and separate the shape of segment s into the $T+1$ stripe shapes which acquired at $t = 0, 1, \cdots, T$.

4 Results

4.1 Experiments for Accuracy Evaluation

The proposed method require at least only three markers for acquiring the rigid motion of each segment s. However, we put a lot of markers $M_k^s(k = 1, \cdots, N^s)$ and measure their 3D position $M_k^s(t)$ with the above procedure (mentioned in 3.1) at all times $t = 0, \cdots, T$ for evaluating the accuracy. We evaluate 4 kinds of accuracy in this experiment:

- Accuracy of marker position measurement
- Non-rigid deformation of the human body segments while standing still
- Accuracy of the light stripe triangulation (with distortion)
- Accuracy of our method.

Non-rigidity of human body segments. To validate the assumption that the whole body can be divided into rigid segments s, we evaluate the rigidity for each human body segment with standing still. Non-rigidity is evaluated as a residual of the eq. (2) for estimating the rigid transformation $W_{i,j}^s$ from a set of marker positions $M_k^s(i)$ to a set of $M_k^s(j)$ for all pairs of time (i, j). Let

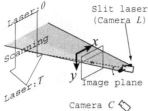
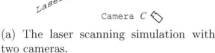

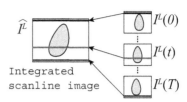

(a) The laser scanning simulation with two cameras.

(b) Scanline integration from the camera images.

Fig. 4. The simulation of the light stripe triangulation

$\widetilde{\boldsymbol{W}}_{i,j}^{s}$ denote the estimation of $\boldsymbol{W}_{i,j}^{s}$ from minimizing eq. (2). We evaluate the non-rigidity of segment s as an average residual $E^s(\widetilde{\boldsymbol{W}}_{i,j}^{s})$, E_W^s, which is defined as follows:

$$E_W^s = \frac{1}{T(T+1)} \sum_{\substack{i=0 \\ i \neq j}}^{T} \sum_{j=0}^{T} E^s(\widetilde{\boldsymbol{W}}_{i,j}^{s}). \tag{4}$$

Accuracy of the marker position measurement. Besides non-rigid deformation of segment s, error in measuring the marker position $M_k^s(t)$ will also influence the average residual E_W^s. We evaluate error in the measuring using the average residual of using a rigid object instead of a human body. As the rigid object, we use a mannequin which is held by a human to make the same motion as a trunk sway. We evaluate an accuracy of the marker position measurement as the average residual of $E^s(\widetilde{\boldsymbol{W}}_{i,j}^{s})$ for the rigid object, $\overline{E_W}$.

Accuracy of the light stripe triangulation. To evaluate the influence of the trunk sway on the light stripe triangulation, we simulate the measurement using the markers M_k^s and acquire the distorted shape.

The simulation is performed using a pair of sequences of images, $I^C(t)$ and $I^L(t)$, from two cameras C and L which observe marker positions. If a laser sheet which goes through lens center of the camera L scans the object, the stripe on the subject is observed as a straight line on camera image $I^L(t)$. Here, the laser plane is parallel to the x-axis of the image plane of camera L and the laser is scanned along the y-axis going from $y=0$ on the image plane at $t=0$ to $y=1$ at $t=T$. The stripe at t is projected to the camera image $I^L(t)$ as the line, $y=t/T (0 \leq x \leq 1, 0 \leq y \leq 1)$ (see Fig.4-a). Therefore, the observation of the laser scanning from the camera L is done by integrating the lines from a sequence of the images $I^L(t)$ into a single image, which we call the *integrated scanline image* $\widehat{I^L}$ (see also Fig.4-b).

With the integrated scanline image $\widehat{I^L}$, we can simulate the markers position, $\widehat{M_k^s}$, on the acquired shape using the light stripe triangulation. When the marker M_k^s is observed on $\widehat{I^L}$ at coordinate $\widehat{m_k^s} = (\hat{x}_k^s, \hat{y}_k^s)$, $\widehat{M_k^s}$ is given by $M_k^s(\hat{y}_k^s/T)$ since the marker would be illuminated by the laser sheet at time $\hat{y}_k^s/T$. For all

t, $M_k^s(t)$ is obtained using the pair of sequences of images $I^C(t)$ and $I^L(t)$, so $\widehat{M_k^s}$ can also be acquired.

Using $\widehat{M_k^s}$ and $M_k^s(t)$, we evaluate the accuracy of the light stripe triangulation for a trunk swaying subject, $E_L^s(t)$, as follows for each segment s:

$$E_L^s(t) = \frac{1}{N^s} \sum_{k=1}^{N_s} ||\widehat{M_k^s} - M_k^s(t)|| = \frac{1}{N^s} \sum_{k=1}^{N_s} ||M_k^s(\hat{y}_k^s/T) - M_k^s(t)||. \quad (5)$$

Accuracy of the proposed method. To evaluate the accuracy of the proposed method, we correct the distorted shape $\widehat{M_k^s}$. We use only 3 of N^s markers for rigid motion estimation and use the other N^s-3 markers for accuracy evaluation. First, we calculate the estimate of the rigid transformation matrix $\widehat{W_{t,0}^s}$ from 3 markers positions $M_k^s(t)$. Then, we transform $\widehat{M_k^s}$ of the remaining markers into their corrected position $\widetilde{M_k^s}(0)$ with $\widehat{W_{t,0}^s}$. Finally, we evaluate the accuracy, E_S^s, by comparing $\widetilde{M_k^s}(0)$ and $M_k^s(0)$ as follows:

$$E_S^s = \frac{1}{N^s} \sum_{k=1}^{N_s} ||\widetilde{M_k^s}(0) - M_k^s(0)|| = \frac{1}{N^s} \sum_{k=1}^{N_s} ||\widehat{W_{\hat{y}_k^s/T,0}^s} M_k^s(\hat{y}_k^s/T) - M_k^s(0)||. \quad (6)$$

4.2   Accuracy Evaluation Results

First, we show the result of evaluating the accuracy of the marker position measurement. We put fifty-eight 3-mm-square markers on a mannequin with about 20mm grid spacing (see Fig.5-a), and measure their 3D position for 10 seconds with 15fps cameras, that is $T = 150$. Fig.5-b illustrates the markers position with wire-frame at $t = 18, 123$. We calculated the marker measurement accuracy from all pairs of time t, $\overline{E_W}$ was 0.73mm. Fig.5-c also illustrates markers position at $t = 123$ transformed into markers at $t = 18$ using the estimated rigid transformation matrix. This figure shows that the rigid transformation matrix is estimated properly.

Next, we show the result of evaluating the non-rigidity of human body E_W^s, the accuracy of the light stripe triangulation $E_L^s(t)$ and the accuracy of the proposed method E_S^s. As mentioned above, we put about 70 markers on the breast and waist, and about 30 markers on the head, upper arms, forearms, thighs and legs and measured the marker positions for 30 seconds, $T = 450$. Also, the subject makes an effort to keep standing still and stop breathing to avoid non-rigid deformation.

We show the camera image at $t=0$, $I^L(0)$, and the integrated scanline image $\widehat{I^L}$ from an upper arm observation in Fig.6. Fig.6-b shows how the trunk sway of the subject will distort the acquired shape.

To evaluate the accuracy, we measure the marker positions at $t=0$, $M_k^s(0)$, the marker positions acquired with simulated the light stripe triangulation, $\widehat{M_k^s}$, and the positions as corrected by the proposed method, $\widetilde{M_k^s}(0)$. Fig.7 illustrates

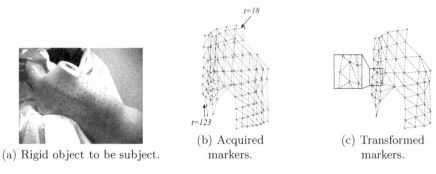

(a) Rigid object to be subject.

(b) Acquired markers.

(c) Transformed markers.

Fig. 5. Experiment to evaluate the accuracy of marker position measurement

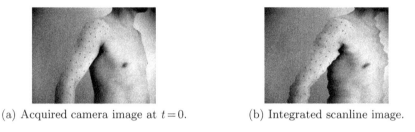

(a) Acquired camera image at $t=0$.

(b) Integrated scanline image.

Fig. 6. Experimental result of integrated scanline image

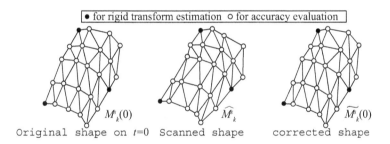

Fig. 7. Experiment for markers position measurement and correction

acquired marker positions $M_k^s(0)$, $\widehat{M_k^s}$, $\widetilde{M}_k^s(0)$ as measured from Fig.6. We chose 3 markers to estimate rigid motion (the black markers in Fig.7) and evaluate the accuracy of the correction using the remaining markers (the white markers).

We show the E_W^s, $E_L^s(0)$ and E_S^s calculated for each segment s in Table 1. From the results, we conclude that:

- In standing still, each segment of the body will deform non-rigidly less than about 1mm (E_W^s).
- Trunk sway degrades the measurement accuracy $E_L^s(0)$ to about 10mm.
- The proposed method maintains the accuracy within about 2mm (E_S^s) with distortion correction.

Table 1. Measurement accuracy evaluation for different body-parts (unit:mm)

Segment s	Non-rigidity E_W^s	Distortion $E_L^s(0)$	Correction E_S^s
head	0.69	10.32	1.09
breast	0.70	7.48	1.47
waist	0.89	6.56	1.56
upper arm	1.54	31.50	1.86
forearm	1.14	7.16	1.99
thigh	1.16	3.94	1.25
leg	1.87	3.35	2.64
Average	1.14	10.04	1.69

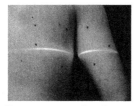   

(a) Camera image for the marker position measurement.   (b) Camera image for the light stripe triangulation.

Fig. 8. Synchronous observations of the markers and the laser scans

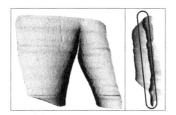   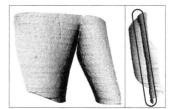

(a) A distorted shape.   (b) Result of the proposed method.

Fig. 9. Comparison of contemporary and proposed method for shape reconstruction

4.3   Measurement Result

We show the acquired shape of a right upper arm and breast with two methods, the light stripe triangulation and the proposed method. We reconstruct the surface from acquired point-cloud by making Delaunay mesh. Fig.8 illustrates the camera images for the marker position measurement and the light stripe triangulation. Fig.9 illustrates the shape acquired with the light stripe triangulation and the result of the proposed method. The distortion which we can see in encircled area of Fig.9-a is corrected by the proposed method, Fig.9-b.

5   Conclusion and Future works

In this paper, we discussed that the trunk sway distorts the 3D shape of a human body acquired with the light stripe triangulation and proposed a method which corrects the distortion using measured body motion. We presented how each segment of the human body undergoes less than 1mm of non-rigid deformation in standing still. Nevertheless, experimental results show that the accuracy of the light stripe triangulation is degraded from less than 1mm of error to about 10mm distortion due to the trunk sway. Our method allows for trunk swaying during the measurement with about 2mm accuracy.

We will apply our method to shape measurement of the whole body. Furthermore, all manual procedures in our method have to be automated in future.

References

1. Cyberware Inc., http://www.cyberware.com/
2. VOXELAN Inc., http://www.voxelan.co.jp/
3. Hamamatsu Inc., http://www.hpk.co.jp/
4. Y. Oike, M. Ikeda, K. Asada. "A COMS Image Sensor for High-Speed Active Range Finding Using Column-Parallel Time-Domain ADC and Position Encoder," IEEE Trans. on electron devices, vol.50 no.1, pp.152-853, 2003.
5. P. Vuylsteke, A. Oosterlinck. "Range Image Acquisition with a Single Binary-Encoded Light Pattern," IEEE Trans. on Pattern Analysis and Machine Intelligence, vol. 12, no. 2, pp. 148-164, 1990.
6. C. Sinlapeecheewa, K. Takamasu. "3D Profile Measurement by Color Pattern Projection and System Calibration," Proc.of ICIT'02, pp.405-410, 2002.
7. K. Hattori, Y. Sato. "Accurate Rangefinder with Laser Pattern Shifting," Proc.of ICPR, vol.3 no.3, pp.849-853, 1996.
8. Winter DA, Patla AE, Prince F, Ishac M, Gielo-Perczak K. "Stiffness Control of Balance in Quiet Standing," J. Neurophysiology, vol. 80, no. 3, pp. 1211 - 1221, 1998.
9. Z. Zhang. "A Flexible New Technique for Camera Calibration," Microsoft Research, MSR-TR-98-71, 1998.
10. T. Ueshiba, F. Tomita. "A Factorization Method for Projective and Euclidean Reconstruction for Multiple Perspective views via iterative depth estimation," Proc. European Conf. Computer Vision, vol.1, pp.296-310, 1998.
11. W.H. Press, B.P. Flannery, S.A. Teukolsky, W.T. Vetterling. "Numerical Recipes in C, the Art of Scientific Computing, Second Edition," Cambridge University Press, 1992.

Combined Head, Lips, Eyebrows, and Eyelids Tracking Using Adaptive Appearance Models*

Fadi Dornaika, Javier Orozco, and Jordi Gonzàlez

Computer Vision Center
Edifici O, Campus UAB
08193 Bellaterra, Barcelona, Spain
{dornaika, orozco, gonzalez}@cvc.uab.es

Abstract. The ability to detect and track human heads and faces in video sequences is useful in a great number of applications, such as human-computer interaction and gesture recognition. Recently, we have proposed a real-time tracker that simultaneously tracks the 3D head pose and facial actions associated with the lips and the eyebrows in monocular video sequences. The developed approach relies on Online Appearance Models where the facial texture is learned during the tracking. This paper extends our previous work in two directions. First, we show that by adopting a non-occluded facial texture model more accurate and stable 3D head pose parameters can be obtained. Second, unlike previous approaches to eyelid tracking, we show that the Online Appearance Models can be used for this purpose. Neither color information nor intensity edges are used by our proposed approach. Moreover, our eyelids tracking does not rely on any eye feature extraction which may lead to erroneous results whenever the eye feature detector fails. Experiments on real videos show the feasibility and usefulness of the proposed approach.

1 Introduction

The ability to detect and track human heads and facial features in video sequences is useful in a great number of applications, such as human-computer interaction and gesture recognition. Vision-based tracker systems provide an attractive alternative since vision sensors are not invasive. Of particular interest are vision-based markerless head and/or face trackers. Since these trackers do not require any artificial markers to be placed on the face, comfortable and natural motions can be achieved. On the other hand, building robust and real-time markerless trackers for head and facial features is a difficult task due to the high variability of the face and the facial features in videos.

To overcome the problem of appearance changes recent works on faces adopted statistical facial textures. For example, the Active Appearance Models have been proposed as a powerful tool for analyzing facial images [1]. Deterministic and

---

* This work was supported by the Government of Spain under the CICYT project TIN2005-09026 and The Ramón y Cajal Program.

F.J. Perales and R.B. Fisher (Eds.): AMDO 2006, LNCS 4069, pp. 110–119, 2006.

statistical appearance-based tracking methods have been proposed and used by some researchers [2,3,4]. These methods can successfully tackle the image variability and drift problems by using deterministic or statistical models for the global appearance of a special object class: the face. A few algorithms exist which attempt to track both the head and the facial features in real time, e.g. [3] and [4]. These works have addressed the combined head and facial feature tracking using the Active Appearance Models principles. However, [3] and [4] require tedious learning stages that should be performed beforehand and should be repeated whenever the imaging conditions change. Recently, we have developed a head and facial feature tracking method based on Online Appearance Models (OAMs) [5]. Unlike the Active Appearance Models, the OAMs offer a lot of flexibility and efficiency since they do not require any facial texture model that should be computed beforehand. Instead the texture model is built online from the tracked sequence.

This paper extends a previous work [5] in two directions. First, we show that by adopting a non-occluded shape-free facial texture that excludes the eyes region more accurate and stable 3D head pose parameters can be obtained. Second, unlike feature-based eyelid trackers, we show that the Online Appearance Models can be used to track the eyelids. Thus, we can infer the eye state without detecting the eye features such as the irises and the eye corners.

Tracking the eyelids and the irises can be used in many applications such as drowsiness detection and interfaces for handicapped individuals. Detecting and tracking the eye and its features has been addressed by many researchers. A variety of methodologies have been applied to the problem of eye tracking. There are many methods for detecting eye features such as eye corners, irises, and eyelids [6,7,8,9]. However, most of the proposed approaches rely on intensity edges and are time consuming. In [8], detecting the state of the eye is based on the iris detection in the sense that the iris detection results will directly decide the state of the eye. In [6], the eyelid state is inferred from the relative distance between the eyelid apex and the iris center. For each frame in the video, the eyelid contour is detected using edge pixels and normal flow. The authors reported that when the eyes were fully or partially open, the eyelids were successfully located and tracked 90% of the time. Their proposed approach depends heavily on the extracted intensity edges. Moreover, it assumes high resolution images depicting an essentially frontal face. In our study, we do not use any edges and there is no assumption on the head pose. In our work, the eyelid motion is inferred at the same time with the 3D head pose and other facial actions, that is, the eyelid state does not rely on the detection results of other features such as the eye corners and irises. Tracking the rapid eyelid motion is not a straightforward task. In our case, we like to track the eyelid motion using the principles of OAMs. The challenges are as follows. First, the upper eyelid is a highly deformable facial feature since it has a great freedom of motion. Second, the eyelid can completely occludes the iris and sclera, that is, a facial texture model will have two different appearances at the same locations. Third, the eyelid motion is very fast compared to the motion of other facial features.

The remainder of this paper proceeds as follows. Section 2 introduces our deformable 3D facial model. Section 3 states the problem we are focusing on, and describes the online adaptive appearance model. Section 4 summarizes the adaptive appearance-based tracker that tracks in real-time the 3D head pose and some facial actions. It gives some comparisons obtained with different facial texture models. In Section 5, we present some tracking results associated with the head, lips, eyebrows and eyelids.

2   Modeling Faces

A deformable 3D model. In our study, we use the 3D face model *Candide* [10]. This 3D deformable wireframe model was first developed for the purpose of model-based image coding and computer animation. The 3D shape of this wireframe model is directly recorded in coordinate form. It is given by the coordinates of the 3D vertices $\mathbf{P}_i, i = 1, \ldots, n$ where n is the number of vertices. Thus, the shape up to a global scale can be fully described by the $3n$-vector $\mathbf{g}$; the concatenation of the 3D coordinates of all vertices $\mathbf{P}_i$. The vector $\mathbf{g}$ is written as:

$$\mathbf{g} = \mathbf{g}_s + \mathbf{A}\,\boldsymbol{\tau}_a \tag{1}$$

where $\mathbf{g}_s$ is the static shape of the model, $\boldsymbol{\tau}_a$ the animation control vector, and the columns of $\mathbf{A}$ are the Animation Units. In this study, we use seven modes for the facial Animation Units (AUs) matrix $\mathbf{A}$. We have chosen the seven following AUs: lower lip depressor, lip stretcher, lip corner depressor, upper lip raiser, eyebrow lowerer, outer eyebrow raiser and eyelid lowerer. These AUs are enough to cover most common facial animations. Moreover, they are essential for conveying emotions. Thus, the lips are controlled by four parameters, the eyebrows are controlled by two parameters, and the eyelids by one parameter.

In equation (1), the 3D shape is expressed in a local coordinate system. However, one should relate the 3D coordinates to the image coordinate system. To this end, we adopt the weak perspective projection model. We neglect the perspective effects since the depth variation of the face can be considered as small compared to its absolute depth. Thus, the state of the 3D wireframe model is given by the 3D head pose parameters (three rotations and three translations) and the internal face animation control vector $\boldsymbol{\tau}_a$. This is given by the 13-dimensional vector $\mathbf{b}$:

$$\mathbf{b} = [\theta_x,\, \theta_y,\, \theta_z,\, t_x,\, t_y,\, t_z,\, \boldsymbol{\tau_a}^T\,]^T \tag{2}$$

Shape-free facial textures. A face texture is represented as a shape-free texture (geometrically normalized image). The geometry of this image is obtained by projecting the static shape $\mathbf{g}_s$ (neutral shape) using a centered frontal 3D pose onto an image with a given resolution. The texture of this geometrically normalized image is obtained by texture mapping from the triangular 2D mesh in the input image (see figure 1) using a piece-wise affine transform, $\mathcal{W}$ (see [10] for more details). The warping process applied to an input image $\mathbf{y}$ is denoted by:

$$\mathbf{x}(\mathbf{b}) = \mathcal{W}(\mathbf{y}, \mathbf{b}) \tag{3}$$

where $\mathbf{x}$ denotes the shape-free texture and $\mathbf{b}$ denotes the geometrical para-meters. Several resolution levels can be chosen for the shape-free textures. The reported results are obtained with a shape-free patch of 5392 pixels. Regarding photometric transformations, a zero-mean unit-variance normalization is used to partially compensate for contrast variations. The complete image transfor-mation is implemented as follows: (i) transfer the texture $\mathbf{y}$ using the piece-wise affine transform associated with the vector $\mathbf{b}$, and (ii) perform the grey-level normalization of the obtained patch. Figure 1 illustrates two shape-free patches associated with an input image.

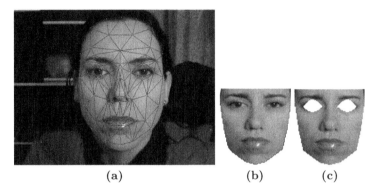

(a)   (b)   (c)

Fig. 1. (a) an input image with correct adaptation. (b) the corresponding shape-free facial image. (c) the same patch without the eyes region.

3   Problem Formulation and Adaptive Appearance Models

Given a video sequence depicting a moving head/face, we would like to recover, for each frame, the 3D head pose and the facial actions encoded by the control vector τ_a. In other words, we would like to estimate the vector $\mathbf{b}_t$ (2) at time t given all the observed data until time t, denoted $\mathbf{y}_{1:t} \equiv \{\mathbf{y}_1, \ldots, \mathbf{y}_t\}$. In a tracking context, the model parameters associated with the current frame will be handed over to the next frame.

For each input frame $\mathbf{y}_t$, the observation is simply the warped texture patch (the shape-free patch) associated with the geometric parameters $\mathbf{b}_t$. We use the HAT symbol for the tracked parameters and textures. For a given frame t, $\hat{\mathbf{b}}_t$ represents the computed geometric parameters and $\hat{\mathbf{x}}_t$ the corresponding shape-free patch, that is,

$$\hat{\mathbf{x}}_t = \mathbf{x}(\hat{\mathbf{b}}_t) = \mathcal{W}(\mathbf{y}_t, \hat{\mathbf{b}}_t) \qquad (4)$$

The estimation of the current parameters $\hat{\mathbf{b}}_t$ from the previous ones $\hat{\mathbf{b}}_{t-1}$ and from the sequence of images will be presented in Section 4. In our work, the initial parameters $\hat{\mathbf{b}}_1$ corresponding to the first frame are manually provided. The automatic initialization can be obtained using the statistical technique proposed in [3].

By assuming that the pixels within the shape-free patch are independent, we can model the appearance of the shape-free facial patch using a multivariate Gaussian with a diagonal covariance matrix Σ. Let μ be the Gaussian center and σ the vector containing the square root of the diagonal elements of the covariance matrix Σ. μ and σ are d-vectors (d is the size of $\mathbf{x}$) representing the appearance parameters. In summary, the observation likelihood at time t is written as

$$p(\mathbf{y}_t|\mathbf{b}_t) = p(\mathbf{x}_t|\mathbf{b}_t) = \prod_{i=1}^{d} \mathbf{N}(x_i; \mu_i, \sigma_i)_t \tag{5}$$

where $\mathbf{N}(x_i; \mu_i, \sigma_i)$ is a normal density:

$$\mathbf{N}(x_i; \mu_i, \sigma_i) = (2\pi\sigma_i^2)^{-1/2} \exp\left[-\rho\left(\frac{x_i - \mu_i}{\sigma_i}\right)\right], \quad \rho(x) = \frac{1}{2}x^2 \tag{6}$$

We assume that the appearance model summarizes the past observations under an exponential envelope, that is, the past observations are exponentially forgotten with respect to the current texture. When the appearance is tracked for the current input image, *i.e.* the texture $\hat{\mathbf{x}}_t$ is available, we can update the appearance and use it to track in the next frame. It can be shown that the appearance model parameters, *i.e.*, μ and σ can be updated using the following equations (see [11] for more details on Online Appearance Models):

$$\mu_{i_{(t+1)}} = (1 - \alpha)\,\mu_{i_{(t)}} + \alpha\,\hat{x}_{i_{(t)}} \tag{7}$$

$$\sigma^2_{i_{(t+1)}} = (1 - \alpha)\,\sigma^2_{i_{(t)}} + \alpha\,(\hat{x}_{i_{(t)}} - \mu_{i_{(t)}})^2 \tag{8}$$

In the above equations, the subscript i denotes a pixel in the patch $\hat{\mathbf{x}}$. This technique, also called recursive filtering, is simple, time-efficient and therefore, suitable for real-time applications. The appearance parameters reflect the most recent observations within a roughly $L = 1/\alpha$ window with exponential decay.

Note that μ is initialized with the first patch $\hat{\mathbf{x}}_1$ corresponding to the geometrical parameters $\hat{\mathbf{b}}_1$. However, equation (8) is not used until the number of frames reaches a given value (*e.g.*, the first 40 frames). For these frames, the classical variance is used, that is, equation (8) is used with α being set to $\frac{1}{t}$.

4   Tracking Using Adaptive Appearance Registration

We consider the state vector $\mathbf{b} = [\theta_x, \theta_y, \theta_z, t_x, t_y, t_z, \boldsymbol{\tau_a}^T]^T$ encapsulating the 3D head pose and the facial actions. In this section, we will show how this state can be recovered for time t using the previous known state $\hat{\mathbf{b}}_{t-1}$, the current input image $\mathbf{y}_t$, and the current appearance parameters. The vector $\boldsymbol{\tau_a}$ may have 6 facial actions (lips and eyebrows) or 7 facial actions (lips, eyebrows, and eyelids).

The sought geometrical parameters $\mathbf{b}_t$ at time t are related to the previous parameters by the following equation ($\hat{\mathbf{b}}_{t-1}$ is known):

$$\mathbf{b}_t = \hat{\mathbf{b}}_{t-1} + \Delta\mathbf{b}_t \tag{9}$$

where $\Delta\mathbf{b}_t$ is the unknown shift in the geometric parameters. This shift is estimated using a region-based registration technique that does not need any image feature extraction. In other words, $\Delta\mathbf{b}_t$ is estimated such that the warped texture will be as close as possible to the facial appearance given by the Gaussian parameters. For this purpose, we minimize the *Mahalanobis* distance between the warped texture and the current appearance mean,

$$\min_{\mathbf{b}_t} e(\mathbf{b}_t) = \min_{\mathbf{b}_t} D(\mathbf{x}(\mathbf{b}_t), \boldsymbol{\mu}_t) = \sum_{i=1}^{d} \left(\frac{x_i - \mu_i}{\sigma_i} \right)^2 \tag{10}$$

The above criterion can be minimized using iterative first-order linear approximation which is equivalent to a Gauss-Newton method. It is worthwhile noting that minimizing the above criterion is equivalent to maximizing the likelihood measure given by (5). Moreover, the above optimization is made robust by using robust statistics [5]. In the above optimization, the gradient matrix $\frac{\partial \mathcal{W}(\mathbf{y}_t, \mathbf{b}_t)}{\partial \mathbf{b}} = \frac{\partial \mathbf{x}_t}{\partial \mathbf{b}}$ is approximated by numerical differences. More details about this optimization technique can be found in [5].

On a 3.2 GHz PC, a non-optimized C code of the approach computes the 3D head pose and the seven facial actions in 70 ms.

5   Tracking Comparisons

In this Section, we compare the 3D head pose estimates obtained with different shape-free patches using the same robust optimization technique described above. To this end, we use the two shape-free patches depicted in Figure 1.(b) and 1.(c). Note that the second patch is obtained from the first one by removing the eyes region. We assume that the state vector $\mathbf{b}$ is given by the six head pose parameters and the six facial actions associated with the lips and eyebrows.

We have used a 1000-frame long sequence featuring a talking subject[1] as a test video. Note that talking is a spontaneous activity. Figure 2 illustrates the estimates of the 3D head pose parameters associated with a 150-frame long segment using the two different shape-free facial patches (this segment starts at frame 500). This video segment contains three blinks at frames 10, 104, and 145. As can be seen, the most significant deviations in the 3D head pose parameters occur at those frames (e.g., see the scale plot). Whenever eye blinking occurs the patch without the eyes region has provided more accurate and stable parameters than the patch with the eyes region. This is explained by the fact that despite the use of robust statistics the estimation of the 3D head pose with a texture model

---

[1] http://www-prima.inrialpes.fr/FGnet/html/benchmarks.html

containing the eyes region (sclera and iris) is affected by the eyelids motion. One can notice that the rotational deviations/errors seem to be small. However, the vertical and in-depth translation errors can be large. For example, at frame 145 the obtained scale deviation/error is about 0.025 which corresponds to an in-depth error of about 3 centimeters[2].

6   Head, Lips, Eyebrows, and Eyelids Tracking

In the previous Section, we have shown that the accuracy of the 3D head pose can be affected by the eyelids motion/blinking if the sclera and iris region is included in the texture model. This is not surprising since eye blinking corresponds to a sudden occlusion of a small part of the face. Thus, if the eyelids motion is tracked one can expect that the 3D head pose parameters can be more stable. Also, we have shown that the estimated 12 degrees of freedom associated with the head, lips ad eyebrows together with the used deformable 3D model are enough to track the eye boundaries in a video sequence. However, one needs to do more to track the eyelids motion. As we have mentioned earlier, tracking the eyelids motion is a very challenging task, and most of the proposed approaches for locating and tracking the eyelids rely on the extracted intensity edges.

To tackle the difficulties associated with the eyelids motion, we use the following. First, we adopt a shape-free facial texture model whose eyes region corresponds to closed eyes configuration (see Figure 3), which implicitly excludes the iris and sclera regions. Second, we use the same registration technique described in Section 4 where the facial action vector τ_a is now given by 7 facial actions (lips, eyebrows, and eyelids). Note that when the eyes are open in the input image, the shape-free texture corresponding to the eyelids region (associated with a correct eyelid facial action) will be a distorted version of a very small area in the input image. However, the global appearance of the eyelid is still preserved since the eyelids have the skin appearance.

We have tracked the head, lips, eyebrows, and eyelid using the 1000-frame long sequence. Figure 4 displays the tracking results (13 degrees of freedom) associated with frames 280, 284, and 975. The middle displays zoomed views of those frames. Notice how the eyelids are correctly tracked. The upper left corner of each image shows the current appearance (μ_t) and the current shape-free texture ($\hat{x}_t$). The bottom of this figure displays the estimated eyelid facial action as a function of time where the zero value corresponds to a closed eyelid and the one value to a wide open eyelid. Eye blinking is a discrete and important facial action [12,13]. In our case, it can be directly detected and segmented by thresholding the continuous eyelid facial action. As can be seen, the dual state of the eye can easily be inferred from the continuous curve. For the tracked sequence, all blinks are correctly detected and segmented.

Figure 5 displays the tracking results obtained with another two videos.

---

[2] The exact value depends on the camera intrinsic parameters and the absolute depth.

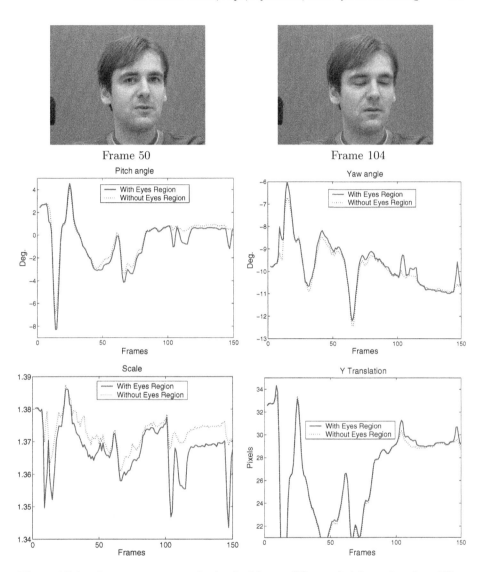

Fig. 2. 3D head pose parameters obtained with two different facial patches that differs by the eyes region

Fig. 3. The shape-free texture used to track 13 degrees of freedom including the eyelid motion

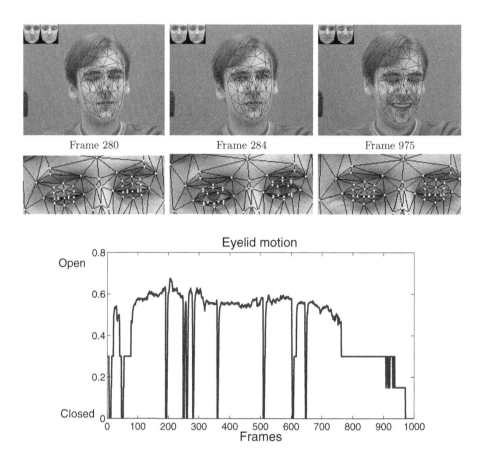

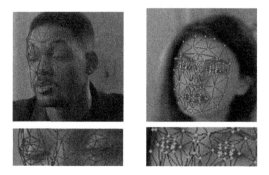

Fig. 4. Tracking the 3D head pose, the lips, the eyebrows and the eyelids associated with a 1000-frame long sequence. Only frames 280, 284, 975 are shown. The plot depicts the estimated eyelid facial action as a function of time.

Fig. 5. Two test sequences

7   Conclusion

In this paper, we have extended our appearance-based 3D head and facial action tracker to deal with eyelid motions. The 3D head pose and the facial actions associated with the lips, eyebrows, and eyelids are simultaneously estimated in real-time using Online Appearance Models. Compared to other eyelid tracking techniques our proposed approach has several advantages. First, computing and segmenting intensity edges has been avoided. Second, the eyelid is tracked with other facial actions at the same time, and hence it does not depend on the detection of other eye features. Third, the eyelid motion is tracked using a continuous facial action. Experiments on real video sequences indicate that the eye state can be detected using the eyelid tracking results.

References

1. Cootes, T., Edwards, G., Taylor, C.: Active appearance models. IEEE Transactions on Pattern Analysis and Machine Intelligence **23**(6) (2001) 681–684
2. Cascia, M., Sclaroff, S., Athitsos, V.: Fast, reliable head tracking under varying illumination: An approach based on registration of texture-mapped 3D models. IEEE Transactions on Pattern Analysis and Machine Intelligence **22**(4) (2000) 322–336
3. Ahlberg, J.: An active model for facial feature tracking. EURASIP Journal on Applied Signal Processing **2002**(6) (2002) 566–571
4. Matthews, I., Baker, S.: Active appearance models revisited. International Journal of Computer Vision **60**(2) (2004) 135–164
5. Dornaika, F., Davoine, F.: On appearance based face and facial action tracking. IEEE Transactions on Circuits and Systems for Video Technology (In press)
6. Sirohey, S., Rosenfeld, A., Duric, Z.: A method of detecting and tracking irises and eyelids in video. Pattern Recognition **35**(6) (2002) 1389–1401
7. Liu, H., Wu, Y., Zha., H.: Eye states detection from color facial image sequence. In: SPIE International Conference on Image and Graphics, vol. 4875. (2002) 693–698
8. Tian, Y., Kanade, T., Cohn, J.F.: Dual-state parametric eye tracking. In: International Conference on Automatic Face and Gesture Recognition. (2000)
9. Zhu, J., Yang, J.: Subpixel eye gaze tracking. In: International Conference on Automatic Face and Gesture Recognition. (2002)
10. Ahlberg, J.: Model-based coding: Extraction, coding, and evaluation of face model parameters. PhD thesis, No. 761, Linköping University, Sweden (2002)
11. Jepson, A., Fleet, D., El-Maraghi, T.: Robust online appearance models for visual tracking. IEEE Transactions on Pattern Analysis and Machine Intelligence **25**(10) (2003) 1296–1311
12. Grauman, K., Betke, M., Gips, J., Bradski, G.R.: Communication via eye blinks - Detection and duration analysis in real time. In: International Conference on Computer Vision and Pattern Recognition. (2001)
13. Moriyama, T., Kanade, T., Cohn, J., Xiao, J., Ambadar, Z., Gao, J., Imamura, H.: Automatic recognition of eye blinking in spontaneously occuring behavior. In: International Conference on Pattern Recognition. (2002)

Mobile Path and Spin 3D Tracking and Reconstruction

Federico Cristina[1], Sebastián H. Dapoto[1], Claudia Russo[1], Armando Degiusti[1],
and María José Abásolo[2]

[1] Instituto de Investigación en Informática LIDI
Facultad de Informática Universidad Nacional de La Plata
La Plata, Buenos Aires, Argentina
{fcristina, sdapoto, crusso, degiusti}@lidi.info.unlp.edu.ar
[2] Departamento de Matemática e Informática de la Universidad
de las Islas Baleares
Palma, Baleares, España
{mjabasolo}@uib.es

Abstract. The branch of Computer Science known as digital image processing includes different topics of Investigation and Development, as well as applications encompassing different stages that go from data acquisition, enhancement, and segmentation, up to the analysis, classification and interpretation of images [1]. Particularly, the reconstruction of 3D movements from 2D images (photos, filming) is a complex area, which becomes significant when it is a matter of obtaining real time responses. [1, 2, 3]. This project aim is developing a three-dimensional analysis system considering the processing of a soccer ball trajectory and rotational speed for its later computer-generated graphical modeling. The objective of the system is to improve the player's skills and the training methodology, and is framed within the research line of this Institute and within the area of signal and image processing.

Keywords: Image processing, objects tracking, path, spin.

1 Introduction

Path tracking and analysis is of particular importance in industrial environments, especially robotics. [4]

Focusing now on the subject matters of this project, we shall mention those robot applications called car-like robots. These vehicles have to move in unknown environments and avoid obstacles fast and effectively.

They are used, for instance, in games employing robots, which move in a small scenario taking the ball towards the rival goal. They have also been found in some tests with games of several sports, in which the ball is tracked in order to analyze shots [5, 6].

Path tracking requires a previous retrieval of the environment, be it manual or automatic, in order to obtain the information on the location and dimension of potential obstacles. On the other hand, if the generated path is to be tracked, we need to detect the specific object within the environment, so as to place it along the path and make the corresponding decisions. [5, 7]

F.J. Perales and R.B. Fisher (Eds.): AMDO 2006, LNCS 4069, pp. 120–131, 2006.

The system aims at improving the players' free-shot technique by means of the immediate display of the results obtained after each attempt. It also allows qualifying each shot according to the achieved precision and speed, showing comparatives among the different attempts. Thanks to this, each player will have its history, which will let us make note of their evolution.

3D reconstruction of the moving object (the ball) is of utmost importance since not only can the observation point vary but also other effects of sports importance can be studied (for example, ball spin on its axis over a lineal path). This requires identifying the points of the mobile object and reconstructing the spin path simultaneously with the advance path [4, 8].

This aspect presents a particular complexity since the ball's translational movement should be properly isolated from that of rotation. We should also take into account the labeling criteria over the surface in order to obtain the proper results.

In order to carry out the system development, several steps had to be followed, including camera calibration, image filtering, point triangulation in space, path obtaining, and ball spin. The following section presents a theoretical explanation of each technique used and the developed implementation for its solution.

2 Camera Calibration

In order to obtain a proper triangulation of the object in space, we have to know first the characteristics of the camera to be used [8, 11, 12, 14].

There exist two sets of parameters that should be obtained by the camera calibration process. These are the intrinsic and extrinsic parameters.

2.1 Intrinsic Camera Calibration

Camera intrinsic calibration allows us to obtain its intrinsic parameters. These do not depend on the orientation and position of the camera within the 3D world; they are typical of this camera as optical device. The intrinsic parameters are the following:

- Principal point or position of image center with respect to the camera reference system. It is the intersection point between the camera optical axis and the image plane.
- Focal length: distance separating the image plane optical center.
- Scale factors for x and y axis, to convert pixels into units.
- Distortion coefficients. Geometric distortion affects the points in the image plane, as a result of a series of imperfections in the manufacture and assemblage of the lenses of the optical system. There are three types of distortion: radial, decentering, and prismatic.

2.2 Extrinsic Camera Calibration

Extrinsic calibration of a camera allows us to obtain its extrinsic parameters. These define the orientation and position of the camera in relation to a determined coordinate system, which is known as the world coordinate system. Three parameters define the movement and another three parameters (three angles with respect to axis x and y) define orientation.

2.3 Calibration Methodology in the Developed System

A camera intrinsic and extrinsic calibration module has been developed. This has the following features: left and right camera calibration, and stereo camera.

2.3.1 Left and Right Camera Calibration
In order to obtain the intrinsic calibration, we have used a known-size calibration grid, as Figure 1 shows. A series of shots are obtained with different positions and the grid's intersections are detected.

Figure 2 shows how the left and right camera were calibrated. For this, it was necessary to inform the system about the size of the frames of the grid (in millimeters) and the quantity of internal points of intersections (both horizontal and vertical).

Fig. 1. Different shots of the Calibration Grid

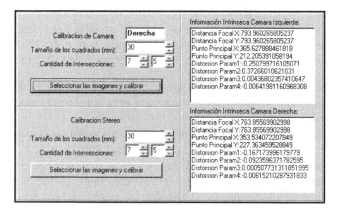

Fig. 2. Information obtained after Camera Calibration

2.3.2 Stereo Calibration
Once both cameras are calibrated, the following step entails the stereo or extrinsic calibration. For this, it is necessary to inform once again the features of the grid used. Once this is finished, a stereo image of the left camera and a stereo image of the right

Fig. 3. Images corresponding to Stereo Calibration

camera are selected. Both images should be correspondent to one another, as Figure 3 shows.

3   Filtering of the Object of Interest

Since a color filtering technique is used, the corresponding module is developed in order to detect without mistakes the red ball in each of the squares making up the videos to process. Such module allows setting up a configuration of the maximum and minimum allowable color thresholds, such as follows:

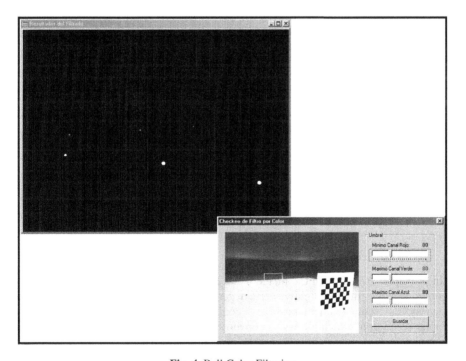

Fig. 4. Ball Color Filtering

- Red Channel Minimum: it represents the minimum allowable red intensity of the image. Those pixels with a red intensity lower than such value will not be taken into account.
- Green Channel Maximum: it represents the maximum allowable green intensity of the image. Those pixels with a green intensity higher than such value will not be taken into account.
- Blue Channel Maximum: it represents the maximum allowable blue intensity of the image. Those pixels with a blue intensity higher than such value will not be taken into account

4 Path Computation and Visualization

Once each stereo pair corresponding to each other and making up the video sequence are filtered, the ball triangulation is to be carried out. This technique is referred to as stereovision. [9, 16].

4.1 Stereovision

The correspondence problem is the most difficult to solve within stereovision. It means deciding which points of two images are the projection of the same real point. Once I_1 and I_2 are established to be the projection of the same point P in the two image planes R_1 and R_2, it is possible to obtain the 3D coordinates of such point by triangulation.

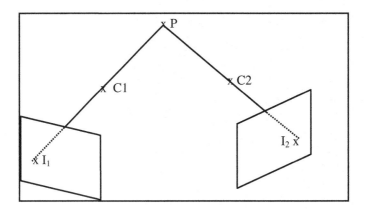

Fig. 5. Corresponding Points in Two Stereo Images

In principle, any point in the image plane R_2 could correspond to any point in R_1. In order to solve this ambiguity, certain geometrical restrictions depending on the image system setup (camera positions) could be used. The most important is the epipolar restriction, which allows us converting a two-dimensional search into a one-dimensional.

4.2 Object-of-Interest Triangulation Methodology in the Developed System

The ball triangulation is carried out by the corresponding video processing. The processing time will mainly depend on the quantity of squares per second of the videos (the higher the quantity of squares per second, the longer will be the processing time) and the resolution of the images making up the video (the higher the resolution, the larger the volume of information to be processed, and thus the longer the processing time).

Once the video sequence is processed, enough information is obtained to render the following results:

1. Numerical Information:
    a. Initial ball acceleration.
    b. Point-to-point ball speeds along the path.
    c. Maximum ball height.
    d. Average shot speed.
    e. Ball location in space.
2. Visual Information:
    a. Shot starting point.
    b. Impact point in the barrier or arrival at the goal line.
    c. Real path description.
    d. Estimated path description
    e. Comparison between the real and the estimated path.

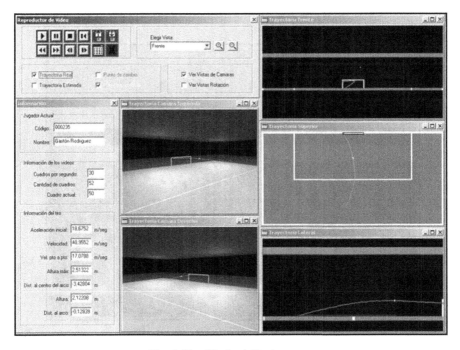

Fig. 6. Shot Playback Environment

The shot playback environment allows functionalities similar to those of a video player with different views (front, upper, lateral) as well as shot numerical data, such as figure 6 shows.

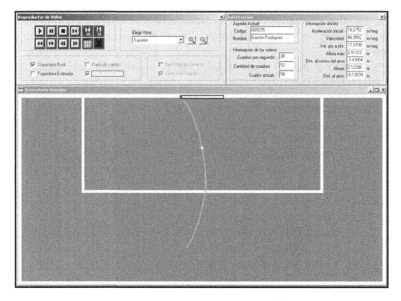

Fig. 7a. Zooming in of the upper view in the Shot Playback environment

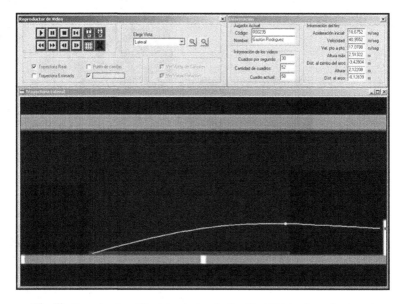

Fig. 7b. Zooming in of the lateral view in the Shot Playback environment

The shot playback environment also presents the possibilities of storing the shots, for a later load and playback of them if necessary, without the need of re-processing. It also provides the possibility of zooming in one of the views for a greater detail of the path traced by the ball, such as figure 7 shows.

5 Spin Computation

In order to determine the ball spin speed, it is necessary to analyze the movement made by the ball between one frame and the next one. In these cases, movement estimation or optical flow techniques are used, which allows us to detect the movements generated along the video sequence. [18, 19].

5.1 Movement Estimation

It is a process by means of which the object (or pixels) movement between two images is measured. Figure 8 shows that the moving image can be expressed in a three-dimensional space resulting from moving two consecutive images through the time axis.

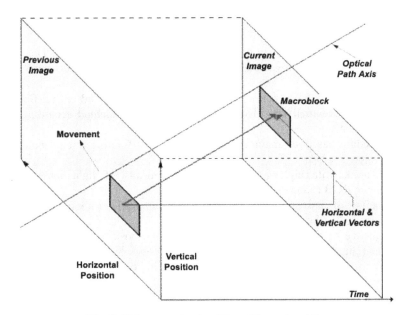

Fig. 8. Objects moving in a Three-Dimensional Space

In the case in which the object is static, its movement is only seen over the time axis. However, when an object is moving, it moves over the optical path axis (horizontal and vertical axis in time) which is not parallel to the time axis.

5.2   Object-of-Interest Spin Computation Methodology in the Developed System

The main problem to solve in this case entailed determining the correct labeling over the ball surface in order to know the movement the ball is making at all times.

Several alternatives [10] have been analyzed and we found that the best option – according to the project's requirements – is to make marks with a distinctive color. In this case, yellow marks are used to distinguish them from the ball, the goal, and the field. The distribution consists of two marks per axial axis, such as figure 9 shows.

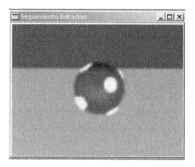

Fig. 9. Display of marks in the ball

Thus, there exists the problem of identifying each mark individually. This means, given an image and a mark, determining the new location of such mark in the following image.

Techniques of both movement estimation (block matching) and optical flow have been tested. We eventually decided to develop an ad-hoc method according to the posed requirements.

The procedure has three main stages: yellow marks filtering, their labeling, and label tracking.

Yellow marks filtering was carried out by means of light intensity level thresholding in RGB channels.

The labeling of marks consists in assigning an identifier (label) to each of the marks obtained after the filtering.

The objective of label tracking is to determine the position of each label in the previous and subsequent images of the referential one. Knowing the distance the marks have traveled between a frame and the following of the video sequence and its capture speed (FPS), we are able to determine the ball spin speed.

In order to obtain a higher precision when estimating the rotation, the procedure searches the frame along the video in which the ball shows a defined mark in the center. The three previously mentioned stages are carried out over the central mark.

The case this mark does not have any clear movement over the capture view point, or no defined central mark is found along the video may arise. That is why perimeter marks are taken into account.

The algorithm assures the existence of the selected mark along the frames to be used for the spin computation.

Fig. 10. Filtering and Labeling

Figure 10 shows the mark filtering and labeling process over the optimum image found along the video sequence.

A camera has been exclusively placed in order to carry out the ball spin computation at the time this comes closer to the goal.

6   Used Resources

6.1   Software

In order to ease the initial tests, a virtual model was made with the 3D Studio program. Thanks to this model, we were able to determine the technical requirements to be fulfilled by the cameras and their optimal position.

Then a ToolBox for MatLab [15] was used in order to understand the camera calibration process, the involved variables (focal length, aberrations, etc), and carry out real calibration tests.

An optimum language was then determined in order to carry out the application. The OpenCV library ("Open Computer Vision") [17] was selected as adequate together with the C++Builder development environment.

It is important to mention that certain changes to the libraries making up OpenCV were made in order to adapt it to the project's requirements. Due the considerably long distance between the cameras and the calibration board, the empiric bound for minimal allowed perimeter for squares and the minimal distance between image etalon points were changed to more suitable values.

6.2   Hardware

6.2.1   Cameras
After a detailed analysis, the optimum setup of the cameras making up the stereo system was determined. The cameras should have the following characteristics:

- 640x480 pixel resolution
- 100 Frame Per Second (FPS)
- 1/1000 of Shutter Speed

Using images of 640x480 pixels, we can attain a reasonable precision, taking into account that the greatest distance between the camera and the ball will be of approximately 20 meters.

 Capturing 100 frames per second, the ball traces a path no bigger than 20 centimeters between a frame and the other.

With a shutter speed of 1/1000, the problem of capturing images in which the ball appears in the form of a tail will be avoided.

We opted to use two stereo systems instead of one in order to avoid occlusion problems and obtain a higher precision in the triangulation computations.

6.2.2 Capturing System

The digital capture system should allow large quantities of information per second. Using four cameras for the path computation and one camera for the spin computation, we will need a storage speed of approximately 450 Megabytes per second.

7 Achieved Results

As regards the path computation, a precision with a 10 cm maximum error at a maximum distance was obtained, taking into account the specified hardware - being able to minimize such error if we counted with images of higher resolution.

Each shot processing time is closely related to two main factors: quantity of frames per second (FPS) of the video and its resolution. The higher the FPS and/or resolution, the larger will be the required processing time. The tests carried out rendered the following results: it takes 20 seconds approximately to process the 5 videos without compression of 300 frames (3 seconds).

8 Current Research Lines

There exists an attempt to improve the shot playback environment and take it to a 3D playback environment. This aims at providing a visualization of the shots from any point in the space, thus allowing placing virtual cameras in endless locations for a better interpretation of results. [13]

9 Conclusions

An analysis and computer graphic modeling system was developed providing detailed information on the path and a ball spin computation, thus being able to obtain results allowing the technical improvement of players and their training methodology.

In order to develop it, several techniques, tools, and computer vision methods have been used. A customized spin computation method was also developed. In addition, a shots capturing, processing, and visualization environment was developed.

A future expansion of the system will be the three-dimensional representation of the path from any point of view, which will allow the analysis from strategic points of view, such as the goalkeeper's vision, the shooter player' vision, etc.

References

[1] Digital Video Processing – A. Murat Tekalp – Prentice Hall - 1995
[2] Visión por Computador, Fundamentos y Métodos – Arturo de la Escalera – Prentice Hall - 2001
[3] Machine Vision – Ramesh Jain, Rangachar Kasturi, Brian G. Schunck – Mac Graw-Hill Internacional Edition - 1995
[4] Real-time 3D Soccer Ball Tracking from Multiple Cameras. Jinchang Ren, James Orwell, Graeme Jones, Ming Xu. Digital Imaging Research Centre, Kingston University. Surrey, KT1 2EE, U. K. - 2004
[5] Estimating the Position of a Football from Multiple Image Sequences. Jinchang Ren, James Orwell and Graeme A. Jones. Digital Imaging Research Center, Kingston University. Penrhyn Road, Kingston upon Thames, Surrey, KT1 2EE, UK - 2003
[6] Fútbol de Robots Uruguayo para Torneos. Alvaro Castromán & Ernesto Copello. Tesis de Grado de la Carrera de Ingeniería en Computación. Facultad de Ingeniería - Universidad de la República - 2004
[7] Tracking Players and a Ball in Video Image Sequence for Retrieving Scenes in Soccer Games. Akihito Yamada, Yoshiaki Shirai and Jun Miura. Dept. of Computer-Controlled Mechanical Systems, Osaka University. 2-1, Yamadaoka, Suita, Osaka 565-0871, JAPAN - 2000
[8] Introductory Techniques for 3D Computer Vision – Emanuele Trucco, Alessandro Verri - Prentice Hall - 1998
[9] An Effective and Fast Soccer Ball Detection and Tracking Method. Xiao-Feng Tong, Han-Qing Lu, Qing-Shan Liu. National Laboratory of Pattern Recognition, Institute of Automation, Chinese Academy of Sciences - 2003
[10] An image recognition system for the measurement of soccer ball spin characteristics. Paul Neilson1, Roy Jones, David Kerr1 and Chris Sumpter. Institute of physics publishing - LE11 3EH, UK - 2004
[11] Estereoscopía y Calibración de Cámaras. María Jose Abásolo - 2003
[12] A compact algorithm for rectification of stereo pairs. Andrea Fusiello, Emanuele Trucco, Alessandro Verri. Machine Vision and Applications - 2000
[13] 3D Polygon Rendering Pipeline. Greg Humphreys. University of Virginia CS 445 - 2003
[14] A Flexible New Technique for Camera Calibration. Zhengyou Zhang. Technical Report MSR-TR-98-71 - 2002
[15] Camera Calibration Toolbox for Matlab. Last access: Jul 2005. www.vision.caltech.edu \bouguetj \calib_doc\index.html
[16] Seguimiento tridimensional usando dos cámaras. Pablo Barrera González, José María Cañas Plaza - 2004
[17] OpenCV - Open Source Computer Vision Library Community. Last access: Feb 2006. http://groups.yahoo.com/group/OpenCV
[18] Search Algorithms for Block-Matching in Motion Estimation. Deepak Turaga, Mohamed Alkanhal. Last access: Feb 2006. http://www.ece.cmu.edu/~ee899/project/deepak_mid.htm
[19] Optical Flow. David Marshall. Last access: Oct 2005. http://www.cs.cf.ac.uk/Dave/ Vision_lecture/node45.html

Generalized SCODEF Deformations
on Subdivision Surfaces

Sandrine Lanquetin[1], Romain Raffin[2], and Marc Neveu[1]

[1] LE2I, UMR CNRS 5158
UFR des Sciences et Techniques,
Université de Bourgogne, BP 47870
21078 DIJON Cedex, France
{slanquet, mneveu}@u-bourgogne.fr
[2] LSIS, UMR CNRS 6168
Université de Provence,
13288 MARSEILLE Cedex 9, France
romain.raffin@up.univ-mrs.fr

Abstract. This paper proposes to define a generalized SCODEF deformation method on a subdivision surface. It combines an "easy-to-use" free-form deformation with a Loop subdivision algorithm. The deformation method processes only on vertices of an object and permits the satisfaction of geometrical constraints given by the user. The method controls the resulting shape, defining the range (i.e. the impact) of the deformation on an object before applying it. The deformation takes into account the Loop properties to follow the subdivision scheme, allowing the user to fix some constraints at the subdivision-level he works on and to render the final object at the level he wants to. We also propose an adaptive subdivision of the object driven by the deformation influence.

1 Introduction

Subdivision surfaces are now widely used in computer graphics. It allows the generation of smooth surfaces, as well in geometric modelers, CAD or animation movies. On the other hand, handling such surfaces is not so easy, due to the subdivision process which can modify the object from one level to another. Large parts of modeling actions are made by the user, implying up and down changeover from the modeling subdivision level to the smooth rendering one. We present in this paper a tool to define deformations on a subdivision surface, guaranteeing the respect of the deformation whatever the refinement level.

In the existing methods to modify or deform subdivision surfaces, Schweitzer [17] proposes a mathematical formulation for the subdivision surfaces and the displacement of the mesh vertices. This method is non intuitive and non interactive. Lee defines a deformation of the surface normals, Ehmann and Khodakovsky use respectively methods based on weight linked to the surface vertices or a perturbation curve which modifies the successive subdivisions process ([14], [9], [10]). However, these methods are based on the mathematical definition of the subdivision surfaces which is not trivial for a common user.

F.J. Perales and R.B. Fisher (Eds.): AMDO 2006, LNCS 4069, pp. 132–142, 2006.

Agron [1] works on Free Form Deformation (FFD, cf. [18]) of subdivision surface. He gives an easy way to interact with the subdivision mesh since the FFD hides the description of the surface. Other methods based on FFD can be used to facilitate the interaction of the user ([3], [16], [19]). The user working with these methods chooses a point to be deformed, eventually a neighborhood influence of the deformation or a displacement path, and the deformation model insures the satisfaction of these constraints. The *a priori* perception of the resulting object is very intuitive and its computation is very fast.

The first part of this paper deals with a brief recall on the subdivision surfaces and the deformation model used, then we define the principle and the process to deform a subdivision surface with the free form deformation method (including adaptive subdivision linked to the influence of the deformation). The last section will present some significant results.

2   Loop Subdivision Surfaces and Deformation Methods

2.1   Subdivision Surfaces

Subdivision surfaces were introduced in 1978 by Catmull-Clark [5] and Doo-Sabin [8] as an extension of the Chaikin algorithm [6]. These surfaces are widely used in character animation (such as Geri's Game$^{©}$ or Finding Nemo$^{©}$[1]) to smooth models. Indeed, successive refinements of a coarse mesh give finer meshes. A sequence of subdivided meshes converges towards a smooth surface called the "limit surface". Since the beginning of subdivision surfaces, many subdivision schemes were proposed. Some of them are approximating and others are interpolating (i.e. control vertices of successive meshes belong to the limit surface).

Fig. 1. Example of subdivision surface with a Loop scheme

Subdivision surfaces are among the easiest ways to generate smooth surfaces. They preserve both advantages of NURBS and polygonal meshes. We choose Loop scheme, defined in [15], to apply our results because most of the meshes are currently triangular (triangular meshes provided by geometric modelers, triangulated meshes reconstructed from laser range images…). An example of Loop subdivision is shown at Figure 1. Loop scheme generalizes quadratic triangular B-splines and the limit

---

[1] Pixar Animation Studios http://www.pixar.com/

surface obtained is a quartic Box-spline. This scheme is based on splitting faces: each face of the control mesh at the refinement level n is subdivided into four new triangular faces at the level $n+1$. This first step is illustrated in Figure 2. Consider a face: new vertices -named odd vertices- are inserted in the middle of each edge, and those of the initial face are named even vertices. In the second step, all vertices are displaced by computing a weighted average of the vertex and its neighbouring vertices ([15]).

Fig. 2. Left, an initial face. Right, the 4 new faces

2.2 Deformation Model

Once the deformation model is chosen, let us provide a deformation process. If a wide range of deformation methods exists, the major parts of them are linked to the representation of the object to be modified. The Free Form Deformations model on which we base our works wish to be generic. It consists of a space deformation, acting only on points without taking into account topology, geometry or neighborhood informations. The first method developed by Barr [2], is an explicit formulation of simple deformations (bend, taper, twist). A frequently used method, Sederberg's FFD [18], embeds the object to be deformed in a parallelepipedical lattice of control points, expressing any object point in vertices coordinates of the lattice and allowing the user to deform the initial object by modifying this control grid. The deformation can be local if the lattice is only surrounding a part of the object. An extension has been made to support lattice of arbitrary topology by Coquillart [7].

Fig. 3. The *Scodef* method in action: a constraint C_i with an influence radius R_i is applied on a plane

The same general principle gives the DOGME model where punctual deformation constraints are defined [3]. The initial object is embedded in a space of higher degree to solve the constraints set and then projected in 3D or 4D space to obtain the deformed object. This method has been made more practical by the definition of a radius of influence surrounding the constraint point and a deformation function $\tilde{f}$ [4]. Using this, the closest an object point is to the deformation constraint and the more it is deformed (see Figure 3). If an object point lies at the constraint point location, it is deformed by the deformation constraint vector. Conversely if a point lies outside the influence, it is not deformed. To follow the decreasing deformation from the constraint point to the influence boundary, authors use a non linear function $\tilde{f}$ (Bspline basis). An object point may be influenced by several constraint points C_i, $i = 1, \ldots, n_c$ where n_c is the number of constraints. Then, the mathematical expression of the *Scodef* model is defined by: C_i, D_i, the displacement associated to this point (i.e. the deformation constraint), R_i, the radius of influence of the ith constraint C_i and n_c (see Figure 3). The deformation of a point Q is given by:

$$\forall Q \in \mathbb{R}^n : d(Q) = \sum_{i=1}^{n_c} M_i.\tilde{f}_i(Q) \, M_i f_i(Q), \text{ with } \tilde{f}_i(Q) = B_i \left(\frac{\|Q - C_i\|}{R_i} \right) \qquad (2.2.1)$$

The deformation function $\tilde{f}_i$ is the contribution of the ith constraint to the displacement of a point Q. It is a scalar function of C_i and R_i. M_i is the matrix obtained by the inverse resolution of the constraints, satisfying the set of constraints.

Raffin et al. extends in [16] this deformation model with the definition of constraint curves, various influence sets (star-shaped solids) called influence hulls and paths of deformation that replace the initial vector between the constraint point and its deformed location. The following works are based on this method and applied on subdivision surfaces.

3 Our Method

In this section, we apply the deformation method on subdivision surfaces, taking into accounts some interesting properties of these surfaces. The chosen deformation is a constrained free form deformation. So, the user defines a constraint, an influence zone and a path of deformation. From these constraints, two methods of deformation are possible. The first method consists in deforming the mesh at a given level of subdivision and then subdividing the deformed mesh. The second method respects the deformation fixed by the user for any subdivision level. It implies to follow the constraint points from a level to the next one.

3.1 First Method

The first method is straightforward. Free form deformations can be applied to any object since the point coordinates, the constraint point, the path of deformation and the influence zone are known. Indeed, once the constraint is defined, every point of the mesh is treated as shown in Figure 3 Figure 4.a shows an initial object deformed to obtain the resulting mesh of the Figure 4.b.

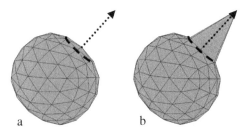

Fig. 4. Control mesh deformation by a SCODEF constraint at a given level (the influence zone is in pointed line and the path of the deformation is a vector in dotted line)

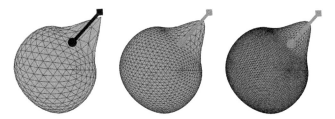

Fig. 5. Successive subdivisions of the mesh deformed in Figure 4

Figure 5 illustrates meshes obtained by subdividing three times the deformed mesh and the loss of the constraint satisfaction. As the Loop scheme is approximating, the deformation is gradually eroded.

In the simple example shown on Figure 4, only the constraint point belongs to the influence zone, it is the only point to be moved when the deformation is applied. Figure 6 shows the deformation obtained on a more complex example. According to the definition of constrained free form deformation, the constraint point undergoes the deformation imposed by the user. The displacement of the points in the influence zone grows when the points get closer to the constraint point. The points lying out of the influence zone are not moved.

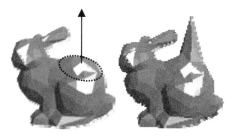

Fig. 6. Deformation of the bunny model

The obtained deformation does not correspond any more to the one fixed by the user; it is much less significant. This deformation can be sufficient if the user does not want to insure that the mesh interpolates one point. If the size of the deformation must absolutely correspond to the constraints fixed by the user, it is necessary to proceed differently. We have to keep the deformation constraints (constraint point, displacement, influence) along the successive subdivision levels. A solution consists in performing the deformation on each subdivision level. This will preserve the displacement amplitude but the constraint point is not lying anymore on the mesh due to the Loop subdivision (the constraint point "escapes"). Thus, the influence zone is not centered any more on the mesh and consequently, the number of vertices influenced by the deformation is much less significant. Even if the deformation can be performed, the resulting mesh does not satisfy the constraint (Figure 7). Figure 7.a. shows the initial mesh (a cube) and the deformation constraint. After five subdivisions, as the mesh is eroded by subdivision, Figure 7.b. illustrates that the influence zone is not centered any more on the mesh and there are fewer vertices influenced. It is easy to see that the deformation is much less significant than the one given by the user.

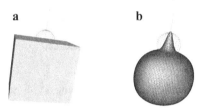

a   b

Fig. 7.a. the initial control mesh and the deformation constraint. b. deformation of the mesh defined in a. at the 5th level of subdivision, keeping the same deformation settings.

So, we need to compute the image of the constraint point at any level of the subdivided mesh to avoid the "escape" of the constraint point. We will use this image as the new constraint point and the initial displacement constraint will be preserved. The main advantage of our method compared to interpolating subdivision schemes lies in the fact that the path of deformation can be simple or complex. Indeed, the path of deformation can follow a Bspline curve for example [16].

3.2   Image of the Constraint Point at Successive Subdivision Levels

The method presented in [11, 12], based on a Loop scheme, permits the follow-up of a point lying on the surface from one subdivision level to the next one.

If we consider a point I_0^0 on the mesh surface (i.e. I_0^0 belongs to a face but is not necessarily a mesh vertex), we have first to determine to which face of the control mesh the point I_0^0 belongs (Figure 8.a). For this purpose, we use the classical area property of triangles[2]. Then we subdivide this face $\left(P_0^0, P_1^0, P_2^0 \right)$ into sub-faces,

---

[2] $P \in \left(ABC \right)$ if and only if

$Area\left(ABP \right) + Area\left(BCP \right) + Area\left(CAP \right) = Area\left(ABC \right)$.

adding the middle-point of edges: N_0^0, N_1^0, N_2^0 (Figure 8.b). The triangle surface property is again applied to determine the sub-face to which the constraint point I_0^0 belongs. We can find the barycentric coordinates of I_0^0 in the sub-face F_i, $i \in [1,4]$. For the example of Figure 8.b, the point I_0^0 belongs to the face F_1, and it depends on P_0^0, N_0^0, N_2^0. Finally, we compute the new coordinates of I_0^0 with Loop masks, keeping the barycentric coefficients previously found. The result is a new point, I_0^1 (image of I_0^0), which lies on the mesh (Figure 8.c).

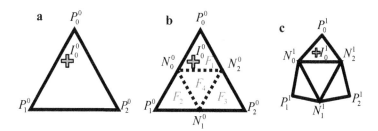

Fig 8. a. step 1: determination of the face F containing I_0^0 . b. step 2 : splitting the face F , inserting the new vertices: N_0^0, N_1^0, N_2^0. c. step 3 : image I_0^1 of I_0^0 in the next subdivision level.

The process can be iterated on successive subdivision levels to follow any point on the mesh. From this, the user can define a deformation at a given level, and this deformation will stick on the successive meshes obtained by subdivision. The resulting shape will thus correspond to the user request.

3.3 Algorithm

Let the object be subdivided at level k (k is chosen by the user, k is arbitrary)
   Step 1:
   Definition of the constraints (C_i, D_i, R_i, n_c)
   Step 2:
   if the user wants the deformation to be performed (and visualized) at this level
   then
   | the deformation is computed according to (2.2.1)
   else (the user wants the deformation at the level $k + n$, n chosen by the user)
     for i = 1 to i = n
       | the object is subdivided and the images of constraints are computed (see 3.2)
     endfor
   | the deformation is computed according to (2.2.1)
   endif

4 Discussion and Results

Once the method to track the constraint point from a level to the next one is defined, we can easily deform a subdivision surface. Let us consider the example introduced in Figure 6, a deformation which follows the levels of subdivision can now be performed. Thus, Figure 9 shows deformed meshes obtained at three different levels of subdivision.

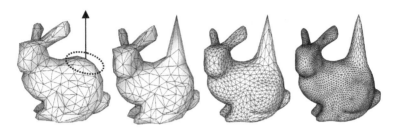

Fig. 9. Three deformed meshes obtained in following the constraint point on successive subdivision of the bunny model

If the user wishes to visualize the effect of the deformation for every consecutive level, we have to compute and visualize the deformation in the loop of the algorithm (3.3). In this case, we have to compute n deformations. This could be avoided by using an interpolating subdivision scheme after deformation. Indeed, the constraint free form deformation can be performed at the initial level and then the mesh can be subdivided as many times as needed. The two main disadvantages of this interpolating method are the following: the first one comes from the non commutativity of interpolation and deformation. Performing a deformation at each subdivision level is heavy but really uses the shape of the deformation function $\tilde{f}$ whereas interpolation at successive levels after only one deformation does not respect the shape of $\tilde{f}$ (although both methods give the same deformation amplitude). The second comes from the interpolating scheme itself: interpolating schemes creates well known artifacts as illustrated in Figure 10.

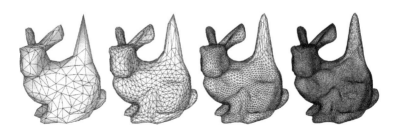

Fig. 10. From the bunny model deformed Figure 6, the butterfly scheme is applied twice

Despite of this, this interpolating solution can be appropriate in particular cases according to the wish of the user.

The main advantages of our method are the following. First, the constraint point can be any point on the mesh (not necessarily a mesh control vertex). Moreover, the displacement can be more complex, as shown in Figure 11 and can follow a displacement path. This result is obtained by using properties of the deformation model [16]. In this example, the displaced points of the mesh follow a 3D curve (Bspline). Faces in the influence zone, which is non-isotropic, are first geometrically refined because of the important number of vertices needed to draw the curved shape. Finally, the deformation is performed as previously.

Instead of refining the faces of the influence zone, the user can choose to subdivide only these faces by using a local scheme Figure 12 illustrates a Bspline deformation where faces in the influence zone are subdivided with the non uniform Loop scheme introduced in [13].

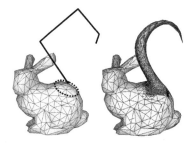

Fig. 11. A complex deformation on a bunny mesh. The deformation is defined by a constraint point and a curvilinear path of displacement. The influence hull (circle on the left image) is a superellipsoïd.

Fig. 12. An adaptive subdivision is performed on faces of the influence zone before applying the deformation

5 Conclusion and Future Works

In this paper, we proposed a new deformation tool to model complex objects with subdivision surfaces. This method is easy to perform and leaves a great freedom in the choice of the constraint point and of the path of deformation. Indeed, the constraint point can be arbitrarily chosen on the mesh and the path can be complex such as a B-spline curve. The deformation enables to fix geometric deformation constraints that are satisfied after computation and exactly kept in the subdivision levels. Finally, we can use a better deformed mesh, which can be first locally subdivided in the influence zone of the constraint point. If the user wishes the deformation to reach a fixed point, the solution is to perform the deformation at each subdivision level. As the deformation acts only on points of the mesh, it is not time consuming compared to subdivision. Thus, even if the user wishes to visualize the deformation at each subdivision step, this not a drawback. Extending the model is foreseen because the deformations used in this paper are punctual whereas the deformation model [16] defines curves or surfaces constraints.

References

1. P. Agron. Free Form Deformation of Subdivision Surfaces. *Course paper; Spring 2002*, SUNY Stony Brook.
2. A.H. Barr. Global and local deformations of solid primitives. *Computer Graphics*, vol. 18 , no. 3, pp. 21-30, 1984.
3. P. Borrel and D. Bechmann. Deformations of n-dimensional objects. *Research Report*, IBM Research Division, 1990.
4. P. Borrel and A. Rappoport. Simple Constrained Deformations for Geometric Modeling and Interactive Design. *ACM Transactions on Graphics*, vol. 13, no. 2, pp . 137-155, 1994.
5. E. Catmull and J. Clark. Recursively generated B-spline surfaces on arbitrary topological meshes. *Computer Aided Design*, 1978. **9**(6): p. 350-355.
6. Chaikin, G. (1974). "An algorithm for High Speed Curve Generation." CGIP 3, p. 346 - 349.
7. S. Coquillart. Extended Free-Form Deformation : a Sculpturing tool for 3D Geometric Modeling. *ACM Computer Graphics*, vol. 24, no. 4, 1990.
8. D. Doo and M. Sabin. Behaviour of recursive subdivision surfaces near extraordinary points. *Computer Aided Design*, 1978. **9**(6): p. 356-360.
9. S. Ehmann, A. Gregory, and M. Lin. A Touch-Enabled System for Multiresolution Modeling and 3D Painting. *Journal of Visualization and Computer Animation*, 2001.
10. A. Khodakovsky and P. Schröder. Fine level feature editing for subdivision surfaces. *Symposium on Solid Modeling and Applications 1999*, pp. 203-211.
11. S. Lanquetin. Study of subdivision surfaces: intersection, accuracy and depth of subdivision. *PhD thesis*, University of Burgundy, France, 2004 (in french).
12. S. Lanquetin et R. Raffin. ***Constrained free form deformation on subdivision surfaces***, Advances in Computational Methods in Sciences and Engineering 2005 , Selected papers from the international conference of computational methods in sciences and engineering volume 4A,, Theodore Simos, Loutraki, Greece, pp. 311-314, 2005.
13. S. Lanquetin et M. Neveu. ***A new non-uniform Loop scheme,*** International Conference on Computer Graphics Theory and Applications (GRAPP) , Setúbal, Portugal, 2006 (to appear).
14. A. Lee, H. Moreton and H. Hoppe. Displaced Subdivision Surfaces. *Proceedings of SIGGRAPH 2000*, pp. 85–94, 2000.
15. C. Loop. Smooth Subdivision Surfaces Based on Triangles. *Department of Mathematics: Master's thesis*, University of Utah, 1987.

16. R. Raffin, M. Neveu, F. Jaar ``Extended constrained deformations : a new sculpturing tool", in: International Conference on Shape Modeling and Applications, University of Aizu, Japan, pp. 219-224, IEEE Computer Society, March 1999. ISBN 0-7695-0065-X.

17. J.E. Schweitzer. Analysis and Application of Subdivision Surfaces. *PhD thesis*, Department of Computer Science and Engineering, University of Washington, 1996.

18. T.W. Sederberg and S.R. Parry. Free-Form Deformation of Solid Geometric Models. *Proceedings of Siggraph'86*, vol. 20, no. 4, 1986.

19. Shi-Min H.,Hui Z., Chiew-LanT., Jia-Guang S.. Direct manipulation of FFD: efficient explicit solutions and decomposible multiple point constraints, The Visual Computer 17, pp. 370–379, 2001.

Viewpoint Insensitive Posture Representation for Action Recognition

Feiyue Huang, Huijun Di, and Guangyou Xu

Department of Computer Science and Technology,
Tsinghua University, 100084, Beijing, China
{hfy01, dhj98}@mails.tsinghua.edu.cn,
xgy-dcs@mail.tsinghua.edu.cn

Abstract. Human action recognition is a popular research area while it is changeling when facing various conditions related to viewpoint, subject, background, illumination and so on. Among all the variances, viewpoint variant is one of the most urgent problems to deal with. To this end, some view invariance approaches have been proposed, but they suffered from some weaknesses, such as lack of abundant information for recognition, dependency on robust meaningful feature detection or point correspondence. We propose a novel representation named "Envelop Shape". We prove it from both theory and experiments that such representation is viewpoint insensitive. "Envelop Shape" is easy to acquire. It conveys abundant information enough for supporting action recognition directly. It also gets ride of the burdens such as feature detection and point correspondence, which are often difficult and error prone. In order to validate our proposed approach, we also present some experiments. With the help of "Envelop Shape", our system achieves an impressive distinguishable result under different viewpoints.

Keywords: View Invariant, Affine Projection Model, Action Recognition, Envelop Shape.

1 Introduction

Human action recognition is an active area of research in computer vision. There have been several surveys which tried to summarize and classify previous existing approaches for this problem [1], [2], [3], [4]. According to [3]'s opinion, a general system for human motion analysis can be made up of four subparts: Initialization, Tracking, Pose Estimation and Recognition. Among them, the first two parts are preprocessing of images to get low level representation for pose estimation, the Pose estimation is the process of identifying how a human body and/or individual limbs are configured in a given frame, while the Recognition part uses the results of pose estimation of frames to classify actions.

In our research work, we divide human action recognition system into three subparts: Preprocessing, Posture Estimation and Action recognition. Preprocessing part includes human detection and tracking. Posture Estimation part includes posture representation and estimation. Here, posture just means a kind of representation of

F.J. Perales and R.B. Fisher (Eds.): AMDO 2006, LNCS 4069, pp. 143–152, 2006.

human body in a single frame, for example, horizontal and vertical histograms of silhouette [5], vector of distances from boundary pixels to the centroid [6]. In our opinion, posture representation is one of the most basic and key problems in action recognition system.

It is well known that a good representation for classification should have such measurement property whose values are similar for objects in the same category while very different for objects in the different categories. So this leads to the idea of seeking distinguishing features that are invariant to irrelevant transformations of the input [7]. In the case of recognition of human action, we argue that a good feature representation should be able to resist the variations in viewpoint, human subject, background, illumination and so on. Among all the invariance, the most important invariance is view invariance. We can perform training and recognition according to specialized environments and specialized persons. But in order to perform natural human action recognition, we can't limit human body's movement and rotation at any time which means observing viewpoint changes.

It is a challenge to find a view invariant posture representation for action recognition. There have been some proposed approaches on view invariant action recognition. Campbell et al. proposed a complex 3D gesture recognition system based on stereo data [8]. Seitz and Dyer described an approach to detect cyclic motion that is affine invariant [9]. Cen Rao had done a lot of researches on view invariant analysis of human activities in his Ph.D work [10], [11]. He used trajectory of hand centroid to describe an action performed by a hand. He discovered affine invariance of trajectory and his system can work automatically. Vasu Parameswaran had also focused on approaches for view invariant human action recognition in his Ph.D work [12], [13]. He chose six joints of the body and calculated their 3D invariants of each posture. So each posture can be represented by a parametric surface in 3D invariance space.

Though there have been so many research works on view invariant action recognition, there are still many problems to solve. For example, most approaches depend on robust meaningful feature detection or point correspondence, which, as we know, are often hard to realize. The price paid by view invariant representation for its insensitive to the view angle is the losing of some useful information for discriminating the different actions. As the result, how to make the representation insensitive to the view-angle while keeping appropriate discriminating information for recognition is the key point. In this regard, we propose a novel posture representation named "Envelop Shape". Under the assumption of affine camera projection model, we prove it from both theory and experiments that such representation is viewpoint insensitive for action recognition. "Envelop Shape" is easy to acquire from low level features, which can be obtained from silhouettes of subjects by using two orthogonal cameras. It conveys more abundant information compared to previous view invariant representation for action recognition. And it does not rely on any meaningful feature detection and point correspondence, which as we know are often difficult and sensitive to errors. Also in order to validate our proposed approach, we present some experiments. With the help of "Envelop Shape" representation, our system achieved an impressive distinguishable result facing different actions under different viewpoints.

The remainder of this paper is organized as follows. In section 2, we present our novel view insensitive representation. We first present our thought of this research work, then we derivate this representation. In section 3, we propose the experiments based on our representation and give our conclusions.

2 View Invariant Representation

In human action recognition, representation is the basic and key issue. Here we call all kinds of representation of human body in a single frame as posture representation. Viewpoint invariance of representation means the measurements using this representation are keeping almost the same even under different viewpoints. Our research work aims for discovering viewpoint invariant representation for natural human action.

2.1 Preliminaries

Viewpoint transformation can be separated into two parts, translation and rotation. Almost all representations have translation invariance, so we only consider rotation invariance. Figure 1 shows the coordinate in our system. In this coordinate, the Y-axis is vertical. There are three kinds of rotation terms used to describe the rotation in the coordinate: roll, pitch and yaw. Roll, pitch and yaw describe the rotation around the Z-axis (α), X-axis (β), and Y-axis (γ), respectively. It is quite often that the subject makes some kind of actions, while roaming in front of the fixed camera, for example the actors on the stage or teachers are conducting the class. In this case the yaw motion of the body is caused by the variations of the view angle, but due to the meaningful gesture. In this regard, we classify human postures in a same category if only yaw rotation exists and we classify human postures in different categories if there exist other two kinds of rotation terms, roll or pitch. For example, when a human is standing compared with lying on the ground, the rotation term is roll or pitch, and we regard them as different postures. While if a human only turns his body facing another direction, we think he is acting the same posture. So with the above discussion, we can conclude that for most viewpoint invariance in human action recognition, we need only to consider the invariance on yaw rotation.

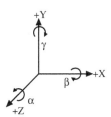

Fig. 1. Coordinate in our system

In the practical situation of human action recognition, because the depth range of human body is usually small compared with the distance between human and the camera, the affine camera model can be used. Let us give one form of affine epipolar constraint [14]:

$$\alpha\mu + \beta v + \alpha' \mu' + \beta' v' + \delta = 0 \tag{1}$$

Where (μ, v) and (μ', v') are image coordinates of a same point P on image pair of two cameras, and α, β, α', β', δ are constants depending on the two cameras' parameters, as Figure 2. Then for a point pair (μ, v) and (μ', v'), we can also give a equivalent transformation as following,

$$Y_1 = \alpha\mu + \beta v + \delta_1 \ ; \ Y_2 = \alpha'\mu' + \beta'v' + \delta_2 \qquad (2)$$

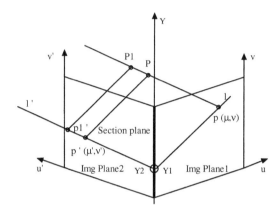

Fig. 2. Two cameras' configuration in affine geometry

When we assign proper values to δ_1 and δ_2, Y1 is equal to Y2 for any point pairs. So with this transformation, trajectory of a moving point can be projected to a one dimension direction. This projection direction is parallel to intersection line of the two image planes. Since such projection of a trajectory is a one dimension value in a direction, it is view invariant in the other two orthogonal directions. So we get a direct representation: "two trajectories match if and only if their 1D projection curves match, the projection direction is parallel to intersection line of the two image planes." It is the same as "two trajectories match if and only if M is of rank at most 3", which is proposed as a theorem in [11]. Here M is an observation matrix configured as:

$$\begin{bmatrix} \mu_1^i & \mu_2^i & \cdots & \mu_n^i \\ v_1^i & \mu_1^i & \cdots & \mu_1^i \\ \mu_1^j & \mu_2^j & \cdots & \mu_n^j \\ v_1^j & v_2^j & \cdots & v_n^j \end{bmatrix}.$$

Where $((\mu_1^i, v_1^i), (\mu_2^i, v_2^i), ...(\mu_n^i, v_n^i))$ and $((\mu_1^j, v_1^j), (\mu_2^j, v_2^j), ...(\mu_n^j, v_n^j))$ are two set of image coordinates of correspondent points from the two different viewpoints.

Based on above analysis, we can define a direct and convenient view invariant representation for human action recognition. If the camera coordination system is fixed as the following: the image plane of camera is parallel to the vertical axis Y, then the projection of pixels of images on axis Y is view invariant on yaw rotation. Then we can recognize some actions effectively disregarding its rotation around Y axis. For example, we can classify action "Raising hand" and "Waving". The price paid for the convenience is that it only records the trajectory on Y axis. Therefore it loses other two axis motion information, so it can not distinguish the motion characteristics on horizontal plane. For example, we can not distinguish hand moving on a line or on a circle on the horizontal plane. There is also another shortcoming, that is, we should detect the exact meaningful points and track their trajectories as input, for example, centroid or joints of human body, which as we know are often hard to realize.

2.2 Envelop Shape

To overcome the shortcoming mentioned above, a two camera scheme is proposed as the following: the image planes of two cameras are both parallel to the vertical axis Y, and the optical axes are orthogonal, as Figure 2. Let us consider a horizontal section plane of human body, projections of all points on this section plane into the image plane 1 are on the line l and projections of all points on this section into the image plane 2 are on the line l' . The line l are the epipolar line of point p1' and the line l' are the epipolar line of point p. To discover the yaw rotation invariance, we need only to analysis a 2D shape's projection on X-axis and Y-axis in different rotations. See Figure 3.

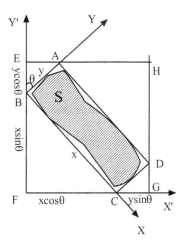

Fig. 3. 2D Shape's projection on X-axis and Y-axis in different rotations

Let us suppose a 2D shape "S" whose projection segments in original coordinate XY are AB and BC, so it is in the rectangle ABCD. In another coordinate X'Y' which rotates at an angle of θ, its projection segments will be in segment EF and FG. Let us define the original projection segments length as x and y, the new projection segments length as x' and y'. So we can get the following formulas:

$$x' \leq x\cos\theta + y\sin\theta , \quad y' \leq y\cos\theta + x\sin\theta \tag{3}$$

Now let us define a value r as following,

$$r = \sqrt{x^2 + y^2}\,,\tag{4}$$

then

$$r' = \sqrt{x'^2 + y'^2} \leq \sqrt{x^2 + y^2 + 2xy\sin 2\theta} \leq \sqrt{x^2 + y^2 + 2xy} \leq \sqrt{2}r\tag{5}$$

Let r_0 be the minimal value of "r" s among all rotations, then at any rotation, the r value will meet the following inequation:

$$r_0 \leq r \leq \sqrt{2}r_0\tag{6}$$

This is a quite small value range compared to the unlimited ranges of ratios between x' and x or y' and y. What's more, in order to get the upper boundary, following requirements should be met:

$$x=y \text{ and } \sin2\theta=1\tag{7}$$

If x and y differs a lot, the value of r' and r will remains almost the same. As in the case of our human body analysis, for most horizontal section plane, x and y differs a lot, so the value of r keeps a small change while human body only performs yaw rotation. That is to say, we get a view insensitive representation of human body. At each horizontal section plane, we can calculate an "r" value with formula (4). For a single frame of human posture, we get a vector of "r" value. Since this vector can envelop the human body silhouette inside, we call this representation of vector of r value as "Envelop Shape". Here we give some "Envelop Shape" images of some synthesized human body model data at different viewpoints. Figure 4, Figure 5 and Figure 6 shows three kinds of postures rotated on Vertical axis Y at eight different angles, the first rows are silhouettes of images in the first camera, the second rows are silhouettes of images in the other camera, and the third rows are "Envelop Shape" images. We can see that the Envelop Shapes does really change only few facing viewpoint changes.

Though we propose our representation in a configuration such as Figure 2, that is, two cameras should be placed with image planes both parallel to the vertical axis Y

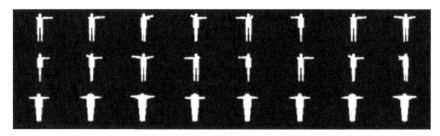

Fig. 4. Posture 1 at different viewpoints

Fig. 5. Posture 2 at different viewpoints

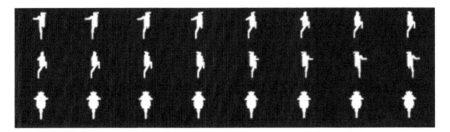

Fig. 6. Posture 3 at different viewpoints

and optical axes orthogonal. It does not need accurate calibration. As we know, accurate calibration is often complex. It is enough when the cameras are placed approximately meeting this kind of placement requirement. That means we do not need to spend a lot of time on configuring the accurate placement. As we mentioned above, this kind of representation is just view insensitive, so approximate value can also do. We have done our experiments with just rough placement of cameras, while we can see that the result is alright.

Here is a brief description of approaches to get Envelop Shapes.

1. Extract two silhouettes of human body from image pairs.
2. Perform a scale transformation to make that the silhouettes are of same height.
3. Use formula (4) to calculate "r" value at each height of the silhouettes, the x and y are the corresponding width of the two silhouettes at this height.

This new representation has following advantages:

1. It keeps information on two dimension degrees of freedom, vertical axis and horizontal plane. It has one more dimension of information than the simple view invariance representation of trajectory. This means it has stronger distinguish ability, at the same time, it is view insensitive.

2. It is Easy to obtain. Only silhouette is required as input, which is easier to get than meaningful feature points detection, tracking and correspondence.

3   Experiments and Conclusions

In order to validate our proposed approach, we have also done some experiments. We have recorded video data of one actor's action data using two cameras placed roughly orthogonal. We segmented the videos into 6 actions which are "Raise Hand", "Fetch", "Communication", "Walk", "Bow" and "Touch head". Each action is repeated six times at arbitrary viewpoints. Figure 7 to 10 show two kinds of actions' experiment

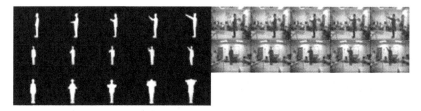

Fig. 7. Sample frames of "Fetch" segment1

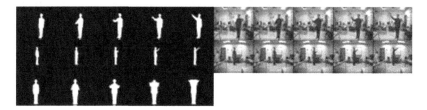

Fig. 8. Sample frames of "Fetch" segment2

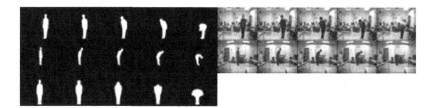

Fig. 9. Sample frames of "Bow" segment1

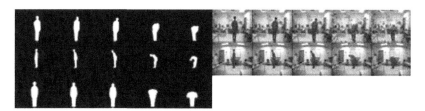

Fig. 10. Sample frames of "Bow" segment2

result. Figure 7 shows one segment of "Fetch" action and Figure 8 show another segment of "Fetch" action at a different viewpoint. Figure 9 shows one segment of "Fetch" action and Figure 10 show another segment of "Bow" action at a different viewpoint. In each figure, the first row shows the silhouettes and real images from one camera and the second row shows the silhouettes and real images from the other camera, while the third row shows their "Envelop Shape" images.

We then used the "Envelop Shape" to perform action classification. First we sampled five frames from each video segment equally. Then we calculated such five frames' "Envelop Shape" as input vectors, and we also performed length normalization on the "Envelop Shape". We used the sum of five input vector pairs' distances to measure two video segments' disagreement. Then we applied the Nearest Neighbor method to classify them. Table 1 show the classify result. The number in each cell means the counts of action in the first column classified by system to the action category in the first row. We can see with the help of "Envelop Shape" representation, our system achieves an impressive distinguishable result facing different actions under different viewpoints though the classify method is simple.

Table 1. Action Classify Results

	RaiseHand	Fetch	Comm.	Walk	Bow	TouchHead
RaiseHand	5	1	0	0	0	0
Fetch	0	6	0	0	0	0
Comm.	0	0	6	0	0	0
Walk	0	0	0	6	0	0
Bow	0	0	0	0	6	0
TouchHead	1	0	0	0	0	5

From the above presentation of our proposed approach and experiments, we can find that the "Envelop Shape" representation do have many advantages in applications facing view variant problems. It is view insensitive, and compared to previous approaches, it is easy to acquire and has abundant information. It does not need any meaningful feature detection and point correspondence, which as we know are often difficult to get and sensitive to errors. While, there is still quite a lot of work to accomplish further. The first thing is that although this kind of representation is view insensitive and has comparatively abundant information, it still loses some view variant information sometimes important for action recognition. For example, only with this representation we can not distinguish left and right hand. Some view variant information may help in solving this kind of problem. How to combine both this representation and other view variant information is a question. The second thing is that now we focus on representation of posture, while in fact representation and recognition are always in a whole, we should consider further how to make better use of this representation in recognition dynamic posture sequences of actions with context while not just simply recognize them as static posture sequences.

References

1. C. Cedras, M. Shah, Motion-based recognition: a survey, Image and Vision Computing, 13 (2) (1995) 129-155.
2. J.K. Aggarwal, Q. Cai, Human motion analysis: a review, Computer Vision and Image Understanding, 73 (3) (1999) 428-440
3. T.B. Moeslund, E. Granum, A survey of computer vision-based human motion capture, Computer Vision and Image Understanding, 81 (3) (2001) 231-268.
4. Liang Wang, Weiming Hu, Tieniu Tan, Recent Developments in Human Motion Analysis, Pattern Recognition, Vol. 36, No. 3, pp.585-601, 2003
5. M. Leo,T. D'Orazio,P. Spagnolo,International Multimedia Conference,Proceedings of the ACM 2nd international workshop on Video surveillance & sensor networks,(2004), 124-130
6. Liang Wang, Tieniu Tan, Huazhong Ning, Weiming Hu, Silhouette analysis-based gait recognition for human identification, IEEE Trans on Pattern Analysis and Machine Intelligence,Vol25,No 12,pp 1505 - 1518,Dec. 2003
7. R. O. Duda, P.E. Hart, D. G. Stock, Pattern Classification, pp 11
8. L.W. Campbell, D.A. Becker, A. Azarbayejani, A.F. Bobick,and A. Pentland, In-variant Features for 3D Gesture Recognition,in Proceedings of International Conference on Automatic Face and Gesture Recognition, pp. 157-162, 1996.
9. Steven M. Seitz1 and Charles R. Dyer1,View-Invariant Analysis of Cyclic Motion, International Journal of Computer Vision, 1997
10. Cen Rao, A. Yilmaz,M. Shah,View-Invariant Representation And Recognition of Actions,International Journal of Computer Vision, Vol. 50, Issue 2, 2002
11. Cen Rao,M. Shah,T. S. Mahmood,Action Rectionition based onView Invariant Spatiotemporal Analysis ,ACM Multimedia 2003, Nov 2-8, Berkeley, CA USA
12. Parameswaran, V., Chellappa, R, Using 2D Projective Invariance for Human Action Recognition, International Journal of Computer Vision,2005
13. Parameswaran, V., Chellappa, R., Human Action Recognition Using Mutual Invariants, Computer Vision and Image Understanding, 2005
14. David A. Forsyth, Jean Ponce, Computer Vision, A Modern Approach, pp260-263

Ballistic Hand Movements

V. Shiv Naga Prasad[1], Vili Kellokumpu[2], and Larry S. Davis[1],[*]

[1] Perceptual Interfaces and Reality Laboratory,
Univ. of Maryland - College Park, College Park, MD 20742, USA
[2] Machine Vision Group,
Univ. of Oulu, Oulu, Finland

Abstract. Common movements like reaching, striking, etc. observed during surveillance have highly variable target locations. This puts appearance-based techniques at a disadvantage for modelling and recognizing them. Psychological studies indicate that these actions are ballistic in nature. Their trajectories have simple structures and are determined to a great degree by the starting and ending positions. We present an approach for movement recognition that explicitly considers their ballistic nature. This enables the decoupling of recognition from the movement's trajectory, allowing generalization over a range of target-positions. A given movement is first analyzed to determine if it is ballistic. Ballistic movements are further classified into reaching, striking, etc. The proposed approach was tested with motion capture data obtained from the CMU MoCap database.

1 Introduction

We consider the problem of recognizing human actions commonly observed in surveillance situations. Computer vision research on recognizing movements has focused on appearance or position based approaches. Commonly observed movements like reaching, striking, waving, etc., have highly variable target locations - the subject can reach above the head, to the left/right, bend to reach for the floor, etc. Such spatial variability makes the projective 2D as well as 3D shape of the subject highly variable. The resulting intra-class variation puts appearance-based recognition techniques at a disadvantage. Either a large variety of training examples, or specialized models for different target locations are needed.

It seems conceivable that there is a factor common to reach movements that is independent of the target's location. Psychological studies indicate that one of these factors is the manner in which forces are applied to the hands during these movements [1,2]. We explore this possibility for recognizing common movements like reach, strike, etc.

Psychologists studying human movements have identified two models for limb propulsion [1]: ballistic movements and mass-spring movements, which form two ends of a spectrum of human movements. Ballistic movements involve impulsive propulsion of the limbs. There is an initial impulse accelerating the hand/foot towards the target, followed by a decelerating impulse to stop the movement. There is no mid-course correction. Reaching, striking, kicking have characteristically ballistic movements [1,2]. In

---

[*] We thank the U.S. Government for supporting the research described in this paper. We also acknowledge Yiannis Aloimonos and Yaser Yacoob for helpful discussions about the work.

F.J. Perales and R.B. Fisher (Eds.): AMDO 2006, LNCS 4069, pp. 153–164, 2006.

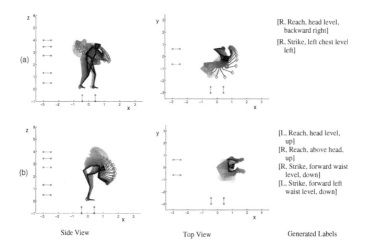

Side View   Top View   Generated Labels

Fig. 1. Two instances of striking: (a) slapping someone's back, (b) banging on a table with both hands. In both cases, the subjects first draw back their hands before striking. Skeletons at different time instants are plotted - older ones have faded colors. Red diamonds correspond to the right hand and leg; blue asterisks are for the left hand and leg. The blue stubs placed along the axes mark front/back, left/right, and height reference points for the subjects. The labels generated by the proposed system are listed alongside in the order generated.

the mass-spring model, the limb is modelled as a mass connected to springs (the muscles). The actuating force is applied over a period of time rather than impulsively [1,3]. Steady pushing, pulling, and many communicative gestures fall under this category.

There are two differences between ballistic and mass-spring movements that are relevant for recognizing human actions:

1. Ballistic movements have a simpler structure. Often, the starting and ending positions of the limbs are enough to describe the trajectory of a ballistic movement. In contrast, the mass-spring model allows for complicated trajectories. For example, drawing a figure '8' with the hand, moving the hand in a circle to signal "start engine", etc.
2. Reaching, striking, waving, kicking, etc., which are predominantly ballistic, are the most common actions encountered during surveillance. These have highly variable target locations. Mass-spring movements, especially communicative gestures, have higher spatial consistency.

Our study focuses on reach and strike movements as they are the ones most commonly observed in surveillance. We explicitly consider the ballistic nature of these movements. Psychological studies indicate that the hand movements for these cases have distinctive velocity profiles [1,2,4]. The recognition proceeds in two stages: First a given sequence is segmented into ballistic and mass-spring movement segments. Next, ballistic movement segments are further classified into reaching, striking, etc. We present a model for ballistic movement actuation that is independent of the target's location - varying its parameters varies the nature of the movement from that of reaching to striking. Eliminating the direct dependence on positional information enables generalization over all possible target locations. After recognizing the movement, the target's location and other motion features are used to generate additional labels. For the strike instances shown in Figure 1, the movements are first recognized to be strikes. Then additional labels like "above head", "at chest level", etc., are generated. The format for the labels is: [<*R/L hand*>, <*action name*>, <*target location*>, <*direction*>].

We assume that the 3D coordinates of different points on the subject's body (e.g. hands, elbows, feet, etc.) are given. The 3D motion capture data we employ was obtained from the CMU MoCap database. We consider reach and strike movements. The sequences for each class were obtained from at least 3 or 4 subjects, and the targets of the movements are highly variable. The segments for striking were collected while subjects pretended to be boxing. Although the original database contains data at 60/120 f.p.s., we down-sample this to 15 f.p.s. in order to simulate typical video capture rates.

Many approaches have been proposed for recognizing human movements [5]. There are two generic categories based on how appearance is represented:

1. Approaches which use points located at specific parts of the body, e.g. on the hands, elbows, etc. These points could be 2D projections or in 3D space (obtained using motion capture techniques). Recognition is accomplished by comparing trajectories of these points using Hidden Markov Models (HMMs) [6], shape invariants [7], Support Vector Machines (SVMs) [8], [9] etc.

2. Approaches which use body shape contours and articulated models to recognize the pose in each frame and then model the dynamics of these poses. The recognition is accomplished using HMMs [10], Space Time Volumes (STVs) [11], motion-history images [12], etc.

Interestingly, it has been observed that the locations of the hands and feet w.r.t. the torso capture most of the information needed to discriminate between basic human actions like reaching, striking, kicking, jumping, etc. [13,1]. Thus, tracking the whole body of the subject might not be needed for recognizing simple movements.

Wilson and Bobick proposed a parametric HMM to handle variability in gestures [6]. Parametric HMMs would need a sufficient variety of training examples to be able to generalize over all possible target locations. However, as they model the trajectory of movement, their approach can be used for recognizing different mass-spring movements like communicative gestures. In this respect, our work and parametric HMMs complement each other.

Bregler presented an approach for recognizing complex actions as a sequence of simpler actions [14]. At the lowest level, actions are considered to be atomic, called movemes. It is interesting to note that actions having ballistic movement are atomic by nature. Once started, they run their course and their trajectory is fixed. Our work can be considered as an approach for representing and recognizing movemes that are ballistic movements. Closely related to this, there have been studies using Switching Linear Dynamical Systems (SLDSs) for characterizing human movement e.g. [15], [16], etc. Our work compliments these approaches by explicitly studying the ballistic nature of movements like reach, strike, etc. This prevents incorrect application of the proposed ballistic movement model.

2   Human Movements

Figure 2(a) shows velocity profiles of some mass-spring and ballistic hand movements. The plots are shown in different colors for discernibility. The mass-spring movements were observed when the subjects moved as if directing traffic. The hand was moving in smooth circles - in case (1) the circles were big, in case(2) they were smaller. The velocity remains low and constant during mass-spring movements, going to 0 only at the end of the movement. The other two plots show velocity profiles of movements during reaching and striking. The ballistic movements have a characteristic "bell" shaped profile. The secondary bells occurring in the case of reaching correspond to the retraction phase of the movement. As there is higher acceleration and deceleration during striking compared to reaching, the bells in the profiles in the case of striking are more convex than those for reaching.

Ballistic Movements

Consider the following simple model for force actuation during a ballistic movement. Let m be the mass of the body part, f^+ the accelerating force and f^- be the decelerating force. Starting at time $t = 0$, f^+ acts on m for time t_1. After this, the body part moves ballistically for time t_2. Finally, the deceleration force, f^-, acts on m for time t_3. As the body part comes to a near stop at the end of a ballistic movement like reach, etc., f^+ and f^- oppose each other. For simplicity, we ignore gravitational force.

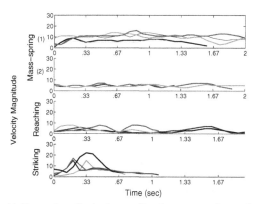

(a) Examples of velocity profiles for mass-spring and ballistic movements.

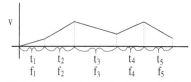

(b) Schematic of the velocity profile during a mass-spring movement.

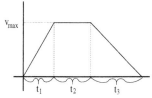

(c) Schematic of the velocity profile during a ballistic movement.

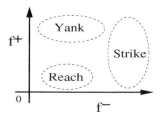

(d) Low f^+ and f^- for reach, high f^- for strike, and high f^+ for yanking.

Fig. 2. Models for ballistic and mass-spring movements

Let $T = t_1 + t_2 + t_3$ be the total duration of the movement and D be the total distance. Figure 2(c) shows a schematic of the velocity profile. The plan for the movement, called the execution plan, would be specified by t_1, t_2, t_3, f^+ and f^-.

Depending upon the values of f^+ and f^-, a ballistic movement could act as a reach, strike, etc. Figure 2(d) shows a schematic of a two dimensional space formed by the possible magnitudes of f^+ and f^-. Reach movements have low acceleration and deceleration. Strike movements, by definition, have high deceleration. There is also the possibility of yanking - the initial acceleration is high and the decelerating force may vary in magnitude. The present study considers reach and strike movements.

For each type of movement, the motion parameters are further tuned to suit the task at hand. For example, during reaching, if the target is small or fragile, t_3 is considerably longer and f^- is relatively low. This increases the precision in homing onto the target and provides more time for adjusting the wrist and finger positions during the final approach [2].

The problem with these movement parameters is that they are not observable from the hand/foot trajectories. Let $v(t)$ be the velocity magnitude of the hand/foot during a movement. The execution plan can be described implicitly in terms of the following observable quantities:

1. The peak velocity reached during the movement - $v_{\max}$
2. The second derivative of the velocity at the location of the peak - $\ddot{v}(t_p)$.
3. The total time duration of the movement, T.
4. The total distance travelled during the movement, D.

Note that there are additional morphological constraints imposed on the motion parameters. For example, the hand cannot travel in one direction beyond an arm length without torso movement, etc. We neglect these constraints.

Mass-Spring Movements

Since our focus is on ballistic movements - the model for mass-spring movements is only used for distinguishing them from ballistic cases. Therefore, the mass-spring model is simply a sequence of forces $f_1, f_2, \ldots$ acting on the limb for times $t_1, t_2, \ldots$. Figure 2(b) shows a schematic of the velocity profile. In contrast to the "bell" observed in ballistic cases, there is no fixed pattern here. The speed remains low and fairly steady through the movement.

Reference Frame for Describing Movement

We define the movement's coordinate system as the subject's reference frame at the time the movement commences. As this is the time and location when the subject planned and began execution, the generated description would be consistent not only with his/her viewpoint, but also with similar movements executed at other times and locations. A 3D orthogonal coordinate system is used - the x-axis is along the front-back direction, the y-axis is along the left-right direction, and the z-axis is always vertical. The origin is kept on the ground plane. The azimuthal orientation and the x and y coordinates of the origin are computed using 4 motion-capture markers fixed to the subject's waist. See Figure 3(a) for an illustration. Let $T(t_0)$ be the 3D translation and $R(t_0)$, the rotation, needed for shifting the reference frame w.r.t. the movement commencing at time t_0. $T(t_0) = -[x_o(t_0), y_o(t_0), z_o(t_0)]^T$, where x_o and y_o are as shown in

Figure 3(a), and z_o is the height of the toes of the subject in the world-centric frame. The rotation matrix $R(t_0)$ defines a clockwise rotation by θ (see Figure 3(a)).

Let $\mathbf{x}(t)$ be the 3D coordinates of a body part as given by motion capture, where $t \in [t_0, t_1]$. These would be in world-centric coordinates. The analysis is done on the transformed coordinates $\tilde{\mathbf{x}}(t) = R(t_0)[\mathbf{x}(t) + T(t_0)]$.

3   Recognizing Ballistic Hand Movements

The 3D motion capture data consists of unsegmented sequences of 3D coordinates of the hands, feet and other body parts. Given a sequence of 3D positions of a hand, segments with possible ballistic movements are detected - described in detail in section 3.2. For each segment, a 3D transformation shifts the reference frame w.r.t. the movement being portrayed. The segment is then classified into ballistic and mass-spring movement segments. Ballistic movements are subsequently analyzed to detect reaching and striking.

To highlight the utility of the proposed features, experiments on classifying movements are presented. In each experiment, the classification was done using Support Vector Machines (SVMs). Half of the available data was randomly chosen for training and the remaining was used for testing. This was repeated for 100 trials in each experiment to verify the stability of the features' distributions.

3.1   Location of Target and Direction of Movement

Location: A 3D orthogonal coordinate system is employed for representing the target's location. This could simply be the target's 3D Cartesian coordinates in the movement's reference frame. However, comparing the similarity/dissimilarity of the target locations of the movements would be difficult. Instead, we quantize the space around the subject in terms of his/her morphology. For example, the dimension along the height axis is quantized into regions such as "at feet level", "below knee level", "at knee level", etc. The reasoning is that, in the absence of external reference points obtained from the environment, humans reference their immediate neighborhood in terms of their own morphology [1]. The regions overlap and are of different sizes. Examples of the volumes obtained are: in front of the chest, in front of the left half of the chest, etc. See Figure 3(b) for a schematic of the spatial quantization.

Direction: Similar to spatial location, the movement direction is also described using labels. Let $\mathbf{d}(t)$ be the unit direction vector of movement at time t, $\mathbf{d}(t) = \frac{\tilde{\mathbf{x}}(t+1) - \tilde{\mathbf{x}}(t)}{\|\tilde{\mathbf{x}}(t+1) - \tilde{\mathbf{x}}(t)\|}$. The x component of $\mathbf{d}(t)$ is divided into forward, negligible and backward motion, the y component into leftward, negligible and rightward motion, and the z component into upward, negligible and downward motion. Therefore, each component of the unit direction vector is quantized into three bins having angular width of $120°$ - shown in Figure 3(c). Let $\hat{\mathbf{d}}_x(t)$ denote a 3×1 vector quantifying the membership values of the x component of the direction vector in the 3 bins. The membership values vary continuously from 0 to 1. Similarly, $\hat{\mathbf{d}}_y(t)$ and $\hat{\mathbf{d}}_z(t)$ are defined for the y and z components respectively. The complete quantization is denoted by $\hat{\mathbf{d}}(t) = [\hat{\mathbf{d}}_x(t) \ \hat{\mathbf{d}}_y(t) \ \hat{\mathbf{d}}_z(t)]$.

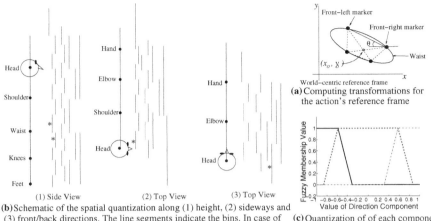

(a) Computing transformations for the action's reference frame

(b) Schematic of the spatial quantization along (1) height, (2) sideways and (3) front/back directions. The line segments indicate the bins. In case of sideways and front/back directions, the shown bins are reflected about the head to allow for locations on the right and at the back. Bins marked with a '*' define the resting position for the hands. Movements with targets located in these bins are considered to be irrelevant.

(c) Quantization of of each component of the unit direction vector into 3 bins. The 3 plots (solid, dashed and dot–dashed) show the membership values assigned to each bin.

Fig. 3. (a) Computing the movement's reference frame, (b) Spatial Quantization, and (c) Direction quantization

3.2 Segmenting the Capture Sequences

A given continuous capture sequence is segmented into subsequences such that each of them is likely to have a ballistic movement. Thus, each ballistic movement actually occurring during the motion capture would be put into a segment, but not all segments might be ballistic; some might be segments of a mass-spring movement. Ideally, the velocity profile of each segment would have a monotonically non-decreasing phase followed by a monotonically non-increasing phase. However, noise in the observations may cause false extrema in the velocity profile. Instead of explicitly modelling the noise, we treat this as a problem of classifying local minima that actually demarcate ballistic subsequences from those caused by noisy observations. Each local minima was characterized by the decelerating impulse preceding it, the time duration of this impulse, the speed at the minima, the accelerating impulse following it and its duration.

In addition to segments exhibiting motion, there are segments with little or no motion. These are characterized by their maximum velocities being below a certain threshold (≤ 2). Given confidence values for each time instant to be a starting, ending or negligible movement, we compute the most likely segmentation of the capture sequence using the Maximum Likelihood (ML) principle. As we are interested in ballistic movements - which are atomic in nature - we assume the mutual independence of the individual segment likelihoods. This allows an efficient dynamic programming approach to computing the most likely segmentation - similar to the Forward-Backwards algorithm [17].

Let $p^*(t)$ denote the likelihood of segmentation such that the last segment ends at t. Let $\alpha_t(t_s)$ be the likelihood for the most likely segmentation whose last segment starts at t_s and ends at t. Let $\beta_t(t_s)$ be the likelihood for the most likely segmentation whose last segment starts at t_s and *continues beyond* t. Let $s(t)$ be the likelihood for t to be a start of a ballistic movement, and $e(t)$, for t to be an ending. Let $\delta_t(t_s)$ be the likelihood for the most likely segmentation such that the last segment has negligible movement, starts at t_s and ends at t. A negligible segment must be preceded by a non-negligible segment. We have the following recursive relations:

$$\beta_t(t_s) = \begin{cases} p^*(t-1)\,s(t) & t_s = t \\ \beta_{t-1}(t_s)(1-e(t)) & t_s < t \end{cases}; \qquad u(t) = \max_{t'=0}^{t-1} \alpha_t(t');$$

$$\alpha_t(t_s) = \begin{cases} p^*(t-1)\,s(t)e(t) & t_s = t \\ \beta_{t-1}(t_s)e(t) & t_s < t \end{cases}; \qquad \delta_t(t_s) = u(t_s)\Psi\left(v_t^*(t_s)\right);$$

$$v_t^*(t_s) = \begin{cases} v(t) & t_s = t \\ \max\left(v_{t-1}^*(t_s), v(t)\right) & t_s < t \end{cases}; \qquad p^*(t) = \max_{t'=0}^{t-1}\left(\max(\alpha_t(t'), \delta_t(t'))\right)$$

$$\tag{1}$$

Here $\Psi(v) = [v \le 2]$ - it maps velocity magnitudes to likelihoods for being negligible. The mentioned recursive functions can be computed with linear time and space complexity[1]. For the first step in the computation, i.e. for $t = 1$, we keep $p^*(0) = 1$ and $v^*(0) = 0$. For an optimal segmentation whose last segment starts at t_s, let $prev_t(t_s)$ point to the segment preceding the last segment.

$$prev_t(t_s) = \begin{cases} \arg\max_{t'=0}^{t-1}\left(\max(\alpha_t(t'), \delta_t(t'))\right) & t_s = t \\ prev_{t-1}(t_s) & t_s < t \end{cases} \tag{2}$$

Let $\phi_s(i)$ and $\phi_e(i)$ denote the start and end of the ith segment in the optimal segmentation. After the set of relations (1) and (2) are computed for $t = 1 \ldots T$, the optimal segments are recovered recursively as:

$$\phi_s(n) = \begin{cases} \arg\max_{t=0}^{T-1}[\alpha_T(t), \delta_T(t)] & n = N \\ prev_T(\phi_s(n+1)) & n < N \end{cases}; \qquad \phi_e(n) = \begin{cases} T & n = N \\ \phi_s(n+1) & n < N \end{cases} \tag{3}$$

Here N is the number of segments in the optimal segmentation. (This need not be known a priori and is simply used to describe the computation.) The obtained segments are post-processed to eliminate irrelevant movements. Only movements in which the hand moves by a distance greater than the length of the subject's forearm are considered relevant. In addition, the spatial quantization described previously is used to define a volume around the waist of the subject in which the hands are usually located when at rest. Movements with target locations in this volume are considered to be irrelevant. The quantization bins lying in this volume are marked with '*' in Figure 3(b).

3.3 Distinguishing Between Mass-Spring and Ballistic Movements

Each segment containing an accelerating impulse followed by a decelerating impulse is classified into ballistic and mass-spring movement. Three features are used for the classification:

1. The convexity of the peak in the velocity profile of the segment. This characterizes the acceleration and deceleration during the movement. It has a greater magnitude for ballistic movements. Let $v(t) = at^2 + bt + c$ be the velocity magnitude during the segment, convexity is measured by a.

---

[1] The time complexity is made linear by assuming that valid segments cannot be greater than a certain length (2 secs.).

2. Because ballistic movements are well-practised, they have greater impulsive propulsion. We approximate the impulse with $m(v_{\max} - v_{\min})$. In order to be able to compare its values across different capture sequences, it is normalized by the maximum momentum attained during movement. The normalized value would be $1 - \frac{v_{\min}}{v_{\max}}$. For ballistic movements, $v_{\min}$ is almost 0, so the feature's value is close to 1. In mass-spring movements, $v_{\min} \approx v_{\max}$ making the feature close to 0.

3. Mass-spring movements can have more complex trajectories than ballistic movements. The instantaneous change in direction is $\rho(t) = \frac{\|(\tilde{\mathbf{x}}(t) - \tilde{\mathbf{x}}(t_s)) \times (\tilde{\mathbf{x}}(t_e) - \tilde{\mathbf{x}}(t_s))\|}{\|\tilde{\mathbf{x}}(t_e) - \tilde{\mathbf{x}}(t_s)\|}$. The complexity is measured by $\max_t \rho(t)$ - greater for more change in direction.

In order to evaluate the utility of the features, segments obtained using the peak-detection were hand-labelled into three categories (the first being mass-spring, the other two being ballistic):

1. Mass-spring movements - these consisted of movements along big circles and those used for indicating someone to move forward (77 segments).

2. Ballistic movements - reaching (64 segments) and striking (83 segments).

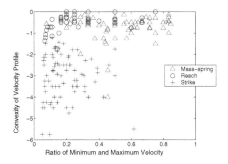

Fig. 4. Scatter plot of the normalized minimum velocity w.r.t. convexity of velocity profile, for mass-spring movements, reaching and striking

No constraint was imposed on the target of the movements. Subjects were moving around naturally when trying to direct traffic. The reach movements had highly variable target locations - above the head, on the floor, at waist level, left, right, etc. The segments for striking were for boxing sequences, with the subjects jumping around and dodging. Figure 4 shows a 2D plot of normalized minimum velocity w.r.t. convexity of the velocity profile.

Support Vector Machines (SVMs) were employed to classify movements into mass-spring and ballistic movements. Reaching and striking movements were combined into the same class, i.e. ballistic. Table 1 shows the classification results. The classification accuracies are fairly high and the variance due to sampling for constructing the training sets is low.

3.4   Distinguishing Reach from Strike

Section 2 described four features for characterizing execution plans of ballistic movements. Figure 5 shows scatter-plots of the $\ddot{v}(t_p)$ vs. T, and $\ddot{v}(t_p)$ vs. $v_{\max}$, for the reach and strike segments. As strike movements have greater acceleration and deceleration, their velocity peaks are more convex (more -ive). Moreover, they are faster, so their time durations are small and the maximum velocities are higher than those of reach movements. There is a significant separation in the distributions of the two types of movements.

An SVM was used to distinguish between reaching and striking. The 64 samples collected for reaching and 83 for striking were used. Each sample was represented by a

Table 1. Means and standard deviations of the classification accuracies for mass-spring vs. ballistic over 100 trials of SVM training and testing

	Mean	Std. Dev.
Mass-Spring	0.8323	0.0582
Reach	0.8915	0.0456
Strike	0.9763	0.0244

Table 2. Means and standard deviations of the classification accuracies for reaching vs. striking over 100 trials of SVM training and testing

	Mean	Std. Dev.
Reach	0.9478	0.0449
Strike	0.9690	0.0377

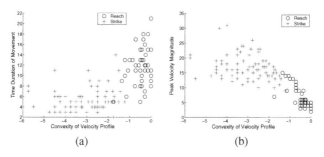

Fig. 5. Scatter-plot of (a) $\ddot{v}(t_p)$ vs. T, (b) $\ddot{v}(t_p)$ vs. $v_{\max}$

3D vector consisting of $\ddot{v}(t_p)$, T and $v_{\max}$. Table 2 shows the classification results. The high accuracies indicate that the features adequately characterize the ballistic nature of reaching and striking movements.

4   Experimental Results

The proposed approach was tested with several capture sequences of reach and strike movements. These included cases in which a subject assembles and uses a vacuum-cleaner, moves around objects, climbs a ladder, etc. For the strike movements, the subjects pretended as if boxing - they stepped around, dodged and executed combinations of punches, jabs, hooks, etc. The duration of the sequences varied from 3 sec. to approximately 40 sec. The data used for training and testing was obtained from different subjects so as to observe the generalization ability of the approach. The ground truth for each sequence was manually observed. Out of 55 instances of reach movements, 44 (80%) were detected correctly and there were 2 false detections. Some of the reach movements were missed due insubstantial movement of the hands. There were also cases during the vacuum-cleaner assembly in which it was not clear if the movements were ballistic - these were still considered as reaches in the ground truth. Out of 78 instances of strike movements, 71 (91%) were detected correctly and there were 6 false detections. The 6 false strike detections were for cases when the subject made rapid hand movement before executing a "hook". Figures 1 and 6 show the labels generated for some instances of striking and reaching. For Figure 6, the movements were: (a) Subject takes a step forward and reaches out forward with right hand near knee level, (b) Subject turns around and takes a couple of steps to reach out behind with right

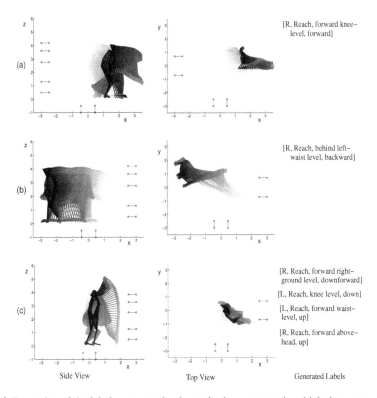

Fig. 6. Examples of the labels generated - shown in the sequence in which they were output

hand, and (c) Subject reaches for the floor and then above the head. As is illustrated in the figures, the target labels generated by the proposed approach are coherent.

5   Conclusion

An approach for recognizing human movements commonly encountered during surveillance was presented. Explicitly considering the ballistic nature of movements like reaching, striking, etc. allows the decoupling of positional/appearance information from the recognition. This enables generalization over a large range of target locations. Experiments were presented to illustrate the utility of the proposed approach.

References

1. Smyth, I., Wing, M., eds.: The Psychology of Human Movement. Academic Press Inc., Orlando, FL 32887 (1984)
2. Marteniuk, R.G., MacKenzie, C.L., Jeannerod, M., Athenes, S., Dugas, C.: Constraints on human arm movement trajectories. Canadian Jnl. Psychology **41** (1987) 365–378
3. Asatryan, D.G., Fel'dman, A.G.: Functional tuning of the nervous system with control of movement or maintenance of a steady posture. Biophysics **1** (1965) 925–935

4. Cooke, J.D.: The organization of simple, skilled movements. In Stelmach, G.E., Requin, J., eds.: Tutorials in Motor Behavior. (1980) 199–211
5. Gavrila, D.M.: The visual analysis of human movement: A survey. Computer Vision and Image Understanding **73** (1999) 82–98
6. Wilson, A.D., Bobick, A.F.: Parametric hidden markov models for gesture recognition. IEEE Trans. Pattern Anal. and Machine Intell. **21** (1999) 884–900
7. Parameswaran, V., Chellappa, R.: View invariants for human action recognition. In: Proc. IEEE Conf. Computer Vision and Pattern Recognition (CVPR-2003). Volume 2. (2003) 613–619
8. Arikan, O., Forsyth, D.A., O'Brien, J.F.: Motion synthesis from annotations. ACM Trans. Graph. **22** (2003) 402–408
9. Yilmaz, A., Shah, M.: Recognizing human action in videos acquired by uncalibrated moving cameras. In: Proc. IEEE Int'l Conf. Computer Vision (ICCV-2005). (2005)
10. Elgammal, A., Shet, V.D., Yacoob, Y., Davis, L.S.: Learning dynamics for exemplar-based gesture recognition. In: Proc. IEEE Conf. Computer Vision and Pattern Recognition (CVPR-2003). Volume 1. (June 18-20, 2003) 571–578
11. Yilmaz, A., Shah, M.: Actions as objects: A nover action representation. In: Proc. IEEE Conf. Computer Vision and Pattern Recognition (CVPR-2005). (2005)
12. Bobick, A.F., Davis, J.W.: The recognition of human movement using temporal templates. IEEE Trans. Pattern Anal. and Machine Intell. **23** (2001) 257–267
13. Johansson, G.: Visual perception of biological motion and a model for its analysis. Perception and Psychophysics **14** (1973) 201–211
14. Bregler, C.: Learning and recognizing human dynamics in video sequences. In: Proc. IEEE Conf. Computer Vision and Pattern Recognition (CVPR-1997). (1997)
15. Pavlovic, V., Rehg, J.M., MacCormick, J.: Learning switching linear models for human motion. In: Proc. Neural Information Processing Systems (NIPS-2000). (2000) 981–987
16. Ren, L., Patrick, A., Efros, A.A., Hodgins, J.K., Rehg, J.M.: A data-driven approach to quantifying natural human motion. ACM Trans. Graph. **24** (2005) 1090–1097
17. Rabiner, L.R.: A tutorial on hidden markov models and selected applications in speech recognition. In: Proc. IEEE. Volume 77. (Feb. 1989) 257–286

Collision Detection Trough Deconstruction of Articulated Objects[*]

Roberto Therón, Vidal Moreno, Belén Curto, and Francisco J. Blanco

Departamento de Informática y Automática
Universidad de Salamanca, Salamanca, 37008, Spain
theron@usal.es, vmoreno@abedul.usal.es,
bcurto@abedul.usal.es, jblanco@abedul.usal.es

Abstract. Many applications in computer graphics require fast and robust collision detection algorithms. The problem of simulating motion in an articulated chain has been well studied using both dynamic and kinematics techniques. This paper describes an efficient method for obstacle representation in the configuration space (C-space) for articulated chains. The method is based on the analytical deconstruction of the C-space, i.e., the separated evaluation of the C-space portion contributed by the collisions of each link. The Deconstruction method is not limited to particular kinematic topologies and allows good collision detection times. The systematic application of a simple convolution of two functions describing each link in the kinematic chain and the workspace, respectively, is applied. The proposed method can naturally face the evaluation of high-dimensional C-spaces, since only non-colliding configurations are considered for the evaluation of the next link in the chain.

Keywords: collision detection, interference tests, motion planning.

1 Introduction

This paper presents a novel and efficient method for the evaluation of possible collisions of any articulated body in an environment of obstacles.

Collision detection is a classical problem in computer graphics, robotics, manufacturing, animation and computer simulated environments. The goal of collision detection (also known as interference detection or contact determination) is to automatically report a geometric contact when is about to occur or has actually occurred. In many of these application areas, collision detection is considered a major computational bottleneck. This problem has been widely studied; [1],[2] and [3] provide recent surveys.

The motion of articulated bodies has been a subject of considerable literature using both dynamic and kinematics techniques. While inverse kinematics models are computationally less expensive, dynamics models achieve a greater degree of realism due to underlying physical basis. On the other hand, inverse kinematics,

---

[*] This work was supported by the MCyT of Spain under Integrated Action (Spain-France) HF2004-0277 and by the Junta de Castilla y León under project SA042/02.

F.J. Perales and R.B. Fisher (Eds.): AMDO 2006, LNCS 4069, pp. 165–174, 2006.
© Springer-Verlag Berlin Heidelberg 2006

owing to kinematic constrains, enable more direct animations than in purely dynamic models. Usually the emphasis is on simulating an articulated figure as realistic as possible. Although realism is a worthy goal, designing interactive environments requires efficient performance [4]. With this goal in mind, Bandi and Thalmann [4] propose a configuration space approach for efficient animation of human figures, where the configuration space is splitted into various regions, mapped onto 2D, and a search is carried out to avoid obstacles. [5][6] also perform a configuration space search in order to achieve collision avoidance.

The concept of configuration space was introduced by Lozano-Pérez [7] and has been widely used in motion planning. The goal of motion planning is to generate a collision-free path for a robot. Thus, collision-free planners must be able to perform some kind of geometric reasoning concerning collision detection between the robot and the obstacles [8]. In general, the configuration of a robot is given by a set of parameters, or degrees of freedom, that determine its location and orientation. The space defined by the ranges of allowed values for these parameters is usually called configuration space (C-space).

An obstacle in C-space (C-obstacle) is defined as the connected set of configurations where a given mobile object intersects with an obstacle in workspace. C-obstacle generation can be viewed as a further generalization of the static interference and collision detection problems: here objects are not tested for interference at a particular configuration nor even along a given parameterized trajectory, but rather at all possible configurations in the workspace. Thus, once C-obstacles are obtained, all information concerning interferences is captured[1].

Concisely, we propose a fast method for the evaluation of the configuration space of articulated bodies (kinematic chains) based on the analytical deconstruction of the C-obstacles [9], that can be further exploited in computer graphics and animation. Some benefits of the proposed method are: it is valid for any kind of structure (including highly articulated bodies), the evaluation of obstacles is performed locally for every element of the articulated chain, the anticipation of collisions due to each link permits to diminish the portion of evaluated space and the method is inherently parallel.

2   Evaluating C-Obstacles as a Convolution

In this section, the method proposed by Curto et al. in [10] is reviewed, as it is the basis for the method presented in this paper.

The representation of the C-obstacles is proposed based on the integral of the product of two functions: one that represents the kinematic chain A and another one that represents the obstacles in the workspace, B. W will designate the workspace and C the C-space. Thus,

Definition 1. *Let* $A : C \times W \rightarrow R$ *be the function defined by*

$$A(q, x) = \begin{cases} 1 \text{ if } x \in \mathbf{A}(q) \\ 0 \text{ if } x \notin \mathbf{A}(q) \end{cases} \tag{1}$$

where $\mathbf{A}(q)$ *is the subset of* W *that represents the chain at configuration* q.

Definition 2. *Let* $B : W \rightarrow R$ *be the function defined by*

$$B(x) = \begin{cases} 1 \text{ if } x \in \mathbf{B} \\ 0 \text{ if } x \notin \mathbf{B} \end{cases} \tag{2}$$

where $\mathbf{B}$ *is the subset of* W *formed by the obstacles.*

Using both A and B, a new definition for calculating C-obstacles is proposed:

Definition 3. *Let* $CB : C \rightarrow R$ *be the function defined by*

$$CB(q) = \int A(q, x) B(x) dx \quad \forall q \in C, \quad \forall x \in W \tag{3}$$

The region $\mathbf{CB_f}$ *is defined as the subset of* C *that verifies*

$$\mathbf{CB_f} = \{q \in C / CB(q) > 0\} \tag{4}$$

The previous expressions were defined without considering any specific parameterization of W and C.

Now, a representation of W and C is given by selecting two frames F_W and F_A for the workspace and for the kinematic chain, respectively, where F_W is fixed and F_A is attached to the kinematic chain. In this way, a point $x \in W$ is given by $(x_1, x_2, \cdots, x_n)$ where n is the workspace dimension, and a configuration $q \in C$ is represented by $(q_1, q_2, \cdots, q_m)$ that specify the position and orientation of F_A respect to F_W, where m is the dimension of C. Thus, the expression (3) becomes

$$CB(q_1, \cdots, q_m) = \int A(q_1, \cdots, q_m, x_1, \cdots, x_n) B(x_1, \cdots, x_n) dx_1 \cdots dx_n \tag{5}$$

3   Superposition Principle of C-Obstacles

In this paper, an articulated body is considered as a kinematic chain. In this way, a body $\mathbf{A}$ is viewed as a set of r rigid objects. The kinematics of this chain, i.e., the movement restrictions imposed by the joint to each element, $\mathbf{A}_i$ —the degrees of freedom, DOFs—, would determine some regions of the C-space.

This principle is the basis of the evaluation of the C-space for bodies that consist of several links connected by means of different types of joints.

Considering that a body consists of r rigid objects, the resulting C-obstacles will follow the Superposition Principle:

Theorem 1. *Let* $\mathbf{A}$ *be an articulated body formed by* r *links* $\mathbf{A}_1, \ldots, \mathbf{A}_r$. *If* $\mathbf{CB}_1, \ldots, \mathbf{CB}_r$ *are, respectively, the C-obstacle regions for the* $\mathbf{A}_1, \ldots, \mathbf{A}_r$ *objects in the space where the obstacle* $\mathbf{B}$ *is projected, then, the C-obstacle* $\mathbf{CB}$ *due to* $\mathbf{B}$ *for the articulated body* $\mathbf{A}$ *can be obtained as*

$$\mathbf{CB} = \bigcup_{k=1}^{r} \mathbf{CB}_k \tag{6}$$

The expression (6) reflects the fact that the union of these subsets equals the configuration space for $\mathbf{A}$. The idea of C-obstacles superposition is the key principle that enables the deconstruction approach.

4   The Deconstruction Method

The Deconstruction method tries to independently evaluate portions of the C-space in order to find the C-obstacles due to each link in the kinematic chain.

4.1   Applying the Superposition Principle

Taking into account (6), the calculation of **CB** for a body **A**, a kinematic chain of r links, is done through the union of all the $\mathbf{CB}_k$ related to each of the links of the chain. The computation of every C-obstacle region must be done through the evaluation of the associated CB_k functions.

$$CB_k(q_{1_k}, \cdots, q_{s_k}), \ \forall k \in \{1, \ldots, r\} \tag{7}$$

with $\{q_{1_k}, \cdots, q_{s_k}\} \subseteq \{q_1, \cdots, q_m\}$, where $\{q_1, \cdots, q_m\}$ are the DOFs associated to the articulated body **A**. That is, for the $k\text{-}th$ element only the subset of configuration variables associated to it are considered, and, analogously to (5), each of the $CB_k(q_{1_k}, \cdots, q_{s_k})$ functions is evaluated as follows

$$\int A_k(q_{1_k}, \cdots, q_{s_k}, x_1, \cdots, x_n) B(x_1, \cdots, x_n) dx_1 \cdots dx_n \tag{8}$$

4.2   Choosing the Frames

When solving the integral (8), the function $A_k(q_{1_k}, \cdots, q_{s_k}, x_1, \cdots, x_n)$, representing the articulated body, is difficult to evaluate, due to its dependency on all of the DOFs related to itself and to the previous links in the chain. Thus, we will try to reduce this difficulty by choosing the proper frames.

In order to do that, let's consider the body formed by the kinematic chain of figure 4.2. As one can see, following the Denavit-Hartenberg method [11], a frame is associated with each link, placing the origin at the end of the link; the orientation of axes depends on the position and orientation of the link.

Following the Denavit-Hartenberg procedure, the Deconstruction method proposes to use the frame determined by the previous link for the $k\text{-}th$ element. Thus, for link 1 the frame F_{A_0} —which coincides with the workspace frame, F_W— is used; similarly, for the $k\text{-}th$ link, frame $F_{A_{k-1}}$ will be used (figure 4.2).

Now, if we have a look to $A_k(q_{1_k}, \cdots, q_{s_k}, x_1, \cdots, x_n)$, the expression we are evaluating, it can be written as follows

$$A_k(\underbrace{q_{1_k}, \cdots, q_{u_k}}_{DOF_{(1,\ldots,k-1)}}, \underbrace{q_{(u+1)_k}, \cdots, q_{s_k}}_{DOF_k}, x_1, \cdots, x_n) \tag{9}$$

where $\{q_{1_k}, \cdots, q_{u_k}\}$ are the degrees of freedom associated to the elements preceding the $k\text{-}th$ element, whose DOFs are $\{q_{(u+1)_k}, \cdots, q_{s_k}\}$.

At this point, the position and orientation of the element $\mathbf{A}_k$ is expressed related to the frame F_{A_0}. The position, just like the frame $F_{A_{k-1}}$, is determined by the associated degrees of freedom of the previous links in the chain, that is

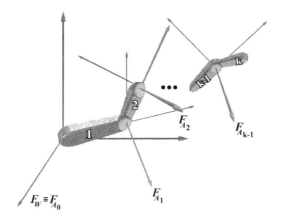

Fig. 1. Frames in the kinematic chain of an articulated body

to say, some of the parameters related to each $\mathbf{A}_i$ —previous elements— in that subchain, $(a_i,\, \alpha_i,\, d_i$ and θ_i, the Denavit-Hartenberg parameters).

Thus, if the position and orientation of the element $\mathbf{A}_k$ are expressed taking as origin the frame $F_{A_{k-1}}$, its evaluation will be much simpler. An homogeneous transformation $\mathbf{T}$ is needed to perform this operation.

Definition 4. *Let* ${}_0^{k-1}\mathbf{T}$ *be the transformation that permits to move the frame* F_{A_0} *to such point that it will coincide with* $F_{A_{k-1}}$.

It is important to point out that this homogeneous transformation depends on the configuration parameters related to the previous elements in the chain, that is to say, ${}_0^{k-1}\mathbf{T} = f(q_{1_k}, \cdots, q_{u_k})$. At this point, the position and orientation of the link $\mathbf{A}_k$, expressed related to the frame $F_{A_{k-1}}$, will only depend on its associated degrees of freedom, that is, $\{q_{(u+1)_k}, \cdots, q_{s_k}\}$.

However, this homogeneous transformation has a consequence: it will be necessary to express the workspace as a function of the new frame, $F_{A_{k-1}}$:

$$B'(x'_1, \cdots, x'_n) = {}_0^{k-1}\mathbf{T}B(x_1, \cdots, x_n) \tag{10}$$

In this way, the evaluation of (9) is equivalent to the following one

$$A'_k(q_{(u+1)_k}, \cdots, q_{s_k}, x'_1, \cdots, x'_n) \tag{11}$$

Finally, (8), which is used to calculate the C-obstacle portion pertaining to the element $\mathbf{A}_k$, becomes

$$\int A'_k(q_{(u+1)_k}, \cdots, q_{s_k}, x'_1, \cdots, x'_n)B'(x'_1, \cdots, x'_n)dx'_1 \cdots dx'_n \tag{12}$$

Now, after the proper frame is chosen, as it can be seen in (12), it is possible to study individually each one of the links.

4.3 Choosing the Coordinate Functions

Kavraki [12] and Curto [10] propose the simplification of the C-space calculation by using of the Convolution theorem (and the Fast Fourieer Transform). We shall now expose how this is applicable inside the new proposed formalism by means of the introduction of a coordinate functions change.

As demonstrated in [10], it is sufficient to choose the proper coordinate functions, $(\xi_1, \cdots, \xi_n)$, that will permit to find one or more relationships between some of the configuration variables and some of the coordinate functions, which will allow to find the convolution.

Thus, a new function, $\bar{A}'_k$, is introduced; the idea is to find a simpler functional dependency in function A'_k, in such a way that element $\mathbf{A}_k$ becomes independent of a subset of $\left\{q_{(u+1)_k}, \cdots, q_{s_k}\right\}$, depending only on $\left\{q_{(v+1)_k}, \cdots, q_{s_k}\right\}$.

Having this new function $\bar{A}'_k$, (12) will be defined as

$$\int long A\ long B\ d\xi_1 \cdots d\xi_n$$

$$long A = \bar{A}'_k(0, \cdots, 0, q_{(v+1)_k}, \cdots, q_{s_k}, \xi_1 - q_{(u+1)_k}, \cdots, \xi_v - q_{v_k}, \xi_{(v+1)_k}, \cdots, \xi_n)$$
$$long B = B'(\xi_1, \cdots, \xi_n) \tag{13}$$

which leads to a function $\bar{A}'_k$ that depends only on $\left\{q_{(v+1)_k}, \cdots, q_{s_k}\right\}$. Now, for variables $\left\{q_{(u+1)_k}, \cdots, q_{v_k}\right\}$ the following convolution product appears.

$$\int (\bar{A}'_{k(0,\cdots,0,q_{(v+1)_k}, \cdots, q_{s_k})} * B)_{(\xi_1, \cdots, \xi_{v_k})}(\xi_{(v+1)_k}, \cdots, \xi_n)\, d\xi_{(v+1)_k} \cdots d\xi_n \tag{14}$$

where subindices $(\xi_1, \cdots, \xi_{v_k})$ denote that the convolution product is calculated for all of the values of these variables.

5 Case Study: Deconstruction of an Arm in 3D

For simplicity's sake a simple example of a 3-DOF arm is considered.

Let's consider the following articulated arm, $\mathbf{A}$, consisting of 3 rigid objects, $\mathbf{A}_1$, $\mathbf{A}_2$ and $\mathbf{A}_3$, moving in R^3 by means of revolution joints. The three DOF are $(\theta_1, \theta_2, \theta_3) \in [-\pi, \pi)$. Being the waist ($\theta_1$), shoulder ($\theta_2$) and elbow ($\theta_3$).

Choosing the Frames. The frames are chosen following the Denavit-Hartenberg method, with the objective of obtaining certain symmetries that will simplify the calculation of the C-obstacles. F_W and F_{A_0} frames have their origins located at the intersection point of the two elements $\mathbf{A}_1$ and $\mathbf{A}_2$.

Choosing the Coordinate Functions and CB Calculation. Together with the frame choosing step, this will produce great simplification in the evaluation.

Indeed, the degrees of freedom associated to the second element are the two turning angles in the three-dimensional space, so the election of spherical coordinates $(r, \varphi_1, \varphi_2)$ within $[0, l_2 + l_3] \times [-\pi, \pi) \times \left[\frac{-\pi}{2}, \frac{\pi}{2}\right]$ (with l_2 and l_3, the

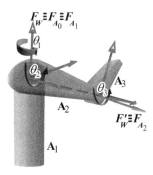

Fig. 2. A 3-DOF arm in 3D workspace

longitudes of the second and third element, respectively) is the best option, since θ_1 will be related to φ_1 and θ_2 to φ_2.

Following the deconstruction idea, we want to solve separately the group of collisions associated to each one of the three links of the chain.

$$\mathbf{CB} = \mathbf{CB}_1 \cup \mathbf{CB}_2 \cup \mathbf{CB}_3 \tag{15}$$

this way, three functions (expression 7) must be evaluated, and, according to expression 8, this can be done as follows

$$CB_1(\theta_1) = \int A_1(\theta_1, r, \varphi_1, \varphi_2) B(r, \varphi_1, \varphi_2) dr d\varphi_1 d\varphi_2 \tag{16}$$

$$CB_2(\theta_1, \theta_2) = \int A_2(\theta_1, \theta_2, r, \varphi_1, \varphi_2) B(r, \varphi_1, \varphi_2) dr d\varphi_1 d\varphi_2 \tag{17}$$

$$CB_3(\theta_1, \theta_2, \theta_3) = \int A_3(\theta_1, \theta_2, \theta_3, r, \varphi_1, \varphi_2) B(r, \varphi_1, \varphi_2) dr d\varphi_1 d\varphi_2 \tag{18}$$

where functions A_k and B of the formalism proposed in section 4 are parameterized for this case as $q = (\theta_1, \theta_2, \theta_3)$ and $x = (r, \varphi_1, \varphi_2)$.

At this point, we have considered that element $\mathbf{A}_1$, the waist, is only responsible of another degree of freedom for the shoulder, but we are only interested in the collisions of the arm. This way, expression 16 is null; in other case it should be computed. The evaluation of other CB follows.

Use of Convolution for CB_2 Calculation. In the first place, the relationships of φ_1 with θ_1 and φ_2 with θ_2 are important, since we can introduce the following expression.

$$A_2(\theta_1, \theta_2, r, \varphi_1, \varphi_2) = A_2(0, 0, r, \varphi_1 - \theta_1, \varphi_2 - \theta_2) \tag{19}$$

and changing the notation for element $\mathbf{A}_2$ at *zero* configuration ($\theta_1 = 0, \theta_2 = 0$) we have

$$A_2(0, 0, r, \varphi_1 - \theta_1, \varphi_2 - \theta_2) = A_{2_{(0,0)}}(r, \varphi_1 - \theta_1, \varphi_2 - \theta_2) \tag{20}$$

With this simple change an enormous advantage is gained, since the evaluation of the function A_2 is reduced to considering the element at configuration ($\theta_1 = 0, \theta_2 = 0$), instead of evaluating for each value $\theta_1, \theta_2 \in [-\pi, \pi)$.

So $CB_2(\theta_1, \theta_2)$ calculation is carried out by the following integral

$$\int A_{2_{(0,0)}}(r, \varphi_1 - \theta_1, \varphi_2 - \theta_2) B(r, \varphi_1, \varphi_2) dr d\varphi_1 d\varphi_2 \tag{21}$$

And, considering the convolution of both functions defined in R^3 over the θ_1 and θ_2 variables, it is obtained

$$CB_2(\theta_1, \theta_2) = \int (\bar{A}_{2_{(0,0)}} * B)_{(\varphi_1, \varphi_2)}(r, \theta_1, \theta_2) dr \tag{22}$$

where subindex (φ_1, φ_2) means that the convolution product of functions $\bar{A}_2$ and B is carried out for all the values of variables $(\varphi_1, \varphi_2) \in [-\pi, \pi)$, and function $\bar{A}_{2_{(0,0)}}$ is defined by

$$\bar{A}_{2_{(0,0)}}(r, \varphi_1, \varphi_2) = A_{2_{(0,0)}}(r, -\varphi_1, -\varphi_2) \tag{23}$$

Finally, the convolution theorem can be applied, so now the expression 22 is calculated with the inverse Fourier transform (over two dimensions) of

$$\int \mathcal{F}\left[\bar{A}_{1_{(0,0)}}(r, \theta_1, \theta_2)\right]_{(\varphi_1, \varphi_2)} \mathcal{F}\left[B(r, \theta_1, \theta_2)\right]_{(\varphi_1, \varphi_2)} dr \tag{24}$$

Using Homogeneous Transformation (D-H Method) for CB_3. Taking into account that we are working on spherical coordinates, the frames of figure 5, where a new frame F'_W is established, which is equal to F_{A_2}, are the best election.

The idea is to perform the transformation of the workspace points related to F_W, to the ones related to F_{A_2} (F'_W) (see figure 5); that is, change from $(r, \varphi_1, \varphi_2)$ coordinates to $(r', \varphi'_1, \varphi'_2)$ coordinates.

Using the Denavit-Hartenberg method, we have $p' = {}^0_2\mathbf{T}^{-1} \cdot p$, and after the proper calculations we obtain the following expressions:

$$r' = \sqrt{l_2^2 + r^2 - 2rl_2(C\theta_1 C\theta_2 C\varphi_1 C\varphi_2 + S\theta_1 C\theta_2 S\varphi_1 C\varphi_2 + S\theta_2 S\varphi_2)}$$

$$\varphi'_1 = artg\left(\frac{-r(C\theta_1 S\theta_2 C\varphi_1 C\varphi_2 + S\theta_1 S\theta_2 S\varphi_1 C\varphi_2 - C\theta_2 S\varphi_2)}{r(C\theta_1 C\theta_2 C\varphi_1 C\varphi_2 + S\theta_1 C\theta_2 S\varphi_1 C\varphi_2 + S\theta_2 S\varphi_2) - l_2}\right)$$

$$\varphi'_2 = artg\left(\frac{z'}{\sqrt{x'^2 + y'^2}}\right)$$

with

$$x' = r(C\theta_1 C\theta_2 C\varphi_1 C\varphi_2 + S\theta_1 C\theta_2 S\varphi_1 C\varphi_2 + S\theta_2 S\varphi_2) - l_2$$

$$y' = -r(C\theta_1 S\theta_2 C\varphi_1 C\varphi_2 + S\theta_1 S\theta_2 S\varphi_1 C\varphi_2 - C\theta_2 S\varphi_2)$$

$$z' = r(S\theta_1 C\varphi_1 C\varphi_2 - C\theta_1 S\varphi_1 C\varphi_2)$$

Furthermore, since the elbow is a revolution articulation with the turning axis parallel to that of the shoulder articulation (figure 5), within the sphere covered

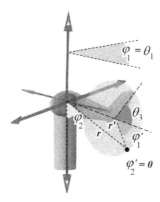

Fig. 3. Any point with $\varphi_1 = \theta_1$ pertains to the disk of interest

by $(r, \varphi_1, \varphi_2)$, only the obstacles within the disk of l_3 radius, i.e. the longitude of the third element, and φ_1' angle in $[-\pi, \pi]$, can be obstacles for $\mathbf{A}_3$. In this situation, it is more efficient to transform only those points that are in the disk of interest, that is to say, with $\varphi_1 = \theta_1$ (related to original frame) and $r' < l_3$ (related to the transformed one). This concept is illustrated in figure 5.

With the introduced frame change, instead of working in the 3D space, we work in the plane, and so, now the expression 18 can be evaluated as

$$CB_3(\theta_1, \theta_2, \theta_3) = \int A_3'(\theta_3, r', \varphi_1')B'(r', \varphi_1')dr'd\varphi_1' \qquad (25)$$

Use of Convolution for CB_3 Calculation. As it can be seen, since there is a relationship between θ_3 and φ_1', expression 25 can be written as

$$CB_3(\theta_1, \theta_2, \theta_3) = \int A_{3_{(0)}}'(r', \varphi_1' - \theta_3)B'(r', \varphi_1')dr'd\varphi_1' \qquad (26)$$

that can be simplified, applying the convolution theorem, and obtain the final expression:

$$\mathcal{F}[CB_3(\theta_1, \theta_2, \theta_3)] = \int \mathcal{F}\left[\bar{A}_{3_{(0)}}'(r', \theta_3)\right]_{\varphi_1'} \mathcal{F}[B'(r', \theta_3)]_{\varphi_1'} dr' \qquad (27)$$

It must be noted that, on the contrary to the previous expression, where it was necessary to perform bidimensional Fourier transforms, in this case the Fourier transforms are one-dimensional, since it is only necessary to *sweep* disks.

Finally, note that, in order to use the Deconstruction method, a discretization must be performed.

6   Conclusions

A fast and new general method for the evaluation of the configuration space of any kinematic chain was presented. The possibility of simplification of the

C-space evaluating process by means of the application of a simple and repetitive operation for each link in the kinematic chain was shown. As case study, the proposed method was applied to a 3-DOFs arm, showing its potential for collision detection of articulated bodies such as human figures.

References

1. Jimenez, P., Thomas, F., Torras, C.: 3d collision detection: A survey. Computers and Graphics **25** (2001) 269–285
2. Lin, M.C., Manocha, D.: Collision and proximity queries. In: Handbook of Discrete and Computational Geometry. CRC Press (2003) 787–808
3. van der Bergen, G.: Collision Detection in Interactive 3d Environments. Morgan Kaufmann Publishers (2004)
4. Bandi, S., Thalmann, D.: A configuration space approach for effcient animation of human figures. In: IEEE Workshop on Motion of Non-Rigid and Articulated Objects. (1997) 38–45
5. Badler, N., Bindiganavale, R., Granieri, J., Wei, S., Zhao, X.: Posture interpolation with collision avoidance. In: Proceedings of. Computer Animation. (1994) 13–20
6. Koga, Y., Kondo, K., Kuffner, J., Latombe, J.C.: Planning motions with intentions. Computer Graphics **28** (1994) 395–408
7. Lozano-Pérez, T.: Spatial planning: A configuration space approach. IEEE Transactions on Computers **32** (1983) 108–120
8. Canny, J.F.: The complexity of robot motion planning. MIT Press, Cambridge (1988)
9. Theron, R., Moreno, V., Curto, B., Blanco, F.J.: A mathematical formalism for the evaluation of the c-space for redundat robots. In: Computer Aided Systems Theory - EUROCAST 2005. Volume 3643 of LNCS., Springer-Verlag (2005) 596–601
10. Curto, B., Moreno, V., Blanco, F.J.: A general method for c-space evaluation and its application to articulated robots. IEEE Transactions on Robotics and Automation **18** (2002) 24–31
11. Denavit, J., Hartenberg, R.S.: A kinematic notation for lower-pair mechanisms on matrices. Journal of Applied Mathematics (1955) 215–221
12. Kavraki, L.E.: Computation of configuration space obstacles using the fast fourier transform. IEEE Tr. on Robotics and Automation **11** (1995) 408–413

Probabilistic Spatio-temporal 2D-Model for Pedestrian Motion Analysis in Monocular Sequences*

Grégory Rogez**, Carlos Orrite, Jesús Martínez***, and J. Elías Herrero

CVLab, Aragon Institute for Engineering Research, University of Zaragoza, Spain
{grogez, corrite, jesmar, jelias}@unizar.es
http://www.cv.i3a.unizar.es

Abstract. This paper addresses the problem of probabilistic modelling of human motion by combining several 2D views. This method takes advantage of 3D information avoiding the use of a complex 3D model. Considering that the main disadvantage of 2D models is their restriction to the camera angle, a solution to this limitation is proposed in this paper. A multi-view Gaussian Mixture Model (GMM) is therefore fitted to a feature space made of Shapes and Stick figures manually labelled. Temporal and spatial constraints are considered to build a probabilistic transition matrix. During the fitting, this matrix limits the feature space only to the most probable models from the GMM. Preliminary results have demonstrated the ability of this approach to adequately estimate postures independently of the direction of motion during the sequence.

1 Introduction

In recent years, human motion analysis has grown to become one of the most active research areas in computer vision [1]. It has a wide spectrum of promising applications in many fields, especially in video-surveillance where the possibility of automatic video understanding and activity recognition would enable a single human operator to monitor wide areas. The most efficient systems are based on the use of a model [2], which is, most of the time, a representation of the human body. The election of an appropriate model is a critical issue. The use of an explicit body model is not simple, given the high number of degrees of freedom of the human body and the self-occlusions, direct consequences of the monocular observation. In previous works, the structure of human body has been represented as 2D or 3D Stick figure [3], 2D (Active) Contour or Shape [4] or 3D volumetric model [5]. The benefits from using a more sophisticated and appropriate model can be reduced or annihilated by poor parameter estimates.

In this paper we present a probabilistic 2D model for pedestrian motion analysis in monocular sequences. The disadvantage of 2D models is their restriction

* This work is supported by grant TIC2003-08382-C05-05 from Spanish Ministry of Science and Technology (MCyT) and FEDER.
** Funded by FPU grant AP2003-2257 from Spanish Ministry of Education.
*** Supported by Spanish Ministry of Education under FPI grant BES-2004-3741.

F.J. Perales and R.B. Fisher (Eds.): AMDO 2006, LNCS 4069, pp. 175–184, 2006.
© Springer-Verlag Berlin Heidelberg 2006

to the camera's angle. We therefore propose to construct 2D dynamical models independent of the orientation of the person with respect to the camera and that can respond robustly to any change of direction during the sequence.

To carry out this goal, we follow the methodology proposed by Bowden [6]. We construct a human model encapsulating within a Point Distribution Model (PDM) the information of the full body silhouette (given by the 2D Shape made of a series of landmarks located along the human contour) and the structural information (given by the corresponding 2D Stick figure). Both training and testing sets comprise of hand-labelled data. The CMU Mobo database [7] has been used for training and real video-surveillance sequences for testing.

The method is based on learning dynamical models. A series of local motion models is learnt by clustering the Stick figure subspace. Using this structure-based partitioning, correspondences between several different views of the same walking sequences are established. This leads to a clustering in the global Shape-Skeleton feature space where all the views considered are projected together. The different clusters correspond in terms of dynamic or view-point. We consider in this work the use of Gaussian Mixture Models (GMM) to cope with the problem of non-linearity of the model as proposed in various papers [8,9]. GMM are fitted to the total Shape-Skeleton training data using the Expectation Maximization (EM) algorithm [8,9]. Temporal and spatial constraints are considered to build a probabilistic transition matrix. This enables a frame to frame prediction of the most probable local models from the GMM that have to be considered.

Once the model has been generated (off-line), it can be applied (on-line) to real sequences. Given an input human blob provided by a motion detection algorithm, the model is fitted for inferring both body shape and posture.

The structure of the paper is as follows: in Sect. 2, we introduce probabilistic modelling. Model construction and fitting are respectively explained in Sect. 3 and Sect. 4. Results are presented in Sect. 5 and conclusions drawn in Sect. 6.

2   Probabilistic Modelling

Our Point Distribution Model (PDM) consists of 2D Shape landmarks concatenated with 2D Skeleton joints. The total space will be clustered following temporal approach (clusters C_j) as well as spatial approach (clusters R_j) as described in Section 3. The first one will partition the dynamic of the motion, and the second one, the direction of motion. The purpose of this probabilistic dynamic model is to obtain a transition matrix combining both constraints.

2.1   Markov Chain for Modelling Temporal Constraint

Following the standard formulation of probabilistic motion model [3], the temporal prior $p(S_t|S_{t-1})$ satisfies a first-order Markov assumption where the choice of the present state S_t is made upon the basis of the previous state S_{t-1}. In the same way, if we partition the state space into N clusters $\mathcal{C} = \{C_1, ..., C_N\}$, the conditional probability mass function defined as $p(C_j^t|C_k^{t-1})$ corresponds to the probability of being in cluster j at time t conditional on being in cluster k at time t-1 [10]. A NxN State Transition Matrix (STM) that gives the probabilities density function (pdf) is then constructed, using the procedure described in [11]. Each cluster corresponds to a state in the Markov chain.

2.2 Modelling Spatial Constraint

In this paper, we introduce a novel spatial prior $p(D_t|D_{t-1,t-2,...t-m})$ for modelling spatial constraint. It expresses the statement that D_t (the present direction of motion of the observed pedestrian in the image) can be predicted given his m previous directions of motion $(D_{t-1}, D_{t-2}, ..., D_{t-m})$. In this approach, the continuous values of all possible directions of motion in the image plane are discretized. This leads to a discrete set of M particular directions of motion corresponding to M clusters $\mathcal{R} = \{R_1, ..., R_M\}$ in the feature space.

Let $\Delta_t = [R_{k_0}^t, R_{k_1}^{t-1}, ..., R_{k_m}^{t-m}]$ be the m+1-dimensional vector representing the sequence of the m+1 cluster labels (denoted by k_i) up to and containing the one at time t. Note that some of these k_i labels might be the same. We call $p(R_j^t|\Delta_{t-1})$ the probability of being in R_j at time t, conditional on being in R_{k_1} at time t-1, in R_{k_2} at time t-2, etc. (i.e. conditional on the m preceding clusters). In this work, we consider a reasonable approach making this probability a normal distribution, with expected value equal to the local mean trajectory angle $\bar{\theta}_t$ and, variance calculated as a function of the sampling rate.

$$p(R_j^t|\Delta_{t-1}) = p(R_j^t|R_{k_1}^{t-1}, R_{k_2}^{t-2}, ..., R_{k_m}^{t-m}) \sim \mathcal{N}(\bar{\theta}_t, \sigma), \tag{1}$$

where $\bar{\theta}_t = \frac{1}{m+1} \sum_{i=t}^{t-m} \theta_i$, being m a function of the sampling frequency.

2.3 Combining Spatial and Temporal Constraints

Let T be the NxM "Toroidal Transition Matrix" (TTM), whose columns represent the N temporal clusters and rows correspond to the M spatial clusters (See Fig.1). Thus the probability $p(C_j^t \cap R_r^t) = p(T_{j,r}^t)$ denotes the unconditional probability of being in C_j and in R_r at time t.

The conditional spatio-temporal transition probability is therefore defined as $p(T_{j,r}^t|C_k^{t-1}, \Delta_{t-1})$, the probability of being in C_j and in R_r at time t conditional on being in temporal cluster k at time t-1 and conditional on the m preceding spatial clusters. In this paper, the assumption is made that the two considered events, state and direction changes, are independent, even if it is not strictly true. Some comments about this assumption will be made in Sections 5 and 6. This leads to the following simplified equation:

$$p_{j,r} = p(T_{j,r}^t|C_k^{t-1}, \Delta_{t-1}) \propto p(C_j^t|C_k^{t-1}).p(R_r^t|\Delta_{t-1}). \tag{2}$$

The resulting NxM toroidal matrix is the Probabilistic Transition Matrix (PTM) that gives, at each time instant, the discrete probability density function (pdf). Its content can be visualized by converting it to grey scale image as will be shown in the Section 5.

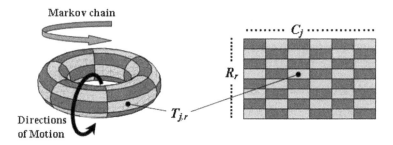

Fig. 1. 3D and 2D representations of the Toroidal Transition Matrix (TTM)

3   Pedestrian Models and Spatio-temporal Transitions

Once we have introduced some theoretical aspects, next we will describe the construction of the model and the transition matrix.

Training Data Base Construction. Precise training human shapes are extracted from Mobo database sequences [7] considering two walking speeds (high and low) and 8 different views (4 manual and 4 interpolated from the previous ones). These views directly provide the spatial clustering. Simultaneously, we labelled 13 fundamental points corresponding to a Stick model. By this process we generated a training database encompassing 21600 Shape-Skeleton vectors, SS-vector (2700 vectors for each different viewpoint).

Training Data Base Normalization. Reliable correspondences between members of the training set have to be established. The case of walking human silhouettes is a very difficult one since pedestrians take a very large number of different poses that affect the contour appearance. We propose to divide the contour into 4 segments (head, right arm, left arm and legs), delimited by a series of Fixed Points (FP), and assign them a fixed number of landmarks equally spaced. The FP are automatically selected with horizontal cutting lines placed at 1/3 and 2/3 of the height. The Shapes are normalized to 100 points. The training set (SS-vectors) is then aligned using Procrustes Analysis to avoid bad effects of position, size and rotation. and PCA is applied for dimension reduction.

Skeleton Clustering. The approach consists in clustering the training set using only the skeleton information that describes more adequately the dynamic of the motion. Thus 2D Skeletons corresponding to the 8 views are concatenated. In this way, the resultant vectors contain the 3D structural information. The set is then pre-processed by PCA and clustered by Kmeans. In this paper, we consider K=6 (when clustering presents the better visual aspect) and leave as suggestion for further research the determination of the optimal K. To make the clustering independent from the initial seeds, we run the K-means algorithm many times and proceed to cluster the results. This leads to the recognition of basic gait cycle phases [12], as illustrated by Fig.2, in an unsupervised way. The patches are ordered according to the logic of the cyclic motion: C1 starts with the Right Mid-Swing and ends with the double support phase, then C3 starts until the

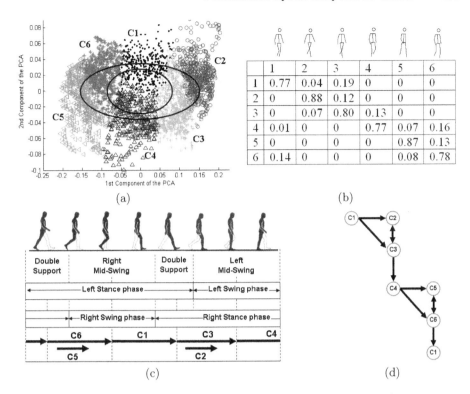

Fig. 2. (a) Skeleton Clustering in the PCA-plane defined by 1st and 2nd components, typical short and long cycles can be observed. (b) Markov State Transition Matrix. (c) Correspondences between Gait cycle and the 6 clusters obtained, (d) State Diagram.

Left Mid-Swing. C4 follows until the second double support of the cycle which ends with C6. C2 and C5 complete C3 and C6 phases in case of a higher speed gait with larger steps. A Markov State Transition Matrix (STM) [9,11] is then constructed (Fig.2b), associating each sample to one of the 6 patches. This gives the state transition probabilities, valid for the 8 sets (views) of SS-vectors.

Shape-Skeleton Gaussian Mixture Model (GMM). The SS-vectors corresponding to the 8 views are grouped following the cluster labels previously obtained, leading to 8 x 6 = 48 clusters in the global SS-PCA space. Following the procedure of [9] a GMM is fitted to the Data by applying EM. Local PCAs are then applied on each cluster [6] leading to the extraction of local modes of variation, in which both Shape and Skeleton deform (see Fig. 3).

Toroidal Transition Matrix. All the different models are ordered and classified according to the direction of motion and the states. This process leads to the creation of the Toroidal Transition Matrix (TTM) which 2D representation is illustrated in Fig.3: the 6 columns correspond to the 6 temporal clusters C_i while the 8 rows represent the 8 spatial clusters R_j. Spatial and temporal relations can be appreciated between local models from adjacent cells.

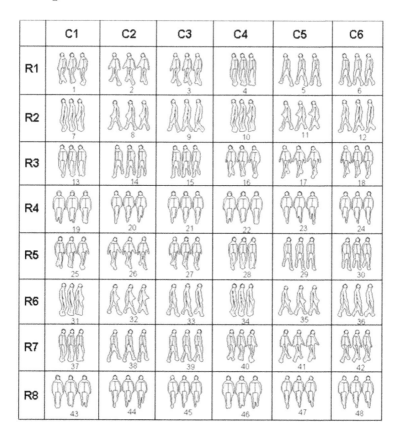

Fig. 3. Toroidal Transition Matrix: 1st Variation Modes of the 48 local Models

4   Model Fitting for Body Pose Inferring

Given an input human blob provided by a motion detection algorithm and the previous m states (poses and trajectory angles), the prediction of the most probable models from the GMM can be estimated by means of the PTM defined in Sect 2.3. It allows a substantial reduction in computational cost since only few models have to be considered. Assuming we have an initial estimate for the Shape parameters the matching process follows these steps:

1. A Shape S is extracted from the blob, looking along straight lines through each model point, following the methodology presented in [8].
2. S and an estimate for the Skeleton (e.g. initially mean Skeleton $\overline{K}$) are concatenated in $V = [S\overline{K}]$ and projected into the SS-PCA obtaining X.
3. Find the nearest cluster by calculating the distance between X and each one of the most probable clusters given by the PTM.
4. Update the parameters to best fit the "local model" defined by its mean $\overline{X}$, eigenvectors Φ and eigenvalues λ_i ,obtaining X^* [8].

5. We project the vector X^* back to the feature space obtaining V^* which contains a new estimation of both Shape S^* and Skeleton K^*: $V^* = [S^* K^*]$.
6. A new background subtraction with an adaptive threshold inside the Contour S^* is applied, leading to an improved human blob detection.
7. Repeat until convergence and store useful data: θ_t, $T_{j,r}^t$, S_t^* and K_t^*.

This leads to an accurate silhouette segmentation and posture estimation directly obtained from the mapping created between Contours and Stick figures.

5   Results

The model is now evaluated with a series of testing sequences that illustrate different situations which may occur in the analysis of pedestrian motion: straight line walking, changes of direction, of speed, etc. Since we want to test both model fitting and pose estimation, and not the tracking in the image, we provide the system with the bounding-box manually selected avoiding the possible problems due to the tracking. The process begins with a manual initialization: indicating the adequate model in the first frame. In the PTM matrices from Fig.4, 6 and 7, the colored cells represent the probability $p_{j,r}$ from (2). The obscured cell is the "winning one": the local model that best fits the silhouette. For each frame, the row of the "winning" model in the TTM indicates the orientation of the pedestrian with respect to the camera. Additionally, both trajectory and previous states are respectively plotted in the image/matrix with a white line.

As illustrated in Fig.4, the resultant vectors from a pedestrian crossing the scene straight ahead without stopping or turning towards anything all belong to

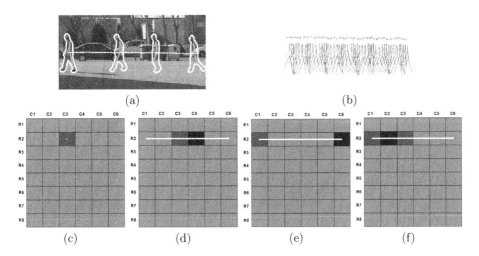

Fig. 4. (a) Outdoor straight line walking sequence at constant speed. (b) Estimated Stick figures. (c, d, e & f) PTM corresponding to the 4 silhouettes depicted in (a).

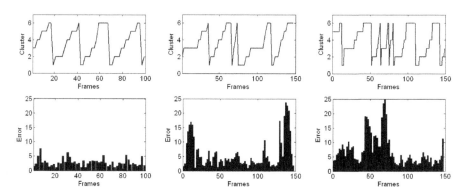

Fig. 5. Feet position error in pixels (bottom) and temporal clusters (top) - given by the column of the TTM corresponding to the "winning" model - of the Straight line walking (left), Indoor (centre) and "Walk-circle" (right) sequences

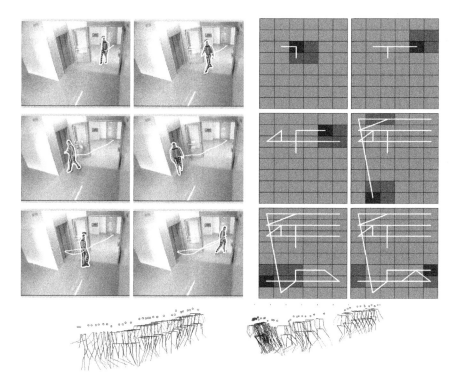

Fig. 6. Indoor sequence with orientation changes and estimated Stick figures

models from the same row of the TTM. Any change of direction is observed as a progressive change of row (See Fig.6 and Fig.7).

Fig.5 shows the pose estimation results for the 3 tested sequences. The mean position error (in pixels) is calculated as the feet-distance between the Skeleton

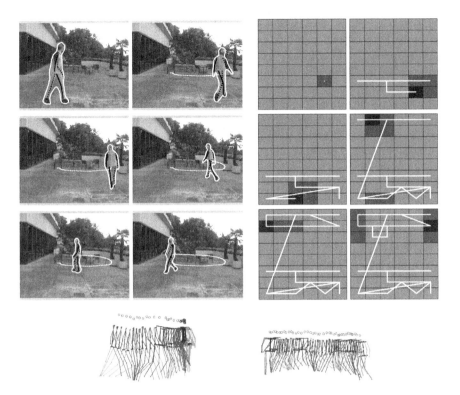

Fig. 7. "Walk-circle" sequence from www.nada.kth.se/~hedvig/data.html and estimated Stick figures

estimated by the algorithm and the hand-labelled one. Some peaks can be noticed in this figure. For instance, in the indoor sequence (centre) the model failed because of the excessive difference of viewpoint-angle between training and input images, when the subject goes in and out of the scene. In the "walk-circle" sequences (right) the model fails because of the stationary behaviour of the tracking that stays stuck in a cluster during too many frames and then can hardly get out of it. It needs to wait until the next cycle to recuperate the dynamic behaviour of the input motion. For the rest of the frames, the results are globally very satisfactory which means that the model is conveniently tuned to the suitable viewpoints and that the assumption made in Section 2.3 is reasonable.

6   Conclusions and Work-in-Progress

This paper describes new probabilistic spatio-temporal models for human motion analysis. Temporal and spatial constraints are considered to build a Probabilistic Transition Matrix (PTM) that gives a frame to frame prediction of the most probable models from a multi-view GMM.

The proposed fitting algorithm, combined with the new probabilistic models, allows a faster and more reliable estimation of both pedestrian Silhouette and

Stick figure in real monocular sequences. Preliminary results have demonstrated that it works independently of the direction of motion in the image, and that it also responds quite robustly to any change of direction during the sequence. However, further work must be done.

For instance, the fitting process has been initialized providing a good model in the first frame. In order to develop a non-supervised system an automatic initialization has to be considered. Moreover, we have made the assumption that temporal and spatial events are independent. In future research this assumption have to be evaluated in detail since it is not strictly true: a pedestrian can change direction only during the second part of the Swing phases of the gait cycle.

Future work relies on combining this approach with a particle filtering framework in order to obtain a robust human motion tracker in feature space. On the other hand, a perspective correction could be applied to avoid the problem of viewpoint correspondences. Finally, more complicated cases such as various pedestrians with partial occlusions will be considered, and others kinds of motion should be taken into account in more complete models that could be built synthetically from a 3D motion capture system.

References

1. Wang, L., Hu, W., Tan, T.: Recent developments in human motion analysis. Pattern Recognition **36** (2003) 585–601
2. Kakadiaris, I.A., Metaxas, D.N.: Model-based estimation of 3d human motion. IEEE Trans. Pattern Anal. Mach. Intell. **22** (2000) 1453–1459
3. Sidenbladh, H., Black, M.J., Sigal, L.: Implicit probabilistic models of human motion for synthesis and tracking. In: ECCV (1). (2002) 784–800
4. Baumberg, A., Hogg, D.: Learning flexible models from image sequences. In: ECCV (1). (1994) 299–308
5. Sminchisescu, C., Triggs, B.: Kinematic jump processes for monocular 3d human tracking. In: CVPR (1). (2003) 69–76
6. Bowden, R., Mitchell, T.A., Sarhadi, M.: Reconstructing 3d pose and motion from a single camera view. In: BMVC. (1998)
7. Gross, R., Shi, J.: The cmu motion of body (mobo) database, Robotics Institute, Carnegie Mellon University, Pittsburgh, PA (2001)
8. Cootes, T., Taylor, C.: A mixture model for representing shape variation. (1997)
9. Ponsa, D., Roca, F.X.: A novel approach to generate multiple shape models for tracking applications. In: AMDO. (2002) 80–91
10. Bowden, R., Sarhadi, M.: Building temporal models for gesture recognition. In: BMVC. (2000)
11. Heap, T., Hogg, D.: Wormholes in shape space: Tracking through discontinuous changes in shape. In: ICCV. (1998) 344–349
12. Inman, V.T., Ralston, H.J., Todd, F.: Human Walking. Williams and Wilkins, Baltimore, USA (1981)

Predicting 3D People from 2D Pictures

Leonid Sigal and Michael J. Black

Department of Computer Science, Brown University, Providence, RI 02912
{ls, black}@cs.brown.edu

Abstract. We propose a hierarchical process for inferring the 3D pose of a person from monocular images. First we infer a learned view-based 2D body model from a single image using non-parametric belief propagation. This approach integrates information from bottom-up body-part proposal processes and deals with self-occlusion to compute distributions over limb poses. Then, we exploit a learned Mixture of Experts model to infer a distribution of 3D poses conditioned on 2D poses. This approach is more general than recent work on inferring 3D pose directly from silhouettes since the 2D body model provides a richer representation that includes the 2D joint angles and the poses of limbs that may be unobserved in the silhouette. We demonstrate the method in a laboratory setting where we evaluate the accuracy of the 3D poses against ground truth data. We also estimate 3D body pose in a monocular image sequence. The resulting 3D estimates are sufficiently accurate to serve as proposals for the Bayesian inference of 3D human motion over time.

1 Introduction

The estimation of 3D human pose and motion is relatively well understood in controlled laboratory settings with multiple cameras where any number of Bayesian inference methods can recover 3D human motion (e.g. [4]). All of these methods rely on accurate background subtraction and edge information; this is a strong limitation that prevents their use in more realistic and complex environments. When the background is changing or the camera is moving, reliable background subtraction is difficult to achieve. The problems become particularly acute in the case of monocular tracking where the mapping from the 2D image to the 3D body model is highly ambiguous. Solutions to the monocular (static camera) case have relied on strong prior models [18], manual initialization [23] and/or accurate silhouettes [1,2,19,23]. The fully automatic case involving a monocular camera is the focus of this paper.

Recent work on 2D body pose estimation and tracking treats the body as a "cardboard person" [9] in which the limbs are represented by 2D planar (or affine) patches connected by joints. Such models are lower-dimensional than the full 3D model and recent work has shown that they can be estimated from 2D images [5,14,15]. The results are typically noisy and imprecise but they provide exactly the kind of information necessary to generate *proposals* for the probabilistic inference of 3D human pose. Thus we simplify the 3D problem by introducing an intermediate 2D estimation stage.

To infer 2D body pose we adopt an iterative bottom-up process. Simple body part detectors provide noisy probabilistic proposals for the location and 2D pose (orientation and foreshortening) of visible limbs (Fig. 1 (**b**)). To estimate the pose of the body

F.J. Perales and R.B. Fisher (Eds.): AMDO 2006, LNCS 4069, pp. 185–195, 2006.

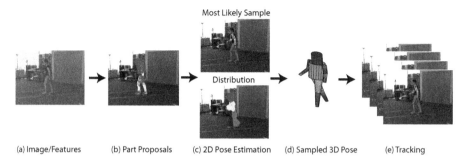

Most Likely Sample

Distribution

(a) Image/Features   (b) Part Proposals   (c) 2D Pose Estimation   (d) Sampled 3D Pose   (e) Tracking

Fig. 1. Example of the hierarchical inference process. (a) monocular input image with bottom up limb proposals overlaid **(b)**; **(c)** distribution over 2D limb poses computed using nonparametric belief propagation; **(d)** sample of a 3D body pose generated from the 2D pose; **(e)** illustration of tracking.

we exploit the idea of a 2D "loose-limbed" body model [20] which has been previously used for 2D articulated pose estimation [21] and 3D pose estimation and body tracking [20]. In particular, we adopt the view-based approach of [21]. We use a variant of non-parametric belief propagation (NBP) [8,25] to infer probability distributions representing the belief in the 2D pose of each limb (Fig. 1 (**c**)). The inference algorithm also introduces hidden binary occlusion variables and marginalizes over them to account for occlusion relationships between body parts. The conditional distributions linking 2D body parts are learned from examples.

This process (limb proposals, NBP) provides reasonable guesses for 2D body pose from which to estimate 3D pose. Agarwal and Triggs [1,2] learned a probabilistic mapping from 2D silhouettes to 3D pose using a Mixture of Experts (MoE) model. We generalize their approach to learn a mapping from 2D poses (including joint angles and foreshortening information) to 3D poses. Sampling from this model provides predicted 3D poses (Fig. 1 (**d**)), that are appropriate as proposals for a Bayesian temporal inference process (Fig. 1 (**e**)). Our multi-stage approach overcomes many of the problems inherent in inferring 3D pose directly from image features. We quantitatively evaluate the 3D proposals using ground truth 2D poses. We also test the method on the monocular sequence in Fig. 1.

2   Previous Work

There are now numerous methods for detecting the 2D pose of people in static images (with [5,21] and without [7,12,13,14,15,16] background subtraction). For example dynamic programming (DP) or other search methods can be used to compute possible 2D poses [5,13,14,15]. While efficient DP methods exist [5], they require a discretization of the state space of 2D limb poses and simple forms for the conditional distributions relating connected limbs. They also require a tree structure, which does not allow longrange interactions between parts that are required for occlusion reasoning.

Alternatively, we adopt a graphical model representation of the body [21] that, in addition to kinematic constraints, also encodes the possible occlusion relationships between limbs (this leads to loops in the graph representation of the body). Pose estimation is formulated as inference in this loopy graphical model and is solved using a variant of Non-parametric Belief Propagation (NBP) [8,25]. This leads to a number of advantages over DP methods. For example, limb positions and orientations need not be discretized as in [5]. Unlike previous methods [5,21] we infer 2D pose as an intermediate step to inferring the full 3D articulated body pose.

Lee and Cohen [11] also use a bottom-up proposal process and infer 3D pose parameters using a data-driven MCMC procedure. Our approach differs in that we break the problem into simpler pieces: generate 2D proposals, inference of 2D pose, and prediction from 2D to 3D.

This final stage has received a good deal of attention with a variety of geometric [13,26] and machine learning methods [1,2,17,19,22] being employed. These previous approaches have focused on directly inferring 3D pose from 2D silhouettes which may be difficult to obtain in general. Additionally silhouettes contain less information than our 2D models which represent all the limbs, the joint angles, and foreshortening. This helps reduce the ambiguities found in matching silhouettes to 3D models [23] but does not remove ambiguities altogether. Consequently we learn a conditional distribution using a MoE model similar to that of Agarwal and Triggs [1,2]. Our work is similar in spirit to [6] in which 3D poses are inferred from 2D tracking results, but our approach can infer 3D pose from a single image and does not require manual initialization.

3   Modeling a Person

We model a 3D human body using a set of P (here $P = 10$) tapered cylinders corresponding to body parts and connected by revolute joints (see Fig. 3 (**a**)). Each part has an associated set of fixed parameters that are assumed to be known (e.g. length and cross-sectional radius at the two joints). We represent the overall pose of the body $Y_t = [\Xi, \Gamma, \theta]^T$ at time t using a set of joint angles θ, a global position Ξ, and global orientation Γ in 3D. Joint angles are represented with respect to the kinematic chain along which they are defined using unit quaternions. For our body model, this results in $Y_t \in R^{47}$, or $Y_t \in R^{55}$ depending on whether one chooses to model the clavicle joints.

In 2D the limbs in the image plane are modeled by trapezoids, and the overall body pose is defined using a redundant representation $X = \{X_1, X_2, ..., X_P\}$ in terms of 2D position, rotation, scale and foreshortening of parts, $X_i \in R^5$. This redundant representation stems from the inference algorithm that we will employ to infer the pose of the body in 2D. Notice we drop the temporal sub-script t for convenience.

4   Finding a Person in 2D

4.1   Limb Proposals

At the lowest level of our hierarchical approach are body part proposals. We need plausible poses/states for some or all the parts of the body to localize the search. There exist a number of approaches for detecting body parts in an image. Among them are approaches for face detection, skin-color-based limb segmentation [11], and color-based

Fig. 2. Proposals and NBP. Example of the belief propagation process. Left: bottom-up proposals for the limbs. Center: 100 samples from the belief at each node/limb after 5 iterations of NBP (NBP was run with 100 particles, producing messages represented by 800-component kernel densities). Right: most likely sample drawn form the belief at each node.

segmentation exploiting the homogeneity and the relative spatial extent of body parts [11,13,16]. In this paper we took a simpler approach, and constructed our set of proposals by simply discretizing the state space and evaluating the likelihood function (below) at these discrete locations, choosing the 100 most likely states as a particle based proposal distribution for belief propagation (BP). It is important to note that not all parts need to be detected. An example of the proposals for various parts of the body are shown in Fig. 1 **(b)** and 2.

4.2   Likelihoods

The likelihood model for an individual limb is built to account for possible occlusions between body parts for a given view-based 2D model. To simplify the occlusion reasoning as in [21], we assume that for a given view there is a fixed and known depth ordering of parts. Assuming pixel independence, we can then write the local image likelihood $\phi(I|X_i)$, for part i as a product of individual pixel probabilities defined over disjoint image regions. For a more detailed description of the occlusion-sensitive likelihoods, and how one can approximate the global likelihood $\phi(I|X)$ with a product of local terms $\phi(I|X_i)$, we refer the reader to [21,24]. In defining $\phi(I|X_i)$ we use silhouette and color features and combine them using an independence assumption.

4.3   2D Loose-Limbed Body Model

Following the framework of [20,21] we implement the search for the 2D body using a spatial undirected graphical model, where each node i in a graph represents a body part (limb), and links between nodes represent the kinematic and occlusion constraints encoded statistically using conditional distributions. Each body part has an associated state vector $X_i \in R^5$ that encodes 2D position, rotation, scale, and foreshortening. The joint probability for this spatial graphical model with P body parts, can be written as $p(X_1, X_2, ..., X_P|I, V) \propto \prod_{ij} \psi_{ij}^K(X_i, X_j|V) \prod_{ij} \psi_{ij}^O(X_i, X_j|V) \prod_i \phi(I|X_i)$, where X_i represents the state of the limb i; $V \in \{1..8\}$ the discrete view; $\psi_{ij}^K(X_i, X_j|V)$ and $\psi_{ij}^O(X_i, X_j|V)$ are the kinematic and occlusion constraints between the connected or potentially occluding nodes i and j for view V and $\phi(I|X_i)$ is the local image likelihood defined above. This model has a number of advantages [21] and has been shown to produce favorable results for the 3D body estimation in a multi-view setting [20]. The graphical model structure corresponding to our model can be seen in Fig. 3 (**b**).

Inferring the state of the 2D body in our graphical model representation corresponds to estimating the belief (marginal) at each node in a graph. We use a form of continuous non-parametric belief propagation [8], Particle Message Passing (PAMPAS), to deal with this task. The approach is a generalization of particle filtering which allows inference over arbitrary graphs rather then a simple chain. In this generalization the message used in standard belief propagation is approximated using a kernel density (formed by propagating particles through a conditional density represented by a mixture model [20,21]). For the details on how the message updates can be carried out using the stratified sampling from the products of messages and proposal distribution see [20].

5 Proposing 3D Body Model from 2D

In order to produce estimates for the body in 3D from the 2D body poses, we need to model the conditional distribution $p(Y|X)$ of the 3D body state Y given 2D body state X. Intuitively this conditional mapping should be related to the inverse of the camera projection matrix and, as with many inverse problems, is highly ambiguous.

To model this non-linear relationship we use a Mixtures of Experts (MoE) model to represent the conditionals [1,2,22]. The parameters of the MoE model are learned by maximizing the log-likelihood of the training data set $D = \{X^1, ..., X^N, Y^1, ..., Y^N\}$ consisting of N input-output pairs (X^i, Y^i). We use an iterative Bayesian EM algorithm, based on type-II maximum likelihood, to learn parameters of the MoE. Our model for the conditional can be written as:

$$p(Y|X) \propto \sum_{k=1}^{M} p_{e,k}(Y|X, \Theta_{e,k}) p_{g,k}(k|X, \Theta_{g,k}) \tag{1}$$

where $p_{e,k}$ is the probability of choosing pose Y given the input X according to the k-th expert, and $p_{g,k}$ is the probability of that input being assigned to the k-th expert using an input sensitive gating network; in both cases Θ represents the parameters of the mixture and gate distributions.

For simplicity and to reduce complexity of the experts we choose linear regression with constant offset $Y = AX + C$ as our expert model, which allows us to solve for the parameters $\Theta_{e,k} = \{A_k, C_k, \Lambda_k\}$ analytically using the weighted linear regression, where $p_{e,k}(Y|X, \Theta_{e,k}) = \frac{1}{\sqrt{(2\pi)^n |\Lambda_k|}} \exp^{-\frac{1}{2}\Delta_k^T \Lambda_k^{-1} \Delta_k}$, and $\Delta_k = Y - A_k X - C_k$.

Pose estimation is a high dimensional and ill-conditioned problem, so simple least squares estimation of the linear regression matrix parameters typically produces severe over-fitting and poor generalization. To reduce this, we add smoothness constraints on the learned mapping. We use a damped regularization term $R(A) = \lambda ||A||^2$ that penalizes large values in the coefficient matrix A, where λ is a regularization parameter. Larger values of λ will result in overdamping, where the solution will be underestimated, small values of λ will result in overfitting and possibly ill-conditioning. Since the solution of the ridge regressors is not symmetric under the scaling of the inputs, we normalize the inputs $\{X^1, X^2, ..., X^N\}$ by the standard deviation in each dimension

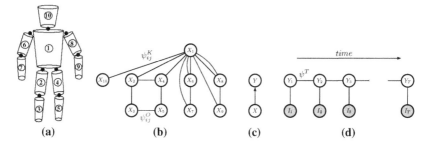

Fig. 3. Hierarchical Inference. Graphical model representation of the hierarchical inference process; **(a)** illustrates the 3D body model; **(b)** the corresponding 2D body model used for inference of the 2D pose at every frame, with kinematic constraints marked in black, and occlusion constraints in blue, and **(d)** the Hidden Markov Model (HMM) used for inferring and tracking the state of the 3D body, Y_t, over time $t \in \{1..T\}$, using the hierarchical inference proposed, in which proposals for each node, Y, are constructed from 2D body pose X using the model in **(c)**.

respectively before solving[1]. We omit the details of weighted ridge regression due to space limitations, and refer readers to [2,22].

Maximization for the gate parameters can be done analytically as well. Given the gate model, $p_{g,k}(k|X,\Theta_{g,k}) = \frac{1}{\sqrt{(2\pi)^n |\Sigma_k|}} \exp^{-\frac{1}{2}(X-\mu_k)^T \Sigma_k^{-1}(X-\mu_k)}$ maximization of the gate parameters $\Theta_{g,k} = (\Sigma_k, \mu_k)$ becomes similar to the mixture of Gaussians estimation, where $\mu_k = \sum_{n=1}^{N} z_k^n X^n / \sum_{n=1}^{N} z_k^n$, $\Sigma_k = \frac{1}{\sum_{n=1}^{N} z_k^n} \sum_{n=1}^{N} z_k^n (X^n - \mu_k)(X^n - \mu_k)^T$, and z_k^n is the the estimated ownership weight of the example n by the expert k estimated by expectation $z_k^n = \frac{p_{e,k}(Y^n|X^n,\Theta_{e,k})p_{g,k}(k|X^n,\Theta_{g,k})}{\sum_{j=1}^{M} p_{e,j}(Y^n|X^n,\Theta_{e,j})p_{g,j}(j|X^n,\Theta_{g,j})}$.

The above outlines the full EM procedure for the MoE model. We learn MoE models for two classes of actions: walking and dancing. Examples of the ground truth 2D query pose with corresponding expected 3D body pose can be seen in Fig. 4 **(a)** and **(b)** respectively. Similar to [1,2] we initialize the EM learning by clustering the output 3D poses using the K-means procedure.

Implementation Details. Instead of learning the full conditional model $p(Y|X)$, we learn two independent models $p(\Gamma|X)$ and $p(\theta|X)$ one for the pose of the 3D body $p(\theta|X)$ given the 2D body pose X, and one for the global orientation of the body $p(\Gamma|X)$. The reasoning for this is two fold. First, this partitions the learned mapping into a fully camera-independent model for the pose $p(\theta|X)$, and the more specific camera-dependent model for the orientation of the body in the world $p(\Gamma|X)$. Second, we found that the optimal damping coefficient is significantly different for the two models that imposing a single joint conditional model (and hence a single coefficient)

---

[1] To avoid problems with 2D and 3D angles that wrap around at 2π, we actually regress the $(cos(\theta), sin(\theta))$ representation for 2D angles and unit quaternion $q = (x,y,z,w)$ representation for 3D angles. After the 3D pose is reconstructed we normalize the not-necessarily normalized quaternions to valid 3D rotations. Since quaternions also suffer from the double cover problem, where two unit quaternions correspond to every rotation, care must be taken to ensure that consistent parameterization is used.

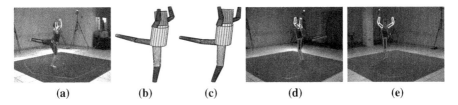

(a)　　　　　(b)　　　　(c)　　　　　(d)　　　　　(e)

Fig. 4. Proposed 3D pose. (a) Query 2D body pose; **(b)** expected 3D pose produced by the learned Mixture of Experts (MoE) model. **(c)** Ground-truth 3D body pose; **(d)** and **(e)** illustrate the projection of the expected 3D pose shown in **(b)** onto two alternative image views.

would result in somewhat larger reconstruction error. Estimation of the depth $p(\Xi|X)$ is done analytically by considering the estimated overall scale of the 2D body.

6   Tracking in 3D

Once the distribution for the 3D body pose at every frame is inferred using the conditional MoE model described, we can incorporate temporal constraints to regularize the individual 3D pose estimates by tracking. We exploit the relatively standard [10] Hidden Markov Model (HMM) shown in Fig. 3 **(d)**. To infer the state of Y_t at every frame t given the temporal constraints $\psi^T(Y_t|Y_{t+1}) = \psi^T(Y_{t+1}|Y_t) \sim N(0, \Sigma_T)$ with learned covariance matrix Σ_T, we use the same inference framework of Non-parametric BP introduced in Section 4.3. Unlike many competing approaches, we allow the model to optimize the pose estimates not only forward but also backward in time in a batch.

The likelihood, $\phi(I_t|Y_t)$, of observing the 3D pose Y_t at time t given image evidence I_t is defined in terms of Chamfer distance of the projected pose Y_t to the silhouettes and edges obtained from I_t using standard techniques. Further details are omitted, and the reader is referred to [4] and [23] for similar likelihood model formulations.

7   Experiments

Datasets. For all experiments presented in this paper we used two datasets that exhibit two different types of actions: **walking** and **dancing**. Both datasets contain a number of motion capture examples used for training, and a single synchronized motion capture example with multi-view video used for testing. Video was captured using 4 stationary grayscale cameras at 60 Hz, and 3D pose was captured using a Vicon system at 120 Hz. The motion capture (mocap) was aligned to video and sub-sampled to 60 Hz, to produce synchronous video/mocap streams. All cameras were calibrated using standard calibration procedures. **Walking** dataset [20] contains 4587 training and 1398 testing poses/frames; **dancing**: 4151 training and 2074 testing poses/frames.

Quantitative Evaluation of 2D to 3D Pose Mapping. Learning the mapping from 2D kinematic pose to 3D kinematic pose is one of the key contributions of this paper. We learned two action-specific MoE models $p(Y|X)$. For each of the action types we first looked at how sensitive our learned mapping is to the parameters of the model (i.e. the

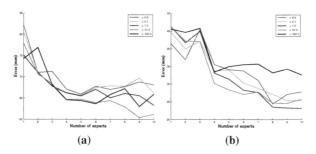

(a)   (b)

Fig. 5. Quantitative evaluation of action-specific **dancing** conditional model $p(Y|X) = p(\Xi|X)p(\Gamma|X)p(\theta|X)$, computed by comparing the expectation of the **(a)** 3D pose $E[p(\theta|X)]$, and of the **(b)** global orientation $E[p(\Gamma|X)]$ to ground truth data. Error is averaged over 4 trained MoE models learned with parameters specified. In both cases, **(a)** and **(b)**, it is clear that there is benefit in using large number of mixture components (> 5), and a moderate value for λ.

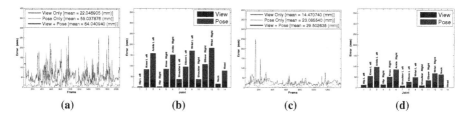

(a)   (b)   (c)   (d)

Fig. 6. Quantitative evaluation of action-specific conditional model $p(Y|X) = p(\Xi|X)p(\Gamma|X)p(\theta|X)$, computed by comparing the expectation to ground truth data for two classes of motion. Per frame error for the reconstructed 3D pose θ, global orientation Γ, and the full 3D state of the body Y are shown for **(a) dancing** and **(c) walking**; the average per joint error as compared to the ground truth is shown in **(b)** and **(d)** respectively.

number of mixture components, and the regularization term λ). The results for **dancing** can be seen in Fig. 5. To quantitatively evaluate the performance we use the measure of [20] computed by choosing 15 virtual markers corresponding to joints and "ends" of limbs, and computing an expected absolute distance in (mm) over all the markers. Once the optimal set of parameters was chosen, the resulting MoE models were applied to the test data, and the error for the reconstructed 3D poses[2] analyzed (see Fig. 6).

The key observation is that **walking**, being considerably simpler of the two action types, can be recovered significantly better (with 50% less error), than the more complex **dancing**. The peaks in the error in both cases often correspond to singular or close to singular cases where foreshortening in the pose of 2D limbs for example is severe.

Hierarchical Inference from Monocular Image Sequence. We also tested the full hierarchical inference on the first 50 frames from the **walking** test sequence. The 3D proposals obtained using the hierarchical inference process (Fig. 7) are accurate, and sufficient to allow reliable Bayesian temporal inference (Fig. 8).

---

[2] Supplementary videos are available from http://www.cs.brown.edu/people/ls/.

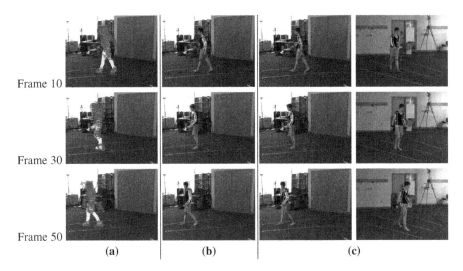

Frame 10

Frame 30

Frame 50

(a)   (b)   (c)

Fig. 7. Hierarchical 3D Pose Estimation. (a) bottom-up proposals for the limbs, (b) most likely sample from the marginals for each limb after 2D pose estimated by NBP, and (c) most likely 3D pose obtained by propagating 2D poses through a conditional $p(Y|X)$ model.

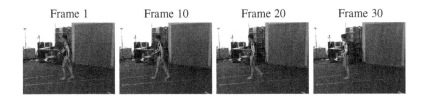

Frame 1   Frame 10   Frame 20   Frame 30

Fig. 8. Tracking in 3D. Tracking based on the 3D proposals (Fig. 7) at 10 frame increments. The 3D poses are projected into the image for clarity. The mean tracking error of 66 (*mm*), computed over first 50 frames of the test sequence, is 77% lower then the error reported for the same dataset using single-view Annealed Particle Filter (APF) with manual initialization in [3]. The best reported result in the literature on this data of 41 (*mm*) was obtained using 4-view APF [3].

8   Summary and Conclusions

The automatic estimation of human pose and motion in monocular image data remains a challenging problem. This is particularly so in the unconstrained environment where good background subtraction is unavailable. Here we have proposed a system to address this problem that uses a hierarchal Bayesian inference framework to go from crude body part detections to a distribution over 3D body pose. We make modest assumptions about the availability of noisy body part detectors and a reasonable image likelihood model. We use belief propagation to infer 2D limb poses that are consistent with the human body model. Our approach extends recent work on inferring 3D body models from 2D silhouettes by using the inferred 2D articulated model instead. This provides a richer representation which reduces ambiguities in the 2D to 3D mapping. We also show that the 3D pose proposals can be used in a tracking framework, that can further regularize the 3D pose estimates.

Acknowledgments. This work was partially supported by Intel Corporation and NSF IGERT award #9870676.

References

1. A. Agarwal and B. Triggs. Learning to track 3D human motion from silhouettes. *ICML*, pp. 9–16, 2004.
2. A. Agarwal and B. Triggs. 3D human pose from silhouettes by relevance vector regression. *CVPR*, vol. 2, pp. 882–888, 2004.
3. A. Balan, L. Sigal and M. Black. A quantitative evaluation of video-based 3D person tracking. *VS-PETS*, pp. 349–356, 2005.
4. J. Deutscher and I. Reid. Articulated body motion capture by stochastic search. *IJCV*, 61(2):185–205, 2004.
5. P. Felzenszwalb and D. Huttenlocher. Pictorial structures for object recognition. *IJCV*, 61(1):55-79, Jan. 2005.
6. N. R. Howe, M. E. Leventon and W. T. Freeman. Bayesian reconstruction of (3D) human motion from single-camera video. *NIPS*, pp. 820–826, 1999.
7. G. Hua, M.-H. Yang and Y. Wu. Learning to estimate human pose with data driven belief propagation. *CVPR*, vol. 2, pp. 747–754, 2005.
8. M. Isard. Pampas: Real-valued graphical models for computer vision. *CVPR*, vol. 1, pp. 613–620, 2003.
9. S. Ju, M. Black and Y. Yacoob. Cardboard people: A parametrized model of articulated motion. *Int. Conf. on Automatic Face and Gesture Recognition*, pp. 38–44, 1996.
10. X. Lan and D. Huttenlocher. A unified spatio-temporal articulated model for tracking. *CVPR*, vol. 1, pp. 722–729, 2004.
11. M. Lee and I. Cohen. Proposal maps driven MCMC for estimating human body pose in static images. *CVPR*, vol. 2, pp. 334–341, 2004.
12. G. Mori. Guiding model search using segmentation. *ICCV*, pp. 1417–1423, 2005.
13. G. Mori, X. Ren, A. Efros and J. Malik. Recovering human body configurations: Combining segmentation and recognition. *CVPR* vol. 2, pp. 326–333, 2004.
14. D. Ramanan, D. Forsyth and A. Zisserman. Strike a pose: Tracking people by finding stylized poses. *CVPR*, vol. 1, pp. 271–278, 2005.
15. D. Ramanan and D. Forsyth. Finding and tracking people from the bottom up. *CVPR*, vol. 2, pp. 467–474, 2003.
16. T. Roberts, S. McKenna and I. Ricketts. Human pose estimation using learnt probabilistic region similarities and partial configurations. *ECCV*, vol. 4, pp. 291–303, 2004.
17. R. Rosales and S. Sclaroff. Inferring body pose without tracking body parts. *CVPR*, vol. 2, pp. 721–727, 2000.
18. H. Sidenbladh, M. Black and D. Fleet. Stochastic tracking of 3D human figures using 2D image motion. *ECCV*, vol. 2, pp. 702–718, 2000.
19. G. Shakhnarovich, P. Viola and T. Darrell. Fast pose estimation with parameter-sensitive hashing. *ICCV*, vol.2, pp. 750–759, 2003.
20. L. Sigal, S. Bhatia, S. Roth, M. Black and M. Isard. Tracking loose-limbed people. *CVPR*, vol. 1, pp. 421–428, 2004.
21. L. Sigal and M. Black. Measure Locally, Reason Globally: Occlusion-sensitive articulated pose estimation. *CVPR*, 2006.

22. C. Sminchisescu, A. Kanaujia, Z. Li and D. Metaxas. Discriminative density propagation for 3D human motion estimation. *CVPR*, vol. 1, pp. 390–397, 2005.
23. C. Sminchisescu and B. Triggs. Estimating articulated human motion with covariance scaled sampling. *IJRR*, 22(6), pp. 371–391, 2003.
24. E. Sudderth, M. Mandel, W. Freeman and A. Willsky. Distributed occlusion reasoning for tracking with nonparametric belief propagation. *NIPS*, pp. 1369–1376, 2004.
25. E. Sudderth, A. Ihler, W. Freeman and A. Willsky. Nonparametric belief propagation. *CVPR*, vol. 1, pp. 605–612, 2003.
26. C. J. Taylor. Reconstruction of articulated objects from point correspondences in a single image. *CVIU*, 80(3):349–363, 2000.

Certain Object Segmentation Based on AdaBoost Learning and Nodes Aggregation Iterative Graph-Cuts*

Dongfeng Han[1], Wenhui Li[1], Xiaosuo Lu[1], Yi Wang[1], and Xiaoqiang Zou[2]

[1] College of Computer Science and Technology, Key Laboratory of Symbol Computation and Knowledge Engineering of the Ministry of Education, Jilin University, Changchun, 130012, P.R. China
handongfeng@gmail.com
[2] College of Transportation, Jilin University, Changchun, 130025, P.R. China

Abstract. In this paper, a fast automatic segmentation algorithm based on AdaBoost learning and iterative Graph-Cuts are shown. AdaBoost learning method is introduced for automatically finding the approximate location of certain object. Then an iterative Graph-Cuts method is used to model the segmentation problem. We call our algorithm as AdaBoost Aggregation Iterative Graph-Cuts (AAIGC). Compared to previous methods based on Graph-Cuts, our method is automatic. Once certain object is trained, our algorithm can cut it out from an image containing the certain object. The segmentation process is reliably computed automatically no additional users' efforts are required. Experiments are given and the outputs are encouraging.

1 Introduction

Image segmentation is a process of grouping together neighboring pixel whose properties are coherent. It is an integral part of image processing applications such as accident disposal, medical images analysis and photo editing. Many algorithms have been proposed (such as Intelligent Paint [1], Intelligent Scissors [2], Graph-Cuts [3], Grab-Cuts [4], Mean Shift [5], Normalized Cuts [6, 7]). In the analysis of the object in images it is essential that we can distinguish between the object of interest and the rest. This latter group is also referred to as the background. The techniques that are used to find the object of interest are usually referred to as segmentation techniques: segmenting the foreground from background. Semi-automatic segmentation techniques that allow solving moderate and hard segmentation tasks by modest effort on the part of the user are becoming more and more popular. However in some situation, we need automatic segmentation for certain object. Previous automatic segmentation methods have two major drawbacks:

1. The final segmentation results are far from users' expectations.
2. The running time is so slow that it can't meet the real-time demands.

In order to overcome the disadvantages of automatic and semi-automatic segmentation algorithms, an AdaBoost learning and iterative Graph-Cuts segmentation algorithm is proposed.

---

* This work has been supported by NSFC Project 60573182, 69883004 and 50338030.

F.J. Perales and R.B. Fisher (Eds.): AMDO 2006, LNCS 4069, pp. 196–202, 2006.

In section 2, we give the details of our algorithm. Experiences and comparisons are given in section 3. In section 4, we give the conclusions and future work.

2 Our Method

Our segmentation algorithm includes four stages: AdaBoost learning for determining object location; expanding location for segmentation; nodes aggregation; iterative Graph-Cuts segmentation for final results. Below we will describe them in detail.

2.1 AdaBoost Learning

The object detector based on AdaBoost learning has been initially proposed by Paul Viola [8] and improved by Rainer Lienhart [9]. First, a classifier (namely a cascade of boosted classifiers working with haar-like features) is trained with a few hundreds of sample views of a particular object, called positive examples, which are scaled to the same size, and negative examples - arbitrary images of the same size. After a classifier is trained, it can be applied to a region of interest (of the same size as used during the training) in an input image. The resultant classifier consists of several simpler classifiers (stages) that are applied subsequently to a region of interest until at some stage the candidate is rejected or all the stages are passed. The classifiers at every stage of the cascade are complex themselves and they are built out of basic classifiers using AdaBoost learning techniques.

The learning algorithm boosts the classification performance by combining a collection of weak classifiers to form a stronger classifier. In each step of AdaBoost, the classifier with the best performance is selected and a higher weight is put on the miss-classified training data. In this way, the classifier will gradually focus on the difficult examples to be classified correctly. The formal guarantees provided by the AdaBoost learning procedure are quite strong. In theory, it is proved that AdaBoost could minimize the margin between positive and negative examples. The conventional AdaBoost procedure can be easily interpreted as a greedy feature selection process. Consider the general problem of boosting, in which a large set of classification functions are combined using a weighted majority vote. The challenge is to associate a large weight with each good classification function and a smaller weight with poor functions. AdaBoost is an aggressive mechanism for selecting a small set of good classification functions which nevertheless have significant variety. Drawing an analogy between weak classifiers and features, AdaBoost is an effective procedure for searching out a small number of good "features" which nevertheless have significant variety. Our procedure is similar with the face detection method. Using AdaBoost learning we can specify the location of certain object in an image.

2.2 Basic Segmentation Method

We briefly introduce some of the basic terminology used throughout the paper. An image that contains $N = n \times n$ pixels, we construct a graph $G = (V, E, W)$ in which each node $v_i \in V$ represents a pixel and every two nodes v_i, v_j representing neighboring pixels are connected by an edge $e_{i,j} \in E$. Each edge has a weight $w_{i,j} \in W$ reflecting the contrast in the corresponding location in the image. We can connect each node to the four or eight neighbors of the respective pixel, producing a graph. Because only background pixels can be determined by AdaBoost, the graph can be partitioned into three disjoint node sets, "U", "B" and "O", where $U \bigcup B \bigcup O = V$, $U \bigcap B \bigcap O = \phi$. U means uncertain pixels and B and O mean background and object pixels. At first $O = \phi$. Finding the most likely labeling translates to optimizing an energy function. In vision and image processing, these labels often tend to vary smoothly within the image, except at boundaries. Because a pixel always has the similar value with its neighbors, we can model the optimization problem as a MRF. In [3], the authors find the most likely labeling for some given data is equivalent to seeking the MAP (maximum a posteriori) estimate. A graph is constructed and the Potts Energy Model (1) is used as the minimization target.

$$E(G) = \underset{v_i \in V}{E_{data}(v_i)} + \underset{\{v_i, v_j\} \in N}{E_{smooth}(v_i, v_j)} \tag{1}$$

The graph G contains two kinds of vertices: p-vertices (pixels which are the sites in the associated MRF) and l-vertices (which coincide with the labels and will be terminals in the graph cut problem). All the edges present in the neighborhood system N are edges in G. These edges are called n-links. Edges between the p-vertices and the l-vertices called t-links are added to the graph. t-links are assigned weights based on the data term (first term in Equations 1 reflecting individual label-preferences of pixels based on observed intensity and pre-specified likelihood function) while n-links are assigned weights based on the interaction term (second term in Equation 1 encouraging spatial coherence by penalizing discontinuities between neighboring pixels). While n-links are bi-directional, t-links are un-directional, leaving the source and entering the sink.

2.3 Nodes Aggregation and Iterative Segmentation by Graph-Cuts

For a large image, it will be slow to segment the whole graph straightly. We introduce a multi-scale nodes aggregation method to construct a pyramid structure over the image. Each procedure produces a coarser graph with about half size, and such that Graph-Cuts segmentation in the coarse graph can be used to compute precision segmentation in the fine graph.

Algorithm proposed in [3] uses a Graph-Cuts based optimization approach to extract foregrounds from images according to a small amount of user input, such as a few strokes. Previous natural image segmentation approaches heavily rely on the user specified trimap. In our situation, only background trimap can be initialized. We use an iterative Graph-Cuts procedure for image matting inspired by [4].

The object of segmentation is to minimize the energy function (1). The first term reflects individual label-preferences of pixels based on observed intensity and pre-specified likelihood function. The second term encourages spatial coherence by penalizing discontinuities between neighboring pixels. So our goal is minimize the energy function and make it adapt to human vision system. In [3] authors give the construction

1.	Applying AdaBoost to find the location of certain object.
2.	Expanding the location for the following operation.
3.	Applying node aggregation to build a pyramid for improving the running speed.
4.	Initially, set the pixels outside the rectangle specified by AdaBoost in B and the rest pixels in U.
5.	Initializing $\beta_i=0$ for $v_i \in B$ and $\beta_i=1$ for $v_i \in U$.
6.	Initializing object and background GMMS from β.
7.	Repeat until convergence (a) Assign GMM components to pixels if pixels $\in U$. (b) Training parameters from data. (c) minimization Gibbs energy using Graph-Cuts. End Repeat
8.	Applying top-down reassembling to get the segmentation result.
9.	Applying post-segmentation methods such as small regions mergence and border repair to improve the performance.

Fig. 1. The whole process of the algorithm proposed in this paper

of the graph in detail. In order to finish the automatic segmentation, a different way is used to construct the graph in this paper.

We use the pixels inside and outside the rectangle specified by AdaBoost to build two Gaussian mixture models (GMM), one for object and the other for background, which are similar with the method described in [3], [4] and [10]. Each GMM is taken to be a full-covariance Gaussian mixture with K=5 components. The Potts Energy Model (1) is equivalent with the Gibbs energy (2)

$$E = \sum_i D(v_i, k_i, \theta, \beta_i) + \sum_{\{v_i, v_j\} \in N} V(v_i, v_j, \beta) \tag{2}$$

$$D(v_i, k_i, \theta, \beta_i) = -\log \pi(k_i, \beta_i) + \frac{1}{2} \log \det \sum (k_i, \beta_i) + \frac{1}{2}[v_i - \mu(k_i, \beta_i)]^T \sum (k_i, \beta_i)^{-1}[v_i - \mu(k_i, \beta_i)] \tag{3}$$

Where $\pi(.)$, $\mu(.)$ and $\sum(.)$ are the mixture weighting coefficients, means and covariance of the 2K Gaussian components for the object and background pixels distributions. So the parameter θ has the form as

$$\theta = \left\{ \pi(k,\beta), \mu(k,\beta), \sum(k,\beta) \right\} \quad k = 1...K = 5; \ \beta = 1 \ or \ 0 \tag{4}$$

The second term of Gibbs energy is

$$\underset{\{v_i, v_j\} \in N}{V}(v_i, v_j) = 1 - \exp(-(v_i - v_j)^2 / \sigma^2) \tag{5}$$

We set σ empirically to be 0.2 in our system.

We use a similar way with [4] to iterative minimize the Gibbs energy which can guarantee the convergence. A more detail can be fond in [4]. The whole procedure of the segmentation algorithm is shown in Fig .1.

3 Experiments

Fig. 3 is a part of training dataset for detection car and flower. There are some positive and negative examples for training. Of course in order to detect other objects we should use others example images. In Fig. 4, the detection results and the iterative segmentation results are shown. In Fig .4 (a) is the car segmentation for gray image. Fig .4 (b) is the segmentation experiments for nature color image. The segmentation results are good enough for some practical applications and the running time is fast enough to meet the real-time demands because we use nodes aggregation to reduce the number of nodes. There are some methods for nodes aggregation. We use a simply but efficient method. For more accurate result we can develop new methods for nodes aggregation. Also the running time comparison between non-nodes aggregation and nodes aggregation is given in Fig. 2. The average ratio of running time is about 20 times faster than non-nodes aggregation.

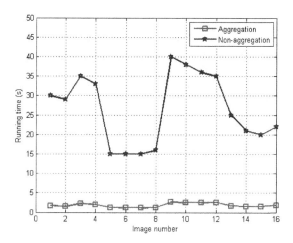

Fig. 2. Running time for aggregation method and non-aggregation method

(a)

(b)

Fig. 3. A part of training image database for car and flower detection

(a)

(b)

Fig. 4. (a) and (b) are the segmentation results by AdaBoost and iterative Graph-Cuts corresponding to four stages of the algorithm

4 Conclusions

This paper proposes a machine learning based image segmentation method. Comparing to previous methods, our scheme is automatic and accurate. AdaBoost learning concept is used to locate the position of certain object. Then nodes aggregation and iterative Graph-Cuts are used to solve the segmentation problems.

On the other hand, how to choose the training images is an important issue for the proposed algorithm. Now we just use experimental parameters which perhaps fail under some situations. In the next step, we should give a reliable parameters based on experiments. Also, In the future, we plan to develop new method to reduce the number of training examples.

References

1. Reese, L.: Intelligent Paint: Region-Based Interactive Image Segmentation, Master's thesis. Department of Computer Science, Brigham Young University, Provo, UT, (1999)
2. Mortensen, E. N., AND Barrett, W. A.: Interactive segmentation with intelligent scissors. Graphical Models and Image Processing, 60, 5 (1998) 349–384
3. Boykov, Y, And Jolly, M.: Interactive graph cuts for optimal boundary & region segmentation of objects in n-d images. In Proceedings of ICCV (2001) 105-112
4. Rother, C, Blake, A, And Kolmogorov, V.: Grabcut-interactive foreground extraction using iterated graph cuts. In Proceedings of ACM SIGGRAPH (2004)
5. D. Comanicu, P. Meer.: Mean shift: A robust approach toward feature space analysis. IEEE Trans. Pattern Anal. Machine Intell, May (2002)
6. J. Shi and J. Malik.: Normalized Cuts and Image Segmentation. Proc. IEEE Conf. Computer Vision and Pattern Recognition (1997) 731-737
7. J. Shi and J. Malik.: Normalized cuts and image segmentation. PAMI, 22(8) (2000) 888–905
8. P. Viola and M. Jones.: Rapid object detection using a boosted cascade of simple features, Proc. CVPR, vol. 1 (2001) 511-518
9. Rainer Lienhart and Jochen Maydt.: An Extended Set of Haar-like Features for Rapid Object Detection. IEEE ICIP 2002, Vol. 1 (Sep. 2002) 900-903
10. Y. Li, J. Sun, C.K. Tang and H.Y. Shum.: Lazy snapping. Proc. of ACM SIGGRAPH (2004) 303-308

Learning Deformations of Human Arm Movement to Adapt to Environmental Constraints

Stephan Al-Zubi and Gerald Sommer

Cognitive Systems, Christian Albrechts University, Kiel, Germany

Abstract. We propose a model for learning the articulated motion of human arm. The goal is to generate plausible trajectories of joints that mimic the human movement using deformation information. The trajectories are then mapped to constraint space. These constraints can be the space of start and end configuration of the human body and task-specific constraints such as avoiding an obstacle, picking up and putting down objects. This movement generalization is a step forward from existing systems that can learn single gestures only. Such a model can be used to develop humanoid robots that move in a human-like way in reaction to diverse changes in their environment. The model proposed to accomplish this uses a combination of principal component analysis (PCA) and a special type of a topological map called the dynamic cell structure (DCS) network. Experiments on a kinematic chain of 2 joints show that this model is able to successfully generalize movement using a few training samples for both free movement and obstacle avoidance.

1 Introduction

Human motion is characterized as being smooth, efficient and adaptive to the state of the environment. In recent years a lot of work has been done in the fields of robotics and computer animation to capture, analyze and synthesize this movement with different purposes [1,2,3]. In robotics there has been a large body of research concerning humanoid robots. These robots are designed to have a one to one mapping to the joints of the human body but are still less flexible. The ultimate goal is to develop a humanoid robot that is able to react and move in its environment like a human being. So far the work that has been done is concerned with learning single gestures like drumming or pole balancing which involves restricted movements primitives in a simple environment or a preprogrammed movement sequence like a dance. An example where more adaptivity is needed would be a humanoid tennis robot which, given its current position and pose and the trajectory of the incoming ball, is able to move in a human-like way to intercept it. This idea enables us to categorize human movement learning from simple to complex as follows: (A) Imitate a simple gesture, (B) learn a sequence of gestures to form a more complex movement, (C) generalize movement over the range allowed by the human body, and (D) learn different categories of movement specialized for specific tasks (e.g. grasping, pulling, etc.).

F.J. Perales and R.B. Fisher (Eds.): AMDO 2006, LNCS 4069, pp. 203–212, 2006.

This paper introduces two small applications for learning movement of type (C) and (D). The learning components of the proposed model are not by themselves new. Our contribution is presenting a supervised learning algorithm which learns to imitate human movement that is specifically more adaptive to constraints and tasks than other models. We will call the state of the environment and the body which affects the movement as constraint space. This may be as simple as object positions which we must reach or avoid, a target body pose or more complex attributes such as the object's orientation and size when garbing it. The first case we present is generating realistic trajectories of a simple kinematic chain representing a human arm. These trajectories are adapted to a constraint space which consists of start and end positions of the arm as shown in fig. 1. The second case demonstrates how the learning algorithm can be adapted to the specific task of avoiding an obstacle where the position of the obstacle varies.

The model accomplishes this by aligning trajectories. A trajectory is the sequence of body poses which change in time from the start to the end of a movement. Aligning trajectories is done by scaling and rotation transforms in angular space which minimizes the distance between similar poses between trajectories. After alignment we can analyze their deformation modes which describe the principal variations of the shape of trajectories. The constraint space is mapped to these deformation modes using a topological map. This map reconstructs a realistic trajectory given a constraint using the deformation information and the transforms.

Next, we describe an overview of the work done related to movement learning and compare them with the proposed model.

2   State of the Art

There are two representations for movements: Pose based and trajectory based. We will describe next pose based methods.

Generative models of motion have been used in [2,1] in which a nonlinear dimensionality reducing method called Scaled Gaussian Latent Variable Model (SGPLVM) is used on training samples in pose space to learn a nonlinear latent space which represents the probability distribution of each pose. Such a likelihood function was used as a prior for tracking in [1] and finding more natural poses for computer animation in [2] that satisfy constraints such as that the hand has to touch some points in space. Another example of using a generative model for tracking is [4] in which a Bayesian formulation is used to define a probability distribution of a pose in a given time frame as a function of the previous poses and current image measurements. This prior model acts as a constraint which enables a robust tracking algorithm for monocular images of a walking motion. Another approach using Bayesian priors and nonlinear dimension reduction is used in [5] for tracking.

After reviewing pose probabilistic methods, we describe in the following trajectory based methods. Schaal [3] has contributed to the field of learning movement for humanoid robots. He describes complex movements as a set of movement primitives (DMP). From these a nonlinear dynamic system of equations are defined that generate complex movement trajectories. He described a reinforcement learning algorithm that can efficiently optimize the parameters (weights) of DMPs to learn to imitate a human in a high dimensional space. He demonstrated his learning algorithm for applications like drumming and a tennis swing.

To go beyond a gesture imitation, In [6] a model for segmenting and morphing complex movement sequences was proposed. The complex movement sequence is divided into subsequences at points where one of the joints reaches zero velocity. Dynamic programming is used to match different subsequences in which some of these key movement features are missing. Matched movement segments are then combined with each other to build a morphable motion trajectory by calculating spatial and temporal displacement between them. For example, morphable movements are able to naturally represent movement transitions between different people performing martial arts with different styles.

Another aspect of motion adaptation and morphing with respect to constraints comes from computer graphics on the topic of re-targeting. As an example, Gleicher [7] proposed a nonlinear optimization method to re-target a movement sequence from one character to another with an identical structure but different segment lengths. The problem is to follow the physical constraints and the smoothness of movement. Physical constraints are contact with other objects like holding the box.

The closest work to the model presented in this paper is done by Banarer [8]. He described a method for learning movement adaptive to start and end positions. His idea is to use a topological map called Dynamic Cell Structure (DCS) network [9]. The DCS network learns the space of valid arm configurations. The shortest path of valid configurations between the start and end positions represents the learned movement. He demonstrated his algorithm to learn a single gesture and also obstacle avoidance for a single fixed obstacle.

3 Contribution

The main difference between pose based methods and our approach is that instead of learning the probability distribution in pose space, we model the variation in trajectory space (each trajectory being a sequence of poses). This representation enables us to generate trajectories that vary as a function of environmental constraints and to find a more compact representation of variations than allowed by pdfs in pose space alone. pose pdfs would model large variations in trajectories as a widely spread distribution which makes it difficult to trace the sequence of legal poses that satisfy the constraints the human actually makes without some external reference like motion sequence data.

Our approach models movement variation as a function of the constraint space. However, style based inverse kinematics as in [2] selects the most likely poses that satisfy these constraints. This works well as long as the pose

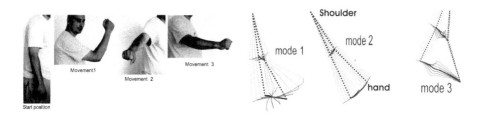

Fig. 1. Movements of the arm

Fig. 2. Movement modes of the arm constructed in 3D space

constraints don't deviate much from the training data. This may be suitable for animation applications but our goal here is to represent realistic trajectories adapted to constraints without any explicit modeling. Banarer [8] uses also a pose based method and the model he proposed does not generalize well because as new paths are learned between new start and end positions the DCS network grows very quickly and cannot cope with the curse of dimensionality. Our DCS network generalizes over the space of trajectories and not poses which enables more generalization.

Gleicher [7] defines an explicit adaptation model is suitable to generate a visually appealing movement but requires fine tuning by the animator because it may appear unrealistic. This is because it explicitly morphs movement using a prior model rather than learning how it varies in reality as done in [2].

In the case of Schaal [3], we see that DMPs although flexible are not designed to handle large variations in trajectory space. This is because reinforcement learning adapts to a specific target human trajectory.

Morphable movements [6] define explicitly the transition function between two or more movements without considering constraint space. Our method can learn the nonlinear mapping between constraint space and movements by training from many samples. The transition between movements is learned and not explicitly pr-defined.

To sum up, we have a trajectory based learning model which learns the mapping between constraints and movements. The movement can be more adaptive and generalizable over constraint space. It learns movements from samples and avoids explicit modeling which may generate unrealistic trajectories.

4   Learning Model

After describing the problem, the concept for learning movement will be explained and how this model is implemented.

In order to develop a system which is able to generalize movement, we need a representation of movement space. The first step is to learn the deformations of the articulated movement itself and the second is to learn how movement changes with start and end configuration and environmental constraints. The mechanics of movement are called *intrinsic features*. The changes of intrinsic features with respect to absolute position and environment are called *extrinsic features*. The intrinsic features describe movement primitives that are characteristic for a human being. These features are the relative coordination of joints in space and time. Extrinsic features can be characterized as the variation of intrinsic features in the space of all possible absolute start and end positions of the joints and any environmental constraints such as obstacle positions.

The difference between intrinsic and extrinsic features that characterizes movement enables the formulation of a learning model. This model consists of two parts: The first part is responsible for learning intrinsic features which uses principal component analysis (PCA). It is applied on the aligned trajectories of the joints to reduce the dimensionality. The second part models the extrinsic features using a special type of an adaptive topological map called the dynamic cell structure (DCS) network. The DCS learns the nonlinear mapping from the extrinsic features to intrinsic features that are used to construct the correct movement that satisfies these extrinsic features.

4.1   Intrinsic Features Using PCA

We assume throughout this paper a kinematic chain representing a human arm shown in Fig. 1. It consists of 2 joints: shoulder and elbow. Each joint has 2 degrees of freedom (ϕ, θ) which represent the direction of the corresponding limb in spherical coordinates.

To perform statistical analysis, we record several samples of motion sequences. In each motion sequence the 3D positions of the joints are recorded with their time. The first step is to interpolate between the 3D points from the stereo cameras of each movement sequence. We end up with a set of parametric curves $\{\mathbf{p}_k(t)\}$ for each motion sequence k where $\mathbf{p}_k(t)$ returns the position vector of all the joints at time t. After that, each $\mathbf{p}_k(t)$ is sampled at n equal time intervals from the start of the sequence k to its end forming a vector of positions $\mathbf{v}_k = [\mathbf{p}_{1,k}, \mathbf{p}_{2,k} \cdots \mathbf{p}_{n,k}]$. By Using the time t as an interpolate variable, the trajectory is sampled such that there are many points at high curvature regions because the arm slows down and less points at low curvature regions because the arm speeds up. Then the Euclidean coordinates of each $\mathbf{v}_k$ are converted to relative orientation angles of all joints $\mathbf{s}_{j,k} = (\phi_{j,k}, \theta_{j,k}), j = 1 \ldots n$ in spherical coordinates: $\mathbf{S}_k = [\mathbf{s}_{1,k}, \mathbf{s}_{2,k}, \ldots \mathbf{s}_{n,k}]$. After this we align the trajectories taken by all the joints with respect to each other. Alignment means to find rotation and scaling transformations on trajectories that minimize the distances between them. This alignment makes trajectories comparable with each other in the sense that all extrinsic features are eliminated leaving only deformation information. The distance measure between two trajectories is the mean radial distance between corresponding direction vectors formed from the orientation angles of the joints. Two transformations are applied on trajectories to minimize the distance between them: 3D rotation R and angular scaling between the trajectory's direction vectors by a scale factor s centered at any point on the trajectory. Fig. 5 shows an example of aligning one trajectory to another one on a unit sphere. We can extend this method to align many sample trajectories with respect to their mean until the mean converges. An example of aligning a group of trajectories is in Fig. 3. The left image shows hand and elbow direction trajectories before alignment and the right is after. We see how the hand trajectories cluster together. The p aligned trajectories are represented as $X = [\mathbf{S}_1^T \ldots \mathbf{S}_k^T \ldots \mathbf{S}_p^T]^T$. Principal component analysis is applied on X yielding latent vectors $\mathbf{\Psi} = [\psi_1 \psi_2 \ldots \psi_n]$. Only the first q components are used where q is chosen such that the components cover a large percentage of the data $\mathbf{\Psi}_q = [\psi_1 \psi_2 \ldots \psi_q]$. Any point in eigenspace can then be converted to the nearest plausible data sample using the following equation

$$\mathbf{S} = \overline{\mathbf{S}} + \mathbf{\Psi}_q \mathbf{b} \tag{1}$$

where $\overline{\mathbf{S}} = \frac{1}{p} \sum_{k=1}^{p} \mathbf{S}_k$ and $\mathbf{b}$ is an eigenpoint.

The latent coordinates $\mathbf{b}$ represent the linear combination of deformations from the average paths taken by the joints. An example of that can be seen in Fig. 2. In this example, the thick lines represent the mean path and the others represent ± 3 standard deviations in the direction of each eigenvector which are called modes. The first mode (left) represents the twisting of the hand's path around the elbow and shoulder. The second mode (middle) shows the coordination of angles when moving the hand and elbow together. The third mode (right) represent the curvatures of the path taken by the hand and shoulder. The reason for using a linear subspace method like PCA in this paper is because the number of trajectories per movement is (for now) only two and because the trajectories are highly covariant since they change in direct response to a low dimensional constraint space. The advantage of this representation is that the dimension reduction depends only on the dimension of the constraint space and not on the dimension of the trajectory which is much higher. As a result we do not require many training samples to extract the deformation modes but only enough samples to cover the constraint space.

4.2   Extrinsic Features Using DCS

PCA performs a linear transform (i.e. rotation and projection in (1)) which maps the trajectory space into the eigenspace. The mapping between constraint space and eigenspace is generally nonlinear. To learn this mapping we use a special type of self organizing maps called Dynamic Cell Structure which is a hybrid between radial basis networks and topologically preserving maps [9]. DCS networks have many advantages: They have a simple structure which makes it easy to interpret results, they adapt efficiently to training data and they can cope with changing distributions. They consist of neurons that are connected to each other locally by a graph distributed over the input space. These neurons also have radial basis functions which are Gaussian functions used to interpolate between these neighbors. The DCS network adapts to the nonlinear distribution by growing dynamically to fit the samples until some error measure is minimized. When a DCS network is trained, the output $\mathbf{b}(\mathbf{x})$ which is a point in eigenspace can be computed by summing the activations of the best matching neuron (i.e. closest) to the input vector $\mathbf{x}$ representing a point in constraint space and the local

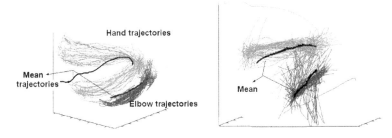

Fig. 3. Example of aligning a training set of trajectories represented as direction vectors tracing curves on a unit sphere

neighbors to which it is connected by an edge which is defined by the function $A_p(\mathbf{x})$. The output is defined as

$$\mathbf{b}(\mathbf{x}) = f_P^{nrbf}(\mathbf{x}) = \frac{\sum_{i \in A_p(\mathbf{x})} \mathbf{b}_i h(\| \mathbf{x} - \mathbf{c}_i \| / \sigma_i)}{\sum_{j \in A_p(\mathbf{x})} h(\| \mathbf{x} - \mathbf{c}_j \| / \sigma_j)}, \tag{2}$$

where $\mathbf{c}_i$ is the receptive center of the neuron i, $\mathbf{b}_i$ is represents a point in eigenspace which is the output of neuron i, h is the gaussian kernel and σ_i is the width of the kernel at neuron i.

The combination of DCS to learn nonlinear mapping and PCA to reduce dimension enables us to reconstruct trajectories from $\mathbf{b}(\mathbf{x})$ using (1) which are then fitted to the constraint space by using scale and rotation transformations. For example, a constructed trajectory is fitted to a start and end position.

5   Experiments

In order to record movements, a marker-based stereo tracker was developed in which two cameras track the 3D position of three markers placed at the shoulder, elbow and hand at a rate of 8 frames per second. This was used to record trajectory samples. Two experiments were conducted to show two learning cases: moving between two positions and avoiding an obstacle.

The first experiment demonstrates that our learning model reconstructs the nonlinear trajectories in the space of start-end positions. For evaluation, we have to measure how close the model-generated trajectories are to the human's. For this purpose it is useful to compare the distance between the model and the human to some worst case trajectory. The mean trajectory is chosen for comparison because it corresponds to the zero vector in eigenspace $\mathbf{b} = 0$ in (1) and represents a path with no deformations. The zero vector of $\mathbf{b}$ is what the DCS network outputs when it has not learned anything. Next, we describe the experiment and the validation using the mean.

A set of 100 measurements were made for an arm movement consisting of three joints. The movements had the same start position but different end positions as shown in Fig. 1.

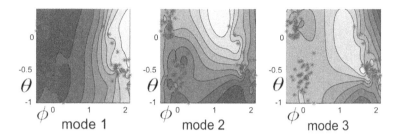

Fig. 4. Distribution of eigenvalues (bright regions represent maxima) in the angular space of the end position of the hand

Fig. 4 shows a contour plot of each eigencoordinate corresponding to the modes in Fig. 2 distributed over the input space which in this figure is the orientation angles of the hand. We see that the first three eigenvalues have a smooth distribution with a single global maximum. The first component explained 72% of the training samples, the second 11% and the third 3%. All subsequent components are noise due to measuring errors. Each distribution is unimodal and nonlinear. The points represent the samples. If more samples are added to cover the space, distributions will become more crisp but will not change significantly because the deformation modes are trained with a representative training set.

The performance of the DCS network was first tested by a k-fold cross validation on randomized 100 samples. This was repeated for $k = 10$ runs. In each run the DCS network was trained and the number of neurons varied between 6 to 11. In 80% of the cases the DCS-trajectory was closer to the sample trajectory than to the mean trajectory. Fig. 6 shows an example where the DCS trajectory was better than the mean. The average distance between the DCS-trajectory and the data sample was 3.9° and the standard deviation was 2.1°. The average distance between the mean trajectory and the data samples was 7.9° and the standard deviation was 3.5°. This shows that the DCS network was able to generalize well using only a small sample size (about 100).

We can compare with Banarer [8] who fixed the DCS network with an upper bound of 15 neurons to learn a single gesture and not many as in our experiment. He used simulated data of 70 samples with a random noise of up to 5° and the mean error was 4.3° compared to our result of 3.9° on real data. The measurement error of the tracker is estimated to be 4.6° standard deviation which accounts for the similar mean errors. This shows that our model scales well with variation.

Finally, we demonstrate the algorithm for obstacle avoidance. In this case 100 measurements were taken for the arm movement with different obstacle positions as shown in fig 7. The black lines show the 3D trajectory of the arm avoiding the obstacle which has a variable position determined by the distance B. We see how the hand backs away from the obstacle and the elbow goes down and then upward to guide the hand to its target. A is the Euclidian distance between the start and end positions of the hand. The grey lines represent a free path without obstacles. In this case we need to only take the first eigenvector from PCA to

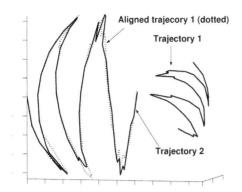

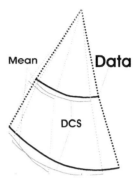

Fig. 5. Alignment of two trajectories by scale and rotation. The curves are traced by a direction vector on a unit sphere.

Fig. 6. DCS trajectory and mean compared to a data sample (in 3D space). The DCS trajectory is closer to the data than the mean.

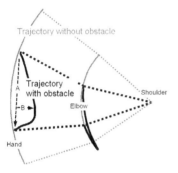

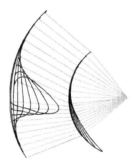

Fig. 7. Trajectory for obstacle avoidance in 3D space

Fig. 8. Variation of arm trajectory with respect to the obstacle

capture the variation of trajectories due to obstacle position. This deformation mode is shown in Fig. 8 We define the relative position of the obstacle to the movement as simply $p = \frac{B}{A}$. The DCS network learns the mapping between p and the eigenvalue with only 5 neurons. The learned movement can thus be used to avoid any obstacle between the start and end positions regardless of orientation or movement scale. This demonstrates how relatively easy it is to learn new specialized movements that are adaptive to contraints.

6   Conclusion

We proposed a learning model for generation of realistic articulated motion. The model characterizes deformation modes that vary according to constraint space. A combination of DCS network to learn the nonlinear mapping and PCA to reduce dimensionality enables us to find a representation that can adapt to constraint space with a few samples. This trajectory based method is more suited for movement generation than pose based methods which are concerned with defining priors for good fitting with image data such as tracking. The proposed method models variation of movement with respect to constraints in a more clear way than the previously proposed methods. In the case of [8] this is true because Banarer learns single poses in the DCS network but in our case we learn complete trajectories in the DCS netwrok. The potential uses of our method is in developing humanoid robots that react more intelligently to there environment. Two small applications towards that goal were experimentally validated. In the future we will improve the algorithm to adapt to new cases with more complicated constraints.

Acknowledgments. The work presented here was supported by the the European Union, grant COSPAL (IST-2003-004176). However, this paper does not necessarily represent the opinion of the European Community, and the European Community is not responsible for any use which may be made of its contents.

References

1. Urtasun, R., Fleet, D.J., Hertzmann, A., Fua, P.: Priors for people tracking from small training sets. In: International Conference on Computer Vision (ICCV). (2005) 403–410
2. Grochow, K., Martin, S.L., Hertzmann, A., Popovic;, Z.: Style-based inverse kinematics. ACM Trans. Graph. **23**(3) (2004) 522–531
3. Schaal, S., Peters, J., Nakanishi, J., Ijspeert, A.: Learning movement primitives. In: International Symposium on Robotics Research (ISPR2003), Springer Tracts in Advanced Robotics, Ciena, Italy (2004)
4. Sidenbladh, H., Black, M.J., Fleet, D.J.: Stochastic tracking of 3d human figures using 2d image motion. In: Proceedings of the 6th European Conference on Computer Vision (ECCV '00), London, UK, Springer-Verlag (2000) 702–718
5. Sminchisescu, C., Jepson, A.: Generative modeling for continuous non-linearly embedded visual inference. In: Proceedings of the twenty-first International Conference on Machine Learning (ICML '04), New York, NY, USA, ACM Press (2004)
6. Ilg, W., Bakir, G.H., Mezger, J., Giese, M.A.: On the repersenation, learning and transfer of spatio-temporal movement characteristics. International Journal of Humanoid Robotics (2004)
7. Gleicher, M.: Retargeting motion to new characters. In: Proceedings of the 25th Annual Conference on Computer Graphics and Interactive Techniques (SIGGRAPH '98), New York, NY, USA, ACM Press (1998) 33–42
8. Banarer, V.: Struktureller bias in neuronalen netzen mittels clifford-algebren. Technical Report 0501, Technische Fakultät der Christian-Albrechts-Universität zu Kiel, Kiel (2005)
9. Bruske, J., Sommer, G.: Dynamic cell structure learns perfectly topology preserving map. Neural Computation **7**(4) (1995) 845–865

Three-Dimensional Mapping from Stereo Images with Geometrical Rectification

A.J. Gallego Sánchez, R. Molina Carmona, and C. Villagrá Arnedo

Grupo de Informática Industrial e Inteligencia Artificial
Universidad de Alicante, Ap.99, E-03080, Alicante, Spain
{ajgallego, rmolina, villagra}@dccia.ua.es

Abstract. In this paper we present a method for mapping 3D unknown environments from stereo images. It is based on a dense disparity image obtained by a process of window correlation. To each image in the sequence a geometrical rectification process is applied, which is essential to remove the conical perspective of the images obtained with a photographic camera. This process corrects the errors in coordinates x and y to obtain a better matching for the map information. The mapping method is an application of the geometrical rectification and the 3D reconstruction, whose main purpose is to obtain a realistic appearance of the scene.

Keywords: Disparity images, Geometrical rectification, 3D mapping.

1   Introduction

Nowadays, a central aspect in artificial intelligence research is the perception of the environment by artificial systems. It is a critical element in robot navigation tasks like map building (mapping) and self-location. Specifically, stereoscopic vision opens new paths that in the future will allow these systems to capture the three-dimensional structure of their environment without any physical contact. Moreover, range sensors can also acquire very detailed models [1], but these types of sensors are more expensive and they cannot provide information of both range and appearance, which is useful for navigation algorithms and texture mapping. For these reasons we will focus on stereo vision.

Several authors use stereo vision and disparity images to solve the 3D mapping problem. For instance, a first solution to three-dimensional reconstruction with stereo technology was developed at Carnegie Mellon University. The possibility of composing several three-dimensional views from the camera transforms is set out, to build the so-called "3D evidence grid" [2]. There are other approaches which infer 3D grids from stereo vision, due to the fact that appearance information is not provided by range finders. Hence, they add an additional camera to their mobile robots [3,4]. Moreover, a module of 3D recognition could be added to identify some objects. This technique is not exclusive of robotics, but it could be used in other applications such as automatic machine guidance or also for detection and estimation of vehicle movement [5].

F.J. Perales and R.B. Fisher (Eds.): AMDO 2006, LNCS 4069, pp. 213–222, 2006.

Stereo vision can improve the perception of scenes and world modelling, so there are some methods which work with disparity images due to their advantages. The problem is that these algorithms cannot be applied in a widespread manner with all types of structures; because the images (or the objects) obtained from a camera have no real size, since they are deformed by the conical perspective effect.

We present an original mapping method which reconstructs the environment from a sequence of geometrically rectified images. For each pair of stereo images in the sequence a dense disparity map is calculated (the map contains depth information for every pixel in the image) and next it is geometrically rectified in order to show the same aspect as the real scene. This process is essential to remove the conical perspective of the images obtained with a binocular camera. Other simpler geometrical rectifications have already been used in other fields, like in [6] to rectify roads and to obtain their real appearance.

2   Proposed Model

2.1   Process Scheme

Stereo vision techniques are based on the possibility of extracting 3D information from a scene using two or more images taken from different view points. We will focus on the basic case of two images of a scene, obtained with a stereo camera with parallel objectives. In order to gather this 3D information, a function that computes the correspondence between the pixels from the left camera (reference image) and those from the right camera must be defined. The positional difference between each of these pairs of pixels is a value called disparity. This information can be displayed as an image, and is known as depth or disparity image. Depending on the camera geometry, the distance can be transformed to coordinates in an Euclidean space, where the centre is placed in the camera position. [7,8,9]

In this work a 3D reconstruction method and a scene mapping algorithm are presented. For the 3D reconstruction several steps are followed: First, the disparity map is calculated starting from the images captured by the stereo camera. Then, a geometrical rectification process is applied in order to remove the effect of the conical perspective (see section 2.2). And finally, the 3D reconstruction is obtained (see section 2.3). The mapping algorithm is an application of this reconstruction method. It is based on a sequence of stereo images. For each image of this sequence its disparity map and its geometrical rectification are calculated. Once their space occupation matrix has been obtained, the mapping process is applied (see section 2.4).

Camera calibration and disparity algorithm are not the purpose of this paper. The disparity image is computed using multi-resolution and energy function [10,11]. Moreover, it is important to note that the quality of the three-dimensional reconstruction depends on the quality of the disparity map. Errors in the disparity map can cause mistaken shapes and incorrect depth values, so errors will be transferred to the reconstruction.

2.2   Geometrical Rectification

In order to correct the perspective in the images a rectification is needed. An image taken with a camera is in conical perspective, such that all parallel lines converge at a point. As an example, figure 1(a) shows an image of a corridor, in which, due to the perspective effect induced by the acquisition conditions, the size of all the elements changes according to their distance from the camera. In this example, a pixel in the lower part of the image represents a small volume of the scene (it represents a part of the scene in the foreground); while a pixel in the centre of the same image represents a larger volume (because the part of the scene represented by the pixel is in the background). So, to correctly perform the 3D reconstruction the perspective must be rectified, thus the obtained result shows the same aspect as the real scene. [12,13]

Figure 1 shows the scheme for the rectification process: figure 1(b) shows a non-rectified scene in 3D, in figure 1(c) the scene is seen from above (with only x and z coordinates shown), and figure 1(d) shows the result which are desired after rectification.

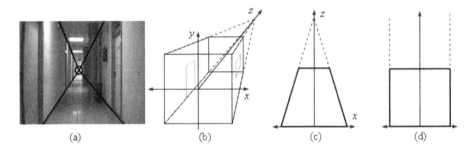

(a)   (b)   (c)   (d)

Fig. 1. Rectification scheme

After the analysis of variables implied in geometrical rectification, it can be concluded that the process of rectification depends on the depth and difference between x, y and centre coordinates. As a result, the so called **Linear Rectification** is obtained. The coordinates are linearly corrected, so that the rectification directly depends on grey level (that is, z coordinate) and position (x and y coordinates). In an ideal situation, the Linear Rectification would rectify the scene to obtain the result given in figure 1(d), but with real images some problems arise. The rectification equation is:

$$\begin{cases} x' := x + f\left(\frac{D(x,y)}{D_{max}}\right) \times \alpha \times w \\ y' := y + f\left(\frac{D(x,y)}{D_{max}}\right) \times \alpha \times w \\ z' := z \end{cases} \qquad (1)$$

Where:

- f is a depth modifier. In the original equation it is a linear function but other functions can also be applied (explained below).

- $D(x, y)$ contains the grey level or the depth corresponding to the pixel of coordinates x and y.
- D_{max} is the maximum value of depth.
- α is a value in the range $[0, 1]$ which measures the filter proportion.
- $w := \begin{cases} -x & \dots \text{ if } x < width/2 \\ width - x & \dots \text{ if } x \geq width/2 \end{cases}$
- $h := \begin{cases} -y & \dots \text{ if } y < height/2 \\ height - y & \dots \text{ if } y \geq height/2 \end{cases}$

It is important to note that in the previous equation the new coordinates of a pixel are obtained from the former value of the coordinates, the depth value and the x, y position of the pixel. Variables w and h contain the highest displacement that can be performed to place one pixel at the borders of the scene, that is, if the pixel is placed at the centre, the highest displacement is half the image. The value of $D(x, y)/D_{max}$ is in the range $[0, 1]$, and depends on the depth: it is 0 if the pixel is in the foreground, and 1 if it is in the background (in this case, if the pixel is in the centre of the image, the rectification is maximum, so the pixel is moved to the border of the image).

The most important drawback is the fact that this method does not distinguish whether the figure is very close, and therefore, errors occur with some images, especially if the main object is too far from the camera. In fact, pixels corresponding to a distant object are split, leaving a hole whose dimensions increase as the distance to the object increases. So, important far non-centred objects can have holes and be dispersed.

In order to minimize these problems, a **Logarithmic Rectification** is proposed. In this case, a logarithmic function is applied to the depth value, substituting the function f. The logarithm has the property of reducing the rectification when the object is close to the camera, and of magnifying the rectification when the object is far away. So, objects in the background suffer a higher correction than those in the foreground.

2.3   Discrete Three-Dimensional Reconstruction

The reconstruction is based on a dense disparity image obtained through a process of window correlation (the correspondence between pixels from both images is carried out using a window correlation criterion, in order to identify similar areas in both images). This depth image contains the disparity which is associated to each pixel in the reference image (left image). Therefore, for every pixel in the original image, we can find the disparity value in $D(x, y)$. Horizontal and vertical components for each point are directly obtained from the row and the column in which the point is located in the image [9,12,13,14]. In this way, a three-dimensional matrix M_{3D} which represents the space occupation of the scene can be filled.

To perform a simple three-dimensional reconstruction process four basic steps are taken: firstly the disparity map (D) is stored in a two-dimensional matrix (M_{2D}) which has the same size as the disparity map $(m \times n)$, and then some smooth filters can be applied if needed (average and/or median filters). Next, a geometrical rectification process (see section 2.2) is applied, which takes the 2D matrix (M_{2D}) and returns a 3D matrix (M_{3D}) containing the result. In this way, the matrix M_{3D} (which is initialized to zero) is filled, making $M_{3D}(x', y', D(x, y)) = 1$ where $x = 0, 1, ..., m - 1$ and $y = 0, 1, ..., n - 1$, which will indicate the space occupation of the final result. Starting from each of the M_{3D} depth values, their equivalence in real units (metres) is calculated and, finally, the result is shown.

1. $M_{2D} := ObtainDisparityData(D)$
2. $M_{2D} := ApplySmoothFilters(M_{2D})$
3. $M_{3D} := ApplyRectification(M_{2D})$
4. $Display(ObtainRealUnits(M_{3D}))$

The most important drawback is the fact that when the geometrical rectification equation (1) is applied, holes are produced in the 3D representation. This is due to the discreteness of disparity maps. In fact, pixels corresponding to a distant object are split, leaving a hole whose dimensions increase as the distance to the object increases. To minimize these problems the geometrical rectification filters which use a logarithmic function were introduced.

2.4   Mapping Algorithm

In this section a novel mapping algorithm is presented. It demonstrates the utility of the geometrical rectification and the advantages of its application to this kind of problem.

In order to do the 3D mapping of the scene, N stereo images $I_0, I_1, ..., I_{N-1}$ of the environment are taken. Each of these images is captured at a fixed distance. Once a stereo pair ($I_i, i = 0, 1, ..., N - 1$) is obtained, its corresponding disparity map D_i is calculated and added to the Σ list which stores all the disparity maps. Next, the algorithm of geometrical rectification (explained in the previous section) is used in order to compute the rectified matrix $M3D_i$ of each disparity map. For each matrix $M3D_i$ its intersection with the previous matrix is calculated ($M3D_{i-1} \cap M3D_i$), and its result is added to the main matrix M_{map} which represents the mapping of the scene. A cubic filter F (explained below) is applied to the whole matrix M_{map}, which discretizes the three-dimensional matrix and transforms it into a grid of rectangular cubes. Lastly, the result (M_{map}) is represented according to the space occupation of this matrix and calculating its equivalence in real units (metres). All these steps could be summarized as follows:

1. **for each** $D_k \in \Sigma$ **do**
   (a) $M_{2D} := ObtainDisparityData(D_k)$
   (b) $M_{2D} := ApplySmoothFilters(M_{2D})$
   (c) $M_{3D} := ApplyRectification(M_{2D})$
   (d) $M_{map} := M_{map} \cap M_{3D}$
2. $M_{map} := ApplyCubicFilter(M_{map})$
3. $Display(ObtainRealUnits(M_{map}))$

Cubic filter F applies the equation $g(x, y, z) := \Sigma_{(i,j,k) \in S} f(i, j, k)$ to each cube of the matrix, where S represents the set of point coordinates which are located in the neighbourhood of $g(x, y, z)$, including the point in question. In this way the space occupation of each cube is in the centre, and each cell contains the set of readings of that portion of the space. The number of readings is referred to as "votes", and represents the probability of space occupation.

Figure 2 shows the scheme for the mapping process: figure 2(a) represents the first image of the sequence, in figure 2(b) the scene is seen from above (with only x and z coordinates shown), and figure 2(c) shows the union of this image with the following image in the sequence; also, the intersection area of both can be seen.

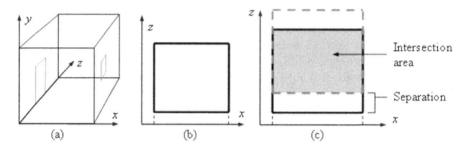

Fig. 2. Mapping scheme

3   Experiment Results

In this section the experiment results are shown. Figure 3 shows a reconstruction comparison using a synthetic disparity map (a) which simulates a corridor. It clearly shows the effect of the geometrical rectification. In figure 3(b) no rectification is applied and in (c) the result of the rectification is shown. As can be seen in (c), the walls are perfectly rectified, becoming parallel as expected.

To do the mapping experimentation we took a sequence of 25 images of a corridor with a resolution of 320x240 pixels. Figure 4 shows three images of the sequence as well as their disparity maps, and the corridor plan is shown below. The main objective is that the walls, floor and roof appear without slope in the reconstruction; it is also important, that columns (represented by circles in the plan) are detected correctly and that there should not be any obstacle in the corridor.

In figure 5 the results of the corridor mapping are shown; a comparison between the different types of rectification can be seen. For all of them a cubic filter size of 3x3x3, and a number of votes of 5 have been used.

In figure 5(a) there is no geometrical rectification, and a wrong result is obtained: the in-between space of the corridor is not clear. In figure 5(b) the Logarithmic Rectification has been applied, but only with a factor of 50%. This result is better than the previous one, because the walls are limited and the in-between

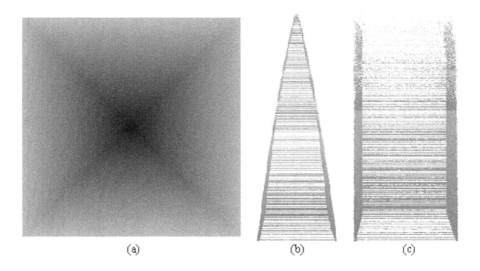

Fig. 3. Effect of the geometrical rectification on a corridor

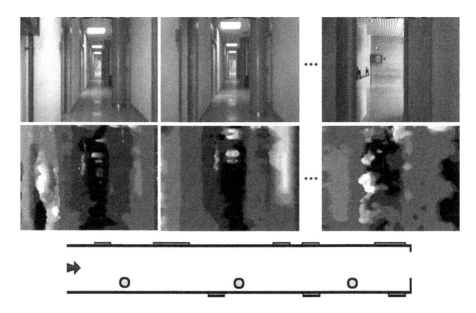

Fig. 4. Sequence of images for the mapping

area of the corridor can be seen. In (c) the same type of rectification has been used, but increasing the factor to 100%. The result is similar to the previous one, although the corridor appears clearer. In figures 5(d) and (e) the Linear Rectification (without applying the logarithm function to the depth value) has been made. These results show a better definition of the corridor and a clearer

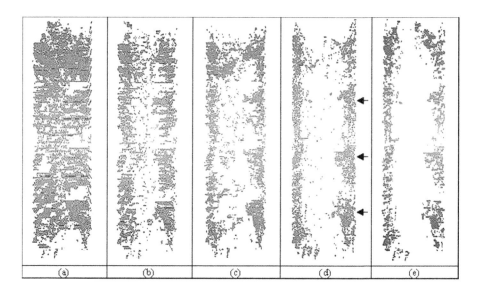

Fig. 5. Mapping results of the corridor

Fig. 6. Lateral views of the corridor

in-between space, moreover, the columns can be distinguished on the right hand side (they are marked with an arrow). Figure 6 shows a pair of lateral views of the result 5(e).

To conduct the experiments, a Pentium IV 3,20GHz with 2GB of RAM and a 512MB graphic card has been used. The reconstruction of the map has been made using a 320x240x256 voxels matrix and disparity maps with a size of 320x240 pixels. Moreover, it is important to note that only the pixels which have some value in the disparity map are processed. In other words, the black pixels whose distance is considered infinite will not be processed. To process the sequence of 25 images (each image has a level of 70% of processed data) the algorithm takes approximately 8 seconds. This time depends on the precision of the final 3D reconstruction. So, the process time of an individual reconstruction is less than 0.3 seconds.

4   Conclusions and Future Work

This paper has presented a novel mapping algorithm which works with disparity maps in order to reconstruct unknown environments. It is an application based on a previous 3D reconstruction work. This method uses geometrical rectification to eliminate the effect of conical perspective, with the intention of obtaining a real aspect in the final result. The cubic filter is very useful to solve odometry problems; if it is not applied the number of coincidences would be too small. Nevertheless, the final quality of the reconstructed image depends on the quality of the disparity map. In future experiments, better disparity images will improve the final result.

These methods have several advantages. Firstly, due to the fact that in the reconstructed scene each position represents the same size, the matching of the mapping algorithm is improved, and also it would be possible to process the information in parallel, allowing a homogeneous distribution of the information among all the image pixels. For instance, as geometrical rectification is applied to all the pixels in the image, a SIMD massively parallel system could be used. Moreover, it can take advantage of the parallel processing to carry out more elaborate operations.

Current work is focused on applying textures to the reconstruction in order to give a more realistic aspect to the final result. Furthermore, we will try to improve the geometrical rectification, calculating the point of view and considering the used camera characteristics [1]. As future work, the obtained results will be used in an Augmented Reality system and in an autonomous robot system. It could solve the occlusion problem using the depth information from the disparity map, and it could take advantage of the scene reconstruction to recognize their geometry, objects, and so on.

References

1. Jose M. Sanchiz, Robert Burns Fisher: Viewpoint Estimation in Three-Dimensional Images Taken with Perspective Range Sensors. IEEE Transactions on Pattern Analysis and Machine Intelligence, vol. 22, no. 11 (2000) 1324–1329
2. Hans P. Moravec: Robot spatial perception by stereoscopic vision and 3D evidence grids. The Robotics Institute Carnegie Mellon University. Pittsburgh, Pennsylvania (1996)

3. Stephen Se, D. Lowe, J. Little: Vision-based mobile robot localization and mapping using scale-invariant features. Proc. of IEEE International Conference on Robotics and Automation. Seoul, Korea (2001)
4. C. Martin and S. Thrun: Real-time acquisition of compact volumetric maps with mobile robots. In Proceedings of ICRA'02: IEEE International Conference on Robotics and Automation (2002)
5. Gonzalo Pajares Martinsanz, Jesús M. de la Cruz García: Visión por computador: imágenes digitales y aplicaciones. Ed. Ra-Ma, D.L. Madrid (2001)
6. Alberto Broggi: Robust Real-Time Lane and Road Detection in Critical Shadow Conditions. In Proceedings IEEE International Symposium on Computer Vision, Coral Gables, Florida. IEEE Computer Society (1995)
7. E. Trucco and A. Verri: Introductory techniques for 3-D Computer Vision. Prentice Hall (1998)
8. I. Cox, S. Ignoran, and S. Rao: A maximum lilelihood stereo algorithm. Computer Vision and Image Understanding, 63 (1996)
9. Oliver Faugeras: Three-dimensional computer vision: a geometric viewpoint. The MIT Press. Cambridge, Massachusetts (1993)
10. Compañ, P.; Satorre, R.; Rizo, R.: Disparity estimation in stereoscopic vision by simulated annealing. Artificial Intelligence research and development. IOS Press. (2003) 160–167
11. Patricia Compañ, Rosana Satorre, Ramón Rizo, Rafael Molina: Inproving depth estimation using colour information in stereo vision. IASTED International Conference on Visualization, Imaging and Image Processing (VIIP 2005), Benidorm (Spain) (2005) 377–389
12. Antonio Javier Gallego Sánchez, Rafael Molina Carmona, Carlos Villagrá Arnedo: Scene reconstruction and geometrical rectification from stereo images. World Multi-Conference on Systemics, Cybernetics and Informatics (WMSCI), Orlando (2005)
13. Antonio Javier Gallego Sánchez, Rafael Molina Carmona, Carlos Villagrá Arnedo: Discrete and Continuous Reconstruction of 3D Scenes from Disparity Maps. IASTED International Conference on Visualization, Imaging, and Image Processing, Benidorm (Spain) (2005) 366–371
14. M. Pollefeys, R. Koch and L. Van Gool: A simple and efficient rectification method for general motion. Proc. International Conference on Computer Vision, Corfu (Greece) (1999) 496–501

Transferring a Labeled Generic Rig to Animate Face Models

Verónica Costa Teixeira Orvalho[1], Ernesto Zacur[2], and Antonio Susin[1]

[1] Laboratorio de Simulación Dinámica (Univ. Politècnica de Catalunya)
veronica.costa@upc.edu, toni.susin@upc.edu
[2] Universitat Pompeu Fabra
ernesto.zacur@upf.edu

Abstract. We present a facial deformation system that adapts a generic facial rig into different face models. The deformation is based on labels and allows transferring specific facial features between the generic rig and face models. High quality physics-based animation is achieved by combining different deformation methods with our labeling system, which adapts muscles and skeletons from a generic rig to individual face models. We describe how to find the correspondence of the main attributes of the generic rig, transfer them to different 3D face models and generate a sophisticated facial rig based on human anatomy. We show how to apply the same deformation parameters to different face models and obtain unique expressions. Our goal is to ease the character setup process and provide digital artists with a tool that allows manipulating models as if they were using a puppet. We end with different examples that show the strength of our proposal.

1 Introduction

Facial animation is related to the interaction of muscles and skeletons beneath the skin. It is the key element to transmit individuality and personality to a character in films and video games. Therefore, to obtain physically-based animations, it is crucial to develop systems that simulate the anatomical structure of the face. Recent advances in facial synthesis show an increased interest in physics-based approaches [23] [15] [22]. Today, to animate a character, an experienced CG artist has to model each facial rig by hand, making it impossible to re-use the same rig in different facial models. The task is further complicated when a minor artistic change on the facial topology leads to the restarting of the rigging process from scratch. This creates a bottleneck in any CG production and leads to the research of automated methods to accelerate the process [14].

Modeling and animation of deformable objects have been applied to different fields [1] [3]. *Noh et al.* [17] proposed several methods for transferring animations between different face models. The surface correspondence is obtained by specifying the corresponding point pairs on the models. *Pighin et al.* [7] presented a method to interactively mark corresponding facial features in several photographs of an individual, to deform a generic face model using radial basis function. *Sederberg and Parry* [20] first introduced Free-Form Deformation

F.J. Perales and R.B. Fisher (Eds.): AMDO 2006, LNCS 4069, pp. 223–233, 2006.
© Springer-Verlag Berlin Heidelberg 2006

(FFD) in 1986; the method does not require setting the corresponding features on the geometries. Other interesting approaches for high level geometric control and deformation over 3D model were introduced [5] [12] [21].

We propose a deformation method to transfer the inner structure of a generic rig to individual face models, based on thin-plate splines [2] and the use of facial features labels. We tag the generic rig with landmarks on its surface (the skin) and automatically deform it, together with the muscle and skeleton structure, to fit different face models. Because all models share the same generic set of attributes, we don't need to develop unique scripts for each face. We can transfer generic rig parameters, enabling re-use of existing animation scripts. We can build models with underlying anatomical structure, skin, muscle and skeleton, for human heads or other type of creatures. The models are suitable for real-time animation based on simulation of facial anatomy.

2   The Generic Rig

Our method builds on a sophisticated 3D face model we call generic rig $\mathcal{R}$ (see figure 4), designed for use within a facial animation production pipeline to accelerate the rigging process. The model is formed by different layers of abstraction: skin surface $\mathcal{R}_S$, muscles surfaces $\mathcal{R}_M$, skeleton joints $\mathcal{R}_B$, facial feature landmarks λ, skinning system and other components for representing the eyes, teeth and tongue. We can assign different attributes to each of these layers, like: weight, texture, muscle stress, etc. [10]

The **generic rig** $\mathcal{R}$ has been modeled manually and is a highly deformable structure of a face model based on physical anatomy. During the modeling process, we used facial features and regions to guarantee realistic animation and reduce artifacts.

The **surface** $\mathcal{R}_S$ is the external geometry of the character, determining the skin of the face using polygonal surfaces composed by a set of vertices $\mathbf{r}$ and a topology that connects them.

The generic rig is tagged with **landmarks** λ, distributed as a set of sparse anthropometric points. We use these landmarks to define specific facial features to guarantee correspondence between models. Our rig has 44 landmarks placed on the surface (see figure 4c) [9] [6].

The **skeleton** $\mathcal{R}_B$ is a group of bones positioned under the skin. It defines the pose of the head and controls lower level surface deformation.

The **muscles** $\mathcal{R}_M$ are a group of volumes, surfaces or curves located under the skin, which control higher level surface deformation. To build our muscle structure, we selected eleven key muscles (see figure 4d) responsible for facial expressions [8], out of the twenty-six that move the face.

3   Transferring the Generic Rig Structure

We introduce a method to automatically transfer the generic rig structure and components to individual 3D face models, which can be divided in three main steps: first, we deform the generic rig surface to match the topology of the face model we want to control; then, we adapt the muscles, skeleton and attributes of the generic rig to the 3D model; finally, we bind the transferred elements to the model, obtaining an anatomic structure prepared for physically-based animation.

The face model that inherits the generic rig setup is referred as $\mathcal{F}$. It is defined by a face surface $\mathcal{F}_S$, which determines the face geometry and shape, and a set of landmarks ϕ placed on $\mathcal{F}_S$. Like $\mathcal{R}_S$ from the generic rig, $\mathcal{F}_S$ is defined by a set of vertices $\mathbf{f}$ and a topology that connects them. The landmarks are positioned manually by the artist, to guarantee correspondence with the generic rig landmarks (see section 2). Even though the generic rig has 44 landmarks, it is not necessary to use them all to transfer the rig (see results in figure 5). Starting with a landmarked face model $\mathcal{F}$, the rest of the structure transfer is automated as it will be detailed next.

3.1   Geometric Transformations

To deform the rig $\mathcal{R}$ into $\mathcal{F}$ we use linear and non-linear global transformations and local deformation. Linear transformations in combination with non-linear transformations, give us enough degrees of freedom (DOF) to ensure the correct match between the geometries.

Equation 1 describes the generic form of the transformations:

$$\mathbf{x}' = \begin{pmatrix} x' \\ y' \\ z' \end{pmatrix} = \begin{pmatrix} \sum_{i=1}^{n} w_{xi} U(\mathbf{x}, \mathbf{p}_i) + a_{x0} + a_{xx}\, x + a_{xy}\, y + a_{xz}\, z \\ \sum_{i=1}^{n} w_{yi} U(\mathbf{x}, \mathbf{p}_i) + a_{y0} + a_{yx}\, x + a_{yy}\, y + a_{yz}\, z \\ \sum_{i=1}^{n} w_{zi} U(\mathbf{x}, \mathbf{p}_i) + a_{z0} + a_{zx}\, x + a_{zy}\, y + a_{zz}\, z \end{pmatrix} \qquad (1)$$

Following Bookstein [2] [18], we use the kernel function $U(\mathbf{x}, \mathbf{p}_i) = \|\mathbf{x} - \mathbf{p}_i\|$ that minimizes the bending energy of the deformation. This transformation is called Thin Plate Spline Warping (TPS) and it is a special case of Radial Basis Function Warping [4].

Solving the linear system of equations 2, we obtain $\mathbf{w}$ and $\mathbf{a}$ coefficients, using $\mathbf{p}$ and $\mathbf{q}$ correspondence, where $\mathbf{p}$ are surface origin coordinates and $\mathbf{q}$ are surface target coordinates. The TPS wrapping ensures the exact point matching and interpolates the deformation of other points smoothly.

$$\left(\begin{array}{cccc|cccc} 0 & U(\mathbf{p}_1, \mathbf{p}_2) & \cdots & U(\mathbf{p}_1, \mathbf{p}_n) & p_{x1} & p_{y1} & p_{z1} & 1 \\ U(\mathbf{p}_2, \mathbf{p}1) & 0 & \cdots & U(\mathbf{p}_2, \mathbf{p}_n) & p_{x2} & p_{y2} & p_{z2} & 1 \\ \vdots & \vdots & \ddots & \vdots & \vdots & \vdots & \vdots & \vdots \\ U(\mathbf{p}_n, \mathbf{p}1) & U(\mathbf{p}_n, \mathbf{p}_2) & \cdots & 0 & p_{xn} & p_{yn} & p_{zn} & 1 \\ p_{x1} & p_{x2} & \cdots & p_{xn} & 0 & 0 & 0 & 0 \\ p_{y1} & p_{y2} & \cdots & p_{yn} & 0 & 0 & 0 & 0 \\ p_{z1} & p_{z2} & \cdots & p_{zn} & 0 & 0 & 0 & 0 \\ 1 & 1 & \cdots & 1 & 0 & 0 & 0 & 0 \end{array} \right) \left(\begin{array}{c} w_1 \\ w_2 \\ \vdots \\ w_n \\ a_x \\ a_x \\ a_x \\ a_0 \end{array} \right) = \left(\begin{array}{c} q_1 \\ q_2 \\ \vdots \\ q_n \\ 0 \\ 0 \\ 0 \\ 0 \end{array} \right) \qquad (2)$$

3.2   Surface Deformation

Given $\mathbf{p}$ and $\mathbf{q}$, we define the operation:

$$\mathbf{x}' = TPS_{\mathbf{p}}^{\mathbf{q}}(\mathbf{x}) \qquad (3)$$

that minimizes the energy of the surface deformation. We use the following notation, $\mathbf{q} = \mathbf{p}|_S$, where $\mathbf{q}_i$ is the position of the correspondent point to $\mathbf{p}_i$ in the geometry S.

Figure 1a shows the deformation of a surface uniformly sampled into another surface, using a reduced set of sparse landmarks. Only these landmarks will result on an exact deformation, while the rest of the surface points lay outside the target surface. Figure 2 shows the deformation of the generic rig into a face model using 10 anthropometric landmarks.

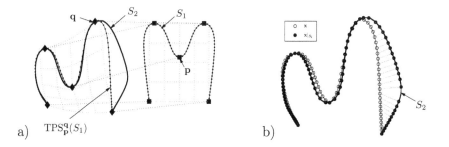

Fig. 1. a) TPS wrap of a generic surface based on reduced set of sparse landmarks (S_1: original surface, S_2: target surface, $\mathbf{p}$: origin landmarks, $\mathbf{q}$: target landmarks); b) Sticking of the original surface to the target surface after applying the TPS (see section 3.3)

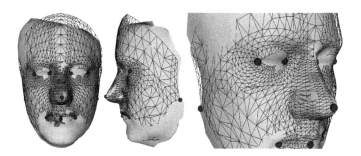

Fig. 2. Human Face wraping process using 10 landmarks

3.3 Obtaining a Dense Correspondence Between Surfaces

To obtain an exact deformation of every surface point, where the origin surface matches the target surface, we apply a local deformation to every point of the origin surface. Then, we project every point of the wrapped surface to the closest point of the target surface. As a result, we get the correspondent point in the target surface for every vertex of the origin surface. This is called *dense correspondence* [13] between surfaces.

We define in our pipeline an operation called *Stick* (STK) that computes the dense correspondence of points $\mathbf{r}$, between the generic rig $\mathcal{R}$ and the face model $\mathcal{F}$:

$$\mathbf{r}|_{\mathcal{F}} = STK_{\mathcal{F}_S}\left(TPS_\lambda^\phi\left(\mathbf{r}\right)\right) \tag{4}$$

This operation can present undesirable folds in areas with high curvature or if the distance between origin and target points is large. Lorenz and Hilger worked on solutions to avoid these folds [16] [11]. Fortunately, we didn't came across this problem in the many tests we performed on different face models: human and cartoon.

3.4 Deforming Layer Structures

Based on the dense correspondence between $\mathcal{R}_S$ and $\mathcal{F}_S$, we can deform the generic rig muscles $\mathcal{R}_M$ and skeleton $\mathcal{R}_B$. This correspondence avoids placing additional landmarks on the muscles or on the skeleton structure. Figure 3 shows that the wrap based on dense correspondence keeps the relationship between the structure and the surfaces better than the wrap based on sparse landmarks.

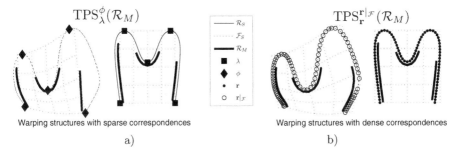

Warping structures with sparse correspondences

a)

Warping structures with dense correspondences

b)

Fig. 3. Wrap based on a) landmarks; b) dense correspondence

3.5 Attribute Transfer

The generic rig $\mathcal{R}$ has a set of attributes on the surface nodes $\mathbf{r}$ defined as scalar or vectorial fields. We have to transfer each of these attributes to surface $\mathcal{F}_S$. For each surface vertex $\mathbf{f}_i$, we find its closest point on $\mathcal{R}_S|_{\mathcal{F}}$, get the interpolated value and assign it to $\mathbf{f}_i$.

Figure 9a shows the transferred weights that influence the movement of the jaw bone. Figure 9b shows a region labeling transfer. Both figures show the attributes transfer from the generic rig to the cartoon, with different triangulations.

3.6 Skinning

In animation, skinning is the process of binding deformable objects to a skeleton [19]. In some software packages it is also known as envelope or birail. After skinning, the deformable object that makes up the surface is called the character's skin, and the deformable objects under the skin, which influence and shape it, are called the muscles.

The output of the skinning process is a character model setup, with the skeleton and muscles controlling the deformations. The positioning of the muscles has two goals: build an inner structure that correctly reflects the character's appearance and enable the projected facial animations with minimum effort. The deformations of the character's skin, produced by the movements of the skeleton and muscles, allows physically-based animation.

Our skinning method uses the generic rig weight to automatically attach the previously deformed skeleton and muscles to the face model $\mathcal{F}$.

3.7   Method Overview

Next, we describe the method pipeline:

$\mathcal{R} \leftarrow$ Generic Rig
$\mathcal{F} \leftarrow$ Face Model
$\lambda \leftarrow$ Generic Rig Landmarks
$\phi \leftarrow$ Face Model Landmarks

$\mathcal{R}'_S \leftarrow \mathrm{TPS}^\phi_\lambda(\mathcal{R}_S)$
$\mathbf{r}|_\mathcal{F} \leftarrow \mathrm{STK}_\mathcal{F}(\mathcal{R}'_S)$
$\mathcal{F}_M \leftarrow \mathrm{TPS}^{\mathbf{r}|_\mathcal{F}}_\mathbf{r}(\mathcal{R}_M)$
$\mathcal{F}_B \leftarrow \mathrm{TPS}^{\mathbf{r}|_\mathcal{F}}_\mathbf{r}(\mathcal{R}_B)$
$\mathbf{f} \leftarrow attributeTransfer(\mathbf{r}|_\mathcal{F})$
$\mathcal{F} \leftarrow skinning(\mathcal{F}_S, \mathcal{F}_M, \mathcal{F}_B)$

4   Results and Conclusion

The deformation methods have been implemented in C++ as a plug-in for Maya 7.0 software. Our method speeds up the character setup and animation pipeline, since we drive all face models by deformation of the same generic rig. This allows using the facial expressions created in the rig on different models. To obtain unique deformation in each face, both generic rig's muscles and skeleton can be adjusted in the different facial regions.

In contrast with other methods [15] that landmark the skin, muscle and skull, we only landmark the skin surface because we obtain dense correspondence. This simplifies and eases the setup of the character. Our results indicate that anthropometric modeling is a good approach to generate physically-based animations.

Our *generic rig* has 1800 points, 44 landmarks, 4 bones and 11 muscles, and is based on human anatomy (see figure 4). The *human model* is a 3D scan of a human face. It has 1260 points and 10 landmarks (see figure 5). Figure 5b displays the wireframe mesh. We use 10 landmarks to transfer the rig structure (see figure 5d). Figure 12 shows the wrapping process.

The *cartoon model* has 1550 points and 44 landmarks (see figure 6). Figure 6 shows the muscle transfer and figure 9 shows the attribute transfer of the weight and region label. Based on the weights of figure 9a, figure 10 shows the transfer of a facial expression. The graphics on figure 8 display the distance between the muscle and the skin surface points, on the generic rig (solid line) and on the face model (dots). Results show that the wrapping works better for human faces. To explore the limits of our method, figure 7 confirms that the wrapping and landmarks fitting work robustly in non-human faces with extreme facial appearance. We use 12 landmarks to transfer the rig structure to a goat (see figure 7d).

For further automation we will create a set of facial expression templates and an intuitive GUI running in Maya. Our generic rig will include different type of muscles. We will add support on our plug-in for NURBS surfaces. We will allow the models to inherit the animation controls from the generic rig. The purpose of these animation controls is to reduce: the complexity to obtain facial motion, the effort required by artist and computation time.

Our final goal is to automate the character setup process within an animation pipeline, without changing the input model, enabling the artists to manipulate it as if they were using a puppet. The model can be created by an artist or scan generated. This will further speed up the creation of animations, because it will require no additional rigging.

Acknowledgement

Special thanks goes to João Orvalho for his review, unconditional support and motivation. We also thank Dani Fornaguera, Marco Romeo and Carlos for their valuable comments and 3D Models. This research is partially supported by CI-CYT grant TIN2004-08065-C02-01.

References

[1] A. Angelidis, M. Cani, G. Wyvill, and S. King, *Swirling-sweepers: Constant-volume modeling*, Pacific Graphics 2004, 2004.

[2] F. Bookstein, *Principal warps: Thin-plate splines and the decomposition of deformations*, IEEE Trans. on Pattern Anaylsis and Machine Intelligence, vol. 11, no. 6, 1989, pp. 567–585.

[3] M. Botsch and L. Kobbelt, *An intuitive framework for real-time freeform modeling*, ACM Transactions on Graphics (TOG), SIGGRAPH '04, 2004, pp. 23(3), 630–634.

[4] J. Carr, W. Fright, and R. Beatson, *Surface interpolation with radial basis functions for medical imaging*, vol. 16, IEEE Trans. on Medical Imaging, 1997.

[5] S. Coquillart, *Extended free-form deformations: A sculpturing tool for 3d geometric modeling*, Proc. SIGGRAPH 90' Conf., ACM Computer Graphics, 1990, pp. 187–196.

[6] D. Metaxas D. DeCarlo and Matthew Stone, *An anthropometric face model using variational techniques*, Proc. SIGGRAPH '98, 1987, pp. 67–74.

[7] R. Szeliski D.H. Salesin F. Pighin, D. Lischinski and J.Hecker, *Synthesizing realistic facial expressions from photographs*, Proc. SIGGRAPH '98 Conf, 1998, pp. 75–84.

[8] G. Faigin, *The artist's complete guide to facial expressions*, Watson-Guptill Publications, New York, 1987, pp. 67–74.

[9] Munro Farkas, Leslie and Ian, *Anthropometric facial proportions in medicine*, Charles Thomas publisher ltd., USA, 1987.

[10] J. Haber, *Anatomy of the human head*, SIGGRAPH 2004, Course Notes: Facial Modeling and Animation, 2004.

[11] K. B. Hilger, R. R. Paulsen, and R. Larsen, *Markov random field restoration of point correspondences for active shape modelling*, SPIE - Medical Imaging, 2004.

[12] W.M. Hsu, J.F. Hugues, and H. Kaufman, *Direct manipulation of free-form deformation*, Proc. SIGGRAPH '92, ACM Press, 1992, pp. 177–184.

[13] T. Hutton, B. Buxton, and P. Hammond, *Dense surface point distribution models of the human face*, IEEE Workshop on Mathematical Methods in Biomedical Image Analysis, 2001, pp. 153–160.

[14] P. Joshi, W. Tien, M. Desbrun, and F. Pighin, *Learning controls for blend shape based realistic facial animation*, Eurographics/SIGGRAPH Symposium on Computer Animation, ACM Press, 2003, pp. 187–192.

[15] H. Yamauchi H. Seidel K. Kahler, J. Haber, *Head shop: Generating animated head models with anatomical structure*, ACM, 2002.

[16] C. Lorenz and N. Krahnstöver, *Generation of point-based 3d statistical shape models for anatomical objects*, vol. 77, Computer Vision and Image Understanding: CVIU, 2000, pp. 175–191.

[17] J. Noh and U. Neumann, *Expression cloning*, Proc. SIGGRAPH '01 Conf, ACM SIGGRAPH, 2001, pp. 277–288.

[18] K. Rohr, H.S. Stiehl, R. Sprengel, T.M. Buzug, J. Weese, and M.H. Kuhn, *Landmark-based elastic registration using approximating thin-plate splines*, vol. 20, IEEE Trans. on Medical Imaging, 2001, pp. 526–534.

[19] J. Schleifer, *Character setup from rig mechanics to skin deformations: A practical approach*, Proc. SIGGRAPH '02, Course Note, 2002.

[20] T. Sederberg and S. Parry, *Free-form deformation of solid geometric models*, Proc. SIGGRAPH 86' Conf., ACM Computer Graphics, 1986, pp. 151–160.

[21] K. Singh and E. L. Fiume, *Wires: a geometric deformation technique*, Proc. SIGGRAPH 98' Conf., ACM Computer Graphics, 1998, pp. 405–414.

[22] R. Szeliski and S. Lavallee, *Matching 3d anatomical surfaces with non-rigid deformation using octree splines*, Internatinal Journal of Computer Vision 18,2, 1996, pp. 171–186.

[23] K. Waters and J. Frisbie, *A coordinated muscle model for speech animation*, Proc. Graphics Interface '95, 1995, pp. 163–170.

Transferring a Labeled Generic Rig to Animate Face Models

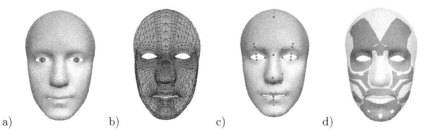

Fig. 4. Generic Rig a)textured; b)wireframe; c)44 landmarks; d)muscles

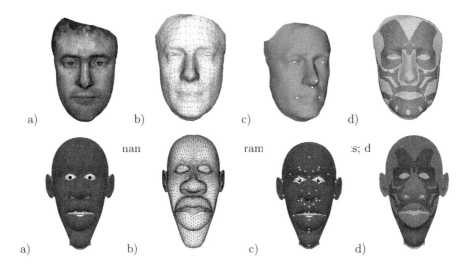

Fig. 6. Cartoon a)textured; b)wireframe; c)44 landmarks; d)muscles

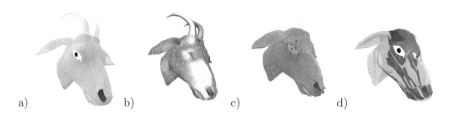

Fig. 7. Animal a)textured; b)wireframe; c)44 landmarks; d)muscles

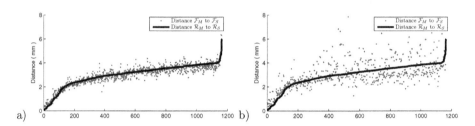

Fig. 8. Distance between muscle and skin surfaces on the generic rig and on the model a) Human model; b) Cartoon model

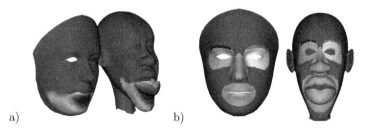

Fig. 9. Attribute transfer from generic rig to cartoon model a) weight of the jaw bone (red is $w = 0$, blue is $w = 1$); b) region labels

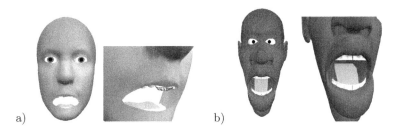

Fig. 10. Facial Expression a) Generic Rig and close up; b) Cartoon and close up

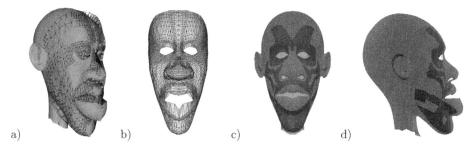

Fig. 11. Cartoon Deformation a) TPS and Stick Lines; b) Cartoon after STK; c) Muscles transfer front view; d) Muscles transfer side view

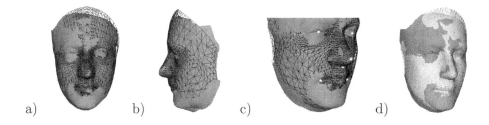

Fig. 12. Human Face Deformation with 10 landmakrs a) TPS front view; b) TPS side view; c) close up; d) dense correspondence after STK

Virtual Characters as Emotional Interaction Element in the User Interfaces

Amalia Ortiz[1], David Oyarzun[1],
María del Puy Carretero[1], and Nestor Garay-Vitoria[2]

[1] VICOMTech Research Centre. Paseo Mikeletegi 57, E-20011 Donostia
[2] University of the Basque Country. Manuel Lardizabal 1 E-20018 Donostia
aortiz@vicomtech.es

Abstract. Virtual assistants, also called Avatars, are virtual characters making the communication between the user and the machine more natural and interactive. In this research we have given avatars the capacity of having and expressing emotions by means of a computational emotional model based on the cognitive perspective. Once the system knows the emotional expressiveness that the virtual character will show to the user, we also have worked in how to express it through facial animation techniques.

Keywords: Affective computing, appraisal theory of emotion, virtual characters, facial animation.

1 Introduction

Emotions affect in many aspects of our live and many researchers have been studying trying to understand the fundamental aspects of them. They affect in the evaluative judgement, in the memory, in the creative thinking and in the decision making process, where some authors as Picard [1] estimated the computers would improve their decisions if they had emotions or emotional mechanisms which work with the computer rule systems.

The emotions also affect in the communication and social interactions. This was studied by Mehrabian [2], who shows in his research, the 93% of our message goes through non-verbal language (55%), mainly based on facial and corporal motions, and the use of the voice (38%). Furthermore, according to the Reeves and Nass research [3], people present social behaviour even when they are interacting with computers. However, at the moment, the person-device interaction is not based on the communication between people. People speak, gesticulate and feel in our interactions. Hence, the interaction should be totally different to the present desktop paradigm based on keyboard, mouse and screen. Therefore, it appears a new research field, which centres its work in the area of conversational user interfaces, including virtual assistants. These assistants, also called avatars, are virtual characters making the communication between user and machine more natural and interactive due to anthropomorphic issues. This will be achieved by mimicking human communication that is, among others, giving the avatar emotional components.

F.J. Perales and R.B. Fisher (Eds.): AMDO 2006, LNCS 4069, pp. 234–243, 2006.

According to Goleman [4] the emotional intelligence consists in the capacity of recognizing, expressing and having emotions. If we translate this concept to the affective computing, not every computer need all of these capacities all the time [1]. Although the recognition field is very important for the creation of the emotional computers, in the frame of this research we are going to focus in the possession and expression. First of all, regarding to the possession field, the system should detect the emotion that is going to show. This is the reason why there exist several emotional models which are explained in section 2. In section 3 two if these emotional models are compared in order to find which one fits better with our approach. Section 4 explains how the selected emotional model is implemented. At the time to express emotions, Picard exposes that the sentic modulation, such as the voice intonation, the facial expression and the pose, is the physical mean to express an emotional state and it is the primary way of communicating human emotions. Regarding to facial expression, in section 5 we study how emotions should be expressed and in section 6 we explain the animation techniques used in order to execute each emotion. In order to get a conversational avatar we use the voice intonation through the integration of a commercial synthesizer explained in 6. At the end of this paper we explain the conclusion and future work produced by this work.

2   Emotional Models

There are principally four different perspectives on emotion: the Darwinian, the Jamesian, the social constructivist, and the cognitive. For the implementation of emotional computers, the most followed perspective is the fourth one. In this case, emotions are considered as responses to the meaning of events with regard to the individual's goals and motivations. There are a lot of emotional models which follows this perspective. We tried to find which one is the emotional model that better fits with an interface depending on the application requirements.

In general, the *appraisal theories* indicate that the result of an emotional reply comes from a dynamic assessment process of the needs, beliefs, objectives, worries or environmental demands. Each emotional model use different appraisals. Therefore, for choosing an emotional model that fits with the application in which it is going to be integrated, it is very important to know what kind of information about the user and system we have; which are the application requirements, how the user will interact and communicate with the system and what will be the avatar role. In the framework of HIZKING21 project [5] we made a research about the use of virtual characters in the current interfaces. We concluded that they can play three different roles:

Interaction element: The avatar acts as the main interaction element between the user and the application. The user has the illusion of being interacting with a real person. Both, the avatar and the user, are an active element in the system. Examples of this kind of role are virtual assistants: e.g. teachers in e-learning environments or shop assistant in e-commerce.

Person representation: Another kind of role is the user representation in the virtual environment. In this case the user is an active element in the system but he/she does not interact with the avatar. The avatar acts according to the user orders. These kind of avatars are used in virtual communities or chats.

Virtual presenter: In another applications the avatar can be a virtual presenter. Its main function is to present information. The user is a passive member of the audience. These kind of avatars are used in applications for Digital TV or in information web pages.

For this work we have the following requirements about the system: The avatar is an emotional interaction element in the interface and we do not have any previous information about the user, just the ones that are generating during the interaction and are implicit in the application (such as pass an exam, win a game or buy a product). At this point we tried to find the emotional model that better fits for a system with this characteristics.

Inside the cognitive emotional models to study, the OCC [6] and Roseman's model [7] were explicitly thought for its integration in computers and they give us a mechanism based on rules for the emotion cognitive generation. Hence, in this research we were focussed in the study of these two emotional models.

The OCC model groups the emotions depending on the cognitive conditions in which they are generated. In this model emotions are reactions to events, agents or objects. These events, agents or objects are appraised according to an individual's goals, standards and attitudes.

In another hand, Roseman specifies a cognitive structure associated with emotions based on the assessment that different people have about the events which cause emotions. He developed a model, in which six cognitive dimensions determine whether an emotion arises and which one it is. From the combination of this dimensions and their values a table can be arranged (Fig.1), from which, according to Roseman, emotions can be predicted.

Several authors have developed computational systems following these both emotional models in order to give emotions to avatars. For example, the Roseman's model was implemented by Velasquez in Cathexis [8]. The OCC model has been extensive implemented. The most outstanding ones have been developed by Elliot [9] and by Bates [10]. Some other authors, who find some lacks in both models, decided to use a combination of them, such as FLAME [11] or ParleE [12].

As it is shown, we found in the state of the art more computational emotional models based on OCC than on Roseman. Many developers of such avatars believe that this model will be all they ever need to equip their character with emotions. Bartneck [13] points out what the OCC model is able to do and what is not for an embodied emotional character. He found a lot of limitations such as the lack of the surprise emotion or the need of having into account the history of events, actions and objects. In this work we compared both models in order to find the one which fits better with a system where we do not have any previous information about the user and the avatar acts as the main emotional interaction element (section 3).

3   Comparison Between OCC and Roseman

We found the following main differences comparing OCC model with Roseman's one:

1. **Surprise Emotion:** Roseman's model has surprise emotion while the OCC model do not consider it. However, some authors as Elliot[9] or Buy [12], who use this model, have included it. For example, Buy mixed both model in order to achieve surprise. The target of this research is to use one of the models just as the psychologists defined.

2. **Appraisals:** In Roseman's model, events are appraised only according to goals. This way, attitude and standard related emotions such as like/dislike or anger are not defined in a reasonable way [12]. This fact, which at the beginning can seem a Roseman's model limitation, can become in some cases positive depending on the application requirements. In this case we do not have any previous information about the user and we do not know the attitudes or standards so the use of Roseman's model could be more appropiate.

3. **Historical:** Bartneck studied the viability of the OCC model for being integrated in a Virtual Character. He concludes that the history function is not described in the original OCC model, but it plays an important role for the believability of the character. The history function will help to calculate the likelihood, realization and effort of events. In Roseman's model one of the dimensions involved is the situational and motivational state. Moreover, the event outcome probability and the potential an individual has to control the situation are used to further sort out emotions in this category. This forces having a historic function in order to assess an event.

4. **Number of Emotions:** Initially the OCC model generates 22 different emotions. Bartneck considers that, if a character uses the emotional model only changing its facial expressions then its emotion categories should be limited to the ones it can express. This is a problem in two models because both have more emotions that the avatar can facially reproduce. Some authors as Elliot implemented all 22 emotional categories in his agents, but this was because he developed a character-character interaction. Others modified the emotional models, but this is not the focus of this work. For solving this problem we assign each emotion to its facial expression following the concept explain in section 5.

5. **Simplicity:** Bartneck concluded that the OCC model contains a sufficient level of complexity and detail to cover most situations an emotional interface character might have to deal with. However, Roseman's model received positive feedback from the AI society because of its simple structure that can be translated quickly into rules to define which appraisal triggers which emotion.

Mainly due to the lack of surprise emotion and the history function in the OCC model, and because of the Roseman's model generate emotions just based on the assessment of an event, which is the only information that we have in the system, we decided to implement the Roseman's model (Fig.1) for the application with the requirements explained above and that is going to be presented in section 4.

4   A Computational Roseman's Model

We implement Roseman's model by means of a rule-based system based on the table shown in Fig.1. In this table are presented the six cognitive dimensions which determine whether an emotion arises and which one it is; 1)if the event is self-caused, other-caused or circumstance caused, 2)if the event is unexpected, 3)if the event is a motive consistent or motive inconsistent, 4) if the person can control of the situation (in case the event is motive inconsistent), 5) if the event is certain or uncertain and 6) if the event is noticed as negative because it blocks a goal or because it is negative in its nature.

		Positive emotions		Negative emotions		
		Motive-Consistent		Motive-Inconsistent		
		Appetitive	Aversive	Appetitive	Aversive	
	Unknown	Surprise				
	Uncertain	Hope		Fear		Weak
Circumstance - Caused	Certain	Joy	Relief	Sadness	Distress	
	Uncertain	Hope		Frustration	Disgust	Strong
	Certain	Joy	Relief			
	Uncertain	Dislike				Weak
Other - Caused	Certain	Liking				
	Uncertain			Anger	Contempt	Strong
	Certain					
	Uncertain	Regret				Weak
Self - Caused	Certain	Pride				
	Uncertain			Guilt	Shame	Strong
	Certain					

Fig. 1. Roseman's model [7]

The implemented model has been integrated in a prototype with the required requirements in order to prove it in a real application. This application consists in a quiz-game in which the avatar gives to the user emotional feedback related with its results. The interface of the game (Fig.2) is composed by an emotional avatar, which expresses the emotions given the Roseman's model, by a clock, which controls the time, and by a questions zone, which are taken from a XML file. When the quiz-game begins the emotional module starts to assess the event following the Roseman's appraisals described above.

The first appraisal is the agency, this means whereas the event is self-caused, other-caused or circumstance caused. An event is circumstance-caused whether the user has been started and the system gets the first user reply. Then, the first thing to do is to ascertain if the answer is correct.

If it is correct, the system checks the **second appraisal** of Roseman's model; whether this is unexpected or not. For achieving this information we use the relative frequency ($f_s = n_s \div n$) which is a number that describes the proportion of successes happening in a given play. If the system gets an unexpected reply, the avatar will show the *SURPRISE* emotion.

If this is an expected response, the **third appraisal** to treat is whether it is motive-consistent or not. An event is motive-consistent whereas it helps to achieve one of the subject's goals and it is motive-inconsistent if it threatens it. Anyway, the main goal here is winning the game. As we are evaluating a correct answer, the user will be in a motive-consistent. Inside the set of emotions generated by motive-consistent event we get *JOY* if the event is motivated by the desire to obtain a reward (the player is wining) or *RELIEF* if the desire to avoid punishment. If the answer is not correct, the event is motive-inconsistent. It follows the same sequence rules than above. If it is unexpected, then we get *SURPRISE*. If not, the system checks whether it is appetitive or not.

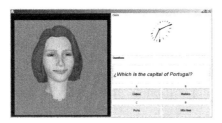

Fig. 2. Quiz-game interface

In the case of a failed reply the emotion is also affected by the **forth appraisal**, the user potential to control the situation. For guessing it (if he/she can still win) we use the Eq. 1. For achieving this equation we start with the binomial distribution function $(P(X = k) = \binom{N}{k}P_{ok}^k(1 - P_{ok})^{N-k})$ which gives us the discrete probability distribution of obtaining exactly k successes out of N trials, taking into account that the probability of getting right one question is P_{ok}. Knowing that the user goal is to answer k correct questions for winning the game and he/she answered n questions, we need to calculate the winning probability at each point of the game, depending on the x previous correct answers. We follow the Eq. 1. If the user can control the situation and the event is appetitive, then we get the *FRUSTRATION* emotion. If he/she can not control the situation, the avatar will show the *SADNESS* emotion. In the case that the event is aversive we get the *DISTRESS* emotion if he/she has not potential control and again *FRUSTRATION* if he/she has it.

$$\sum_{i=k-x}^{N-n} \binom{N-n}{i}P_{ok}^i(1 - P_{ok})^{N-n-i} \tag{1}$$

All of this occurs when the event is certain (the player has already answered the question). Whereas the event is certain or not, is the **fifth Roseman's appraisal**. For assessing this appraisal, the system calculates the time that the player has to answer by means of a clock the player can visualize in the quiz-game interface (Fig.2). While the user is not answering, the system gets an uncertain event. In this case, the computational emotional model looks at the success probability which is also calculated through the relative frequency. If the user has a high probability of getting right then the system gives us the *HOPE* emotion. If not, then the control potencial is achieving again through the equation 1. If the user could not control the situation, then the avatar will show the *FEAR* emotion, if not, we will get *FRUSTRATION*.

The first Roseman's appraisal that we assessed is the agency of an event. At this point we got the events caused by the circumstances but Roseman contemplates two more kinds of event-causes, the other-caused events and the self-caused. The emotions generated by the assessments of this kind of events will appear when the system know if the player wins or not. The first ones will show the avatar feeling about the user game and the other ones will be the avatar prediction about the user feeling. The rules followed for obtaining this emotions are the ones related with the appetitive and control potential appraisals. Then we will get the *LIKING*, *DISLIKE* and *ANGER* emotions for other-caused events and *PRIDE*, *GUILT* and *REGRET* for self-caused events.

The last appraisal, the kind of problem, describes whether an event is noticed as negative because it blocks a goal or because it is negative in its nature. In this kind of application we always get the first kind of problem.

5   The Expression of Emotions

Several researches have been centred in defining how the human express the emotions he/she is experimenting. Darwin was one of the pioneers in studying it. His studies made an emotional theory which have followed researchers as Ekman [14]. The Ekman's theory is maybe the most successful and most followed for representing facial expressions. In 1978 he developed a system for coding the facial actions called FACS (The Facial Action Coding System). FACS is a comprehensive, anatomically based system for measuring all visually discernible facial movement. FACS describes all visually distinguishable facial activity on the basis of 44 unique action units (AUs), as well as several categories of head and eye positions and movements.

In our work we transfer these studies to the emotional dramatization of the avatars. The animation techniques used for performing the facial expressions are explained in chapter 6. For the animation models required we use the 14 AUs (Fig.3) which describe the facial activity in each emotion.

The first problem we found for using the Ekman work is that he defined only six basic emotions and we get 17 from the Roseman model. The main reason of

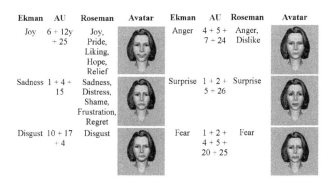

Ekman	AU	Roseman	Avatar	Ekman	AU	Roseman	Avatar
Joy	6 + 12y + 25	Joy, Pride, Liking, Hope, Relief		Anger	4 + 5 + 7 + 24	Anger, Dislike	
Sadness	1 + 4 + 15	Sadness, Distress, Shame, Frustration, Regret		Surprise	1 + 2 + 5 + 26	Surprise	
Disgust	10 + 17 + 4	Disgust		Fear	1 + 2 + 4 + 5 + 20 + 25	Fear	

Fig. 3. Relation between Ekman's emotions, AUs and Roseman's emotions

using this six basic emotions is that Ekman and his colleagues gathered evidence of the universality of this six facial expressions of emotion and they can be combined to obtain other expressions. One of our goals [15] is that the avatar must be multilingual so it should not express emotions dependents on the culture. Kshirsagar in [16] grouped OCC and Ekmans emotions within 6 expressions to represent the emotional states and to reduce the computational complexity. He also makes this categorization using the basic expressions as a layer between visible facial expressions and invisible mood. Following this research, we make the same relations with the Roseman's emotions shown in Fig.3.

6   Facial Animation

Facial expressions are obtained through the animation of the head, lips, eyes, pupils, eyebrows and eyelids. These animations are easily mapped for humanoids. Some animations are generated making individual deformations or translations over the object in a determined trajectory. This technique is used for the pupils or the global head pose. Some other animations, like lip motion, are achieved using the morphing techniques developed by Alexa [17]. Let us briefly summarize the morphing technique used: first, we establish an appropriate set of basic objects (B_i in Fig.4 and Eq. 2), in such a way that all face expressions necessary to produce the animation can be obtained from combinations of these basic objects. We use a set of basic objects made by the the 14 Ekman's AUs defined in Fig.3 and another one called default face which shows the neutral face of the avatar.

$$V(i) = \sum_{j=1}^{n-1} a_i B_i = (\sum_{j=1}^{n-1} a_i B_{ij}) \tag{2}$$

The animations are represented by one geometric base and a set of key frames (defined by a vector of weights). Each value of this vector corresponds to the interpolated value (a_i in the facial animation engine module shown in Fig.4 and Eq. 2). The sequences of animations are set defining the operations in eq. 2 with the required input values. The facial animation engine module in Fig.4 illustrates this process.

   The architecture works as follows: First, Roseman's model receives the application goal (in this case it recibes the percentage of the successes that the player should get right in order to win the game). When the interaction starts, Roseman's model is receiving each user input (in this case, it recibes the reply to each question). Following the rules described in section 4, the output of this module is the emotion that the avatar should express. In this point, the system asks if the interaction should be verbal or non-verbal. If the interaction is non-verbal, then the emotion tag goes directly to the animation engine. For a verbal interaction we have a short database of predefined markup text for some emotions. The markup text is transferring to the pre-process module, which interprets the text and extracts the emotions, gestures and the precise moment when they have to be reproduced. This information is transferred to the graphic

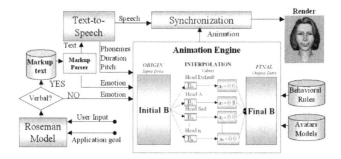

Fig. 4. System Architecture

platform for controlling facial expressions. The text to vocalize, the emotions and events related to them are also transferred to the Text to Phoneme module. The Text to Phoneme module calculates the chain of phonemes necessary to vocalize the message contained in the text with the indicated emotion, assigning to each phoneme its prosodic characteristics, mainly its duration and pitch. These prosodic characteristics are transferred to the graphic platform. In the graphic platform, with these prosodic data, each phoneme will be associated to its corresponding viseme (visual representation of the phoneme) by means of morphing techniques. The vocalized facial animation is based on the parameters coming from the Text to Phoneme module and a set of internal behavior rules (associated with emotions).

7   Conclusions and Future Work

In this research we worked in giving avatars the capacity of having and expressing emotions. Concretely, we implemented a computational emotional model based on the cognitive perspective for an application that has an avatar as the main emotional interaction element (such as, a virtual teacher or virtual shop assistant), and it does not have any information about user's preferences or standards. Most authors found and mentioned in this paper use the OCC model for having a computational emotional model. However, after a comparison of both models, we conclude that Roseman's model fits better for an application with the above mentioned requirements, while maybe the OCC model would fit better when the avatar is interacting with another avatar and a user model is available.

In this work, the avatar produces an emotional expression through facial animation engine based on morphing techniques. This kind of technique fits well with the Ekman AUs, which defined how an emotion should be expressed.

Although the system is able to reproduce emotional verbal communication, text reproduced is always predefined. As future work we plan to extend this module in order to have a more intelligent verbal communication. Additionally, we will work in the avatar personality and emotion intensities because the personality of each person influences in the way of assessing the events that occur in our environment.

References

1. Picard, R.: Affective Computing. The MIT Press (1997)
2. Mehrabian, A.: Communication without words. Psychology Today **2** (1968) 53–56
3. Reeves, B., Nass, C.: The media equation: how people treat computers, television, and new media like real people anda places. Cambridge MA (1996)
4. Goleman, D.: Inteligencia Emocional. Kairs (1996)
5. HIZKING21 Project-Human Language Technologies in 21st century. Avatars state of the art. Internal Report. 2005
6. Ortony, A., C.G.L., Collins, A.: The Cognitive Structure of Emotions. Cambridge University Press, Cambridge, England. (1998)
7. Roseman, I. Antoniou, A., Jose, P.: Appraisal determinants of emotions: Constructing a more accurate and comprehensive theory. Cognition and Emotion, 10 (1996)
8. Velsquez, J.: Cathexis–a computational model for the generation of emotions and their influence in the behavior of autonomous agents. Master's thesis, Massachusetts Institute of Technology. Dept. of Electrical Engineering and Computer Science (1996) Plublisher, Massachusetts Institute of Technology.
9. Elliott, C.: I picked up catapia and other stories: A multimodal approach to expressivity for emotionally intelligent agents. In: International Conference on Autonomous Agents, Chicago, IL (1997) 451 – 457
10. Bates, J.: The role of emotion in believable agents. Source Communications of the ACM archive **37** (1994) 122 – 125
11. El-Nasr, M., Yen, J., Ioerger, T.: Flame:fuzzy logic adaptive model of emotions. Autonomous Agents and Multi-Agent Systems **3** (2000) 219 – 257
12. Buy, D.: Creating emotions and facial expressions for embodied agents. PhD thesis, University of Twente (2004)
13. Bartneck, C.: Integrating the occ model of emotions in embodied characters. (2002)
14. Ekman, P.: Facial expression and emotion. American Psychologist **48** (1993) 384–392
15. I. Aizpurua, A. Ortiz, D.O.I.A.J.A.A., I.Iurgel: Adaptation of mesh morphing techniques for avatars used in web applications. In: AMDO2004, Palma de Mallorca, Spain (2004) 26–39
16. Kshirsagar, S.: A multilayer personality model. In Press, A., ed.: 2nd international symposium on Smart graphics, New York, NY, USA (2002) 107–115
17. M. Alexa, J. Behr, W.M.: The morph node. In: Web3d/VRML. (2000) 29–34

Face Modeling and Wrinkle Simulation Using Convolution Surface

Qing He, Minglei Tong, and Yuncai Liu

Institute of Image Processing and Pattern Recognition
Shanghai Jiaotong University, Shanghai, 200240, China
{heqing118, tongminglei, whomliu}@sjtu.edu.cn

Abstract. This paper presents a new method to simulate wrinkles on individual face model, applying convolution surface to face modeling. A generic face mesh is deformed and the texture image is computed using image-based modeling technique. The deformed mesh is then convolved with a kernel function to generate a convolution surface, and wrinkles are generated by modulating the surface with a designed profile function. The pre-computed texture is mapped onto the convolution surface to enhance the realism. Experimental results show that our method can generate wrinkles with different patterns by regulating some parameters of the profile function.

1 Introduction

One of the most aspiring goals in computer animation is the realistic animation of the human face. Human face modeling and animation is a strenuous task because of the physical structure of the face and the dynamics involving the psychological and behavioral aspects. Two classes of models have been developed, which are geometric models and physically based models, according to the way of simulating the behaveiors of facial components.

Facial aging is one of the natural phenomena which will happen in a person's face. Modeling of skin aging has wide applications in virtual reality, entertainment, medical surgery and criminal objects detection. However, simulating the aging process is quite cumbersome and remains a lot to be desired. The geometric methods model wrinkles by displacing vertices at certain positions where wrinkles appear, but a simple model with a relatively small number of vertices can't accurately model the subtleties of facial deformation of wrinkles unless a carefully designed subdivision is implemented. On the other hand, the physically based methods simulate wrinkles by approximating the biomechanical properties of real skin. The results are realistic, but the process is complicated and computational expensive due to the modeling of the mass-spring or finite element system.

Our method takes an alternative by modeling the human face with convolution surface. This method deals with facial deformation from a completely different point of view. We only need a rough triangular mesh as the skeleton, and instead of painstakingly subdividing the mesh, we get a smooth surface by convolving the skeleton with a kernel function. The facial deformation is obtained by adjusting the width of the kernel and/or adding some profile function, without explicitly computing the displacement of each vertex.

F.J. Perales and R.B. Fisher (Eds.): AMDO 2006, LNCS 4069, pp. 244–251, 2006.

The paper is organized as follows. Section 2 briefly reviews some of the previous work of skin aging. Section 3 presents a simple geometric model which has been widely used in individual face modeling. Section 4 describes the way to generate the convolution surface model using the previous model as skeleton. Section 5 shows how we flexibly model wrinkles based on the newly generated model. Section 6 shows the results and section 7 concludes.

2 Related Work

There are a few works for simulating wrinkles using geometrical models. Volino and Thalrnann [8] animate wrinkles on deformable models by modulating the amplitude of a given wrinkle pattern on a per triangular basis. Bando et al. [11] propose a simple method to dynamically modulate wrinkle amplitudes on the body part. Yu Zhang and Terence Sim [14] present a geometric wrinkle model based on facial muscles.

Physically based models have been studied more widely [6,12,13]. Although these methods differ from each other, they almost animate the plastic and visco-elastic properties of the skin based on the three-layered structure: skin, muscle and skull.

Our work is most inspired by Andrei Sherstyuk [2] and differs from the above ones. The concept of convolution surface was first proposed by J. Bloomenthal and K. Shoemake [5], in which a convolution surface was obtained by convolving a skeleton with a three-dimensional, low-pass Gaussian filter kernel. As a powerful and flexible tool to model complex objects, convolution surface still faced the problems of limited choices of kernel functions and skeleton primitives that can be convolved together analytically. Sherstyuk [2] addressed this weakness by introducing a new kernel function called Cauchy function and deduced analytical solutions for several useful primitives, namely, points, line segments, arcs, triangles and planes. Jin [10] extends the work by using line skeletons with polynomial density distributions. Steffen Oeltze [9] uses line skeletons to model vasculature and J. Bloomenthal [4] uses the combination of points, line segments and triangles as skeletons to make a hand model. Up to now, little has been done to model human faces using convolution surface except the work in [2], which presents several modeling techniques to model different objects, including human faces. Our work is an extension of Sherstyuk [2]. However, we use a simpler skeleton and propose the way to generate realistic wrinkles on the surface.

3 Initial Face Model

We adopt modified Candide3 model [3] as a generic face mesh. It is to be deformed to an individual face and then used as triangular skeletons to render convolution surface. The original Candide3 (Figure 1 (a), (b)) does not include the back part of a head. In this paper, we manually add some vertices to let it cover the whole head, as shown in Figure 1 (c), (d). The modified model contains 122 vertices and 216 triangles. There are also other 3D generic face models available in the literature, which consist of more vertices and can display more accurate face shape, but we use Candide3 for less computational cost. Moreover, it will be demonstrated later that this simple model is sufficient as convolution skeleton.

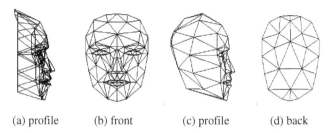

(a) profile   (b) front   (c) profile   (d) back

Fig 1. (a),(b) Original Candide 3 model. (c),(d) Modified Candide 3 model

To deform the Candide3 model to a personalized 3D face mesh, we use an image-based modeling technique [1,15]. The feature points on the model are displaced to match those chosen from a front and a profile image of a person, and the positions of other points are interpolated using RBF function. The flatten texture is generated by projecting the deformed face mesh onto cylinder surface and then blending the frontal and profile images [15]. Mapping the texture onto the personalized face mesh produces the final facial model. The images and the model are shown in Figure 2.

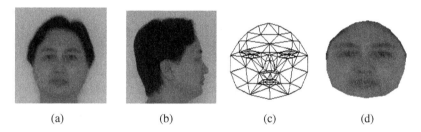

(a)   (b)   (c)   (d)

Fig. 2. (a),(b) Front and profile images. (c) Deformed face mesh. (d) Textured face model.

Thanks to the simplicity of the face mesh, the whole process takes little computational time. While the triangular mesh is going to be convolved to produce a smoother surface, the texture can be mapped onto the new surface without any change.

4   Modeling with Convolution Surfaces

In this section we first briefly introduce the concept of convolution surface, and then we use the above face mesh as triangular skeletons to render the convolution surface.

4.1   Basic Concept

A convolution surface is an isosurface in a scalar field defined by convolving a skeleton, which comprises points, line segments, curves, polygons or other geometrical primitives, with a kernel function. Sherstyuk [2] proposed a new kernel function called Cauchy function and derived the field functions for several basic primitives. This kernel is:

$$h(r) = \frac{1}{(1 + s^2 r^2)^2} \tag{1}$$

where r is the distance from an arbitrary point on the convolution surface to the skeleton, and s controls the width of the kernel. The main advantage of this kernel over other kernels is that it has analytical solutions for a number of primitives without consideration of integration boundary problems. This remarkably reduces the complexity of convolution with triangular primitives, which are used in our model. Therefore, we convolve a triangle primitive with this kernel function. First, a triangle is split along the longest edge into two right-angled triangles (figure 3). Next, the field function [2] for the right half is obtained:

$$F_{right}(x, y) = \int_{y=0}^{h - \frac{hx}{a_2}} \int_{x=0}^{a_2} \frac{dxdy}{(1 + s^2 r^2(x, y))^2} \tag{2}$$

and F_{left} is derived from F_{right} by replacing x by $-x$ and a_2 by a_1. Finally, F_{left} and F_{right} are added together to satisfy the equation:

$$F_{right}(x, y) + F_{left}(x, y) - T = 0 \tag{3}$$

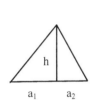
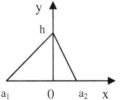
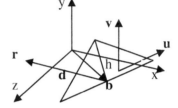

Fig. 3. Integration parameters   **Fig. 4.** Triangle modeling primitive

For an arbitrarily positioned triangle (Figure 4), **r** is a point on the surface and the following parameters are introduced: a point **b**, the projection onto the longest edge of the opposite vertex; vectors **u** and **v** that form the local surface coordinate system, with **b** as its origin and **u** aligned in the direction of the longest edge; h that is the distance from **b** to the apex of the triangle; **d=r-b**; scalar u=**du** and v=**dv**. The analytical form of the field function can be found in [2].

4.2   Convolution Surface of the Face Model

We use the face mesh derived in section 3 as triangular skeletons (Figure 2(c)), and convolve them with the above Cauchy function. The convolved result is shown in Figure 5, which is similar to that in [2], but the number of our skeletons is far less than theirs, which greatly reduces the rendering time.

We can see after convolving process the model remains its original shape except for some inflation. However, the great change is not in appearance but in the way of controlling the appearance. The convolved model allows a number of modeling

Fig. 5. Convolution surface of the model   **Fig. 6.** Wrinkle area

techniques [2] to adjust its shape without changing the initial skeletons. The next section will describe in detail some of the techniques.

5   Wrinkle Simulation and Facial Deformation

The convolution surface of the face model is discretized into numerous triangles for implementation, thus it can also be viewed as a subdivided fine mesh. While modeling the shape change, we look it as an entire surface thus we need not explicitly know the displacement of each vertex. On the other hand, we can map the texture image generated in section 3 onto the new surface, where the convolution surface is viewed as a triangle mesh in order to compute texture coordinate for each vertex. The following will describe the two steps in detail.

5.1   Wrinkle Simulation

We define the wrinkle area where wrinkles are most likely to appear with aging. The area covers certain triangle patches on the forehead of the initial mesh, shown in Figure 6. We then manipulate these triangles by multiplying a profile function [2] with the field function of each triangle.

Bloomenthal [13] modulated an arc skeleton by a sine wave to produce wrinkles on a seanorse's tail. As to the triangular primitive, a similar profile function can be used to model wrinkles, but the variables are more complex. We derive a profile function to modulate triangle primitives, which is:

$$k_1(\sin(k_2(a_1u + a_2v)/\sqrt{a_1^2 + a_2^2}) + c) \tag{4}$$

where u and v are scalars defined in section 4. c is a positive constant to offset the negative value of the sin function, and we choose c=1.5 in our experiment. k1 and k2 are scale factors used to control the depth and density of wrinkles. a1 and a2 are coefficients of a direction vector on the triangle. We choose the coefficients to make the vector $\mathbf{v'}=a_1\mathbf{u}+ a_2\mathbf{v}$ perpendicular to the wrinkle direction. Similar to the definition of u and v, we define a scalar:

$$v' = d\mathbf{v'} = d(a_1\mathbf{u} + a_2\mathbf{v}) = a_1u + a_2v$$

The item $\sqrt{a_1^2 + a_2^2}$ in (4) is for normalization purpose. Therefore, the expression in the parenthesis of sin function is just the coordinate of **d** on the new axis **v'** multiplied by a scale, and the sin function which takes the new coordinate as variable will produce waves along this axis.

We suppose the wrinkle lines lie on the horizontal plan, which is a reasonable approximation of the direction of natural wrinkles. Then for each triangle in the wrinkle area, it is not difficult to compute the values of a_1, a_2. Let l be the intersection line of the triangle plan and the plan y=0. We rotate l 90 degree inside the triangle plan to get v', and the rotation axis is $n=u\times v$. Clearly, $a_1=v'u$ and $a_2=v'v$ are the desired results. Since v' is just an indication of direction, it does not matter what exact values a_1 and a_2 take as long as they satisfy a desired ratio. Besides, the sin function is periodical in the whole definition area, so it does not make difference if l or v' takes the opposite direction. The remained parameters k_1 and k_2 can be regulated by users to simulate wrinkles with different depth and width.

Note that we can take an alternative to add line primitives to the original triangle skeletons as done in [4], but it needs manually defining the precise location of the line segments, which is a difficult and cumbersome task. The main advantage of our method is we can control the appearance of the model surface implicitly without computing exact position of the skeleton.

5.2 Texture Mapping

We map the texture onto the convolution surface to enhance the realism of the model. This time we look the model as a refined triangular mesh and compute texture coordinate of each vertex using the same method in section 3. The mapped results can be seen in Figure 8-10.

6 Experimental Results

We have implemented our experiments by using Visual C++ and matlab. The calculations and rendering were carried out on a Pentium 4, 512M PC. The convolution surface of each face model comprises about 10000 triangles.

Figure 7 shows different wrinkle patterns on the same person. We achieve this by regulating parameters k1 and k2 in (3). There should be some constraints on the values of k1 and k2, since the area and depth of each convolved triangle is finite. In our experiment, k1 ranges from 0.1 to 10 and k2 from 50 to 90. Figure 8 shows the textured model of the case in Figure 7 (a). We can see wrinkles on the forehead under proper illumination. Figure 9 and Figure 10 show the experimental results with other two persons. Note that the dark area on the top of the head is due to poor lighting.

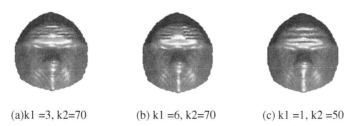

(a)k1 =3, k2=70   (b) k1 =6, k2=70   (c) k1 =1, k2 =50

Fig. 7. Different wrinkle patterns

Fig. 8. Textured model with wrinkles

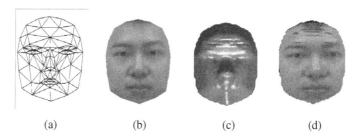

(a)   (b)   (c)   (d)

Fig. 9. (a) face mesh (b) textured model (c) convolution surface with wrinkles (d) textured model with wrinkles

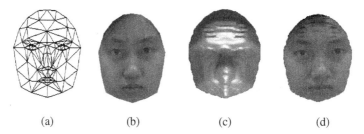

(a)   (b)   (c)   (d)

Fig. 10. (a) face mesh (b) textured model (c) convolution surface with wrinkles (d) textured model with wrinkles

7   Conclusion and Future Work

This paper has presented a new method to simulate wrinkles on the face model. A rough model is convolved with a function to generate a convolution surface, and modulating the surface with a profile function produces wrinkles. Textures are mapped onto the surface to enhance the realism. The original contribution of this paper is a new kind of face model which allows implicit and flexible adjustment of its shape.

Modeling with convolution surface is a potential tool and we have just explored a small portion of various modeling techniques. For future work we intend to design more profile functions adapted to other parts of the face. Besides, we would like to model other facial deformations by regulating the width of the kernel function. Currently we just keep the width to a fixed value. Finally, we plan to build a convolution surface model of a generic face and deform it to an individual face by some optimization approaches.

References

[1] A.N Ansari, M. Abdel-Mottaleb. 3D Face Modeling Using Two Orthogonal Views and A Generic Face Model. *Proceedings of 2003 International Conference on Multimedia and Expo,* 2003: 289-92

[2] A. Sherstyuk. Convolution Surfaces in Computer Graphics. *PhD dissertation*, Monash University, School Of Computer Science and Software Engineering, 1999

[3] J. Ahlberg. CANDIDE-3 -- an updated parameterized face, Report No. LiTH-ISY-R-2326, Department. of Electrical Engineering, Linköping University, Sweden, 2001

[4] J.Bloomenthal, Chek Lim. Skeletal methods of shape manipulation. *Proceedings of International Conference on Shape Modeling and Applications 1999,* 1999:44 - 47, 267

[5] J. Bloomenthal, K. Shoemake. Convolution Surfaces. *SIGGRAPH Proceedings*, 1991, 25(4): 251-256

[6] L. Boissieux, G..Kiss, N. M. Thalmann and P. Kalra. Simulation of Skin Aging and Wrinkles with Cosmetics Insight. *Proc Eurographics Workshop on Computer Animation and Simulation 2000*, 2000:15-27

[7] M. Tong, Y. Liu, T. Huang. Recover Human Pose from Monocular Image Under Weak Perspective Projection. *Lecture Notes in Computer Science*, Springer-Verlag GmbH 2005, 3766

[8] P. Volino and N. M. Thalmann. Fast Geometrical Wrinkles on Animated Surfaces. *Proc. WSCG'99*, 1999.

[9] Steffen Oeltze, Bernhard Preim.Visualization of Vasculature with Convolution Surfaces: Method, Validation and Evaluation. *IEEE Transactions on Medical Imaging*, 2005, 24(4):540-548

[10] Xiaogang Jin, Chiew-Lan Tai. Convolution surfaces for Line Skeletons with Polynomial Weight Distributions. *Journal of Grapgics Tools ACM Press*, 2001, 6(3): 17-28

[11] Y. Bando, T. Kuratate and T. Nishita. A Simple Method for Modeling Wrinkles on Human Skin. *Proc. Pacific Graphics 2002*, 2002:166-175

[12] Y. Wu, P.Kalra and N. M. Thalmann. Physically-based Wrinkle Simulation & Skin Rendering. *Proc Eurographics Workshop on Computer Animation and Simulation'97*, 1997:69-79

[13] Y. Wu, N. M. Thalmann and D. Thalmann. A dynamic wrinkle model in facial animation and skin aging. *J. Visualization and Computer Animation,* 1998, 6: 195-202

[14] Y. Zhang, T. Sim. Realistic and efficient wrinkle simulation using an anatomy-based face model with adaptive refinement. *Proceedings of Computer Graphics International 2005*, 2005:3-10

[15] Y. Zhuang, C. Su, L. Huang and F. Wu. Subdivision Feedback Based 3D Facial Modeling for E-learning. *Lecture Notes in Computer Science*. 2003,2783: 218-229

Cascade of Fusion for Adaptive Classifier Combination Using Context-Awareness

Mi Young Nam, Suman Sedai, and Phill Kyu Rhee

Dept. of Computer Science & Engineering, Inha University
253, Yong-Hyun Dong, Incheon, Korea
{rera, suman}im.inha.ac.kr, pkrhee@inha.ac.kr

Abstract. This paper proposes a novel adaptive classifier combination scheme based on the cascade of classifier selection and fusion, called adaptive classifier combination scheme (ACCS). In the proposed scheme, system working environment is learned and the environmental context is identified. GA is used to search most effective classifier systems for each identified environmental context. The group of selected classifiers is combined based on GA model for reliable fusion. The knowledge of individual context and its associated chromosomes representing the optimal classifier combination is stored in the context knowledge base. Once the context knowledge is accumulated the system can react to dynamic environment in real time. The proposed scheme has been tested in area of face recognition using standard FERET database, taking illumination as an environmental context. Experimental result showed that using context awareness in classifier combination provides robustness to varying environmental conditions.

1 Introduction

We present a classifier combination method based on adaptive cascading of selection and fusion of different classifiers using Genetic Algorithm (GA), hence aiming high performance. For a given input pattern, the best classifiers are those that are more likely to classify the pattern correctly. Then most effective classifier fusion is achieved by combining the best chosen classifiers. In general, a combined classifier system is expected to produce superior performance to a single classifier system in terms of accuracy and reliability [1].Classifier combination can be divided into classifier selection and classifier fusion [1, 2]. During classifier selection, proper classifiers that are most likely to produce accurate output for a local area of feature space are selected. Whereas during classifier fusion, individual classifiers are activated in parallel and group decision is made to combine the output of the classifiers. The proposed method primarily aims at robust object recognition under uneven environments. The method explores the group of most effective classifier system for each identified environmental context using GA and combines the result using popular fusion methods. In this paper, the idea of such single classifier component optimizations using GA[5, 6] is extended to multiple classifiers components. The proposed method has been tested for face recognition using FERET

F.J. Perales and R.B. Fisher (Eds.): AMDO 2006, LNCS 4069, pp. 252–261, 2006.
© Springer-Verlag Berlin Heidelberg 2006

database where face images are exposed to different lighting environments. We achieve encouraging experimental results showing that performance of the proposed method is superior to those of most popular methods.

2   Model of Adaptive Classifier Combination Scheme

Classifier combination can be thought as the generation of candidate classifiers and decision aggregation of candidate classifiers. For the simplicity of explanation, we assume that a classifier combination consists of four stages: preprocessing, feature representation class decision, and aggregation stages. As an example of face recognition area, the preprocessing components may be the histogram equalization, feature representation component may be Gabor wavelet and class decision can be done by ecludian distance measurement of feature vectors. If we have s preprocessing, t different feature representation and u class decision components, then there combination produces total $k=(s{\times}t{\times}u)$ classifiers. In general, the total number of classifiers k is too huge to be evaluated for finding an optimal output, so context awareness is used reduce the classifier space. GA is used to select a group of best classifier combinations for each identified context, and then selected best classifiers are combined as shown in Figure 1.Figure 1 shows that context aware unit, working on GA, finds the optimal classifier sets for a data context y from the total classifiers set. In proposed ACCS two types of data inputs are used. The action data, denoted by **x**, is normal data which is finally to be classified. The context data, denoted by **y**, is used to identify environmental context of system and to control classifier combination based on the identified context. We assume that the context data can be modeled in association with the input action data, and can be identified easily compared to the original classification problem.

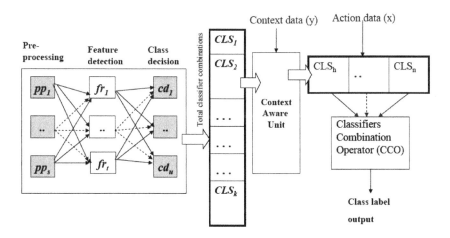

Fig. 1. Model of Adaptive Classifier Combination Scheme (ACCS)

3 Framework of Adaptive Classifier Combination Scheme (ACCS)

In this section, we will discuss about the architecture of ACCS and describe working of ACCS on evolution mode and action mode separately.

3.1 Architecture of ACCS

The proposed scheme operates in two modes: the learning and the action mode. In learning mode :a)context learning is performed by an unsupervised learning method and b)the knowledge of most effective subset of classifier systems for an identified context is accumulated and stored in the context knowledge base (CKB) in terms of associated artificial chromosomes. In action mode: a) Context identification of context data y of action data x is implemented by a normal classification method. b) the most effective subset of classifier systems for an identified context (which is learned and stored in CKB) is combined to classify the action data x.

The proposed scheme architecture consists of the context-aware unit (CAU), the context knowledge base (CKB), the evolution control unit (ECU), the action control unit (ACU) and the action unit (AU) as shown in Fig.2. The CAU performs the functions of modeling and identifying environmental contexts. The ECU accumulates the knowledge of the most effective group of classifiers systems for each identified context using the GA, and stores the knowledge in the CKB. The accumulated knowledge of an effective classifier group and the corresponding identified context is stored in the CKB. During operation period, the ACU searches for a most effective group of classifier systems, for identified context using the previously accumulated knowledge in the CKB. The AU is a normal classifier fusion scheme configured from the encoding of the selected effective classifier systems using ACU.

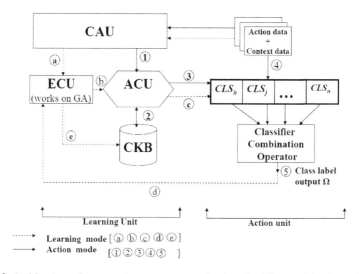

Fig. 2. Architecture of proposed context aware adaptive classifier combination scheme

3.2 Context Modeling and Identification

Context data is defined as any observable and relevant attributes, and its interaction with surrounding environment at an instance of time [8]. Context learning, also referred as context modeling, basically implies clustering context data into context categories. So the result of context learning is several context categories where each category represents the context to which an environment can be associated at given timestamp, see Fig.3. Context learning can be performed by an unsupervised learning algorithm such as SOM, Fuzzy Art, K-means etc. Context identification is to determine the context category of a given context data y. It can be carried out employing a normal classification method such as NN, K-NN, SVM, etc.

3.3 Evolution Mode and Context Knowledge Accumulation Using GA

In the evolutionary mode, the scheme learns application's environmental contexts bye clustering the training data into data context categories by the CAU see Fig. 3.ⓐ. Evolution process is controlled by ECU and it accumulates the knowledge of context-action associations, and stores them in the CKB as shown in Fig.3ⓔ. The detail of context knowledge accumulation steps are given below.

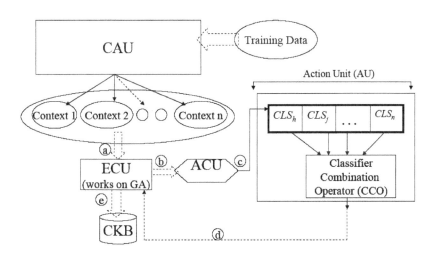

Fig. 3. ACCS working on evolution mode

Step1. The AU configuration is encoded by the chromosome encoding (describes all possible combination of classifier).

Step2. The context data associated with application environment are clustered (learned) as context categories by the CAU.

Step3. The most effective subset of classifier systems for each identified context is decided by ECU using GA and the associated training set as follows.

    3.1 Generate a random population of the chromosome.

    3.2 Evaluate the fitness of each chromosome vector of the population.

3.3 Select only a portion of the best population as the population of next generation.

3.4 Repeat 3.2 and 3.3 until a most effective classifier is reached.

Step4. The classifier system chromosomes and the fusion structure with their associated contexts are stored in the CKB see Fig. 2 (e).

Note that fitness of chromosome vector is calculated from recognition rate of the fusion of the classifiers chromosomes and is described in section 5.2.

3.4 Action Mode

In the action mode, the scheme identifies the application's environmental context, searches the knowledge of context-action association i.e. best classifiers for an identified context in the CKB, and produces a combined classifiers response. The operation scenario of the ACSS is outlined as follows.

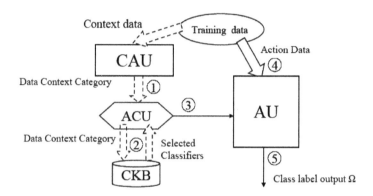

Fig. 4. ACSS working on action mode

Step1. Environmental context is identified using input context data by CAU. The output of CAU is an identified context of an input data sees Fig 4 ①.

Step2. If the environmental context is changed, the chromosomes of most effective group of classifier systems for the newly identified environmental context are searched from the CKB by ACU. Otherwise, Go to Step 4.

Step3. AU is configured by ACU (see Fig 4 ③) using the searched chromosomes.

Step4. The combines configured classifiers by adopting a fusion method described in section 4, using the action data Fig 4 ④ and produce the response Fig 4 ⑤.

Step5. The CKB can be updated whenever the system performance is measured to fall down below the predefined criterion by activating the evolution mode described above.

4 Classifiers Fusion

Once best classifiers are chosen by evolutionary learning described above, individual classifiers are activated in parallel and group decision is made to combine the output of the classifiers. Here we use four fusion methods namely Decision Templates (DT) [2]. Majority Voting (MV) [9], Product (PRO) and and Average (AVG) [9].

5 Design Example and Experiments

The proposed method was tested in the area of face recognition using standard FERET database. Its performance was evaluated through extensive experiments, and shown to be reliable and superior to those of most popular methods, especially under changing illumination.

5.1 Face Recognition Scheme Using ACCS

Face images are used as context data as well as action input data. The changes in image data under changing illumination are modeled as environmental contexts. Context aware Unit (CAU) clusters face data into several distinguishable   contexts according to illumination variations, considering light direction and brightness. The CAU is implemented by Kohnen's self-organizing map (SOM) [9] and Radial basis function (RBF). SOM has the capability of unsupervised learning. It models illumination environment as several context categories. The RBF neural network is trained using the clustered face data in order to identify the context category of an input image. In the AU, histogram equalization (HE) is used for preprocessing components and gabor wavelet is used as feature representation. Gabor wavelet is proved to be biologically motivated convolution kernels in the shape of plane waves restricted by Gabor kernel [10]. Gabor wavelet also shows desirable characteristics in orientation selectivity and special locality. As an example, Gabor13 is generated using 13 fiducial points as shown Fig. 5.

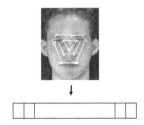

Fig. 5. An example of 13 feature points for face recognition

The learning module of the ACCS is implemented by GA which explores the structure of the AU adaptive to a given image data subset and stores in CKB. In the recognition mode, the system searches for a most effective classifier combination based on the identified context category in CKB. The knowledge of effective classifiers structure for a data context is described by the pair of data context category and corresponding artificial chromosome.

5.2 Chromosome Encoding and Fitness Function

GA is employed to search among the different combinations of feature representations and combining structure of classifiers. The optimality of the chromosome is defined by classification accuracy and generalization capability. Fig. 6 shows a possible encoding of chromosome description.

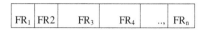

Fig. 6. Chromosome encoding for the face recognition using ACCS

Each feature representation FRi denotes the set of weights values for the fiducial points. GA needs a salient fitness function to evaluate current population and choose offspring for the next generation by which evolution will be guided. The learning module generates the classifier being balanced between successful recognition rate and generalization capability by the fitness function defined as follows:

$$\eta(V) = \lambda_1 \eta_s(V) + \lambda_2 \eta_g(V) \qquad (6)$$

where $\eta_s(V)$ is the term for the system correctness, i.e., successful recognition rate and $\eta_g(V)$ is the term for class generalization[10, 11, 12]. λ_1 and λ_2 are positive parameters that indicate the weight of each term, respectively. The recognition system learns the optimal structures of classifier systems and Gabor representation using the context knowledge accumulation procedure discussed in section 3.3.

5.3 Experimental Results

The feasibility of the proposed method has been tested using FERET [10] database. The data set has 2,182 frontal face images from 1091 people. The data set divided in two parts, training set called probe set and test set called gallery set. One image is used for registration or training for each people in training set containing 1,091 images. The remaining 1091 images are used as the test images. First of all the training data are divided into the data context categories or clusters (six, nine and

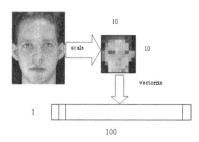

Fig. 7. Face data vectorization is 1x100 dimensions for context modeling

Fig. 8. Face data clustered according to illumination

twelve clusters are investigated separately). This is done by unsupervised learning. Each training face image is scaled as 10 x 10 window and normalized using min-max normalization. 1 x100 dimensional vectors are generated using vertical scanning of image to provide context data for the CAU as shown in Fig 7. SOM is used for context modeling and RBF is used for context identification. An example of different context of face data identified using SOM is shown Fig. 8. It can be seen that, each cluster consists of group of faces having similar intensity and direction of light.

GA is used by Evolution control unit to search the best classifiers for each identified context. After several iterations of evolution, the ECU results the best sets of weight values for each fiducial points minimizing the classification error. These best sets are considered here as selected best classifiers. GA generates the weight set by assigning more weight value to the to the fiducial points at face where intensity is high and small weight to fiducial points where the intensity is low. Hence error due to bad illumination is expected to be minimum. After the evolution best three classifiers are selected for each identified context. Experiment is conducted on two sets of classifiers from same feature weight representation for each context. First set uses Euclidian distance as the distance, measure in feature space and second used cosine distance as the distance measure as shown in Fig. 9.The result of classifiers are combined using fusion method stated in section 4.

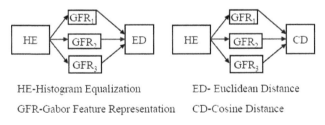

HE-Histogram Equalization   ED- Euclidean Distance

GFR-Gabor Feature Representation   CD-Cosine Distance

Fig. 9. Two sets of classifiers for each context

Table 1 shows the result of experiments done on 6, 9 and 12 context mode. (6 context mode means context is modeled as 6 clusters).For each cluster, result of fusion of each two sets of classifier is shown (Euclidian and Cosine distance).For each classifier its recognition accuracy (A) and rank(R) comparing different fusion methods is shown. Result shown suggests that face recognition rate is different according context number. It shows that the face recognition accuracy of nine cluster mode is 92.1% and hence it is better than other cluster mode. Therefore, the cluster number is important   for efficient face recognition. Since we use huge search space to select the best diverse classifiers by GA, the result of fusion is superior in all context models. Again recognition rate is appreciably high even though test data set we used contains face images with various illumination conditions. This is because best classifiers are selected and fused for every illumination condition encountered. Decision Template (DT) and Majority voting (MV) fusion methods gives better performance than Product(PRO) and Average(AVG) fusion methods.

Table 1. Result of 6 and 9 and 12 cluster models conducted on classifiers using different fusion methods

Cont-ext	6-Cluster				9 Clusters				12-Cluster			
Classifier	Eucl.		Cosine		Eucl.		Cosine		Eucl.		Cosine	
Combiner	A	R	A	R	A	R	A	R	A	R	A	R
DT	90.3	7	91.5	5.5	89.1	7	92.1	6	88.8	3	91.1	8
MV	91.6	9	91.4	8	88.7	3	92.1	6	89.4	9	90.7	2
PRO	90.3	7	91.5	5.5	89.0	5	92.1	6	88.8	3	91.1	8
AVR	90.3	7	91.5	5.5	89.0	5	92.1	6	88.8	3	91.1	8

Table 2. Recognition rate of proposed method and comparison with other methods

	Method	6 Clusters	9 Clusters	12 Clusters
Selection	Best	91.56	92.11	90.74
Kuncheva[1]	DT	91.10	91.93	91.01
	MV	91.47	92.20	90.92
	Product	91.10	91.93	91.01
	Average	91.10	91.93	91.01
Proposed Method	GA based fusion	91.47	92.11	91.10

Experiment is performed on face recognition by using similar methodology Kuncheva [1] and result is compared to our systems as shown in Table 2. It is found that our proposed system is better than [1].

6   Conclusion

GA is used as classifier selector which chooses best classifiers for the respective region or data sample that belongs to particular context. Selected classifiers are combined using four fusion methods (DT, MV, PRO and AVG) to classify. Our experimental results shows that cascading of such selection and fusion gives superior performance The proposed method tested on face recognition system shows the reliable result across varying environmental context. We trained and examined the system for three context models, in each model the number of context clusters were 6, 9 and 12 respectively. We found almost consistent result across different illumination is face image and across various experiments we conducted. In future, we will research on clustering method taking facial expression and appearance as an environmental context.

References

[1] L.I. Kuncheva, Switching between selection and fusion in combining classifiers: An experiment, *IEEE Transactions On Systems Man And Cybernetics, Part B-cybernetics*, vol. 32, no.2, (2002) 146-156.

[2] L. I. Kuncheva, J. C. Bezdek, and R. P. W. Duin, "Decision templates for multiple classifier fusion: An experimental comparison," Pattern Recognit., Vol. 34, No. 2, (2001) 299–314.

[3] M.Y. Nam and P.K. Rhee, A Novel Image Preprocessing by Evolvable Neural Network, LNAI3214, Vol.3, (2004) 843-854.

[4] M.Y. Nam and P.K. Rhee, An Efficient Face Recognition for Variant Illumination Condition, ISPACS2005, vol.1 (2004) 111-115.

[5] F. Roli, S. Raudys, G.L. Marcialis, An experimental comparison of fixed and trained fusion rules for crisp classifiers outputs, in: J. Kittler, F. Roli (eds.), Multiple Classifier Systems (Proc.Third International Workshop, MCS 2002, Cagliari, Italy), Lecture Notes in Computer Science, Springer, Berlin, (2002).

[6] D. E. Goldberg,"Genetic Algorirhnis iri Search. Optimiation, arid Machine Leaniirrg," Addison-Wesley (1989)

[7] Y.S. Huang and C.Y. Suen, "A Method of Combining Multiple Classifiers—A Neural Network Approach," Proc. of IWFHR-3, (1993) 11-20.

[8] X. Wang and X. Tang, "A Unified Framework for Subspace Face Recognition," IEEE Trans. on PAMI, Vol. 26, No. 9 (2004) 1222- 1228.

[9] Ludmila I. Kuncheva, "A Theoretical Study on Six Classifier Fusion Strategies." IEEE on PAMI, Vol. 24, No. 2, (2002).

[10] Inja Jeon, Eun-Sung Jung and Phill Kyu Rhee, "Adaptive Normalization based Highly Efficient Face Recognition under Uneven Environments ", ,KES 2005, LNCS 3682,(2005).759-768.

[11] Mi Young Nam, Phill Kyu Rhee, "Adaptive Classifier Combination for Visual Information Processing using Data Context-Awareness," IDA 2005, LNCS 3646, (2005) 260-271.

[12] E. Pe₊kalska and R.P.W. Duin, Dissimilarity representations allow for building good classifiers, *Pattern Recognition Letters*, Vol. 23, No. 8, (2002) 943-956.

Modeling Relaxed Hand Shape for Character Animation

Michael Neff and Hans-Peter Seidel

MPI Informatik, Stuhlsatzenhausweg 85, 66123 Saarbrücken, Germany
{neff, hpseidel}@mpi-inf.mpg.de
http://www.mpi-inf.mpg.de/~neff

Abstract. We present a technique for modeling the deformations that occur to hand pose under the influence of gravity when the hand is kept in a relaxed state. A dynamic model of the hand is built using Proportional-Derivative controllers as a first order approximation to muscles. A process for tuning the model to match the relaxed hand shape of subjects is discussed. Once the model is tuned, it can be used to sample the space of all possible arm orientations and samples of wrist and finger angles are taken. From these samples, a kinematic model of passive hand deformation is built. Either the tuned dynamic model or the kinematic model can be used to generate final animations. These techniques increase the realism of gesture animation, where the character often maintains a relaxed hand.

1 Introduction

People will often allow their hands and wrists to relax without exerting active control. When this occurs, the angles of the wrist and fingers will vary due to the influence of gravity as the arm moves. These subtle variations add important realism to an animated character. This is particularly important in gesture animation, where sometimes the hand is actively adjusted to a particular, meaningful pose while other times it is simply left relaxed as the arm moves.

In this work, we model this relaxed, passive variation in wrist and finger angles. Our approach is to first build and tune a dynamic model of the hand. This model is then used to automatically generate a large quantity of sample data, from which a kinematic model is built. Either the tuned dynamic model or the generated kinematic model can be used in the generation of final animations, depending on the requirements of the application.

This work makes the following contributions:

- A simple, low-cost tuning method that offers sufficient accuracy for generating natural animations,
- an approach for building a kinematic model from dynamic simulation,
- a model of relaxed hand shape that can improve the realism of animations.

F.J. Perales and R.B. Fisher (Eds.): AMDO 2006, LNCS 4069, pp. 262–270, 2006.

2   Previous Work

The human hand has been a significant focus of research in the computer graphics community, but to our knowledge, no one has focused on passive hand shape nor used a dynamic model to build a kinematic hand model.

Much graphics hand research has focused on the problem of grasping. Rijpkema and Girard present a knowledge-based approach to grasp planning [1]. Sanso and Thalmann present a system that decides on an appropriate grasp type for a given task and uses forward and inverse kinematics (IK) to solve for hand shape [2]. Pollard and Zordan use motion capture data in building a physics-based controller for grasping [3]. In a related problem, ElKoura and Singh model finger coordination for guitar playing, using motion capture data to model joint correlations and introducing a multiple kinematic chain IK routine [4].

Physics-based simulation has been a recent research focus. Sibille et al. model bone movement and soft tissue deformation. They represent muscles as angular springs and minimize potential energy in order to solve for the joint equilibrium points [5]. Albrecht et al. present a system in which *pseudo* muscles are used to move bones and *geometric* muscles are used to deform skin tissue [6]. Tsang et al. present a physical simulation system in which the activation of individual muscles can be calculated and muscle bundles can be visually separated for anatomical study [7]. Pollard and Zordan employ a Proportional Derivative controller system, similar to the one employed here [3].

Research has also focused on improving other aspects of hand models. Lin et al. model constraints on hand motion, including joint limits and inter-joint constraints, such as the DIP angle being 2/3 the PIP angle (see Figure 1 for acronyms)[8]. Braido and Zhang conducted an experimental study to measure joint coordination patterns of fingers during grasping and flexion of individual fingers [9]. We do not explicitly model joint correlations. McDonald et al. focus on improving the articulation of hand models and apply their work to animating American Sign Language [10]. Kry et al. present a method for compactly representing skin deformations that can then be animated using graphics hardware [11]. Kurihara and Miyata use CT scans to generate a high quality model of skin deformations [12].

The idea of using physical simulation to generate a kinematic model has been applied previously by Yu and Terzopoulos who created a kinematic model of biomechanically based fish motion from a spring-mass-damper model of the fish [13].

Two previous works are particularly relevant to this paper. Zordan and Pollard [3] present a similar physical hand model, but whereas they actively compensate for torques induced by gravity, we make use of these torques to deform our model. Neff and Fiume [14] model tension and relaxation, including gravity based deformations, also using a PD-based control strategy, but they do not explicitly deal with hands, present a tuning methodology or generate a kinematic model from their simulations.

3   Dynamic Model of the Hand

We use a rigid-body hand model consisting of 23 Degrees of Freedom (DOFs), as shown in Figure 1. Each of the PIP and DIP joints of the fingers and thumb IP and MCP have one DOF for flexion. The MCP joints of the fingers each have an additional DOF to support abduction/adduction (spreading of the fingers). The CMC joint of the thumb has three DOFs. The wrist has two DOFs allowing the hand to be moved up and down and side-to-side. Axial rotation of the whole hand is accomplished by a rotational DOF associated with the forearm, which is not part of this model.

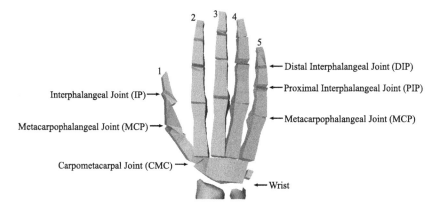

Fig. 1. Hand model illustrating the joints and finger numbering used in our system

We use a forward-simulation approach to dynamics, in which at each time step, torques are applied to each DOF and the resulting accelerations are twice integrated to update the hand's position. Our torques are generated by a simple Proportional-Derivative (PD) controller, common in the literature. PD control can be thought of as a spring and damper arranged in parallel and the control law is given as:

$$\tau = k_s(\theta_{desired} - \theta) - k_d\dot{\theta}, \tag{1}$$

where τ is the resulting torque, θ is the current angle of the DOF, $\theta_{desired}$ is the desired angle of the DOF, $\dot{\theta}$ is the velocity of the DOF, and k_s and k_d are the spring and damper gains respectively. Essentially, the controller generates torque in order to minimize the error between the desired value and the actual value of the DOF. Note though, that even at steady-state, there will normally be some error between the actual and desired value of the DOF in the presence of external forces such as gravity. Intuition for this can be developed by considering a mass hanging from a spring. At steady-state, the spring will deviate from its rest length due to the force of gravity pulling on the mass. Other approaches compensate for this error [14,3], but exploiting this "error" to generate natural hand deformations is the central idea of this work. We use SD/Fast [15] to generate the equations of motion for our simulation.

Joint limits proved important to prevent unnatural looking backwards bend of the fingers when the palm was facing up. Limits were maintained by adding additional limit terms to the PD-controller, a technique similar to that used in [3]:

$$\tau = k_s(\theta_{desired} - \theta) + c_0 k_{lim}(\theta_{low} - \theta) + c_1 k_{lim}(\theta_{high} - \theta) - k_d\dot{\theta}, \qquad (2)$$

where k_{lim} is the limit gain, many times higher than the normal gain, θ_{low} and θ_{high} are the low and high limits respectively and

$$c_0 = \begin{cases} 1 \text{ if } \theta_{low} - \theta > 0 \\ 0 \text{ otherwise} \end{cases} \quad c_1 = \begin{cases} 1 \text{ if } \theta_{high} - \theta < 0 \\ 0 \text{ otherwise} \end{cases} \qquad (3)$$

3.1   Tuning the Model

A proportional-derivative controller has three free parameters: the proportional gain, or stiffness k_s; the damping gain k_d; and the set point $\theta_{desired}$. We tune each of these parameters to match observed passive hand deformations. The set point is used to define the desired rest posture of the hand. This is the pose the hand would assume without the influence of gravity. The proportional gains are adjusted to determine how far the joints move from this rest pose under the influence of gravity. The damping gain is tuned to control the duration of relaxation movements under the influence of gravity. Each of these tuning processes will be explained in detail.

The rest pose of the hand will vary from subject to subject and is likely a parameter animators will want to control. Mount et al. [16] measured the neutral postures of astronauts in space, giving an indication of rest pose in the absence of gravity. They found flexion varied from 21 to 60 degrees across six subjects, further indicating the potential need for customization. We apply a simple measurement approach to a test subject in order to determine a sample rest pose. We ask the subject to relax his hand and hold it so that the plane of finger flexion is horizontal, thus minimizing deflection due to gravity. We photograph the hand and estimate joint angles from this. The angles used in our experiment are included in the appendix and these define the $\theta_{desired}$ parameters for each of the PD controllers. This process can be repeated with different values to model different hand behaviour, as desired by the animator.

The gain values, k_s, are determined so that the hand will have a desired shape under the influence of gravity when in a particular orientation. At steady state, the PD control law can be rewritten as:

$$k_s = \frac{T}{(\theta_{desired} - \theta)} \qquad (4)$$

where $\theta_{desired}$ is the rest pose defined above and T is the torque acting on the joint due to the force of gravity pulling on the limb and each limb lower down in the kinematic chain. For a given pose, T can be calculated, so if we can define the vector of θ values that define an observed pose, we can solve for k_s.

Table 1. Mean relaxation times

Body Part	Time to Relaxed Pose	Standard Deviation
Wrist Y	0.48	0.06
Wrist Z	0.41	0.06
Fingers	0.38	0.13

The hand orientation in which we define this vector of θ values must have two properties: it must allow the theta values to be easily determined and there must be a significant torque due to gravity acting on the measured joints in order to obtain meaningful k_s values. We use three different orientations. For the fingers, we hang the hand straight down, allowing gravity to partially straighten the fingers. For the wrist forward rotation, we hold the forearm horizontal with the palm down and allow the hand to sag downwards. This is also used for the downward rotation of the thumb CMC joint. Similarly, we simply rotate the palm to vertical with the arm horizontal for the sideways wrist rotation and the remaining thumb DOFs. The angles in these poses are once again determined by photographs and measurements of our test subject and are summarized in the appendix. The MCP DOFs related to abduction/adduction were not tuned as their deformations were considered to be too small to be worth modeling.

The third free parameter, k_d, is used to control the timing of motion under the influence of gravity. Like moving in molasses, as k_d increases, it will slow the movement. k_d values that are too small will allow the joints to move too quickly and oscillate too much. We define k_d as a factor of the k_s value for the corresponding joint and solve for three different factors: one for each wrist DOF, and one for the thumb and fingers. These factors are determined by matching animation timing to video of the subject. For the two wrist orientations, we ask the subject to hold his wrist straight and then instantly release tension so that the wrist falls to its relaxed orientation, as per above. For the fingers, we ask him to curl them into a loose fist, and then instantly release tension so that again, they relax to the default orientations above. These tests were performed multiple times and ten samples of each were chosen in which the movement appeared natural. The mean times for each movement are summarized in Table 1. Since it is difficult to precisely judge the start and stop frame of a motion, there will be some error in these values. Precise measurements do not appear to be needed, however, for the animation application. The damping factors were calculated by recreating the scenarios under simulation and adjusting the damping factor to match the original timing. The three damping factors ranged from five to seven ($k_d \approx k_s * 5$ for our low proportional gains).

4   Building a Kinematic Model

The goal of our kinematic model is to automatically set the values for the wrist and finger DOFs based on the world orientation of the forearm. The model is built by using dynamic simulation to sample the space of possible forearm orientations. We only attempt to capture the static pose deformation caused by gravity, not dynamic deformations resulting from inertial effects.

The orientation of the forearm in world-space can be captured by two parameters, which we refer to as *inclination* and *rotation*. Inclination is the angle of the arm relative to the horizontal plane; essentially its latitude on a sphere. Rotation refers to the amount of twist around the axis of the arm. Note that the rotation of the arm around the vertical axis can be ignored as the effect of gravity will not change under this transformation.

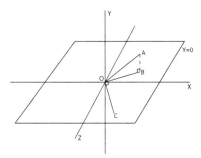

Fig. 2. Vector OA represents the arm orientation. The angle between OA and OB defines *inclination*. The cross product of OA and OC is used in determing arm *rotation*.

The process for calculating the two arm values is shown in Figure 2. The vector OA defines the current forearm orientation in world coordinates. This vector is projected onto the plane $Y = 0$ to yield the vector OB. The angle between these vectors is the *inclination*. A vector OC is calculated which is perpendicular to OB and lies in the $Y = 0$ plane. Taking the cross-product of OA and OC yields a vector OD that is perpendicular to OA and lies in the plane containing the points O, A, B. We define a vector in local forearm coordinates that is perpendicular to the forearm and points straight up in the forearm local frame. This up direction is then converted to world coordinates. The angle between this vector and OD defines the *rotation* of the arm.

4.1   Sampling Process

For ease of look up, we would like to store our data points on a grid (2D array) where the coordinates of the grid correspond to arm inclination and rotation. This is facilitated by a sampling process that computes one column of this grid on each iteration. We begin with the arm hanging down, held back behind the character and bring it forward and up, bending the elbow, until the hand is about head height and the forearm is again leaning backwards. This gives a complete sampling of the inclinations of interest. This movement is done over 8s to minimize inertial effects. Each iteration is completed with a specified world space arm rotation. The actual forearm axial rotation is varied at each time step in order to achieve this desired orientation. We have tried spacing the rotation sampling by two and six degrees, with no noticeable reduction in visual quality in the reconstructed motion. Note that since we are using PD controllers with reasonable stiffness to control the arm orientation, there will be some error between the actual orientation and the desired orientation. This error is less than our sampling spacing and we simply store the actual orientation and use this in our reconstruction. Each sample consists of the actual inclination and rotation along with values for the 23 DOFs defining the hand and wrist pose. The sample file used to build our model is available online via the first author's home page. It would be difficult, if not impossible, to complete such a controlled sampling procedure using motion capture and a human actor.

4.2   Reconstruction

Once the data has been collected, there are several ways in which it can be used for kinematic animation. The data is quite smooth, so 2D functions could be fit to each DOF to limit storage or the data could be queried for hand poses at pre-set keyframes. We use a very simple reconstruction process: At each time step, we calculate the current orientation of the arm. We then use this value as a pointer into our samples to determine the values for the 23 DOFs associated with the hand.

As stated above, the samples are stored in a grid indexed by inclination and orientation values. For a forearm orientation input, we find the four surrounding grid points. Bilinear interpolation of these vectors is performed to determine the final DOF values. Note that the interpolation is based on the actual inclination and rotation values stored with each sample, not their grid indices. This process is very fast and can be used in interactive applications where the hand pose is automatically updated as the animator moves the character's arm.

5   Results and Conclusion

Figure 3 shows frames from a kinematic animation sequence without and with the relaxed hand model applied. The more natural hand and wrist posture with the relaxed hand model is clearly evident. The video accompanying the submission includes this sequence and also a dynamic sequence using the tuned values for our model developed with the above procedure. The dynamic sequence shows subtle inertial effects that are missing in the kinematic sequence, however, when the hand is brought up to head height at a reasonable speed, the fully relaxed wrist appears slightly too loose to provide a realistic motion in this area given the inertial effects. This is not surprising, as it is rare for a person to have their wrist fully relaxed in this position. The relaxed hand model represents a baseline for hand stiffness values and they should be increased for less loose movements.

There are other effects that would be interesting to model, in particular, correlations between finger joints and the impact of wrist movement on finger deflection; for instance, a severe downward movement of the wrist will cause some straightening of the fingers as the tendons are stretched over the wrist. It would be possible to model this effect by varying the set point of the controller if a model for the correct amount of variation was available.

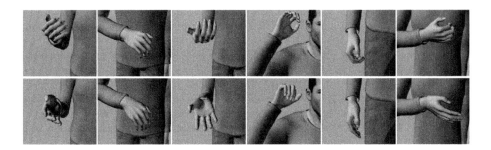

Fig. 3. The top row shows frames from an animation sequence in which the hand is held at its rest pose. The bottom row shows frames from the same kinematic animation sequence, but with our passive hand model applied.

In summary, we have presented a simple method for tuning hand parameters that is inexpensive and appears to offer sufficient accuracy for computer animation. We have also built a kinematic model of passive hand shape that provides real-time performance and that significantly improves the naturalness of character animation.

References

1. Rijpkema, H., Girard, M.: Computer animation of knowledge-based human grasping. In: Computer Graphics (Proceedings of SIGGRAPH 91). Volume 25. (1991) 339–348
2. Sanso, R.M., Thalmann, D.: A hand control and automatic grasping system for synthetic actors. Computer Graphics Forum **13**(3) (1994) 167–177
3. Pollard, N.S., Zordan, V.B.: Physically based grasping control from example. In: 2005 ACM SIGGRAPH / Eurographics Symposium on Computer Animation. (2005) 311–318
4. ElKoura, G., Singh, K.: Handrix: animating the human hand. In: 2003 ACM SIGGRAPH / Eurographics Symposium on Computer Animation. (2003) 110–119
5. Sibille, L., Teschner, M., Srivastava, S., Latombe, J.C.: Interactive simulation of the human hand. In: CARS 2002. (2002) 7–12
6. Albrecht, I., Haber, J., Seidel, H.P.: Construction and animation of anatomically based human hand models. In: 2003 ACM SIGGRAPH / Eurographics Symposium on Computer Animation. (2003) 98–109
7. Tsang, W., Singh, K., Fiume, E.: Helping hand: An anatomically accurate inverse dynamics solution for unconstrained hand motion. In: 2005 ACM SIGGRAPH / Eurographics Symposium on Computer Animation. (2005) 319–328
8. Lin, J., Wu, Y., Huang, T.S.: Modeling the constraints of human hand motion. In: Proc. Workshop on Human Motion. (2000) 121–126
9. Peter Braido, X.Z.: Quantitative analysis of finger motion coordination in hand manipulative and gestic acts. ACM Transactions on Graphics **22** (2004) 661–678
10. McDonald, J., Toro, J., Alkoby, K., Berthiaume, A., Carter, R., Chomwong, P., Christopher, J., Davidson, M.J., Furst, J., Konie, B., Lancaster, G., Roychoudhuri, L., Sedgwick, E., Tomuro, N., Wolfe, R.: An improved articulated model of the human hand. The Visual Computer **17**(3) (2001) 158–166

11. Kry, P.G., James, D.L., Pai, D.K.: Eigenskin: Real time large deformation character skinning in hardware. In: ACM SIGGRAPH Symposium on Computer Animation. (2002) 153–160
12. Kurihara, T., Miyata, N.: Modeling deformable human hands from medical images. In: 2004 ACM SIGGRAPH / Eurographics Symposium on Computer Animation. (2004) 355–363
13. Yu, Q., Terzopoulos, D.: Synthetic motion capture: Implementing an interactive virtual marine world. The Visual Computer **15**(7/8) (1999) 377–394
14. Neff, M., Fiume, E.: Modeling tension and relaxation for computer animation. In: ACM SIGGRAPH Symposium on Computer Animation. (2002) 81–88
15. Hollars, M.G., Rosenthal, D.E., Sherman, M.A.: SD/FAST User's Manual. Symbolic Dynamics Inc. (1994)
16. Mount, F.E., Whitmore, M., Stealey, S.L.: Evaluation of neutral body posture on shuttle mission sts-57 (spacehab-1). Technical Report TM-2003-104805, NASA (2003)

Appendix

Table 2. Angles used to calibrate our dynamic hand model. The "Angle" column defines the rest pose of the hand. "Deviation" refers to the difference between the rest angle and the angle of the DOF that is used to calculate gain values with the specified arm orientation.

Finger	DOF	Angle	Deviation	DOF	Finger	Angle	Deviation
1	CMC Abduction	42	-2	1	CMC Flexion	28	+6
1	MCP Flexion	36	+2	1	IP Flexion	24	+2
2	MCP Abduction	1	N/A	2	MCP Flexion	40	-21
2	PIP Flexion	50	-30	2	DIP Flexion	35	-34
3	MCP Abduction	0	N/A	3	MCP Flexion	42	-21
3	PIP Flexion	50	-25	3	DIP Flexion	38	-35
4	MCP Abduction	-1.5	N/A	4	MCP Flexion	42	-21
4	PIP Flexion	50	-25	4	DIP Flexion	38	-35
5	MCP Abduction	-6	N/A	5	MCP Flexion	29	-14
5	PIP Flexion	42	-24	5	DIP Flexion	40	-28
-	Wrist Side	0	+29	-	Wrist Forward	0	+22

Boundary Fragment Matching and Articulated Pose Under Occlusion

Nicholas R. Howe

Smith College, Northampton, Massachusetts, USA

Abstract. Silhouette recognition can reconstruct the three-dimensional pose of a human subject in monocular video so long as the camera's view remains unoccluded by other objects. This paper develops a shape representation that can describe and compare partial shapes, extending the silhouette recognition technique to apply to video with occlusions. The new method operates without human intervention, and experiments demonstrate that it can reconstruct accurate three-dimensional articulated pose tracks from single-camera walking video despite occlusion of one-third to one-half of the subject.

1 Introduction

Intense research interest has focused lately on the recovery of articulated pose information from monocular video [1,2,3]. Despite great progress, current methods commonly assume that subjects remain fully visible apart from self-occlusion of one body part by another. Yet outside of controlled studio conditions, extraneous objects can often block a camera's view either momentarily or for an extended period of time. This paper develops techniques to handle situations where some portion of a subject's body passes either behind a stationary object or out of the video frame.

Silhouette shape matching has already proven itself well suited for recovering articulated pose in a variety of applications [4,5].[1] Previous work with silhouette-based pose recovery has assumed that full silhouettes are available, and employed similarity measures that require complete shape information. This paper develops a novel approach to shape comparison that can operate with either full or partial shape information. Under occlusion, the visible portion of the shape boundary can thus be extracted and used for pose recovery. Reconstructions based upon this technique can recover the articulated pose trace (3D joint positions over time) of a walking human subject undergoing either episodic or extended partial occlusion by stationary objects.

1.1 Related Work

Much research has looked at recovery of articulated three-dimensional pose from monocular video without external occlusion [1]. Recent work in this area includes

---

[1] Although the silhouette-to-pose relationship is many-to-one, enforcing temporal continuity can disambiguate the true pose.

F.J. Perales and R.B. Fisher (Eds.): AMDO 2006, LNCS 4069, pp. 271–280, 2006.

several alternatives to silhouette-based reconstruction [2,3], as well as other related results that stop short of recovering full 3D pose [6,7]. Another body of research has examined the problem of non-articulated object tracking under intermittent occlusion [8,9]. The combination problem of single-camera articulated pose reconstruction with occlusion has received very little attention. One alternative to the method presented here would be to track the silhouettes using an occlusion-resistant deformable shape tracker [10] followed by ordinary silhouette recognition, but this would require a good prior model on the possible shapes of human silhouettes. Prior models on human motion can also guide tracking under occlusion [11]

A number of works have examined techniques specialized for partial shape matching; one recent paper gives an excellent survey [12]. The approach used herein resembles the B-spline technique of Salari and Balaji [13], but the use of the EMD embedding here improves on that work by allowing arbitrarily dense sampling of the shape boundary without increasing the complexity of the final representation. The method also somewhat resembles the curvature scale space [14,15] and the fast correspondence of Adamek and O'Connor [16], but these do not address partial matching. The use of EMD embedding herein is adapted from work using the shape context and various other features.[17,18].

2   Shape Matching: Sets of Boundary Fragments

This paper develops a measurement of shape similarity based upon matching many small, overlapping fragments of the shape boundary. Because each boundary fragment can be parameterized in only one dimension, the set of fragments is potentially simpler than other sets of localized descriptors such as the shape context [19], and also less affected by occlusions.

Simple metrics like Euclidean distance cannot properly compute similarity between sets. Fortunately, recent work provides a means of embedding sets of fragment descriptors in a high-dimensional metric space, such that the L_1 distance in the embedding space approximates the earth-movers distance (*EMD*) for the local shape or boundary descriptors [17]. Such an embedding will be referred to as an *EMD embedding*. The EMD corresponds to the sum error in the best global matching between the boundary fragments of the two images. The EMD embedding of a set of boundary fragments thus constitutes a practical representation for computing a meaningful similarity measure on binary shape images.

2.1   Extracting Boundary Fragments

To describe a binary image using boundary fragments, begin by representing the boundary as a sequence of points with roughly equal spacing. Extract multiple overlapping subsequences spaced uniformly along the boundary and of similar length, then express these in a uniform representation. The EMD embedding transforms the set of fragment representations into a form offering better computational efficiency, as described in Section 2.2.

The specific application will determine the best choice of boundary segment lengt, based upon one or more heuristics. A fixed scaled length is best when the scale of the shape can be known; most pose tracking applications fall into this category once tracking has begun. Alternately, properties of the shape itself may be used to estimate a scale. For example, the fragment length may be set at some fraction of the total perimeter length.

Once identified, boundary fragments must be described in a concise numeric format. Suppose that a fragment is parameterized by s, where $s = 0$ at one end of the fragment and $s = 1$ at the other end, and $\tau(s)$ gives the tangent to the boundary at s. Sample $\tau(s)$ at uniform intervals, compute the discrete cosine transform (DCT), then zero the constant term and truncate high-order terms beyond k. The inverse DCT then yields a k-dimensional representation of the fragment shape that is rotation invariant and effectively low-pass filtered.

Rotational information can be restored to the descriptor if desired by including $\sin(\tau(0.5))$ and $\cos(\tau(0.5))$ as additional features. Using two features for rotation information avoids circular anomalies when comparing values such as 0 and 2π. Including rotation information makes sense when shapes can be oriented *a priori*, as for example in video where the the y axis aligns with gravity.

2.2   Embedding the Boundary Fragments

In order to efficiently compute the best matching between shapes, the EMD embedding takes the set of fragment descriptors and creates a high-dimensional vector describing the shape as a whole. Each component of the embedded vector covers a region of the fragment descriptor space, with the magnitude of the component depending upon the size of the region and on how many fragments lie within it. The full embedding algorithm is too involved to give here, but follows Grauman and Darrell [17], with several modifications. To ensure that new shapes can be embedded within the same framework as existing ones, the embedding covers a fixed region of the fragment descriptor space: $[-2\pi, 2\pi]$ for the sampled features, and $[-1, 1]$ for the rotation-dependent features. Furthermore, the hierarchical subdivision of the feature space into component regions stops after five levels.

2.3   Partial Shape Matching with the Boundary Fragments

Under occlusion, some portion of a shape is unobservable. Define a *partial shape* as the result of hiding some part of a binary shape image with a mask. Note that a partial shape is not equivalent to the smaller shape made by deleting the masked portion; instead, the masked portion is simply undefined. Instead of a closed contour, the boundary of a partial shape becomes one or more open curves.

Many traditional shape descriptors simply cannot be computed for shape fragments due to the undefined region. Those comprising sets of localized descriptors, such as boundary fragments and the shape context, can still compute descriptors for regions that do not overlap with the undefined area. However, the shape context runs into problems: because it is defined on a circular area, its descriptors easily overlap unknown areas even when centered on a visible point. Consider frames 55-60 in Figure 3.3, where the entire shape lies close to the occlusion, but there are nonetheless long boundaries visible. Without sufficient local descriptors, the shape context cannot match accurately and becomes inviable for occluded pose recovery.

Given a partial shape as described above, straightforward computation yields an EMD-embedded descriptor that incorporates all fully-defined boundary fragments. For matching purposes, the components of this descriptor should be normalized to sum up to the fraction α of contour segments fully visible, while descriptors of complete shapes are all normalized to sum to one. For pose recovery, Section 3 describes how to estimate α when it is unknown. Experiments on retrieval tasks show low sensitivity to errors in α: retrieval sets overlap by up to 80% for α values varying by as much as 30%.

2.4   Benchmark Experiments with Boundary Fragment Matching

Boundary fragments shows reasonable performance as a general shape matching tool on standard test sets. For example, on the MPEG7 CE-Shape-1 test set, boundary fragments score 68.01% on the standard "bullseye" criterion [20]. Experiments in the same framework show a similar result for the shape context (68.11%). Other work has reported better results for shape context when combined iteratively with geometric warping [19]. Presumably boundary fragment matching would also benefit from such a treatment, although the procedure is too slow for application to pose recovery.

3   Pose Recovery Under Occlusion

Monocular video provides only limited cues for reconstructing the full 3D pose of a subject. Silhouette recognition offers a simple yet effective way to apply background knowledge to the problem. Silhouettes observed in the video serve as keys to look up known 3D poses with similar silhouettes for further consideration [4]. The approach does have drawbacks; most commonly noted is the difficulty of identifying accurate silhouettes. Although this remains an area of research, current performance is adequate in some applications [21].

This paper addresses a different problem, occurring when part of a subject's body is occluded by stationary objects situated along the camera's line of sight, or by the frame boundary. In either case, it becomes impossible to determine the shape of the entire silhouette, and thus to retrieve the 3D pose directly.

3.1   Boundary Fragments for Silhouette Lookup

EMD-embedded boundary fragment matching provides the framework for silhouette lookup. Because other sources describe silhouette-based pose recovery in detail [4], only an outline appears here. After background stabilization (if necessary) and modeling, change detection yields a silhouette in each video frame [21]. Each silhouette becomes a query into a database of silhouettes with known 3D poses, acquired via motion capture. The most likely pose-silhouette pairs are retained and registered to the video frame. A temporal synchronization step then searches for the sequence of poses that simultaneously maximizes the similarity to the observed silhouettes while minimizing the energy of pose changes from frame to frame. Further postprocessing smooths the results and optimizes their fidelity to the observations. Boundary fragment matching provides a convenient mechanism for the silhouette lookup stage of the algorithm; other portions remain unchanged.

Because fragment matching handles both complete and partial shapes, the method applies easily to the partial shapes that arise during external occlusion. However, the algorithm must know what portions of the shape are occluded so that it can distinguish the real silhouette boundaries from the occlusion edges. The discussion below begins by assuming that an operator provides a manually created "occlusion map" identifying areas containing potential occluding objects (Figure 1). Section 3.3 addresses how to generate such maps automatically.

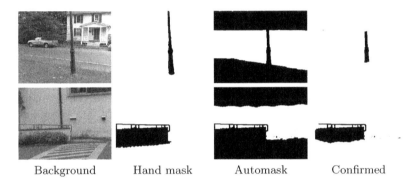

Background   Hand mask   Automask   Confirmed

Fig. 1. Static background with manually provided and automatically generated occlusion maps for two sample videos. The automatic masks are more conservative in the visible areas they identify. Rightmost column shows confirmed occluded areas after algorithm has run.

Given an occlusion map, the lookup process first determines whether the observed silhouette touches any occluded areas. If it does not, then normal lookup proceeds. If occluded areas overlap the silhouette, then the visible portions of the silhouette generate a partial shape consisting of one or more boundary contours. The scale of the figure (for boundary section length) and the visibility α may be estimated in most cases from neighboring frames with silhouettes already registered. In this case, the partial shape query returns candidate poses from the database just as a full image query would. Section 3.3 discusses how to bootstrap scale and visibility estimates for clips consisting entirely of occluded frames.

Registering a retrieved silhouette with its video frame becomes slightly more complicated when working with occlusion. One or more boundary contours will be visible in the frame. These must be matched to equivalent portions on the border of the retrieved silhouette. Phase matching between sequences of equally-space points extracted along both boundaries yields the desired correspondence.

The registration scale and translation then minimize the Euclidean distance between the corresponding sequence points. Once the retrieved silhouettes are registered, the remainder of the computation proceeds as before.

3.2 Experiments with Occluded Video

The evaluation test set comprises two short videos involving significant occlusion. The first, *Pole*, shows a walking subject passing completely behind a lightpost. The second, *Ramp*, shows the subject walking up a handicapped access ramp. A low wall at the edge of the ramp obscures the view of the subject's legs in the latter half of this video, making pose recovery much more challenging.

The reconstruction of the *Pole* video entirely avoids any major errors. Occlusions by the post and the frame edges are handled gracefully. There is some small error in the arm positions and in the hip orientation, similar to those occurring in silhouette-based reconstruction without occlusion. Space constraints preclude reproducing the results here, as they are similar to those presented later. This clip shows boundary fragment matching easily handling transient external occlusions of this sort. Note that the figure can be tracked outside the frame boundary only so long as a sufficient amount of the boundary is visible; the outer limit for getting reasonable results seems to be about $\alpha = 0.3$.

The extended occlusion of the legs in the *Ramp* video makes pose reconstruction much more difficult in the second half of the clip. The system must infer what the legs are doing from the motions of the upper body. When the arms are visible this is somewhat easier, but there are points in the stride where the upper body shape appears more or less as an undifferentiated pillar. Despite this, the shape-fragment matching reconstructs the *Ramp* motion with only one significant error, a stutter-step near the very end of the clip. Errors near the beginning and end of a clip sometimes occur due to the lack of corroborating observations from neighboring frames on one side.

3.3 Fully Automatic Reconstruction

Manual occlusion maps are a crutch that preclude fully automatic operation. This section describes an algorithm to automatically determine the non-occluded areas, using no more information than the silhouette observations already employed for pose retrieval (as derived from background modeling and change detection). The composition of all the areas where the subject silhouette is observed over time forms a map of known unoccluded areas. The complement of this set is the union of two pieces: true occlusion zones and areas of background that are indistinguishable from occlusion zones because the subject was never observed there.

Figure 1 shows for each test video the regions containing no observation of the subject. Although these masks cover much more area than the manually created occlusion masks, these masks may nevertheless function in the same role. Treating zero-silhouette regions as occlusion zones will disregard some valid silhouette boundaries that cannot be verified as real. A typical silhouette will now have undefined regions above the head and below the feet, because the subject was never observed in these areas. This increases the challenge of database retrieval: since occlusions cannot be distinguished from unidentified background, in practice all frames must use partial shapes for retrieval.

Atomatic occlusion maps may not be error-free, and the penalties for error are not symmetric. Marking a visible area as occluded merely makes retrieval slightly more difficult by reducing the length of boundary available as a query. This is generally much less serious than counting an occluded area as visible, which will usually introduce spurious boundaries that are more likely to interfere with both retrieval and registration. For example, the railing at the top of the wall in the *Ramp* clip is not always segmented properly in the silhouette of every frame. To prevent such problems, a special high-threshold foreground segmentation generates the occlusion map, biasing the result against mistakenly labeling occlusion zones as visible areas.

Estimating the parameter relating library scales to observed silhouette dimensions becomes more difficult without frames known to be unoccluded. This work adopts a heuristic approach, assuming that the silhouettes with maximal vertical extent are unoccluded or nearly so, and estimating scale based upon their height. Allowing slow (0.5%) changes in scale between neighboring frames causes each silhouette to impose a minimum scale on all other frames. Silhouettes whose vertical extent indicates a scale greater than the minimum imposed by all other frames are considered reliable indicators of the true scale. Interpolation gives the estimated scale of the remaining frames. While effective for the clips tested here, this heuristic is not universally reliable and might be less successful in some cases than a technique based upon boundary curvature or limb thickness.

Estimating the visibility α is also more difficult without known occlusion-free frames. The silhouette dimensions for the indicator frames described above can give a very rough estimate of α. Unoccluded silhouette perimiters average around four times the figure height, although this ratio can vary by up to 30% in either direction. In most cases this suffices for adequate retrieval. Nevertheless, once an initial frame has been solved, using the visibility of registered silhouettes in a neighboring frame is generally more accurate and therefore preferable.

Figures 3.3 and 3 show the reconstruction results under fully automatic operation. Despite the increased difficulty of retrieving and registering correct candidate silhouettes from partial shapes at every frame, the boundary fragment matching reconstructs both clips without major errors. The automatic reconstructions capture the qualitative features of the walk nearly as well as the result using the manual occlusion map, but exhibit somewhat larger transient deviations in scale and body orientation. Interestingly, this reconstruction avoids stutter-steps in the *Ramp* clip.

Although 3D pose ground truth is unavailable for these clips, the results can be evaluated in comparison to 2D tracking points hand-entered by two individuals. For the *Pole* clip, the difference between the two humans in placement of control points averaged 1.9 pixels; the automatic result differed from the human mean by 6.1 pixels (roughly four inches). No increase in error was observed during the occlusion by the lamp pole. The *Ramp* clip is more difficult for humans to

Fig. 2. Automatic reconstruction of *Pole* clip shown at selected frames

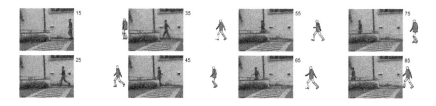

Fig. 3. Automatic reconstruction of *Ramp* clip shown at periodic frames

annotate due to the extended occlusion, and disagreement between human point placements averaged 4.4 pixels. The disagreement between the automatic and human results averaged 7.4 pixels. On this clip, occlusion causes a noticable decrease in accuracy for both the humans and the computer algorithm: the error averaged for the frames before and after frame 40 are 2.1 vs. 6.6 pixels for humans, and 5.8 vs. 8.7 pixels for the computer.

While walking motions arguably make for a simple evaluation choice, they are nevertheless of interest in many applications. Furthermore, these experiments indisputably provedemonstrate the utility of shape fragment matching for handling occlusion. Perhaps this will spur the development of additional occlusion-handling techniques for other pose reconstruction modalities.

3.4 Refined Occlusion Maps

The automatic reconstruction can proceed one step further to refine the original automatic occlusion map, distinguishing between true occlusion zones and areas with no data. With pose reconstruction in hand, animation and rendering reveals the region swept out by the moving subject in the image frame. The reconstruction registration may not be entirely accurate, so the outer edge of this region should be thrown out using morphological erosion. The intersection of the remaining area and the original occlusion map yields a set of pixels held to be occupied by occluding objects. Storing these locations may help in subsequent pose reconstructions, or in other scene interpretation tasks. Figure 1 shows the refined automatic occlusion maps for the two clips.

4   Conclusion

This paper has described an extension of silhouette-based monocular 3D pose reconstruction to handle partial occlusions by stationary objects. One enabling development is EMD-embedded boundary fragments, a novel contour-based description of shape that allows comparison of partial shapes. The other key is the explicit use of an occlusion/visibility map, allowing the algorithm to discriminate between valid silhouette boundaries and spurious ones arising from occlusion. The occlusion map may be created by hand, but it can also be generated through an automatic process with surprisingly little decrease in the quality of the final result.

Acknowledgements

This material is based upon work supported by the National Science Foundation under Grant No. IIS-0328741.

References

1. T. B. Moeslund and E. Granum, "A survey of computer vision-based human motion capture", *Computer Vision and Image Understanding*, vol. 81, pp. 231–268, March 2001.
2. L. Sigal, S. Bhatia, S. Roth, M. Black, and M. Isard, "Tracking loose-limbed people", *in IEEE Computer Society Conference on Computer Vision and Pattern Recognition*, vol. I, pp. 421–428, 2004.
3. C. Sminchisescu, A. Kanaujia, Z. Li, and D. Metaxas, "Learning to reconstruct 3d human motion from bayesian mixtures of experts: A probabilistic discriminative approach", Technical Report CSRG-502, University of Toronto, October 2004.
4. N. Howe, "Silhouette lookup for monocular 3d pose tracking", *Image and Vision Computing*, 2006, (to appear).
5. G. Mori and J. Malik, "Estimating human body configurations using shape context matching", *in European Conference on Computer Vision*, 2002.
6. R. Fablet and M. Black, "Automatic detection and tracking of human motion with a view-based representation", *in European Conference on Computer Vision*, pp. 476–491, 2002.
7. D. Ramanan, D. A. Forsyth, and A. Zisserman, "Strike a pose: Tracking people by finding stylized poses", *in IEEE Computer Society Conference on Computer Vision and Pattern Recognition*, pp. 271–278, 2005.
8. P Gabriel, J. Verly, J. Piater, and A. Genon, "The state of the art in multiple object tracking under occlusion in video sequences", *in Advanced Concepts for Intelligent Vision Systems*, pp. 166–173, 2003.
9. O. Lanz and R. Manduchi, "Hybrid joint-separable multibody tracking", *in IEEE Computer Society Conference on Computer Vision and Pattern Recognition*, pp. 413–420, 2005.
10. Y. Rathi, N. Vaswani, A. Tannenbaum, and A. Yezzi, "Particle filtering for geometric active contours with application to tracking moving and deforming objects", *in IEEE Computer Society Conference on Computer Vision and Pattern Recognition*, pp. 2–9, 2005.

11. R. Urtasun, D. Fleet, and P. Fua, "3d people tracking with gaussian process dynamical models", *in IEEE Computer Society Conference on Computer Vision and Pattern Recognition*, 2006.
12. E. Saber, Y. Xu, and A. M. Tekalp, "Partial shape recognition by sub-matrix matching for partial matching guided image labeling,", *Pattern Recognition*, vol. 38, pp. 1560–1573, 2005.
13. E. Salari and S. Balaji, "Recognition of partially occluded objects using b-spline representation", *in Proc. SPIE, High-Speed Inspection Architectures, Barcoding, and Character Recognition*, vol. 1384, pp. 115–123, 1991.
14. F. Mokhtarian, "Silhouette-based object recognition with occlusion through curvature scale space", *in Proceedings of the European Conference on Computer Vision*, pp. 566–578, 1996.
15. F. Mokhtarian, S. Abbasi, and J. Kittler, "Robust and efficient shape indexing through curvature scale space", *in Proceedings of the British Machine Vision Conferenc*, pp. 53–62, 1996.
16. T. Adamek and N. O'Connor, "Efficient contour-based shape representation and matching", *in Multimedia Information Retrieval*, pp. 138–143, 2003.
17. K. Grauman and T. Darrell, "Fast contour matching using approximate earth mover's distance", *in IEEE Computer Society Conference on Computer Vision and Pattern Recognition*, vol. I, pp. 220–227, 2004.
18. K. Grauman and T. Darrell, "Efficient image matching with distributions of local invariant features", *in IEEE Computer Society Conference on Computer Vision and Pattern Recognition*, vol. II, pp. 627–634, 2005.
19. M. Belongie, J. Malik, and J. Puzicha, "Shape matching and object recognition using shape contexts", *IEEE Transactions on Pattern Analysis and Machine Intelligence*, vol. 24, pp. 509–522, April 2002.
20. L. J. Latecki, R. Lakämper, and U. Eckhardt, "Shape descriptors for non-rigid shapes with a single closed contour", *in IEEE Computer Society Conference on Computer Vision and Pattern Recognition*, pp. 424–429, 2000.
21. N. Howe and A. Deschamps, "Better foreground segmentation through graph cuts", Technical report, Smith College, 2004, `http://arxiv.org/abs/cs.CV/0401017`.

Object Tracking and Elimination Using Level-of-Detail Canny Edge Maps

Jihun Park

Department of Computer Engineering
Hongik University, Seoul, Korea
jhpark@cs.hongik.ac.kr

Abstract. We propose a method for tracking a nonparameterized subject contour in a single video stream with a moving camera. Then we eliminate the tracked contour object by replacing the background scene we get from other frame that is not occluded by the tracked object. Our method consists of two parts: first we track the object using LOD (Level-of-Detail) canny edge maps, then we generate background of each image frame and replace the tracked object in a scene by a background image from other frame. In order to track a contour object, LOD Canny edge maps are generated by changing scale parameters for a given image. A *simple (strong)* Canny edge map has the smallest number of edge pixels while the most detailed Canny edge map, $Wcanny_N$, has the largest number of edge pixels. To reduce side-effects because of irrelevant edges, we start our basic tracking by using *simple (strong)* Canny edges generated from large image intensity gradients of an input image, called *Scanny* edges. Starting from *Scanny* edges, we get more edge pixels ranging from simple Canny edge maps until the most detailed (weaker) Canny edge maps, called *Wcanny* maps along LOD hierarchy. LOD Canny edge pixels become nodes in routing, and LOD values of adjacent edge pixels determine routing costs between the nodes. We find the *best* route to follow Canny edge pixels favoring stronger Canny edge pixels. In order to remove the tracked object, we generate approximated background for the first frame. Background images for subsequent frames are based on the first frame background or previous frame images. This approach is based on computing *camera motion*, camera movement between two image frames. Our method works nice for moderate camera movement with small object shape changes.

1 Introduction and Related Works

The tracking of moving subjects is a hot issue because of a wide variety of applications in motion capturing for computer animation, video coding, video surveillance, monitoring, and augmented reality. We track a highly textured subject moving in a complex scene compared to a relatively simple subject tracking done by others. We mean *complex* because both tracked subject and background scene leave many edges after the edge detection. We assume our subject is never occluded by any background objects, but it occludes other objects in the background while the camera is moving. Our background generation

F.J. Perales and R.B. Fisher (Eds.): AMDO 2006, LNCS 4069, pp. 281–290, 2006.

assumes all background objects are static. This paper is an extension of our previous work[1]. We can classify the methods of representing a subject contour into two categories depending on the method used; parameterized contour or nonparameterized contour. In tracking a parameterized contour, a subject contour estimating the motion is represented by using parameters. In general, these methods use the Snake model[2]; Kalman Snake[3] and Adaptive Motion Snake[4] are popular Snake models.

In the method of tracking a nonparameterized contour, a subject contour as a subject border is represented. The contour created by these algorithms is represented as a set of pixels. Paragios's algorithm[5] and Nguyen's algorithm[6] are popular in these approaches. Recently, Nguyen proposed a method[6] for tracking a nonparameterized subject contour in a single video stream with a moving camera and a changing background. Nguyen's approach combined the outputs of two steps: creating a predicted contour and removing background edges. Nguyen's approach removed background edges by computing object motion. But Nguyen's approach left many irrelevant edges that prohibit accurate contour tracking because removing the background edges is difficult. In Nguyen's algorithm[6], a watershed line that was determined by using the watershed segmentation[7] and the watershed line smoothing energy[6,8] becomes the new contour of a tracked subject. In other words, the watershed line is generated by combining the previous frame contour and the current frame Canny edges that do not always make a closed edge contour. Nguyen's method[6] of combining the predicted contour computed from the previous frame accumulates tracking error, because tracking errors are accumulated by always including the previous contour regardless of the intensity of the current Canny edges. Predicted contour that is computed from the previous frame is usually different from the exact contour for the current frame. A big change between the previous and current contour shapes makes this kind of contour tracking difficult. We remove redundant edges by modifying Canny edge generation, one of major contribution of this paper.

There is another interesting method for color based segmentation, called Mean shift[9]. This method use parameters to adjust segmented regions of an image. This method works excellent if the adjacent color area in the image are

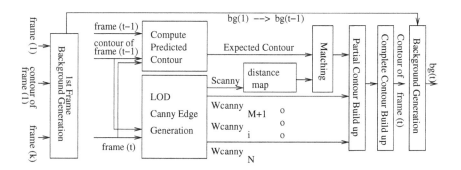

Fig. 1. Overview of our single frame tracking and background generation

distinct each other. But ordinary video images have blurred colors and is usually indistinguishable at segment boundaries. Another drawback is that the segmented boundary severely changes according to the parameters, while we get *LOD Canny edges* at the same spot consistently.

2   Overview of Our System

Figure 1 shows an overview of our system for tracking and eliminating an object (to make a background image) in a single image frame. First, we generate the first frame background scene that will be explained in Section 3. Then we compute a tracked object contour for the next frame. As inputs to compute an object contour, we get a previous image frame, denoted as $frame\ (t-1)$ and the corresponding tracked subject contour of input $frame\ (t-1)$, and a current image frame, denoted as $frame\ (t)$. From $frame\ (t-1)$, contour of $frame\ (t-1)$, and $frame\ (t)$, we compute a predicted contour, $\partial\Omega^{(p,t)}$, for $frame\ (t)$ using object motion[6]. Then, we generate various detailed levels of modified Canny edge image maps for the input $frame\ (t)$. We select *Scanny* edges from the LOD Canny edge maps. From a *Scanny* edge map, we derive a corresponding distance map. Using the predicted contour, the best matching is then found between the predicted contour and the *Scanny* distance map. *Scanny* edge pixels matching with the predicted contour become the frame of the contour build up. We call these pixels *selected Scanny contour pixels*. *Selected Scanny contour pixels*, generated using *Scanny* and predicted contour, are the most reliable (but not closed) contour pixels to start building a closed tracked contour, and are stored in the *selected Scanny found list*. We then route a path to connect adjacent *selected Scanny contour pixels* in the found list using LOD Canny edge pixels. If we finish connecting every adjacent *selected Scanny contour pixel* pair, we get a set of *partial contours* although not guaranteed to be the *best* closed contour. We mean *best* because the contour is four-neighbor connected and follows every possible *Scanny* edge.

To build a *best* closed contour for the $frame\ (t)$, we use LOD Canny edge maps around the predicted contour. We run a final routing using the computed

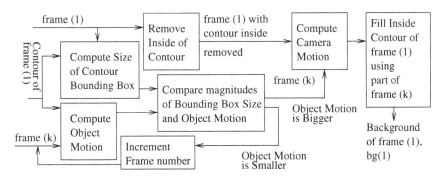

Fig. 2. Process of generating the first frame background

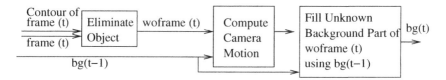

Fig. 3. Process of generating the tth frame background using $(t-1)$th frame background

segments of partial contours and *Scanny* edges around it to find the best contour. In this process, we fix the wrong computed basic contour. The resulting contour becomes the contour of $frame$ (t), and it is used to generate background of $frame$ (t). Our method to generate the background (tracked object eliminated) image is using the previous frame background image, as presented in Figure 3, while the approach for computing the first frame presented in Figure 2 produces higher quality background images.

3   Object Elimination and Background Generation

This approach is based on the assumptions that the background objects are static and camera movement is neither violent nor stationary. Because the actual input video has moving camera, there are minor errors which cause accumulated errors if the approach is used in tracking using background elimination. Figure 2 shows a process to determine the first frame background given a sequence of video stream. As inputs, we get the kth frame denoted as $frame$ (k), the first image frame denoted as $frame$ (1) and the corresponding tracked subject contour of input $frame$ (1). The first frame consists of the tracked object as well as background. The kth frame is the earliest frame, in video sequence, that has the background information for the part occluded by the tracked object in $frame$ (1). But sometimes it is possible that we cannot get the part of scene information occluded by the tracked object. From $frame$ (1) and contour of $frame$ (1), we compute a size of the bounding box of the tracked contour, and remove inside of the tracked object contour, the part of the image frame occluded by the tracked object. The resulting image frame is denoted as $woframe(1)$. By filling the occluded/removed part using background image from $frame$ (k), we build a background image of $frame$ (1), denoted as bg (1). The process to determine the exact frame to fill occluded part is as follows. First we try with an arbitrary frame, say $frame$ (k). In order to verify that the frame actually contains the missing background part of the first image frame, we compute object motion between $frame$ (1) and $frame$ (k)[6]. If the object motion magnitudes in both x and y direction are bigger than the width and height of the bounding box of the first frame respectively, we are done in finding the exact frame to fill the missing part of $frame$ (1). Otherwise we try with the next image frame until the exact frame is found. Then we compute *camera motion* between the first frame and the kth frame, and the computation result is used in generating a background image of the first frame denoted as bg(1). $woframe$ (1) denotes the first frame with the contour inside removed. In order to compute *camera motion*, we find the best matching displacement between $woframe(1)$ and $frame\ (k)$. We mean *camera motion*, a computation for camera movement, to be the image displacement between two image frames. In order to fill the occluded part of $woframe(1)$, we use computed *camera motion* and take corresponding image part from $frame\ (k)$. As a result, we get the background image of the first frame, denoted as $bg(1)$.

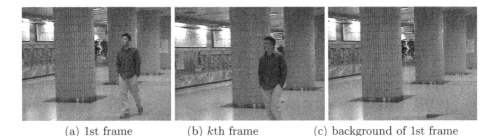

(a) 1st frame   (b) kth frame   (c) background of 1st frame

Fig. 4. The result of generating background of the first frame

Figure 3 shows a process to determine the tth frame background especially for early image frames. After early image frames, we can get occluded background information from previous image frames, and the algorithm is similar to Figure 2. This approach should be used for early frames, but if the tracked object is fairly away from the occluded backgrounds, then the background image generation can be done using a modified version of algorithm presented in Figure 2.

As inputs, we get a tth image frame, denoted as $frame\ (t)$, the corresponding tracked subject contour of input $frame\ (t)$, and the computed background image of $frame\ (t-1)$, denoted as $bg(t-1)$. Given $frame\ (t)$ and the contour of $frame\ (t)$, we eliminate inside the contour, the tracked object. The resulting image frame is denoted as $woframe\ (t)$. Using $woframe\ (t)$ and $bg(t-1)$, we compute the *camera motion* between the $frame\ (t-1)$ and the $frame\ (t)$. Using the computed *camera motion*, we fill the occluded part of $woframe\ (t)$ using $bg(t-1)$. As a result, we get the background image for $frame\ (t)$, denoted as $bg(t)$.

Figure 4 shows an example of generating the background image for the first frame. The inputs were a sequence of video, the first frame, and the contour for the full tracked body of the first frame. Figure 4(a) shows the first frame, Figure 4(b) is the selected kth frame which has the background image for the occluded part of the first frame, and Figure 4(c) is the computed background image for the first frame. The tracked object size is significantly different between two image frames, Figure 4(a,b), but this does not disturb correct *camera motion* computation because we compute matching with the known tracked object removed, say $woframe(1)$. As you may find, there are some dark image areas that do not have any corresponding background image available. It is impossible to fill this missing background information.

4   LOD Canny Edge Maps, Matching for Selecting Reference Contour Pixels, Reference Contour Pixel Connection by Routing

A *strong Canny edge map* is generated by a pixel-wise union of the simplest Canny edge maps out of various scaled Canny edge maps. Contrary to Nguyen's approach, we do not remove background edges that are difficult to remove. Our new method selects only the Canny edges with large image intensity gradient values, *Scanny* edges. A *Scanny* edge map does not have noisy background edges and looks simple, meaning there are less edges in the Canny edge map of the scene. Working on Scanny has an effect of background removal. Our accurate tracking is based on reducing the effects from irrelevant edges by only selecting strongest edge pixels, and relying on the current frame edge pixels as much as possible contrary to Nguyen's approach of always combining the previous contour.

For Canny edge maps generated with smaller image intensity gradient values, we call $Wcanny_i$, $i = M + 1, \cdots, N$ where N is the number of LOD Canny edge maps, M is the number of Canny edge maps used in computing *Scanny* edge map. $Wcanny_{M+1}$ has the simplest Canny edges generated from a set of large *(strongest)* intensity gradient value edges. $Wcanny_N$ has the most detailed Canny edges generated by an accumulation from largest *(strongest)* till to the smallest *(weakest)* intensity gradient valued edges. Figure 5(a,b) shows an example of *Scanny* and $Wcanny_N$ Canny edge maps respectively.

By varying control parameters, we can get various Canny edge maps of different scales given a single image. The resulting Canny edge maps are mainly affected by the image intensity changes between pixels. We take advantage of the fact that we can get various Canny edge maps by varying these control parameters. Usually, very detailed Canny edge maps confuses us in finding the exact outline, but simple Canny edge maps generated from large image intensity changes do not have enough detail to make a closed contour for the tracked subject. But simple Canny edge maps are very reliable because they are generated only if there are big intensity changes in the image. We need both simple and detailed Canny edge maps for the best subject tracking. Various detailed Canny edge maps are generated by varying the values of control parameters. We totally order the resulting Canny edge maps by counting the number of edge pixels in each edge map.

Let $\Phi_i^{(I,t)}$, where $i = 1, \cdots, N$, be a totally ordered set of Canny edge maps of an input image frame (t). The ordering is done by counting the number of edge pixels. $\Phi_1^{(I,t)}$ has the smallest number of edge pixels while $\Phi_N^{(I,t)}$ has the largest number of edge pixels. N is the total number of Canny edge maps generated for the input image. Then, we take the top 10 percent to 30 percent of the simple Canny edge maps and union into pixel-level to make a *Scanny* edge map, $S\Phi^{(I,t)}$. M is the total number of Canny edge maps used to make a $S\Phi^{(I,t)}$. The rest of the Canny edge maps are used to generate $Wcanny_i$, $W\Phi_i^{(I,t)}$.

$$S\Phi^{(I,t)} = \bigcup_{i=1}^{M} \Phi_i^{(I,t)}$$
$$W\Phi_i^{(I,t)} = S\Phi^{(I,t)} \bigcup \left(\bigcup_{j=M+1}^{i} \Phi_j^{(I,t)}\right), i = (M+1),\cdots,N \tag{1}$$

where $\bigcup$ is pixel-wise union of bitmaps. $Wcanny_{M+1}$ is a pixel-wise union of *Scanny* and the next detailed sets of Canny edge maps. $Wcanny_i$ is generated by unioning $Wcanny_{(i-1)}$ and the next detailed sets of Canny edge maps, etc. $Wcanny_N$ has the union of all levels of detail Canny edges generated by an accumulation from *highest-to-lowest* intensity gradient value edges.

LOD Canny edge map, $L\Phi^{(I,t)}$, is generated using $S\Phi^{(I,t)}$ and $W\Phi_i^{(I,t)}$s edge pixels around $\partial\Omega^{(p,t)}$. $\Gamma(L\Phi^{(I,t)}(x,y))$ is a function returning an LOD value given an edge pixel (x,y) of an LOD edge map, $L\Phi^{(I,t)}$. To build a $L\Phi^{(I,t)}$, we search $S\Phi^{(I,t)}$ and $W\Phi_i^{(I,t)}$s from the simplest edge map to the most detailed edge map.

Basically, we rely only on a *Scanny* edge map and a predicted contour from the previous frame to find reference pixels, called *selected* Scanny pixels, for building a basic (but not closed) tracked contour frame. Then, we seek additional edge pixels from $Wcanny_i$s according to the descending sequence of multi-level detailed edge pixels, following LOD in edge maps. These *selected* Scanny pixels become start nodes and end nodes in routing. LOD Canny edge pixels become nodes in routing, and LOD values of adjacent edge pixels determine routing costs between the nodes.

Rather than removing background edges, we start with a *Scanny* edge map, as presented in Figure 5(a), that has simple edges in a scene. Figure 5(c-f) shows a process of computing *selected Scanny pixels*, and the selection result is presented in Figure 5(g). *Selected Scanny pixels* are denoted as green pixels in Figure 5(g),

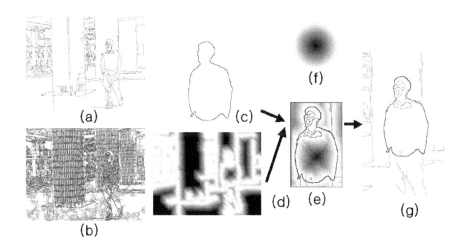

Fig. 5. *Scanny* edge map (a), LOD $Wcanny_N$ edge map (b), predicted contour from frame $(t-1)$ (c), distance map generated from *Scanny* (d), matching between predicted contour and *Scanny* distance map (e), circular distance map used in matching (f)

along the predicted contour, while red pixels mean a failure in finding a matching *Scanny* pixel. By using an image matching as used by others[6], we can get a predicted contour, $\partial\Omega^{(p,t)}$, as presented in Figure 5(a). Then, we generate a distance map of *Scanny*, $DS\Phi^{(I,t)}$, as in Figure 5(d).

From a set of adjacent *selected* Scanny edge pixels, we find segments of contours, called *partial contour*. In finding a *partial contour*, we find the *best* route to follow Canny edge pixels favoring stronger Canny edge pixels. We do a routing between two disconnected *Scanny* edge pixels using LOD *Wcanny* edge maps favoring stronger edge maps. The disconnected contour is connected using Dijkstra's minimum cost routing. We consider *Scanny* edges around a predicted contour, computed from the previous frame contour, to likely be a part of the new contour. To make a closed contour, we do a final routing using the above segments of *partial contours* and *Scanny* edges around the predicted contour.

We route a path to connect *adjacent selected Scanny contour pixels* in the *found list* using LOD Canny edge pixels, $LS\Phi^{(I,t)}$. We mean *adjacent* to be adjacent in the *found list*. If we finish connecting every adjacent *selected Scanny contour pixel* pairs, we get a set of *partial contours* although they are not guaranteed to be complete. We mean *complete* because the contour is four-neighbor connected and follows every possible *Scanny* edge. These *selected Scanny contour pixels* become start and end nodes in routing.

LOD Canny edge pixels become nodes in routing, and LOD values of adjacent edge pixels determine routing costs between the nodes. In finding a *partial contour*, we find the *best* route to follow Canny edge pixels favoring stronger Canny edge pixels. We mean *best* because building an optimal partial contour route by taking possible strongest Canny edges (minimizing routing cost) according to the descending sequence of multi-level detailed edge pixels, following LOD in edge maps.

5   Experimental Results

We have experimented with easily available video sequences either available on the Internet or generated with a home camcorder, SONY DCR-PC3. Recall our background generation and tracked object removal assume all background objects are static, but major sequences of our experimental input video has moving background objects. In tracking an object, neither Nguyen's nor our approach can handle big change in contour shape, but our approach performs better in tracking a highly textured object. In deleting the tracked object and replacing it by the background scene, we deleted bigger than the actually computed contour in order to remove accumulation errors in generating the background scene. We have generated 64 different LOD Canny edge maps, ordered them according to the number of Canny edge pixels, and union simplest 18 (top 30 percent) Canny edge maps to make *Scanny* Canny edge map. Figure 6[a-j] show a man walking in a subway hall, and Figure 6[k-t] are corresponding background generated images. We tracked the upper body of the man because his pants color is similar to that of the subway station floor (Figure 6[a]). Extremely difficult

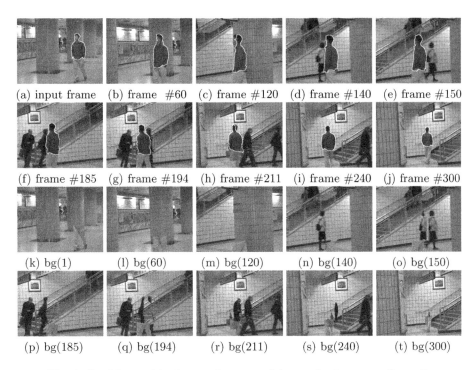

(a) input frame   (b) frame #60   (c) frame #120   (d) frame #140   (e) frame #150

(f) frame #185   (g) frame #194   (h) frame #211   (i) frame #240   (j) frame #300

(k) bg(1)   (l) bg(60)   (m) bg(120)   (n) bg(140)   (o) bg(150)

(p) bg(185)   (q) bg(194)   (r) bg(211)   (s) bg(240)   (t) bg(300)

Fig. 6. Tracking and background generated (upper body removed) result

job is tracking walking legs because the contour shape changes heavily. The hall tiles as well as a cross stripe shirt generate many complicated Canny edges. The tracked contour shape and color changes as the man with a cross stripe shirt rotates from facing the front to the back as he comes closer to a camera and then moves away from it. There are many edge pixels in the background and the subject has many edges inside the tracked contour. There are other people moving in different directions (Figure 6[f-h]), in the background, causing errors in background image generation(Figure 6[o-s]). To make tracking more difficult, the face color of the tacked subject is similar to the hall wall color (Figure 6[a-c]) while his shirt color is similar to that of stairs (Figure 6[f,g]), and tracked body black hair is interfered with by a walking woman in Figure 6(f,g) and a man with a black suit in Figure 6(h). Our tracked contour is bothered by these interferences, but recovers as soon as we get *Scanny* edges for the interfered part. Even under this complex circumstance, our boundary edge-based tracking and background generation was successful. Full tracking movies can be downloaded from http://www.cs.hongik.ac.kr/~jhpark .

6   Conclusion

In this paper, we proposed a method of improving accuracy in tracking a highly textured object and eliminating it to generate corresponding background scene.

We start by selecting a boundary edge pixel from the *simple (strong) Canny edge map*, referring to the most detailed edge map to get edge information along the LOD Canny edge maps. Our basic tracking frame is determined from the strong Canny edge map, and the missing edges are filled by the detailed Canny edges along the LOD hierarchy. We minimize the possibility of accumulated tracking errors by relying on the current Canny edge map only. If there is no edge present, we may have a tracking error for the part. Whenever we get *Scanny* edge information, the tracking error disappears, and we can restart accurate tracking for the erroneous part. Our tracking condition is tougher to track compared to Nguyen's. Our experimental results show that our tracking approach is more reliable in handling a bigger change of the tracked subject shape in a complex scene, compared to Nguyen's approach. Our background generation approach is based on an attempt to use the result in detecting a moving object at the current frame. Our current approach to handle big contour shape change is to use model body based matching combined with the contour based approach presented in this paper.[1]

References

1. Park, J.: Contour tracking using modified canny edge maps with level-of-detail. Lecture Notes in Computer Science (CAIP 2005) **3691** (2005) 1–8
2. Kass, M., Witkin, A., Terzopoulos, D.: Snakes: Active contour models. International Journal of Computer Vision **1** (1987) 321–331
3. Peterfreund, N.: Robust tracking of position and velocity with kalman snakes. IEEE Trans. on Pattern Analysis and Machine Intelligence **21** (1999) 564–569
4. Fu, Y., Erdem, A.T., Tekalp, A.M.: Tracking visible boundary of objects using occlusion adaptive motion snake. IEEE Trans. on Image Processing **9** (2000) 2051–2060
5. Paragios, N., Deriche, R.: Geodesic active contours and level sets for the detection and tracking of moving objects. IEEE Trans. on Pattern Analysis and Machine Intelligence **22** (2000) 266–280
6. Nguyen, H.T., Worring, M., van den Boomgaard, R., Smeulders, A.W.M.: Tracking nonparameterized object contours in video. IEEE Trans. on Image Processing **11** (2002) 1081–1091
7. Roerdink, J.B.T.M., Meijster, A.: The watershed transform: Definition, algorithms and parallelization strategies. Fundamenta Informaticae **41** (2000) 187–228
8. Nguyen, H.T., Worring, M., van den Boomgaard, R.: Watersnakes: energy-driven watershed segmentation. IEEE Trans. on Pattern Analysis and Machine Intelligence **25** (2003) 330–342
9. Comaniciu, D., Meer, P.: Mean shift: A robust approach toward feature space analysis. IEEE Transactions on Pattern Analysis and Machine Intelligence **24** (2002) 603–619

---

[1] This research was supported by the 2006 Hongik University Academic Research Support Fund.

Facial Expression Recognition in Various Internal States Using Independent Component Analysis

Young-suk Shin

Department of Information and telecommunication Engineering, Chosun University, #375
Seosuk-dong, Dong-gu, Gwangju, 501-759, Korea
ysshin@chosun.ac.kr

Abstract. This paper presents a new approach method to recognize facial expressions in various internal states using independent component analysis (ICA). We developed a representation of facial expression images based on independent component analysis for feature extraction of facial expressions. This representation consists of two steps. In the first step, we present a representation based on principal component analysis (PCA) excluded the first 2 principal components to reflect well the changes in facial expressions. Second, ICA representation from this PCA representation was developed. Finally, classification of facial expressions in various internal states was created on two dimensional structure of emotion with pleasure/displeasure dimension and arousal/sleep dimension. The proposed algorithm demonstrates the ability to discriminate the changes of facial expressions in various internal states. This system is possible to use in cognitive processes, social interaction and behavioral investigations of emotion.

1 Introduction

Most research on facial expression recognition includes studies using six basic emotions of Ekman[1, 2, 3, 4, 5]. The six basic emotions are fear, anger, sadness, happiness, disgust and surprise. Such studies provide a convenient framework. But these studies have limitations for recognition of natural facial expressions which consist of several other emotions and many combinations of emotions.

The dimensions of emotion can be overcome this limitation. The two most common dimensions are "arousal" (calm/excited), and "valence" (negative/positive). The study of Peter Lang has assembled an international archives of imagery rated by arousal and valence with image content [6]. Russell who argued that the dimension model can be applied to emotion recognition [7]. To recognize facial expressions in various internal states, we worked with dimensions of emotion instead of with basic emotions or discrete emotion categories. The dimensions of emotion proposed are pleasure/displeasure dimension and arousal/sleep dimension.

Methods [8, 9, 10] for representing facial expression images have been proposed such as Optic flow and Geometric tracking method, Gabor representation, PCA (Principal Component Analysis) and ICA (Independent Component Analysis). At recently study, PCA representation excluded the first 1 principal component in full face was

F.J. Perales and R.B. Fisher (Eds.): AMDO 2006, LNCS 4069, pp. 291–299, 2006.
© Springer-Verlag Berlin Heidelberg 2006

applied to input features of neural network classifier in work for facial expression recognition[10], and ICA filters was demonstrated the successful classifying twelve facial actions of the upper and lower face [11]. PCA representation excluded the first 1 principal component can remove neutral expressions. ICA is a generalization of PCA which learns the high-order moments of the data in addition to the second-order moments [12]. We thought that ICA representation using PCA images excluded neutral expression components in full face could be used effectively in the facial expression recognition as well.

We present an approach to recognize facial expressions in various internal states using independent component analysis. We developed a representation of facial expression images based on independent component analysis for feature extraction of facial expressions. This representation consists of two steps. Firstly, we present a representation based on principal component analysis excluded the first 2 principal components to reflect well the changes in facial expressions. Secondly, ICA representation from this PCA images was developed. Finally, classification of facial expressions in various internal states was created on two dimensional structure of emotion having pleasure/displeasure dimension and arousal/sleep dimension.

2   Image Database

The face images used for this research were a subset of the Korean facial expression database based on dimension model of emotion [13]. The dimension model explains that the emotion states are not independent one another and related to each other in a systematic way. This model was proposed by Russell [7]. The dimension model also has cultural universals and it was proved by Osgood, May & Morrison and Russell, Lewicka & Niit [14, 15].

The data set with two dimension structure of emotion contained 498 images, 3 females and 3 males, each image using 640 by 480 pixels. Expressions were divided into two dimensions(Pleasure/Displeasure and Arousal/Sleep dimension) according to the study of internal states through the semantic analysis of words related with emotion by Younga et al. using 83 expressive words [16]. Each expressor of females and males posed 83 internal emotional state expressions when 83 words of emotion are presented. 51 experimental subjects rated pictures on the degrees of expression in each of the two dimensions on a nine-point scale. The images were labeled with a rating averaged over all subjects. Examples of the images are shown in figure 1. Figure 2 shows a result of the dimension analysis of 44 emotion words related to internal emotion states.

Fig. 1. Examples from the facial expression database in various internal emotional state expressions

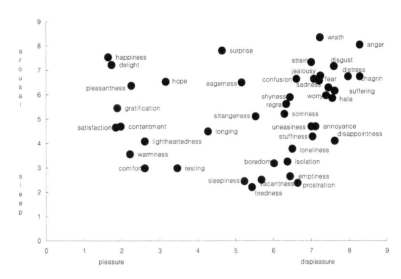

Fig. 2. The dimension analysis of 44 emotion words related to internal emotion states

3 Independent Component Representation of Facial Expressions

This section develops a representation of facial expression images based on independent component analysis for feature extraction. This representation consists of two steps. In the first step, we present a representation based on PCA excluded the first 2 principal components. Second, ICA representation from this PCA representation was developed.

3.1 PCA Representation Excluded Neutral Expressions

The face images used for this research were centered the face images with coordinates for eye and mouth locations, and then cropped and scaled to 20x20 pixels. The luminance was normalized in two steps. The rows of the images were concatenated to produce 1×400 dimensional vectors. The row means are subtracted from the dataset, X. Then X is passed through the zero-phase whitening filter, V, which is the inverse square root of the covariance matrix:

$$V = E\{ XX^T \}^{-\frac{1}{2}}, \quad Z = XV \tag{1}$$

From this process, Z removes much of the variability due to lightening. Atick and Redlich [17] have argued for such compact, decorrelated representations as a general coding strategy for the visual system. Redundancy reduction has been discussed in relation to the visual system at several levels. A first-order redundancy is mean luminance. The variance, a second order statistic, is the luminance contrast. PCA is a way of encoding second order dependencies in the input by rotating the axes to corresponding to directions of maximum covariance.

The first 1 or 2 principal components of PCA do not address the changes of facial expressions. It just displays the neutral face. That is to say, the neutral face means redundant codes in facial expressions. Figure 3(a) shows PCA representation that included the first 2 principal components. But selecting intermediate ranges of components that excluded the first 2 principal components of PCA do address well the changes in facial expression (Figure 3(b)).

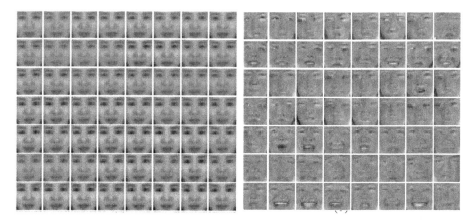

Fig. 3. (a) PCA representation only included the first 2 principal components (b) PCA representation excluded the first 2 principal components

To extract information of facial expression excluded redundant codes such as neutral expressions in facial expressions, we employed the 200 PCA coefficients, P_n, excluded the first 2 principal components of PCA of the face images. The principal component representation of the set of images in Z in Equation(1) based on P_n is defined as $Y_n = Z * P_n$. The approximation of Z is obtained as:

$$\overline{Z} = Y_n * P_n^T . \tag{2}$$

The columns of Y_n consist of input data $\hat{X}$ for ICA representation.

3.2 Independent Component Analysis Representation

Independent component analysis (ICA) is a generalization of principal component analysis, which decorrelates the high-order moments of the input [12]. Much of the important information is contained in the high-order statistics of the images. In a task such as facial expression recognition, a representational basis in which the high-order statistics are decorrelated should consider changes in facial expressions. Therefore, we applied images after excluding the high-order statistics such as neutral expressions for feature extraction of facial expressions to ICA representation.

The images were converted to vectors and comprised the rows of a 252x200 data matrix, $\hat{X}$. We assume the facial images in $\hat{X}$ to be a linear mixture of an known set of statistically independent source images U, where $A = W^{-1}$ is an unknown mixing matrix. The sources, U are gained by a matrix of learned filters, W. ICA representation is generated according to the following linear model

$$U = W \hat{X} \tag{3}$$

This model was based on the image synthesis model of Olshausen and Field [18], and was also employed by Bell and Sejnowski [19]. The weight matrix, W, was obtained by using the FastICA algorithm [20]. The FastICA algorithm computes the independent components that become uncorrelated by a whitening process and then maximizes non-Gaussianity of data distribution by using kurtosis maximization. The columns of the ICA output matrix, $W\hat{X} = U$ provided a factorial code for the training images in $\hat{X}$. Each column of U contained the coefficients of the basis images in A for reconstructing each images in $\hat{X}$. Figure 4 shows the factorial code representation in facial expression image. The columns of $A = W^{-1}$ consist of basis images for the ICA factorial representation(Fig. 5).

The representational code for the test images was found by $W\hat{X}_{test} = U_{test}$.

$\hat{X}_{test}$ was the matrix excluded the first 2 principal components of test images and W was the weight matrix gained by performed ICA on the training images.

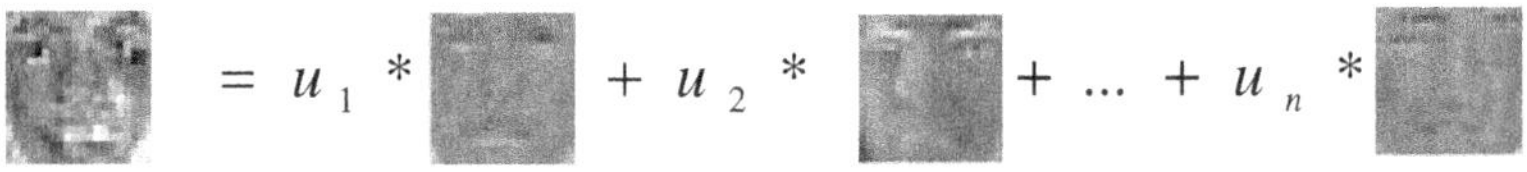

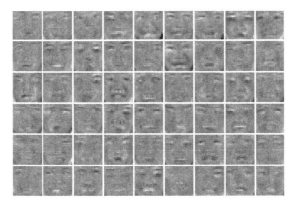

Fig. 4. ICA factorial representation=$(u_1, u_2, ..., u_n)$

Fig. 5. Basis images for the ICA factorial representation $(A = W^{-1})$

4   Recognition Performance

Facial expression recognition in various internal states was evaluated by the similarity measure on two dimensional structure of emotion having pleasure/displeasure dimension and arousal/sleep dimension. The coefficient vectors U in each of the two dimensions are given as vectors of U_{train} and U_{test}. Coefficient vectors in each test set were assigned to the class label of the coefficient vector in the training set that was most similar as evaluated by S:

$$S = \frac{U_{train} \cdot U_{test}}{\|U_{train}\|\|U_{test}\|} \min(\frac{\|U_{train}\|}{\|U_{test}\|}, \frac{\|U_{test}\|}{\|U_{train}\|}) . \tag{4}$$

252 images for training and 66 images excluded from the training set for testing are used. The first test verified with 252 facial images trained already. The recognition result by 252 images trained previously showed 100% recognition rates. The 66 images for test include 11 expression images of each six people. The class label consists of four sections on two dimensional structure of emotion. Figure 6 shows the sections of each class label.

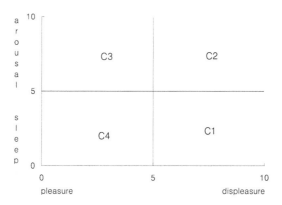

Fig. 6. The class region on two dimensional structure of emotion

Table 1 gives a result of facial expression recognition recognized by proposed algorithm on two dimensions of emotion and indicates a part of all. The recognition result in the Pleasure/Displeasure dimension of test set showed 90.9% and 66.6% in the Arousal/Sleep dimension. In Table 1, the first column indicates the emotion words of 11 expression images used for testing, the second and third columns include each dimension value on bipolar dimensions of test data. The fourth column in Table 1 indicates the class label(C1,C2,C3,C4) of test data and the classification results recognized by proposed algorithm are shown in the fifth column.

Table 1. A result data of facial expression recognition recognized by proposed algorithm (Abbreviation: P-D,pleasure/displeasure;A-S,arousal/sleep;)

Emotion word (person)	Test data P – D	A – S	Class label of test data	Recognized class label on proposed algorithm
depression(a)	6.23	4.43	1	4
crying(a)	6.47	4.10	1	1
gloomy(a)	7.37	5.53	2	1
strange(a)	6.17	5.17	1	1
proud(a)	3.07	4.47	4	4
confident(a)	3.47	4.57	4	1
despair(a)	6.23	5.97	2	2
sleepiness(a)	5.00	1.80	1	1
likable(a)	1.97	4.23	3	3
delight(a)	1.17	4.20	3	3
boredom(a)	6.77	5.50	2	2
pleasantness (b)	1.40	5.47	3	3
depression (b)	6.00	4.23	1	1
crying(b)	7.13	6.17	2	2
gloomy(b)	5.90	3.67	1	1
strangeness(b)	6.13	6.47	2	1
proud(b)	2.97	5.17	3	3
confident(b)	2.90	4.07	4	2
despair(b)	7.80	5.67	1	2
sleepiness(b)	6.00	1.93	4	3
likable(b)	2.07	4.27	4	2
delight(b)	1.70	5.70	3	2
gloomy(c)	6.60	3.83	1	1
strangeness(c)	6.03	5.67	2	2
proud(c)	2.00	4.53	4	4
confident(c)	2.47	5.27	4	4
despair (c)	6.47	5.03	2	2
sleepiness(c)	6.50	3.80	1	1
likable(c)	1.83	4.97	4	4
delight(c)	2.10	5.63	3	3
boredom(c)	6.47	5.73	2	1
tedious(c)	6.73	4.77	1	1
Jealousy(c)	6.87	6.80	2	2

5 Discussion

This paper presents a new approach method to recognize facial expressions in various internal states using independent component analysis. The recognition results of each dimension through similarity measure were significant 90.9% in Pleasure/Displeasure dimension and 66.6% in the Arousal/Sleep dimension. The two dimensional structure of emotion in the facial expression recognition appears as a stabled structure for the facial expression recognition.

Pleasure/Displeasure dimension was significant 90.9%, while Arousal-Sleep dimension was significant 66.6%. Pleasure-Displeasure dimension is analyzed as a more stable dimension than Arousal-Sleep dimension. When the full face was presented, facial expressions based ICA were successfully recognized. This findings means that holistic analysis is important for facial expression recognition. It may be reflected by PCA-based representation excluded the first 2 PCs components. Our result may be analyzed that the inference of emotional states within a subject from facial expressions may depends more on the Pleasure/Displeasure dimension than Arousal/Sleep dimension.

Our current results tested different expressions of same person. In the future work, we will consider real-time recognition on sequences of images and work in the person-independent mode recognizing new person's expressions.

Acknowledgements. This work was supported by the Korea Research Foundation Grant funded by the Korean Government (KRF-2005-042-D00285).

References

1. Bartlett, M., Viola, P., Sejnowski, T., Larsen, J., Hager, J., Ekman, P.: Classfying Facial Action. In: Advances in Neural Information Processing Systems 8. D. Touretzky et al. editors, MIT Press, Cambridge, MA (1996)
2. Essa, I., Pentland, A.:Coding, analysis, interpretation, and recognition of facial expressions. IEEE Transactions on Pattern Analysis and Machine Intelligence, **19** (1997) 757-763
3. Lien, J.: Automatic recognition of facial expressions using hidden Markov models and estimation of expression intensity. Ph.D. Thesis, Carnegie Mellon University, (1998)
4. Oliver, N. Pentland, A., Berard, F.: LAFTER:a real-time face and lips tracker with facial expression recognition. Pattern Recognition **33** (2000) 1369-1382
5. Cohen, I., Sebe, N., Garg, A., Chen, L. S., Huang, T. S.: Facial expression recognition from video sequence. Proc. Int'l Conf. Multimedia and Exp(ICME) (2002) 121-124
6. Peter J. L.: The emotion probe: Studies of motivation and attention. American Psychologist, 50(5) (1995) 372-385
7. Russell, J. A.: Evidence of convergent validity on the dimension of affect. Journal of Personality and Social Psychology, **30**, (1978) 1152-1168
8. Donato, G., Bartlett, M., Hager, J., Ekman, P. and Sejnowski, T.: Classifying facial actions, IEEE PAMI, 21(10) (1999) 974-989
9. Pantic, M., Rothkrantz, L.J.M.: Towards an Affect-Sensitive Multimodal Human Computer Interaction, Proc. Of IEEE. 91 1370-1390
10. Youngsuk S., Youngjoon A.: Facial expression recognition based on two dimensions without neutral expressions, LNCS(3711) (2005) 215-222
11. Bartlett, M.: Face Image analysis by unsupervised learning, Kluwer Academic Publishers (2001)
12. Comon, P.: Independent component analysis - a new concept? Signal processing 36 (1994) 287-314
13. Saebum, B., Jaehyun, H., Chansub, C.: Facial expression database for mapping facial expression onto internal state. '97 Emotion Conference of Korea, (1997) 215-219
14. Osgood, C. E., May, W.H. and Miron, M.S.: Cross-curtral universals of affective meaning. Urbana:University of Illinoise Press, (1975)
15. Russell, J. A., Lewicka, M. and Nitt, T.: A cross-cultural study of a circumplex model of affect. Journal of Personality and Social Psychology, 57, (1989) 848-856

16. Younga, K., Jinkwan, K., Sukyung, P., Kyungja, O., Chansub, C.: The study of dimension of internal states through word analysis about emotion. Korean Journal of the Science of Emotion and Sensibility, **1** (1998) 145-152
17. Atick, J., Redlich, A.: What does the retina know about natural scenes?, Neural Computation (4) (1992) 196-210
18. Olshasen, B. Field, D.: Natural image statistics and efficient coding, Network:computation in neural systems, 7(2) (1996) 333-340
19. Bell,A. Sejnowski, T.: The independent components of natural scenes areedge filters, Vision Research, 37(23) (1997) 3327-3338
20. Hyvarinen, A., Karhunen, J., Oja, E.: Independent component analysis, John Wiley & Sons, Inc. (2001)

Gender Identification on the Teeth Based on Principal Component Analysis Representation

Young-suk Shin

Department of Information and telecommunication Engineering, Chosun University, #375
Seosuk-dong, Dong-gu, Gwangju, 501-759, Korea
ysshin@chosun.ac.kr

Abstract. We present a new approach method for gender identification on the teeth based on PCA (principal component analysis) representation using geometric features of teeth such as the size and shape of the jaws, size of the teeth and teeth structure. In this paper we try to set forth the foundations of a biometric system for automatic evaluation of gender identification using dental geometric features. To create a gender identification system, a template based on PCA is created from dental data collected the plaster figures of teeth which were done at dental hospital, department of oral medicine. Templates of dental images based on PCA representation include the 18 principal components as the features for gender identification. The PCA basis vectors reflects well the features for gender identification in the whole of teeth. The classification for gender identification is generated based on the nearest neighbor (NN) algorithm. The gender identification performance in dental images of 50 person was 76%. The identified values in females and males were 79.3% and 71.4%, respectively.

1 Introduction

Gender differences in terms of structure and size of the teeth are frequently emphasized [1,2,3,4].

McCord et al. attempted to determine whether patients, dental students and prosthodontists could distinguish age and sex from photographs of trial arrangements. It was reported that they were difficult to distinguish sex or age [5]. Sellen et al. studied the fact that the outline forms through superimposition had an correlation among face, arch and tooth forms [6]. Semih et al. stated the experts were difficult to distinguish the gender by the visual assessment [4]. All of these approaches seem to provide a much improved method by anterior tooth selection, tooth face and arch form [4,6]. But these methods were unsuccessful in distinguishing the actual sex. Our algorithm utilizes information about differences in the size and shape of the jaws, size of the teeth and teeth structure.

In this paper, we present a new approach method for gender identification based on PCA (principal component analysis) using geometric features of teeth like the size and shape of the jaws, size of the teeth and teeth structure. First, we collected the plaster figures of teeth from the department of oral medicine in dental hospital. Second, we developed a representation of dental images based on PCA included the 18

F.J. Perales and R.B. Fisher (Eds.): AMDO 2006, LNCS 4069, pp. 300–304, 2006.
© Springer-Verlag Berlin Heidelberg 2006

principal components as the features for gender identification. Finally, the nearest neighbor (NN) algorithm for gender identification was applied.

2   PCA Representation for Gender Identification

2.1   Preprocessing

Dental data was a database of the plaster figures of teeth which were done at Chosun University dental hospital, department of oral medicine. The data set contained images of 350 individuals of males and females. Each person has two images in a upper jaw and lower jaw. The data set used for research contained 347 gray level images in a upper jaw, each image using 800 by 600 pixels. Examples of the original images are shown in figure 1.

The dental images were centered with fixed coordinates locations, and then cropped and dug the palatine by semi-automatic method with a teeth template. Finally, The images were scaled to 30x30 pixels. Figure 2(b) shows the image dug the palatine with a teeth template(Figure 2(a)).

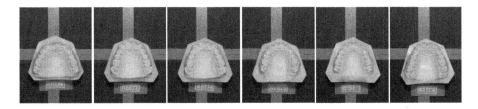

Fig. 1. Examples in a upper jaw from the dental database

(a)   (b)

Fig. 2. (a) A teeth template (b) A dental image dug by a teeth template (a)

The luminance was normalized in two steps. First, a "sphering" step prior to principal component analysis is performed. The rows of the images were concatenated to produce 1×900 dimensional vectors. The row means are subtracted from the dataset, X. Then X is passed through the zero-phase whitening filter, V, which is the inverse square root of the covariance matrix:

$$V = E\{XX^T\}^{-\frac{1}{2}}$$

$$W = XV$$

(1)

This indicates that the mean is set to zero and the variances are equalized as unit variances. Secondly, we subtract the local mean gray-scale value from the sphered each patch. From this process, W removes much of the variability due to lightening.

2.2 PCA Representation

PCA provides a dimensionality-reduced code that separates the correlations in the input. Atick and Redlich[7] have argued for such compact, decorrelated representations as a general coding strategy for the visual system. Redundancy reduction has been discussed in relation to the visual system at several levels. A first-order redundancy is mean luminance. The variance, a second order statistic, is the luminance contrast. PCA is a way of encoding second order dependencies in the input by rotating the axes to corresponding to directions of maximum covariance.

For gender identification based on dental feature, we employed the first 18 PCA coefficients, P_n. The principal component representation of the set of images in W in Equation(1) based on P_n is defined as $Y_n = W * P_n$. The approximation of W is obtained as:

$$\overline{W} = Y_n * P_n^T.$$ (2)

The columns of Y_n contains the representational codes for the training images. The representational code for the test images was found by $Y_{test} = W_{test} * P_n^T$ (see figure 3). Best performance for gender identification based on dental feature was obtained using the first 18 principal components.

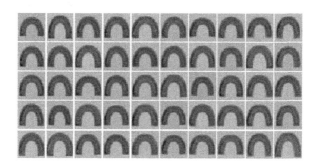

Fig. 3. PCA representation included the first 18 principal components

3 Results

Recognition performance for gender identification was evaluated by the coefficient vectors Y by the nearest neighbor (NN) algorithm. The principle of the NN algorithm is that of comparing input image patterns against a number of paradigms and then classifying the input pattern according to the class of the paradigm that gives the closest match.

The coefficient vectors Y are given as vectors of Y_{train} and Y_{test}. Coefficient vectors in each test set were assigned the class label of the coefficient vector in the training set that was most similar as evaluated by S:

$$S = \frac{Y_{train} \cdot Y_{test}}{\|Y_{train}\| \|Y_{test}\|} \min\left(\frac{\|Y_{train}\|}{\|Y_{test}\|}, \frac{\|Y_{test}\|}{\|Y_{train}\|}\right). \tag{3}$$

The first test verifies with 297 person images of upper jaw trained already. The recognition result was produced by 297 images trained previously showed 100% recognition rates. For testing, 50 person images excluded in the training set were used. The gender identification performance in 50 person dental images was 76%. The identified values in females and males were 79.3% and 71.4%, respectively.

4 Discussion and Conclusions

This paper propose a new approach method for gender identification based on principal component analysis using geometric features of teeth such as the size and shape of the jaws, size of the teeth and teeth structure. This simulation demonstrates that PCA representation included the first 18 principal components can solve a challenging problem for distinguishing the actual sex by the visual assessment from person. This result means PCA representation could detect some characteristic features for distinguishing teeth between female and male.

Our system extracts PCA representation included only the first 18 principal components from image scaled to 30x30 image and gender identification was produced over 76% recognition rates. It can reflect the fact that the global feature is important for gender identification based on geometric features of teeth such as the size and shape of the jaws, size of the teeth and teeth structure. The proportions of females and males identified 79.3% and 71.4%, respectively.

We suggest that PCA-based gender identification could identify the actual sex of the subjects correctly and the same in both evaluations. This can be explained by the fact that the experts, instead of basing on some objective parameters, usually make their decisions depending on their simultaneous perception and according to the accepted assumptions regarding the sex related differences of tooth forms.

References

1. Zarb, G., Bolender, C., Carlsson, G.: Boucher's prosthodontic treatment for edentulous patients, 11th ed. St. Louis:CV Mosby (1997) 326-328
2. Winker, S.: Essentials complete denture prosthodontics, 2nd ed. Massachusetts:PSG Publishing Comp (1998) 205-207
3. Hyde, T. McCord, F. Macfarlane, T., Smith, J.: Gender esthetics in the natural dentition, Eur J Prosthodont Rest Dent (1999) 27-30
4. Semih, B., Ufuk H., Burak, G.: Computer-based evaluation of gender identification and morphologic classification of tooth face and arch forms, Journal of prosthetic dentistry 88(6) (2002) 578-584

5. McCord J. Burke, T. Roberts, C., Deakin, M.: Perceptions of denture aesthetics: a two-centre study of denture wearers and denture providers, Aust Dent J. 39 (1994) 365-367
6. Sellen, P. Jagger, D. Harrison, A.: Computer-generated study of the correlation between tooth, face, arch form, and palatal contour, J. ProsthetDent, 80 (1998) 163-168
7. Atic, J., Redlich, A.: What does the retina know about natural scenes?, Neural Computation (4) (1992) 196-210

Grasp Motion Synthesis
Based on Object Features

Yoshihiro Yasumuro, Masayuki Yamazaki, Masataka Imura,
Yoshitsugu Manabe, and Kunihiro Chihara

Graduate School of Information Science, Nara Institute of Science and Technology,
8916-5, Takayama, Ikoma, Nara, 630-0192 Japan
{yasumuro, masayu-y, imura, manabe, chihara}@is.naist.jp
http://chihara.naist.jp

Abstract. This paper presents a new scheme for synthesizing hand motion to grasp various objects. Hand motion has a variety of expression with its high degrees of freedom and the functional motions are especially complex and difficult to synthesize. This paper focuses on a fact that actual grasp motion varies depending on the features of the object including its size and shape, which give important clues for reproducing a proper hand motion to manipulate them. Based on this idea, we propose a scheme to sample grasp motions and synthesize the whole hand motion including approach to the object, preparation of the hand shape and grab motion. Synthesized animation demonstrated a potential for easily designing functional motions for hand animation.

Keywords: Hand motion, grasp, motion capture, animation.

1 Introduction

Hand motion is one of the key aspects to provide reality for computer generated human figures, which may act in movies, video games and so forth. They may even show how to fasten your seatbelt on monitor displays when you are board on an aircraft. Computer graphics (CG) effectively shows instructions including some motions, while even just a simple and easy motion is hard to design sometimes.

We consider that the active hand motion can be roughly divided into gesture type and functional one. The gesture motion is used for showing some signs by specific hand's shapes or motion patterns. Whereas the most typical examples are finger alphabets and sign languages which have established systems, we use a lot of common gestures in daily life as well. While the gesture motions are performed with nothing in the hand, functional motions involve physical contacts and interactions with other objects when drinking a glass of water, opening the door, and every single behavior in the life. Grasp is one of the most fundamental and mostly initial motions among those quite a number of functional ones.

As for synthesizing the motion, linguistic systems and typical patterns in gesture type motion have advantages for systematically preparing the motion data and reusing them for generating a new motion [1,2,3]. On the other hand, a

F.J. Perales and R.B. Fisher (Eds.): AMDO 2006, LNCS 4069, pp. 305–314, 2006.
© Springer-Verlag Berlin Heidelberg 2006

functional motion varies so heavily depends on each object to be manipulated that systematic motion synthesis is difficult. This paper proposes a new systematic scheme for data preparation and synthesis of grasp motion, focusing on the target objects' features such as rough geometries and sizes.

2   Proposed Framework

Keyframing is one of the traditional and still powerful methods to create human motion. To prepare natural keyframes, constrain-based approaches are proposed for generating human-like postures [4,5]. In terms of dynamics of the hand motion and the task which involves physical interactions between the hand and the object, physical simulation is also effective method [6]. In either approaches, initial motion path is necessary for simulation in many cases. Minimization of a energy cost function can be also applied for planning a natural motion path.

This paper focuses especially on observations of actual human motion to grasp objects. It can be assumed that we intentionally/unintentionally comprehend the objects' information including shapes, sizes, functions, surface textures etc [7]. in the daily life and such comprehension leads us to select a proper way to grab the objects naturally. In fact, many objects' shapes are designed by expecting how to handle them; e.g. doorknobs, mug cups, switches in electronic products, and many other commodities.

Observation-based approach has been introduced in robotics researches for task learning by articulated robots [8,9]. Yahya captured whole body motions and stored them in a database, which is used for synthesizing motions of a virtual human who takes objects in a computer generated world [10]. Kitamura gathered hand motion data and categorized them by kinematics similarity for reusing to synthesize hand motions [11]. Ying focused hand shapes and object surface shapes and proposed a fast algorithm for shape feature matching between possible hand shape and the object surface [12]. Storing variety hand shape data allows producing suitable hand postures for arbitrary object to be grasped.

Our targeting framework is similar to that of the knowledge-based motion planning approach[13] and our approach to acquire the life-like motion rules is based on observing whole motions of the actual grasp. To record the various grasp behaviors for different geometry types of objects we employ optical motion capturing techniques, too. The target motion scenarios are categorized and prepared based on fundamental geometrical features of the objects and relative hand direction to approach them. As far as the shape of every single object can be approximated as combination of limited types of primitive geometry, it is possible to apply the sampled motion data to new motion synthesis. To adjust the synthesized data so as to grasp a new object properly, categorized motion pattern sets are available to refer for interpolating with respect to the feature parameter. Grasp motion is completed when the finger tips contact the surface of the object. This procedure can be achieved by collision detection techniques effectively.

3   Storing Grab Motion

3.1   Motion Capture

One of the popular devices for capturing hand postures and motions is glove type sensor, in which the finger motions are mainly considered as flexion and extension. However, especially for grasp motion, destinations of the finger tips are concentrated according to the object size. This motion requires a combination of adduction and flexion for each finger. We employed an optical motion capturing system (MAC3D System by Motion Analysis inc. [14]) to capture the precise differences of the finger motion arisen from variations of object's features. We settled the vision sensors as shown in Fig.1. As the optical markers are directly attached on the hand surface, whole hand motion is captured as time sequences of each markers position in an identical 3D space with less physical constraints. Additionally, we also put 3 markers on the wrist to record the approach path toward the object.

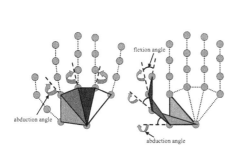

Fig. 1. Optical markers (left) and hand motion capture setup (right)

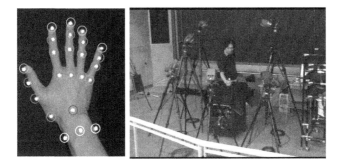

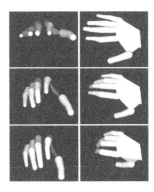

Fig. 2. Skeletal posture model

Fig. 3. Grasp motion with the proposed Model

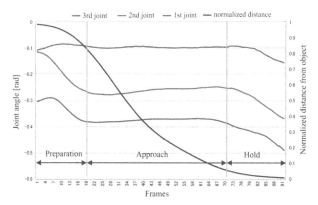

Fig. 4. Grasp motion phases

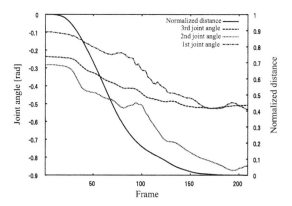

Fig. 5. Motion data for grasping cubic objects from the side

3.2 Hand Posture Model

Many traditional hand skeletal models have about 23 degrees of freedom (DOFs) [15]. They miss information about deformation of the back of the hand (equivalent to palm deformation) and twisting motion for the fingers. The directions of the rotation axes are varying during the flexion of the fingers[16]. To cover these DOFs and to allow flexible reusability of the captured motion data, we designed a skeletal model shown in Fig.2.

Fig.3 shows an example of sampled data for grasping a cylindrical object. As bending the fingers, palm shape is rounded and each rotational axis of the flexion slightly changed so that tips are gathered toward the middle finger and natural motion can be expressed by the skeletal model we prepared.

3.3 Captured Motion

Phases in Grasp Motion. Fig.4 shows flexion angles of an index finger and normalized distance from the object in a case of grasping top part of a cylinder shaped object. We recorded the motion from the same starting point in the

measurement setup and the distance from the wrist to the object can be normalized so that the start to the end is mapped as 1 to 0.

We divided the whole sequence of the grasp motion into three phases; prepare,
approach and hold. In the prepare phase, according to the targeted object's shape
and size, the whole shape of the hand and wrist direction are roughly determined.
Then approach phase gets close to the object, adjusting the hand shape. Finally,
each finger contacts the object with further flexion in the hold phase.

Grasp Patterns. We observed that the different object features lead different
grasp patterns for whole motion. Previously, a grasp motion profile in the case
of targeting the top of a cylinder (Fig.4) showed earlier preparation of the hand
shape to hold the target. In the case for targeting the side of the same cylinder
(Fig.5), hand is gradually opening during the approach. Fig. 6 shows profiles of
joint angles of index finger in grasping cubic objects. In the case of targeting a
larger cube (130mm width), 1st joint moves quickly to open the hand, adjusting

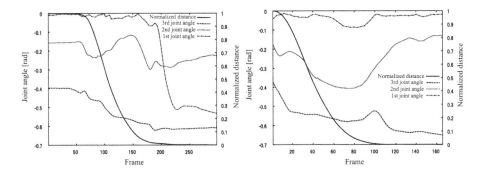

Fig. 6. Grasp data for different sizes of cubic objects (right: 45mm width, left: 130mm
width)

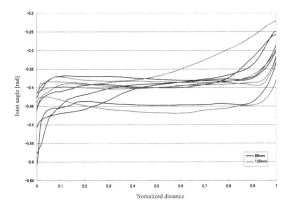

Fig. 7. Similar grasp patterns for the same object with different sizes

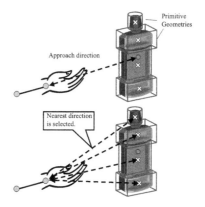

Fig. 8. Conceptural scheme for grasp generation

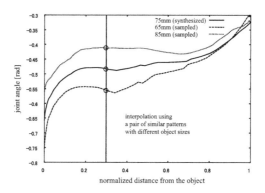

Fig. 9. Joint trajectory generation by interpolation among similar patterns

to the size of the target. For smaller cube (45mm width), 2nd joint is dominantly moved to adjust to the target size in grasp phase. We assured that motion pattern differences due to the type of object shape.

Fig.7 shows the cases for grasping top part of the cylinders of 95mm ϕ and 120 mm ϕ. X axis shows normalized distance. This profile represents similarity of the grasp pattern for the same shape object. Final finger shapes are different due to the sizes but analogy can be seen in each of the phase sequences.

4   Grab Motion Synthesis

4.1   Process

For synthesizing the grasp motion, the geometry of every virtual (CG) object are approximated as a single primitive or a combination of multiple primitives. Each grasp motion pattern is recorded in real motion capture. As shown in Fig. 8, the approach direction of the virtual hand indicates the primitive to be targeted. Thus the natural motion can be synthesized by referring similar patterns for grasping the same primitive type stored in the system beforehand. The

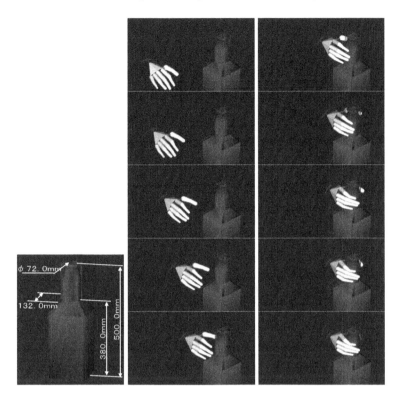

Fig. 10. A bottle object(left) and synthesized grasp for thin part of a bottle (right)

primitives are simple polyhedrons circumscribing the CG objects. Interpolating among the similar motion patterns for the different sizes of the same type of the primitive targets allows adjusting to any newly targeted primitive (Fig. 9). To complete the grasp motion, hold phase motion is extrapolated till every finger contacts the surface of the actual object, using collision detection technique. Fig. 9 shows synthesizing grasp for a 75mm ϕ cylinder primitive by interpolating the motion patterns of grasping a 65mm ϕ and a 85mm ϕ cylinder. For implementing collision detection process[17,18], we used a open library called ColDet[19].

4.2   Animation Synthesis

Fig.10(left) shows a target model of a bottle we used for demonstrating the proposed method. This target has 3 different primitives. Fig. ?? shows an animation sequence when grasping upper part of the bottle. Fig. 12 shows grasping lower part. On each figures, left row shows the wrist trajectory we gave to the system as an input. In this implementation, we manually assigned the primitives to the bottle objects. One of our future works is addressed to automatic process for estimating the rough topology, splitting into primitive parts and assigning the circumscribing polyhedron to the CG object. Many foregoing works for mesh

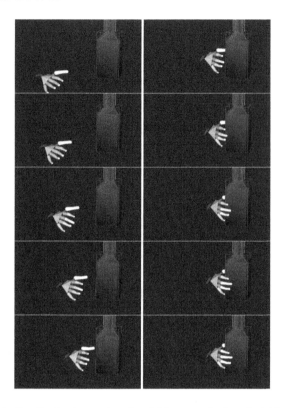

Fig. 11. Synthesized grasping for thick part of a bottle (side view)

simplification and polygon reduction techniques[20,21] can be applied for taking care of variety of CG objects to be grasped.

5   Discussion and Conclusion

This paper presented a new approach for reusing motion data for synthesizing grasp motion including approaching trajectory and grab motion. This approach gives an effective scheme for sampling and storing actual grasp motion as well. The proposed method is applicable for any polygonal CG object by assigning primitive geometry. Collision detection process also functions effectively to adjust the detailed shape of the object. We observed that some unnatural motions were generated when the contact timing of finger tips were too different. This is caused by extrapolation of the sampled motion data in grasp phase. Motion generation of each finger is basically terminated when contacting the surface of the object. However, earlier terminated finger motion is also to be extrapolated till all the other fingers reach the object surface in our current implementation. This force to extrapolate the measured position of a finger staying still and thus the finger may be bent in impossible direction by extrapolated (magnified) measurement noise. This situation can be avoided by independent control for terminating the motion synthesis for each finger.

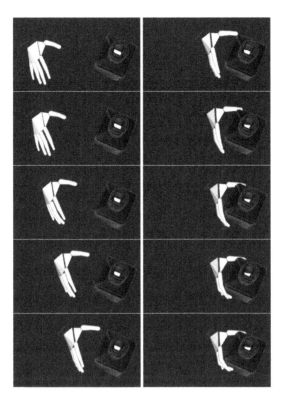

Fig. 12. Synthesized grasping for thick part of a bottle (top view)

Actually the measured data patterns are not always the same as we defined 3 phases even for the same person with the same object, however the motion itself is so natural in a way that this is one of the real grasp motions. However, our current implementation is not so flexible to synthesize various motion pattern for one condition. Our future work is to extend the proposed frame work to generate variation of possible motion patterns for the same object so that the user can adjust to the desired motion.

Acknowledgment

This work has been partly supported by a Grant-in-Aid for Scientific Research (B)(16700180) from the Ministry of Education, Culture, Sports, Science and Technology.

References

1. Vassilis Athitsos and Stan Sclaroff: Estimating 3D Hand Pose from a Cluttered Image, Boston University Computer Science Tech. Report, No.2003-009, 2003.
2. Vassilis Athitsos and Stan Sclaroff: Database Indexing Methods for 3D Hand Pose Estimation, Boston University Computer Science Tech. Report, No.2003-010, 2003.

3. Mikako Murakami, Yoshihiro Yasumuro, Tomohiro Kuroda, Yoshitsugu Manabe, Kunihiro Chihara: Modifier Representation in Sign Animation, Concurent Engineering: Advanced Design, Production and Management Systems, pp.989-994, 2003.
4. Jintae Lee, Tosiyasu L.Kunii: Constraint-Based Hand Animation, Springer-Varlag, Models and Techniques in Computaer Animation,Tokyo, pp.110-127, Jan.1993.
5. Yoshihiro Yasumuro, Qian Chen and Kunihiro Chihara: Three-dimensional Modeling of the Human Hand with Motion Constraints, Image and Vision Computing, Vol.17, No.2, pp.149-156, 1999.
6. Nancy S.Pollard and Victor B.Zordan: Physically Based Grasping Control from Example, ACM SIGGRAPH Symposium on Computer Animation, 2005.
7. Hiroshi Fukuda,Naohiro Fukumura,Masazumi Katayama and Yoji Uno: Relation between Object Recognition and Formation of Hand Shape - Computational Approach to the Human Grasping Movements -, Systems and Computers in JAPAN, Vol. 31,Issue 12,pp. 11-22, 2000.
8. Koichi Ogawara, Jun Takamatsu, Hiroshi Kimura, Katsushi Ikeuchi: Extraction of Essential Interactions Through Multiple Observations of Human Demonstrations, IEEE Trans. on Industrial Electronics, Vol.50, No.4, pp.667-675, 2003.
9. Yoshihiro Sato,Keni Bernardin,Hiroshi Kimura,Katsushi Ikeuchi:Task analysis based on observing hands and objects by vision, Proc.of 2002 IEEE/RSJ International Conference on Intelligent Robots and Systems, pp.1208-1213, 2002.
10. Yaha AYDIN,Masayuki NAKAJIMA: Database Guided Realistic Grasping Posture Generation Using Inverse Kinematics, IEICE TRANS.INF.& SYST., Vol.E81-D No.11, pp.1272-1280,Nov,1998.
11. Yoshifumi Kitamura, Tomohiko Higashi, Takayuki Iida, Fumio Kishino: Interactive computer animation of hand gestures using status estimation with multiple regression analysis, Computer Graphics Forum, Vol. 20, No. 3 (Proceedings of Eurographics 2001, 3-7 September 2001 Manchester, United Kingdom), pp. 251-259, 2001.
12. Ying Li,Nancy S.Pollard: A Shape Matching Algorithm for Synthesizing Humanlike Enveloping Grasps, IEEE-RAS International Conference on Humanoid Robots (Humanoids 2005), Tsukuba, Japan, 2005.
13. Hans Rijpkema, Michael Girard: hComputer Animation of Knowledge- Based Human Graspingh, ACM Computer Graphics, Vol.25, No.4, 1991.
14. MotionAnalysis: http://www.motionanalysis.com/
15. : Etsuko Ueda, Yoshio Matsumoto, Masakazu Imai, Tsukasa Ogasawara: Hand Pose Estimation Using Multi-Viewpoint Silhouette Images, Proceedings of 2001 IEEE/RSJ International Conference on Intelligent Robots and Systems (IROS'2001), pp.1989-1996, 2001.
16. Finger Joint Kinematics from MR Images: Natsuki MIYATA, Makiko KOUCHI, Masaaki MOCHIMARU, Tsuneya KURIHARA Proceedings of the 2005 IEEE/RSJ International Conference on Intelligent Robots and Systems, pp. 4110-4115, 2005.
17. G. van den Bergen: Efficient Collision Detection of Complex Deformable Models using AABB Trees. Journal of Graphics Tools, 2(4):1-13, 1997.
18. S. Gottschalk, M. C. Lin and D. Manocha: OBBTree: A Hierarchical Structure for Rapid Interference Detection, Proc. of ACM Siggraph'96, 1996.
19. ColDet Free 3D Collision Detection Library: http://photoneffect.com/coldet/
20. H.Hoppe: Progressive meshes, ACM SIGGRAPH 1996, pp.99-108,1996
21. J. Popovic,H. Hoppe: Progressive simplicial complexes, ACM SIGGRAPH 1997,pp.217-224,1997

Carrying Object Detection Using Pose Preserving Dynamic Shape Models

Chan-Su Lee and Ahmed Elgammal

Department of Computer Science,
Rutgers University, Piscataway, NJ, USA
{chansu, elgammal}@cs.rutgers.edu

Abstract. In this paper, we introduce a framework for carrying object detection in different people from different views using pose preserving dynamic shape models. We model dynamic shape deformations in different people using kinematics manifold embedding and decomposable generative models by kernel map and multilinear analysis. The generative model supports pose-preserving shape reconstruction in different people, views and body poses. Iterative estimation of shape style and view with pose preserving generative model allows estimation of outlier in addition to accurate body pose. The model is also used for hole filling in the background-subtracted silhouettes using mask generated from the best fitting shape model. Experimental results show accurate estimation of carrying objects with hole filling in discrete and continuous view variations.

1   Introduction

This paper presents a new approach for carrying object detection using a dynamic shape model of human motion with decomposition of body pose, shape style and view. To model nonlinear shape deformations by multiple factors, we propose kinematics manifold embedding and kernel mapping in addition to multilinear analysis of collected nonlinear mappings. The kinematics manifold embedding, which represents body configuration invariant to different people and views in low dimensional space based on motion captured data, is used to model dynamics of shape deformation according to intrinsic body configuration. The intrinsic body configuration has one-to-one correspondence with kinematics manifold (Sec. 2.1). Using this kinematics manifold embedding, individual differences of shape deformations can be solely contained in nonlinear mappings between manifold embedding points and observed shapes. By utilizing multilinear analysis for collection of these nonlinear mappings in different people and views, we can achieve decompositions of shape styles and views in addition to the body poses (Sec. 2.2). Iterative estimation of body pose, shape style and view parameters for the given decomposable generative model provides pose preserving, style preserving reconstruction of shape in different view human motion (Sec. 2.3).

The proposed pose preserving, dynamic shape models are used to detect carrying objects from sequences of silhouette images. The detection of carrying objects is one of the key element in visual surveillance systems [7]. The performance of gait recognition is degraded dramatically when people carry objects like briefcases [13]. Our pose-preserving dynamic shape model detects carrying objects as outliers. By removing

F.J. Perales and R.B. Fisher (Eds.): AMDO 2006, LNCS 4069, pp. 315–325, 2006.

outliers from extracted shape, we can estimate body pose and other factors accurately in spite of variations of shapes due to carrying objects (Sec. 3.3). Hole filling based on signed distance representation of shape (Sec. 3.1) also helps correcting shapes from inaccurate background subtraction (Sec. 3.2). Iterative procedure of hole filling and outlier detection using pose preserving shape reconstruction achieves gradual hole filling and advance in precision of carrying objects detection in iterations (Sec. 3.4). Experimental results using CMU Mobo gait database [6] and our own dataset from multiple views show accurate estimation of carrying object with correction of silhouettes from multiple people and multiple view silhouettes with holes (Sec. 4).

1.1 Related Work

There have been a lot of work on contour tracking from cluttered environment such as active shape models (ASM) [2], active contours [8], and exemplar-based tracking [15]. However, there are few works to model shape variations in different people and views as a generative model with capturing nonlinear shape deformations. The framework to separate the motion from the style in a generative fashion was introduced in [5] where the motion is represented in a low dimensional nonlinear manifold. Nonlinear manifold learning technique can be used to find intrinsic body configuration space [18,5]. However, discovered manifolds are twisted differently according to person styles, views, and other factors like clothes in image sequences [4]. We propose kinematics manifold embedding as an alternative uniform representation of intrinsic body configuration (Sec. 2.1).

In spite of the importance of carrying objects detection in visual surveillance system, there has been few works focused on carrying objects detection due to difficulties in modeling variations of shape due to carrying objects. By analyzing symmetry in silhouette model, carrying objects can be detected by aperiodic outlier regions [7]. Amplitude of the shape feature and the location of detected objects are constrained in [1] to improve accuracy of carrying object detection. Detecting outlier accurately and removing noise and filling hole in extracted silhouette still remains unresolved.

Shape models are used for segmentation and tracking using level sets [16,11]. Shape priors can be used for pose-preserving shape estimation. However, previous shape prior models like [11] cannot represent dynamic characteristics of shape deformations in human motion. This paper proposes gradual detection of outlier, and correction of noise silhouette by hole filling and outlier removal using pose-preserving dynamic shape model.

2   Pose Preserving Dynamic Shape Models

We can think of the shape of a dynamic object as instances driven from a generative model. Let $y_t \in \mathbb{R}^d$ be the shape of the object at time instance t represented as a point in a d-dimensional space. This instance of the shape is driven from a model in the form

$$y_t = \gamma(b_t; s, v), \tag{1}$$

where the $\gamma(\cdot)$ is a nonlinear mapping function that maps from a representation of the body pose b_t into the observation space given a mapping parameter s, v that characterizes shape style and view variations in a way independent of the configuration. Given this generative model, we can fully describe observation instance y_t by state parameters b_t, s, and v. In the generative model, we model body pose b_t invariant to the view and shape style. We need a unified representation for body configuration invariant to the variation of observation in different person and in different view. Kinematics manifold embedding is used for intrinsic manifold representation of body configuration b_t.

2.1 Kinematics Manifold Embedding

We find low dimensional representation of kinematics manifold by applying nonlinear dimensionality reduction techniques for motion captured data. We first convert joint angles of motion capture data into joint locations in three dimensional spaces. We align global transformation in advance in order to model motions only due to body configuration change. Locally linear embedding (LLE) [12] is applied to find low dimensional intrinsic representation from the high dimensional data (collections of joint locations). The discovered manifold is one-dimensional twisted circular manifold in three-dimensional spaces.

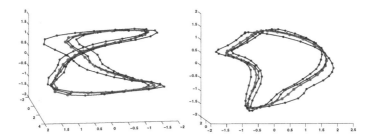

Fig. 1. Kinematics manifold embedding and its mean manifold: two different views in 3D space

The discovered manifold is represented using a one-dimensional parameter by spline fitting. We use multiple cycles to find kinematics intrinsic manifold representation by LLE. For the parametrization of kinematics manifold, we use mean-manifold representation from the multiple cycle manifold. The mean manifold can be found by averaging multiple cycles after detecting cycles by measuring geodesic distance along the manifold. The mean-manifold is parameterized by spline fitting by a one-dimensional parameter $\beta_t \in \mathbb{R}$ and a spline fitting function $g : \mathbb{R} \to \mathbb{R}^3$ that satisfies $b_t = g(\beta_t)$, which is used to map from the parameter space into the three dimensional embedding space. Fig. 1 shows a low dimensional manifold from multiple cycles motion captured data and their kinematics mean manifold representation.

2.2 Modeling Shape Variations Using Decomposable Generative Models

Individual variations of shape deformations can be discovered in the nonlinear mapping space between the kinematics manifold embedding and the observation in different people. If we have pose-aligned shapes for all the people, then it becomes relatively easy to model shape variations in different people. Similarly, as we have common representation of the body pose, all the differences of the shape deformation can be contained in the mapping between the embedding points and observation sequences. We employ nonlinear mapping based on empirical kernel map [14] to capture nonlinear deformation in difference body pose. There are three steps to model shape deformations in decomposable nonlinear generative models. Here we focus on walking sequence but the framework can be applicable to other motion analysis in different variation factors.

First, for a given shape deformation sequence, we detect gait cycles and embed collected shape deformation data to the intrinsic manifold. In our case, kinematics manifold is used for embedding in each detected gait cycle. As the kinematics manifold comes from constant speed walking motion captured data, we embed the shape sequence in equally spaced points along the manifold. Second, we learn nonlinear mappings between the kinematics embedding space and shape sequences. According to the representer theorem [9], we can find a nonlinear mapping that minimizes the regularized risk in the following form:

$$f(x) = \sum_{i=1}^{m} \alpha_i k(x_i, x),$$ (2)

for given patterns x_i and target values $y_i = f(x_i)$. The solutions lie on the linear span of kernels centered on data points. The theorem shows that any nonlinear mapping is equivalent to a linear projection from a kernel map space. In our case, this kernel map allows modeling of motion sequence with different number of frames as a common linear projection from the kernel map space. The mapping coefficients of the linear projection can be obtained by solving the linear system

$$[y_1^{sv} \cdots y_{N_{sv}}^{sv}] = C^{sv}[\psi(x_1^{sv}) \cdots \psi(x_{N_{sv}}^{sv})].$$ (3)

Given motion sequences with N_s shape styles and N_v views, we obtain $N_s \times N_v$ number of mapping coefficients. Third, multi-linear tensor analysis is applied to decompose the gait motion mappings into orthogonal factors. Tensor decomposition is achieved by higher-order singular value decomposition (HOSVD) [17], which is a generalization of SVD. All the coefficient vectors can be arranged in an order-three gait motion coefficient tensor $\mathscr{C}$ with a dimension of $N_s \times N_v \times N_c$, where N_c is the dimension of the mapping coefficients. The coefficient tensor can be decomposed as $\mathscr{C} = \mathscr{A} \times_1 S \times_2 V \times_3 F$ where S is the collection of the orthogonal basis for the shape style subspace. V represents the orthogonal basis of the view space and F represents the basis of the mapping coefficient space. $\mathscr{A}$ is a core tensor which governs the interactions among different mode bases.

The overall generative model can be expressed as

$$y_t = \mathscr{A} \times s \times v \times \psi(b_t).$$ (4)

The pose preserving reconstruction problem using this generative model is the estimation of parameter b_t, s, and v at each new frame given shape y^t.

2.3   Pose Preserving Reconstruction

When we know the state of the decomposable generative model, we can synthesize the corresponding dynamic shape. For given body pose parameter, we can reconstruct best fitting shape by estimating style parameter and view parameter with preserving the body pose. Similarly, when we know body pose parameter and view parameter, we can reconstruct best fitting shape by estimating style parameter with preserving view and body pose. If we want to synthesize new shape at time t for a given shape normalized input y_t, we need to estimate the body pose x_t, the view v, and the shape style s which minimize the reconstruction error

$$E(x_t, v, s) = || y_t - \mathcal{A} \times v \times s \times \psi(x_t) || . \tag{5}$$

We assume that the estimated optimal style can be written as a linear combination of style class vectors in the training model. Therefore, we need to solve for linear regression weights α such that $s^{est} = \sum_{k=1}^{K_s} \alpha_k s^k$ where each s^k is one of the K_s shape style vectors in the training data. Similarly for the view, we need to solve for weights β such that $v^{est} = \sum_{k=1}^{K_v} \beta_k v^k$ where each v^k is one of the K_v view class vectors.

If the shape style and view factors are known, then equation 5 reduces to a nonlinear 1-dimensional search problem for a body pose b_t on the kinematics manifold that minimizes the error. On the other hand, if the body pose and the shape style factor are known, we can obtain view conditional class probabilities $p(v^k|y_t, b_t, s)$ which is proportional to the observation likelihood $p(y_t | b_t, s, v^k)$. Such the likelihood can be estimated assuming a Gaussian density centered around $\mathcal{A} \times v^k \times s \times \psi(b_t)$, i.e., $p(y | b_t, s, v^k) \approx \mathcal{N}(\mathscr{C} \times v^k \times s \times \psi(b_t), \Sigma^{v^k})$.

Given view class probabilities we can set the weights to $\beta_k = p(v^k | y, b_t, s)$. Similarly, if the body pose and the view factor are known, we can obtain the shape style weights by evaluating the shape factor given each shape style class vector s^k assuming a Gaussian density centered at $C \times v \times s^k \times \psi(b_t)$. An iterative procedure similar to a deterministic annealing where in the beginning the each view and shape style weights are forced to be close to uniform weights to avoid hard decisions about view and shape style classes, is used to estimate x_t, v, s from given input y_t. To achieve this, we use variables, view and style class variances, that are uniform to all classes and are defined as $\Sigma^e = T_v \sigma_v^2 I$ and $\Sigma^s = T_s \sigma_s^2 I$ respectively. The parameters T_v and T_s start with large values and are gradually reduced and in each step and a new configuration estimate is computed.

3   Carrying Object Detection

We can detect carrying objects by iterative estimation of outlier using the generative model that can synthesize pose-preserving shapes. In order to achieve better alignment in normalized shape representation, we performed hole filling and outlier removal for the extracted shape iteratively.

3.1   Shape Representation

For consistent representation of shape deformations in variant factors, we normalize silhouette shapes by resizing and re-centering. To be invariant to the distance from camera and different height in each subject, we normalized the extracted silhouette height from background-subtracted silhouettes. In addition, the horizontal center of the shape is re-centered by the center of gravity of silhouette blocks. We use silhouette blocks whose sizes are larger than a specific threshold value for consistent centering of shape in spite of small incorrect background block due to noise and shadow. we perform normalization after morphological operation and filtering to remove noise spot and small holes.

We parameterize the motion shape contour using signed distance function with limitation of maximum distance for robust shape representation in learning and matching shape contour. Implicit function $z(x)$ at each pixel x such that $z(x) = 0$ on the contour, $z(x) > 0$ inside the contour, and $z(x) < 0$ outside the contour are used, which is typically used in level-set methods [10]. We add threshold values $d_c^{TH_p} - d_c^{TH_n}$ as follows,

$$z(x) = \begin{cases} d_c^{TH_p} & d_c(x) \geq d_c^{TH_p} \\ d_c(x) & x \text{ inside } c \\ 0 & x \text{ on } c \\ -d_c(x) & x \text{ outside } c \\ -d_c^{TH_n} & -d_c(x) \leq -d_c^{TH_n} \end{cases} \tag{6}$$

where the $d_c(x)$ is the distance to the closest point on the contour c with a positive sign inside the contour and a negative sign outside the contour. We threshold distance value $d_c(x)$ by $d_c^{TH_p}$ and $-d_c^{TH_n}$ as the distance value beyond certain distance does not contain meaningful shape information in similarity measurements. Such representation imposes smoothness on the distance between shapes and robustness to noise and outlier. In addition, by changing threshold value gradually, we can generate mask to represent inside of the shape, which is useful in gradual hole filling. Given such representation, an input shape sequence is points in a d dimensional space, $y_i \in \mathbb{R}^d, i = 1, \cdots, N$ where all the input shapes are normalized and registered and d is the dimensionality of the input shape vector , and N is the number of frame in the sequence.

3.2   Hole Filling

We fill holes in the background-subtracted shape to attain more accurate normalized shape representation. When the foreground color and the background color are the same, most of the background subtracted shape silhouettes have holes inside the extracted shape. This can cause inaccurate description of shape in normalization and in signed distance representation. A Hole can induce misalignment in normalized shape as the hole can cause shifting the center of gravity for the horizontal axis alignment. In addition, holes inside shape result in inaccurate shape description in signed distance representation. So, holes can cause incorrect estimations of the best fitting shape to the given observation.

We utilize *inside shape mask* generated from shape models to fill holes in the original shape. We can generate the mask to represent inside of the shape for estimated style, view, and body pose parameters by threshold in the signed distance representation.

$$h(x)_{hole\,mask} = \begin{cases} 1 & d_c(x) \geq d_c^{TH_{hole}} \\ 0 & \text{otherwise} \end{cases}, \tag{7}$$

where $d_c^{TH_{hole}} \geq 0$ is the threshold value for the inner shape mask for hole filling. If the threshold value is zero, the mask will be the same as the silhouette image generated by the nonlinear shape model for the given style, view and configuration. As we don't know the exact shape style, view and configuration at the beginning, and as holes can causes misalignments, we start from a large threshold value, which generates a small mask of the inner shape area in order to be robust to any misalignment and inaccurate state estimation. We reduce the threshold value as estimated model parameters get more accurate.

The hole filling operation can be described by $y_{hole\ filling} = z(\text{bin}(y) \oplus h(y^{est}))$, where $\oplus$ is logical OR operator to combine extracted foreground silhouette and mask area, $\text{bin}(\cdot)$ converts signed distance shape representation into binary representation, and $z(\cdot)$ convert binary representation into signed distance representation with threshold. Fig. 2 shows an initial shape normalized silhouette with holes (a), the best estimated shape model (b) which is generated from the generative model with estimated style and view parameters and body configuration, and the hole mask (c) when $d_c^{TH_{hole}} = 3$, and a new shape after hole filling (d). We improve the best matching shape by excluding mask area in the computation of the similarity measurement for generated samples in searching the best fitting body pose. Re-alignment of the shape and re-computation of the shape representation after hole filling provide better shape description for next iteration.

(a)   (b)   (c)   (d)   (e)   (f)   (g)   (h)

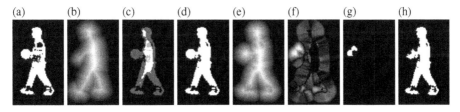

Fig. 2. Hole filling using mask from the best fitting model : (a) Initial normalized shape with holes. (b) The best matching shape. (c) Overlapping with initial silhouette and mask from the best matching shape. (d) New shape with hole filling. (e) A normalized shape for outlier detection. (f) Euclidian distance error. (g) Detected outliers. (h) A new shape after outlier removal.

3.3 Carrying Object Detection

Carrying objects are detected by estimating outliers from the best matching normal dynamic shape from the given input shape. Outliers of a shape silhouette with carrying objects are mismatching parts in input shape compared with the best matching normal walking shape. Carrying objects are the major source of mismatching when we compare with normal walking shape even though other factors such as inaccurate shape extraction, shape misalignment can also cause mismatches. For accurate detection of carrying objects from outliers, we need to remove other source of outlier such as holes and misalignment in shapes. Hole filling and outlier removal are performed iteratively to improve shape representation for better estimation of the matching shape.

We gradually reduce the threshold value for outlier detection to get more precise estimation of outlier progressively. The mismatching error $e(x)$ is measured by Euclidian distance between signed distance input shape and best matching shape generated from the dynamic shape model,

$$e_c(x) = ||z_c(x) - z_c^{est}(x)|| \,. \qquad (8)$$

The error $e(x)$ increases linearly as the outlier goes away from the matching shape contour due to signed distance representation. By threshold the error distance, we can detect outliers.

$$O(x)_{outlier\,mask} = \begin{cases} 1 & e_c(x) \geq e_c^{TH_{outlier}} \\ 0 & \text{otherwise} \end{cases}, \qquad (9)$$

At the beginning, we start from large $e_c^{TH_{outlier}}$ value. We reduce the threshold value gradually. Whenever we detect outliers, we remove the detected outlier areas and perform realignment to reduce misalignment due to the outliers. In Fig. 2, for given signed distance input shape (e), we measure mismatching error (f) by comparing with best matching shape (b). Outlier is detected (g) with given threshold value $e_c^{TH_{outlier}} = 5$, and new shape for next iteration is generated by removing outlier (h). This outlier detection and removal procedure is combined with hole filling as both of them help accurate alignment of shape and estimation of the best matching shape.

3.4   Iterative Estimation of Outliers with Hole Filling

An iterative gradual estimation of outliers, hole filling and outlier removal is performed by threshold value control. The threshold value for hole filling and the threshold value for outlier detection need to be decreased to get more precise in the outlier detection and hole filling in each iteration. In addition, we control the number of samples to search body pose for estimated view and shape style. At the initial stage, as we don't know accurate shape style and view, we use small number of samples along the equally distant manifold points. As the estimation progress, we increase accuracy of body pose estmation with increased number of samples. We summarize the iterative estimation as follows:

Input: image shape y_b, estimated view v, estimated style s, core tensor $\mathscr{A}$

Initialization: – initialize sample num N_{sp}, $d_c^{TH_{hole}}$, $e_c^{TH_{outlier}}$

Iterate: – Generate N_{sp} samples y_i^{sp} $b_i, i = 1, \cdots, N_{sp}$
   • Coefficient $C = \mathscr{A} \times s \times v$
   • embedding $b_i = g(\beta_i)$, $\beta_i = \frac{i}{M_{sp}}$
  – Generate hole filling mask $h_i = h(y_i^{sp})$
  – Update input with hole filling $y_{hole\,filling} = z(\text{bin}(y) \oplus h_i(y^{est}))$
  – Estimate best fitting shape with hole filling mask: 1-D search for y^{est} that minimizes $E(b_i) = ||y_{hole\,filling} - h_i(C\psi(b_i))||$
  – Compute outlier error $e_c(x) = ||y_{hole\,filling} - y^{est}(x)||$
  – Estimate outlier $o_{outlier}(x) = e_c(x) \geq e_c^{TH_{outlier}}$

Update: – reduce $d_c^{TH_{hole}}$, $e_c^{TH_{outlier}}$
  – increase N_{sp}

Based on the best matching shape, we compute outliers from the initial source after re-centering initial source.

4   Experimental Results

We evaluated our method using two gait-database. One is from CMU Mobo data set and the other is our own dataset with multiple view gait sequences. Robust outlier detection in spite of holes in the silhouette images was shown clearly in CMU database. We collected our own data set to show carrying object detection in continuous view variations.

4.1   Carrying Ball Detection from Multiple Views

The CMU Mobo database contains 25 subjects with 6 different views walking on the treadmill to study human locomotion as a biometric [6]. The database provides silhouette sequences extracted using one background image. Most of the sequences have holes in the background subtracted silhouette sequences. We collected $12(= 4 \times 3)$ cycles to learn dynamic shape models with view and style variations from normal slow walking sequences of 4 subjects with 3 different views. For the training sequences, we corrected holes manually. Fig. 3 shows detected carrying objects in two different views from different people. The initial normalized shape has holes with a carrying ball (a)(e). Still the best fitting shape models recover correct body pose after iterative estimations of view and shape style with hole filling and outlier removal (b)(f). Fig. 3 (c)(g) show examples of generated masks during iteration for hole filling. Fig. 3 (d) (h) show detected outlier after iteration. In Fig. 3 (h), the outlier in bottom right corner comes from the inaccurate background subtraction outside the subject, which cannot be managed by hole filling. The verification routine based on temporal characteristics of the outlier similar to [1] can be used to exclude such a outlier from detected carrying objects.

(a)   (b)   (c)   (d)   (e)   (f)   (g)   (h)

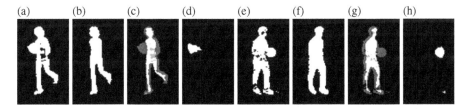

Fig. 3. Outlier detection in different view: (a) Initial normalized shape for outlier detection. (b) The best fitting model from the generative model. (c) Overlapping initial input and hole filling mask at the last iteration. (d) Detected outlier. (e) (f) (g) (h) : Another view in different person.

4.2   Carrying Object Detection with Continuous View Variations

We collected 4 people with 7 different views to learn the nonlinear decomposable dynamic shape model of normal walking for detection of carrying objects in continuous view variations. In order to achieve reasonable multiple view interpolation, we captured normal gait sequence on the treadmill with the same height camera position in our lab. The test sequence is captured separately in outdoor using commercial camcorder. Fig. 4 shows an example sequence of carrying object detection in continuous change of walking direction. The first row shows original input images from the camcorder. The second

Frame 1   Frame 15   Frame 30   Frame 45   Frame 60   Frame 75   Frame 90   Frame 105

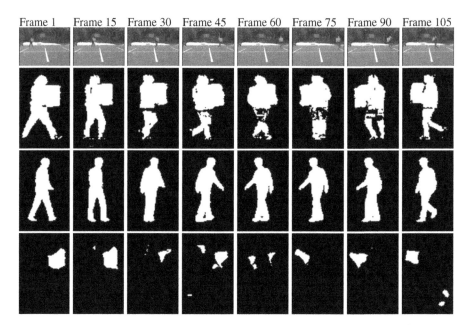

Fig. 4. Outlier detection in continuous view variations: First row: Input image. Second row: Extracted silhouette shape. Third row: Best matching shape. Fourth row: Detected carrying objects.

row shows normalized shape after background subtraction. We used the nonparametric kernel density estimation method for per-pixel background models, which is proposed in [3]. The third row shows best matching shape estimated after hole filling and outlier removal using dynamic shape models with multiple views. The fourth row shows detected outliers. Most of the dominant outliers come from the carrying objects.

5   Conclusions

We presented a new framework for carrying object detection from given silhouette images based on pose preserving dynamic shape model. The signed distance representation of shape helps robust matching in spite of small misalignment and hole. To enhance the accuracy of alignment and matching, we preformed hole filling and outlier detection iteratively with threshold control. Experimental results from CMU Mobo data set show accurate detection of outliers in multiple fixed views. We also showed the estimation of outliers in continuous view variations from our collected data set. The removal of outlier or carrying object will be useful for gait recognition as it helps recovering high quality original silhouette, which is important in gait recognition. We plan to apply the proposed method to test gait recognition with carrying objects.

Acknowledgement. This research is partially funded by NSF award IIS-0328991.

References

1. C. BenAbdelkader and L. S. Davis. Detection of people carrying objects: A motion-based recognition approach. In *Proc. of FGR*, pages 378–383, 2002.
2. T. F. Cootes, C. J. Taylor, D. H. Cooper, and J. Graham. Active shape models: Their training and applications. *CVIU*, 61(1):38–59, 1995.
3. A. Elgammal, D. Harwood, and L. Davis. Background and foreground modeling using non-parametric kernel density estimation for visual surveillance. *IEEE Proceedings*, 90(7):1151–1163, 2002.
4. A. Elgammal and C.-S. Lee. Inferring 3d body pose from silhouettes using activity manifold learning. In *Proc. CVPR*, volume 2, pages 681–688, 2004.
5. A. Elgammal and C.-S. Lee. Separating style and content on a nonlinear manifold. In *Proc. CVPR*, volume 1, pages 478–485, 2004.
6. R. Gross and J. Shi. The cmu motion of body (mobo) database. Technical Report TR-01-18, Carnegie Mellon University, 2001.
7. I. Haritaoglu, R. Cutler, D. Harwood, and L. S. Davis. Packpack: Detection of people carrying objects using silhouettes. In *Proc. of ICCV*, pages 102–107, 1999.
8. M. Isard and A. Blake. Condensation–conditional density propagation for visual tracking. *Int.J.Computer Vision*, 29(1):5–28, 1998.
9. G. Kimeldorf and G. Wahba. Some results on tchebycheffian spline functions. *J. Math. Anal. Applic.*, 33:82–95, 1971.
10. S. Osher and N. Paragios. *Geometric Level Set Methods*. Springer, 2003.
11. M. Rousson and N. Paragios. Shape priors for level set representations. In *Proc. ECCV, LNCS 2351*, pages 78–92, 2002.
12. S. Roweis and L. Saul. Nonlinear dimensionality reduction by locally linar embedding. *Science*, 290(5500):2323–2326, 2000.
13. S. Sarkar, P. J. Phillips, Z. Liu, I. R. Vega, P. Grother, and K. W. Bowyer. The humanid gait challenge problem: Data sets, performance, and analysis. *IEEE Trans. PAMI*, 27(2):162–177, 2005.
14. B. Schlkopf and A. Smola. *Learning with Kernels: Support Vector Machines, Regularization, Optimization and Beyond*. MIT Press, 2002.
15. K. Toyama and A. Blake. Probabilistic tracking in a metric space. In *ICCV*, pages 50–59, 2001.
16. A. Tsai, A. Yezzi, W. Wells, C. Tempany, D. Tucker, A. Fan, and W. E. Grimson. A shape-based approach to the segmentation of medical imagery using level sets. *IEEE Trans. on Medical Imaging*, 22(2), 2003.
17. M. A. O. Vasilescu and D. Terzopoulos. Multilinear subspace analysis of image ensembles. In *Proc. of CVPR*, 2003.
18. Q. Wang, G. Xu, and H. Ai. Learning object intrinsic structure for robust visual tracking. In *CVPR*, volume 2, pages 227–233, 2003.

Person Recognition Using Human Head Motion Information

Federico Matta and Jean-Luc Dugelay

Eurecom Institute,
2229 route des Cretes, B.P. 193
06904 Sophia Antipolis, France
Federico.Matta@eurecom.fr, Jean-Luc.Dugelay@eurecom.fr

Abstract. This paper describes a new approach for identity recognition using video sequences. While most image and video recognition systems discriminate identities using physical information only, our approach exploits the behavioural information of head dynamics; in particular the displacement signals of few head features directly extracted at the image plane level. Due to the lack of standard video database, identification and verification scores have been obtained using a small collection of video sequences; the results for this new approach are nevertheless promising.

1 Introduction

In the past few decades, there has been intensive research and great strides in designing and developing algorithms for face recognition from still images; only recently the problem of recognizing people using video sequences has started to attract the attention of the research community. Compared with conventional still image face recognition, video person recognition offers several new challenges and opportunities; in fact, image sequences not only provide aboundant data for pixel-based techniques, but also record the temporal information and evolution of the individual.

The area of automatic face recognition has been dominated by systems using physical information, such as greylevel values; while these systems have indeed produced very low error rates, they ignore the behavioural information that can be used for discriminating identities. Then, most of these strategies have been developed using perfectly normalized image databases, but for actual applications it would be better to work on common data; for example, low quality compressed sequences or video surveillance shots.

In this paper, we propose a new person recognition system based on displacement signals of a few head features, automatically extracted from a short video sequence. Instead of tracking the head as a whole, its movement is analysed by retrieving the displacements of the eyes, nose and mouth in each video frame. Statistical features are then computed from these signals, in order to extract the motion information from the video, and used for discriminating identities; the classification task is done using a Gaussian Mixture Model (GMM) approximation and Bayesian classifier.

F.J. Perales and R.B. Fisher (Eds.): AMDO 2006, LNCS 4069, pp. 326–335, 2006.
© Springer-Verlag Berlin Heidelberg 2006

The rest of the paper is organized as follows: we briefly cite the most relevant works in section 2, then we detail our recognition system in section 3, after that we report and comment our experiments in section 4 and finally we conclude this paper with remarks and future works in section 5.

2   Related Works

While numerous tracking and recognition algorithms have been proposed in the computer vision community, these two topics were usually studied separately. For human face tracking, many different techniques have been developed, such as subspace-based methods [1], pixel-based tracking algorithms [2], contour-based tracking algorithms [3,4,5], and global statistics of color histograms [3,6]. Likewise, there is a rich literature on face recognition published in the last 15 years [7,8]; however, most of these works deal mainly with still images. Moreover, a great part of the video face recognition techniques are straightforward generalizations of image face recognition algorithms: in these systems, the still image recognition strategy is applied independently for each frame, without taking into account the temporal information enclosed in the sequence. Among the few attempts aiming to address the problem of video person recognition in a more systematic and unified manner, the methods by Li & Chellappa [9], Zhou *et al.* [10] and Lee *et al.* [11] are the most relevant: all of them develop a tracking and recognition method using a unified probabilistic framework.

Our work is also closely related to the visual analysis of human motion, in particular with the automatic gait recognition (field of research). It is possible to classify the most important techniques in two distinct areas: holisitic approaches [12,13], which aim to extract statistical features from a subject's silhouette in order to differentiate between individuals, and model-based approaches [14,15], which aim to model human gait explicitly.

3   Recognition Using Head Displacements

Our person recognition system is mainly composed by three parts: a video analyser for obtaining displacement signals, a feature extractor for computing feature vectors, and a person classifier for retrieving identities.

3.1   Video Analyser Module

The video analyser module takes as an input a video shot, representing few seconds of a speaker. The head detection part is done semi-automatically: the user must manually click on the (face) features of interest in the first frame, then a tracking algorithm continues until the end of the sequence. In fact, the displacement signals are automatically retrieved using a template matching technique in the RGB color space. The similarity measure is obtained by computing an Euclidean or city-block distance for each color component, then adding them (equal component weighting). If $\mathbf{T}_k$ is the actual template, $\mathbf{T}_{k-1}$ the previous one, $\mathbf{M}_{k-1}$ the latest match and α a weighting constant, then the template is updated with the following rule: $\mathbf{T}_k = \alpha \mathbf{M}_{k-1} + (1 - \alpha) \mathbf{T}_{k-1}$. One can easily verify that the actual template is a weighted sum of all the previous ones and it can be set to include the limit cases of no update ($\alpha = 0$) and full update ($\alpha = 1$).

3.2   Feature Extractor Module

The feature extractor module deals with rough displacement signals of different head features, extracted from the video sequence.

In order to compute the feature vector, the system applies some global transformations to the displacement signals, that are likely to normalize them and provide a better representation for the classification task. By default, this module centers the signals and scales them, in order to remove any dependence on absolute head position and video resolution; it is also possible to impose an uniform variance, exploit polar coordinates or compute derivatives (like velocities or accelerations). It is important to notice that each signal has two components, usually the horizontal and vertical displacements, so the total number of different features F is the double of the number of face elements analyzed. In the following part, we are going to express all the feature vectors of a person q, extracted from his r-th video, with the following notation:

$$\mathbf{X}^{(q,r)} = \begin{bmatrix} \mathbf{x}_1^{(q,r)} \\ \vdots \\ \mathbf{x}_K^{(q,r)} \end{bmatrix}$$

where K is the total number of frames and $\mathbf{x}_k$ is a row vector representing the feature values computed from frame k.

3.3   Person Recogniser Module

The last module exploits the feature vectors computed from video sequences for classification purposes.

The processed head displacements are used for training a Gaussian Mixture Model (GMM) for each person in the database, in order to model the characteristic displacements (or its derivatives) for that user; more precisely, the algorithm estimates the class-conditional probability density functions in a Bayesian classifier. Formally, the posterior probability for class ω_q is:

$$P\left(\omega_q \mid \mathbf{x}_k\right) = \frac{P\left(\mathbf{x}_k \mid \omega_q\right) P\left(\omega_q\right)}{P\left(\mathbf{x}_k\right)}$$

In our case, where each user has the same amount of videos, the priors and scaling factors are uniform and does not affect the posterior probability computation. The global video score is computed by making the assumption that displacements are independent (which is actually not true for our case) and by taking the product of individual probabilities,

$$P(\omega_q \mid \mathbf{X}) \simeq \prod_{k=1}^{K} P(\omega_q \mid \mathbf{x}_k)$$

The class-conditional probability functions of each frame, $P(\omega_q \mid \mathbf{x}_k)$, are approximated using a Gaussian Mixture Model (GMM); in formulas:

$$P(\omega_q \mid \mathbf{x}_k) = \sum_{c=1}^{C} \alpha_c \aleph(\mathbf{x}_k; \mu_c, \mathbf{\Sigma}_c)$$

where α_c is the weight of the c-th Gaussian component, $\aleph(\mathbf{x}_k; \mu_c, \mathbf{\Sigma}_c)$.

It is important to underline that a part of the videos in the database is used for training those models, while the remaining sequences are used as tests for assessing the recognition performances (identification and verification scores).

4   Experiments and Results

4.1   Data Collection

Due to the lack of any standard video database for evaluating video person recognition algorithms, we collected a set of 144 video sequences of 9 different persons, for the task of training and testing our system. The video chunks are showing TV speakers, announcing the news of the day: they have been extracted from different clips during a period of 6 months. A typical sequence has a spatial resolution of $352 \times 288\,pixels$ and a temporal resolution of $23.97\,frames/second$, and lasts almost $14\,seconds$ (refer to Figure 1 for an example). Even though the videos are low quality, compressed at $300\,Kbits/second$ (including audio), the behavioural approach of our system is less affected by the visual errors, introduced during the compression process, than the pixel-based methods. Moreover, the videos are taken from a real case: the behaviour of the speakers is natural, without any constraint imposed to their movement, pose or action.

4.2   Experimental Set-Up

For our experiments, we selected 72 video sequences for training (8 for each of the 9 individuals), and the remaining 72 (out of 144) were left for testing. It is important to point out that there are no theoretical constraints concerning the number of videos per user and the total video chunks; on the other hand, it is necessary to have a few minutes for each individual for being able to learn the characteristical head motion and to train the individual GMMs.

We chose to extract the displacements of 4 head features - the eyes, nose and mouth - providing then 8 signals in total. During our experiments, we tested multiple configurations concerning the number of features to extract. The experimental results obtained using only two signals, like the eye displacements,

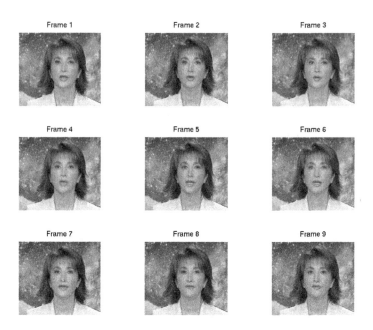

Fig. 1. The first 9 frames of a video sequence

were not as good as the actual choice of 4. We believe that even if our algorithm tracks the head in the image plane, the originating $3D$ movement - which can be represented with six parameters in the $3D$ space - needs more than just two points for proper estimation; moreover, more feature points may provide a higher precision for the global motion and can be sensible to small local deformations of the face (due to relative movement of the features).

As stated in section 3.1, the head detection part is done semi-automatically: the user must manually click on the (face) features of interest in the first frame, then then a tracking algorithm continues until the end of the sequence. After the localization of the head features - the eyes, nose and mouth - four templates of fixed size ($19 \times 25\,pixels$) are computed using the update formula. For the automatic tracking process, keeping the initial template ($\alpha = 0$) has showed the best discriminating properties, even if the algorithms is not always returning the correct match (absence of update); knowing the computational burden of a full template matching, we optimized the search window by taking into account the position of each feature and consequently analysing only small regions of the video frame ($74 \times 74\,pixels$).

Concerning the signal normalization, the most relevant results have been obtained using zero-mean; in fact, stronger constraints, like an uniform range or fixed variance, reduced the discriminating power and were abandoned. It is important to notice that in our case all the videos have almost equal head sizes and zooms, so there is no need for spatial scaling. We also tried to compute our feature vectors using first and second derivatives of the displacement signals - as velocities and accelerations - but the resulting recognition scores were not better than using only the original displacements.

For training the individual GMMs, we obtained the best results using a classical Expectation-Maximization (EM) algorithm and considering 4 Gaussian components for each model. In our experiments, we were not able to add more than 9 components, because our small video database was insufficient for a reliable training of the GMMs; moreover, more complicated algorithms, which are automatically selecting the optimal number of components like the Figueiredo-Jain or the Greedy-EM [16], did not provide any advantage over the standard EM.

4.3 Identification and Verification Scores

Figure 2 shows the identification scores of our system: it is possible to notice that the identification rate is 95.8%, when considering the best match ($NBest = 1$), and 98.6%, when considering the three best matches ($NBest = 3$). Figure 3 shows the Receiver Operating Characteristic (ROC) curve of our system, with False Rejection Rates (FRR) plotted as a function of False Acceptance Rates (FAR): the Equal Error Rate (EER) value is 1.13%.

For providing a general reference to our experiments, we tested our video database using a pixel-based recognition system that implements a classic eigenface algorithm. The face database for the enrollment was built from the respective video database, by extracting 14 keyframes from each video chunk; on the other hand, only one keyframe was used in the testing phase. It's important to underline that the original keyframes have been manually normalized, by cropping

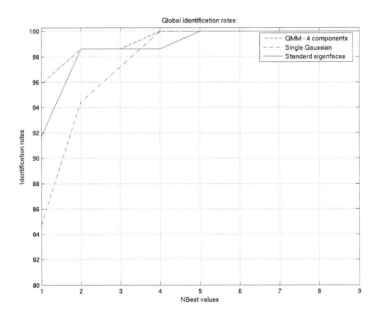

Fig. 2. Identification rates as a function of NBest values; for computing the scores, an individual is correctly identified if it is within the NBest matches

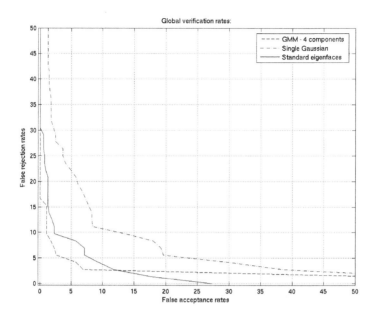

Fig. 3. Verification scores: False Rejection Rates (FRR) plotted as a function of False Acceptance Rates (FAR)

the face region, then aligning and (in-plane) rotating the heads. The results have been obtained considering an eigenspace of dimension 25 and some light preprocessing. The identification rate for the best match is 91.7%, rising up to 98.6% when considering the best three matches; the equal error rate of the system is 7.03%.

The previous experiments for recognising people from their head displacements are interesting; in fact, even if these signals could be considered as weak modalities and can not be as performing as the latest pixel-based techniques, they show that the behaviour of people can be a possible biometric. Moreover, our system is applied in real cases, with compressed video sequences and no constraints on movements or actions; our behavioural approach also showed a great tolerance to face changes, due to presence of glasses and beard, or difference in haircuts, illumination and skin color. On the other hand, our technique is sensible to within-subject variations: individuals may change their characteristic head motion when placed in different contexts or affected by particular emotional states.

4.4   Robustness to Noise

In order to evaluate the robustness of our method from input noise, we artificially add a Gaussian noise with zero mean and variable standard deviation to all displacement signals (both training and testing sets), retrieved by the tracking module. In Figure 4, we report the identification scores as a function of the noise power; in order to relate the energy of the signal with the one of the noise,

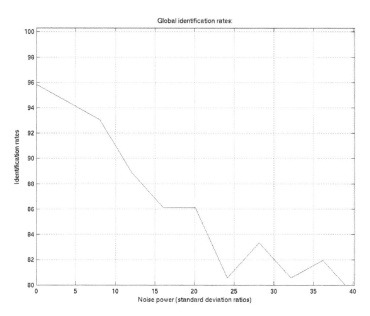

Fig. 4. Identification rates as a function of the noise power; in order to relate the energy of the signal with the one of the noise, the noise power is defined as the ratio between the standard deviation of the noise and the mean standard deviation of the signals (expressed in percentages)

the noise power is defined as the ratio (expressed in percentages) between the standard deviation of the noise and the mean standard deviation of the signals. It is possible to notice that initially the identification rate is decreasing rapidly (-10% for noise power between 0 and 20%), then the loss is less important. One possible explaination may be the following: the characteristic small movements, which are really important for discriminating identities, are easily lost for low noise strenghts; after that the noise starts corrupting the global individual movements, less useful in recognition.

5   Conclusion and Future Works

This pioneering work on person recognition using head dynamics, retrieved in the image plane without the need of a complex $3D$ pose estimation, showed that the human behaviour and motion may be useful for discriminating people. Our study on head feature displacements represents a first step in the exploration of the face dynamics and their potential use in real recognition applications, either as an alternative to physical aspects of the face, like its appearance, or jointly with them.

Our system can be improved by researching and implementing different solutions. One way is to use our biometric system, based on head displacements, and integrate it in a multimodal one; for this purpouse it could be possible to couple it with a physical modality, like the appearance of the face, or with another behavioural modality, like eye blinking or lip movements. Considering the low quality of our video database, in which fine details are affected by compression noise, the former case seems more feasible. Another possibility is to refine the signal extraction process, implementing a more robust tracking algorithm than the RGB template matching. Although it is reasonable that more precise signals could provide better classification power, the quality of those already extracted is actually good enough for our algorithm; in fact, by manual inspection we noticed that the tracking points are almost always correct (considering a pixel of tolerance) and that the occasional errors have reduced influence on our statistical approach. It may be also interesting to focus the analysis on individual gestures and exploit that knowledge for classifying identities; as an example, the head dynamics might be analysed in a local way, computing feature vectors in each temporal window. This approach may show more important discriminating power, capturing the details of personal movement, but the lack of prior information on the evolution of the motion and the relatively small size of the training database could be overwhelming. Finally, all our identification and verification results should be validated on a bigger database.

Acknowledgment

The authors would like to thank the anonymous reviewers for their useful comments.

References

1. G. D. Hager and P. N. Belhumeur, "'Efficient region tracking with parametric models of geometry and illumination"', in *Transactions on Pattern Analysis and Machine Intelligence*, vol. 20, no. 10, pp. 1025–1039, October 1998.
2. A. D. Jepson, D. J. Fleet and T. R. El-Maraghi, "'Robust online appearance models for visual tracking"', in *Proceedings of the IEEE Computer Society Conference on Computer Vision and Pattern Recognition (CVPR 2001)*, 8–14 December 2001, Toronto, Canada, vol. 1, pp. 415–422.
3. S. Birchfield, "'Elliptical head tracking using intensity gradients and color histograms"', in *Proceedings of IEEE Computer Society Conference on Computer Vision and Pattern Recognition*, 23–25 June 1998, Stanford, USA, pp. 232–237.
4. Y. Chen, Y. Rui and T. S. Huang, "'JPDAF based HMM for real-time contour tracking"', in *Proceedings of the IEEE Computer Society Conference on Computer Vision and Pattern Recognition (CVPR 2001)*, 8–14 December 2001, Toronto, Canada, vol. 1, pp. 543–550.
5. Y. Wu and T. S. Huang, "'A co-inference approach to robust visual tracking"', in *Proceedings of the Eighth IEEE International Conference on Computer Vision (ICCV 2001)*, 7–14 July 2001, Urbana, USA, vol. 2, pp. 26–33.
6. D. Comaniciu, V. Ramesh and P. Meer, "'Kernel-based object tracking"', in *IEEE Transactions on Pattern Analysis and Machine Intelligence*, vol. 25, no. 5, pp. 564–577, May 2003.

7. R. Chellappa, C. L. Wilson and S. Sirohey, "'Human and machine recognition of faces: a survey"', in *Proceedings of the IEEE*, May 1995, College Park, USA, pp. 705–741.
8. W. Zhao, R. Chellappa, P. J. Phillips and A. Rosenfeld, "'Face Recognition: A Literature Survey"', in *ACM Computing Surveys*, vol. 35, no. 4, pp. 399–458, 2003.
9. B. Li and R. Chellappa, "'A generic approach to simultaneous tracking and verification in video"', in *IEEE Transactions on Image Processing*, vol. 11, no. 5, pp. 530–544, May 2002.
10. S. Zhou, V. Krueger and R. Chellappa, "'Probabilistic recognition of human faces from video"', in *Computer Vision and Image Understanding*, vol. 91, no. 1–2, pp. 214–245, July-August 2003.
11. K. Lee, J. Ho, M. Yang and D. Kriegman, "'Visual tracking and recognition using probabilistic appearance manifolds"', in *Computer Vision and Image Understanding*, vol. 99, no. 3, pp. 303–331, September 2005.
12. P. S. Huang, C. J. Harris and M. S. Nixon, "'Recognising humans by gait via parametric canonical space"', in *Artificial Intelligence in Engineering*, vol. 13, no. 4, pp. 359–366, October 1999.
13. J. B. Hayfron-Acquah, M. S. Nixon and J. N. Carter, "'Automatic gait recognition by symmetry analysis"', in *Pattern Recognition Letters*, vol. 24, no. 13, pp. 2175–2183, September 2003.
14. D. Cunado, M. S. Nixon and J. N. Carter, "'Automatic extraction and description of human gait models for recognition purposes"', in *Computer Vision and Image Understanding*, vol. 90, no. 1, pp. 1–41, April 2003.
15. C. Yam , M. S. Nixon and J. N. Carter, "'Automated person recognition by walking and running via model-based approaches"', in *Pattern Recognition*, vol. 37, no. 5, pp. 1057–1072, May 2004.
16. P. Paalanen, J. K. Kmrinen, J. Ilonen and H. Klviinen, "'Feature Representation and Discrimination Based on Gaussian Mixture Model Probability Densities - Practices and Algorithms"', in *Research report of the Lappeenranta University of Technology*, no. 95, 1995.

Matching Deformable Features Based on Oriented Multi-scale Filter Banks

Manuel J. Marín-Jiménez and Nicolás Pérez de la Blanca

Dpt. Computer Science and Artificial Intelligence, University of Granada
C/ Periodista Daniel Saucedo Aranda s/n,
Granada, 18071, Spain
mjmarin@decsai.ugr.es, nicolas@ugr.es

Abstract. This paper presents a technique to enable deformable objects to be matched throughout video sequences based on the information provided by multi-scale Gaussian derivative filter banks. We show that this technique is robust enough for viewpoint changes, lighting changes, large motions of the matched object and small changes in rotation and scale. Unlike other well-known color-based techniques, this technique only uses the gray level values of the image. The proposed algorithm is mainly based on the definition of a particular multi-scale template model and a similarity measure for template matching. The matching approach has been tested on video sequences acquired with a conventional webcam showing a promising behavior with this kind of low-quality images.

1 Introduction

In this paper, we approach the problem of matching deformable objects through video sequences, based on the information provided by responses of oriented multi-scale filter banks. Our approach is traditional in the sense that we define a template of the object of interest, and we attempt to find the image region that best matches the template. What is new about our approach is the template definition and the similarity measure. Deformable object matching/tracking remains a very challenging problem mainly due to the absence of good templates and similarity measures which are robust enough to handle all the geometrical and lighting deformations that can be present in a matching process. Very recently, object recognition by parts has been suggested as a very efficient approach to recognize deformable object [1][3][2][6]. Different approaches are used in the recognition process from the basic parts, but the matching of salient parts is a common task to all approaches. Region and contour information are the main sources of information from which the location of a part of an object in an image can be estimated (e.g. [7][8]). It has been shown that histograms are robust features for translation, rotation and view point changes [12][10]. However, the main drawback of using the histogram directly as the main feature is the loss of the gray level spatial information [12]. Recent approaches based on the space-scale theory have incorporated the image's spatial information. In [10] multidimensional histograms, which are obtained by applying Gaussian derivative filters to the image, are used. This approach incorporates the image's spatial

F.J. Perales and R.B. Fisher (Eds.): AMDO 2006, LNCS 4069, pp. 336–345, 2006.

information with global histograms. None of the above approaches explicitly addresses the local spatial information present in the image. The ideas presented in [4] suggest the interest in removing the local spatial information in deformable regions matching process. On the other hand, it is well known that local features based on Gaussian derivatives responses are robust in the task of object recognition [15][5][14], and texture description [13]. In this paper, in contrast to the above approaches based on histograms, we impose a better compromise between spatial information and robustness to deformations. In our case, the matching template for each image region is built as a array of combined responses of oriented multi-scale filter banks. On each image, the template is iterated on all the possible locations within it. The matching on each image location is the vector of the similarity matched on each spatial scale. The optimum (minimum or maximum, according to the similarity criterion definition) of this vector defines the saliency value in each image location. The set of these values defines a saliency map associated to the image, which is the input to the final decision criteria defining the optimum location. This paper is organized in the following way: Section 2 introduces the template definition and the similarity measure; Section 3 presents the algorithm; Section 4 shows the experimental results; and finally, Section 5 concludes the paper.

2   Template and Similarity Measure

2.1   Template Definition

Unlike classical templates based on patches of raw gray levels or templates based on histograms, our approach is based on filter responses. In concrete, the template building is addressed by the HMAX model [9][11]. The main idea is to convolve the image with a filter bank compound by oriented filters at diverse scales. We will use four orientations per scale (0, 45, 90 and 135 degrees).

Let $F_{s,o}$ be a filter bank compound by $(s \cdot o)$ filters grouped into s scales (an even number) with o orientations per scale. Let $F_{i,\cdot}$ be the i-th scale of filter bank $F_{s,o}$ compound by o oriented filters.

The steps for processing an image(or building the template) are the following:

1. Convolve the target image with a filter bank $F_{s,o}$, obtaining a set $S_{s,o}$ of $s \cdot o$ convolved images. The filters must be normalized to zero mean and sum of squares equals one, and also each convolution window of the target image. Hence, values of filtered images will be in [-1,1].
2. For $i = \{1, 3, 5, 7, ..., s - 1\}$, in pairs $(i, i + 1)$, subsample $S_{i,\cdot}$ and $S_{i+1,\cdot}$ by using a grid of size g_i and selecting the local max value of each grid. Grids are overlapped by v pixels. This is independently done for each orientation. At the end of this step, the resultant images $\hat{S}_i$ and $\hat{S}_{i+1}$ contain the local max values (of each grid) for the o orientations.
3. Then, combine each pair $\hat{S}_i$ and $\hat{S}_{i+1}$ in a single band C_i by selecting the max value for each position between both scales $(i, i + 1)$. As a result, $s/2$ bands C_i are obtained, where each one is compound by o elements.

Fig. 1. Anisotropic oriented filters: second order Gaussian derivatives

The definition of the template can be done in two different ways:

1. From the gray-scale image, we can extract (by hand or with an automatic method) a region of interest R, and process R with the previous algorithm. Therefore, each C_i is an independent template.
2. On the other hand, we can process an image containing the full model and extract a patch from a C_i band which will be the template. In this case, the template can be extract around a region containing salient points (e.g. global maximums).

We prefer the second option for selecting the template because, as we will see, template matching is carry out in a natural way in the domain of the transformed images $C_{s,o}$.

Note that, by construction, the template is flexible in the sense that it is compound by local maximums, what provides certain invariance to translation, and combination of pairs of scales, what provides some invariance to scale. Moreover, unlike histograms, the template keeps information about local structure. Also, since the template is based on filter responses, invariance to illumination changes is achieved.

The filter bank used in this work is based on second order Gaussian derivatives (as in [13]):

$$G_2(x, y) = \frac{y^2 - \sigma_y^2}{2\pi\sigma_x\sigma_y^5} \exp\left(-\frac{x^2}{2\sigma_x^2} - \frac{y^2}{2\sigma_y^2}\right) \tag{1}$$

Where σ_x and σ_y are the standard deviations in the directions x and y respectively.

Figure 1 shows a sample of $F_{i,\cdot}$ with its four oriented filters.

2.2 Template Matching

Once we have defined our template T, we are interested in locating it in a new image. We will select the position of the new image where the similarity function raises a maximum. The proposed similarity measure M is based on the following expression:

$$M(\mathbf{T}, \mathbf{X}) = \exp(-\gamma \cdot \|F(\mathbf{T}) - F(\mathbf{X})\|^2) \tag{2}$$

Where $\mathbf{T}$ is the template, $\mathbf{X}$ is the comparison region of the same size of $\mathbf{T}$, γ controls the steepness of the exponential function, F is an indicator function and $\|\cdot\|$ is the Euclidean norm. Values of M are in the interval $[0, 1]$.

In our first approach F was defined as the identity function (as [11]), but it showed an undesirable behavior due to the influence of the mean. So, $F(\mathbf{X})$ is defined as $F(\mathbf{X}) = \mathbf{X} - \bar{\mathbf{X}}$, where $\bar{\mathbf{X}}$ is the mean of $\mathbf{X}$. Note than F can become more sophisticated normalizing the energy of the patches or regularizing the standard deviation, however we have empirically checked that it does not worth in the practice.

The problem of find the best matching window $\mathbf{X}_p^i$ with a template $\mathbf{T}$ over an image $C_{s,o}$ can be defined as the optimization function:

$$\mathbf{X}_p^i = \arg \max_{i \in s, p \in N_i} \{M(\mathbf{T}, \mathbf{X}_p^i)\}$$

Where N_i is the set of all possible positions in C_i.

Therefore, the procedure for locating the best matching window is:

1. For all bands C_i and for all possible windows $\mathbf{X}_p^i$ in C_i, compute the similarity measure $M_{i,p}$.
2. Choose the position p at scale i where $M_{i,p}$ is maximum.
3. Transform p to image coordinates.

Since each C_i has been built by subsampling, coordinates p must be transformed to image coordinates to find the actual region in the image where template is found.

3   The Algorithm

The previous steps can be summarized as follows:

---

1. Fix the scales for the filter bank $F_{s,o}$.
2. Build the template $\mathbf{T}$, following the previously explained method, using $F_{s,o}$.
3. Transform the target image I with $F_{s,o}$ obtaining $C_{s,o}^I$.
4. Compute the similarity maps M.
5. Locate the coordinates p of the global maximum over all positions and bands.
6. Transform p to image coordinates.

When more than a maximum is found, we have decided to choose the position closer to the origin of coordinates. However, other criterions can be defined. For example, if we are working on a video sequence we could choose the position closer to the one in the previous frame.

4   Experimental Results

Several experiments have been performed in order to assess the effectiveness of the proposed approach. Firstly, we focus our experiments to show how robust our approach is to diverse perturbations introduced to an object. Secondly, we study the capability of generalization of the templates between different poses and different instances of the objects.

4.1 Parameters for the Experiments

For our experiments, the anisotropic second order Gaussian derivatives (with aspect-ratio equals 0.25) are oriented at 0, 45, 90 and 135. All the filter banks contain 8 scales. The standard deviation used for the filter banks is equal to a quarter of the filter-mask size. Table 1 shows the value of the parameters for the filter banks, where FS is the size (in pixels) of the 8 mask-filters and σ is the related standard deviation of the functions. For the subsampling step (see sec. 2.1), grid size g_i is in $\{8, 10, 12, 14\}$ and overlap v is equal to 3.

Table 1. Parameters of the four bands (B): filter mask size (FS) and filter width (σ) for second order Gaussian derivative filter bank, and grid size (GS) used in subsampling step

B	C_1		C_2		C_3		C_4	
FS	7	9	11	13	15	17	19	21
σ	1.75	2.25	2.75	3.25	3.75	4.25	4.75	5.25
GS	8		10		12		14	

Note that, the value of the grid size will depend on the size of the object we are considering (e.g. faces). So, the value of overlap depends on the minimum value of grid size.

4.2 Measuring Robustness

In this section a target image is altered in different ways in order to test the capability of our approach to perform a correct matching in adverse conditions. The experiments has been carried out with functions included in ©*Matlab* 7.0. The six kinds of alterations are:

1. Lighting change: pixel values are raised to an exponent each time.
2. Addition of multiplicative noise (speckle): mean zero and increasing variance in [0.02:0.07:0.702].
3. Blurring: iteratively, a gaussian filter of size 5x5, with mean 0 and variance 1, is applied to the image obtained in the previous iteration.
4. Unsharping: iteratively, an unsharp filter (for local contrast enhancement) of size 3x3 and α (controls shape of the Laplacian) equals 0.1, is applied to the image obtained in the previous iteration.
5. Motion noise: iteratively, a motion filter (pixels displacement in a fixed direction) with a displacement of 5 pixels in the 45 degrees direction, is applied to the image obtained in the previous iteration.
6. In-plane rotation: several rotations θ are applied to the original image. With values $\theta = [5 : 5 : 50]$.

A template of size 8x8 (with the four orientations) is extracted around the left eye, and the aim is to find its position in the diverse test images. The battery of

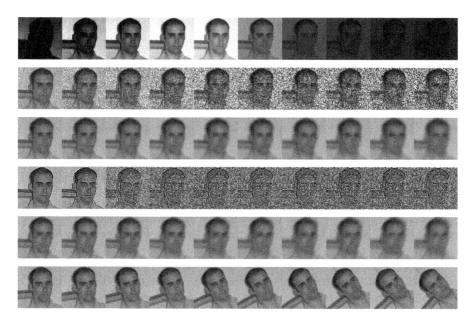

Fig. 2. The six test. From top to bottom: lighting, speckle, blurred, unsharp, motion, rotation.

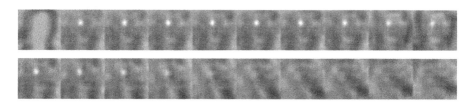

Fig. 3. Responses of similarity measure. Lighter pixels correspond to higher responses. Top row: lighting test. Bottom row: rotation test.

altered images is shown in figure 2. Each row is compound by ten images. Note that, even for us, some images are really hard.

In figure 3, we see the similarity maps obtained for the lighting and rotation test. The lightest pixel is the position chosen by our method as the best matching position.

For evaluating the test, the matching is considered correct if the proposed template position is not far from the real one more than 1 unit (in C_i coordinates). The percentages of correct matching for the different cases are shown in table 2.

In blurring, unsharping and motion test the results are really satisfactory, template has been always precisely matched. Matching in lighting test fails only for the first image (left in fig. 2). On the other hand, in speckle test, matching begins failing when variance of noise is greater than 0.5 (the seventh image in

Table 2. Percentage of correct matching for each test

Test	Lighting	Speckle	Blurring	Unsharp	Motion	Rotation
% Hit	90	60	100	100	100	50

the second row, fig. 2); and matching in rotation test fails when angle is near 30 degrees. However, these results suggest the interesting properties of robustness of this kind of templates for matching in adverse noisy conditions.

4.3 Tracking Facial Features in Webcam Video Sequences

Since nowadays webcams are widely extended and used in diverse environments, and they can be used as input in user-interfaces, in this section we deal with sequences of images taken from a conventional webcam. These sequences contain human heads in motion. Very different poses are present in the images as well as different facial gestures. The size of each frame is 240x320 pixels and they are encoded with ©*Indeo video 5* codec[1]. We have converted each frame to gray-scale images and resized to 120x160 pixels for the experiments.

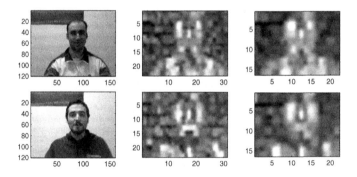

Fig. 4. Webcam images (first column), with C1 maps (from filter oriented at 90) at two scales. Top row: subject A. Bottom row: subject B.

Two templates have been taken from a single frame, and we are interested in locate them in all the remaining frames by using the proposed matching approach. In figure 4 we can see two frames of different subjects and two maps processed at level C_1 and C_2 with a filter oriented at 90 degrees.

The templates shown in figure 5 have been extracted from the first band of subject A (fig. 4), and represents zones around the eye and the mouth. The size of the templates is 6x6 (per 4 orientations). Note that these templates cover a region about 25x25 image pixels (remember the subsampling step in sec. 2.1). They are matched in sequences of more than 150 frames (each one), obtaining results as shown in figure 6. Green square and yellow circle refers to region

---

[1] 24 bits color frames, 15 fps, 114 kbps.

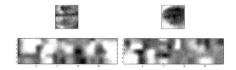

Fig. 5. Two templates from subject A (fig. 4). Left: mouth. Right: eye. Size: 6x6. The four orientations are joint for representational purposes.

Fig. 6. Result images with the located position of the two templates (fig. 5). Green square is eye, and yellow circle is mouth. Top row: subject A. Bottom row: subject B.

Fig. 7. Incorrect detection. Result images with the proposed position of the two templates (fig. 5). Green square is eye, and yellow circle is mouth. Top row: subject A. Bottom row: subject B.

where eye and mouth are matched respectively. The templates not only have been searched for the subject A sequences, but they have been matched in the sequences of subject B. For both subjects the majority of the time matching is correct. It is remarkable the capacity of the templates to generalize between different poses and subjects. However, and what was predictable, figure 7 shows incorrect detections due to large pose changes or big shadows in the regions of interest. In concrete, if face rotates around the Y-axis, it works well[2] until face is near profile. When face rotates around the Z-axis (in-plane rotation), it works well up to approximately 30 degrees, what supports the results shown in Sec.4.2. And finally, if face rotates around the X-axis (facing up and down), matching performs correctly up to 45 degrees, approximately. Also, there are moments

---

[2] When we say that it works well, we mean that maybe one spurious local maximum appears in some of the intermediate frames.

in which the subject approaches to the camera or moves backward, in these situations, where scale changes, matching continues performing well.

Although the quality of the images taken with the webcam is poor, great noise is present and the sequence is compressed the results are promising. Note that none temporal information is used between frames, what can improve the results. Moreover, template is never updated.

5   Summary and Conclusions

A scheme for matching deformable regions is proposed and evaluated over human faces. The first experiment shows how our approach is stable and robust enough for different kinds of alterations over the images: changes in illumination, blurring, motion noise, rotation, etc. Then, in the second experiment, templates have been matched along sequences of images taken with a conventional webcam. In these sequences, human faces in motion are present with different points of view and facial gestures. The results show the capability of the approach to match the selected templates in the different frames for the same subject, and for different subjects, showing this way the capability of generalization of the templates. Even though, images acquired with conventional webcams are low-quality, as multiple sources of noise are present, the algorithm as shown quite robust. On the other hand, matching is wrong when too large pose variation is present or huge lighting variation occurs. Nevertheless, this approach is intended to be utilized as tracker initialization or tracker recovery, where temporal information can be used to reduce this problem improving the results. As future work, we intend to compare our proposed scheme with the one based on SIFT features [7].

Acknowledgments

Thanks to Dr. Jordi Vitrià for his helpful comments, and to the referees for their suggestions. This work was partially supported by the Spanish Ministry of Education and Science (grant AP2003-2405), and project TIN2005-01665.

References

1. Shivani Agarwal, Aatif Awan, and Dan Roth. Learning to detect objects in images via a sparse, part-based representation. *IEEE PAMI*, 26(11):1475–1490, Nov. 2004.
2. R. Fergus, P. Perona, and A. Zisserman. Object class recognition by unsupervised scale-invariant learning. *IEEE CVPR'03*, 2:264–271, Feb 2003.
3. B. Heisele, P. Ho, J. Wu, and T. Poggio. Face recognition: component-based versus global approaches. *Computer Vision and Image Understanding*, 91:6–21, 2003.
4. J. Koenderink and A. van Doorn. The structure of locally orderless images. *Int. Journal of Comp. Vision*, (318273):159–168, 1999.
5. J.J. Koenderink and A.J. van Doorn. Representation of local geometry in the visual system. *Biological Cybernetics*, 55:367–375, 1987.

6. Bastian Leibe. *Interleaved Object Categorization and Segmentation.* PhD thesis, ETH Zurich, October 2004.
7. David G. Lowe. Distinctive image features from scale-invariant keypoints. *International Journal of Computer Vision*, 2(60):91–110, 2004.
8. Krystian Mikolajczyk and Cordelia Schmid. Scale and affine invariant interest point detectors. *International Journal of Computer Vision*, 60(1):63–86, 2004.
9. M. Riesenhuber and T. Poggio. Hierarchical models of object recognition in cortex. *Nature Neuroscience*, 2(11):1019–1025, 1999.
10. Bernt Schiele and James L. Crowley. Object recognition using multidimensional receptive field histograms. In *ECCV (1)*, pages 610–619, 1996.
11. T. Serre, L. Wolf, and T. Poggio. Object recognition with features inspired by visual cortex. In *IEEE CSC on CVPR*, June 2005.
12. M.J. Swain and D.H. Ballard. Color indexing. *Int. Journal Comp. Vision*, 1(7):11–32, 1991.
13. M. Varma and A. Zisserman. Unifying statistical texture classification frameworks. *Image and Vision Computing*, 22(14):1175–1183, 2005.
14. J. J. Yokono and T. Poggio. Oriented filters for object recognition: an empirical study. In *Proc. of the Sixth IEEE FGR*, May 2004.
15. Richard A. Young. The gaussian derivative model for spatial vision: I. Retinal mechanisms. *Spatial Vision*, 2(4):273–293, 1987.

Principal Spine Shape Deformation Modes Using Riemannian Geometry and Articulated Models

Jonathan Boisvert[1,2,3], Xavier Pennec[2], Hubert Labelle[3],
Farida Cheriet[1,3], and Nicholas Ayache[2]

[1] École Polytechnique de Montréal
P.O. Box 6079, Station Centre-Ville, Montréal H3C 3A7, Canada
`jonathan.boisvert@polymtl.ca`
[2] INRIA, Asclepios Project Team - 2004 route des Lucioles - BP 93
06902 Sophia Antipolis Cedex, France
[3] Sainte-Justine Hospital, 3175, Chemin de la Côte-Ste-Catherine, Montréal, Canada

Abstract. We present a method to extract principal deformation modes from a set of articulated models describing the human spine. The spine was expressed as a set of rigid transforms that superpose local coordinates systems of neighbouring vertebrae. To take into account the fact that rigid transforms belong to a Riemannian manifold, the Fréchet mean and a generalized covariance computed in the exponential chart of the Fréchet mean were used to construct a statistical shape model. The principal deformation modes were then extracted by performing a principal component analysis (PCA) on the generalized covariance matrix. Principal deformations modes were computed for a large database of untreated scoliotic patients and the obtained results indicate that combining rotation and translation into a unified framework leads to an effective and meaningful method of dimensionality reduction for articulated anatomical structures. The computed deformation modes also revealed clinically relevant information. For instance, the first mode of deformation appeared to be associated with patients' growth, the second is a double thoraco-lumbar curve and the third is a thoracic curve.

1 Introduction

Most of the statistical shapes models currently used to describe anatomical structures are based on point to point correspondences extracted from images ([1,2] for example). However, points are not always the best choice of primitives. To deal with articulated anatomical structures a more natural choice would be to use frames (points associated with three orthogonal axes). The main reason for this choice is that frames enable a more natural analysis of the relative orientations and positions of the models.

The spine is one of the anatomical structures that is better described using frames instead of points. In this context, a frame is associated to each vertebra and the deformations of the spine are then described in terms of rigid transforms applied to those frames.

However, conventional statistical methods usually apply only in vector spaces, while rigid transforms naturally belong to a Lie group. Therefore, concepts as

F.J. Perales and R.B. Fisher (Eds.): AMDO 2006, LNCS 4069, pp. 346–355, 2006.

simple as the mean and the covariance had to be generalized because addition and scalar multiplication are not defined in Lie groups. Probability and statistics applied to Riemannian manifolds [3] offer an elegant way to deal with those difficulties and variability models based on Lie groups can now be built. The Riemannian framework was also used in the context of statistical shape modelling to perform PGA (principal geodesic analysis) on medial axis representations (m-reps) [4].

Thus, it is now possible to compute a variability model of the spine based on the tools from the Riemannian geometry [5]. But a rigid transform has 6 DOF (degrees of freedom) and there are 5 lumbar and 12 thoracic vertebrae for a total of 102 DOF (excluding cervical vertebrae). The analysis of such large variability model can hardly be performed by a clinician. It is therefore necessary to find a way to reduce the dimensionality of the variability model and to extract only the most meaningful modes of variability.

Dimensionality reduction applied to the spine or to articulated models is not a new idea and methods were proposed in the past. As a part of a method that aim to predict the geometry of the spine based on the geometry of the trunk, Bergeron et al. [6] performed a principal component analysis on the 3D coordinates of vertebrae's center in the frequency domain. Principal components analysis was also used to process articulated body models (see, for instance, Gonzalez et al. [7] and Jiang and Motiai [8]). In that context, classical PCA was used on a representation that was either only based on 3D coordinates or only based on an angular description of the articulated body. However, using both positions and orientations would allow a better separation of different physiological phenomena such as pathological deformations and normal growth.

The main contributions of this paper will therefore be to propose a method based on Riemannian geometry to perform principal components analysis on an articulated model of the spine and to apply that method to a large database of scoliotic patients in order to construct the first statistical atlas of 3D deformation patterns for idiopathic scoliosis (a pathology that causes spine deformations).

2   Material and Methods

This section will be divided into four subsections. Firstly, elements of probability and statistics on Riemannian manifolds will be introduced. Secondly, a generalization of principal component analysis on Riemannian manifolds will be described. Then, the specialization of this method for articulated models will be tackled in the third subsection. Finally, the fourth subsection will explain how the extraction of articulated models is performed from spine radiographs.

2.1   Elements of Probability and Statistics on Riemannian Manifolds

Because there is no addition or scalar multiplication operations readily defined on rigid transforms, we need a way to generalize the notions of mean and directional dispersion. The distance is a general concept that can be used to perform those generalisations and Riemannian geometry offers a mathematical framework to work with primitives when only a distance function is available.

In a complete Riemannian manifold $\mathcal{M}$ the smallest smooth curve $\gamma(t)$ such that $\gamma(0) = x$ and $\gamma(1) = y$ is called a geodesic and the length of that curve is the distance between x and y. Two important maps can be defined from the geodesics: the exponential map Exp_x which maps a vector ∂_x of the tangent plane $T_x\mathcal{M}$ to the element reached in a unit time by the geodesic that starts at x with an initial tangent vector ∂_x and the logarithmic map Log_x which is the inverse function of Exp_x. In other words, these two maps enable us to "unfold" the manifold on the tangent plane (which is a vector space) and to project an element of the tangent plane to the manifold.

With the knowledge of Exp_x and Log_x, it is possible to compute the generalisations of the conventional mean and covariance. The following subsections will introduce those generalisations in the univariate and multivariate cases.

Fréchet Mean. For a given distance, the generalization of the usual mean can be obtained by defining the mean as the element μ of a manifold $\mathcal{M}$ that minimizes the sum of the distances with a set of elements $x_{0...N}$ of the same manifold $\mathcal{M}$:

$$\mu = \arg\min_{x \in \mathcal{M}} \sum_{i=0}^{N} d(x, x_i)^2$$

This generalization of the mean is called the Fréchet mean. Since it is defined using a minimization, it is difficult to compute it directly from the definition. However, it can be computed using a gradient descent performed on the summation. The following recurrent equation summarizes this operation:

$$\mu_{n+1} = \mathrm{Exp}_{\mu_n}\left(\frac{1}{N} \sum_{i=0}^{N} \mathrm{Log}_{\mu_n}(x_i)\right) \tag{1}$$

Generalized Covariance. The variance (as it is usually defined on real vector spaces) is the expectation of the L_2 norm of the difference between the mean and the measures. An intuitive generalization of the variance on Riemannian manifolds is thus given by the expectation of a squared distance:

$$\sigma^2 = \frac{1}{N} \sum_{i=0}^{N} d(\mu, x_i)^2 \tag{2}$$

To create statistical shape models it is necessary to have a directional dispersion measure since the anatomical variability of the spine is anisotropic [5]. The covariance is usually defined as the expectation of the matricial product of the vectors from the mean to the elements on which the covariance is computed. Thus, a similar definition for Riemannian manifolds would be to compute the expectation in the tangent plane of the mean using the log map:

$$\Sigma = \frac{1}{N} \sum_{i=0}^{N} \mathrm{Log}_\mu(x)\mathrm{Log}_\mu(x)^T \tag{3}$$

Multivariate Case. The Fréchet mean and the generalized covariance make it possible to study the centrality and dispersion of one primitive belonging to a Riemannian manifold. However, to build complete statistical shape models, it would be most desirable to study multiple primitives altogether. Therefore, a generalized cross-covariance Σ_{fg} is needed.

$$\Sigma_{fg} = \frac{1}{N} \sum_{i=0}^{N} \text{Log}_{\mu_f}(f_i)\text{Log}_{\mu_g}(g_i)^T$$

A natural extension is to create a multivariate vector $f = [f_1, f_2, f_3, \ldots, f_k]^T$ where each element corresponds to a part of a model made of several primitives. The mean and the covariance of this multivariate vector will thus be:

$$\mu = \begin{bmatrix} \mu_1 \\ \mu_2 \\ \vdots \\ \mu_k \end{bmatrix} \quad \text{and} \quad \Sigma = \begin{bmatrix} \Sigma_{f_1 f_1} & \Sigma_{f_1 f_2} & \cdots & \Sigma_{f_1 f_k} \\ \Sigma_{f_2 f_1} & \Sigma_{f_2 f_2} & \cdots & \Sigma_{f_2 f_k} \\ \vdots & \vdots & & \vdots \\ \Sigma_{f_k f_1} & \Sigma_{f_k f_2} & \cdots & \Sigma_{f_k f_k} \end{bmatrix} \quad (4)$$

This is very similar to the conventional multivariate mean and covariance except that the Fréchet mean and the generalized cross-covariance are used in the computations.

2.2 Extraction of the Principal Deformations

The equation 4 allows us to compute a statistical shape model for a group of models made of several primitives. However, the different primitives will most likely be correlated which makes the variability analysis very difficult. Furthermore, the dimensionality of the model is also a concern and we would like to select only a few important uncorrelated components.

Unlike the manifold itself, the tangent plane is a vector space and its basis could be changed using a simple linear transformation. Thus, we seek an orthonormal matrix A $(AA^T = I)$ to linearly transform the tangent plane ($\text{Log}_\mu(g) = A\text{Log}_\mu(f)$) such as the generalized covariance in the transformed tangent space is a diagonal matrix ($\Sigma_{gg} = \text{diag}(\lambda_1, \lambda_2, \ldots, \lambda_k)$). The covariances of the transformed tangent space and of the original tangent space are connected by the following equation:

$$\Sigma_{gg} = \text{diag}(\lambda_1, \lambda_2, \ldots, \lambda_k) = A\Sigma_{ff}A^T$$

If A is rewritten as $A = [a_1, a_2, \ldots, a_k]^T$, then it is easy to show that:

$$[\lambda_1 a_1, \lambda_2 a_2, \ldots, \lambda_k a_k] = [\Sigma_{ff}a_1, \Sigma_{ff}a_2, \ldots, \Sigma_{ff}a_k] \quad (5)$$

The line vectors of the matrix A are therefore the eigenvectors of the original covariance matrix and the elements of the covariance matrix in the transformed space are the eigenvalues of the original covariance. This is the exact same procedure that is used to perform PCA in real vector spaces. Like for real vector spaces, the variance is left unchanged since $\sigma^2 = \mathrm{Tr}(\Sigma_{ff}) = \mathrm{Tr}(\Sigma_{gg})$ and the cumulative fraction of the variance explained by the first n components is:

$$p = \frac{1}{\sigma^2} \sum_{i=1...n} \lambda_i$$

A shape model can be re-created from coordinates of the transformed tangent space simply by going back to the original tangent space and projecting the model on the manifold using the exponential map. So if α_i is the coordinate associated with the ith principal component, the following equation can be used to re-create a shape model:

$$S = \mathrm{Exp}_\mu \left(\sum_{i=1}^{k} \alpha_i a_i \right)$$

2.3   Application to Articulated Models of the Spine

In this paper, the spine is modelled as a set of frames associated to local coordinates systems of vertebrae. The modifications of the spine geometry are thus modelled as rigid transforms that are applied to those frames. In order to compute the principal deformations modes (from equation 5), the exponential and logarithmic maps associated with a distance function on rigid transforms are needed.

A rigid transform is the combination of a rotation and a translation. Defining a suitable distance on the translational part is not difficult since 3D translations belong to a real vector space. However, the choice of a distance function between rotations is more complex.

To define a suitable distance function between rigid transforms, another representation of the rotations called the rotation vector is needed. This representation is based on the fact that a 3D rotation can be

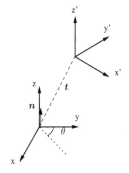

Fig. 1. Rigid transform expressed by an axis of rotation n, an angle of rotation θ and a translation vector t

fully described by an axis of rotation supported by a unit vector n and an angle of rotation θ (see figure 1). The rotation vector r is then defined as the product of n and θ.

The conversion from the rotation vector to the rotation matrix is performed using the Rodrigues equation:

$$R = I + \sin(\theta).S(n) + (1 - \cos(\theta)).S(n)^2 \quad \text{with} \quad S(n) = \begin{bmatrix} 0 & -n_z & n_y \\ n_z & 0 & n_x \\ -n_y & n_x & 0 \end{bmatrix}$$

And the inverse map (from a rotation matrix to a rotation vector) is given by the following equations:

$$\theta = \arccos(\frac{Tr(R) - 1}{2}) \quad \text{and} \quad S(n) = \frac{R - R^T}{2\sin(\theta)} \tag{6}$$

Using the rotation vector representation, a left-invariant distance $(d(T_3 \circ T_1, T_3 \circ T_2) = d(T_1, T_2))$ between two rigid transformations can easily be defined:

$$d(T_1, T_2) = N_\omega(T_2^{-1} \circ T_1) \quad \text{with} \quad N_\omega(T)^2 = N_\omega(\{r, t\})^2 = \|r\|^2 + \|\omega t\|^2 \quad (7)$$

Where ω is used to weight the relative effect of rotation and translation, r is the rotation vector and t the translation vector. Because the selected distance function is left-invariant, we have $\text{Exp}_\mu(T) = \text{Exp}_{Id}(\mu^{-1} \circ T)$ and $\text{Log}_\mu(T) = \text{Log}_{Id}(\mu^{-1} \circ T)$. Furthermore, it can be demonstrated that the exponential and log map associated with the distance of equation 7 are the mappings (up to a scale) between the combination of the translation vector and rotation vector and the combination of the rotation matrix and the translation vector [9].

$$\text{Exp}_{Id}(\boldsymbol{T}) = \begin{vmatrix} R(r) \\ \omega^{-1}t \end{vmatrix} \quad \text{and} \quad \text{Log}_{Id}(T) = \begin{vmatrix} r(R) \\ \omega t \end{vmatrix}$$

2.4 Extraction of Articulated Model of the Spine from Radiographs

The 3D geometry of the spine is digitized using a posterior-anterior and a lateral radiograph. Radiographs are used because it allows the patients to stand up during the acquisition (which is important since a large proportion of the spine deformation is hidden when patients lie down). Six anatomical landmarks are identified on the two radiographs. The 3D coordinates of the landmarks are computed using a triangulation algorithm and the deformation of a high-resolution template using dual kriging yields 16 additional reconstructed landmarks. The accuracy of this method was previously established to 2.6mm [10].

Once the landmarks are reconstructed in 3D, each vertebra is rigidly registered to its first upper neighbour and the resulting rigid transforms are recorded. By doing so, the spine is represented by a set of rigid transforms (see the figure 2). This set of inter-vertebral transforms will be used to compute the mean and covariance of the spine shape.

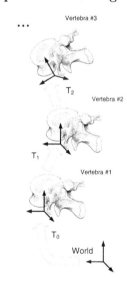

Fig. 2. Frames and transforms used to express the spine as a articulated model

3   Results and Discussion

The method described in the previous sections was applied to a group of 307 scoliotic patients. The patients selected for this study had not been treated with

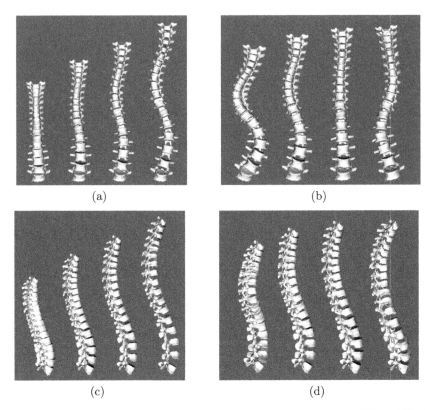

(a)   (b)

(c)   (d)

Fig. 3. First principal deformation mode (reconstructions for $-3\sqrt{\lambda_1}, -\sqrt{\lambda_1}, \sqrt{\lambda_1},$ $3\sqrt{\lambda_1}$), posterior-anterior view (a) and lateral view (c). Second principal deformation mode (reconstructions for $-3\sqrt{\lambda_2}, -\sqrt{\lambda_2}, \sqrt{\lambda_2}, 3\sqrt{\lambda_2}$), posterior-anterior view (b) and lateral view (d).

any kind of orthopaedic treatment when radiographs were taken. Therefore, the inter-patients variability observed was mainly caused by anatomical differences and not by any treatments. The ω constant was set to 0.05 because this value leads to approximatively equal contributions of the rotation and the translation to the variance.

To illustrate the different deformation modes retrieved using the proposed method, four models were reconstructed for each of the first four principal deformation modes. Those models were reconstructed by setting α_k to $-3\sqrt{\lambda_k}$, $-\sqrt{\lambda_k}$, $\sqrt{\lambda_k}$ and $3\sqrt{\lambda_k}$ for $k = 1\ldots4$ while all others components (α_i with $i \neq k$) were set to zero (see figures 3 and 4).

A visual inspection reveals that the first four principal deformation modes have clinical meanings. The first appears to be associated with the patient growth because it is mainly characterized by an elongation of the spine and also includes a mild thoracic curve. The second principal deformation mode could be described as a double thoraco-lumbar curve, because there are two curves: one in the thoracic segment (upper spine) and another in the lumbar segment (lower spine).

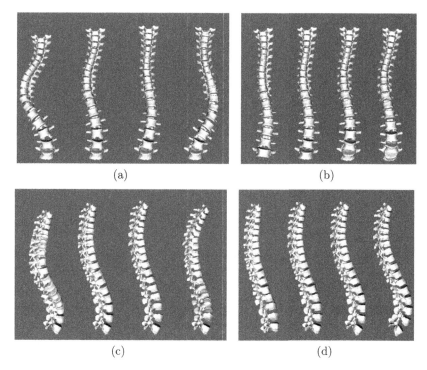

Fig. 4. Third principal deformation mode (reconstructions for $-3\sqrt{\lambda_3}, -\sqrt{\lambda_3}, \sqrt{\lambda_3}$, $3\sqrt{\lambda_3}$), posterior-anterior view (a) and lateral view (c). Fourth principal deformation mode (reconstructions for $-3\sqrt{\lambda_4}, -\sqrt{\lambda_4}, \sqrt{\lambda_4}, 3\sqrt{\lambda_4}$), posterior-anterior view (b) and lateral view (d).

The third principal mode of deformation is a simple thoracic curve (the apex of the curve is in the thoracic spine), but it is longer than the thoracic curve observed in the first principal component. It is also interesting to note that, in addition to the curves visible on the posterior-anterior view, the second and third principal deformation modes are also associated with the development of a kyphosis (back hump) on the lateral view. Finally, the fourth component is a lumbar lordosis (lateral curve of the lumbar spine).

Those curve patterns are routinely used in different clinical classifications of scoliosis (used to plan surgeries). For instance, the reconstructions built from the first principal deformation mode would be classified using King's classification [11] as a type II or III (depending on which reconstruction is evaluated), the second deformation mode would be associated to King's type I or III and the third principal deformation could be associated to King's type IV.

Previouly those patterns were derived from surgeons' intuition using 2D images and clinical indices, whereas it is now possible to automatically compute those patterns from statistics based only on 3D geometries. This also makes it possible, for example, to compare principal deformation modes of different subgroups of scoliotic patients.

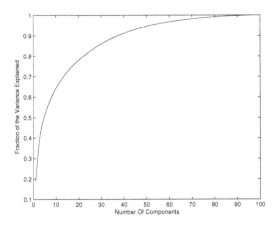

Fig. 5. Fraction of the variance explained by the nth most important principal deformation modes

Furthermore, the cumulative variance explained by an increasing number of principal deformations modes (illustrated at figure 5) shows the capacity of the proposed method to reduce the dimensionality of the model while keeping a large part of the original variance.

Finally, the algorithm is not very sensitive to the exact value of ω (values between 0.01 and 0.25 were tried and yielded similar results with our database), but setting a value considerably too high or too low would discard either the rotation or translation part of the rigid transforms from the analysis.

4   Conclusion

A method to extract the principal modes of deformation from articulated models was described. The method consists in performing a principal component analysis in the tangent space of a Riemannian manifold (the Lie group of rigid transforms equipped with a metric). We applied this method to a database of scoliotic patients reconstructed in 3D using stereo radiographs. Clinically relevant patterns of deformations were extracted from that database and dimensionality reduction was successfully achieved. Results also suggest that PCA applied to a suitable representation of the spine, namely a set of rigid transforms, leads to an algorithm that can expose natural modes of deformation of the spine. However, it might be interesting to validate the method using an high accuracy imaging apparus and a deformable spine phantom.

One of the reasons to perform dimensionality reduction on statistical shape models is to reduce the number of DOF that needs to be optimized during model registration. The proposed method will therefore be integrated to a spine registration algorithm in the future. It might also be useful for the integration of a large number of rigid structures in non-rigid registration procedures [12] of the whole human torso.

Also, the current method takes only into account the shape of the spine and not the shape of the individual vertebrae. But the deformations of individual vertebrae are connected to the deformations of the whole spine (see, for example, the vicious cycle described by Stokes et al. [13]). Thus, future developments might include the construction of hybrid models where the global shape of the spine would be modelled using inter-vertebral rigid transforms and the shape of individual vertebrae would be taken into account using spherical harmonics or medial axis representations (for instance).

References

1. Lorenz, C., Krahnstover, N.: Generation of point-based 3d statistical shape models for anatomical objects. Comput. Vis. Image Underst. **77** (2000) 175 – 91
2. Benameur, S., Mignotte, M., Parent, S., Labelle, H., Skalli, W., de Guise, J.: 3D/2D registration and segmentation of scoliotic vertebrae using statistical models. Computerized Medical Imaging and Graphics **27** (2003) 321–37
3. Pennec, X.: Intrinsic statistics on Riemannian manifolds: Basic tools for geometric measurements. Journal of Mathematical Imaging and Vision (2006)
4. Fletcher, P., Lu, C., Pizer, S., Joshi, S.: Principal geodesic analysis for the study of nonlinear statistics of shape. IEEE Trans. Med. Imaging **23** (2004)
5. Boisvert, J., Pennec, X., Ayache, N., Labelle, H., Cheriet, F.: 3D anatomical variability assessment of the scoliotic spine using statistics on lie groups. In: Proceedings of ISBI. (2006)
6. Bergeron, C., Cheriet, F., Ronsky, J., Zernicke, R., Labelle, H.: Prediction of anterior scoliotic spinal curve from trunk surface using support vector regression. Engineering Applications of Artificial Intelligence **18** (2005) 973 – 82
7. Gonzalez, J., Varona, J., Roca, F., Villanueva, J.: Analysis of human walking based on aspaces. Proc. of Articulated Motion and Deformable Objects (2004) 177 – 88
8. Jiang, X., Motai, Y.: Learning by observation of robotic tasks using on-line pca-based eigen behavior. Proc. International Symposium on Computational Intelligence in Robotics and Automation (2005) 391 – 6
9. Pennec, X.: Computing the mean of geometric features - application to the mean rotation. Research Report RR-3371, INRIA (1998)
10. Aubin, C.E., Dansereau, J., Parent, F., Labelle, H., de Guise, J.: Morphometric evaluations of personalised 3d reconstructions and geometric models of the human spine. Med. Bio. Eng. Comp. **35** (1997)
11. King, H.A.: Selection of fusion levels for posterior instrumentation and fusion in idiopathic scoliosis. Orthop Clin North Am **19** (1988) 247–255
12. Little, J., Hill, D., Hawkes, D.: Deformations incorporating rigid structures. Computer Vision and Image Understanding **66** (1997) 223–32
13. Stokes, I.A., Spence, H., Aronsson, D.D., Kilmer, N.: Mechanical modulation of vertebral body growth. implications for scoliosisprogression. Spine **21** (1996) 1162–1167

Automatic Pose Correction for Local Feature-Based Face Authentication

Daniel González-Jiménez[1], Federico Sukno[2],
José Luis Alba-Castro[1], and Alejandro Frangi[2]

[1] Departamento de Teoría de la Señal y Comunicaciones, Universidad de Vigo, Spain
{danisub, jalba}@gts.tsc.uvigo.es
[2] Departamento de Tecnología, Universidad Pompeu Fabra, Barcelona, Spain
{federico.sukno, alejandro.frangi}@upf.edu

Abstract. In this paper, we present an automatic face authentication system. Accurate segmentation of prominent facial features is accomplished by means of an extension of the Active Shape Model (ASM) approach, the so-called Active Shape Model with Invariant Optimal Features (IOF-ASM). Once the face has been segmented, a pose correction step is applied, so that frontal face images are synthesized. For the generation of these virtual images, we make use of a subset of the shape parameters extracted from a training dataset and Thin Plate Splines texture mapping. Afterwards, sets of local features are computed from these virtual images. The performance of the system is demonstrated on configurations I and II of the XM2VTS database.

Keywords: Face Authentication, Automatic Segmentation, Pose Correction.

1 Introduction

Although many algorithms have been proposed during the last decade, the general face recognition problem still remains unsolved because of several causes that affect the performance of face-based biometric approaches, such as illumination and pose variations, expression changes, etc [19]. Moreover, face recognition algorithms must be supplied with cropped images that ideally contain only face pixels, i.e. there must exist a previous step that locates the face (and perhaps a set of facial features) within the input image. Face authentication contests like [17] have shown that there is a general degradation in performance when changing between manual registration of faces and using automatic detection before authentication. In this paper, we address two aspects of the face authentication problem: automatic face modelling from still images and pose correction.

One of the most popular approaches for statistical modelling are the active models of shape and appearance, introduced by Cootes et al. in [11,12]. These techniques allow for detailed modelling of a wide range of objects, as long as an appropriate training set is available. Their application to facial images has been previously exploited [16,15] to locate the main facial features (e.g. eyes,

F.J. Perales and R.B. Fisher (Eds.): AMDO 2006, LNCS 4069, pp. 356–365, 2006.

nose, lips) and recover shape and texture parameters. In this work we use the Active Shape Models with Invariant Optimal Features (IOF-ASM), an extension of Active Shape Models (ASM) that improves segmentation accuracy by means of a non-linear texture model based on local image structure [21].

As stated above, the presence of pose differences within the input images is one of the main factors that degrades the performance of face recognition systems. Up to now, the most practical and successful algorithms dealing with pose-invariant face recognition are those which make use of prior knowledge of the class of faces such as [1], where an individual eigenspace is constructed for each pose. Another approach is presented in [2], where from a single image of a subject and making use of face class information, virtual views facing different poses are synthesized, which are then used in a view-based recognizer. In [3], a morphable 3D face model was fitted to the input images. Among others, the parameters that account for pose are subject to modification, so that virtual images facing the adequate pose can be synthesized. The main drawbacks of this method are the need of a 3D face training database and the high computational complexity. Using a training dataset of face images, we built a Point Distribution Model and, from the main modes of variation, the parameters responsible for the pose of the face (namely the pose parameters) were identified. Using the segmentation results provided by the IOF-ASM approach, our system compensates for pose variations by normalizing these pose parameters and synthesizing virtual frontal images through texture mapping. Sets of local features are extracted from these virtual images by means of a two-stage approach. Experiments on the XM2VTS database showed how this simple strategy softens (moderated) pose effects, achieving error rates comparable to the state of the art.

The paper is organized as follows: Section 2 presents the statistical modelling of the face and the approach used for segmenting facial features. In Section 3, the synthesis of pose corrected face images is addressed, while section 4 explains the two stages of feature extraction. In Section 5, we show our experimental results over the XM2VTS database [18]. Finally, conclusions are drawn in Section 6.

2   Statistical Face Modelling

2.1   A Point Distribution Model for Faces

A Point Distribution Model (PDM) of a face is generated from a set of training examples. For each training image I_i, N landmarks are located and their coordinates are stored, conforming a vector $\mathbf{X}_i = (x_{1i}, x_{2i}, \ldots, x_{Ni}, y_{1i}, y_{2i}, \ldots, y_{Ni})$. The pair (x_{ji}, y_{ji}) represents the coordinates of the j-th landmark in the i-th training image. After aligning all training examples, a Principal Components Analysis is performed in order to find the most important modes of shape variation. As a consequence, any training shape $\mathbf{X}_i$ can be approximately reconstructed as:

$$\mathbf{X}_i = \bar{\mathbf{X}} + \mathbf{Pb}, \tag{1}$$

where $\bar{\mathbf{X}}$ stands for the mean shape, $\mathbf{P}$ is a matrix whose columns are unit eigenvectors of the first t modes of variation found in the training set, and $\mathbf{b}$ is the

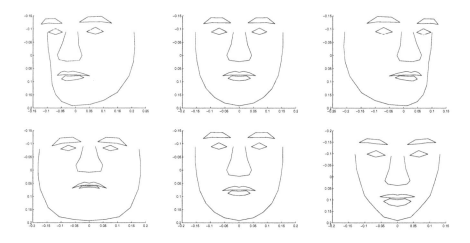

Fig. 1. Effect of varying pose parameters. rotations in depth parameter (first row) and elevation parameter (second row). The middle column shows the average face shape, while the left and right columns are generated displacing the corresponding parameters by ± 5 times the standard deviation of the training set.

vector of parameters that define the actual shape of $\mathbf{X}_i$. Notice that the k-th component from $\mathbf{b}$ $(b_k, k = 1, 2, \ldots, t)$ weighs the k-th mode of variation. Examining the shapes generated by varying b_k within suitable limits, we find those parameters responsible for pose, as indicated in figure 1. Note that, although a given eigenvector should not be assigned to an unique mode of facial variation, it is clear that the eigenvectors shown in this figure are mainly related to pose changes. Let $\mathbf{b}^{pose}$ be the set of parameters which accounts for pose variation. Since $\mathbf{P}^T \mathbf{P} = \mathbf{I}$, then

$$\mathbf{b} = \mathbf{P}^T \left(\mathbf{X}_i - \bar{\mathbf{X}} \right), \tag{2}$$

i.e. given any shape, it is possible to obtain its vector of parameters $\mathbf{b}$ and, in particular, we are able to find its pose (i.e. $\mathbf{b}^{pose}$).

We built a 62-point PDM using the set of manual annotated landmarks[1] from the training images shared by both configurations I and II [9] of the XM2VTS database[18].

2.2   IOF-ASM

When a new image containing a face is presented to the system, the vector of shape parameters that fits the data, $\mathbf{b}$, should be computed automatically. Active Shape Models with Invariant Optimal Features (IOF-ASM) is a statistical modelling method specifically designed and tested to handle the complexities of facial images. The algorithm learns the shape statistics as in the original ASMs [11] but improves the local texture description by using a set of differential

---

[1] http://www-prima.inrialpes.fr/FGnet/data/07-XM2VTS/xm2vts-markup.html

---

Algorithm 1. IOF-ASM matching to a new image

1: Compute invariants for the whole image
2: $\mathbf{T}$ = Initial transformation guess for face position and size
3: $\mathbf{X} = \overline{\mathbf{X}}$ (*modelShape = meanShape*)
4: **for** $i = 1$ to number_of_iterations **do**
5:    Project shape to image coordinates: $\mathbf{Y} = \mathbf{TX}$
6:    **for** $l = 1$ to number_of_landmarks **do**
7:       Sample invariants around *l-th* landmark
8:       Determine best candidate point to place the landmark
9:       **if** the best candidate is good enough **then**
10:          Move the landmark to the best candidate point
11:       **else**
12:          Keep previous landmark position (do not move)
13:       **end if**
14:    **end for**
15:    Let the shape with new positions be $\widetilde{\mathbf{Y}}$
16:    Update $\mathbf{T}$ and PDM parameters: $\widetilde{\mathbf{b}} = \mathbf{P}^T(\mathbf{T}^{-1}\widetilde{\mathbf{Y}} - \mathbf{X})$
17:    Apply PDM constraints: $\mathbf{b} = PdmConstrain(\widetilde{\mathbf{b}}, \beta)$
18:    Get new model shape: $\mathbf{X} = \overline{\mathbf{X}} + \mathbf{Pb}$
19: **end for**

---

invariants combined with non-linear classifiers. As a result, IOF-ASM produces a more accurate segmentation of the facial features [21].

The matching procedure is summarized in Algorithm 1. In line 1 the image is preprocessed to obtain a set of differential invariants. These invariants are the core of the method and they consist on combinations of partial derivatives that result invariant to rigid transformations [22,20]. Moreover, IOF-ASM uses a *minimal set* of order K so that any other algebraic invariant up to order K can be reduced to a linear combination of elements of this minimal set [13].

The other key point of the algorithm is between lines 1 and 1. For each landmark, an image-driven search is performed to determine the best position for it to be placed. The process starts by sampling the invariants in a neighborhood of the landmark (line 1). In IOF-ASM this neighborhood is represented by a rectangular grid, whose dimensions are parameters of the model. A non-linear texture classifier analyzes the sampled data to determine if the local structure of the image is compatible with the one learnt during training for this landmark. A predefined number of displacements are allowed for the position of the landmark (perpendicularly to the boundary, as in [11]), so that the texture classifier analyzes several *candidate positions*. Once the best candidate is found, say (x_B, y_B), the matching between its local image structure and the one learnt during training is verified (line 1) by means of a robust metric [14]. The applied metric consists on the evaluation of the sampled data grouped according to its distance perpendicularly to the shape boundary. Grouping this way, the samples can be organized in a one-dimensional *profile* of length l_P. Based on the output from the texture classifier, each position on this profile will result as a *supporting point* or an *outlier* (the *supporting points* are those profile points suggesting that (x_B, y_B) is the best position for the landmark to be placed, while *outliers* indicate a different position and, therefore, suggest that (x_B, y_B) is incorrect). If the supporting points are (at least) two thirds of l_P, then the matching is considered accurate and the landmark is moved to the new position. Otherwise the matching is not trustworthy (i.e. the image structure does not clearly suggests a landmark) and the landmark position is kept unchanged (see [21] for details).

The PDM constraints of line 1 ensure that the obtained shape is *plausible* according to the learnt statistics (i.e. it looks like a face). For this purpose, each component of **b** is limited so that $|b_k| \leq \beta\sqrt{\lambda_k}$, $(1 \leq k \leq t)$; where t is the number of modes of variation of the PDM, λ_k is the eigenvalue associated to the *k-th* mode and β is a constant, usually set between 1 and 3, that controls the degree of flexibility of the PDM (see [11]).

3   Correcting Pose Variations in Face Images

Once the flexible shape model (with coordinates X) has been fitted to the face image I, the shape parameters **b** are extracted using equation (2). In particular, we are interested in the subset of parameters describing the pose ($\mathbf{b}^{pose}$). In order to generate a frontal mesh, these parameters are set to zero[2]. Hence, we obtain a new vector of parameters $\hat{\mathbf{b}}$ and, through equation 1, the frontal face mesh $\hat{X}$.

Given the original face I, the coordinates of its respective fitted flexible shape model, X, and the new set of coordinates, $\hat{X}$, a virtual face image $\hat{I}$ must be synthesized by warping the original face onto the new shape. For this purpose, we used a method developed in [4], based on thin plate splines. Provided the set of correspondences between X and $\hat{X}$, the original face I is allowed to be deformed so that the original landmarks are moved to fit the new shape. The full procedure of pose normalization is shown in figure 2.

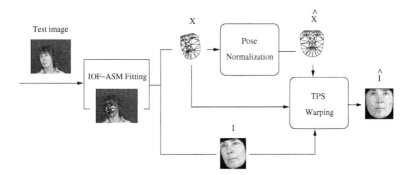

Fig. 2. Block diagram for pose normalization. TPS stands for Thin Plate Splines.

---

[2] We will use the term *frontal* when referring to the pose of the mean shape of the PDM. However, the only requirement of the method is that all shapes can be mapped to a common view, then there is not a need for a strictly frontal mean-shape.

3.1   Advantages over Warping onto a Mean Shape

When warping an image onto the average shape ($\bar{X}$) of a training set, all shape parameters are set to zero. In other words, the fitted flexible shape model is forced to be moved to the coordinates of $\bar{X}$. Holistic approaches such as PCA need all images to be embedded into a given reference frame (an average shape for instance), in order to represent these images as vectors of ordered pixels. The problem arises when the subject's shape differs enough from the average shape, as the warped image may appear geometrically distorted, and subject-specific information may be removed. Given that our method is not holistic but uses local features instead, the reference-frame constraint is avoided and the distortion is minimized by modifying only pose parameters rather than the whole shape.

4   Feature Extraction

Once the normalization process has finished, we must proceed to extract features from the virtual frontal images $\hat{I}$. Up to now, most algorithms encoding local information have been based on localizing a pre-defined set of landmarks and extracting features from the regions surrounding those points. The key idea behind our approach relies on selecting an *own* and discriminative set of points per client, where features should be extracted. The choice of this set is accomplished through a two-layer strategy, whose stages are explained below.

Layer I: Shape-driven selection and matching. In the first step, a preliminary selection of facial points is accomplished through the use of shape information [5]. Lines depicting face structure are extracted by thresholding the response

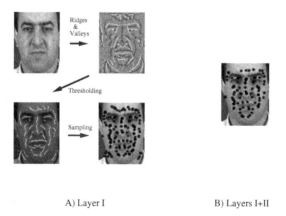

A) Layer I   B) Layers I+II

Fig. 3. A) Layer I: A ridge and valley detector is applied to the original image (top left), and its response is shown on the right. Thresholding this representation leads to a set of lines depicting face structure (bottom left). The set of points $\mathcal{P}$ is obtained by sampling from these lines (bottom right). **B) Layers I+II:** Final set of points after layer II is applied.

of a ridge and valley detector, and a set of points $\mathcal{P} = \{\boldsymbol{p}_1, \boldsymbol{p}_2, \ldots, \boldsymbol{p}_n\}$ is chosen automatically by sampling from these lines. Figure 3-A illustrates this procedure. Then, a set of multi-scale and multi-orientation Gabor features (so-called jet) is computed at each shape driven point. Let $\mathcal{J}_{\boldsymbol{p}_i}$ be the jet obtained from point $\boldsymbol{p}_i$. Given the two faces to be compared, say $\hat{I}_{train}$ and $\hat{I}_{test}$, their respective sets of points are computed: $\mathcal{P}_{train} = \{\boldsymbol{p}_1, \boldsymbol{p}_2, \ldots, \boldsymbol{p}_n\}$ and $\mathcal{P}_{test} = \{\boldsymbol{q}_1, \boldsymbol{q}_2, \ldots, \boldsymbol{q}_n\}$, and a shape matching algorithm based on shape contexts [6] is used to calculate the correspondences between the two sets of points, $\xi(i) : \boldsymbol{p}_i \Longrightarrow \boldsymbol{q}_{\xi(i)}$. Hence, jet $\mathcal{J}_{\boldsymbol{p}_i}$ will be compared to $\mathcal{J}_{\boldsymbol{q}_{\xi(i)}}$. The comparison between $\mathcal{J}_{\boldsymbol{p}_i}$ and $\mathcal{J}_{\boldsymbol{q}_{\xi(i)}}$ is given by the normalized dot product ($< \mathcal{J}_{\boldsymbol{p}_i}, \mathcal{J}_{\boldsymbol{q}_{\xi(i)}} >$), but taking into account that only the moduli of jet coefficients are used.

Layer II: Accuracy-based selection. Some previous approaches have been focused on identifying which features were the most important for authentication purposes. Among others, [8], [7] have selected and weighted the nodes from a rectangular grid based on a Linear Discriminant Analysis (LDA). This kind of analysis is possible due to the fact that a given node represents the same facial region in every image. In our case, we can not assume this, so a different method is needed in order to select the most discriminative points. The problem can be formulated as follows. Given:

- a training image for client C, say $\hat{I}_{train}$,
- a set of images of the same client $\left\{\hat{I}_j^c\right\}, j = 1, \ldots, N_c$, and
- a set of imposter images $\left\{\hat{I}_j^{im}\right\}, j = 1, \ldots, N_{im}$,

we want to find which subset, $\mathcal{P}^* \subset \mathcal{P}_{train}$, is the most discriminative. As long as each $\boldsymbol{p}_i$ from $\mathcal{P}_{train}$ has a correspondent point in any other image, we evaluate the individual classification accuracy of its associated jet $\mathcal{J}_{\boldsymbol{p}_i}$, so that only the locations whose jets are good at discriminating between clients and imposters are preserved. With the set of images given above, we have N_c client accesses and N_{im} imposter trials for jet $\mathcal{J}_{\boldsymbol{p}_i}$ to classify. We measure the False Acceptance Rate (FAR$_i$) and the False Rejection Rate (FRR$_i$) for this jet and, if the Total Error Rate (TER$_i$ = FAR$_i$ + FRR$_i$) exceeds a threshold τ, jet $\mathcal{J}_{\boldsymbol{p}_i}$ will be discarded. Finally, only a subset of points, $\mathcal{P}^*$, is chosen per image, and the score between $\hat{I}_{train}$ and $\hat{I}_{test}$ is given by:

$$\mathcal{S} = f_{n^*}\left\{< \mathcal{J}_{\boldsymbol{p}_i}, \mathcal{J}_{\boldsymbol{q}_{\xi(i)}} >\right\}_{\boldsymbol{p}_i \in \mathcal{P}^*} \tag{3}$$

where f_{n^*} stands for a generic combination rule of the n^* dot products. Figure 3-B presents the set of points that was chosen after both layer selection.

5 Experimental Results on the XM2VTS Database

The proposed method was tested using the XM2VTS database on configurations I and II of the Lausanne protocol [9]. The XM2VTS database contains image

Table 1. False Acceptance Rate (FAR), False Rejection Rate (FRR) and Total Error Rate (TER) over the test set for our method and automatic approaches from [17]

	Conf. I			Conf. II		
	FAR(%)	FRR(%)	**TER(%)**	FAR(%)	FRR(%)	**TER(%)**
UPV	1.23	2.75	3.98 ± 1.35	1.55	0.75	2.30 ± 0.71
UNIS-NC	1.36	2.5	3.86 ± 1.29	1.36	2	3.36 ± 1.15
IDIAP	1.95	2.75	4.70 ± 1.35	1.35	0.75	2.10 ± 0.71
Pose Corr.(Auto)	0.83	2.75	3.58 ± 1.35	0.85	2	2.85 ± 1.15
Pose Corr.(Manual)	0.46	2.75	3.21 ± 1.35	0.72	1.50	2.22 ± 1.00
No Pose Corr.(Auto)	0.65	3.75	4.40 ± 1.56	0.74	2.5	3.24 ± 1.28
No Pose Corr.(Manual)	0.89	4	4.89 ± 1.61	0.75	2.5	3.25 ± 1.28

data recorded on 295 subjects (200 clients, 25 evaluation imposters, and 70 test imposters).The database is divided into three sets: training, evaluation and test. The training set was used to build client models, the PDM, and the IOF-ASM[3], while the evaluation set was used to select the best features and estimate thresholds. Finally, the test set was employed to assess system performance.

In all the experiments, $n = 130$ shape-driven points are computed for every image. However, only $n^* \leq 130$ local scores are computed, because of the feature selection explained in Section 4. The median rule [10] was used to fuse these scores, i.e. $f_{n^*} \equiv median$. Configurations I and II of the Lausanne protocol differ in the distribution of client training and client evaluation data, representing configuration II the most realistic case. In configuration I, there are 3 training images per client, while in configuration II, 4 training images are available. Hence, for a given test image, we get 3 and 4 scores respectively, which can be fused in order to obtain better results. Again, the median rule was used to combine these values, obtaining a final score ready for verification.

Table 1 shows a comparison between the proposed method (*Pose Corr.(Auto)*) and a set of algorithms that entered the competition held in conjunction with the Audio- and Video-based Biometric Person Authentication (AVBPA) conference in 2003 [17]. All these algorithms are automatic. In this table, and derived from the work in [24], 90% confidence intervals for the TER measures are also given. As we can see, our approach offers competitive error rates in both configurations (with no statistically significant differences between methods). Furthermore, the last three rows from this table show baseline results:

- *Pose Corr.(Manual)*: The automatic segmentation provided by IOF-ASM is replaced by manual annotation of landmarks.
- *No Pose Corr.(Auto)*: Automatic segmentation without pose correction (only in-plane rotations are corrected).
- *No Pose Corr.(Manual)*: Manual segmentation without pose correction (only in-plane rotations are corrected).

---

[3] The IOF-ASM was built with the same parameters detailed in [21].

It is clear that the use of IOF-ASM offers accurate results for our task, as the degradation between the error rates with manual and automatic segmentation is small. Moreover, the comparison between lines 4 and 6-7, shows that the use of pose-corrected images improves the performance of the system (even if manual landmarks are used to segment the original faces).

6   Conclusions

We have presented an automatic face authentication system that reduces the effect of pose variations by synthesizing frontal face images. The segmentation of the face in the original image is accomplished by means of the IOF-ASM approach. A set of discriminative points and features is then selected in two steps: the shape-driven location stage and the accuracy-based selection step.

The quality of the synthesized face (and thus, system performance) mainly depends on the segmentation accuracy, which is intimately related to the degree of pose variation in the input image and the dataset used for training. The achieved results on the XM2VTS database demonstrate the usefulness of the method in a limited range of pose variations, offering state-of-the-art error rates. As a main future research line, we plan to work on video-sequences in which facial features will be tracked in a frame-by-frame basis through the combination of IOF-ASM segmentation and a robust face tracker [25].

Acknowledgments

This work is framed within the RAVIV project from Biosecure NoE, and has also been partially funded by grants TEC2005-07212, TIC2002-04495-C02 and FIT-390000-2004-30 from the Spanish Ministry of Science and Technology. FS is supported by a BSCH grant. AF holds a Ramón y Cajal Research Fellowship.

References

1. Pentland, A. et al. View-based and Modular Eigenspaces for Face Recognition. In *Proc. IEEE Conference on Computer Vision and Pattern Recognition,* 1994, pp. 84–91.
2. Beymer, D.J. and Poggio, T. Face Recognition from One Example View. In *Proc. International Conference on Computer Vision,* 1995, pp. 500–507.
3. Blanz, V. and Vetter, T. A Morphable model for the synthesis of 3D faces. In *Proc. SIGGRAPH,* 1999, pp. 187-194.
4. Bookstein, Fred L. Principal Warps: Thin-Plate Splines and the Decomposition of Deformations. In *IEEE Transactions on Pattern Analysis and Machine Intelligence 11,* 6 (1989), 567–585.
5. González-Jiménez, D., Alba-Castro, J.L., "Shape Contexts and Gabor Features for Face Description and Authentication," in *Proc. IEEE ICIP 2005,* pp. 962-965.
6. Belongie, S., Malik, J., Puzicha J. Shape Matching and Object Recognition Using Shape Contexts. In *IEEE Transactions on Pattern Analysis and Machine Intelligence 24,* 24 (2002), 509–522.

7. Duc, B., Fischer, S., and Bigun, S. Face authentication with sparse grid gabor information. In *IEEE Proc. ICASSP*, (Munich 1997), vol. 4, pp. 3053–3056.
8. Argones-Rúa, E., Kittler, J., Alba-Castro, J.L., González-Jiménez, D. Information fusion for local Gabor features based frontal face verification. In *Proc. International Conference on Biometrics (ICB)*, Hong Kong 2006, (Springer), pp. 173–181.
9. Luttin, J. and Maître, G. Evaluation protocol for the extended M2VTS database (XM2VTSDB). Technical report RR-21, IDIAP, 1998.
10. Kittler, J., Hatef, M., Duin, R., and Matas, J. On Combining Classifiers. In *IEEE Transactions on Pattern Analysis and Machine Intelligence 20*, 3 (1998), 226–239.
11. Cootes, T., Taylor, C., Cooper, D., and Graham, J. Active shape models - their training and application. *Computer Vision and Image Understanding 61*, 1 (1995), 38–59.
12. Cootes, T., Edwards, G., and Taylor, C. Active appearance models. In *Proc. European Conference on Computer Vision* (Springer, 1998), vol. 2, pp. 484–498.
13. Florack, L. *The Syntactical Structure of Scalar Images*. PhD thesis, Utrecht University, Utrecht, The Nedherlands, 2001.
14. Huber, P. *Robust Statistics*. Wiley, New York, 1981.
15. Kang, H., Cootes, T., and Taylor, C. A comparison of face verification algorithms using appearance models. In *Proc. British Machine Vision Conference* (Cardiff, UK, 2002), vol. 2, pp. 477–486.
16. Lanitis, A., Taylor, C., and Cootes, T. Automatic interpretation and coding of face images using flexible models. *IEEE Transactions on Pattern Analysis and Machine Intelligence 19*, 7 (1997), 743–756.
17. Messer, K., Kittler, J., Sadeghi, M., Marcel, S., Marcel, C., Bengio, S., Cardinaux, F., Sanderson, C., Czyz, J., Vandendorpe, L., and al. Face verification competition on the XM2VTS database. In *Proc. 4th International Conference on Audio- and Video-based Biometric Person Authentication (AVBPA)* Guildford, UK (2003), pp. 964–974.
18. Messer, K., Matas, J., Kittler, J., Luettin, J., and Maitre, G. XM2VTSDB: The extended M2VTS database. In *Proc. International Conference on Audio- and Video-Based Person Authentication* (1999), pp. 72–77.
19. Philips, P., Moon, H., Rizvi, S., and Rauss, P. The FERET evaluation methodology for face recognition algorithms. *IEEE Transactions on Pattern Analysis and Machine Intelligence 22(10)* (2000), 1090–1104.
20. Schmid, C., and Mohr, R. Local greyvalue invariants for image retrieval. *IEEE Transactions on Pattern Analysis and Machine Intelligence 19(5)* (1997), 530–535.
21. Sukno, F., Ordas, S., Butakoff, C., Cruz, S., and Frangi, A. Active shape models with invariant optimal features IOF-ASMs. In *Proc. Audio- and Video-Based Biometric Person Authentication* (New York, USA, 2005), Springer, pp. 365–375.
22. Walker, K., Cootes, T., and Taylor, C. J. Correspondence using distinct points based on image invariants. In *British Machine Vision Conference* (1997), vol. 1, pp. 540–549.
23. Wiskott, L., Fellows, J.-M., Kruger, N., and von der Malsburg, C. Face recognition by elastic bunch graph matching. *IEEE Transactions on Pattern Analysis and Machine Intelligence 19*, 7 (1997), 775–779.
24. Bengio, S. Mariéthoz, J. A statistical significance test for person authentication. In *Proc. Odyssey*, 2004, pp. 237–244.
25. Baker, S. and Matthews, I. Equivalence and Efficiency of Image Alignment Algorithms. In *Proc. IEEE Conference on Computer Vision and Pattern Recognition*, 2001, vol. 1, pp. 1090–1097.

An Adaptive 3D Surface Mesh Cutting Operation

Huynh Quang Huy Viet, Takahiro Kamada, and Hiromi T. Tanaka

Department of Human and Computer Intelligence, Ritsumeikan University
4F Creation Core Building, 1-1-1 Noji-higashi, Kusatsu, Shiga 525-8577, Japan
viet@is.ritsumei.ac.jp

Abstract. The cutting operation of 3D surface meshes plays an important role in surgery simulators. One of the important requirements for surgical simulators is the visual reality. We propose a new strategy for cutting on surface meshes: refinement and separate strategy consisting of the refinement followed by the separation of the refined mesh element.The proposed strategy gives the faithful representation of interaction paths of a surgical tool.

1 Introduction

Surgical simulators have been developed to create environments to help train physicians in learning skills of surgical operations at many research centers. The virtual cutting operation plays an important role in surgery simulators. The virtual cutting methods can be divided into two categories: (i) volume cutting method that consists of cutting methods on a tetrahedral mesh and (ii) surface cutting method that consists of cutting methods on a 3D surface mesh. One of the important requirements for cutting methods is the issue of accuracy representation of the interaction path of a surgical tool.

In addition the cutting techniques may also be classified into two major categories based on the implementation of a cutting operation; those that remove intersected meshes [1] and those that re-mesh intersected meshes [2,3,4,5,6,7,8]. The methods of the first category simply dismiss mesh elements that intersect the cutting tool; the methods of the second category recreate the path passed over by the tool through the intersected mesh elements by way of re-meshing them. The methods of the second category have the disadvantage of the supplemental cost for computing the intersection path but provide a good visual representation of the path passed over by the cutting tool. In order to have the accuracy representation of the intersection path without considerably scarifying the cost of computation of deformation, there is a strategy proposed and implemented on tetrahedral meshes: refinement and remove strategy [9]. This strategy composes of the refinement followed by the elimination of the mesh elements (tetrahedral) on the surface cut. Despite the fact that the sizes of removed mesh elements are small due to the previous mesh refinement process, the approach still has the drawback of creating non-smooth cuts, and hence are still not appropriate for a

F.J. Perales and R.B. Fisher (Eds.): AMDO 2006, LNCS 4069, pp. 366–374, 2006.

realistic simulator. Moreover, there are not the implementations of this strategy on surface meshes.

We propose a new strategy for cutting on surface mesh: refinement and separate strategy consisting of the refinement followed by the separation of the refined mesh element. Since the advantage of the low computational cost (linear time complexity comparing to $O(NlogN)$ time complexity of Delaunay refinement methods), the longest-edge refinement method [10] is utilized for the refinement process. The proposed strategy gives the faithful representation of the interaction path in comparing with the conventional methods.

This paper is organized as follows. Section 2 introduces the longest-edge refinement method which is the base for constructing the proposed method for virtual cutting. Section 3 details the proposed method. Section 4 describes the results. Section 5 is devoted for conclusions and future works.

2   Backward Longest-Size Refinement Algorithm

As a preliminary for presenting the proposed method, in this section we introduce the backward longest-edge refinement algorithm of Rivara [10] for triangular mesh refinement. The requirement of a refinement of a mesh is to satisfy the main properties: conforming, well shaped and smooth. A conforming mesh is a mesh without any "T-junctions". T junction is a non-conforming point which is defined as an interior point of an edge of one triangle and common vertex of two other adjoin triangles. The well shaped mesh is a mesh whose angle of the elements is bounded from 0 and π. Rivara proposed the backward longest-edge bisection refinement algorithm. The method only bisects along the longest-edge of a triangle; this guarantees the construction of non-degenerate and smooth irregular triangulations whose geometrical properties only depend on the initial mesh. In order to maintain a conforming mesh, the local refinement of a given triangle involves refinement of the triangle itself and refinement of its longest edge neighbors.

Longest-side propagation path is a concept utilized in the backward longest-size refinement algorithm. It is defined as follows: For any triangle t_0 of any conforming triangulation T, the longest-side propagation path of t_0 will be the ordered list of all the triangles $t_0, t_1, t_2, ...t_{n-1}, t_n$, such that t_i is the neighbor triangle of t_{i-1}, by the longest-size of t_{i-1}, for $i = 1, 2, ..n$. The longest-side propagation path pf triangle t_0 is denoted as $LSPP(t_0)$.

The following is the backward longest-size refinement algorithm:

Backward Longest-Size Bisection (T, t)
While t remains without being bisected do
    Find the $LSPP(t)$
    If t^*, the last triangle of the $LSPP(t)$, is a terminal boundary triangle, bisect t^*
    Else bisect the (last) pair of terminal triangles of the $LSPP(t)$

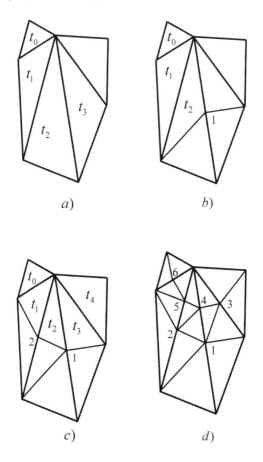

Fig. 1. Backward longest-side bisection of triangle t_0

Figure 1 explains the backward longest-size refinement algorithm: Fig. 1a gives the initial triangulation; Fig. 1b gives the first step of the process; Fig. 1c gives the second step in the process and Fig. 1d gives the final triangulation.

3   Data Structure and Cutting Algorithm

The objects of the surgical simulation are represented by 3D surface meshes. The surface mesh of the object can be taken from laser scanner. The VRML output file of a laser scanner is used in a data structure based on winged-edge data structure, which includes the physical parameters of a damped mass-spring model. The data which is stored at each vertices are their 3D coordinates, the value of mass and the information of an edge adjacent to vertex, the data which is stored at each edge are the start of node, the end of node of vertex, the parameters of a damper and a spring, the previous edge for left face, the next

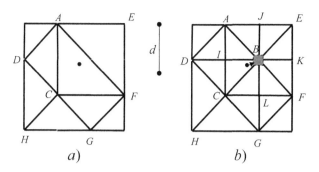

Fig. 2. Initial interacting point

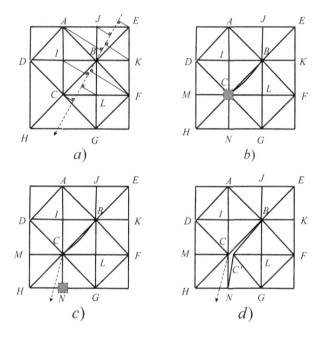

Fig. 3. Remeshing and making new point in a cutting process

edge for left face. This data structure allows quick computation of finding the adjacent triangles for cutting algorithm, and performing of deformation.

There are different approaches for changing the topology of an object such as destroying the mesh elements or dividing them. In our proposed method, to yield accuracy representation of cutting paths, instead of simple dividing the triangles (the mesh elements), we refine them by subdividing into smaller triangles using the longest-edge refinement algorithm mentioned in the previous section. The virtual cut is performed by way of separating the subdivided smaller triangles.

At first the triangle that is collided by the surgical tool is refined by using the backward longest-edge refinement algorithm mentioned in previous section, as

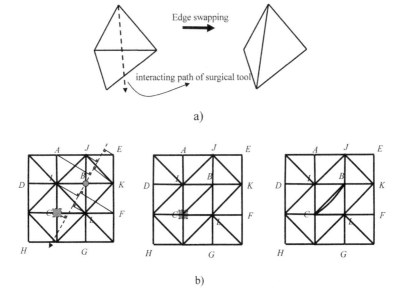

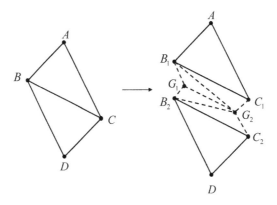

Fig. 4. Swapping an edge in a cutting process

Fig. 5. Groove Generation

showed in the Fig. 2b. The vertex that is nearest the colliding point is considered as the initial vertex for performing cutting.

Suppose that a virtual cut is being carried out at a vertex, we call this vertex as the reference vertex, the cut is performed by repetition of the following steps:

1. Finding the next vertex in cutting path: The next vertex is the neighboring vertex which has the closest distance toward the direction of the motion of a surgical tool. The neighboring vertex is a vertex adjacent to the reference vertex, or is the vertex of a triangle sharing the common edge with the triangle of the reference vertex; and do not lie on the common edge. The edge linking the reference vertex to the next vertex is called reference edge. Figure 3a shows how to choose the next vertex.

2. Changing the topology: The triangles sharing the next vertex from the reference vertex in cutting path are refined by the longest-edge refinement algorithm until the longest-edge l of the subdivided smaller triangles is satisfied the requirement of $d/2 < l < d$, where d is a predefined distance. Notice that the requirement of $l > d/2$ is to assure the termination for a refinement process. Figure 3b. gives an illustration a process of refinement of the triangles sharing the next vertex.

3. Changing the adjacent information of two triangles along the cutting path: The reference vertex is duplicated and the adjacent information of two triangles sharing the reference vertex is updated as not adjacent. Figure 3c and d clarifies this step when considering the vertex C as a reference vertex.

In the case that the next vertex is not belong the same triangle of the reference vertex and the edge which is shared by the two triangles is the longest edge as shown Fig. 4a, this edge is swapped so as the next vertex is connected with the reference vertex by an edge, and the cutting process is continued as described in Step 2 and Step 3 (see Fig. 4b).

It is necessary to have an algorithm for generating the groove of a cutting path. As shown in Fig. 5, when the triangles ABC and BCD are divided and the vertices B_1, B_2, C_1, C_2 are created, the bottom of the groove is generated at the tip positions of the cutting tool G_1 and G_2.

4   Experimental Results

Regarding with the issue of accuracy representation of the interaction path of a surgical tool, it is difficult to compare the proposed method which is based on the refinement and separate strategy with that of the refinement and removal strategy. However, in any situations, the fact that separating process of the refinement and separate strategy do not dismiss mesh elements definitely increases the accuracy much more than that of refinement and removal strategy. Here we show the results of the proposed method. We build the system as showed in Fig. 6 to implement the proposed method. The handling of the virtual object

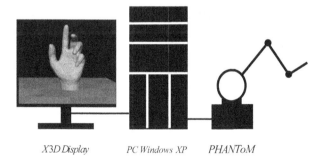

Fig. 6. System diagram

in 3D virtual space is performed by using the haptic interface device Phantom. The visual result is represented realistically in the X3D display screen.

Figure 7 shows the wire frame representation of a virtual cutting of a hand which is model by the 3D surface triangle mesh: Fig.7a gives the original representation of the hand and Fig.7b gives the result of the virtual cutting.

Fig.8a shows the enlargement of the result, the cutting path appears delicately; the very small shakes of the hand handling the Phantom arm are captured and expressed faithfully in zigzags. This show the effectiveness of the proposed method in accurate representation of the motion of the surgical tool. In fact if the friction force in hand surface is considered, the real motion of hand, which handles the Phantom arm, will become smooth. However, this does not affect the effectiveness of the proposed algorithm.

Fig.8b illustrates the case without using mesh refinement algorithm for the same motion of cutting tool of the previous experiment, the cutting path is far

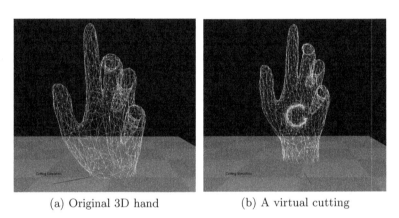

(a) Original 3D hand   (b) A virtual cutting

Fig. 7. Wire frame representation

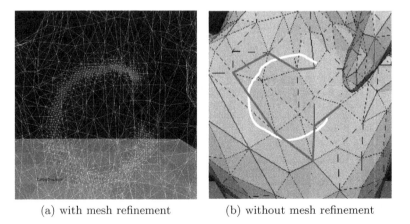

(a) with mesh refinement   (b) without mesh refinement

Fig. 8. Comparison of the algorithm with and without mesh refinement

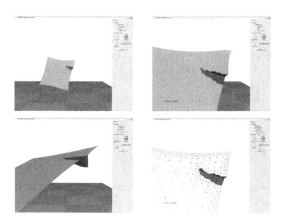

Fig. 9. Cut a groove on a surface

different from the motion of cutting tool (white line). In Fig.9, we show a result of cutting with groove generation.

5   Conclusions

The paper introduces a new method for carrying out a virtual cutting process with high visual effect. The main contribution of the work is a real-time 3D surface cutting algorithm that cooperates with the longest-edge based local refinement algorithm for unstructured meshes of triangle. The experiment results show the performance of the approach. Our closest goal of future work is to render deformation and haptic of highly deformable virtual objects under a virtual cutting.

References

1. S. Cotin, H. Delingette and N. Ayache: "A hybrid elastic model for real-time cutting, deformations, and force feedback for surgery training and simulation.", The Visual Computer, **16**, 7, pp. 437–452 (2000).
2. C. D. Bruyns and S. Senger: "Interactive cutting of 3d surface meshes", Computers & Graphics, **25**, pp. 635–642 (2001).
3. H.-W. Nienhuys and A. F. van der Stappen: "A surgery simulation supporting cuts and finite element deformation", Medical Image Computing and Computer-Assisted Intervention, Utrecht, The Netherlands, pp. 153–160 (2001).
4. C. Basdogan: "Simulation of instrument-tissue interactions and system integration", Medicine Meets Virtual Reality 2001 (2001).
5. D. Bielser, P. Glardon, M. Teschner and M. Gross: "A state machine for real-time cutting of tetrahedral meshes", Journal of Graphical Models, **66**, 6, pp. 398–417 (2004).
6. M. Harders, D. Steinemann, M. Gross and G. Szekely: "A hybrid cutting approach for hysteroscopy simulation", Conference on Medical Image Computing and Computer-Assisted Intervention, Palm Springs, USA (2005).

7. F. Ganovelli, P. Cignoni, C. Montani and R. Scopigno: "Enabling cuts on multiresolution representation", The Visual Computer, **17**, 5, pp. 274–286 (2001).

8. C. Mendoza and C. Laugier: "Simulating soft tissue cutting using finite element models", Proc. of the IEEE Int. Conf. on Robotics and Automation, Taipei, Taiwan, pp. 1109–1114 (2003).

9. C. Forest., H. Delingette and N. Ayache: "Removing tetrahedra from manifold tetrahedralisation : application to real-time surgical simulation", Medical Image Analysis, **9**, 2, pp. 113–122 (2005).

10. M.-C. Rivara: "New mathematical tools and techniques for the refinementand/or improvement of unstructured triangulations", 5th International Meshing Roundtable, pp. 77–86 (1996).

11. C. Bruyns, S. Senger, A. Menon, K. Montgomery, S. Wildermuth and R. Boyle: "A survey of interactive mesh-cutting techniques and a new method for implementing generalized interactive mesh cutting using virtual tools.", Journal of Visualization and Computer Animation, **13**, 1, pp. 21–42 (2002).

12. S. Payandeh, J. Dill and J. Zhang: "A study of level-ofdetail in haptic rendering", ACM Transactions on Applied Perceptions, **2**, 1, pp. 15–34 (2005).

13. H. T.Tanaka and F. Kishino: "Adaptive mesh generation for surface reconstruction: Parallel hierarchical triangulation without discontinuities", Proc. IEEE Conf. Computer Vision Pattern Recognition (CVPR93), New York City, pp. 88–94 (1993).

14. H.-W. Nienhuys and A. F. van der Stappen: "Supporting cuts and finite element deformation in interactive surgery simulation", Tech Report.

15. A. Liu, F. Tendick, K. Cleary and C. Kaufmann: "A survey of surgical simulation: applications, technology, and education", Presence: Teleoperators and Virtual Environments, **12**, 6, pp. 599–614 (2003).

Action Recognition Using Motion Primitives and Probabilistic Edit Distance

P. Fihl, M.B. Holte, T.B. Moeslund, and L. Reng

Laboratory of Computer Vision and Media Technology
Aalborg University, Denmark
tbm@cvmt.dk

Abstract. In this paper we describe a recognition approach based on the notion of primitives. As opposed to recognizing actions based on temporal trajectories or temporal volumes, primitive-based recognition is based on representing a temporal sequence containing an action by only a few characteristic time instances. The human whereabouts at these instances are extracted by double difference images and represented by four features. In each frame the primitive, if any, that best explains the observed data is identified. This leads to a discrete recognition problem since a video sequence will be converted into a string containing a sequence of symbols, each representing a primitives. After pruning the string a probabilistic Edit Distance classifier is applied to identify which action best describes the pruned string. The approach is evaluated on five one-arm gestures and the recognition rate is 91.3%. This is concluded to be a promising result but also leaves room for further improvements.

1 Introduction

In the last decade the focus on automatical analysis of human motion has increased rapidly. This is evident by the number of workshops and special sessions at conferences and special journal issues devoted to this research field. Furthermore, the recent public interest in security issues has increased the interest from the funding agencies leading to even more research in this field. Whereas more and more robust solutions are seen within both tracking and pose estimation, the subfield of automatical recognition of actions and activities is still lacking. One reason being that this field is not only based on advances in signal processing but also in AI. A number of advanced approaches have, however, been reported. The current trend is not as much on first reconstructing the human and the pose of his/her limbs and *then* do the recognition on the joint angle data, but rather to do the recognition directly on the image data, e.g., silhouette data.

Yu *et al.* [19] extract silhouettes and unwrapped their contours. PCA is used to obtain a compact representation. A three-layer feed forward network is used to distinguish actions such as walking and running based on the trajectories in eigenspace. Yilmaz and Shah [17] use spatio-temporal volumes (STV) for action recognition. A person's 3D contour is projected into 2D over time and yields the STV. Differential geometric is used to extract features from the STV and action recognition is carried out as an object matching task by interpreting the STV as rigid 3D objects. Bobick and Davis [4] apply temporal templates based on motion energy images (MEI) and motion history images

F.J. Perales and R.B. Fisher (Eds.): AMDO 2006, LNCS 4069, pp. 375–384, 2006.

(MHI). The MEI is a binary cumulative motion image. The MHI is an enhancement of the MEI where the pixel intensities are a function of the motion history at that pixel. Matching temporal templates is based on Hu moments. Related approaches are to use a 4D motion history volume based on the visual hull [16] or motion flow history [1].

Common for these approaches is that they represent an action by image data from all frames constituting the action, e.g., by a trajectory through some state-space or a spatio-temporal volume. This means that the methods in general require that the applied image information can be extracted reliably in every single frame. In some situations this will not be possible and therefore a different type of approach has been suggested. Here an action is divided into a number of smaller temporal sequences, for example movemes [6], atomic movements [7], states [5], dynamic instants [13], examplars [11], behaviour units [9], key-frames [8], and primitives [14]. The general idea is that approaches based on finding smaller units will be less sensitive compared to approaches based on an entire sequence of information.

For some approaches the union of the units represents the entire temporal sequence, whereas for other approaches the units represent only a subset of the original sequence. In Rao *et al.* [13] dynamic hand gestures are recognized by searching a trajectory in 3D space (x and y-position of the hand, and time) for certain dynamic instants. Gonzalez *et al.* [8] also look for key-frames for recognizing actions, like walking and running. Approaches where the entire trajectory (one action) is represented by a number of sub-sequences, are Barbic *et al.* [2] for full body motion, where probabilistic PCA is used for finding transitions between different behaviors, and Bettinger *et al.* [3] where like-lihoods are used to separate a trajectory into sub-trajectories. These sub-trajectories are modeled by Gaussian distributions each corresponding to a temporal primitive.

In this paper we address action recognition using temporal instances (denoted primitives) that only represent a subset of the original sequence. That is, our aim is to recognize an action by recognizing only a few primitives as opposed to recognition based on the entire sequence (possibly divided into sub-trajectories). The actions that we focus on in this work are one-arm gestures, but the approach can with some modifications be generalized to body actions. Concretely we represent our primitives by four features extracted from a motion-image, yielding simple and yet powerful descriptors for our primitives. In each frame the primitive, if any, that best explains the observed data is identified. This leads to a discrete recognition problem since a video sequence will be converted into a string containing a sequence of symbols, each representing a primitive. After pruning the string a probabilistic Edit Distance classifier is applied to identify which action best describes the pruned string.

The paper is structured as follows. In section 2 we describe our features used to represent the primitives. In section 3 we recognize the actions by first recognizing the primitives and then the actions. In section 4 the approach is evaluated on a number of actions and in section 5 the approach is discussed.

2 Representation of Primitives

Our long term goal is for any given set of actions to be able to automatically find primitives that can be used to represent the actions independent of the viewing angle [14].

In this work, however, we work with arm gestures and assume the torso to be fronto-parallel.

For a given set of training sequences a set of primitives is defined. This set of primitives allows for a representative description of the different actions. Concretely the primitives are each a 3D body configuration and the nature of these primitives will depend on the actions to be recognized. The actual selection of the primitives is presented in section 4 after the test data has been introduced. This and the following section will therefore describe the general principles, whereas implementation details are left for section 4.

Instead of attempting to reconstruct the 2D/3D pose of the human and compare with a 2D/3D action database, we use local motion to describe the whereabouts of the person. This approach is motivated by the notion that image motion is often less sensitive compared to other cues, but yet a powerful cue for inferring information from a sequence of images [4]. The simplest type of local motion is a difference image. Even though this only provides crude information it has the benefit of being rather independent to illumination changes and clothing types and styles. Furthermore, no background model or person model is required. However, difference images suffer from "shadow effects" and we therefore apply double difference images, which are known to be more robust [18]. The idea is to use three successive images in order to create two difference images. These are thresholded and ANDed together. This ensures that only pixels that have changed in both difference images are included in the final output. In figure 1 the principle is illustrated. The effects of outliers and "holes" are addressed using morphology.

When doing arm gestures the respond from the double difference image will roughly speaking be a "motion-cloud", which we model compactly by an ellipse. The length and orientation of the axes of the ellipse are calculated from the Eigen-vectors and Eigen-values of the covariance matrix defined by the motion pixels.

We use four features to represent this cloud. In order to make the features independent of image size and the person's position in the image they are represented as ratios.

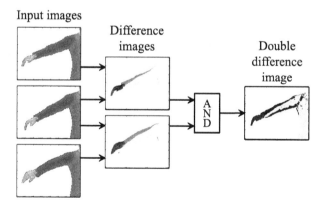

Fig. 1. Principle behind the double difference image. **Left:** Input images. **Middle:** Two (inverted) difference images. **Right:** Double difference image. The silhouette of the input (light gray) has been overlayed for clarification, hence the black pixels are the output.

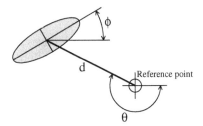

Fig. 2. An illustration of the four features used to describe the primitives

Furthermore, they are defined with respect to a reference point currently defined as the center of gravity of the person (discussed further in section 5). The four features are illustrated in figure 2 and defined as:

1. The eccentricity of the motion cloud defined as the ration between the minor and major axes of the ellipse.

$$\text{Eccentricity} = \frac{\text{Minor axis length}}{\text{Major axis length}} \tag{1}$$

2. The orientation ϕ of the ellipse.
3. The minimum ratio r between the length of the major axis and the distance d from the reference point to the center of the ellipse.

$$r = \min\left(\frac{\text{Major axis length}}{d}, \frac{d}{\text{Major axis length}}\right) \tag{2}$$

4. The angle θ between the reference point and the center of the ellipse.

3   Recognition of Actions

3.1   Recognition of Primitives

For a given set of actions a set of primitives is defined using the four features. To be able to recognize the primitives a Mahalanobis classifier is build by forming the covariance matrix for each primitive based on a set of representative examples. The four features are not equally important and therefore weighted in accordance with their importance. This yields the following classifier for recognizing a primitive at time, t:

$$\text{Primitive}(t) = \arg\min_i \left[(\boldsymbol{W} \cdot (\boldsymbol{f}_t - \boldsymbol{p}_i))^T \Pi_i^{-1}(\boldsymbol{W} \cdot (\boldsymbol{f}_t - \boldsymbol{p}_i))\right] \tag{3}$$

where $\boldsymbol{f}_t$ is the feature vector estimated at time t, $\boldsymbol{p}_i$ is the mean vector of the ith primitive, Π_i is the covariance matrix of the ith primitive, and $\boldsymbol{W}$ contains the weights and are included as an element-wise multiplication.

The classification of a sequence can be viewed as a trajectory through the 4D feature space where, at each time-step, the closest primitive (in terms of Mahalanobis distance) is found. To reduce noise in this process we introduce a minimum Mahalanobis distance in order for a primitive to be considered in the first place. Furthermore, to reduce the flickering observed when the trajectory passes through a border region between two primitives we introduce a hysteresis threshold. It favors the primitive recognized in the preceding frame over all other primitives by modifying the individual distances. The classifier hereby obtains a "sticky" effect, which handles a large part of the flickering.

After processing a sequence the output will be a string with the same length as the sequence. An example is illustrated in equation 4. Each letter corresponds to a recognized primitive and $\emptyset$ corresponds to time instances where no primitives are below the minimum required Mahalanobis distance. The string is pruned by first removing '$\emptyset$'s, isolated instances, and then all repeated letters, see equation 5. A weight is generated to reflect the number of repeated letters (this is used below).

$$\text{String} = \{\emptyset, \emptyset, B, B, B, B, B, E, A, A, F, F, F, F, \emptyset, D, D, G, G, G, G, \emptyset\} \quad (4)$$
$$\text{String} = \{B, A, F, D, G\} \quad (5)$$
$$\text{Weights} = \{5, 2, 4, 2, 4\} \quad (6)$$

3.2 Recognition Using Probabilistic Edit Distance

The result of recognizing the primitives is a string of letters referring to the known primitives. During a training phase a string representation of each action to be recognized is learned. The task is now to compare each of the learned actions (strings) with the detected string. Since the learned strings and the detected strings (possibly including errors!) will in general not have the same length, the standard pattern recognition methods will not suffice. We therefore apply the Edit Distance method [12], which can handle matching of strings of different lengths.

The edit distance is a well known method for comparing words or text strings, e.g., for spell-checking and plagiarism detection. It operates by measuring the distance between two strings in terms of the number of operations needed in order to transform one to the other. There are three possible operations: *insert* a letter from the other string, *delete* a letter, and *exchange* a letter by one from the other string. Whenever one of these operations is required in order to make the strings more similar, the score or distance is increased by one. The algorithm is illustrated in figure 3 where the strings *motions* and *octane* are compared.

The first step is initialization. The two strings are placed along the sides of the matrix, and increasing numbers are place along the borders beside the strings. Hereafter the matrix is filled cell by cell by traversing one column at a time. Each cell is given the smallest value of the following four operations:

Insert: The value of the cell above + 1
Delete: The value of the cell to the left + 1
Exchange: The value of the cell up-left + 1
No change: The value of the cell up-left + 0. This is the case when the letters in question in the two stings are the same.

Using these rules the matrix is filled and the value found at the bottom right corner is the edit distance required in order to map one string into the other, i.e., the distance

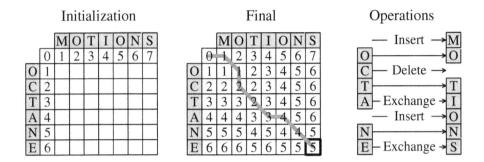

Fig. 3. Measuring the distance between two strings using edit distance

between the two strings. The actual sequence of operations can be found by back-tracing the matrix. Note that often more paths are possible.

When the strings representing the actions are of different lengths, the method tends to favor the shorter strings. Say we have detected the string $\{B, C, D\}$ and want to classify it as being one of the two actions: $\#1 = \{J, C, G\}$ and $\#2 = \{A, B, C, D, H\}$. The edit distance from the detected string to the action-strings will be two in both cases. However, it seems more likely that the correct interpretation is that the detected string comes from action #2 in a situation where the start and end has been corrupted by noise. In fact, 2 out of 3 of the primitives have to be changed for action #1 whereas only 2 out of 5 have to be changed for action #2. We therefore normalize the edit distance by dividing the output by the length of the action-string, yielding 0.67 for action #1 and 0.2 for action #2, i.e., action #2 is recognized.

The edit distance is a deterministic method but by changing the cost of each of the three operations with respect to likelihoods it becomes a probabilistic method[1]. Concretely we apply the weights described above, see equation 6. These to some extent represent the likelihood of a certain primitive being correct. The higher the weight the more likely a primitive will be. We incorporate the weights into the edit distance method by increasing the score by the weight multiplied by β (a scaling factor) whenever a primitive is *deleted* or *exchanged*. The cost of *inserting* remains 1.

The above principle works for situations where the input sequence only contains one action (possibly corrupted by noise). In a real scenario, however, we will have sequences which are potentially much longer than an action and which might include more actions after each other. The action recognition problem is therefore formulated as for each action to find the substring in the detected string, which has the minimum edit distance. The recognized action will then be the one of the substrings with the minimum distance. Denoting the start point and length of the substring, s and l, respectively, we recognize the action present in the detected string as:

$$\text{Action} = \arg \min_{k,s,l} PED(\Lambda, k, s, l) \tag{7}$$

where k index the different actions, Λ is the detected string, and $PED(\cdot)$ is the probabilistic edit distance.

---

[1] This is related to the Weighted Edit Distance method, which however has fixed weights.

4   Results

4.1   Test Setup

To evaluate our approach we use five arm gestures inspired by [10,14], see figure 4. In order to get better insides to our novel recognition approach we apply semi-synthetic data in this work. Another reason for semi-synthetic data is that we need access to the 3D configurations of the test subjects when defining the primitives. Concretely we use a magnetic tracking system with four sensors to capture movements of the test subjects. The sensor placements are: one at the wrist, one at the elbow, one at the shoulder, and one at the upper torso (for reference). The hardware used is the Polhemus FastTrac [15] which gives a maximum sampling rate of 25Hz when using all four sensors. The data is converted into four Euler angles: three at the shoulder and one at the elbow in order

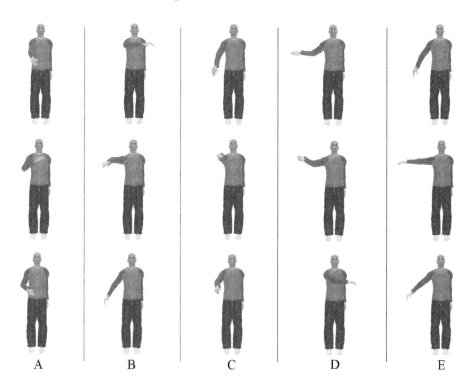

A   B   C   D   E

Fig. 4. Examples of images generated by Poser using real motion captured data. Each column shows samples from the five gestures. **A - Move closer:** A stretched arm is raised to a horizontal position pointing forward while the palm is pointing upwards. The hand is then drawn to the chest, and lowered down. **B - Move right:** Right hand is moved up in front of the left shoulder. The arm is then stretched while moved all the way to the right, and then lowered down. **C - Point forward:** A stretched arm is raised to a horizontal position pointing forward, and then lowered down. **D - Move left:** A stretched arm is raised to a horizontal position pointing right. The arm is then moved in front of the body ending at the right shoulder, and then lowered down. **E - Point right:** A stretched arm is raised to a horizontal position pointing right, and then lowered down.

to make the data invariant to body size. An action corresponds to a trajectory through a 4D space spanned by the Euler angles.

We use seven test subjects, who each perform each gesture 20 times. This leads to 840 synthetic sequences. We manual evaluate the sequences from three of the test subjects and find 10 primitives to describe the five different actions. The criteria for finding the primitives are 1) that they represent characteristic and representative 3D configurations, 2) that their projected 2D configurations contain a certain amount of fronto-parallel motion, and 3) that the primitives are used in the description of as many actions as possible, i.e., fewer primitives are required.

Based on the manually selected primitives we randomly choose 20 sequences for each primitive. The sequences are aligned temporally and the double difference images are calculated and represented by the four features, yielding a 4x4 covariance matrix for each primitive. The maximum Mahalanobis distance for primitive recognition is set to 40, the weighting of the features are $\{1, 2, 1, 2\}$, and $\beta = 1/8$. A string representation of each action is found and since the shortest string contains five primitives and the longest eight primitives, we only perform the probabilistic edit distance calculation for substrings having the lengths $\in [4, 16]$.

4.2 Tests

The tests are performed on the four test subjects not included in the training data. We randomly choose 23 sequences of each gesture, yielding 115 test sequences. For each sequence we add "noise" in both the beginning and end of the sequence. The noise is in the form of approximately half a sequence of a different gesture. This introduces the realistically problem of having no clear idea when an action commence and terminates.

In figure 5 a typical situation is shown for using the probabilistic edit distance to match a detected string with an action. The X-axis represents the frame number. The Y-axis represents the string length. The Z-axis represents the probabilistic edit distance - the smaller the better the match. One point on the surface, e.g., $(4, 5, 1.2)$, corresponds to the distance 1.2 between a substring of the detected string, and an action-string. The substring has length 5 and starts at time instance #4. For this particular figure the best

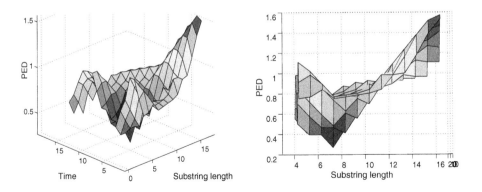

Fig. 5. An example of the probabilistic edit distance. See text for details.

	1	2	3	4	5
1. Point right	23				
2. Point forward		21			2
3. Move left	1		22		
4. Move right				23	
5. Move closer		7			16

Fig. 6. The confusion matrix for the recognition of the different actions

match is found for the substring of length 7 and starting at time instance #7. Its value is compared to the best matches for the other actions and the one with the smallest value defines the recognized action for this sequence. The overall recognition rate is 91.3%. In figure 6 the confusion matrix for the results is shown.

5   Conclusion

In this paper we have presented an action recognition approach based on primitives as opposed to trajectories. Furthermore, we extract features from temporally local motion as opposed to background subtraction or another segmentation method relying on learned models and a relatively controlled environment. We hope this makes our approach less sensitive, but have still to prove so in a more comprehensive test.

The primitives used in this work are found manually. This turned out to be quite an effort due to the massive amount of data. Currently we are therefore working to automate this process [14].

The presented results showed that action #2 and #5 are sometimes confused. This problem might be solved by using better primitives - learned automatically. But this is not certain as the confusions are mainly due to the fact that 1) the two actions are very similar, and that 2) some test subjects did the same action rather differently. Seen from this point of view the recognition rate is quite good.

References

1. R.V. Babu and K.R. Ramakrishnan. Compressed domain human motion recognition using motion history information. In *Proc. Int. Conf. on Acoustics, Speech and Signal Processing*, Hong Kong, April 6-10, 2003.
2. J. Barbic, N.S. Pollard, J.K. Hodgins, C. Faloutsos, J-Y. Pan, and A. Safonova. Segmenting Motion Capture Data into Distinct Behaviors. In *Graphics Interface*, London, Ontario, Canada, May 17-19 2004.
3. F. Bettinger and T.F. Cootes. A Model of Facial Behaviour. In *IEEE International Conference on Automatic Face and Gesture Recognition*, Seoul, Korea, May 17 - 19 2004.
4. A. Bobick and J. Davis. The Recognition of Human Movement Using Temporal Templates. *IEEE Trans. Pattern Analysis and Machine Intelligence*, 23(3):257–267, 2001.
5. A.F. Bobick and J. Davis. A Statebased Approach to the Representation and Recognition of Gestures. *IEEE Trans. on Pattern Analysis and Machine Intelligence*, 19(12):1325 – 1337, 1997.
6. C. Bregler. Learning and Recognizing Human Dynamics in Video Sequences. In *Conference on Computer Vision and Pattern Recognition*, pages 568 – 574, San Juan, Puerto Rico, 1997.

7. L. Campbell and A. Bobick. Recognition of Human Body Motion Using Phase Space Constraints. In *International Conference on Computer Vision*, Cambridge, Massachusetts, 1995.

8. J. Gonzalez, J. Varona, F.X. Roca, and J.J. Villanueva. *aSpaces*: Action spaces for recognition and synthesis of human actions. In *AMDO*, pages 189–200, AMDO02, 2002.

9. O.C. Jenkins and M.J. Mataric. Deriving Action and Behavior Primitives from Human Motion Data. In *Proc. IEEE Int. Conf. on Intelligent Robots and Systems*, pages 2551–2556, Lausanne, Switzerland, Sept.30 – Oct.4, 2002.

10. A. Just and S. Marcel. HMM and IOHMM for the Recognition of Mono- and Bi-Manual 3D Hand Gestures. In *ICPR workshop on Visual Observation of Deictic Gestures (POINTING04)*, Cambridge, UK, August 2004.

11. A. Kale, N. Cuntoor, and R. Chellappa. A Framework for Activity-Specific Human Recognition. In *International Conference on Acoustics, Speech and Signal Processing*, Orlando, Florida, May 2002.

12. V.I. Levenshtein. Binary Codes Capable of Correcting Deletions, Insertions and Reversals. *Doklady Akademii Nauk SSSR*, 163(4):845–848, 1965.

13. C. Rao, A. Yilmaz, and M. Shah. View-Invariant Representation and Recognition of Actions. *Journal of Computer Vision*, 50(2):55 – 63, 2002.

14. L. Reng, T.B. Moeslund, and E. Granum. Finding Motion Primitives in Human Body Gestures. In S. Gibet, N. Courty, and J.-F. Kamps, editors, *GW 2005*, number 3881 in LNAI, pages 133–144. Springer Berlin Heidelberg, 2006.

15. *http://polhemus.com/*, January 2006.

16. D. Weinberg, R. Ronfard, and E. Boyer. Motion History Volumes for Free Viewpoint Action Recognition. In *IEEE Int. Workshop on Modeling People and Human Interaction*, 2005.

17. A. Yilmaz and M. Shah. Actions Sketch: A Novel Action Representation. In *Proc. IEEE Conf. on Computer Vision and Pattern Recognition*, San Diego, CA, June 20-25, 2005.

18. K. Yoshinari and M. Michihito. A Human Motion Estimation Method using 3-Successive Video Frames. In *Int. Conf. on Virtual Systems and Multimedia*, Gifu, Japan, 1996.

19. H. Yu, G.-M. Sun, W.-X. Song, and X. Li. Human Motion Recognition Based on Neural Networks. In *Int. Conf. on Communications, Circuits and Systems*, Hong Kong, May 2005.

Shape-Motion Based Athlete Tracking for Multilevel Action Recognition

Costas Panagiotakis[1], Emmanuel Ramasso[2], Georgios Tziritas[1], Michèle Rombaut[2], and Denis Pellerin[2]

[1] Department of Computer Science, University of Crete, P.O. Box 2208, Heraklion, Greece
{cpanag, tziritas}@csd.uoc.gr
[2] Laboratoire des Images et des Signaux, 46 avenue Félix Viallet, 38031 Grenoble, France
first_name.family_name@lis.inpg.fr

Abstract. An automatic human shape-motion analysis method based on a fusion architecture is proposed for human action recognition in videos. Robust shape-motion features are extracted from human points detection and tracking. The features are combined within the Transferable Belief Model (TBM) framework for action recognition. The TBM-based modelling and fusion process allows to take into account imprecision, uncertainty and conflict inherent to the features. Action recognition is performed by a multilevel analysis. The sequencing is exploited for feedback information extraction in order to improve tracking results. The system is tested on real videos of athletics meetings to recognize four types of jumps: high jump, pole vault, triple jump and long jump.

1 Introduction

Human motion analysis has many applications in many areas, such as analysis of athletic events, surveillance, content-based image storage and retrieval. The main scientific challenges in human motion analysis are to detect, track and identify people and to recognize the human activity [1] from observations coming from video. Wang, Hu and Tan [2] emphasize on three major issues of human motion analysis systems, namely human detection, tracking and activity understanding. There are model based approaches and systems using Shape-From-Silhouette methods to detect and track the human in 2D [3]. The silhouettes are generally of good quality providing valuable information about the position and shape of the person. Camera motion estimation methods [4] can locate the independently moving objects.

Many methods have been proposed for action recognition [2] notably based on *classification*, *template matching* and *neural networks*. Generally, the methods are based on the *Bayesian framework* with *Hidden Markov Models* (HMM) and *Dynamic Bayesian Network* (DBN) [5]. Other methods are developed in Artificial Intelligence community notably *Petri Nets* [6]. In [7], it is proposed an

F.J. Perales and R.B. Fisher (Eds.): AMDO 2006, LNCS 4069, pp. 385–394, 2006.

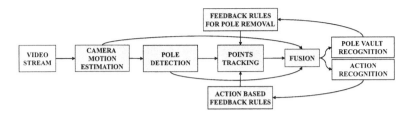

Fig. 1. Schema of the proposed system architecture

architecture for human action recognition using the *Transferable Belief Model* (TBM) which is based on belief theory.

A challenging problem appears when the camera is moving and the estimated human silhouettes are of low quality or extremely wrong (see Fig. 4(a)). In this work we focus on automatic human detection, tracking and action recognition under real and dynamic environments of athletic meetings. We suppose that the camera tracks the athlete and we test the algorithm in sports such as pole vault, high jump, triple jump and long jump.

The proposed architecture consists of several main modules (Fig. 1):

1. Silhouettes are computed using a camera motion estimation method [4], where an affine model is used to describe the camera motion. Such a model is generally sufficient for most of real video sequences. The above method that we use, was implemented by the Vista Team of IRISA.
2. The pole detection procedure, is applied to the human silhouette detecting the pole and extracting features related to it such as its eccentricity and its position.
3. Four major human points are recognized and tracked using the human silhouettes. Shape-motion based features are extracted using the results of the tracking procedure.
4. A fusion architecture, based on TBM, is used for action recognition. The input parameters for the fusion process include camera motion, pole detection and human shape-motion parameters estimated by the corresponding modules.
5. The results of the fusion process can be used as feedback information improving the results of human tracking.

The rest of the paper is organized as follows: Section 2 presents the human shape-motion analysis method. Section 3 describes the action recognition and feedback method. Finally, Sections 4 and 5 provide experimental results and the discussion, respectively.

2   Human Shape-Motion Analysis

The human shape-motion analysis is based on binary silhouettes. They are computed from camera motion estimation as described in [7].

2.1   Pole Detection

The pole is recognized first since it can be easily detected by its shape which has high eccentricity. The eccentricity (ε) is defined by the ratio between the two principal axes of the best fit ellipse, measuring how thin and long a region is. If the detected region has high ε (more than 20) then it is probably a pole. This feature is relevant in the fusion process to recognize the pole vault videos.

First, the highest area object (O_1) is detected. Then, the end of pole point (P_e) is estimated. P_e is defined as the farthest O_1 point from the mass center (C) of O_1 object under the constraint that it is found above the C as the athlete is running. The pole pixels will be detected by a region growing method (RG) starting from P_e point. This method terminates when the area of region exceeds the 50% of the O_1 area or when the number of pixels of the boundary between the region and O_1 exceeds a threshold. The threshold is a percentage (e.g. 40%) of the square root of the O_1 area approximating the double of O_1 mean width. However, the region will have been expanded in the athlete area. Therefore, we have to ignore the last pixels that RG adds, until the region where ε will be maximum (see Fig. 2). Let O_2 be the estimated pole region. We compute the distance d between the farthest point (P_f) of O_2 from P_e and P_e itself. Then, ε can be estimated by the ratio $\varepsilon = \frac{\pi d^2}{O_2\ area}$. P_f can be approximated directly by the last point that the RG method adds.

The proposed pole detection method detects the pole with high accuracy and robustness to silhouette noise (see Fig. 2(e)). The strong point of this method is that it is simple and low cost. The results on our database show a great performance of this detector.

| (a) | (b) | (c) | (d) | (e) |

Fig. 2. Results of pole detection procedure. The light gray pixels denote those that ignored (last added) by the RG method and the gray pixels denote the detected pole region. **(a)** $\varepsilon = 6.08$, **(b)** $\varepsilon = 12.24$, **(c)** $\varepsilon = 31.27$ **(d)** $\varepsilon = 50.01$, **(e)** $\varepsilon = 31.32$.

2.2   Points Detection and Tracking

In this step, four major human points, namely: the head center, the mass center, the left end of leg and the right end of leg (see Fig. 4(b)) are detected and tracked using as input human silhouettes. The above points are selected because they are visible in the whole sequence providing sufficient information for the action recognition. The method is divided into two procedures: the detection procedure and the tracking procedure. Results of this method are illustrated in Fig. 3.

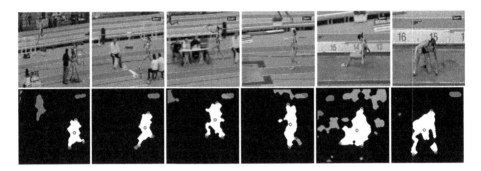

Fig. 3. Results of Major Human Points Tracking method on triple jump sequence

Detection. In this step, the four major human points are automatically detected (see Fig. 4(b)). This procedure is executed just once, in the first silhouette frame of the sequence or when the tracking history is erased by feedback information of the fusion process. The "Human Points Detection" algorithm is described hereafter.

First, the mass center point (C) is computed. This point is defined as the mass center of the foreground pixels. Next, the human body major axis (see Fig. 4(b)) is computed using second order moments. The head point (H) is defined as the farthest major axis point from C, that is found above the C. The first end of leg point (L_1) can be computed by getting the farthest foreground pixel from the C, that is found below the C. Finally, the next end of leg point (L_2) should have the following properties: high distances from C, H and L_1. Moreover, the triangle PCL_1 should be close to an isosceles triangle, where P denotes a candidate L_2 point. The last two constraints are equal to the triangle area $(E(PCL_1))$ maximization. Thus, the maximization of product $(|PH| \cdot |PC| \cdot E(PCL_1))$ provides the L_2 point.

Tracking. In this step, the four major human points are tracked. This procedure is executed in every frame of the sequence, apart from the first one, taking as input the position of the four major human points in the previous frame (history) and the current silhouette image.

First, we reclassify the binary silhouette image pixels reducing the number of wrong classified pixels. We compute the minimum distance of each foreground object from the previous position of the four human points multiplied by the percentage of the foreground pixels that belong to a line segment started on the mass center of the foreground object and ended on the specific major human point. If this distance is higher than a threshold then the foreground pixels will be classified to background class (gray pixels of Fig. 4(b)).

The four major human points can be detected by "Human Points Detection". This method produces two pairs of solutions for the head point and the leg points, as it is unknown if the head point is found above or under the mass center. We choose the pair which is closer to the estimated pair of the previous frame.

2.3   Human Shape-Motion Parameters

Using the results of pole detection and points tracking, we can compute shape-motion features useful for action recognition. The estimated pole eccentricity (ε) is relevant shape feature since we can recognize if the detected region is a pole. It can also be used to detect dropping bar during jumping or falling stages in high jump and pole vault.

The motion based features are computed from the major points trajectories. One important feature concerns the vertical translation of the mass center (P_{msvt}). Then, the angle between the human major axis and the horizontal axis (Θ_1) (see Fig. 4(c)) is of key of importance for action discrimination. If this angle is about 90°, the human is standing or running, whereas important variation occur during the jumping and falling in high jump and pole vault. Moreover, the angle between the legs (Θ_{34}) (see Fig. 4(c)) is another relevant feature. Indeed, the gait period can be measured from its trajectory providing an estimation of the human speed. The camera motion parameters are also exploited for action recognition: the camera horizontal translation (P_{cht}), the camera vertical translation (P_{cvt}), and the camera zoom (P_{cz}).

3   Human Action Sequence Recognition

The parameters described previously are now combined within TBM [8] framework for action recognition. Some parts of the work described in the sequel relies on [7,9].

3.1   From Numerical Parameters to Belief on Actions

An action A is described by two states gathered in the frame of discernment (FoD) $\Omega_A = \{R_A, F_A\}$ with R_A (resp. F_A) stands for "action A is right" (resp. "A is *false*"). A basic belief assignment (BBA) on an A according to a parameter P is defined on the set of propositions $2^{\Omega_A} = \{\emptyset, R_A, F_A, R_A \cup F_A\}$ by $m_P^{\Omega_A} : 2^{\Omega_A} \to [0,1]$, $X \to m_P^{\Omega_A}(X)$ and by construction $m_P^{\Omega_A}(\emptyset) = 0$, and $\sum_{X \subseteq \Omega_A} m_P^{\Omega_A}(X) = 1$. The set $R_A \cup F_A$ explicitly represents the doubt concerning the real state of an action: it does not imply any additional claims regarding the subsets, i.e. neither R_A nor F_A. This is a fundamental difference with a probability measure which is additive. A fuzzy-set inspired method [7] is used

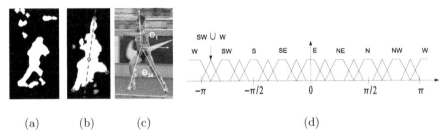

<table>
<tr><td>(a)</td><td>(b)</td><td>(c)</td><td>(d)</td></tr>
</table>

Fig. 4. (a) Low quality silhouette. **(b)** Estimated four major human points. The human body major axis is shown as a red dashed line. **(c)** The human major axis angle (Θ_1) and the angle between legs (Θ_{34}). **(d)** Numeric-to-symbolic conversion of Θ_1.

to convert each numerical parameter described section 2.3 into sources of belief (see Fig. 4(d)).

3.2   Transferable Belief Model Fusion

Belief of several parameters are combined in the axiomatically well-founded Transferable Belief Model (TBM) framework proposed by Smets and Kennes [8] to obtain a belief which takes all parameters into account. The fusion process is performed frame by frame for each action independently by rules of combination defined for two distinct BBAs $m_{P_1}^{\Omega_A}$ and $m_{P_2}^{\Omega_A}$ by:

$$m_{P_1}^{\Omega_A} \bigcirc m_{P_2}^{\Omega_A}(E) = \sum_{C \triangle D = E} m_{P_1}^{\Omega_A}(C).m_{P_2}^{\Omega_A}(D) \qquad (1)$$

with $\triangle = \cap$ (resp. $\cup$) for the conjunctive (resp. disjunctive) rule of combination. The rules of combination can be used in logical rules such as "*if* ... AND ... OR ... *then* ..." for describing actions by means of parameters states. These logical rules are then translated into belief combinations where the logical AND is replaced by the $\bigcirc$-rule and the logical OR by the $\bigcirc$-rule assuming the same FoD [8]. Some reliability factors can also be integrated in equation (1).

3.3   From Action to Sequence of Actions

The Temporal Belief Filter (TBF) proposed in [9] is exploited for *action sequence recognition*. The TBF worked on each action independently taking as input the BBA obtained from parameters fusion and providing a temporally clean and consistent BBA.

The TBF dissociates in an online manner the intervals of frames where an action is *right* to the intervals of frames where the action is *false*. For that, the current state is predicted and conjunctively combined with the measurements resulting in a smooth belief. The state change detection is based on the conflict between prediction and measurements and computed by the conjunctive rule of combination. The state change detector embeds a CUSUM process of the conflict to be more robust. While the CUSUM process does not indicate that the state has to be changed, the state is compelled even if there is conflict between prediction and measurements accounting for a smooth belief.

We assume a sequence $S_n = \{A_1^n \rightarrow A_2^n \rightarrow \ldots \rightarrow A_k^n \rightarrow \ldots \rightarrow A_K^n\}$ made of K actions. The sequences evolutes from an action $\{A_k^n\}$ to $\{A_{k+1}^n\}$ if the TBF indicates that $\{A_k^n\}$ becomes *false* or if $\{A_{k+1}^n\}$ becomes *right*. The action sequencing method ensures that, at each frame of the video, one and only one action is in the *right state* while the others are in the *false state*. The final goal of action sequencing is to find out which sequence better matches the data at each frame of the video. For that, a Quality Performance Criteria (QRP) is proposed.

When the sequence S_n evolutes from $\{A_k^n\}$ to $\{A_{k+1}^n\}$, a Local QRP ($\mathbf{LQRP}_k^n$) is computed for $\{A_k^n\}$. This criterion is computed without reference for a given action thus it is "local" w.r.t the sequence. The $\mathbf{LQRP}_k^n$ is defined by the mean of pignistic probability [8] of action $\{A_k^n\}$ weighted by the contradiction[1] between the data and the state compelled by the TBF. When the entire sequence is covered, K values of $\mathbf{LQRP}_k^n$ are available. A Global QRP ($\mathbf{GQRP}^n$) is computed by the mean of the $\mathbf{LQRP}_k^n$: $\mathbf{GQRP}^n = \sum_{k=1}^{K} \mathbf{LQRP}_k^n / K$. The sequence S_n better corresponds to the data than S_p if $\mathbf{GQRP}^n > \mathbf{GQRP}^p$ and if $\mathbf{GQRP}^n$ is greater than a given required value (e.g. 50%).

3.4   Coarse to Fine Approach and Feedback

The action sequence method consists in two steps: a coarse detection and a fine detection of the actions. The coarse step involves the camera motion parameters and the center of mass. In the fine step, sequencing based on Θ_1 is used to discriminate all actions.

Coarse step. The sequences to recognize concern four types of jump: high jump (S_{hj}), pole vault (S_{pv}), triple jump (S_{tj}) and long jump (S_{lj}). Sequences $S_n, \forall n \in \{hj, pv, lj\}$ are firstly described by a *coarse* action sequence: $S_n = \{R_n \rightarrow J_n \rightarrow F_n \rightarrow U_n\}$, where $\{R_n\}$ is the running action, $\{J_n\}$ is jumping, $\{F_n\}$ is falling and $\{U_n\}$ is standing up in sequence S_n. For triple jump, the coarse sequence is: $S_{tj} = \{R_{tj} \rightarrow J_{tj} \rightarrow F_{tj} \rightarrow J_{tj} \rightarrow F_{tj} \rightarrow J_{tj} \rightarrow F_{tj} \rightarrow U_{tj}\}$. There is no subsequence for triple jump because the coarse one is characteristic and can not be confused with the other types of jump.

All actions $\{R_n, J_n, F_n, U_n\}, \forall n \in \{hj, pv, lj, tj\}$ are detected by a fusion process performed at each frame of the video following these rules (see Section 2.3 for symbols):

IF (P_{cht} is high **OR** P_z is high **OR** P_{msvt} is almost null)
THEN ($\{R_n\}$ is true)
IF (P_{cvt} is highly positive **OR** P_{msvt} is highly positive)
THEN ($\{J_n\}$ and $\{U_n\}$ are true)
IF (P_{cvt} is highly negative **OR** P_{msvt} is highly negative)
THEN ($\{F_n\}$ is true)

---

[1] This information is provided by the TBF, see equation (9) of [9].

Rules are well-managed in the TBM using eq. (1). The coarse definition of a sequence provides the intervals of frame where an action is potentially true but does not allows to distinguish the type of sequence. In order to differentiate the sequences, a fine analysis is required.

Fine step. The fine analysis is performed in the intervals of frame detected by the coarse process by exploiting the parameter Θ_1. The numerical-to-symbolic conversion [7] of Θ_1 is performed by dividing the interval of possible values $[-180°, 180°]$ into 4 main positions $\{N, S, W, E\}$ (North, South, West, East) and 4 intermediate positions $\{NW, SW, SE, NE\}$. The conversion is depicted Fig. 4(d) and shows the explicit modelling of the doubt between two positions, for instance $SW \cup W$. The fuzzy description of the angle value allows to take imprecision and uncertainty of this parameter into account. Notably, each position is modelled by a trapezoidal fuzzy set with a size support of $40°$.

The sequencing of the angle value is performed according to each action sequence. One set of sequences is necessary for both right-to-left and left-to-right translations of the camera. In Table 1, only the first case is described. In Fig. 5(b), the high jump action sequence is pictorially described.

Table 1. Sequences of the angle for each type of jump

sequence name	symbol and action sequence expression
pole vault	$S_{pv} = \{R_{pv} \to J_{pv} \to F_{pv} \to U_{pv}\}$
running	$R_{pv} = \{N \cup (\varepsilon \ is \ high)\}$
jumping	$J_{pv} = \{N \to NE \to E \to SE \to S \to SE \to E\}$
falling	$F_{pv} = \{E \to NE \to N \to NW \to W\}$
standing up	$U_{pv} = \{W \to NW \to N\}$
high jump	$S_{hj} = \{R_{hj} \to J_{hj} \to F_{hj} \to U_{hj}\}$
running	$R_{hj} = \{N\}$
jumping	$J_{hj} = \{N \to NW \to W\}$
falling	$F_{hj} = \{W \to SW \to S\}$
standing up	$U_{hj} = \{S \to SE \to E \to NE \to N\}$
long jump	$S_{lj} = \{R_{lj} \to J_{lj} \to F_{lj} \to U_{lj}\}$
running	$R_{lj} = \{N\}$
jumping	$J_{lj} = \{N\}$
falling	$F_{lj} = \{N \to NE \to E\}$
standing up	$U_{lj} = \{E \to NE \to N\}$

Error detection for feedback. A feedback is a powerful means to adapt a processing chain to varying conditions. In order to illustrate the approach, the example of high jump is presented. In Fig. 5(a), the angle shows an inversion of the human points provided by the tracking due to very bad segmentation when the athlete falls on the air mattress (top foot, down head). This error can be detected by means of action sequencing (Fig. 5(b)). We denote I_{hj} the symbol of the action associated to the inversion in a high jump. Coarsely, the inversion is searched after a falling. Finely, the sequence used to detect this error is close to the sequence used for a standing up: $I_{hj}^{\Theta_1} = \{S, SE, E, SE, E\}$. This sequence is depicted in Figs.5(a) and 5(b). When the error sequence is of high quality,

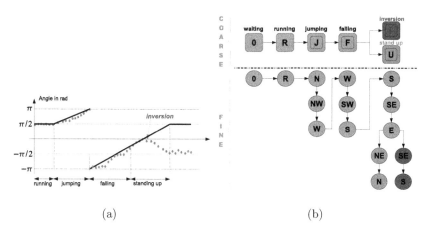

(a)   (b)

Fig. 5. (a) Theoretical angle rough evolution (full line) and observed one (dotted-line). **(b)** Action sequence by a coarse to fine approach for high jump based on angle Θ_1.

i.e. **GQRP** is high, then an error is assumed to be detected and a feedback process is performed onto the tracking algorithm to correct the inversion. The same reasoning can be applied for others jumps, notably for pole vault.

4 Experiments

The database contains 68 videos with four types of jumps: high jump (hj), pole vault (pv), triple jump (tj) and long jump (lj). Each video is analyzed by the four sequences S_n, $\forall n \in \{hj, pv, lj, tj\}$ providing four criteria **GQRP**^{n}. A jump n^* is associated to the current video if $n^* = \max_n$ **GQRP**^{n} (Section 3.3) and if **GQRP**$^{n^*}$ is greater than 50%. One setting per type of jump is provided for the TBF. Then, the obtained results are compared with the manually annotated video to compute a precision index. Using the coarse sequencing, all actions are well detected. However, to discriminate actions, we use the refinement described Section 3.4 and based on the angle.

The *error rates* are: $\mathbf{E}_{hj} = 2/15$, $\mathbf{E}_{pv} = 4/26$, $\mathbf{E}_{tj} = 3/12$ and $\mathbf{E}_{lj} = 4/15$. Concerning *inversion of the tracked points in high jump*, the detection rate is of $\mathbf{C}_{inv-hj} = 6/8$. The reasons have been identified to account for error rates: videos with pure divergence (zoom) with athlete in front of the camera prevent from using the angle, bad pole deletion, video shot changes and bad camera motion estimation in too low quality videos disturb the tracking.

5 Conclusion

An unsupervised-automatic human motion analysis and action sequence recognition (running, jumping and falling, standing up) based on the TBM is proposed and tested on athletics videos. The first main contribution concerns the original robust human shape-motion parameters extractors from camera motion and human silhouette. The color independent silhouette analysis algorithm detects and tracks four major human points. Sometimes, the tracking procedure fails because of wrong previous silhouettes (wrong history) or because of pole appearing in pole vault sequences (wrong shape). We have developed a shape based pole detector, detecting automatically the pole vault videos and removing the pole with great pole detection ratio. The second main contribution concerns the action sequence recognition based on a fusion process using the TBM. A multilevel approach is exploited to refine action detection and recognition. Some action sequences are also used to detect errors in tracking providing feedback information for further corrections.

Acknowledgments

This work is partially supported by SIMILAR European Network of Excellence.

References

1. J. Aggarwal and S. Park, "Human motion: Modeling and recognition of actions and interactions," in *3DPVT04*, 2004, pp. 640–647.
2. L. Wang, W. Hu, and T. Tan, "Recent developments in human motion analysis," *PR*, vol. 36, no. 3, pp. 585–601, 2003.
3. C. Panagiotakis and G. Tziritas, "Recognition and tracking of the members of a moving human body," in *Proc. of AMDO 2004*, 2004, pp. 86–98.
4. J.M. Odobez and P. Bouthemy, "Robust multiresolution estimation of parametric motion models," *J. of Vis. Comm. and Image R.*, vol. 6, no. 4, pp. 348–365, 1995.
5. Y. Luo, T.D. Wu, and J.N. Hwang, "Object-based analysis and interpretation of human motion in sports video sequences by dynamic bayesian networks," *CVIU*, vol. 92, pp. 196–216, 2003.
6. M. Rombaut, I. Jarkass, and T. Denoeux, "State recognition in discrete dynamical systems using petri nets and evidence theory," in *ECSQARU*, June 1999.
7. E. Ramasso, D. Pellerin, C. Panagiotakis, M. Rombaut, G. Tziritas, and W. Lim, "Spatio-temporal information fusion for human action recognition in videos," in *13th European Signal Processing Conf.*, 2005.
8. P. Smets and R. Kennes, "The Transferable Belief Model," *Artificial Intelligence*, vol. 66, no. 2, pp. 191–234, 1994.
9. E. Ramasso, M. Rombaut, and D. Pellerin, "A temporal belief filter improving human action recognition in videos," in *ICASSP*, 2006, to appear.

Finding Articulated Body in Time-Series Volume Data

Tomoyuki Mukasa, Shohei Nobuhara, Atsuto Maki, and Takashi Matsuyama

Graduate School of Infomatics, Kyoto University, Japan

Abstract. This paper presents a new scheme for acquiring 3D kinematic structure and motion from time-series volume data, in particular, focusing on human body. Our basic strategy is to first represent the shape structure of the target in each frame by using aMRG, augmented Multiresolution Reeb Graph [6], and then deform each of the shape structures so that all of them can be identified as a common kinematic structure throughout the input frames. Although the shape structures can be very different from frame to frame, we propose to derive a unique kinematic structure by way of clustering some nodes of graph, based on the fact that they are partly coherent. The only assumption we make is that human body can be approximated by an articulated body with certain number of end-points and branches. We demonstrate the efficacy of the proposed scheme through some experiments.

1 Introduction

The description of moving articulated objects, e.g. human figure, is important in many applications including technical analysis of sports and dance, or production of video contents. Motion-capture system is well-known and available for such purposes. However, the scope of description is limited to the case that the precise structure is given as articulated rigid body. Meanwhile, for the production of video contents, it is desirable to be able to describe non-rigid objects such as human skin or clothes, in motion. Aiming for the realization of comprehensive scheme for describing rigid and non-rigid objects in motion, we thus employ time-series volume data for the input of motion description acquisition scheme. In this paper, we propose a scheme for acquiring kinematic structure of articulated rigid body as an opening outset of above purpose.

Conventional approaches for acquisition of kinematic structure from volume data are either top-down or bottom-up. Top-down approach uses a specific model, cylinder-model for example, to match with volume data. It is impossible to acquire a description of non-rigid motion by this approach. Moreover, in this approach, we need employ a somewhat elaborate model for each observation target. On the other hand, there are some bottom-up methods which acquire kinematic structure from observed motion without specific model [4,3]. In these methods, unit of motion description is voxel or vertex on surface. Therefore, it is impossible to detect correspondence of their motion units before and after an osculation of arthromeres(primitive segments of body). To avoid this problem,

F.J. Perales and R.B. Fisher (Eds.): AMDO 2006, LNCS 4069, pp. 395–404, 2006.

some partial sets should be prepared, to which some units related by closeness belong. However, in each method [4,3], the partial sets are constructed based only on the motion units, and thus there are not always that kind of sets when the osculation occurs.

In the proposed method, we prepare the global description of shape which represents the partial sets described above, and acquire a kinematic structure accordingly. That is, we first represent the shape structure of the target in each frame, and then deform each of the shape structures so that all of them can be identified as a common kinematic structure throughout the input frames.

2   Acquisition of Kinematic Structure

2.1   Overview

We acquire kinematic structure through an off-line process as shown below.

(1) Acquire time-series visual hull [1] from multi-viewpoints videos.
(2) Obtain surface mesh by applying marching cubes method [7] to each visual hull.
(3) Construct Reeb Graphs [5,6] based on geodesic distance on the surface.
(4) As initial models, pick up some graphs that appear to be relatively close to the targeted kinematic structure.
(5) Deform each initial model so that it fits to reeb graphs in a certain number of neighboring frames in what we call "fitting interval". We define the size of the fitting intervals so that the sum of them can cover all the input frames.
(6) For each interval, cluster some nodes of deformed reeb graph based on their motion, and acquire kinematic structure.
(7) Integrate kinematic structures that are acquired for different fitting intervals.

(1),(2),(3) are processes for acquiring global shape structure. (4),(5) are processes for making correlations between shape structure and kinematic structures which enable us to acquire the kinematic structure in process (6). Last of all, by process (7), we can acquire kinematic structure that reflects the diversity of motion in the input visual hull.

2.2   Reeb Graph

We employ the reeb graph for the global shape description. To construct a reeb graph, we first segmentalize surface S of an object on the basis of a continuous function, $\mu(\mathbf{v})$ ($\mathbf{v}$ is an arbitrary vertex on the surface S), defined on the surface, and represent each segmented surface by a node, and finally link the nodes based on the connectivity between the segmented surfaces. We use geodesic function as $\mu(\mathbf{v})$. Now, the surface of the object is represented by a mesh model. The geodesic distance $g(\mathbf{v}, \mathbf{p})$ is defined by shortest path between $\mathbf{v}$ and another vertex $\mathbf{p}$ on the mesh. Then, function $\mu(\mathbf{v})$ can be represented as

$$\mu(\mathbf{v}) = \sum_{\mathbf{p} \in S} g(\mathbf{v}, \mathbf{p}). \tag{1}$$

This indicates the sum of distance from vertex **v** to all vertices on S.

The reeb graph based on the geodesic distance is stable when there are no osculation between any arthromeres. However, even when observing an identical object, the graph structure may easily vary due to an osculation, and the coherence between the graph structure and the kinematic structure will break. Considering this problem, we represent the shape structure by a unique graph structure in a certain definite time range. To acquire such unique graph structure, we regard partial invariability of reeb graph.

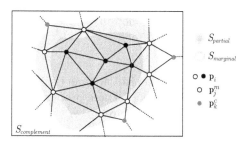

Fig. 1. Partial region on the surface and its mesh structure

We denote the vertices on a partial region surface $S_{partial}$ by $\mathbf{p}_i$, $(i = 0, 1, ..., N_{\mathbf{p}} - 1)$, the vertices on a partial region $S_{complement}$, which is complement region of $S_{partial}$, by $\mathbf{p}_j^c$, $(j = 0, 1, ..., N_{\mathbf{p}^c} - 1)$. We also denote the vertices connected to an arbitrary vertex $\mathbf{p}_i^c$ and also belonging to $S_{partial}$ by $\mathbf{p}_k^m$, $(k = 0, 1, ...N_{\mathbf{p}^m} - 1)$, and represent the partial region to which $\mathbf{p}_k^m$ belonging as $S_{marginal} (\subset S_{partial})$ (see Figure 1) The function $\mu(\mathbf{p})$ defined at arbitrary $\mathbf{p}_i$ can be represented as

$$\mu(\mathbf{p}_i) = \mu_{partial}(\mathbf{p}_i) + \mu_{complement}(\mathbf{p}_i), \tag{2}$$

where $\mu_{partial}(\mathbf{p}_i)$ is caused by $\mathbf{p}_i$, $\mu_{complement}(\mathbf{p}_i)$ is caused by $\mathbf{p}_j^c$, and

$$\mu_{partial}(\mathbf{p}_i) = \sum_{i'=0}^{N_{\mathbf{p}}-1} g(\mathbf{p}_i, \mathbf{p}_{i'}), \tag{3}$$

$$\mu_{complement}(\mathbf{p}_i) = \sum_{j=0}^{N_{\mathbf{p}^m}-1} \mu_{complement}(\mathbf{p}_j^m) = \sum_{j=0}^{N_{\mathbf{p}^m}-1} \sum_{k=0}^{N_{\mathbf{p}^c}-1} g(\mathbf{p}_j^m, \mathbf{p}_k^c). \tag{4}$$

The condition for that arbitrary vertices $\mathbf{p}_{i1}$ and $\mathbf{p}_{i2}$ on $S_{partial}$ correspond to a same node in the reeb graph is represented as

$$|\mu(\mathbf{p}_{i1}) - \mu(\mathbf{p}_{i2})| < \mu_{span}, \tag{5}$$

where μ_{span} is a constant. Regarding Equation (4), this equation can be transformed to

$$|\mu_{partial}(\mathbf{p}_{i1}) - \mu_{partial}(\mathbf{p}_{i2})| < \mu_{span}. \tag{6}$$

Equation (6) means that the structure of the partial reeb graph corresponding to $S_{partial}$ depends only on the vertices in $S_{partial}$. Therefore, the partial reeb graph is stable while all $\mathbf{p}_i$ are identical.

We can find almost invariable structures at the neighborhood of the end-points of the reeb graphs in a certain number of neighboring frames, because there are no osculation between corresponding arthromeres, and all $\mathbf{p}_i$ are thus almost identical. For these reeb graphs, it is reasonable to pick up a reeb graph as an initial model and deform it so that it fits to the other graphs. After this deformation, the shape structure is represented by a unique graph structure.

We thus can estimate the motion of the nodes in the graph, and then acquire the kinematic structure based on the motion.

2.3   Selection of Initial Model

The reeb graph which we select as an initial model should have just an appropriate number of branches and no loop. These properties are equivalent to the following conditions for the graph structure.

(i) "The graph has five end-points".
(ii) "The graph has two branch-points, one has four branches, and the other has three branches", or "The graph has three branch-points each of which has three branchs".

The later is due to the fact that the reeb graph is not necessarily symmetric.

2.4   Deformation of Initial Model

We deform initial models so as to deal with the changes in shape structure over time. In order to deform an initial model and fit it to other reeb graphs, we shift the nodes of initial model to the position where the nodes of other reeb graph are, while maintaining connective relations of the nodes in initial model.

We take the following constraints into account for the movement of nodes.

(a) Maintain the distance between nodes as much as possible
(b) Move a node in initial model to its nearest neighbor node in the target reeb graph

We enforce these constraints to work on each node. (a) can be realized by elastic force between nodes (we call the force as "internal force"), and (b) by the external force to move these nodes. Given these forces working at each nodes, we can compute how initial model deforms its shape by solving Newtonian equation with backward Euler integration method.

External Force. The nodes of the initial model should be moved to the neighborhood of the nearest nodes of the target reeb graph without any crossing in pathways of nodes' movement. We define the external force which urges such nodes' movement based on the point-set deformation algorithm [2].

We denote the reeb graph at time a and b by N and M respectively. First, we find nearest neighbor nodes in M for each node in N, and make a pair (m_a, m_b). We also make another pair (n_a, n_b) for each node in M in a similar way. Note that (m_a, m_b) and (n_a, n_b) are not always identical generally. Now, we denote the distances from an arbitrary point $p(x, y)$ to node n_a and m_a as $d_a(n)$ and $d_b(m)$, respectively. We also denote the drift force of node n_a to n_b, node m_a to m_b by $f_a(n)$ and $f_b(m)$, respectively. Then, we can define the external force $f_{external}(x, y)$ working on $p(x, y)$ as

$$f_{external}(x, y) \equiv \frac{\sum_n \alpha_n f_a(n)}{\sum_n \alpha_n} + \frac{\sum_m \beta_m f_b(m)}{\sum_m \beta_m}, \tag{7}$$

$$\alpha_n = exp(\frac{-d_a(n)}{\sigma}), \qquad \beta_m = exp(\frac{-d_b(m)}{\sigma}). \tag{8}$$

Internal Force. We introduce the internal force, $F_{internal}(v)$, as

$$F_{internal}(v) \equiv \sum_1^n k_j(\|\boldsymbol{q}_{v_j} - \boldsymbol{q}_v\|) \frac{\boldsymbol{q}_{v_j} - \boldsymbol{q}}{\|\boldsymbol{q}_{v_j} - \boldsymbol{q}\|} - k'_j \boldsymbol{q}_v, \tag{9}$$

where k_j denotes a constant, v_j a node connected to v within 2 hops, $\boldsymbol{q}_{v_j}$ its 3D position, and n the number of v_j, respectively. The internal force works so as to maintain the smoothness of reeb graph's shape.

Updating Initial Model Based on Correlation of Reeb Graph. The temporal sampling rate of the input volume date can often be too low to follow the rapid motion of the target object. That is, it is not always true that temporally neighboring graphs are strongly-correlated.

On every deformation, we select a frame in which the reeb graph has the highest correlation to the target reeb graph among the frames in which the reeb graph has already deformed, and use its deformed reeb graph as a new initial model. We utilize a correlation computing method of reeb graphs that is proposed in [6].

2.5   Acquisition of Kinematic Structure Based on the Motions of Nodes

We first acquire kinematic structures in the corresponding fitting intervals, starting with initial models. We call the kinematic structures "piecewise kinematic structure". We then choose the most detailed partial kinematic structures for each branch corresponding to arm, leg, or head. Finally, we deform the partial kinematic structures so as to fit them all over the time-series reeb graphs, and integrate them. This integrated kinematic structure is the result of our method, which reflects various kinematic motion pattern in the input volume data.

Acquisition of Piecewise Kinematic Structure. We acquire kinematic structure by clustering nodes of reeb graph based on cross-correlation of motion between neighboring nodes(see Figure 2). We denote the number of nodes

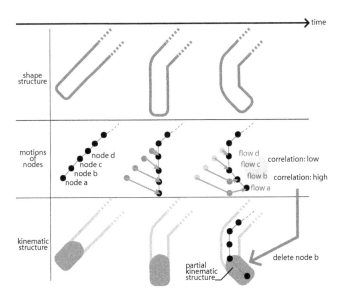

Fig. 2. Clustering of nodes based on their motion

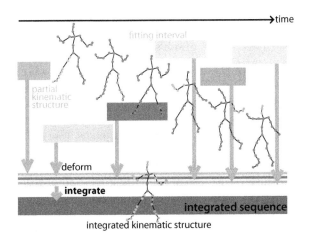

Fig. 3. Integration of piecewise kinematic structures

in the initial model by n, the velocity of node p_i, $(i = 1, 2, ..., n)$ at time t by $\boldsymbol{v}_t^i$, and the cross-correlation function of nodes p_i, p_j at time interval $[t_b, t_e]$ as $r(i, j)$ can then be represented as

$$r(i,j) = \frac{\sum_{k=t_b}^{t_e}(\boldsymbol{v}_k^i - \boldsymbol{v}_{mean}^i)(\boldsymbol{v}_k^j - \boldsymbol{v}_{mean}^j)}{\sqrt{\sum_{k=t_b}^{t_e}(\boldsymbol{v}_k^i - \boldsymbol{v}_{mean}^i)^2}\sqrt{\sum_{k=t_b}^{t_e}(\boldsymbol{v}_k^j - \boldsymbol{v}_{mean}^j)^2}}, \qquad (10)$$

where

$$\boldsymbol{v}_{mean}^i = \frac{\sum_{t=t_b}^{t_e}\boldsymbol{v}_t^i}{t_e - t_b}, \qquad \boldsymbol{v}_{mean}^j = \frac{\sum_{t=t_b}^{t_e}\boldsymbol{v}_t^j}{t_e - t_b}. \qquad (11)$$

Regarding a set of neighboring two nodes, the higher the cross-correlation is, the more probable that both of the nodes belong to the same rigid body.

Integration of Piecewise Kinematic Structure. We choose the most detailed partial kinematic structure for each branch, corresponding to arm, leg, or head. Then, we deform the partial kinematic structures so as to fit them all over the time-series reeb graphs, and integrate them(see Figure 3).

To coordinate partial kinematic structures in different fitting intervals, We use proximity of partial kinematic structures at overlapping fitting intervals.

3   Experiments

3.1   Real Data

We used nine cameras circumnavigating the target object (a dancing lady), and acquired time-series visual hull from multi-viewpoints videos. Applying proposed

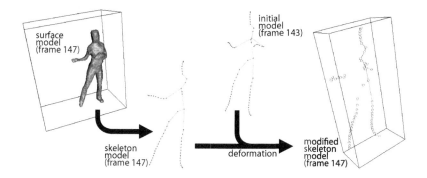

Fig. 4. Modification of reeb graph at frame 147

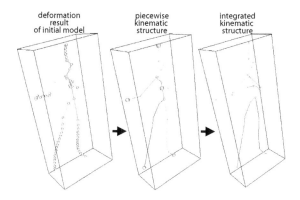

Fig. 5. Acquisition process of kinematic structure at frame 147

method, we acquired the kinematic structure. This acquisition process is exemplified at frame 147 as in Figure 4 and Figure 5. as an example.

In Figure 5, we can observe that human like kinematic structure is acquired from real data by the proposed method.

3.2   CG Data

We generate CG scene of a walking human by applying a motion capture data[1] to a CG model. We then shot the scene by 15 virtual cameras circumnavigating the CG object, and acquired its time-series voxel data using a technique based on visual hull. Finally, we acquired kinematic structure from the time-series visual hull by the proposed method.

We evaluated the acquired kinematic structure by comparing it with the original motion capture data. In this evaluation, as a criterion, we computed the mean value of distance between joint positions in the motion capture data to their nearest neighbor nodes in the acquired kinematic structure. We denote the motion capture data by M, acquired kinematic structure by N, joint points in structures M and N by $m_i, (i = 0, 1, ..., i_{max})$ and $n_j, (j = 0, 1, ..., j_{max})$, respectively. We also denote the distance between the joint points in M and N by $dist(m_i, n_j)$. Then, we can define above described criterion by

$$E_{dist} \equiv \frac{\sum_i dist(m_i, n_{i'})}{i_{max} + 1} \tag{12}$$

while

$$dist(m_i, n_{i'}) = \min\{dist(m_i, n_j)\}. \tag{13}$$

Moreover, we also use another criterion V_{dist}, which is the variance of the distances between the joint points in M and N.

$$V_{dist} = \frac{\sum_i \{dist(m_i, n_{i'}) - E_{dist}\}^2}{i_{max} + 1}. \tag{14}$$

For the purpose of comparative evaluation, we also implemented a simple model-based human posture estimation method. This method employs cylindrical articulated human-figure model. First, the hip position of the cylinder-model is matched with the centroid of voxel data. Then, each joint angle of the model is adjusted so as to maximize the overlapping volume of the voxel data and the group of cylinders corresponding to arthromeres from the hip to each end-points.

In Figure 6, we show examples of kinematic structures acquired by the cylinder-model based method and proposed method, respectively.

Figure 7 and 8 show the evaluated value, E_{dist} and V_{dist}, respectively throughout the input frames. Solid line represents the values of the proposed method, and dot by the cylinder-model based method. In both of Figure 7 and 8, the values by the cylinder-model based method is affected by changes of object's posture

---

[1] The source of data anonymous. Detailed information will be provided in the final draft of this paper.

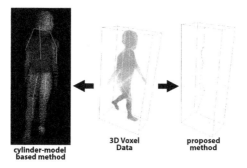

Fig. 6. Acquisition results of kinematic structure

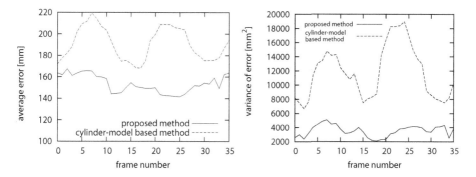

Fig. 7. Evaluation value E_{dist} **Fig. 8.** Evaluation value V_{dist}

whereas those by the proposed method undergo in small range of shifting, showing that the kinematic structure can be acquired by the proposed method more stably.

However, the mean value of estimation error, E_{dist}, hover around 150mm whereas object's height defined by motion capture data is 1800mm. There is a room for improvement in terms of estimation accuracy.

4   Conclusion

In this paper, we proposed a scheme for acquiring kinematic structure from time-series voxel data using the reeb graph for the global shape description. For the case of human figure in motion, we have presented our early results that show the stable characteristic of the proposed scheme compared to a model-based method.

However, it is not guaranteed that the kinematic structure which reflects proper structure of the observed object can be always acquired. Accuracy of the acquired kinematic structure may not be sufficient for practical use. One of the solution to this problem will be to introduce a countermeasure in the presented bottom-up approach, for example, by restricting the edges connecting the nodes to lie inside the volume of the corresponding arthromeres.

Finally, since the proposed method works on time-series voxel data, we plan to expand the scope of the scheme to deal with non-rigid body in motion.

Acknowledgements

This work has been supported by "Foundation of Technology Supporting the Creation of Digital Media Contents" project (CREST, JST).

References

1. A. Laurentini, "How Far 3D Shapes Can Be Understood from 2D Silhouettes" *IEEE Trans. Pattern Analysis and Machine Intelligence, Vol.17, No.2* pp. 188–195, 1995.
2. D.J.Burr, "A Dynamic Model for Image Registration", *Computer Graphics and Image Processing 15*, pp. 102–112, 1981.
3. S. Nobuhara, T. Matsuyama, "Heterogenieous Deformation Model for 3D Shape and Motion Recovery from Multi-Viewpoint Images", *2nd International Symposium on 3D Data Processing, Visualization, and Transmission*, pp. 566–573, 2004.
4. I. Masaaki, K. Yoshinari, M. Michihiko, "Estimation of the Location of Joint Points of Human Body from Successive Volume Data" *ICPR2000*, pp. 699–702, 2002.
5. M. Hilaga, Y. Shinagawa, T. Kohmura, T.L. Kunii, "Topology Matching for Fully Automatic Similarity Estimation of 3D Shapes", *Proc. of SIGGRAPH 2001*, pp. 203–212, 2001.
6. Tony Tung at el., "The augmented multiresolution Reeb graph approach for content-based retrieval of 3D shapes", *International Journal of Shape Modeling (IJSM), Vol.11, No.1*, pp. 91–120, June 2005.
7. Y. Kenmochi, K. Kotani, A. Imiya, "Marching Cubes Method with Connectivity", *Proc. of International Conference on Image Processing*, pp. 361–365, 1999.

Emotional Facial Expression Classification for Multimodal User Interfaces

Eva Cerezo and Isabelle Hupont

Departamento de Informática e Ingeniería de Sistemas, Universidad de Zaragoza
C/Maria de Luna 3, 50018 Zaragoza (Spain)
{ecerezo, 478953}@unizar.es

Abstract. We present a simple and computationally feasible method to perform automatic emotional classification of facial expressions. We propose the use of 10 characteristic points (that are part of the MPEG4 feature points) to extract relevant emotional information (basically five distances, presence of wrinkles and mouth shape). The method defines and detects the six basic emotions (plus the neutral one) in terms of this information and has been fine-tuned with a data-base of 399 images. For the moment, the method is applied to static images. Application to sequences is being now developed. The extraction of such information about the user is of great interest for the development of new multimodal user interfaces.

Keywords: Facial Expression, Multimodal Interface.

1 Introduction

Facial expression is the most powerful, natural and direct way between humans to communicate emotions, valuations and intentions. As pointed out by Bruce [1], human face-to-face communication is an ideal model for designing a multimodal human-computer interface (HCI).

A system capable of extracting emotional information from user's facial expressions would be of great interest for developing new interfaces which follow the human face-to-face communication model in the most realistic way. In particular, the creation of virtual environments populated by 3D virtual characters capable of understanding users' expressions and reacting accordingly represents, nowadays, a challenging but affordable task.

Nevertheless, to develop a system that interprets facial expressions is difficult. Three kinds of problems have to be solved: face detection in a facial image or image sequence, facial expression data extraction and facial expression classification (e.g. into emotional categories). In this paper we are going to deal with the third problem: classification. This implies the definition of the set of categories we want to deal with, and the implementation of the categorization mechanisms.

Facial expression analyzers make use of three different methods of classification: patterns, neuronal networks or rules. If a pattern-based method is used [2,3,4], the face expression found is compared with the patterns defined for each expression category. The best matching decides the classification of the expression. Most of these

F.J. Perales and R.B. Fisher (Eds.): AMDO 2006, LNCS 4069, pp. 405–413, 2006.
© Springer-Verlag Berlin Heidelberg 2006

methods first apply PCA and LDA algorithms to reduce dimensionality. In the systems based on neuronal networks [5,6], the face expression is classified according to a categorization process "learned" by the neuronal network during the training phase. In general, the input to this type of systems is a set of characteristics extracted from the face (points or distances between points). The rule-based methods [7] classify the face expression into basic categories of emotions, according to a set of face actions previously codified. In [8] an excellent state-of-the-art on the subject can be found.

In any case, the development of automatic facial classification systems presents several problems. Most of the studies on automated expression analysis perform an emotional classification. The emotional classification of Ekman [9] is the most followed one. It describes six universal basic emotions: joy, sadness, surprise, fear, disgust and anger. Nevertheless, the use of Ekman's categories for developing automating facial expression emotional classification is difficult. First, his description of the six prototypic facial expressions of emotions is linguistic and, thus, ambiguous. There is no uniquely defined description either in terms of facial actions or in terms of some other universally defined facial codes. Second, classification of facial expressions into multiple emotion categories should be possible (e.g. raised eyebrows and smiling mouth is a blend of surprise and happiness). Another important issue to be considered is individualization. The system should be capable of analyzing any subject, male or female of any age and ethnicity and of any expressivity.

The structure of the paper is as follows: in Section 2 our method is explained whereas in Section 3 results are presented. Conclusions and comments about future work are discussed in Section 4.

2   A Simple Method for the Automatic Analysis of Face Expressions

Our method is based on the work of Hammal et al [10]. They have implemented a facial classification method for static images. The originality of their work consists, on the one hand, in the supposition that all the necessary information for the recognition of expressions is contained in the deformation of certain characteristics of the eyes, mouth and eyebrows and, on the other hand, in the use of the Belief Theory to make the classification. Nevertheless, their method has important restrictions. The most important restriction comes from the fact that it is only able to discern 3 of the 6 basic emotions (without including the neutral one). This is basically due to the little information they handle (only 5 distances). It would not be viable, from a probabilistic point of view, to work with many more data, because the explosion of possible combinations would remarkably increase the computational cost of the algorithm.

2.1   General Description of the Method

Our method studies the variation of a certain number of face parameters (distances and angles between some feature points of the face) with respect to the neutral expression. The objective of our method is to assign a score to each emotion, according to the state acquired by each one of the parameters in the image. The emotion (or emotions in case of draw) chosen will be the one that obtains a greater score.

For example, let's imagine that we study two face parameters (P_1 and P_2) and that each one of them can take three different states (C^+, C^- and S, following the nomenclature of Hammal). State C^+ means that the value of the parameters has increased with respect to the neutral one; state C^- that its value has diminished with respect to the neutral one; and the state S that its value has not varied with respect to the neutral one. First, we build a descriptive table of emotions, according to the state of the parameters, like the one of the Table 1. From this table, a set of logical tables can be built for each parameter (Table 2). That way, two vectors of emotions are defined, according to the state taken by each one of the parameters (C^+, C^- or S) in a specific frame. Once the tables are defined, the implementation of the identification algorithm is simple. When a parameter takes a specific state, it is enough to select the vector of emotions (formed by 1's and 0's) corresponding to this state. If we repeat the procedure for each parameter, we will obtain a matrix of as many rows as parameters we study and 7 columns, corresponding to the 7 emotions. The sum of 1's present in each column of the matrix gives the score obtained by each emotion.

Table 1. Theoretical table of parameters' states for each emotion

	P1	P2
Joy	C-	S/C-
Surprise	C+	C+
Disgust	C-	C-
Anger	C+	C-
Sadness	C-	C+
Fear	S/C+	S/C+
Neutral	S	S

Compared to the method of Hammal, ours is computationally simple. The combinatory explosion and the number of calculations to make are reduced considerably, allowing us to work with more information (more parameters) of the face and to evaluate the seven universal emotions, and not only four of them, as Hammal does.

Table 2. Logical rules table for each parameter

		E1 joy	E2 surprise	E3 disgust	E4 anger	E5 sadness	E6 fear	E7 neutral
P1	C+	0	1	0	1	0	1	0
	C-	1	0	1	0	1	0	0
	S	0	0	0	0	0	1	1

		E1 joy	E2 surprise	E3 disgust	E4 anger	E5 sadness	E6 fear	E7 neutral
P2	C+	0	1	0	0	1	1	0
	C-	1	0	1	1	0	0	0
	S	1	0	0	0	0	1	1

2.2   Feature Selection

The first step of our method consists of extracting the 10 feature points of the face
that will later allow us to analyze the evolution of the face parameters (distances and
angles) that we wish to study. Figure 1 shows the correspondence of these points with
the ones defined by the MPEG-4 standard. For the moment, the extraction of the
points is made manually, by means of a landmarking program made in Matlab. The
manual selection of landmarks is an important drawback in order to perform an automatic system. We are now developing an automatic features extraction, which will
allow us to analyze a greater number of images and to study the evolution of the parameters in video sequences, and not only in static images.

The characteristic points are used to calculate the five distances shown in Figure 2.
These five distances can be translated in terms of MPEG-4 standard, putting them in
relation to the feature points shown in Figure 1 and with some FAPs defined by the
norm. All the distances are normalized with respect to the distance between the eyes
(MPEG FAPU "ESo"), which is a distance independent of the expression. This way,
the values will be consistent, independently of the scale of the image, the distance to
the camera, etc.

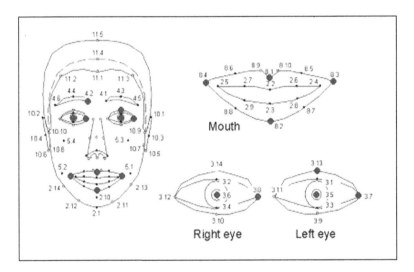

Fig. 1. Facial feature points used for the later definition of the parameters to analyze, according
to MPEG-4 standard

2.3   Database

In order to define the emotions in terms of the parameters states, as well as to find the
thresholds that determine if parameter is in a state or another, it is necessary to work
with a wide database. In this work we have used the facial expressions and emotions
database FG-NET of the University of Munich [11] that provides video sequences of
19 different people showing the 7 universal emotions from Ekman (Fig.3).

MPEG-4 FAPs NAME	FEATURE POINTS USED FOR DISTANCES
close_upper_l_eyelid close_lower_l_eyelid	D1=d(3.5, 3.1)
raise_r_i_eyebrow	D2=d(4.2, 3.8)
stretch_l_cornerlip stretch_r_cornerlip	D3=d(8.4, 8.3)
open_jaw	D4=d(8.1 , 8.2)
raise_r_cornerlip	D5=d(8.3, 3.7)

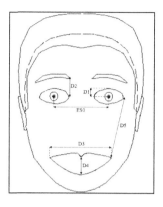

Fig. 2. Characteristic distances used in our method (left). On the right, relationship between the five characteristic distances and the MPEG-4 FAPs and feature points.

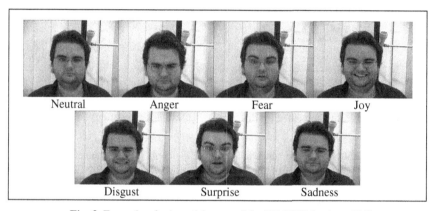

Fig. 3. Example of selected frames of the FG-NET database [11]

3   Results

3.1   Initial Results

First we considered to work with the same parameters as the Hammal method, ie, with the 5 characteristic distances shown in Figure 2. In order to build a descriptive table of each emotion in terms of states of distances, we must determine the value of the states of distances that define each emotion (C^+, C^- or S), as well as evaluate the thresholds that separate a state from another, for each distance. To do this, we studied the variation of each distance with respect to the neutral one, for each person of the database and for each emotion. An example of the results obtained for distance D_4 is shown in Figure 4. From these data, we can make a descriptive table of the emotions according to the value of the states (Table 3).

The last step to complete our algorithm is to define the values of the thresholds that separate a state of another one, for each studied distance. Two types of thresholds exist: the upper threshold (marks the limit between neutral state S and state C^+) and the lower threshold (the one that marks the limit between neutral state S and state C^-). The thresholds' values are determined by means of several tests and statistics on all the subjects and all the expressions of the database. Figure 4 shows an example of thresholds estimation for the distance D_4.

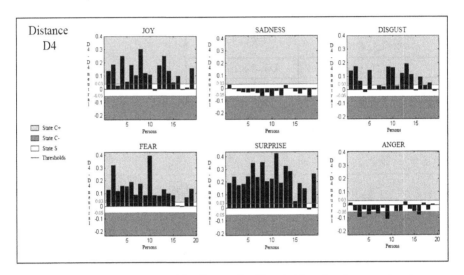

Fig. 4. Statistics results obtained for distance D_4. Thresholds estimations are also shown.

Table 3. Theoretical table of the states taken by the different studied characteristics for each emotion, according to the results of the statistics obtained from the FG-NET database. The distances (D1,..D5) are those shown in Figure 2. Some features do not provide any information of interest for certain emotions (squares in gray) and in these cases they are not considered. The four last columns are explained in sections 3.2 and 3.3 and in Figure 6.

	D_1	D_2	D_3	D_4	D_5	Wrinkles	Ang 1	Ang 2	W/H
Joy	C-	S/C-	C+	C+	C-	No	C+	S/C+/C-	S/C-
Surprise	S/C+	S/C+	S/C-	C+	S/C+	No	C-	C+	C-
Disgust	C-	C-	S/C+/C-	S/C+	S/C-	Yes	S/C+/C-	S/C+	S/C-
Anger	C-	C-	S/C-	S/C-	S/C+/C-	Yes	C+	C-	C+
Sadness	C-	S	S/C-	S	S/C+	No	S/C+/C-	S/C-	S/C+
Fear	S/C+	S/C+/C-	C-	C+	S/C+	No	C-	C+	C-
Neutral	S	S	S	S	S	No	S	S	S

Once the states that characterize each emotion and the value of the thresholds are established, the algorithm has been proved on the 399 images of the database. In the evaluation of results, the recognition is marked as "good" if the decision is coherent with the one taken by a human being. To do this, we have made surveys to 30 different people to classify the expressions shown in the most ambiguous images. For example, in the image shown in Figure 5, the surveyed people recognized it as much "disgust" as "anger", although the FG-NET database classifies it like "disgust" exclusively. Our method obtains a draw.

Fig. 5. Frame classified like "disgust" by the FG-NET database [11]

The obtained results are shown in the third column Table 4. As it can be observed, the percentage of success obtained for the emotions "disgust", "anger", "sadness", "fear" and "neutral" are acceptable and similar to the obtained by Hammal (second column). Nevertheless, for "joy" and "surprise" the results are not very favorable. In fact, the algorithm tends to confuse "joy" with "disgust" and "surprise" with "fear", which comes justified looking at Table 3, where it can be seen that a same combination of states of distances can be given for the mentioned pairs of emotions. The method has also been tested with other databases different from the one used for the threshold establishment, in order to confirm the good performance of the system. Related to classification success, it is interesting to realize that human mechanisms for face detection are very robust, but this is not the case of those for face expressions interpretation. According to Bassili [12], a trained observer can correctly classify faces showing emotions with an average of 87%.

3.2 Addition of Characteristics: Information About the Wrinkles in the Nasal Root

In order to improve the results obtained in "joy", we introduce a new face parameter: the presence or absence of wrinkles in the nasal root, typical of the emotions "disgust" and "anger". This way, we will mark a difference between "joy" and "disgust". The obtained success rates are shown in the forth column in Table 4. We observe, as it was expected, a considerable increase in the rate of successes, especially for "joy" and "disgust". However, the rates still continue being low for "sadness" and "surprise", which makes us think about the necessity to add more characteristics to the method.

3.3 Addition of Characteristics: Information About the Mouth Shape

A key factor to analyze in the recognition of emotions is the mouth shape. For each one of the 7 basic emotions, its contour changes in many different ways. In our method, we have extracted 4 feature points of the mouth that are shown in Figure 6.

Results are shown in the fifth column in Table 4. As it can be seen, the new information has introduced a great improvement in our results. The importance of the mouth shape in the expression of emotions is thus confirmed.

Table 4. Classification rates of Hammal [10] (second column), of our method with the 5 distances (third column), plus wrinkles in the nasal root (fourth column) plus mouth shape information (fifth column)

EMOTION	% SUCCESS HAMMAL METHOD	% SUCCESS OUR METHOD	% SUCCES WRINKLES NASAL ROOT	% SUCCES MOUTH SHAPE
Joy	87,26	36,84	100	100
Surprise	84,44	57,89	63,16	63,16
Disgust	51,20	84,21	94,74	100
Anger	not recognized	73,68	94,74	89,47
Sadness	not recognized	68,42	57,89	94,74
Fear	not recognized	78,95	84,21	89,47
Neutral	88%	100	100	100

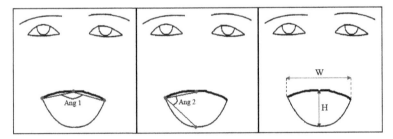

Fig. 6. Extra information added about the mouth shape

4   Conclusions and Future Work

We have presented a simple and effective method for the automatic classification of facial expressions. The introduction of several additional parameters barely increases the computational cost of the algorithm, given its simplicity, and produces very significant rates of improvement. In the future it is hoped to introduce new characteristics, in the form of face distances or angles (for example the angle formed by the eyebrows). Another noticeable objective in the short term is to make the tracking of the landmarks in an automatic way. Thanks to it, we will be able to introduce dynamic information in our method, that is to say, to study the evolution in the time of the evaluated parameters. Every time with more force, the psychological investigation argues that the timing of the facial expressions is a critical factor in the interpretation of expressions. In the midterm, the objective is to add the system to the ambient intelligent applications that the group is developing, to enrich user interaction.

Acknowledgments

This work has been partially financed by the Spanish "Dirección General de Investigación", contract number N° TIN2004-07926 and by the Aragon Government through the WALQA agreement (ref. 2004/04/86).

References

1. V. Bruce: What the Human Face Tells the Human Mind: some Challenges for the Robot-Human Interface. Proc. Int'l workshop Robot and Human Comm.A. (1992) 44-51.
2. G.J. Edwards, T.F. Cootes y C.J. Taylor, "Face Recognition Using Active Appearance Models", Proc. European Conf. Computer Vision, Vol. 2, pp. 581-695, 1998.
3. H. Hong, H. Neven y C. von der Malsburg, "Online Facial Expression Recognition Based on Personalized Galleries", Proc. Int'l Conf. Automatic Face and Gesture Recognition, pp. 354-359, 1998.
4. H. Hong, H. Neven y C. von der Malsburg, "Online Facial Expression Recognition Based on Personalized Galleries", Proc. Int'l Conf. Automatic Face and Gesture Recognition, pp. 354-359, 1998.
5. M.J. Lyons, J. Budynek y S. Akamatsu, "Automatic Classification of Single Facial Images", IEEE Trans. Pattern Analysis and Machine Intelligence, Vol. 21, n°12, pp. 1357-1362, 1999.
6. Z. Zhang, M. Lyons, M. Schuster y S. Akamatsu, "Comparison between Geometry-Based and Gabor Wavelets-Based Facial Expression Recognition Using Multi-Layer Perceptron", Proc. Int'l Conf. Automatic Face and Gesture Recognition, pp. 454-459, 1998.
7. M. Wallace, A. Raouzaiou, N. Tsapatsoulis y S. Kollias, "Facial Expression Classification Based on MPEG-4 FAPs: The Use of Evidence and Prior Knowledge for Uncetainty Removal", IEEE International Conference on Fuzzy Systems (FUZZ-IEEE), Vol. 1, pp. 51-54, Budapest (Hungría), 25-29 de Julio de 2004.
8. M. Pantic y L.J.M. Rothkrantz, "Expert System for Automatic Analysis of Facial Expression", Image and Vision Computing J., Vol. 18, n°. 11, pp. 881-905, 2000.
9. M. Pantic and L.J.M. Rothkrantz: "Automatic Analysis of Facial Expressions: The State of the Art". Pattern Analysis and Machine Intelligence, IEEE Transactions on Volume 22, Issue 12 (December 2000) 1424–1445.
10. P. Ekman: "Facial Expression, the Handbook of Cognition and Emotion". John Wiley et Sons (1999).
11. Z. Hammal, L. Couvreur, A. Caplier and M. Rombaut: "Facial Expressions Recognition Based on the Belief Theory: Comparison with Diferent Classifiers". Proc. 13th International Conference on Image Analysis and Processing (Italy 2005).
12. http://www.mmk.ei.tum.de/~waf/fgnet/feedtum.html (Reviewed in February 2006).
13. J.N. Bassili: "Emotion recognition: The role of facial movement and the relative importance of upper and lower areas of the face". Journal of Personality and Social Psychology n° 37 (1997) 2049-2059.

Posture Constraints for Bayesian Human Motion Tracking

Ignasi Rius[1], Javier Varona[2], Xavier Roca[1], and Jordi Gonzàlez[3]

[1] Centre de Visió per Computador
Edifici O. Campus UAB. 08193, Bellaterra, Spain
irius@cvc.uab.es
[2] Unitat de Gràfics i Visió per Computador
Anselm Turmeda. Campus UIB. 07122, Palma de Mallorca, Spain
[3] Institut de Robòtica i Informàtica Ind. UPC
St. LLorens i Artigas 4-6 08028, Barcelona, Spain

Abstract. One of the most used techniques for full-body human tracking consists of estimating the probability of the parameters of a human
body model over time by means of a particle filter. However, given the
high-dimensionality of the models to be tracked, the number of required
particles to properly populate the space of solutions makes the problem
computationally very expensive. To overcome this, we present an efficient
scheme which makes use of an action-specific model of human postures
to guide the prediction step of the particle filter, so only feasible human
postures are considered. As a result, the prediction step of this model-
based tracking approach samples from a first order motion model only
those postures which are accepted by our action-specific model. In this
manner, particles are propagated to locations in the search space with
most a posteriori information avoiding particle wastage. We show that
this scheme improves the efficiency and accuracy of the overall tracking
approach.

1 Introduction

Full-body 3D human tracking from a monocular image sequence is one of the
most challenging problems from visual human motion analysis. However, the
number of difficulties related to the problem are very large. Among others,
the shape and appearance of a human body in 2D images may change drastically over time due to changing lighting conditions, loose fitting clothes and
background clutter. Additionally, one must deal with 2D-3D projection ambiguities, and self and non-self occlusions of body parts. Hence, only a reduced
number of DOF present in the model are directly observable from 2D images.
Finally, the implied models are very high dimensional, non-linear, and may suffer from kinematic ambiguities and singularities [12]. To overcome these issues,
many approaches make use of Bayesian filtering techniques combined with carefully designed search strategies of the solution space [2,8,11,14,13]. When the
involved distributions are non-Gaussian, the computation of model parameters
over time can be approximated by means of a particle filter [3]. This probabilistic

F.J. Perales and R.B. Fisher (Eds.): AMDO 2006, LNCS 4069, pp. 414–423, 2006.

framework can deal with multiple hypotheses, and brings a principled way to incorporate *a priori* knowledge about human motion into the tracking, so the solution space can be explored in a more efficient manner.

Particle filters supply a powerful tool for representing and propagating complex posterior distributions. However, the number of needed particles grows exponentially as the number of dimensions to be tracked does [7]. This fact is obvious in the human motion tracking case, due to the high DOF needed to represent human postures. For this reason, it is necessary to make particle filters more efficient. For example, the *annealed* particle filter aims to reduce the number of required samples by successively pruning less likely hypotheses [2]. They used it in combination to a smooth motion model in a multi-camera tracking system in order to track generic human motion.

Alternatively, it is possible to use efficient motion models which concentrate particles in areas of interest. Sidenbladh et al. applied the particle filtering framework for full human body tracking in [10] in combination with a cyclic dynamic model designed to improve the performance of the tracker for the walking action. Likewise, Ning. et al [8] tracked a walking sequence of a 12 DOF body model using a particle filter and a dynamic model of walking. The dynamic model included constraints on human motion, and learnt the parameters of motion formulated as independent Gaussian distributions per each joint. In [11], Sidenbladh et al. generalized their approach to include different actions than walking. They learnt the dynamic model from a pre-recorded set of human motions, and predictions were made assuming a Gaussian distribution over subsequences of the learned motions. As a result, particle wastage was avoided by concentrating particles in areas where motion was observed before. However, the model can only predict postures which were present in the motion database.

Recently, Urtasun et al. introduces the use of Scaled Gaussian Process Latent Variable Models (SGPLVM) to learn models of 3D human poses from small training sets [13]. They use this model as a motion prior to constrain the human postures to the learned actions. However, instead of particle filters, they use a deterministic optimization approach to implement the Bayesian filter. Alternatively, for large motion sets it is possible to use the learning scheme of Chai et al. to build a more efficient space of human postures [1].

Likewise, we propose a posture-based human action space for modeling feasible postures within an action. This model is used to constrain human postures within the framework of a particle filter responsible for tracking the human body motion. In such a recursive model-based tracking approach, human postures are projected forward by means of a dynamic model, and they are subsequently updated according to the measurements obtained from images. As a result, we must define both the dynamic model and the fitness function of human postures to images. In this work, predictions are made according to a dynamic model which focuses and constrains human postures only to a set of feasible postures within the performance of a particular action.

The remainder of this paper is organised as follows. In Section 2 we present the training of our action-specific model of human postures using real data acquired with a commercial Motion Capture system. This action model is used to determine whether a human posture belongs to a particular action or not. Section 3 introduces the tracking framework. We define a dynamic model based on a first order motion model constrained to the postures which are accepted by the action model. Moreover, we present a fitness function based on the overlapping area between the projection of the body state and the body region obtained from image segmentation. In Section 4 results of the tracking approach are presented for a performance not considered in the training set. Finally, Section 5 discusses the conclusions and future research.

2   Learning Posture Constraints

The 3D human body model used in this work is composed of 12 limbs with 3 DOF per joint expressed as relative angles in a 3D polar coordinate system. Using a commercial Motion Capture System, we acquired 45 performances, in average, of 9 different actions performed by 9 different actors. We refer the reader to [9] for details on the body model and motion database used. From the observed motion, we aim to automatically learn per each action, which human postures are feasible during the performance of that particular action. Towards this end, we first express all the training postures for action A in a lower dimensional representation called *aSpace* [4] which is computed as follows:

Let ϕ be a 36-dimensional vector representing a particular human posture, and Φ be a sequence of human postures, hereafter performance. Then, for a particular action A, we compute PCA over all the training performances Φ_j for that action. The resulting PCA-like space - called *aSpace* - will be denoted as Ω^A. The projections $\tilde{\Phi}_j$ on the *aSpace* of Φ_j constitute the lower dimensional version from the original data.

Subsequently, we aim to characterize the *shape* of the training performances for action A within the *aSpace*. Since each performance $\tilde{\Phi}_j$ may be composed of a different number of postures and may exhibit different speeds, we need a method for synchronising all the performances from the training set. Hence, we normalise the length of each performance by means of a cubic spline, and compute the mean performance $\bar{g}^A$. Afterwards, a key-frame set $\boldsymbol{K}^A$ is found from $\bar{g}^A$ by selecting the maximum and minimum distant postures from the mean posture in the same fashion than [5]. We look for the most similar postures to the key-frames found in each performance, so we can resample all the performances to have the same number of postures. As a result, we obtain a synchronised version of the training set. Fig. 1 shows the first 4 dimensions of the *aSpace* from the non-synchronised (Fig. 1.(a)) and the synchronised (Fig. 1.(b)) versions of the training set for a bending action.

As a result, we can put in correspondence postures between different training performances. Therefore, we compute the synchronised mean performance $\hat{g}^A$, and the standard deviation σ_k^A for each k-th posture, using all the synchronised performances $\tilde{\Phi}_j$. In Fig.1.(b), we show the synchronised training performances (thin lines) and its mean performance (thick line) for a bending action. The

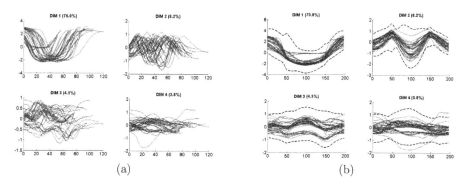

Fig. 1. Before (a) and after (b) synchronization of the training set using key-frames

dashed black line corresponds to three times the standard deviation computed from the mean. Finally, our action model is defined as:

$$\Gamma^A = (\Omega^A, \hat{g}^A, \sigma_k^A), \tag{1}$$

where Ω^A defines the *aSpace*, $\hat{g}^A$ stands for the synchronised version of the mean performance, and σ_k^A is the observed standard deviation.

The learnt action model will be used in the prediction step of the particle filter to probabilistically determine whether a posture belongs to action A or not. The probabilistic framework used to face the tracking problem is described in the next section.

3 Using the Posture Constraints

The Bayesian filter recursively estimates the state of the tracked object at each time step given the evidences (image data) up to that moment. It decomposes the problem in two differentiated steps, i.e. the *prediction* and *update* steps. The prediction step projects forward the model parameters to the next time step by means of a *dynamic model*. Then the update step makes use of a *likelihood* probability function in order to evaluate the fitness of the predictions to the evidences available at each moment.

Formally, within the Bayesian filtering framework, we formulate the computation of the *posterior* distribution $p(\phi_t | \mathbf{I}_t)$ of our model parameters over time as follows:

$$p(\phi_t | \mathbf{I}_t) \propto p(I_t | \phi_t) \int p(\phi_t | \phi_{t-1}) \, p(\phi_{t-1} | \mathbf{I}_{t-1}) \, d\phi_{t-1} \,, \tag{2}$$

where ϕ_t is a 36-dimensional vector from our body model representing a particular pose of the human body at time t, $\mathbf{I}_t$ is the image sequence up to time t, $p(I_t | \phi_t)$ is the *likelihood* of observing the image I_t given the parametrization ϕ_t of our model at time t, and finally $p(\phi_t | \phi_{t-1})$ is the *dynamic model*.

We use particle filtering techniques in order to approximate the true *posterior* pdf by means of a discrete weighted set of samples. Hence, whilst the likelihood function decides which particles are worth to propagate, the dynamic model is responsible for guiding the exploration of the space of solutions. The *posterior* $p(\phi_t|\mathbf{I}_t)$ represents all the current knowledge about the model state we have extracted from image measurements. We can estimate the state ϕ_t at a particular time step by computing the mean of the posterior pdf.

The number of samples -or *particles*- determines the accuracy and the speed of the tracker. However, the computational cost of particle filters mainly comes from the computation of the likelihood function from image measurements [15]. Additionally, the number of needed particles grows exponentially as the number of dimensions of the model to be tracked does [7]. Therefore, given the high-dimensionality present in human motion tracking, we need to design efficient search strategies to lower the number of particles needed. In other words, the dynamic model from the prediction step of the particle filter should be generic enough to track any motion, but specific enough to focus particles only to areas with high a posteriori information.

3.1 Constrained Motion Model

The action-specific posture model constitutes *a priori* knowledge on human motion which can be incorporated into the Bayesian tracking framework by means of the dynamic model $p(\phi_t|\phi_{t-1})$ from Eq. (2). We aim to define a dynamic model which samples only those postures which are feasible during the performance of a particular action A, based on a 1st order motion model. Thus, the prediction step of the particle filter is designed as a two-step process. First, we project forward the particle set $\{\phi_{t-1}^s\}$ following a 1st order motion model plus some Gaussian noise, i.e.,

$$\hat{\phi}_t^s = \phi_{t-1}^s + V_{t-1} + \eta(\sigma_\phi), \tag{3}$$

where ϕ_{t-1}^s denotes the particle s at time $t-1$, and $\hat{\phi}_t^s$ is the prediction for this particle. V_{t-1} is the velocity term computed at time at time $t-1$, and $\eta(\sigma_\phi)$ is a Gaussian diffusion term. To determine σ_ϕ, we used a constant velocity model to predict each performance of the training set. Then, σ_ϕ was computed as the standard deviation of the average error committed. Subsequently, we update the term V_t according to $V_t = \alpha V_{t-1} + (1-\alpha)(\phi_{t-1} - \phi_{t-2})$, where α is a learning coefficient, and ϕ_{t-1}, ϕ_{t-2} correspond to the estimated state of the human body at the two previous time steps.

Secondly, we filter those predictions $\hat{\phi}_t^s$ which are not accepted as feasible postures during the performance of the action A_i by our action-specific model. If a prediction $\hat{\phi}_t^s$ is rejected, we resample from Eq. (3) until a feasible posture is generated for this particle. Finally, the new set of predicted particles $\{\phi_t^s\}$ at time t is constituted by those predictions $\hat{\phi}_t^s$ which were accepted by the action model.

As a result, we reformulate Eq. (2) including the action model into the prediction step as

$$p(\phi_t|\mathbf{I}_t) \propto p(I_t|\phi_t) \int p(\phi_t|\phi_{t-1}, \Gamma^A) \cdot p(\phi_{t-1}|\mathbf{I}_{t-1}) \, d\phi_{t-1}. \tag{4}$$

Now, by applying the Bayes' rule and assuming independence between ϕ_{t-1} and Γ^A, i.e. only current postures are constrained by the action model, we can further decompose Eq. (4) as

$$p(\phi_t|\mathbf{I}_t) \propto p(I_t|\phi_t) \int p(\phi_t|\phi_{t-1}) \, p(\phi_t|\Gamma^A) \cdot p(\phi_{t-1}|\mathbf{I}_{t-1}) \, d\phi_{t-1}, \tag{5}$$

where $p(\phi_t|\Gamma^A)$ is a function which determines whether a particular posture ϕ_t belongs to action A or not defined as follows:

$$p(\phi_t|\Gamma^A) = \begin{cases} 1 & if \ (|\tilde{\phi}_{t,d}, \hat{g}_{j,d}^A| < 2 \cdot \sigma_{j,d}^A), \forall d = 1..D \\ 0 & otherwise \end{cases}, \tag{6}$$

where $\tilde{\phi}_t = (\tilde{\phi}_{t,1}, ..., \tilde{\phi}_{t,D})^T$ is the projection of ϕ_t in the D-dimensional *aSpace*. $\hat{g}_j^A$ is the j-th posture from the mean performance computed for the action A which probabilistically matched $\tilde{\phi}_t$, i.e., we draw $\hat{g}_j^A$ from a Gaussian conditional distribution assuming that $\tilde{\phi}_t = \hat{g}_j^A + \eta(\Delta)$, where Δ is empirically determined from the training set. $\sigma_j^A = (\sigma_{j,1}^A, ..., \sigma_{j,D}^A)$ stands for the learnt standard deviation of the j-th posture for the action A. Notice that the level of filtering depends on the number of dimensions D considered in the *aSpace* representation.

By defining this filtering method, we prune those predictions which are more distant than two times the learnt standard deviation from the matched posture of a particular action. As a result, our dynamic model predicts feasible human postures avoiding particle wastage on postures which are not likely to appear during the performance of a particular action.

3.2   Image Measurements

The *likelihood* function $p(I_t|\phi_t)$ computes how likely is to observe the image I_t given a human body posture ϕ_t. In this paper, we implemented a likelihood function based on the image region filled by the human body. Hence, the human body model has been fleshed out with 3D volumetric primitives consisting in 3D cylinders. As a result, we synthesise an image $\check{I}_{\phi_t^s}$ of the region defined by a particular parametrization ϕ_t^s of the human body model. For simplicity and efficiency, we have simplified the 2D projections onto the image plane from the limbs' cylinders as rectangles.

On the other hand, we extract the true region filled by the body in the current image I_t by applying a background subtraction algorithm from Horprasert et al. [6]. This pixel-wise algorithm needs to be trained with several background-only frames beforehand. Then, for each frame to be segmented, the algorithm

Fig. 2. I_t (a), $\breve{I}_{\phi_t}$ (b), $\hat{I}_t$ (c), I_{t,ϕ_t}^{OV} (d) and I_{t,ϕ_t}^U (e) images from the likelihood computation. See text for details.

computes for each pixel the normalised distortion on chromacity and brightness with respect to the learnt background model. Based on this values, each pixel is classified as background, foreground, shadow, or highlight. We denote the segmented body region image as $\hat{I}_t$. Finally, the *likelihood* is computed based on the overlapping area between the synthesised and the segmented images, i.e.,

$$p(I_t|\phi_t) \propto \frac{\sum_x \sum_y (I_{t,\phi_t}^{OV}(x,y))}{\sum_x \sum_y (I_{t,\phi_t}^U(x,y))}, \qquad (7)$$

where I_{t,ϕ_t}^{OV} refers to the overlapping region between $\breve{I}_{\phi_t}$ and $\hat{I}_t$, I_{t,ϕ_t}^U is the union of both regions. The notation $I(x,y)$ is used to make reference to the pixel of I at column x, row y. As a result, we assign maximum weight to those postures whose synthesised image coincide totally with the segmented one, and lower values otherwise. Fig. 2 shows the images I_t (a), $\breve{I}_{\phi_t}$ (b), $\hat{I}_t$ (c), I_{t,ϕ_t}^{OV} (d) and I_{t,ϕ_t}^U (e) computed at a particular time t of the algorithm.

4   Experimental Results

To test this work we used a training set of 40 performances of a bending action carried out by 9 different actors. However, the approach is easily extensible to other sets of actions. Hence, we have tested the tracking approach using a bending sequence not present in the training set, consisting in 86 frames from which we have 3D ground truth data available.

The number of D dimensions considered when building the *aSpace* representation determines the degree of adaptation of the action model to the training data. Hence, too low values for D result in a poor filtering effect, since too many particles with low a posteriori information will be accepted by the action model. On the other hand, too high values lead to overfitting to the training set, since the action model only accepts particles that are almost equal to postures used to learn the action model. To test this work, we used $D = 13$ dimensions which proved to achieve a good compromise between generality of the model and non-feasible postures rejection.

To test the effectiveness of the approach, we compared the results obtained using our action model against a first order motion model without any filtering method. We repeated the same experiment varying N from 100 to 10000 particles, with $D = 13$ and the learning coefficient of the velocity set to $\alpha = 0.5$. In

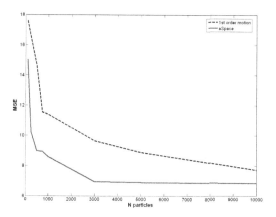

Fig. 3. MSE obtained with both approaches

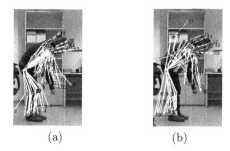

(a)   (b)

Fig. 4. Predictions of the *aSpace* and 1st order motion approaches

Fig.3 we show the obtained error for the *aSpace* filtering method (solid line) and the simple first order motion model (dashed line). The error was computed as the average Mean Square Error (MSE) of the relative angles between the final estimated postures -computed as the expectation of the posterior pdf- and the ground truth data from the sequence. We may observe that the action model overperforms the 1st order motion model in all the experiments. Furthermore, the error for the *aSpace* filtering method quickly stabilises around 7 at $N = 3000$ particles. One may observe that we obtain similar error measures using 2000 particles with the *aSpace* approach than 10000 particles without any filtering. Additionally, with very few particles -below 1000-, our approach quickly lowers the error and tends to stabilise, while the 1st order motion model approach gives very high error rates. Hence, our approach never totally looses the tracked object since it never produces non meaningful postures. This is depicted in Fig.4 where a frame of the tracked sequence is plotted with a randomly selected set of predicted postures projected over it for (a) the *aSpace* approach, and (b) the 1st order motion model approach. One may observe that the latter leads to unlikely and non feasible human postures for this action, while the *aSpace* filtering approach predicts natural and coherent human postures.

Fig. 5. Estimated frames 1, 11, 21, 31, 41, 51, 61, 71 and 81

Finally, selected frames of the final estimated sequence are shown in Fig.5 for $N = 5000$ particles. We may observe, that the left arm is confused with the right arm in the first frames. This is an expected behaviour, since the right arm is totally occluding the left one, so the likelihood function gives us no clue for evaluating the proper arm position. However, in the second half of the sequence, the left arm tends to its correct position since it becomes slightly visible in those frames, so the likelihood function is higher for postures covering the left arm. The ability to handle multiple hypothesis of the particle filtering framework is proved to be very suitable, since it can recover from a self-occluding situation where the likelihood function doesn't provide the right maxima.

5   Conclusion

We have presented an efficient tracking approach based on particle filtering for full-body human tracking, which makes use of an action model to guide the prediction step of the particle filter. Despite the use of a simple likelihood function, the space of possible solutions is explored in an efficient manner since only feasible human postures are generated by our dynamic model. We compared the overall error of our tracking approach against a first order motion model without filtering in the *aSpace*. Results point out that the action model approach drastically reduces the number of particles needed to track a 36 DOF human body model, thus reducing the high computational cost inherent to typical particle filter approaches. Moreover, given the PCA-like definition of the action space, the degree of dependence of the predictions to the training data set can be tuned by considering more or less dimensions when building the space.

Future work relies on extending this approach to a more general set of actions, so we can track any action and transitions between actions. Furthermore, the likelihood function needs to be improved in order to include other image-based cues like color or edges, so it provides more reliable information for evaluating the predicted poses. Moreover, we need to define a method for handling self-occlusions based on predicting which body parts are visible at each time step. Finally, it is possible to improve the action model by considering other formulations which may improve the pruning effect providing more accuracy and efficiency to the overall tracking process.

Acknowledgments. This work has been supported by the Generalitat de Catalunya Research Department, by the EC grant IST-027110 for the HERMES project and by the Spanish MEC under projects TIC2003-08865 and DPI-2004-5414. J. Gonzàlez and J. Varona acknowledge the support of a Juan de la Cierva and Ramon y Cajal postdoctoral fellowships from the Spanish MEC, respectively.

References

1. J. Chai and J.K. Hodgins. Performance animation from low-dimensional control signals. *SIGGRAPH 2005, ACM Trans. Graph.*, 24(3):686–696, 2005.
2. J. Deutscher and I. Reid. Articulated body motion capture by stochastic search. *IJCV*, 61(2):185–205, 2005.
3. A. Doucet, N. de Freitas, and N. Gordon. *Sequential Monte Carlo Methods in Practice.* Springer, 2001.
4. J. Gonzàlez. *Human Sequence Evaluation: the Key-frame Approach.* PhD thesis, Universitat Autònoma de Barcelona, 2004.
5. J. Gonzàlez, J. Varona, X. Roca, and J.J. Villanueva. Analysis of human walking based on aSpaces. *AMDO'04*, September 2004.
6. T. Horprasert, D. Harwood, and L.S. Davis. A robust background subtraction and shadow detection. In *Proc. Asian. Conf. on Comp. Vision*, January 2000.
7. J. MacCormick and M. Isard. Partitioned sampling, articulated objects and interface-quality hand tracking. Dublin, 2000. ECCV'00.
8. H. Ning, T. Tan, L. Wang, and W. Hu. Kinematics-based tracking of human walking in monocular video sequences. *IVC*, 22:429–441, 2004.
9. I. Rius, D. Rowe, J. Gonzàlez, and X. Roca. A 3d dynamic model of human actions for probabilistic image tracking. In *IbPRIA'2005*.
10. H. Sidenbladh, M.J. Black, and D.J. Fleet. Stochastic tracking of 3d human figures using 2d image motion. In *ECCV*, volume 2, pages 702–718, Dublin, 2000.
11. H. Sidenbladh, M.J. Black, and L. Sigal. Implicit probabilistic models of human motion for synthesis and tracking. In *ECCV (1)*, pages 784–800, 2002.
12. W. Stadler. *Analytical Robotics and Mechatronics.* McGraw-Hill, NY, USA., 1995.
13. R. Urtasun, D.J. Fleet, A. Hertzmann, and P. Fua. Priors for people tracking from small training sets. In *IEEE International Conference on Computer Vision (ICCV05)*, volume 1, pages 403–410, 2005.
14. S. Wachter and H. H. Nagel. Tracking persons in monocular image sequences. *CVIU*, 74(3):174–192, June 1999.
15. Y. Wu, J. Lin, and T.S. Huang. Analyzing and capturing articulated hand motion in image sequences. *IEEE Transactions on Pattern Analysis and Machine Intelligence*, 27(12):1910–1922, 2005.

Efficient Incorporation of Motionless Foreground Objects for Adaptive Background Segmentation

I. Huerta[1], D. Rowe[1], J. Gonzàlez[2], and J.J. Villanueva[1]

[1] Computer Vision Centre & Dept. d'Informàtica.
Edifici O. Campus UAB, 08193, Bellaterra, Spain
ivan.huerta@cvc.uab.es
[2] Institut de Robòtica i Informàtica Ind. UPC
Llorens i Artigas 4-6, 08028, Barcelona, Spain

Abstract. In this paper, we want to exploit the knowledge obtained from those detected objects which are incorporated into the background model since they cease their movement. These motionless foreground objects should be handled in security domains such as video surveillance. This paper uses an adaptive background modelling algorithm for moving-object detection. Those detected objects which present no motion are identified and added into the background model, so that they will be part of the new background. Such motionless agents are included for further appearance analysis and agent categorization.

1 Introduction

The analysis of human-motion image sequences involves different tasks, such as movement segmentation and tracking, action recognition and behaviour reasoning [7]. Therefore, the basis for high-level interpretation of observed patterns of human motion relies on *when* and *where* motion is being detected. Consequently, this low-level task still constitutes the most critical step towards Image Sequence Evaluation (ISE) [10].

In this work, the aim is to exploit at the Image Signal Level of the ISE architecture the knowledge obtained from those detected objects which could be incorporate into the background since they cease their movement. These "newly motionless" objects should be handled in security domains such as video surveillance. For example, if a suspicious bag is detected in an airport, some knowledge can be inferred: who left it there, where this bag within in the scene, when the person has left it. In traffic monitoring, if a car is stopped a predefined period of time, the position of this car is inferred within the scene, but also when and (the appearance of) who has left this car. Thus, incorporated objects constitute additional knowledge, which can be represented using feature-based models.

Different techniques have been used for motion segmentation [12], such as temporal differencing, optical flow and background subtraction. The latter consists of a background model used to compare the current image with such a model. Thus, foreground objects in motion are identified. To achieve this objective, many researchers have proposed methods which have been used to solve the

F.J. Perales and R.B. Fisher (Eds.): AMDO 2006, LNCS 4069, pp. 424–433, 2006.

problems found in segmentation, such as gradual or sudden illumination changes, shadows, camouflage, background in motion, or deposited and removed objects from scene, among other problems [8].

Thus, W^4 [4] uses a bimodal distribution, Pfinder [13] uses a single Gaussian to model the background, Stauffer et al. [2,3] use a mixture of Gaussians, and Elgammal et al. [1] present a non-parametric background model. On the other hand, the features used for segmentation vary in the literature: Horprasert et al. [5] use colour information to classify a pixel as foreground, background, shadow or highlighted background, while Wallflower [9] uses a three-level categorization: pixel, region and frame level. Jabri et al. [6] use colour and edge information, and Shen [11] uses a RGB colour space plus fuzzy classification.

These approaches incorporate *gradually* new motionless foreground objects into the background model, that is, the updating rule of the background model incorporates increasingly all the pixel values which constitute the object. Therefore, a suitable representation of motionless objects cannot be built for post-processing tasks, such as object recognition or classification. Moreover, adaptive rules do not usually distinguish between background changes due to illumination than those changes due to left or removed objects.

In particular, W^4 [4] first presented a differentiation between pixel-based and object-based detection: the *pixel-based update* method updates the background model periodically to adapt it to illumination changes, and the *object-based update* method updates the background to adapt it to physical changes, such as those objects deposited or removed into the background scene. Consequently, our work will be based on W^4 in order to obtain a fast background scene modelling and maintenance while considering new incorporated objects. Therefore, such an adaptive background model is updated according to observed developments within the scen e in order to achieve fast and robust segmentation results.

This paper is organized as follows. Section 2 shows how the background model is created. Section 3 describes the foreground region detection, and section 4 how the background model parameters are updated. Section 5 presents our contribution to object incorporation, and section 6 shows the results obtained. Finally, chapter 7 concludes this paper and discusses different alternatives for future research.

2   Initial Background Model

W^4 uses a model of background variation constructed from order statistics of background values during a training period. The background scene is modelled by representing each pixel by three values: its minimum $m(x)$ and maximum $n(x)$ intensity values, and the maximum intensity difference $d(x)$ between consecutive frames observed during this training period. Furthermore, W^4 uses a two-stage method for exclude foreground objects during training period, such as moving people. First, the median filter $|V^z(x) - \lambda(x)| < 2 * \sigma(x)$ distinguishes moving pixels from stationary pixels. $V^z(x)$ is the intensity of a pixel location x in the $z - th$ image of sequence V, $\lambda(x)$ is the median value, and $\sigma(x)$ is the standard

Fig. 1. Detection results in a road sequence with a high number of foreground objects during the training period: (a) foreground detection results using W^4, showing that no detection is achieved; (b) the background is updated using W^4, showing that cars are erroneously incorporated into the background model; (c) foreground detection results; and (d) background model update using our approach

deviation. After that, in the second stage, only stationary pixels are considered for building the initial background model.

However, a training period is not always available, because this period can contain multiple foreground objects in the scene, such as for the road sequence, see Fig. 1 The initial background model can be erroneous if foreground objects are incorporated into the background model. The two-stage method used for W^4 explained above is not sufficient for excluding all foreground objects. Fig. 1.(a) shows a frame with a high number of foregrounds objects during the training period, where foreground regions are shown and no detection is achieved. Consequently, the new background model will be wrong too. Fig. 1.(b) shows a wrong updated background model because of incorporated foreground objects in motion.

To solve the aforementioned problem, the first stage is applied in a recursive way. The median filter is applied until the standard deviation from the new background model is the same as the last background model. Now, the foreground objects are eliminated, as it can be seen in Fig. 1.(c), where foreground objects are detected in contrast to Fig. 1.(a). The background model is well updated as it can be seen in the Fig. 1.(d), and compared to Fig. 1.(b).

3   Foreground Region Detection

W^4 uses a four-stage process to obtain a foreground object: thresholding, noise cleaning, morphological filtering, and object detection. The threshold stage classifies each pixel as either a background or a foreground pixel using the background model. A pixel is a foreground pixel if:

$$B(x) = \begin{cases} 0 \text{ background } \begin{cases} (I^t(x) + m(x)) > k_f * \max(d(x), dmin) \\ \wedge\, I^t(x) - n(x)) < k_f * \max(d(x), dmin) \end{cases} \\ 1 \text{ foreground } \text{ otherwise}. \end{cases} \quad (1)$$

Parameter k_f serves for extend or reduce the detection range[1], and parameter $dmin$ is added to create a minimum background detection range. In this work, all the sequences are processed using only the first stage, i.e. thresholding, in order to evaluate in a better way the overall approach presented here.

4   Updating Background Model Parameters

The background model is updated using the *pixel-based update* and *object-based update* conditions as in W^4. The first condition "$(gS(x) > k * N)$" updates the background model periodically to adapt it to illumination changes in the background scene. And the second one "$(gS(x) < k * N \wedge mS(x) < r * N)$" updates the background model to adapt it to physical changes in the background scene, when new objects are deposited or removed in the background scene.

W^4 uses a detection support map (gS), to represent the number of times a pixel is classified as a background pixel:

$$gS(x,t) = \begin{cases} gS(x, t-1) + 1 \text{ if } x \text{ is background pixel} \\ gS(x, t-1) \quad \text{ if } x \text{ is foreground pixel}. \end{cases} \quad (2)$$

A motion support map (mS) represents the number of times a pixel is classified as moving pixel:

$$mS(x,t) = \begin{cases} mS(x, t-1) + 1 \text{ if } M(x,t) = 1 \\ mS(x, t-1) \quad \text{ if } M(x,t) = 0, \end{cases} \quad (3)$$

where $M(x,t)$ represents moving pixels, computed as:

$$M(x,t) = \begin{cases} 1 \text{ if } (|I(x,t) - I(x, t+1)| > 2 * \sigma) \wedge \\ \quad (|I(x, t-1) - I(x,t)| > 2 * \sigma) \\ 0 \text{ otherwise}. \end{cases} \quad (4)$$

The new background parameters $[m(x), n(x), d(x)]$ are updated after a predetermined number N of frames, and they are determined using the aforementioned maps as follows:

---

[1] The parameter k_f is set to 2, according to our experiments and the results presented in W^4 [4].

$$[m(x), n(x), d(x)] =$$
$$\begin{cases} [m^b(x), n^b(x), d^b(x)] & \text{if } (gS(x) > k * N) \text{ pixel-based update} \\ [m^f(x), n^f(x), d^f(x)] & \text{if } (gS(x) < k * N \wedge mS(x) < r * N) \\ & \text{object-based update} \\ [m^c(x), n^c(x), d^c(x)] & \text{otherwise}, \end{cases} \quad (5)$$

where k and r are typically 0.8 and 0.1, respectively [4]. The parameters $[m^b(x), n^b(x), d^b(x)]$ represent those pixels classified as background in this period of time, $[m^f(x), n^f(x), d^f(x)]$ those pixels classified as foreground pixels, and $[m^c(x), n^c(x), d^c(x)]$ are the value of the background parameters in the last background model. When the background model is updated, the maps are set to zero.

5   Improving Object-Based Update

Achieving a robust object-based updated constitutes a challenging task thereby managing the incorporation of the new objects to the background, and removing the old background objects. The goal is to work with newly motionless foreground objects: detected objects in motion which have exhibited motion up to that moment. They should be identified, and the object-based update should take them into the background model. The first problem is that pixels which are no longer considered as motionless foreground pixels are updated as object-based, since the minimum number of times a particular pixel has been classified as foreground is usually not restrictive enough (according to object-based condition).

In addition, the foreground pixels considered to construct the background model $[m^f(x), n^f(x), d^f(x)]$ do not have to include foreground moving pixels, because these have different intensity values than foreground pixels considered object-based along the updating window.

Furthermore, other problems can be found with those pixels considered as object-based. If these pixels belong to a foreground motionless object which left the scene before the background is updated, such pixels can be included erroneously into the background model. This happens because these pixels also satisfy the object-based condition. Fig. 2.(a) shows a representative example of an background updating intensity value for a given pixel along the updating window with one foreground object which left the scene before the background is updated. Consequently, the pixel is added erroneously in the new background model.

Additionally, different foreground objects can appear at the same place in different times of the same background updating window, and they can be included together. Thus, the object-based parameters may be updated with a minimum intensity value $m(x)$ from one object and a maximum intensity value $n(x)$ from the other. Therefore, as both objects are different, the updating parameters $[m(x), n(x), d(x)]$ will be erroneous. Fig. 2.(b) illustrates the background updating when a new object appears at the same position where another object was before: these two objects will be incorporated into the background model, and the maximum and minimum intensity value from these two objects will wrongly

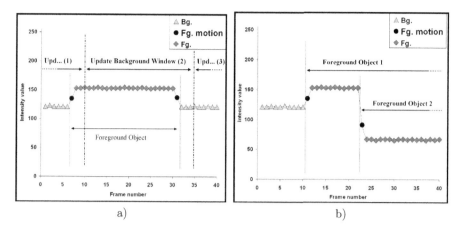

Fig. 2. Problems with object-based update. The pictures represent the background updating model for a given pixel along updating window, where: (a) a foreground object enters (background updating window 1) and leaves the scene before the background is updated (background updating window 2). Consequently, the pixel is incorporated erroneously in the new background model. (b) Background updating when a new object appears at the same position where another object was before: these two objects will be erroneously incorporated into the background model. See text for details.

constitute the new background model. The ghost which appears when an object belongs to the background awakes can present the similar problems above explained.

In order to solve the drawbacks explained above, object-based update is not performed when the pixels belongs to different foreground objects, or belongs to foreground objects that left the scene before the background is updated.

Our algorithm is based on the last detected object. In other words, the number of foreground pixels is computed from the latest foreground pixel in motion or background pixel. A new map is created, called *Foreground History Map*, $fS(x,t)$, which represents the number of times a pixel is detected as foreground continuously without pixels in motion, $M(x,t)$, neither background pixels during its history:

$$fS(x,t) = \begin{cases} fS(x,t-1) + 1 \text{ if } x \text{ is a foreground pixel and } M(x,t) = 0 \\ 0 \qquad\qquad\qquad\quad \text{otherwise.} \end{cases} \tag{6}$$

The Eq. (5) must be changed to include *fS(x,t)* map instead of *gS(x,t)*. The minimum number of foreground pixels which are necessary for considering a pixel as object-based should be within the limits commented above. The foreground history map is more restrictive than gS map, and include this restriction. Furthermore, the use of $M(x,t)$ is avoided in the background updating parameters, because this restriction is already included inside *fS(x,t)*.

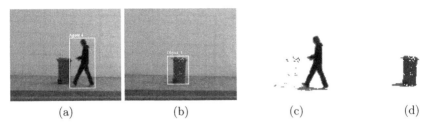

(a)   (b)   (c)   (d)

Fig. 3. Image sequence after background model updating. (a) Original sequence. (b) New background model with motionless foreground object (i.e. a rubbish bin). (c) Foreground detection without motionless foreground object. (d) Newly motionless foreground objects are added to the background model. Results are obtained without any kind of filtering.

The background updating parameters results as follows:

$$[m(x), n(x), d(x)] = \begin{cases} [m^b(x), n^b(x), d^b(x)] & \text{if } (gS(x) > k * N) \text{ pixel-based update} \\ [m^f(x), n^f(x), d^f(x)] & \text{if } (fS(x) > k * N) \text{ object-based update} \\ [m^c(x), n^c(x), d^c(x)] & \text{otherwise.} \end{cases}$$

(7)

With this approach, the problems mentioned above are solved. However, this means that foreground objects which cease their movements are no longer included into the background model. This happens since the pixels from those objects are often considered pixels in motion erroneously. The problem is that $M(x,t)$ map does not distinguish real motion from fluctuations.

A pixel in motion must show an evolution of its intensity value. Presently, $M(x,t)$ compare current intensity value for each pixel with its previous and its posterior intensity value. This can be enhance by comparing its previous value with its posterior one. The new $M(x,t)$ will be computed as follows:

$$M(x,t) = \begin{cases} 1 \text{ if } (|I(x,t) - I(x,t+1)| > 2 * \sigma) \wedge \\ \quad (|I(x,t-1) - I(x,t)| > 2 * \sigma) \wedge \\ \quad (|I(x,t+1) - I(x,t-1)| > 2 * \sigma) \\ 0 \text{ otherwise.} \end{cases}$$

(8)

Thus, the knowledge of motionless foreground objects is incorporated into the background model. Fig. 3.(b) shows a rubbish bin correctly updated as object-based. Furthermore, the problems with ghosts are also solved, see the rubbish bin ghost in Fig. 4.

6   Experimental Results

Our algorithm has been tested with multiple and different sequences which contain different motionless foreground objects and persons who interact with them. Fig.3 shows the scene where a rubbish bin is added to the background model. Fig.3.(a) shows the original image, Fig.3.(b) shows the background model where

Fig. 4. First column shows the original image sequence, second column shows the results of foreground detection using W^4, third column displays the background model using W^4, fourth column shows foreground detection results using our approach and fifth column displays the background model using our approach. Image results are obtained without any kind of filtering. See text for details.

the motionless foreground object (i.e. a rubbish bin) is correctly added. Fig.3.(c) shows the foreground region detection without the motionless foreground object, and Fig.3.(d) shows the newly motionless foreground object which has been properly added to the background model following the object-based criterion. This newly motionless foreground object can then be used for further processing such as object classification or recognition.

Fig. 4 represents the same sequence using the same parameter values. This particular sequence contains 900 frames, and the first 200 frames are used to construct the initial background model, which do not contain any foreground object. The background model is updated every N=100 frames. The sequence corresponds to an agent who leaves a rubbish bin in the middle of the scene. Later on, a new agent enters into the scene. Subsequently, another agent takes the rubbish bin.

In Fig. 4, the first column shows the original image sequence at frame numbers 264, 372, 473, 612, 631, 682, 806. The second column shows the foreground region detection, and the third column shows the background model, and how it is updated using W^4. Fourth and five columns show the foreground region detection and update background model using our approach. In those last two columns can be observed that the foreground person and the object are well segmented, and that the motionless foreground object is incorporated properly into the background model. The agent who passes in front of the incorporated object is also well segmented. After that, when this agent carries the object and leaves the scene, the ghost of this background object is solved and the background model is correctly updated.

7   Conclusions and Future Work

The proposed approach copes with (i) the non-incorporation of erroneous foreground objects to the background model, and (ii) the incorporation of motionless foreground objects. Pixels belonging to false foreground objects, foreground objects in motion, foreground objects that leaves the scene before the background is updated, and multiple foreground objects at the same time have been removed. Finally, a correct detection procedure of motionless foreground objects which have ceased their motion have been presented, and an efficient incorporation of such objects into the background model for a posterior processing have been proposed. Furthermore, the bootstrapping is solved even when many foreground objects are presented.

Future work needs to split the pixel-based and object-based update condition into two separate windows: problems corresponding to the first condition are detected earlier than those physical changes in the scene corresponding to the second one. That is to say, pixel-based update needs to be carried out more periodically than the object-based one. The approach copes with the physical changes in the scene, but the experimental results shows that it is necessary to improve the illumination-change modelling (i.e. the pixel-based update), and background in motion. Likewise, shadows are currently not handled, but these can be eliminated by means of colour information [1,5]. The use of colour will also improve the detection of camouflage. Lastly, objects detected by object-based update should be part of a multilayer background model. In addition, an object appearance model is needed to cover situations involving crowds or multiple objects.

Acknowledgements

This work has been supported by EC grant IST-027110 for the HERMES project and by the Spanish MEC under projects TIC2003-08865 and DPI-2004-5414. Jordi Gonzàlez also acknowledges the support of a Juan de la Cierva Postdoctoral fellowship from the Spanish MEC.

References

1. A. Elgammal, D. Harwood, and L. S. Davis. Nonparametric background model for background subtraction. In *Proceedings European Conference Computer Vision (ECCV'00)*, pages 751–767, Dublin, 2000.
2. W.E.L. Grimson and C.Stauffer. Adaptive background mixture models for real-time tracking. volume 1, pages 22–29, 1999.
3. W.E.L. Grimson, C.Stauffer, and R.Romano. Using adaptive tracking to classify and monitor activities in a site. pages 22–29, 1998.
4. I. Haritaoglu, D. Harwood, and L.S. Davis. W4: Real-time surveillance of people and their activities. *IEEE Trans. Pattern Analysis and Machine Intelligence*, 22(8):809–830, 2000.
5. T. Horprasert, D.Harwood, and L.S.Davis. A statistical approach for real-time robust background subtraction and shadow detection. *IEEE Frame-Rate Applications Workshop*, 1999.
6. H.W.S.Jabri, Z.Duric, and A.Rosenfeld. Detection and location of people in video images using adaptive fusion of color and edge information. volume 4, pages 627–630, September 2000.
7. Jordi Gonzàlez i Sabaté. *Human Sequence Evaluation: the Key-frame Approach*. PhD thesis, May 2004.
8. Mustafa Karaman, Lutz Goldmann, Da Yu, and Thomas Sikora. Comparison of static background segmentation methods. In *Visual Communications and Image Processing (VCIP '05)*, July 2005.
9. K.toyama, J.Krumm, B.Brumitt, and B.Meyers. Wallflower: Principles and practice of background maintenance. volume 1, pages 255–261, 1999.
10. H.-H. Nagel. Steps toward a cognitive vision system. *AI Magazine, Cognitive Vision*, 25(2):31–50, 2004.
11. J. Shen. Motion detection in color image sequence and shadow elimination. *Visual Communications and Image Processing*, 5308:731–740, January 2004.
12. L. Wang, W. Hu, and T. Tan. Recent developments in human motion analysis. *Pattern Recognition*, 36(3):585–601, 2003.
13. C.R. Wren, A. Azarbayejani, T. Darrell, and A.P. Pentland. Pfinder: Real-time tracking of the human body. *IEEE Trans. Pattern Analysis and Machine Intelligence*, 19(7):780–785, 1997.

Interactive Soft Object Simulation with Quadratic Finite Elements

Johannes Mezger and Wolfgang Straßer

University of Tübingen, WSI/GRIS,
72076 Tübingen, Germany
mezger@gris.uni-tuebingen.de, strasser@gris.uni-tuebingen.de

Abstract. We present a new method to simulate deformable volumetric objects interactively using finite elements. With quadratic basis functions and a non-linear strain tensor, we are able to model realistic local compression as well as large global deformation. The construction of the differential equations is described in detail including the Jacobian matrix required to solve the non-linear system. The results show that the bending of solids is reflected more realistically than with the linear refinement previously used in computer graphics. At the same time higher frame rates are achieved as the number of elements can be drastically reduced. Finally, an application to virtual tissue simulation is presented with the objective to improve surgical training.

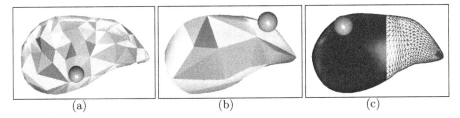

Fig. 1. Interactive liver deformation, (a) 856 linear tetrahedra, (b) 96 quadratic tetrahedra, (c) a high resolution surface mesh attached

1 Introduction and Related Work

Simulating deformable bodies is an important issue in computer animation, because many solid objects in our environment are not rigid but deformable. The animation of such solids by hand is not feasible since they obey complex dynamic behavior with subtle characteristics. The human brain is permanently trained to estimate the motion of soft bodies and to determine their physical properties by touching them. Animations of these objects sometimes look strange, but it is difficult to say why. Therefore, it is preferred to animate them with a physics based simulation that reproduces the reality at the best possible rate. Ideally, the animator should only have to specify some material properties which can

F.J. Perales and R.B. Fisher (Eds.): AMDO 2006, LNCS 4069, pp. 434–443, 2006.

be acquired in real world measurements [1,2], and afterwards the geometric deformation of the object and its interaction with the environment is computed automatically.

With growing demand, applications of such simulations are not only classical computer animations, but also surgery simulations. In the latter case, the requirements on physical realism are especially high, e.g. surgeons often touch tissue to locate diseased parts. A repeated wrong simulation during training could have an impact on his senses and he could accustom wrong actions.

In this paper we present a finite element method which is suited for interactive simulations with high realism. Previously, multi-resolution meshes [3,4] or hierarchical basis [5,6] were used to model local features. However, problems like shear locking can not always be avoided as only linear shape functions are employed. Methods to linearize the differential equations with corotational formulations of the strain were introduced to computer graphics recently [7,8] which cannot be applied to a quadratic basis. A problem we do not address in this paper, nevertheless being very relevant, is collision detection for deformable models [9]. Finally, a complete surgery simulator needs to tackle further important issues [10]. Although the development of mesh-free methods is very promising [11], real-time simulations of real materials are not achieved yet.

2   Continuum Mechanics

Modeling a solid as a continuum, physical laws and real world measurements are directly linked to the problem posed, making continuum mechanics [12] the favorable approach for analysis tasks in engineering and for realistic simulations in medical applications. Subject of solid modeling is the minimization of the total energy Π of the system,

$$\Pi = \Pi_{el} + \Pi_{kin} + \Pi_{ext},$$

composed of the elastic, kinetic and external energy. This problem can be transformed into a variational problem by the principle of virtual work,

$$\delta \Pi = 0. \tag{1}$$

The *elastic force* of a viscoelastic material with linear damping then can be stated as

$$\delta \Pi_{el} = \int_{\Omega} (\delta \epsilon : \sigma + \delta \dot{\epsilon} : \dot{\sigma}) \, d\Omega, \tag{2}$$

where σ is the stress tensor and $\delta \epsilon$ denotes a small virtual variation of the symmetric strain tensor ϵ. Representing the tensors as 3×3 matrices, the double contraction denoted by the operator ":" yields $\delta \epsilon : \sigma = tr(\delta \epsilon^T \sigma)$.

In a general viscoelastic material, σ is function of the strain history $\epsilon(t)$. At this point we restrict to the description of linear elastic materials with $\sigma = C(\epsilon)$, while viscoelastic effects can be added by developing the stress function σ into a Prony series [6].

The strain ϵ itself in general depends non-linearly on the current deformation $\varphi(x,t)$ at time t, with $x \in \Omega$ and Green's strain tensor $\epsilon = \frac{1}{2}(\nabla\varphi^T\nabla\varphi - id)$. The mapping φ transforms the parameter domain Ω to $\mathbb{R}^3$ with the rest state $\varphi_0 = id$ and the displacement field $u = \varphi - id$.

Instead of the non-linear tensor ϵ, many authors employ its linearization, Cauchy's strain tensor, which leads to a linear ODE in the end, but is exact for small deformations only. As in most applications larger deformations have to be handled correctly, we do not adopt this simplification.

The variation of the *inertia* results in the force

$$\delta\Pi_{\text{kin}} = \int_\Omega \delta u^T \, \rho\ddot{u} \, d\Omega \tag{3}$$

with density ρ and acceleration $\ddot{u}$ of the body.

Finally, the *external forces* are defined as

$$\delta\Pi_{\text{ext}} = -\int_\Omega \delta u^T \, f \, d\Omega - \int_{\partial\Omega} \delta u^T \, s \, d\Gamma, \tag{4}$$

where volumetric forces like gravity affect the whole domain Ω and surface forces only act on its boundary $\delta\Omega$.

3   Finite Elements

In order to solve (1), the equation is discretized with finite elements to form an ordinary differential equation. We employ isoparametric tetrahedral elements, where isoparametric means that the interpolation functions of an element are also used to interpolate the geometry of the element. Thus, the finite elements are retrieved by tetrahedralization of the mesh which is to be simulated.

3.1   Element Shape Functions

The shape τ of an element is given in terms of the nodal positions $\mathcal{T}$ together with basis functions $\bar{\Phi}$, $\tau(\xi) = \mathcal{T}^T \bar{\Phi}(\xi)$.

Fig. 2 shows the numbering of a N-node tetrahedron, $N = 4..10$, that we choose for the ease and efficiency of implementing quadratic tetrahedra. For $N < 10$, intermediate nodes are just skipped, resulting in straight edges. With $N = 4$ the linear tetrahedron is obtained, with $N = 10$ the fully quadratic one. The curvilinear coordinates ξ_i, $0 \le \sum_{i=1}^3 \xi_i \le 1$, define the unit tetrahedron $\bar{\mathcal{T}}$ according to the numbering[1] in Fig. 2 with

$$\bar{\mathcal{T}} = \begin{bmatrix} 0 & 1 & 0 & 0 & 1/2 & 0 & 0 & 1/2 & 1/2 & 0 \\ 0 & 0 & 1 & 0 & 0 & 1/2 & 0 & 1/2 & 0 & 1/2 \\ 0 & 0 & 0 & 1 & 0 & 0 & 1/2 & 0 & 1/2 & 1/2 \end{bmatrix}^T .$$

---

[1] With regard of efficient implementation, we write coordinates row-major, thus N vectors v_i give the matrix $[v_{ij}]_{N\times3}$.

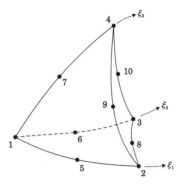

Fig. 2. Numbering of the ten-node tetrahedron

To interpolate the nodes $p_i, i = 1..N$, and to guarantee C_0 continuity, the N shape functions have to meet the requirement $\bar{\Phi}_j(\bar{T}_i) = \delta_{ij}$. Additionally, $\sum \bar{\Phi} = 1$ is required to achieve affine invariance. Altogether, using $N \times N$ shape coefficients $\bar{\alpha}_{ij}$, the quadratic shape functions can be written as

$$\bar{\Phi}_j(\xi) = \sum_{k=1}^{N} \bar{\alpha}_{jk} \, \xi_1^{a_k} \xi_2^{b_k} \xi_3^{c_k}.$$

For $N = 10$, the exponents are $[a\ b\ c] = 2\bar{T}$. Note that the first column of $\bar{\alpha}$ has to be $(1, 0, \ldots, 0)^T$ in order that the $\bar{\Phi}$ sum up to 1 for any ξ. It is equivalent to state

$$\bar{T}_i = \bar{T}^T \, \bar{\Phi}(\bar{T}_i) \tag{5}$$

because of $\bar{T}_0 = (0, 0, 0)$. Therefore, $\bar{\alpha}$ can be computed as

$$\bar{\alpha} = [\mathcal{X}_{ik}]_{i,k=1..N}^{-1}, \quad \mathcal{X}_{ki} := \bar{T}_{i1}^{a_k} \bar{T}_{i2}^{b_k} \bar{T}_{i3}^{c_k}.$$

Likewise, the mapping $\varphi = \mathcal{T}^T \Phi$ for an arbitrary tetrahedron $\mathcal{T}$ is determined by $\mathcal{T}_i = \mathcal{T}^T \, \Phi(\mathcal{T}_i)$, if in (5) $\bar{T}$ is replaced by $\mathcal{T}$. Finally, in order to obtain symmetric system matrices we formulate the variation δu according to the Galerkin method with the same basis Φ,

$$\delta u = \delta \mathcal{U}^T \Phi,$$

and the nodal displacements $\mathcal{U} = \mathcal{T} - \mathcal{T}^0$. The volume integrals of the forces from Sect. 2 then can be approximated by the assembled force matrices of the individual elements. In the following sections we therefore address the integrals of single elements $\mathcal{T}$ only.

3.2   Elastic Forces

Now being able to compute the deformation φ and the gradient $\nabla\varphi = \mathcal{T}^T \, \nabla\Phi$, the symmetric strain tensor ϵ is available. Furthermore, due to the symmetry of σ we get

$$\delta\epsilon : \sigma = (\nabla\varphi^T \, \nabla\delta u) : \sigma.$$

Factoring out the variation, the elastic force matrix $\mathcal{F}$ is retrieved,

$$\delta\epsilon : \sigma = (\nabla\varphi^T \ \delta\mathcal{U}^T \ \nabla\Phi) : \sigma = \delta\mathcal{U} : \mathcal{F},$$

with $\mathcal{F}$ computed optimally as

$$\mathcal{F} = \left[\sum_{k=1}^{3} \nabla\varphi_{jk} \sum_{l=1}^{3} \nabla\Phi_{il}\sigma_{lk} \right]_{i=1..N, \ j=1..3} .$$

If the shape functions Φ are linear, $\nabla\varphi$ and ϵ are constant for the whole element, and therefore the volume integration of the strain energy is trivial. On the one hand, this is a major computational advantage of 4-node tetrahedra, but on the other hand, this causes locking effects and bad convergence.

For quadratic shape functions, ϵ also is quadratic, and the closed form of the volume integral is not appropriate for an efficient implementation. Therefore, it has to be evaluated using numerical integration. For the exact approximation of the quadratic integrals on the tetrahedron, a four point Gauss cubature is needed. We precompute $\nabla\Phi$ at the integration points in the reference tetrahedron T^0 and get $\mathcal{F}$ as the sum of the four force matrices.

The relation of strain and stress is described by the material law $C(\epsilon)$ of the body. An isotropic Hooke material depends on the two engineering constants E (the Young or elasticity modulus) and ν (the Poisson or transverse contraction ratio). It is more efficient to calculate the stress tensor $\sigma = C(\epsilon)$ using Lamé's constants λ and μ [13]:

$$\sigma = \lambda \ tr(\epsilon) \ I + 2\mu\epsilon \ \text{ with } \ \lambda = \frac{E\nu}{(1+\nu)(1-2\nu)} \ \text{ and } \ \mu = \frac{E}{2(1+\nu)}.$$

Likewise, the linear damping $\dot{\sigma} = C(\dot{\epsilon})$ is calculated using $\nabla\dot{\varphi} = \dot{T}^T\Phi$ and the viscous counterparts of λ and μ.

Finally, the Jacobian $\nabla_T\mathcal{F}$ is needed to solve the discrete non-linear system later. An efficient implementation is crucial to achieve high frame rates even when Jacobian updates are required, e.g. in case of large deformations or if dynamic algebraic constraints are applied. Exploiting

$$\frac{\partial}{\partial T_{mn}}(\nabla\varphi)_{ki} = \delta_{nk}(\nabla\Phi)_{mi},$$

the Jacobians of the strain and stress tensors get

$$2\frac{\partial\epsilon_{ij}}{\partial T_{mn}} = (\nabla\Phi)_{mi}(\nabla\varphi)_{nj} + (\nabla\varphi)_{ni}(\nabla\Phi)_{mj}$$

and

$$\frac{\partial\sigma_{ij}}{\partial T_{mn}} = 2\delta_{ij}\lambda \sum_{k=1}^{3} (\nabla\Phi)_{mi}(\nabla\varphi)_{ni} + 2\mu\frac{\partial\epsilon_{ij}}{\partial T_{mn}},$$

which both are symmetric. Hence, the Jacobian of the elastic forces is symmetric and is computed together with (3.2),

$$\frac{\partial \mathcal{F}_{ij}}{\partial \mathcal{T}_{mn}} = \delta_{nj} \sum_{k=1}^{3} (\nabla \Phi)_{mk} \sum_{l=1}^{3} \nabla \Phi_{il} \sigma_{lk} + \sum_{k=1}^{3} \nabla \varphi_{jk} \sum_{l=1}^{3} \nabla \Phi_{il} \frac{\partial \sigma_{lk}}{\partial \mathcal{T}_{mn}},$$

where the first term depends on i and m only. Again, the same calculation is performed to obtain the Jacobian of the viscous forces $\mathcal{F}^v$.

3.3   Inertia and External Forces

The discretization of (3) yields $\delta \Pi_{\text{kin}} \simeq \delta \mathcal{U} M \ddot{\mathcal{U}}$ with the mass matrix $M = \int_\Omega \Phi^T \rho \, \Phi \, d\Omega$. The integrand is quartic for quadratic Φ and thus a 15 node cubature is needed to perform the integration numerically. However, we follow [14] and integrate $\Phi^T \Phi$ at the nodes to obtain a positive definite matrix $\tilde{M}$. Since $\Phi_i(\mathcal{T}_j) = \delta_{ij}$, it is diagonal ("lumped") and can be calculated efficiently on the unit tetrahedron,

$$\tilde{M}_{ii} = \rho(\bar{\mathcal{T}}_i) \, \det(\nabla \bar{\varphi}(\mathcal{T}_i)).$$

If Poisson's ratio $\nu < 0.5$, the material is compressible and ρ depends on the deformation. We recompute $\tilde{M}$ if the Jacobian $\nabla_{\mathcal{T}} \mathcal{F}$ is about to be recomputed as this indicates that the deformation changed noticeably.

The discrete body and surface forces are obtained as

$$\delta \mathcal{U} \mathcal{F}^b = \delta \mathcal{U} \int_\Omega \Phi^T f \, d\Omega \quad \text{and} \quad \delta \mathcal{U} \mathcal{F}^s = \delta \mathcal{U} \int_{\partial \Omega} \Phi^T t \, d\Gamma,$$

where in our application the former is just the constant gravity and the latter connects to the environment.

4   Time-Integration

Altogether, since $\delta \Pi = 0$ has to be met for arbitrary variations $\delta \mathcal{U}$, the discretization proposed in the previous sections results in the ODE

$$\mathcal{F}(\mathcal{U}) + \mathcal{F}^v(\dot{\mathcal{U}}) + M \ddot{\mathcal{U}} - \mathcal{F}^b - \mathcal{F}^s = 0, \tag{6}$$

which is solved at every time-step t_i. We employ the BDF methods (backward differentiation formulas) up to third order for time-integration, discussed in [7], to achieve a simulation which is unconditionally stable. Allowing time-step sizes up to the display refresh period of about $40ms$, the integrators are dedicated for interactive and real-time simulation.

As the BDF methods are implicit, the non-linear equation (6) has to be solved in each step by a Newton method. Observing the convergence of the Newton method, the Jacobians $\nabla_{\mathcal{T}} \mathcal{F}$ and $\nabla_{\mathcal{T}} \mathcal{F}^v$ are updated dynamically. Due to the comparably small number of elements used in interactive simulations, a direct sparse solver is called for the linear part, which turns out to be much more efficient than the commonly used cg method. Boundary conditions of place are embedded directly in the linear system.

5   Results and Conclusions

We show two applications of quadratic elements: a bar bending under gravity and the interactive deformation of a liver model. All tests were performed on a standard PC with an Athlon 64 3500+ processor in 32-bit mode using double precision floating point arithmetics.

Bar under gravity. We simulated the movement of a soft bar with various discretizations under gravity. This experiment shows that our new quadratic elements provide more realism than the linear ones and achieve higher frame rates at the same time. The bar has 25cm × 10cm × 10cm edge length, weighs 0.5kg and is fixed at one side. The elastic material parameters are $E = 20$kPa and $\nu = 0.35$, and for damping $\lambda^v = 0.001\lambda$ and $\mu^v = 0.01\mu$ were used. Released from its horizontal starting position, the bar comes to rest after a few seconds. Fig. 3 shows the simulation results of some discretization examples. It is obvious that the bars with quadratic elements take very similar end states even with very few tetrahedrons, while more than 17000 linear ones are needed to achieve roughly the same result – this effect is known as "shear-locking". However, not only does the linear simulation converge slowly with the number of elements, it also shows wrong dynamic behavior depicted in Fig. 4. The curves denote the vertical displacement of the lower right edge of the bar. As the shear forces can not be reflected sufficiently by the linear elements, oscillations are caused.

In contrast, Fig. 5 demonstrates the fast convergence of the quadratic discretization. An almost optimal solution is already obtained with 156 elements. A benchmark of the simulations is presented in Fig. 6. It shows for each step of the simulation the ratio of computation time versus time-step size. The first two time-steps are needed to setup the solver, afterwards both 156 quadratic and 779 linear tetrahedra give clear real-time performance. However, the 3087 linear

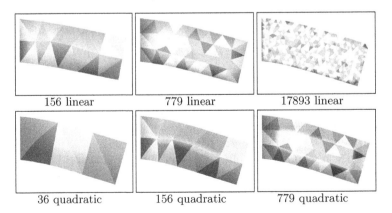

| 156 linear | 779 linear | 17893 linear |
| 36 quadratic | 156 quadratic | 779 quadratic |

Fig. 3. Pictures from the simulations captured after the objects came to rest. The number of tetrahedrons and the element type are quoted.

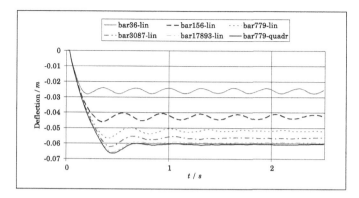

Fig. 4. Vertical oscillation of the bars with linear basis functions bending under gravity. 2.5 seconds are simulated with $20ms$ time-step size. The quadratic bar with 779 elements is added for comparison.

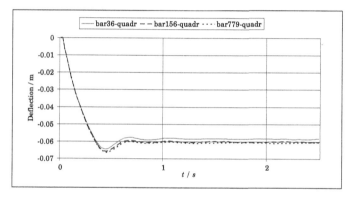

Fig. 5. Vertical oscillation of the bars with quadratic basis functions bending under gravity. The better convergence to the optimum is clearly visible.

tetrahedra, still being far away from achieving realistic bending, are two times slower than real-time.

Verification using a gold standard. To check the correctness of our method, we repeated the simulations with the commercial finite element package ABAQUS using the same discretizations. Fig. 7 shows the deflections at the end state calculated with ABAQUS compared to our simulations. Clearly, the results are almost identical, and again the excellent convergence of quadratic versus linear tetrahedra is revealed.

Simulation of virtual tissue. We simulated a human liver model ($E = 2.5$kPa and $\nu = 0.46$), depicted in Figures 1 and 8, that is touched interactively with a small ball. To obtain a smooth real-time performance, the number of elements is opted to produce an average CPU to simulation time ratio of about 0.2. This is achieved with 856 linear or 96 quadratic tetrahedra. Thus, the quadratic shape

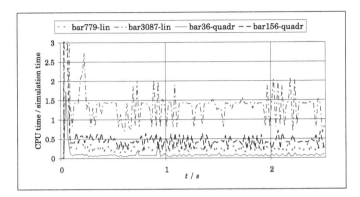

Fig. 6. Ratio of CPU time vs. simulation time during the 2.5s bending simulation. Values below one denote real-time.

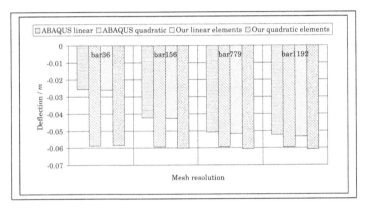

Fig. 7. Comparison of our results with static solutions in ABAQUS using 36, 156, 779 and 1192 tetrahedra. Once more, the slow convergence of linear tetrahedra is evident.

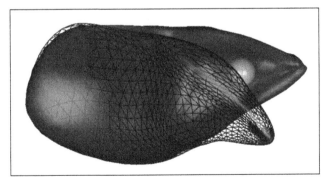

Fig. 8. Large deformation of the liver model. The undeformed state is rendered as wire-frame.

functions are feasible for practical applications like surgery training where an optimum realism has to be achieved. A drawback of using fewer elements is that small geometric features, which cannot be reflected sufficiently by the quadratic element surface, have to be modeled using a dedicated surface mesh.

Conclusions and future work. We introduced a first quadratic finite element model with non-linear strain that is adequate for real-time applications and which shows awesome physical benefits compared to existing methods. In the future, more applications of non-linear shape functions will be exploited. Moreover, the quality of quadratic elements in coarse meshes will be improved.

Acknowledgements

The authors gratefully acknowledge Michael Hauth for many helpful discussions.

References

1. Kerdok, A.E., Cotin, S.M., Ottensmeyer, M.P., Galea, A.M., Howe, R.D., Dawson, S.L.: Truth cube: establishing physical standards for soft tissue simulation. Medical Image Analysis **7**(3) (2003) 283–291
2. Nava, A., Valtorta, D., Mazza, E.: Experimental determination of the mechanical properties of soft biological tissues. In: Int. Conf. on the Mechanical Behavior of Materials. (2003)
3. Debunne, G., Desbrun, M., Cani, M.P., Barr, A.H.: Dynamic real-time deformations using space & time adaptive sampling. In: Proc. of SIGGRAPH. (2001) 31–36
4. Wu, X., Downes, M.S., Goktekin, T., Tendick, F.: Adaptive Nonlinear Finite Elements for Deformable Body Simulation Using Dynamic Progressive Meshes. In: Proc. of Eurographics. (2001)
5. Grinspun, E., Krysl, P., Schröder, P.: Charms: a simple framework for adaptive simulation. In: Proc. of SIGGRAPH. (2002) 281–290
6. Hauth, M., Gross, J., Straßer, W.: Interactive physically based solid dynamics. In: Proc. SIGGRAPH Symposium on Computer Animation 2003, ACM Press (2003)
7. Hauth, M., Strasser, W.: Corotational Simulation of Deformable Solids. In: Proc. WSCG. (2004) 137–145
8. Müller, M., Gross, M.: Interactive Virtual Materials. In: Proc. of Graphics Interface. (2004) 239–246
9. Teschner, M., Kimmerle, S., Heidelberger, B., Zachmann, G., Raghupathi, L., Fuhrmann, A., Cani, M.P., Faure, F., Magnenat-Thalmann, N., Strasser, W., Volino, P.: Collision Detection for Deformable Objects. Computer Graphics Forum **24**(1) (2005)
10. Delingette, H., Ayache, N.: Hepatic surgery simulation. Commun. ACM **48**(2) (2005) 31–36
11. Müller, M., Heidelberger, B., Teschner, M., Gross, M.: Meshless deformations based on shape matching. ACM Trans. Graph. **24**(3) (2005) 471–478
12. Fung, Y.: First Course in Continuum Mechanics. Third edn. Prentice Hall (1993)
13. Ciarlet, P.G.: Three Dimensional Elasticity, Volume I: Mathematical Elasticity. Volume 20 of Studies in Mathematics and its Applications. North-Holland (1988)
14. Zienkiewicz, O.C., Taylor, R.L.: The Finite Element Method. Fifth edn. Butterworth-Heinemann (2000)

An Alternative to Medial Axis for the 3D Reconstruction of Unorganized Set of Points Using Implicit Surfaces

Vincent Bénédet and Dominique Faudot

Le2i Laboratory, University of Burgundy, 21078 Dijon, France
{Vincent.Benedet, Faudot}@u-bourgogne.fr

Abstract. Rebuilding three-dimensional objects represented by a set of points is a classical problem in computer graphics. Multiple applications like medical imaging or industrial techniques require finding shape from scattered data. Therefore, the reconstruction of a set of points that represents a shape has been widely studied, depending on data source and reconstruction's objectives. This purpose of this paper is to provide an automatic reconstruction from an unorganized cloud describing an unknown shape in order to provide a solution that will allow to compute the object's volume and to deform it with constant volume. The main idea in this paper consists in filling the object's interior with an equipotential surface resulting of the fusion of potential field primitives also called metaballs or blobs. Nevertheless, contrary to most of usual rebuilding methods based on implicit primitives blending, we do not compute any medial axis to set the primary objects. Indeed, a fast voxelization is used to find a summary contour from the discrete shape and to determine interior areas. Then, the positioning of implicit primitives rely on a multilayer system. Finally, a controlled fusion of the isosurfaces guarantees the lack of any holes and a respectful contour of the original object, such that we obtain a complete shape filling.

Keywords: Reconstruction, Cloud of dots, Implicit surfaces, Blobs, Voxelization.

1 Introduction

To extend the interest of volume computation of metaballs blending [1] and deformation of them maintaining a constant volume, we focus on rebuilding a scene containing one or more objects which the description is given to us by a set of points, $P = \{P_1, ..., P_n\}$, in order to provide a simple solution for computing the original object's volume. The cloud of dots thus samples the surface of the object (if we consider that there is only one, although it may include several connected components). The points constitute a raw data source for the reconstruction, only coordinates are known; we do not have further information about the vertices, they are neither sorted nor provided with a triangulation. The only assumption, obviously, is that the object (or its related components) is closed, for we will fill it with implicit potential field objects. The underlying principle behind our method is to work as an analogy with the filling of a container by a fluid which finally adopts its shape.

F.J. Perales and R.B. Fisher (Eds.): AMDO 2006, LNCS 4069, pp. 444–452, 2006.

Unfortunately, the problem remains that we do not have a continuous contour. Therefore, we should initially find a summary contour and so, an interior from the sampled shape and then place implicit primitives inside the object until reaching its surface. The fusion property of the these implicit objects, that we will call blobs thereafter by abuse language, is used then to lead to a total filling of the object's volume. Obviously, this fusion must be controlled so that, on the one hand the filling does not include any holes, and on the other hand, the blobs do fit the object's surface.

2 Previous Works

Literature related with computer graphics offers many solutions about reverse engineering problem because of the significant number of practical applications requiring to rebuild a shape whose data source comes from a set of points. Earliest common approaches for reconstruction consist in deforming a surface or a volume in order to fit the set of data points such as "snakes" introduced by Kasset al. [2]. Classical solutions based on Voronoï diagram in three dimensions were widely used to rebuild various topological models [3, 4, 5, 6]. The method of alpha-shapes by Edelsbrunner [7] also makes it possible to find the shape of an object described by whole of points but requires one preliminary Delaunay triangulation. Hoppe et al. 8] provide a solution having the advantage of applying to a raw cloud without any additional information by considering a tangential plan at each point and an implicit function of distance. Recently, Radial Basis Functions have been studied to reconstruct smooth, manifold surfaces from point-cloud data and to repair incomplete Meshes [9, 10, 11]. Nevertheless, all these methods provide solutions to retrieve only the shape of the object and don't consider its volume. Shape reconstruction from a point cloud using implicit surfaces generated by a point-based skeleton was for the first time suggested by Muraki [12] then improved by Tsingos et al. [13]. Nevertheless, this method presents the disadvantage of a manual initialization of the algorithm, which Bittar [14] cures while plunging the point cloud into a binary numerical volume to extract the median axis from it allowing, thereafter, the object reconstruction using implicit surfaces. The computation of the medial axis of two-dimensional or three-dimensional solids is known to be problematic due to its instability: small variations in the boundary of an object result in large variations of its Medial Axis. In our case, the search for the median axis is not interesting because we wish to deform the object, so we should completely recomputed the axis. Although being connected with this form of rebuilding, our approach differs in the sense that the passage from the cloud to binary numerical volume, is not obtained from the median axis, but from the research of the form's interior in order to place our implicit primitives for the rebuilding. For that, it is necessary for us, as a preliminary, to define the discrete contour of the object.

3 Voxelization as a Preliminary Step for Rebuilding

Setting implicit primitives to fill the object's volume is not particularly easy if we consider that its nature isn't known and that our goal is to provide an automatic method. Indeed, talking about interior of an object defined by a set of dots in a continuous three-dimensional space obviously does not have any direction. A solution to alleviate impossibility of distinguishing the interior of the cloud in continuous space is to choose to discretize three-dimensional space by carrying out a voxelization of the cloud's bounding box. The set of points is therefore converted into binary numerical volume in order to obtain an rough continuous shape.

3.1 Finding Contour with an Adequate Voxelization

To obtain an effective voxelization of a unstructured point cloud, in other words to lead to a binary volume correctly describing the topology of the object without creating nor removing overall locally related components, it is advisable to determine an adequate length of voxels.

Indeed, the choice of a significant voxel size will induce a connection of areas which should remain disjoined. Conversely, a too fine voxelization will cause holes and will prevent from obtaining a closed contour. In fact, using mathematical formalism, there must a homotopy between the shape and its voxelization.

For attempting to find a correct voxelization, we use in [14] a qualitative cloud study due to Mary [15] in his thesis to adapt the voxels grid resolution to the characteristics of the set of points. Let $d_{related}$ defines the minimal distance between two points of two different local related components, d_{cloud+} the longest distance between two closest points and d_{cloud-} the smallest distance between two points.

The cloud we wish to rebuild must present characteristics of sufficient uniformity and density to obtain a respectful contour of the original form. In particular, d_{cloud+} distance must obviously be lower than $d_{related}$ to preserve related components, while remaining higher than d_{cloud-} in to obtain a closed surface. In other words, a "good cloud" satisfies two following inequalities for $\varepsilon > 0$:

$$
\begin{aligned}
d_{cloud+} - d_{cloud-} &\leq \varepsilon \\
d_{cloud+} &< d_{related} - \varepsilon
\end{aligned}
\tag{1}
$$

Empirical tests seem proving that a sampling can be considered "good" when :

$$
\varepsilon = d_{cloud-}
\tag{2}
$$

Consequently, the choice for l_v length must be as follows :

$$
d_{cloud+} < l_v < 2\, d_{cloud-}
\tag{3}
$$

3.2 Using Voxelization to Identify Interior and Layers

Once a correct voxelization is defined, a contour is easily found as shown in Fig.1 (green voxels). From there, outer voxels are obtained by propagation ; edge of voxels' box being initialized like outsides with the object (by grid construction), the technique consists in carrying out a sweeping of the voxels on the basis of a corner of the grid by marking the voxels external according to one 2-neighbourhood of voxels already treated. Voxels remaining are inner voxels.

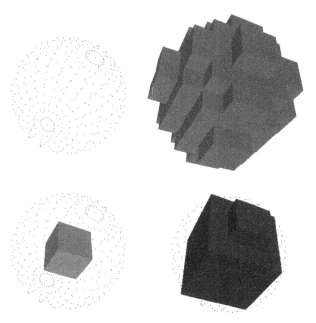

Fig. 1. Contour and layers found from the voxelization of a sphere defined by 424 points

Now, voxels on the inside can be separated into two layers. The *intermediate* voxels are those which remain close to the surface, the *deep* voxels are those located at the heart of the object to be rebuilt. To determine the intermediate voxels, we consider the interior voxels having a surface voxel in their 26-neighbourhood.

Keeping in mind that the voxelization is only one preliminary stage aiming at positioning implicit surfaces inside the object, one will seek to gather the deep voxels per packages in order to obtain voxels of higher size with the goal to minimize the number of blobs intended to replace them for the rebuilding. Our method's objective is to end at an adaptive implicit reconstruction. To obtain packages of voxels, one will carry out coding in octree of inner voxels.

4 Blobs Positioning

Since we seek to fully rebuild the object defined by the point cloud, namely the volume and the surface, the principle of our reconstruction by implicit surfaces breaks up into two parts. The first consists in replacing inner voxels by implicit primitives of significant size, the second to positioning smaller implicit objects close to the surface. At the end, we blend these various elements in order to cover total volume.

Therefore, we consider blobs B_i, based on Muraki's potential field function:

$$F_i = \begin{cases} \left(1 - \left(\dfrac{r}{R_i} \right)^2 \right)^2 & for\ r \in [0, R_i] \\ 0\ otherwise \end{cases} \tag{4}$$

They are implicit primitives with a point-based skeleton whose potential field is a function of the distance from the center. They have moreover a limited influence, R_i, representing the ray of blob's maximum influence.

By considering that the fusion of the blobs is created by the sum of their potential field functions, implicit surface intended to rebuild the object is defined by :

$$F(P) = \sum_{i=1}^{n} \alpha_i F_i(P) \tag{5}$$

This surface must compulsorily pass by all the points of the cloud. Consequently, for a given threshold T, implicit surface must satisfy :

$$\forall\, P_j \in \{P_1, ..., P_N\},\; F(P_j) = \sum_{i=1}^{n} \alpha_i F_i(P_j) = T \tag{6}$$

At first sight, it seems difficult to obtain a whole of blobs checking this condition. Nevertheless, the fact that each blob have a limited influence implies that for a given point P_j, the majority of the F_i will be null in this point. This makes it possible to place blobs close to a zone without calling into question the whole of the rebuilding. One can thus consider a local rebuilding of the cloud independently of the remainder of the blobs that we must place.

The first step of the blobs positioning relates to those inside the cloud but not near to the surface. We choose to replace each deep voxel by a blob sharing the same center and provided with an influence ray equal to half of the size of the considered voxel (computed starting from packaging voxel) added with the size of a basic voxel.

With regard to the intermediate layer of the blobs, one is satisfied to position them in the center of the corresponding voxels and to affect a ray R_i equals to $l_v / 2$. They have a plug role between the deep layer and the blobs placed at surface.

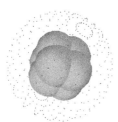 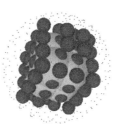 

Fig. 2. Sphere reconstruction with 496 blobs shown with their effective radius (not blended)

To finalize the rebuilding we must blobs close to the surface of the object by ensuring that each point is touched by at least an implicit ball. For that, it is necessary to traverse the whole of the cloud and to create for each point a blob remaining inside the object whose surface touches the point. An intuitive approach of the problem consists, for a given point P, to determine the nearest interior voxel, with center B, then to place the ball in the center of the segment [PB] and to affect a ray with |PB|/2 length. Nevertheless, one realizes that for certain cases ("fold" in the surface corresponding to a local extremum) that the blob created will contain in its interior another point close to that which it is associated, it is thus necessary to re-examine its site. Let us suppose that the P' point is contained in the blob, the new center for the blob must check |C'P'|=|C'P| and be the segment [PB] to remain inside the object.The process of checking the inclusion of points in the blob must be continued until ensuring to obtain a blob not containing any point of the cloud.

Thus created, these three different layers enable us to fill the object which we wish to rebuild. The following step is the fusion of these implicit primitives in order to guarantee a full volume as well as a regular surface.

5 Guaranteed and Controlled Fusion

At this point, the course of our method of rebuilding is incomplete. Indeed, we are satisfied to place the blobs in each considered layer then we blend them without real theoretical justification. However, this fusion deserves a thorough study.

The fusion of the implicit primitives to obtain final volume is subjected to two constraints. First is to secure that the filling is carried out in an exhaustive way, i.e. fusion must be total and not leave voids between the blobs. The second condition is that the primitives have to remains on the surface of the cloud.

5.1 Finding Critical Points to Locate Holes in the Reconstruction

To determine empty spaces resulting of the fusion of implicit primitives consists in fact to study the critical points of the density functions associated with the primitives. That returns to a research of the zeros of the final implicit function F. It is obviously impossible to determine formal solutions, also several analytical methods were developed to determine them. Thus Hart [16] proposes a technique based on the theory of Morse to locally find the critical points which he continues with Stander [17] by using interval Newton's Method.

A critical point of a real function F of one or more variables is a point X whose gradient vanishes. The function's value $F(X)$ at a critical point X is called a critical value. Given l_i i=1, ...,3 the eigenvalues of the function's Hessian, which is the matrix of second partial derivatives, each critical point X can be classified according to the signs of the three eigenvalues.

If any of the eigenvalues is zero, then the critical point is called degenerate, otherwise it is non-degenerate and may be a maximum, a minimum or some kind of saddle point. In three dimensions, saddle points come in two varieties.

We name index of the critical point the number of negative eigenvalues of $H(F)$. It is possible to classify the critical points according to the sign of the three eigenvalues, therefore according to the index.

A maximum point corresponds to a possible center of component, the three eigenvalues are negative. A "2-saddle" point corresponds to a point of possible connection between two components. A "1-saddle" point corresponds to a center of possible torus. A minimum point corresponds to a possible center of an air pocket, the three eigenvalues are positive. It results from this that one can punctually determine the topology of F.

So, in our case, we seek the "1-saddle" points and minima points witnesses to voids in our rebuilding. Thereafter, empty spaces must be filled with blobs.

The search for critical points and filling of voids has been implemented and the algorithm works efficiently with a few blobs (less than 50). However, the cost in memory and computing time grows dramatically using the interval Newton's method. Our program has been able to find a hole in the reconstruction of the sphere (we intentionally do not include deep blobs) and correctly filled it, but fails to find solution with more than 500 blobs (it crashes).

5.2 Controlled Fusion

Given a threshold T for the global implicit surface, we consider each point of the cloud. One considers that only its related blob includes it in its influence radius. So, at a point P_i, we have:

$$F(P_i) = F_i(P_i) = \left(1 - \left(\frac{r}{R_i}\right)^2\right)^2 = T \qquad (7)$$

Knowing the center of the blob and the point coordinates (therefore r), the influence radius can be evaluated:

$$R_i = \frac{r}{\sqrt{1 - \sqrt{T}}} \qquad (8)$$

This choice for R_i guarantees that blob B_i is on the surface at point P_i.

However, the assumption that only one blob includes the point in its influence radius is true for a very small (near to 0) value T. Unfortunately, this condition create an "orange skin" effect on the rebuilt surface.

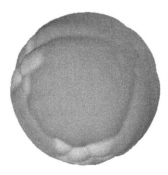

Fig. 3. Sphere reconstruction with 496 blended blobs

6 Some Results

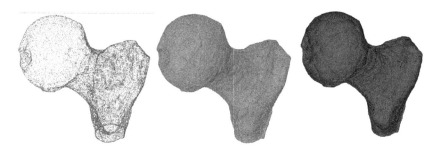

Fig. 4. Ball joint from Cyberware rebuilt with 36211 blobs. Third image is a Pov-Ray rendering.

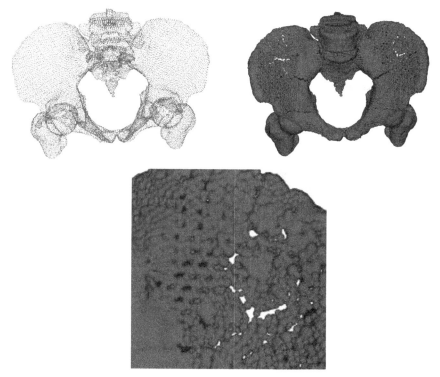

Fig. 5. Pelvis reconstruction encounters usual holes problem due to a large preliminary voxelization

7 Conclusion

We have presented an original method for the reconstruction of an object defined by an unstructured point cloud using the implicit primitives with potential function and their possibility of blending. It constitutes an alternative to the methods based on preliminary research of a skeleton or a median axis which present the disadvantage of their instability. The approach of rebuilding presented in this article has the originality to differ from those existing by its "inside" approach of the object. Moreover, it provides a solution to foresee the possibility of computing the volume of the rebuilt object and its deformation with constant volume, which the other techniques of rebuilding do not allow. Nevertheless, improvements have to be considered concerning holes' detection using Morse theory with largest models.

References

1. D. Faudot, G. Gesquière, L. Garnier. An introduction to an analytical way to compute the volume of blobs. Int. Journal of Pure and Applied Mathematics, vol.11 n°1, 2004, pp 1-20.
2. M. Kass, A. Witkin, and D. Terzopoulos. Snakes: Active contour models. International Journal of Computer Vision, 1:321--331, 1988.
3. N. Amenta, M. Bern, M. Kamvysselisy. A new Voronoï-based surface reconstruction algorithm. Proceedings of ACM Siggraph '98, pages 415-421, 1998.
4. J.D. Boissonnat and B. Geiger. Threedimensional reconstruction of complex shapes based on the Delaunay triangulation. Report 1697, INRIA SophiaAntipolis, Valbonne, France, 1992.
5. D. Attali. r-Regular Shape Reconstruction from Unorganized Points. In Proc. of the 13th ACM Symposium on Computational Geometry, pages 248--253, Nice, France, June 1997.
6. G. Bajaj, F. Bernardini, and G. Xu. Automatic Reconstruction of Surfaces and Scalar Fields from 3D Scans. Proceedings of ACM Siggraph '95, 109-118, 1995.
7. H. Edelsbrunner, E.P. Mücke. Three-dimensional Alpha Shapes. ACM Transactions on Graphics 13:43-72, 1994.
8. H. Hoppe, T. DeRose, T. Duchamp, J. McDonald, W. Stuetzle. Proceedings of ACM Siggraph '92, 71-78, 1992.
9. V. Savchenko, A. Pasko, O. G. Okunev and T. L. Kunii. Function representation of solids reconstructed from scattered surface points and contours. ComputerGraphics Forum, 14(4):181–188 (1995).
10. G. Turk and J. O'Brien. Variational implicit surfaces. In Technical Report GIT-GVU-99-15, Georgia Institute of Technology, page 9 pages (1999b).
11. J. C. Carr, R. K. Beatson, J. B. Cherrie, T.J. Mitchell, W.R. Fright, B.C. McCallum, and T.R. Evans. 2001. Reconstruction and representation of 3D objects with radial basis functions. Proceedings of ACM SIGGRAPH '01. ACM Press, New York, NY, 67-76.
12. S. Muraki. Volumetric shape description of range data using "Blobby Model". Proceedings of ACM Siggraph '91, 227-235, 1991.
13. N. Tsingos and M.P. Gascuel. Implicit surfaces for semi-automatic medical organs reconstruction. Proceedings of Computer Graphics International '95, 3-15, 1995.
14. E. Bittar, N. Tsingos, M.P. Gascuel. Automatic reconstruction of unstructured 3D data: combining medial axis and implicit surfaces. Computer Graphics Forum, 14(3):457-468, 1995.

Modeling Timing Structure in Multimedia Signals

Hiroaki Kawashima, Kimitaka Tsutsumi, and Takashi Matsuyama

Kyoto University, Yoshida-Honmachi Sakyo, Kyoto 6068501, Japan
{kawashima, tm}@i.kyoto-u.ac.jp
http://vision.kuee.kyoto-u.ac.jp/

Abstract. Modeling and describing temporal structure in multimedia signals, which are captured simultaneously by multiple sensors, is important for realizing human machine interaction and motion generation. This paper proposes a method for modeling temporal structure in multimedia signals based on temporal intervals of primitive signal patterns. Using temporal difference between beginning points and the difference between ending points of the intervals, we can explicitly express *timing structure*; that is, synchronization and mutual dependency among media signals. We applied the model to video signal generation from an audio signal to verify the effectiveness.

1 Introduction

Measuring dynamic behavior such as speech, musical performances, and sport actions with multiple sensors, we obtain media signals across different modalities. We often exploit the temporal structure of co-occurrence, synchronization, and temporal difference among temporal patterns in these signals. For example, it is well-known fact that the simultaneity between auditory and visual patterns influences human perception (e.g., the McGurk effect [9]). On the other hand, modeling the cross-modal structure is important to realize the multimedia systems of human computer interaction; for example, audio-visual speech recognition [11] and media signal generation from another related signal (e.g., motion from audio signal)[2]. Motion modeling also exploits this kind of temporal structure, because motion timing among different parts plays an important role in natural motion generation.

State based co-occurrence models, such as coupled hidden Markov models (HMMs) [3], are strong methods for media integration [11]. These models describe a relation between adjacent or co-occurred states that exist in the different media signals (Fig. 1(a)). Although this frame-wise representation enables us to model short term relations or interaction among multiple processes, it is ill-suited to systems in which the features of synchronization and temporal difference between media signal patterns become significant. For example, an opening lip motion is strongly synchronized with an explosive sound /p/; on the other hand, the lip motion is loosely synchronized with a vowel sound /e/, and the motion always precedes the sound. We can see such an organized temporal difference

F.J. Perales and R.B. Fisher (Eds.): AMDO 2006, LNCS 4069, pp. 453–463, 2006.
© Springer-Verlag Berlin Heidelberg 2006

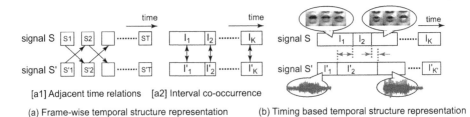

[a1] Adjacent time relations   [a2] Interval co-occurrence

(a) Frame-wise temporal structure representation   (b) Timing based temporal structure representation

Fig. 1. Temporal structure representation in multimedia signals

in music performances also; performers often make preceding motion before the actual sound.

In this paper, we propose a novel model that directly represents this important aspect of temporal relations, what we refer to as *timing structure*, such as synchronization and mutual dependency with organized temporal difference among multiple media signals (Fig. 1(b)).

First, we assume that each media signal is described by a finite set of *modes*: primitive temporal patterns. Segment models [13], which are the generalization of segmental HMMs [7], become popular models in the speech recognition community to describe audio signals based on this assumption. A number of similar models are widely proposed in different communities, for example, hybrid systems [4,6] in the computer vision, and the motion texture [8] in the graphics. These models describe complex temporal variations not only by a physical-time based state transition but also by an event-based state transition that is free from temporal metric space (i.e., it models just the order of events). We refer to these models as *interval models*, because every model provides an interval representation of media signals, where each interval is a temporal region labeled by one of the modes.

Then, we introduce a *timing structure model*, which is a stochastic model for describing temporal structure among intervals in different media signals. Because the model explicitly represents temporal difference between beginning and ending points of intervals, it provides a framework of integrating multiple interval models across modalities. Consequently, we can exploit the model to human machine interaction systems in which media synchronization plays an important role. In the experiments, we verify the effectiveness of the method by applying it to media signal conversion that generate a media signal from another media signal.

2   Modeling Timing Structure in Multimedia Signals

2.1   Temporal Interval Representation of Media Signals

To define timing structure, we assume that each media signal is represented by a single interval model, and the parameters of the interval model are estimated in advance (see [13,8], for example). Then, each media signal is described by an interval sequence. In the following paragraphs, we introduce some terms and notations for the structure and the model definition.

Media signals: Multimedia signals are obtained by measuring dynamic event with N_s sensors simultaneously. Let S_c be a single media signal. Then, multimedia signals become $\mathcal{S} = \{S_1, \cdots, S_{N_s}\}$. We assume that S_c is a discrete signal that is sampled by rate ΔT_c.

Modes and Mode sets: Mode $M_i^{(c)}$ is the property of temporal variation occurred in signal S_c (e.g., "opening mouth" and "closing mouth" in a facial video signal). We define a mode set of S_c as a finite set: $\mathcal{M}^{(c)} = \{M_1^{(c)}, \cdots, M_{N_c}^{(c)}\}$. Each mode is modeled by a sub model of the interval models. For example, hybrid systems, which we use in our experiments, use linear dynamical systems for the mode models.

Intervals: Interval $I_k^{(c)}$ is a temporal region that a single mode represents. Index k denotes a temporal order that the interval appeared in signal S_c. Interval $I_k^{(c)}$ has properties of beginning and ending time $b_k^{(c)}, e_k^{(c)} \in \mathbb{N}$ (the natural number set), and mode label $m_k^{(c)} \in \mathcal{M}^{(c)}$. Note that, we simply refer to the indices of sampled order as "time". We assume signal S_c is partitioned into interval sequence $\mathcal{I}^{(c)} = \{I_1^{(c)}, ..., I_{K_c}^{(c)}\}$ by the interval model, where the intervals have no overlaps or gaps (i.e., $b_{k+1}^{(c)} = e_k^{(c)} + 1$ and $m_k^{(c)} \neq m_{k+1}^{(c)}$).

Interval representation of media signals: Interval representation of multimedia signals is a set of interval sequences: $\{\mathcal{I}^{(1)}, ..., \mathcal{I}^{(N_s)}\}$.

2.2   Definition of Timing Structure

In this paper, we concentrate on modeling timing structure between two media signals S and S'. (We use the mark " ' " to discriminate between the two signals.)

Let us use notation $I_{(i)}$ for an interval I_k that has mode $M_i \in \mathcal{M}$ in signal S (i.e., $m_k = M_i$), and let $b_{(i)}, e_{(i)}$ be its beginning and ending points, respectively. (We omit index k, which denotes the order of the interval.) Similarly, let $I'_{(p)}$ be an interval that has mode $M'_p \in \mathcal{M}'$ in the range $[b'_{(p)}, e'_{(p)}]$ of signal S'. Then, the temporal relation of two modes becomes the quaternary relation of the four temporal points $R(b_{(i)}, e_{(i)}, b'_{(p)}, e'_{(p)})$. If signal S and S' has different sampling rate, we have to consider the relation of continuous time such as $b_{(i)} \Delta T$ on behalf of $b_{(i)}$. In this subsection, we just use $b_{(i)} \in \mathbb{R}$ (the real number set) for both continuous time and the indices of discrete time to simplify the notation.

Let us define timing structure as the relation R that can be determined by four binary relations $R_{bb}(b_{(i)}, b'_{(p)})$, $R_{be}(b_{(i)}, e'_{(p)})$, $R_{eb}(e_{(i)}, b'_{(p)})$, $R_{ee}(e_{(i)}, e'_{(p)})$. In the following, we specify the four binary relations that we focus on this paper.

Considering temporal ordering relations $R_<, R_=, R_>$, which are often used in temporal logic [1], for these binary relations, we get 3^4 relations for R. Because of $b_{(i)} \leq e_{(i)}$ and $b'_{(p)} \leq e'_{(p)}$, it can be reduced to 13 relations as shown in Fig. 2(a). However, temporal metric information is omitted in these 13 relations, which often becomes significant for modeling human behavior with temporal structure (e.g., temporal difference between sound and motion).

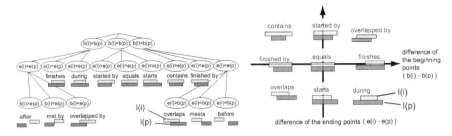

(a) Temporal ordering relations.   (b) Temporal difference relation.

Fig. 2. Temporal relations of two intervals. (a) The temporal order of beginning and ending time provides 13 relations of the two intervals. (b) The horizontal and vertical axes denote the difference between beginning points $b_{(i)} - b'_{(p)}$ and the difference between ending points $e_{(i)} - e'_{(p)}$, respectively.

We therefore introduce metric relations for R_{bb} and R_{ee} by assuming that R_{be} and R_{eb} is $R_<$ and $R_>$, respectively (i.e., the two modes have overlaps). This assumption is natural when the influence of one mode to the other modes with long temporal distance can be ignored. For the metric of R_{bb} and R_{ee}, we use temporal difference $b_{(i)} - b'_{(p)}$ and $e_{(i)} - e'_{(p)}$, respectively; the relation is represented by a point $(D_b, D_e) \in \mathbb{R}^2$ (see also Fig. 2(b)). In the next subsection, we model this type of temporal metric relation by using two-dimensional distributions.

2.3   Modeling Timing Structure

Temporal difference distribution of overlapped mode pairs: To model the metric relations that described in the previous subsection, we introduce the following distribution for every mode pair $(M_i, M'_p) \in \mathcal{M} \times \mathcal{M}'$:

$$P(b_k - b'_{k'} = D_b, e_k - e'_{k'} = D_e | m_k = M_i, m'_{k'} = M'_p, [b_k, e_k] \cap [b'_{k'}, e'_{k'}] \neq \phi). \quad (1)$$

We refer to this distribution as a *temporal difference distribution*. Because the distribution explicitly represent the frequency of the metric relation between two modes (i.e., temporal difference between beginning points and the difference between ending points), it provides significant temporal structure for two media signals. For example, if the peak of distribution comes to the origin, the two modes tend to be synchronized in their beginning and ending points; on the other hand, if $b_k - b_{k'}$ has large variance, the two modes loosely synchronized in their beginning.

As we described in Subsection 2.2, the domain of the distribution is $\mathbb{R}^2$. To estimate the distribution from a finite number of samples (i.e., overlapped mode pairs), we fit a density function such as Gaussian or its mixture models to the samples when we use the model in the real applications.

Co-occurrence distribution of mode pairs: As we see in Eq. (1), the temporal difference distribution is a probability distribution under the condition of the given mode pair. To represent frequency that each mode pair appears in the overlapped interval pairs, we introduce the following distribution:

$$P(m_k = M_i, m_{k'} = M'_p \mid [b_k, e_k] \cap [b'_{k'}, e'_{k'}] \neq \phi). \tag{2}$$

We refer to this distribution as *co-occurrence distribution* of mode pairs. The distribution can be easily estimated by calculating a mode pair histogram from every overlapped interval pairs.

Mode transition probability: Using Eq. (1) and (2), we can represent timing structure that is defined in Subsection 2.2. Although timing structure models temporal metric relations between media signals, temporal relation in each media signal is also important. Therefore, similar to previously introduced interval models, we use the following transition probability of adjacent modes in each signal:

$$P(m_k = M_j \mid m_{k-1} = M_i)\,(M_i, M_j \in \mathcal{M}). \tag{3}$$

3   Media Signal Conversion Based on Timing Structure

Once we estimate the timing structure model that introduced in Section 2 from simultaneously captured multimedia signals, we can exploit the model for generating a media signal from another related signal. We refer to the application as *media signal conversion*, and introduce the algorithm in this section.

The overall flow of media signal conversion from signal S' to S is as follows: (1) a reference (input) media signal S' is partitioned into an interval sequence $\mathcal{I}' = \{I'_1, ..., I'_{K'}\}$, (2) a media interval sequence $\mathcal{I} = \{I_1, ..., I_K\}$ is generated from a reference interval sequence $\mathcal{I}'$, (3) a media signal S is generated from $\mathcal{I}$. (K and K' is the number of intervals in $\mathcal{I}$ and $\mathcal{I}'$, and $K \neq K'$ in general.)

Since the methods of (1) and (3) have been already introduced in some literatures of interval models (see [8,6], for example), we focus on (2), and propose a novel method that generates a media interval sequence from another related media interval sequence based on the timing structure model. In the following subsections, we assume that the two media signals S, S' have the same sampling rate to simplify the algorithm.

3.1   Formulation of Media Signal Conversion Problem

Let Φ be the timing structure model that is estimated in advance. Then, the problem of generating an interval sequence $\mathcal{I}$ from a reference interval sequence $\mathcal{I}'$ can be formulated by the following optimization:

$$\hat{\mathcal{I}} = \arg\max_{\mathcal{I}} P(\mathcal{I} \mid \mathcal{I}', \Phi) \tag{4}$$

In the equation above, we have to determine the number of intervals K and triples (b_k, e_k, m_k) for all the intervals I_k ($k = 1, ..., K$), where $b_k, e_k \in [1, T]$ and $m_k \in \mathcal{M}$. T is the length of signal S', and the mode set $\mathcal{M}$ is estimated simultaneously with the signal segmentation. If we search for all the possible interval sequences $\{\mathcal{I}\}$, the calculation order increases exponentially in the increase of T. We therefore use a dynamic programming method, which is similar to the Viterbi algorithm in HMMs, to solve Eq. (4) (see Subsection 3.2).

We currently do not consider online media signal conversion, because it requires trace back mechanism. If online processing is necessary, one of the simplest method is dividing input stream comparatively longer range than the sampling rate and apply the following method repeatedly.

3.2   Interval Sequence Conversion Via Dynamic Programming

To simplify the notation, we omit the model parameter variable Φ in the following equations. Let us use notation $f_t = 1$ that denotes an interval "finishes" at time t, which follows Murphy's notation that is used in a research note about segment models [10]. Then, $P(m_t = M_j, f_t = 1|\mathcal{I}')$, which is the probability when an interval finishes at time t and the mode of time t becomes M_j in the condition of the given interval sequence $\mathcal{I}'$, can be calculated the following recursive equation:

$$
\begin{aligned}
&P(m_t = M_j, f_t = 1|\mathcal{I}') \\
&= \sum_{\tau} \sum_{p(\neq q)} \left\{ \begin{array}{l} P(m_t = M_j, f_t = 1, l_t = \tau | m_{t-\tau} = M_i, f_{t-\tau} = 1, \mathcal{I}') \\ \times P(m_{t-\tau} = M_i, f_{t-\tau} = 1|\mathcal{I}') \end{array} \right\},
\end{aligned} \quad (5)
$$

l_t is a duration length of an interval (i.e., it continues l_t at time t) and m_t is a mode label at time t. The lattice in Fig. 3 depicts the path of the above recursive calculation. Each pair of arrows from each circle denotes whether the interval "continues" or "finishes", and every bottom circle sums up all the finishing interval probabilities.

The following dynamic programming algorithm is deduced directly from the recursive equation (5):

$$
E_t(j) = \max_{\tau} \max_{i(\neq j)} \underline{P(m_t = M_j, f_t = 1, l_t = \tau | m_{t-\tau} = M_i, f_{t-\tau} = 1, \mathcal{I}')} E_{t-\tau}(i),
$$

$$
\text{where}\quad E_t(j) \triangleq \max_{m_1^{t-1}} P(m_1^{t-1}, m_t = M_j, f_t = 1|\mathcal{I}'). \quad (6)
$$

$E_t(j)$ denotes the maximum probability when the interval of mode M_j finishes at time t, and is optimized for the mode sequence from time 1 to $t-1$ under the condition of given $\mathcal{I}'$. The probability with underline denotes that interval I_k with a triple ($b_k = t - \tau + 1, e_k = t, m_k = M_j$) occurs just after the interval I_{k-1} that has mode $m_{k-1} = M_i$ and ends at $e_{k-1} = t - \tau$. We refer to this probability as *interval transition probability*.

We recursively calculate the maximum probability for every mode that finishes at time $t(t = 1, ..., T)$ using Eq. (6). After the recursive calculation, we find the mode index $j^* = \arg\max_j E_T(j)$. Then, we can get the duration length of the interval that finishes at time T with mode label M_{j*}, if we preserve τ that gives the maximum value at each recursion of Eq. (6). Repeating this trace back, we finally obtain the optimized interval sequence and the number of intervals.

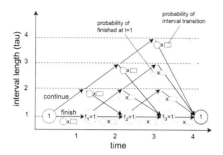 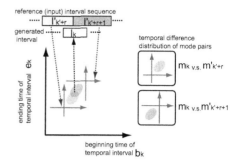

Fig. 3. Lattice to search optimal interval sequence (num. of mode =2). We assume that $\sum_j P(m_T = M_j, f_T = 1|\mathcal{I}') = 1$.

Fig. 4. An interval probability calculation from the trained timing structure model

The remaining problem for the algorithm is the method of calculating the interval transition probability. As we see in the next subsection, this probability can be estimated from the trained timing structure model.

3.3   Calculation of Interval Transition Probability

As we described in previous subsection, the interval transition probability appeared Eq. (6) is the transition from interval I_{k-1} to I_k. To simplify the notation, let us replace $t - \tau + 1$ with B_k. Let $e_{\min} = B_k$ and $e_{\max} = \min(T, B_k + l_{\max} - 1)$ be the minimum and maximum values of e_k, where $l_{\max}$ is the maximum length of the intervals. Let $I'_{k'}, ..., I'_{k'+R} \in \mathcal{I}'$ be reference intervals that are possible to overlap with I_k. Assuming that the reference intervals are independent of each other (this assumption empirically works well), the interval transition probability can be calculated by the following equation:

$$
\begin{aligned}
&P(m_t = M_j, f_t = 1, l_t = \tau | m_{t-\tau} = M_i, f_{t-\tau} = 1, \mathcal{I}') \\
&= P(m_k = M_j, e_k, e_k \in [e_{\min}, e_{\max}] | m_{k-1} = M_i, b_k = B_k, I'_{k'}, ..., I'_{k'+R}) \\
&= \prod_{r=0}^{R} \{ \text{Rect}(e_k, e_k \in [e_{\min}, b'_{k'+r} - 1]) \\
&\quad + \kappa_r P(m_k = M_j, e_k, e_k \in [b'_{k'+r}, e_{\max}] | m_{k-1} = M_i, b_k = B_k, I'_{k'+r}) \},
\end{aligned}
\tag{7}
$$

where $\text{Rect}(e, e \in [a, b]) = 1$ in the range $[a, b]$; else 0. Since the domain of e_k is $[e_{\min}, e_{\max}]$, Rect is out of range when $r = 0$, and $b'_{k'} = e_{\min}$. κ is a normalizing factor: $\kappa_r = 1 \, (r = 0)$ and

$$
\kappa_r = P(m_k = M_j, e_k, e_k \in [b'_{k'+r}, e_{\max}] | b_k = B_k, m_{k-1} = M_i)^{-1} \quad (r = 1, ..., R).
$$

In the experiments, we assume κ_r is uniform for (m_k, e_k); thus, $\kappa_r = N(e_{\max} - e_{\min} + 1)$ (N is the number of modes).

Using some assumption that we will describe later, the probability in Eq. (7) is decomposed as follows:

$$P(m_k = M_j, e_k, e_k \in [b'_{k'+r}, e_{\max}] \,|\, m_{k-1} = M_i, b_k = B_k, I'_{k'+r})$$
$$= P(e_k \,|\, e_k \in [b'_{k'+r}, e_{\max}], m_k = M_j, b_k = B_k, I'_{k'+r})$$
$$\times\, P(m_k = M_j | e_k \in [b'_{k'+r}, e_{\max}], m_{k-1} = M_i, b_k = B_k, I'_{k'+r})$$
$$\times\, P(e_k \in [b'_{k'+r}, e_{\max}] \,|\, m_{k-1} = M_i, b_k = B_k)$$

The first term is the probability of e_k under the condition that I_k overlaps with $I'_{k'+r}$. We assume that it conditionally independent of m_{k-1}. This probability can be calculated from Eq. (1). Here, we omit the details of the deduction, and just make an intuitive explanation using Fig. 4. First, an overlapped mode pair in I_k and $I'_{k'+r}$ provides a relative distribution of $(b_k - b'_{k'+r}, e_k - e'_{k'+r})$. Since $I'_{k'+r}$ is given, the relative distribution is mapped to the absolute time domain (the upper triangle region). Normalizing this distribution of (b_k, e_k) for $e_k \in [b'_{k'+r}, e_{\max}]$, we obtain the probability of the first term. The second term can be calculated using Eq. (2) and (3). For the third term, we assume that the probability of $e_k \geq b'_{k'+r}$ is independent of $I'_{k'+r}$. Then, this term can be calculated by modeling temporal duration length l_t. In the experiments, we assumed uniform distribution of e_k and used $(e_{\max} - b'_{k'+r})/(e_{\max} - e_{\min} + 1)$.

The calculation cost strongly depends on the maximum interval length $l_{\max}$. If we successfully estimate the modes, $l_{\max}$ becomes comparatively small (i.e., balanced among modes); thus, the cost will be reasonable.

4   Experiments

We applied the media conversion method described in Section 3 to the application that generates image sequences from an audio signal.

Feature extraction: First, we captured continuous utterance of five vowels /a/,/i/,/u/,/e/,/o/ (in this order) using a pair of camera and microphone. This utterance was repeated nine times (18 sec.). The resolution of the video data was 720×480 and the frame rate was 60fps. The sampling rate of the audio signal was 48kHz (downsampled to 16kHz in the analysis). Then, we applied short-term Fourier transform to the audio data with the window step of 1/60msec; thus, the frame rate corresponds to the video data. Using filter bank analysis, we obtained 1134 frames of audio feature vectors (dimensionality was 25). For the video feature, we extracted lip region exploiting the Active Appearance Model [5]. Then, we downsampled the lip region to 32×32 pixels and applied principal component analysis (PCA) to the extracted lip image sequence. Finally, we obtained 1134 frames of video feature vectors (dimensionality was 27).

Segmentation and mode estimation of each media signal: Considering the extracted audio and visual feature vector sequences as signal S' and S, we estimated the number of modes, parameters of each mode, and the temporal partitioning of each signal. We used linear dynamical systems for the models of

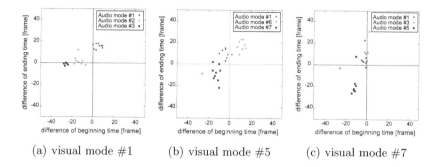

(a) visual mode #1   (b) visual mode #5   (c) visual mode #7

Fig. 5. Scattering plots of temporal difference between overlapped audio and visual modes. Visual mode #1, #5, and #7 corresponds to lip motion /o/ → /a/, /e/ → /o/, and /a/ → /i/, respectively.

modes. To estimate the parameters, we exploited hierarchical clustering of the dynamical systems based on eigenvalue constraints [6]. The estimated number of modes was 13 and 8 for audio and visual modes, respectively. The segmentation results are shown in Fig. 6 (the first and second rows). Because of the noise, some vowel sounds were divided into several audio modes.

Training of the timing structure model between audio and video: Using the two interval sequences obtained by the segmentation, we estimated distributions of Eq. (1), (2), and (3). Figure 5 is the scattered plots of the samples that are temporal difference between beginning points and ending points of overlapped modes. Each chart shows samples of one visual mode to typical (two or three) audio modes. We see that the beginning motion from /a/ to /i/ synchronized with the actual sound (right chart) compared to the motion from /o/ to /a/ (left) and from /e/ to /o/ (middle). Applying Gaussian mixture models to these distributions, we estimated the temporal difference distributions.

Lip image sequence generation from an audio signal: Using the trained timing structure model, we applied the method in Section 3 to the audio signal. To verify the ability of the timing structure model, we input the audio interval sequence that we used in the parameter estimation. First, we generated a visual interval sequence from the input audio interval sequence. Figure 6 (the third row) shows the generated visual interval sequence. We see that the sequence is almost the same as the training data shown in the second row.

Then, we generated visual feature vector sequences using the parameters of modes (linear dynamical systems) estimated in the segmentation process. Finally, we obtained an image sequence by calculating linear combination of principal axes (eigenvectors of PCA). The result of frame 140 to 250 was shown in the fifth row in Fig. 6. The lip motion in the sequence almost corresponds to the original motion (in the sixth row), and we also see the visual motion precedes the actual sound by comparing to the wave data (in the bottom row).

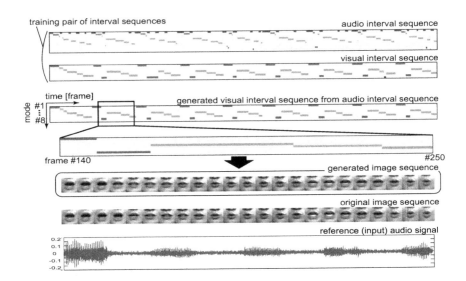

Fig. 6. Generated visual interval sequence and an image sequence from the audio signal

5   Conclusion

We present a timing structure model that explicitly represents the temporal metric relations between multimedia signals. The experiments show that the model can be applied to generate lip motion from speech signal across the modalities. We also applied the method to generate the silhouette motion of piano performance from audio signal. Although the current results is in the stage of the verification of the model, its basic ability for representing temporal synchronization is expected to be useful for wide variety of human machine interaction systems including speaker tracking and audio-visual speech recognition. Moreover, the model provide general framework to integrate variety of signals such as motion in each part of facial deformation [12]. Our future work is to extend the current framework to realize interaction systems that share a sense of time with human.

Acknowledgment. This work is in part supported by Grant-in-Aid for Scientific Research of the Ministry of Education, Culture, Sports, Science and Technology of Japan under the contract of 18049046.

References

1. J. F. Allen. Maintaining knowledge about temporal interval. *Commun. of the ACM*, 26(11):832–843, 1983.
2. M. Brand. Voice puppetry. *Proc. SIGGRAPH*, pages 21–28, 1999.
3. M. Brand, N. Oliver, and A. Pentland. Coupled hidden Markov models for complex action recognition. *Proc. IEEE Conference on Computer Vision and Pattern Recognition*, pages 994–999, 1997.

4. C. Bregler. Learning and recognizing human dynamics in video sequences. *Proc. Int. Conference on Computer Vision and Pattern Recognition*, pages 568–574, 1997.
5. T. F. Cootes, G. J. Edwards, and C. J. Taylor. Active appearance model. *Proc. European Conference on Computer Vision*, 2:484–498, 1998.
6. H. Kawashima and T. Matsuyama. Multiphase learning for an interval-based hybrid dynamical system. *IEICE Trans. Fundamentals*, E88-A(11):3022–3035, 2005.
7. S. E. Levinson. Continuously variable duration hidden Markov models for automatic speech recognition. *Computer Speech and Language*, 1:29–45, 1986.
8. Y. Li, T. Wang, and H.-Y. Shum. Motion texture: A two-level statistical model for character motion synthesis. *Proc. SIGGRAPH*, pages 465–472, 2002.
9. H. McGurk and J. MacDonald. Hearing lips and seeing voices. *Nature*, pages 746–748, 1976.
10. K. P. Murphy. Hidden semi-Markov models (HSMMs). *Informal Notes*, 2002.
11. A. V. Nefian, L. Liang, X. Pi, X. Liu, and K. Murphy. Dynamic Bayesian networks for audio-visual speech recognition. *EURASIP Journal on Applied Signal Processing*, 2002(11):1–15, 2002.
12. M. Nishiyama, H. Kawashima, T. Hirayama, and T. Matsuyama. Facial expression representation based on timing structures in faces. *IEEE Int. Workshop on Analysis and Modeling of Faces and Gestures (LNCS 3723)*, pages 140–154, 2005.
13. M. Ostendorf, V. Digalakis, and O. A. Kimball. From HMMs to segment models: A unified view of stochastic modeling for speech recognition. *IEEE Trans. Speech and Audio Process*, 4(5):360–378, 1996.

Human Motion Synthesis by Motion Manifold Learning and Motion Primitive Segmentation

Chan-Su Lee and Ahmed Elgammal

Rutgers University, Piscataway, NJ, USA
{chansu, elgammal}@cs.rutgers.edu

Abstract. We propose motion manifold learning and motion primitive segmentation framework for human motion synthesis from motion-captured data. High dimensional motion capture date are represented using a low dimensional representation by topology preserving network, which maps similar motion instances to the neighborhood points on the low dimensional motion manifold. Nonlinear manifold learning between a low dimensional manifold representation and high dimensional motion data provides a generative model to synthesize new motion sequence by controlling trajectory on the low dimensional motion manifold. We segment motion primitives by analyzing low dimensional representation of body poses through motion from motion captured data. Clustering techniques like k-means algorithms are used to find motion primitives after dimensionality reduction. Motion dynamics in training sequences can be described by transition characteristics of motion primitives. The transition matrix represents the temporal dynamics of the motion with Markovian assumption. We can generate new motion sequences by perturbing the temporal dynamics.

1 Introductions

In this paper, we present a framework to synthesize human motion by combining motion primitives. Biological study shows that complicated human motions are controlled by linear combination of computational motion primitives called force fields [10]. We learn a generative model with a low dimensional motion manifold representation similar to force fields of motion primitives. To model smooth variations in human motions according to force fields, we learn nonlinear mapping between motion manifold representation and high dimensional motion data. We also model continuous human motion dynamics by sequences of primitive motions.

A low dimensional manifold representation of high dimensional human motion data provides a compact representation for analysis of human motion sequences. It also provides means to control human motion in the low dimensional space after learning a mapping between the low dimensional manifold points and high dimensional motion capture data. We use self organizing maps (SOMs) as a topology preserving network. Using SOMs, we can represent high dimensional human motion data into low dimensional Euclidean space preserving neighborhood relationship. By learning nonlinear mappings between low dimensional manifold points and high dimensional motion capture data, we can generate new motion sequences according to trajectories on the low dimensional motion manifold.

F.J. Perales and R.B. Fisher (Eds.): AMDO 2006, LNCS 4069, pp. 464–473, 2006.

We segment a given sequence of motion into sub-motion primitive by utilizing low dimensional representation of human motion sequence and clustering in the low dimensional space. There are several works related to macro-level motion segmentation, where the motion is segmented into higher level meaningful categories like walk, run, jump and so on. However, we need to find micro-level motion patterns in order to describe simple motion by the combination of the sub-motions. It is not obvious how to define the sub-motion. Recently, huge motion capture data are available in public. Therefore, we find sub-motion primitives by analyzing large motion capture data set. Dimensionality reduction techniques are applied followed by applying clustering to find sub-motion primitive in order to represent intrinsic characteristics of motion efficiently.

To model temporal dynamics of a given motion sequence and to be able to generate new motion sequences that fit to the original motion dynamics, we model motion dynamics by the transition characteristics of sub-motion primitive. Motion dynamics can be captured using transition probabilities from one primitive motion to another primitive transition after segmenting whole sequence of motion into sub-motion primitives. With Markovian assumption, we model the motion dynamics characteristics in a transition matrix of motion primitives.

2   Related Work

Machine-learning techniques are used in increasing number of papers in computer graphics, especially in data-driven motion synthesis. A stylistic hidden Markov model (SHMM), which is an HMM whose parameters are functionally controlled by a style parameter, was used for stylistic motion synthesis [4]. Scaled Gaussian Process Latent Variable Model (SGPLVM) was used to solve inverse kinematics system based on a learned model [8].

There are several different approaches to segment continuous motion sequences. One of the well-known approaches in computer vision is using hidden Markov model (HMM) [5]. Statistical approaches like Principal Component Analysis (PCA), Probabilistic PCA and Gaussian mixture model (GMM), are used to segment motion capture data into distinct behavior segment [1]. Recently there are approaches to use sub-motion sequences for segmentation. Bettinger and Cootes [2] modeled facial motion by segmenting sub-trajectories, grouping similar sub-trajectories and learning temporal relations between groups in order to model facial behavior. Temporal relationship between groups was modeled by variable length Markov model [7]. New sequence can be generated by transition of group from the learned model and sampling principal component in subgroup to find new shape of motion. For the interpolation of two sub-motion, linear model is used to avoid perceptible jumps in the generated video. Clustering techniques are also used to find key-frame in motion analysis [3].

In this paper, we employed also clustering technique similar to [3] to discover motion primitive. However, we use low dimensional motion manifold for the representation of dynamic human motion in low dimensional space, which allows low dimensional representation of high dimensional data. In addition, we learn a nonlinear generative model to synthesize details of the original motions in spite of the low dimensional representation.

3   Learning Low Dimensional Motion Manifold

We represent high dimensional human motion using a low dimensional embedded manifold representation. Then, We learn nonlinear mapping between the low dimensional manifold representation and the original high dimensional motion. The low dimensional manifold representation is motivated by force fields in the biological study of human motion [10]. The motion primitives that we are interested in are relevant to the intrinsic body configuration and irrelevant to the position and orientation of the body. In the preprocessing, we normalize body location and orientation. Now, we can represent body configuration by 3D locations of body joint instead of joint angles. This allows coordinate invariant similarity measure for body pose [9], which may be close to human perception. If we use joint angle, we need to count hierarchy of joint angle in comparison as the small difference of joint angle in higher level can cause large difference of joint location than the same amount of difference in lower level joint angle. Two motion capture datasets are used in the experiments. One is ballet motion and the other is normal walking motion.

3.1   Low-Dimensional Manifold Representation of Human Motion

We applied two manifold learning techniques for motion captured data to find low dimensional manifold representation of motion sequences. First, we find low dimensional representation of each body pose by applying Principal Component Analysis (PCA) using singular value decomposition (SVD). With the first few PCs, we can distinguish each frames with similarity relations.

Second, we applied Kohonen's self organizing map. Kohonen's neural network model was motivated by neurophysiology. The neuron layer acts as a *topographic feature map*, if the location of the most strongly excited neurons is correlated in a regular and continuous fashion with a restricted number of signal features of interest. Neighboring excited locations in the layer then correspond to stimuli with similar features [13]. Figure 1 shows two dimensional representation for walking sequence and ballet motion sequence. We can notice that the representation points spread in all the space (Figure 1 (b)). In Figure 1 (a), We can notice three cycling patterns through the path. However, in SOM, even the similar motion cycles are represented in different locations and are spread in the space. You can see similar patterns in Figure 1 (c) (d), which is the case of complicated ballet motion.

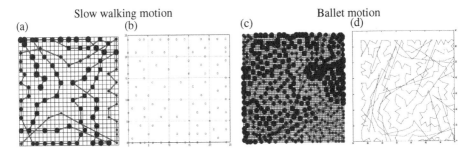

Fig. 1. SOM analysis for simple walking (a) (b) and complicated ballet motion (c) (d)

3.2   Learning Generative Models Using Motion Manifold

We learn nonlinear mapping between the manifold embedding and original motion in order to generate new motions based on embedded manifold points. Suppose that we can learn a nonlinearly embedded representation of the high dimensional motion manifold M in a low dimensional Euclidean embedding space, R^e, then we can learn a set of mapping functions from the embedding space into the input space, i.e., functions $\gamma(x_t) : R^e \rightarrow R^d$ that maps from embedding space with dimensionality e into the input space (observation) with dimensionality d. Since the embedding and the original data are related by nonlinear manifold learning, we need to learn nonlinear mapping in order to capture motion characteristics accurately. In particular we consider nonlinear mapping functions of the form

$$y_t = \gamma(x_t) = B \cdot \psi(x_t) \tag{1}$$

where B is a $d \times N$ linear mapping and $\psi(\cdot) : R^e \rightarrow R^N$ is a nonlinear mapping where N radial basis functions can be used to model the manifold in the embedding space, i.e.,

$$\psi(\cdot) = [\psi_1(\cdot), \cdots, \psi_N(\cdot)]^T$$

For i-th frame y_i, which is sampled data of y_t at time $t = i \cdot \frac{N}{T}$, we can find low dimensional embedding point X_i. Given an embedded manifold representation $x_i, i = 1 \cdots N$ in e dimensional embedding space for $y_i, i = 1 \cdots N$, we can learn nonlinear mappings $f : R^e \rightarrow R^d$ using generalized radial basis function (GRBF) interpolation [12] to the original sequence y_t by solving for multiple interpolants, i.e., $f^l : R^e \rightarrow R$ for each tracking feature l. We can use thin-plate spline ($\phi(u) = u^2 log(u)$) or Gaussian ($\phi(u) = exp(u)$) as the basis function. The whole mapping for sequence k can be written in a matrix form as

$$f_k(x) = B^k \cdot \psi(x) \tag{2}$$

where B^k is a coefficient for the generative model of motion data.

4   Motion Primitive Segmentation and Motion Dynamics Modeling

We segment primitive motions from the low dimensional manifold representation. Based on segmented motion primitive, we can model dynamics of human motion by transition probability of motion primitives.

4.1   Finding Primitive Motion Using Clustering

The representative motion primitive is estimated by clustering of the low dimensional representation of motion sequence. At first, we applied standard k-means algorithm and measured error in a given k clusters. We estimate the natural number of primitive by estimating error in different number of clusters and finding elbow in the error graph for different number of clusters. Based on the reconstruction error according to the number of cluster, we can decide the number of clusters. In our data set, we find that the ballet

(a) ballet dataset: (b) motion primitive(ballet):

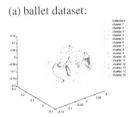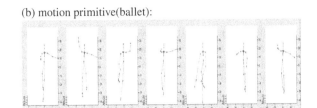

Fig. 2. Clustering motion sequences

motion shows 15 clusters and the walking sequence shows 10 clusters in the estimation of natural number of clusters. After finding natural number of cluster, we applied fuzzy k-means algorithm and Gaussian mixture model clustering using estimated natural cluster number. Fuzzy k-means clustering result shows better clustering result with respect to the inner distance within cluster and separation between clusters. Figure 2 shows clustering result by fuzzy k-means algorithms for ballet motion with 10 clusters (a). Figure 2 (b) shows body poses corresponding to the centers of the first seven clusters in ballet motion dataset. In order to find proper sequence of each cluster for continuous motion generation, we need to model dynamics of the motions.

4.2   Modeling Temporal Dynamics Using Markov Chains

Temporal dynamics of the motions are modeled using Markov chains. A Markov assumption assumes that the next state of a system (S_{t+1}) is only dependent on the previous n states $(S_t, S_{t-1}, S_{t-2}, \cdots, S_{t-n+1})$. By assuming that transition to new motion primitive (new state) depends only on current motion primitive class (current state), we modeled motion dynamics as a first order Markov model. Now, the likelihood of one primitive cluster following another can be expressed as a conditional probability $P(S_{t+1}|S_t)$. Transition probability from state j at time t to state k at time $t+1$

$$p_{k,j} = P(C_k^{t+1}|C_j^t), \tag{3}$$

where $P(C_j^t)$ denotes the unconditional probability of being in cluster j at time t, can be estimated easily by counting two adjacent frames cluster transition in the original data set.

A transition matrix can model the whole dynamics

$$\begin{pmatrix} p_{1,1} & \cdots & p_{1,n} \\ \vdots & \ddots & \vdots \\ p_{n,1} & \cdots & p_{n,n} \end{pmatrix}, \tag{4}$$

where $\sum_j p_{k,j} = 1$ for all j, and n is the number of clusters in the model. Figure 3 shows transition matrices for ballet (a) and walking (b) datasets. The bright color means high probability of transition. The figure show highest probability in the diagonal, which means most likely next frame is within the same cluster. We can estimate most likely

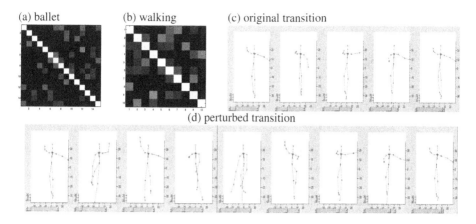

(a) ballet   (b) walking   (c) original transition

(d) perturbed transition

Fig. 3. Transition matrices and transition of motion states

next primitive motion cluster k^* by choosing the next highest probabilistic transition from cluster j.

$$k^* = \arg \max_i p_{i,j}, \; i \neq j \tag{5}$$

in the transition matrix. Figure 3 (c) shows motion transition sequence estimated by the most second likely transition state from one selected primitive motion until it return back to the state. We can get new motion transition sequence by perturbing transition matrix with small noise as shown figure 3 (d).

5 Synthesis of Human Motion Using Motion Manifold and Motion Primitive

We can synthesize a new motion sequence in two ways. First, we can directly synthesize new motion sequence from any low dimensional trajectory since we can generate motion sequences for any given manifold points given the learned nonlinear generative model. Second, we can generate dynamic sequences of motion based on the transition model which is learned from training sequence.

5.1 Direct Motion Synthesis Using Low Dimensional Motion Manifold

We implemented low dimensional representation of ballet motion using SOM. First we learn SOM by 65×65 lattice structure (Actually, we tried smaller number of lattice such as 25×25, 40×40 or 50×50. In these case, some motion fired in the same lattice location, which is not good for learning as the same low dimensional representation point requires learning to reconstruct two different high dimensional data). After finding different lattice representation, we used small number of regular lattice center as the basis center for radial basis function. We used 15×15 number of radial bases for GRBF learning. After that we implemented two kinds of interaction methods: manifold point based synthesis and given key motion based synthesis.

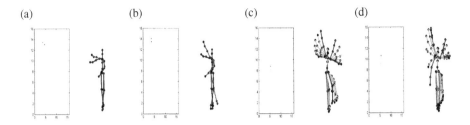

Fig. 4. Motion synthesis: (a) (b) Point interaction in low dimensional space (c) (d) Path interpolation in low dimensional space

In the manifold point-based approach, user selects points on the manifold using mouse. After finding the location of the mouse click point within the given manifold, we can generate motion based on trajectory of selected points. Figure 4 (a) (b) shows last selected point (blue) and newly selected point (red) and their corresponding reconstructed motion. It shows continuous variation of the motion when we interpolate points on the manifold and generate intermediate motion corresponding to intermediate manifold points. When multiple points are selected, we do spline fitting for the selected manifold points for smooth interpolation of intermediate motion. Figure 4 (c) (d) shows examples of the interpolating intermediate motion. Blue color motion is the motion corresponding to the last mouse click. Red color represent new mouse click location. Intermediate motions are generated as shown in the figure (cyan color).

The other method is based on given key motions. Using inverse mapping, we can find a low dimensional representation for a given new key motion. In the case of SOM,

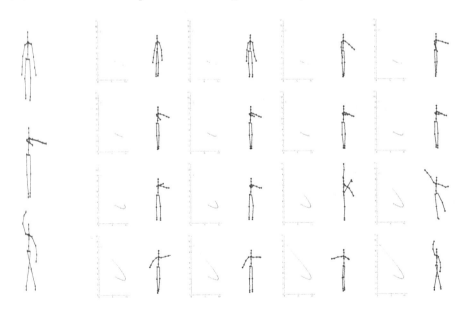

Fig. 5. Path interpolation in low dimensional space

we can find low dimensional manifold representation for given motion frame by finding *Best Matching Unit (BMU)* in the original lattice and scale it to the mapping coordinate space. In other case, we can achieve approximate solution using polynomial terms of GRBF [12].

Figure 5 shows an example of motion synthesis based on given key motions. In the left column, three selected key motions are given. The seletect key motions are the motion we want to generate; we want to generate motion begins from the first motion and then generate second motion in the intermediate frame. Finally the animation needs to be finished in the third key motion. In the right column, we shows low dimensional manifold points and corresponding motion generated. Red markers on the motion manifold represent low dimensional location of the three sample key motions. After spline fitting, we re-sampled the spline curve for a given sample number. As we follow mapping trajectory in the low dimensional space, it shows not just interpolation of three sample points but smooth synthesis of intermediate motions based on training data. The figure shows that there are additional intermediate sub-motions in the synthesis of new motions based on given key motions.

(a) interpolation trajectory:

(b) cluster membership:

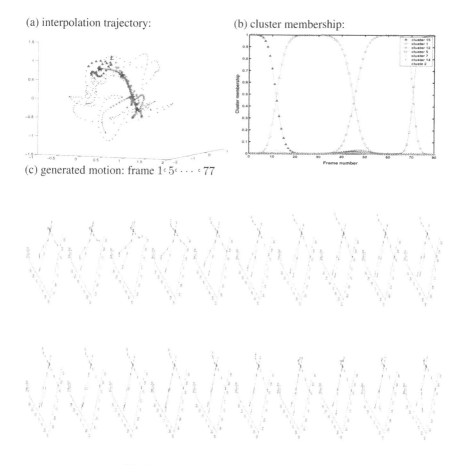

(c) generated motion: frame $1 < 5 < \cdots < 77$

Fig. 6. An example of motion primitive interpolation

5.2   Generation of Continuous Motion Sequence

We can generate new motion sequence for any given initial motion frame with dynamics of original motion. After finding transition sequence for given motion frame, we can define trajectory on the motion manifold by connecting sequence of motion manifold points corresponding to the given motion primitives. The deviation from the original motion sequence can be controlled by the scale factor in the perturbation of transition matrix by superimpose random noise all the transition matrix elements. We find smooth trajectory from the motion primitive sequence by spline fitting of cluster center of each corresponding motion primitives. By sampling points on the manifold points along the spline, we can generate new sequence of motions. Figure 6 shows a generated motion sequence with spline interpolation trajectory and clustering membership in each sampling point along the interpolation trajectory. Possible transition sequence was found from transition matrix and 80 points are resampled after spline fitting to the primitive centers. It shows smooth motion transitions in frame $1, 5, 9, 13, \cdots, 77$. For any given initial pose, we can generate most feasible primitive pose sequence from transition matrix with no perturbation. Figure 7 shows most likely key pose sequence when we start from two different motion frame.

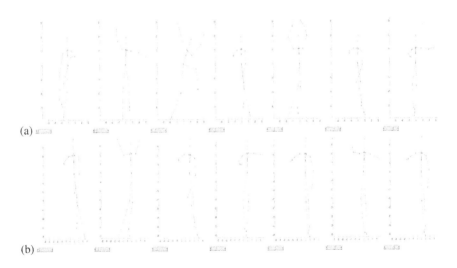

Fig. 7. Generations of following motion for given initial motion frames

6   Conclusions and Future Works

We presented an approach to generate new motion sequences using statistical analysis and learning techniques. This approach is more flexible and close to human motion generation mechanism as it generates sequence of motion based on motion primitive and transition probabilities among motion primitives. Motion primitives found by clustering of given data set is somewhat dependant on the given data set and the number of clusters, even though we find natural number of cluster for the given data set, which may compensate for the dependence of motion primitive to the given data set. However, this motion primitives can summarize whole motion sequence with small motion primitives and it simplifies representation and transition model and makes the problem solvable with simple model. The framework presented in this paper can be applicable in motion analysis in computer vision problem. It will be elegant to combine video data with motion capture data: tracking and recognizing human motion from video sequences with possible motion sequence representation from motion capture data.

For more complicated and general motion primitives, we may need to count hierarchical representation of motion primitive as in [11]. Modeling transition of sub-motion is simplified assuming the first-order Markovian dynamics, which may not enough to capture complicated motion transitions. We may use more rich representation like variable length Markov model [7] or higher order Markov models. We can extend the generative models to cover variations in different person as style factors similar to [6].

References

1. J. Barbic, A. Safonova, J.-Y. Pan, C. Faloutsos, J. K. Hodgins, and N. S. Pollard. Segmenting motion capture data into distinct behaviors. In *Proc. of Graphics Interface*, 2004.
2. F. Bettinger and T. F. Cootes. A model of facial behaviour. In *Proc. of FGR*, pages 123–128, 2004.
3. R. Bowden. Learning statistical models of human motion. In *Proc. of IEEE Workshop on Human Modeling, Analysis & Synthesis*, 2000.
4. M. Brand and A. Hertzmann. Style machines. In *Proc. of SIGGRAPH*, pages 183–192, 2000.
5. M. Brand and V. Kettnaker. Discovery and segmentation of activities in video. *IEEE Trans. on PAMI*, 22(8), 2000.
6. A. Elgammal and C.-S. Lee. Separating style and content on a nonlinear manifold. In *Proc. CVPR*, volume 1, pages 478–485, 2004.
7. A. Galata, N. Johnson, and D. Hogg. Learning variable-length markov models of behavior. *Computer Vision and Image Understanding*, 81:398–413, 2001.
8. K. Grochow, S. L. Martin, A. Hertzmann, and Z. Popovic. Style-based inverse kinematics. *ACM Trans. Graph.*, 23(3):522–531, 2004.
9. L. Kovar and M. Gleicher. Flexible automatic motion blending with registration curves. In *Proc. of SCA*, pages 214 – 224, 2003.
10. F. Mussa-Ivaldi and E. Bizzi. Motor learning through the combination of primitives. *Philosopical Transactions of the Royal Society of London Seris B, Biological Science*, 355:1755–1769, 2000.
11. S. Park and J. K. Aggarwal. Recognition of two-person interactions using a hierarchical bayesian network. In *Proc. of Workshop on Video surveillance*, pages 65–76. ACM Press, 2003.
12. T. Poggio and F. Girosi. Networks for approximation and learning. *Proc. IEEE*, 78(9):1481–1497, 1990.
13. H. Ritter, T. Martinetz, and K. Schulten. *Nueral Computation and Self-Organizing Maps*. Addison-Wesley, 1991.

Towards an Integrated Technological Framework for Modelling Shared Virtual Spaces: Languages and Domotic Applications

Iosu Azkue[1], Alfredo Pina[1], and Michalis Vazirgiannis[2]

[1] Dept of Maths & Computer Science
Univ. Publica de Navarra, Campus de Arrrosadia s/n,
31006 Pamplona, Spain
{iosu.azkue, pina}@unavarra.es
[2] Dept of Informatics,
Athens Univ. of Economics & Business, Patision 76, 10434, Athens
mvazirg@aueb.gr

Abstract. This paper presents an ongoing work which aims to make a step forward in advanced domotic systems and specific intelligent interfaces for shared virtual spaces that represent real world situations. The main contribution is to explain the exploitation and integration of tools and ideas to accomplish this objective, focusing mostly on high level languages - for an integral space design, open source projects like VRML/X3D, JAVA3D or OPENGL - implementation tools, Virtual Reality and Domotics (as domains for application).

Keywords: Shared Virtual worlds, Virtual Reality, Domotics, High-Level Languages, XML.

1 Introduction and Background

If we are talking about a shared virtual world, we are talking about a shared space, used simultaneously by different users, accessible through the Internet, where each user can see all the others and his current context and where some interaction among users is available. In such scenarios we address the following issues considered important:

- need for high level languages to modelling flexible scenarios
- need for representation models for those scenarios (2D or 3D)
- Implementation design capitalizing on available as well as efficient technologies
- need to offer transparent and intuitive systems to the users, that may have low cost equipment
- need to take advantage of current network facilities, such as P2P approaches or database connection for example
- integration with Smart Information Systems within the Internet, such as, Information objects within the semantic web
- definition of rules towards collaboration, coordination, and interaction, within the defined worlds

F.J. Perales and R.B. Fisher (Eds.): AMDO 2006, LNCS 4069, pp. 474–483, 2006.

All the previous aspects should be taken into account when creating such worlds, and what we describe in this paper is how to use several tools and ideas to accomplish this, focusing mostly on high level languages (for an integral space design), open source projects like VRML/X3D, JAVA3D or OPENGL (tools for implementation) and Virtual Reality and Domotics (as domains for application).

Several works in these areas exist already in the literature. Maybe the most recent and significant one is the Croquet project [1] (http://www.opencroquet.org/). This project is a combination of open source computer software and network architecture that supports deep collaboration and resource sharing among large numbers of users. The integrated 2D and 3D Croquet interface allows for co-creativity, knowledge sharing, synchronous deep social telepresence and presence among large numbers of people.

The Web was originally proposed and developed for information sharing within internationally dispersed teams and the dissemination of information by support groups. Emerging technologies like intelligent agents, XML, Web services and Semantic Web (http://www.w3.org/XML/) provide new opportunities for developing Internet-based collaborative design environments, particularly for product information sharing and visualization. Zhang [2] reviews the state of the art in Internet based product information sharing and visualization with a case study to illustrate the emerging technologies used in this area.

Dachselt et al. [3] have demonstrated an abstracted, declarative XML and Schema to model Web3D scene components.

1.1 Our Proposal

We need a 3D information exchange format within the cyberspace. This language should offer at least the following features:

- Sufficient primitives to define and create a scene graph
- tools for both geometric and visual modelling
- tools to for a wide range of animations
- primitives to allow real time interaction between objects and users of the environment
- database access mechanisms, in order to store/retrieve the spatio/temporal state of the shared space
- Tools for defining structured documents with semantics, for example using XML TAG's.

These features can be found in X3D (http://www.web3d.org/x3d/) [4] which adds these other interesting ones:

- It is an international Standard
- Accessibility, versatility and compactness of representation
- Language modularity (with objects easy to re-use)
- Compatibility with widely used browser to visualize scenes
- XML support, thus enabling integration with other web services. XML allows as well interaction between databases and the graphical sub-system
- a real time intuitive user interface to the 3D world similar to the way he will act in real life

Anyway the models have to be easy to access for design or maintenance purposes, and this not only by technicians but also by architects, artists, etc... i.e. final users. Current languages (like X3D) do not allow a high level modelling and they demand specific knowledge to use it. It is possible to make any transform, but using lineal laws. The modelling of objects can be complex, i.e. to specify the position of an object related to another. For example to put an object A "onto" another object B, the user/programmer has to compute coordinates of the centre of A, related to the centre of B. We should have mechanisms that allow us to define virtual worlds in a more natural way (simply A is onto B). So we need a higher-level language to gain abstraction.

We have designed and implemented STEDEL, a system that allows the interactive design of a room, the definition of pieces of furniture and the placement of electrical and electronic appliances. The system works over the WWW offering web-users a tool for designing and visualizing their rooms. The users may define each object in the room, its size, position, and spatial relationships with the room or other objects. Certain integrity constraints are checked during this definition. The system can create on the fly a VRML representation of the specifications and render it to the client. The user may choose to alter and visualise the virtual-world or store it for further reference.

As it will be explained in section 3, we are working on a shared virtual world which is a representation of a domotic house. As it is shown in Figure 1, a world can be modelled with STEDEL (described in the next section) [5] [6].; it is possible to connect to suppliers, in order to include real control objects from the industry in the model. Once the model is validated, it is possible to transform it into an X3D set of files (leveraged in the framework of an XML-based Web, encoding information about the objects in a hierarchical fashion to provide semantics) and a control module (some of the X3D profiles permit programmatic access to objects within our X3D system using SAI, Scene Access Interface), which enables duplex communication with the real house. The scripting environment can receive, process and send events from or to X3D nodes.

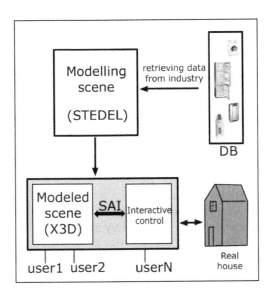

Fig. 1. Overview of the system

The rest of the paper describes this work in progress. Section 2 introduces the as Spatio-Temporal languages and describes the key aspects of STEDEL. Section 3 shows how the kind of system the authors have presented fits well for domotic applications. Section 4 gives some future work ideas.

2   Spatio-temporal Languages & STEDEL

2.1   Introduction to Spatio-temporal Languages

The need for 3D interactive multimedia content in many application areas such as culture, tourism and transportation is profound. The current languages for such content specification i. do not provide database support and ii. are not enough high-level and easy to use.

The mostly used language for 3D specifications is VRML that enables definition of 3D objects of specific geometry. All three geometric transformations are supported (translation, rotations, scaling), but only using linear laws and can be applied to objects. Events can be passed from an object to another object (or list of objects). Though there are some issues which are not covered adequately:

- complex object specification: i.e. it is very tedious to specify in VRML an object A standing "on" object B, since the user/programmer has to calculate the position of A's centre in relation to the centre of B, in order to appear "on" B
- time management: The standard VRML does not support adequately the management of temporal aspects of objects such as: object temporal life (i.e. an object may appear at some point and disappear after some time), temporal relationships among objects presentations (i.e. two objects A, B appear together and disappear when the A's life ends).
- interaction: there is a great diversity in the various interactions that may occur in a virtual world. The interaction can be external (i.e. emanating from the user) or internal (i.e. collisions between objects of the world).
- high level functionality: it is the case in many applications that the authors may want to define a set of interrelated actions

More specifically at the definition lever there are requirements for:

- relationship based specifications, i.e. it more natural to be able to define that an object A is "on" an object B rather that specifying the exact position of A in a world coordinate system.
- handling of temporal aspects, such as
- complex interaction, so that both internal and external events, simple and complex can be handled
- scenario management,
- data base support, the ability to store and retrieve the spatiotemporal structure of a world

2.2 STEDEL

The ideas we have described above are some of the features incorporated in the STEDEL [6] language prototype, a Spatio-Temporal Descriptive Language, and a fully declarative event based language that is suitable for rapid development of VR scenes with dynamic interactive content and for quick prototyping of VR scenes. It is compiled into equivalent VRML97 code, combined with a series of PROTO nodes which we have written which implement the various constructs of the language, corresponding to the primitives of our model outlined in the previous section. The language is not specifically linked to VRML in any way and it can be compiled to other 3D modelling languages. However, due to the prevalence of VRML we have designed STEDEL so as to facilitate the inclusion of VRML code within a STEDEL description. Additionally the VRML content exported by our compiler can be used in a larger project that is done in pure VRML with minimal effort.

STEDEL was designed with two goals in mind. The first and most significant goal is to make life easier for the content developer who is not necessarily either knowledgeable or interested in computer programming. We have thus abstracted away the hows of creating virtual scenes and went fully declarative in the language definition. Users of STEDEL only need to be familiar with basic geometric principles and simple concepts like speed, acceleration, rate of rotation, etc.

Programming effort is thus significantly reduced and trivial syntactic or semantic errors which are frequent in VRML leading to faulty or inconsistent virtual scenes are avoided. Furthermore, in the limited scope of the few virtual scenes that we have implemented ourselves in STEDEL, we have noted that the size of descriptions in our language (in terms of size of code in bytes) is at least a factor of 3 less than the equivalent VRML code.

3 Application to Domotics

The context of this paper is within a wider project which aims to define a global and unified framework with intelligent tri-dimensional agents for the current systems and the future virtual environments. Nowadays electronic communication among persons includes from basic chats and GSM services to virtual immersive sceneries with great realism. The differences are obvious, and virtual immersive sceneries provide mechanisms for interacting virtual elements (avatars, information, passive objects,...) with the sceneries that participate virtually in a universe.

The main goal of the project is to obtain results for applying them in domotic environments with virtual reality domestic systems and 3D agents. The person-home interaction will allow important synergies in both fields. Simultaneously we want to study new communication systems between men-machine, specially directed to disabled persons where their functional limitation can be supported through advanced domotic systems and specific intelligent interfaces.

The term Domotics is associated to the set of elements that, when installed, interconnected and automatically controlled at home, release the user from the routine of intervening in everyday actions and, at the same time, they provide optimized control over comfort, energetic consumption, security and communications [7].

There are three types of domotic elements: sensors, actuators and systems or controllers. The *sensors*, also called receivers, are elements that receive the information from the atmosphere, for example, atmospheric or luminosity variables. They can also obtain information on the actions humans carry out in their daily interaction at home, such as pressing a switch or going into a room. These include sensors of temperature, luminosity, gas, smoke, intrusion, etc. *Actuators* are elements that receive the order to be activated or deactivated. They consist of actions such as switching a light on/off or opening/closing a blind. As in the case of sensors, there are a great variety of actuators. Among these actuators we can include, for example, the heating system, air conditioning, light fittings, the opening/closing of blinds, the alarm, etc. Finally, the *systems* or *controllers* are in charge of processing the information coming from the sensors and, by means of the appropriate programming, they activate or deactivate the actuators.

The domotic elements are grouped by means of links into different *management areas*. Four such areas could be Thermal Comfort, Control over Luminosity, Security and Energy Control. Basically these four areas include most of the domotic elements although their number and functionality is constantly increasing.

A simulation of a domotic home is divided into three sections: *Model* (for describing the phenomenon), *View* or *Graphic Interface* (that permits the visualization of the phenomenon) and *Control*.

In order to specify and organize the general approaches to the solution to the design and control problem of the home, we use Virtual Reality. VR permits a better understanding of spatial and visual aspects of a project of domotic building. This technique will allow users greater interaction possibilities. One of the most interesting aspect in VR is its integration in the Internet. The *Virtual Reality Modelling Language* (VRML), X3D or Java 3D allow building virtual worlds that are accessible via the Internet.

This kind of interfaces adds several advantages to the domotic simulator developed:

- New interaction possibilities.
- A most realistic perception is provided. The purpose of this kind of interfaces is to obtain immersion systems that emulate a real environment and produce a most effective learning.
- Pleasant learning/teaching environments. Users, immersed in 3D simulations, improve their skills thanks to practising real tasks. Operating in this kind of environments is more simple and natural for the users.
- Also, new kind of information is accessible (visual attention and physical movements, position and orientation, …). It will allow us to characterize users.
- Risks are eliminated and costs are reduced.

There are several factors that add a degree of interest to the user that uses a VR application; these are *events*, *realism*, *animation* and *power to answering*.

We have designed and implemented a system for WWW enabled interactive design of a room, definition of pieces of furniture as well as placement of domestic appliances: STEDEL. The user may define for each object, its size, position, and also the inter-object spatial relationships. Certain integrity constraints are checked during this definition. The system generates on the fly a VRML/X3D representation of the specifications and renders it at the client. The user alters and visualizes the world and may save it for further reference.

The STEDEL data model [8] aims at representation of: i. entities present in a room, ii. inter-entity spatial relationships, and iii. spatial constraints so as to produce a coherent, presentable world. Essentially, we used our experience in generalized spatio-temporal modelling to address the simpler issue of developing an authoring tool for rooms. The data model includes objects, spatial relationships between objects and constraints stemming from the real world limitations that the model must address. There are five different object classes. A vector of dimensions fully defines an instance of a class (i.e. actual object). Each object is also placed in the room by an additional vector of placement data.

In Table 1 the reader may see the classes of objects along with their size-related attributes and their domotic attributes:

Another issue is the placement of the objects in the context of the room. We aim at the definition of a set of primitives that define in a declarative way the relative placement of objects. In Table 2 we give the placement attributes describing the inter-object spatial relationship within the room spatial composition.

Table 1. Size and domotic related attributes of object classes

Object-Type	Attributes
Room	Length, Width, Height, Temperature controller, Light controller
Door	Width, Height, opening/closing motor
Window	Width, Height, opening/closing motor, blind opening/closing motor
Furniture	Item Length, Width, Height
Appliance	Length, Width, Height

Table 2. Placement-related attributes of object classes

Object-Type	Attributes
Room	<none>
Door	OnWallName, Distance, FromWallName
Window	OnWallName, Distance, FromWallName, HeightFromFloor
Furniture	Distance1, FromWall1, Distance2, FromWall2, OrientationAngle,HeightChoice, [FromItem	Height]
Appliance	Distance1, FromWall1, Distance2, FromWall2, OrientationAngle,HeightChoice, [FromItem	Height]

The aim is the retrieval of objects and their placement in a virtual room. The authoring tool is used to specify the room (dimensions, colours etc), and the objects in the room (size and placement). The specification of the room is a three-step process: i. definition of the room shape, dimensions and colour, ii. placement of doors and windows and iii. placement of any other object inside the room. In the current version of the room editor, the room is rectangular; thus three parameters (length, width and height) are required. The four walls are identified as front, left, back and right. Doors and windows have size (width and height). Their placement is defined by the wall they are on and the distance from another wall (plus distance from floor for windows). For example: "window W1 is on the left wall and 5m from the front wall, 1m from floor and has the B1 blind controller motor". The list of the available objects (sensors/actuators) is read from the database

By employing a wall identifier and a value that represents distance from the wall in consideration we define the position of Doors and Windows. For window objects, the height with reference to the floor is also required. Furniture Items and Domestic Appliances require the following attributes for their full specification:

· Position of their geometric centre's projection on the ground plan (two distances from perpendicular walls).
· Orientation Angle, a rotation of the object around a vertical axis passing through the object's geometric centre
· Height information: the object is at a specific height, or "on the floor" or "from the ceiling" or "on" another item.

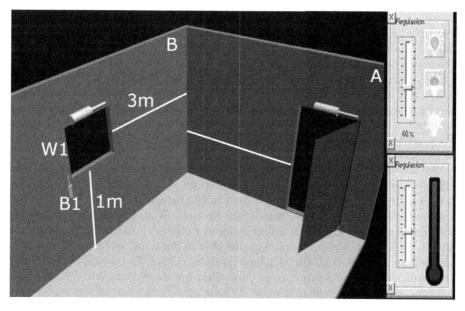

Fig. 2. VRML/X3D obtained scene from an STEDEL file and using controls retrieved from a domotics supplier DB

The use of high-level declarative predicates defined in the STEDEL data model provides expressive power but allows for inconsistencies. Thus we have to consider the related integrity constraints. The constraints arise both from the geometric configuration of the objects and/or from the attached semantics (i.e. some objects are pieces of furniture while others are appliances).

Explicit referential constraints we check in our design are:

1. All object dimensions must be less or equal than the dimensions of the room.

2. The physical dimensions and placement of objects must not allow part of them to be outside the room

3. The intersection of any pair of objects must be either empty or at most of a surface. Objects cannot intrude into one another, since they are solids.

4. Each object must have at least one common surface with another object or with the room (no objects suspended in mid-air).

5. Furniture items may be placed on other furniture items, but not on domestic appliances.

6. Upon removal of an object, all objects that are "on" that object must revert to a consistent position. Our solution was to place all such objects "on the floor".

7. Cyclic placements of objects "on" each other are not allowed.

Figure 2 shows the VRML/X3D obtained scene.

4 Conclusions and Future Work

We have presented ongoing work which aims to make a step forward in advanced domotic systems and specific intelligent interfaces for shared virtual spaces that represent real world situations.

We have designed and implemented STEDEL, a system that allows the interactive design of a room, defining each object in the room, its size, position, and spatial relationships with the room or other objects. Once the model is validated, it is possible to transform it into an X3D set of files (leveraged in the framework of an XML-based Web, encoding information about the objects in a hierarchical fashion to provide semantics) and a control module.

We will work towards integrating sematics in the proposed environment and specifically aspects such as: information organization, and comparability. Encoding information about resources in a manner that can be read and understood by human and software inteligent agents is the basis of the Semantic Web. We consider challenging the transition from a high level language descriptor to a VR modelling language like VRML or X3D, it is also interesting to be able to make the inverse path, that is to obtain from a VRML/X3D file(s), a high level description. This would allow to loose too much detailed information from these files, transform them into related object information files, and to be able to do different operations (comparison, recognition, integration, etc…) with them.

Acknowledgements

This work was supported by the project INEVAI 3D,TIN2004-07926, of Spanish Government.

References

1. A. Kay, D.A. Smith, D. P. Reed, A. Raab, J. Lombardi, M.P. McCahill. *The Croquet Committee,* Web site: http://www.opencroquet.org.
2. Zhang, Z., Shen, W., Ghenniwa, H.: A review of Internet-based product information sharing and visualization. Computers in Industry, Volume 54, Issue 1, (May 2004) 1-15
3. R. Dachselt, M. Hinz and K. Meissner : CONTIGRA: an XML- based architecture for component oriented 3D applications. In Proceedings of the Web3D 2002 Symposium, ACM SIGGRAPH.
4. V. Geroimenko, C. Chen (Eds): Visualizing Information Using SVG and X3D. Springer-Verlag (2005)
5. M. Vazirgiannis.: Interactive Multimedia Documents A Modeling, Authoring and Rendering Approach. Springer-Verlag, LNCS Series (1999)
6. I. Lazaridis, M. Vazirgiannis, T. Sellis.: The STEDEL: a language for interactive spatio-temporal compositions. IEEE International Conference on Multimedia and Expo (2001) 136-139
7. A.I Molina, M.A. Redondo & M. Ortega: Virtual Reality for teaching domotics. IADIS Applied Computing, Lisbon, Portugal (2004)
8. Bruce I. Varlamis, M. Vazirgiannis, I. Lazaridis, M. Papageorgiou, T. Panayiotopoulos: Distributed Virtual Reality Authoring Interfaces for the WWW: the VRSHOP case. IEEE International Conference on Multimedia and Expo,) (2000) 191-194

Agents with Personality for Videogames

Diana Arellano Távara and Andreas Meier

Universidad Simon Bolivar
Sartenejal, Baruta, Miranda State – PC 89000
Caracas, Venezuela
arellano@ldc.usb.ve, meier@usb.ve

Abstract. This paper describes the design and implementation of a module of emotions and personality for synthetic actors. Here are presented the results of previous researches, which were the basis of this project. With this information, a model for emotion generation using personality traits was designed in three stages, and implemented using fuzzy logic, FSMs, and probability theory. Finally, the functionalities of the module were shown using a demo version implemented with the videogame engine *Unreal® 2 Runtime*.

Keywords: artificial intelligence, agents, personality, emotion, motivational state, mood, action, attitude, actor, behavior, fuzzy set, standard, event, interactive narrative, map, Unreal, memory, goal, fuzzy rules.

1 Introduction

During the last years, Arts and Computer Science are two fields that have became more related, giving as a result what has been called, *virtual art.*

VIDGAM is an ambitious project whose objective is to allow the player/user to create stories from the interactions between the characters and their environment, and among the characters. Each story will be different depending on the approach of the player and the course of actions that each character may take. To achieve it, VIDGAM was seen as a videogame with narrative elements. In order to create these stories, it is necessary to provide of psychological features to the videogame characters, so they can act and react in a believable manner.

This paper explains the design and construction of a module of emotions and personality, its components, and finally a short overview of a demonstrative version is given, as well as the conclusions and recommendations for future works.

2 Previous Work

The more important computational models for emotion, personality, and conversational agents simulation used as reference during the development of module of personality and emotions were, among others: OCC Model [8], *OCEAN* Model [4], [6], Oz Project [9], "A Model for Personality and Emotion Simulation", from the University of Geneva [6], *FLAME* [10], and ParleE [5].

F.J. Perales and R.B. Fisher (Eds.): AMDO 2006, LNCS 4069, pp. 484–493, 2006.
© Springer-Verlag Berlin Heidelberg 2006

3   Development Stages

The module of emotions and personality (MEP) was developed in three stages or phases: initial phase, design phase, and construction phase.

For the initial phase the requirements for the project were specified: perception of events occurred in the world, appraisal of these events, generation of emotions, trigger behaviors, interaction among characters, and action taking by the characters.

The techniques that were decided to use were Fuzzy Logic, because it allows decision making and a smooth transition between states; and Finite State Machines (FSM), which allows the simulation of basic animations (running, walking) and the representation of some behaviors. The programming of the AI component was made using *Unreal Script Language*, the programming language of the Unreal engine.

The second phase, the design phase, started with the representation of the problem by doing a conceptual model and a class diagram. Then we defined which emotions, personality traits, and motivational states were going to be implemented in the module. Section 4 gives a detailed explanation of the implementation of the module.

Finally, during the construction phase the elements of the MEP were implemented. These are explained in the following subsections.

3.1   Desirability of an Event

The value of how desire an event is may be inferred from impact of events on goals, and the importance of these goals. The impact and importance are discrete values stored in tables which are defined in the classes that implement the memory of each character. Desirability belongs to a fuzzy set for the aims that are wanted. In order to achieve this, impact and importance values must be fuzzified.

Impact of an event is represented by the fuzzy sets: VERY_POSITIVE, SLIGHTLY_POSITIVE, NO_ IMPACT, SLIGHTLY_NEGATIVE, VERY_NEGATIVE. Importance of goals is represented by the fuzzy sets: NO_IMPORTANT, SLIGHTLY_IMPORTANT, VERY_IMPORTANT.

Desirability values belong to some of these fuzzy sets: VERY_DESIRABLE, SLIGHTLY_DESIRABLE, NEUTRAL, SLIGHTLY_UNDESIRABLE, VERY_UN-DESIRABLE.

As each set is represented by a triangular function, this could be defined with straight lines. Given the straight line equation $y = mx + b$, where m is the gradient, b is the interception point with Y axis, and x is the discrete value of impact of an event; x is evaluated in the straight line equations that form the triangle in the interval of x. The triangular function of the interval is the fuzzy set of x. The value of y is the membership value of x in that set.

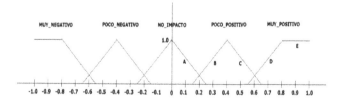

Fig. 1. Fuzzy sets for IMPACT of Events on Goals

The straight line equations used for the Impact of Events sets were:

A: $y = -4x + 1$ **B:** $y = 4x - 0.65$ **C:** $y = -4x + 2.6$ **D:** $y = 4x - 2.2$ **E:** $y = 1.0$ (1)

The following figure shows the triangular functions obtained from equations (**1**): The straight line equations used for the Importance of goals sets were:

A: $y = 1.0$ **B:** $y = -5x + 2$ **C:** $y = 5x - 1.55$

(2)

D: $y = -5x + 3.55$ **E:** $y = 5x - 3.1$ **F:** $y = 1.0$

The following figure shows the triangular functions obtained from equations (**2**):

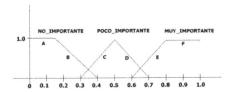

Fig. 2. Fuzzy sets for IMPORTANCE of a Goal

If x is mapped to an interval where two fuzzy sets are overlapped, then x belongs to both sets because it will be evaluated in both straight lines of both sets. The same procedure described before was used for the calculation of Importance of goals.

3.2 Fuzzy Rules

To implement the evaluation of the degree to which each one of these fuzzy rules is "true", we followed a method that assigned a number to each antecedent so that when they are summed in all possible combinations, the result was different in each case. The resulting number corresponds to the number of the fuzzy rule that is going to be evaluated [11]. Fifteen fuzzy rules were defined, which are of the form: *If* Impact = VERY_NEGATIVE AND Importance = NO_IMPORTANT *Then* Desirability = NEUTRAL. They are shown in the following table with the assigned numbers:

Table 1. Fuzzy rules for Desirability of an Event

		IMPACTS				
	Desirability	**VERY_NEG** (0)	**SLIGHTLY_NEG** (1)	**NO_IMPACT** (2)	**SLIGHTLY_POS** (3)	**VERY_POS** (4)
I M P O R T A N C E S	**NO_IMPORTANT** (0)	NEUTRAL (0)	NEUTRAL (1)	NEUTRAL (2)	NEUTRAL (3)	NEUTRAL (4)
	SLIGHTLY_IMPORT (5)	SLIGHTLY_UNDES (5)	SLIGHTLY_UNDES (6)	NEUTRAL (7)	SLIGHTLY_DES (8)	POCO_DES (9)
	VERY_IMPORT (10)	VERY_UNDES (10)	SLIGHTLY_UNDES (11)	NEUTRAL (12)	SLIGHTLY_DES (13)	VERY_DES (14)

3.3 Defuzzification

For defuzzification the "centroid" method was used, in which the "center of mass" of the result provides the crisp value [19]. The formula to find the center of mass is:

$$CM = \frac{\sum_{i=1} mu(i) * output(i)}{\sum_{i=1} mu(i)} \tag{3}$$

Where $mu(i)$ is the truth value of the result membership function for rule i, and $output(i)$ is the value, for rule i. The result membership function is maximum over the output variable fuzzy set range [19].

For this last term the maximum output values were calculated. These were: VERY_UNDESIRABLE = -0.8, SLIGHTLY_UNDESIRABLE = -0.4, VERY_DESI-RABLE = 0.8, SLIGHTLY_DESIRABLE = 0.4, NEUTRAL = 0.0. They represent the highest point of the triangular function that defines each set.

3.4 Expectations of an Event to Occur

To implement the calculation of expectations using probabilities, we created a table in the class that simulates the memory of the character.

When a pattern is observed for the first time, an entry is created in the table, and a counter initialized in 1 ($C = 1$) is assigned to it. Then, every time an event is appraised, the sequences are stored with their respective counter. If a sequence that was already stored is detected, then its counter is incremented in one (+1). This counter is used for the calculation of the probability of a new event Z to occur, given that events X and Y already occurred: $P(Z|X,Y)$ [10].

Table 2. Formulas used in the calculation of emotion

SINGLE EMOTIONS	FORMULA	SIMPLE EMOTIONS	FORMULA
Happiness	$d_i * sqrt(1 - e_i)$	Sadness	$(d_i * (-1)) * (1 - e_i) * (1 - e_i)$
Satisfaction	$d_i * sqrt(1 - e_i)$	Disillusion	$(d_i * -1) * (1 - e_i) * (1 - e_i)$
Pride	$Pride_i = d$	Shame	$Shame_i = d_i * (-1)$
Admiration	$d_i * a(Agent) * (1 - e_i)$	Reprobation	$d_i * (1 - a(Agent)) * (1 - e_i)$
Liking	$Liking_{i-1} + 0.1 * d_i$	Disliking	$Disliking_{i-1} + 0.1 * (d_i * (-1))$
COMPLEX EMOTIONS	FORMULA		
Gratitude	If $abs(Admiration_i - Happiness_i) > 0.2$, then $Gratitude_i = 0$ If not, $Gratitude_i = max(Admiration_i, Happiness_i)$		
Anger	If $abs(Sadness_i - Reprobation_i) > 0.2$, then $Anger_i = 0$ If not, $Anger_i = max(Sadness_i, Reprobation_i)$		
Gratification	If $abs(Pride_i - Happiness_i) > 0.2$, then $Gratification_i = 0$ If not, $Gratification_i = max(Pride_i, Happiness_i)$		
Remorse	If $abs(Sadness_i - Shame_i) > 0.2$, then $Remorse_i = 0$ If not, $Remorse_i = max(Sadness_i, Shame_i)$		

3.5 Intensity of Emotions

For the calculation of this value some formulas were used, based on the values of desirability (d_i) and expectation of an event to occur (e_i), giving as a result a number between 0.0 and 1.0. Some of these formulas were obtained from [5], [10], and [7].

3.6 Behaviors and Actions of the Videogame Actors

The behavior of a character is a fuzzy set: GOOD, REGULAR, or BAD. At the end of the cycle, a vector with four (4) emotions is obtained. To decide the behavior of the agent, the two emotions with stronger intensities are considered. If both are positive emotions, then the behavior is GOOD. If one is positive and the other is negative, then the behavior is REGULAR. If both are negatives, then the behavior is BAD.

We also implemented short dialogues of the form *(f, e, r, i)*, to demonstrate verbally how the actor is behaving. *f* is the *phrase* that is going to be said, *e* is the speaker, *r* is the audience, and if what is said is a question or an answer is *i*. The content of the dialogues is maintained in the memory of the characters.

3.7 3D Scenarios and Characters

Here are shown the actors and the 3D scenarios, modeled using 3D software Maya®, inside the Unreal engine. The model of the soccer player was taken from Unreal's website, which was a mesh modeled using 3D Studio Max®.

Fig. 3. Chef Melanie (left), Soccer Player Estelle (right)

Fig. 4. Views of kitchen (left), living room (middle), bedroom(right)

4 Module of Emotions and Personality

One of the first decisions to make was to choose which emotions and personality traits the agents were going to have. Single emotions are: happiness, sadness, satisfaction, disillusion, pride, shame, admiration, reprobation, liking, and disliking.

Complex emotions, which are the combination of two single emotions are: gratitude (happiness + admiration), anger (sadness + reprobation), gratification (happiness + pride), and remorse (sadness + shame).

The motivational states used were: Hunger, Fatigue, Thirst, and Surprise.

Concerning to personality, it was decided to use *OCEAN* model [4] because of its simplicity, completeness, and because it is very used by psychologists, which guarantees its efficiency. The values set for each personality characteristic of the actors of the game are shown in table 3.

Table 3. Personality Dimensions of both actors

PERSONALITY CHARACTERISTICS		
Dimension	Melanie (Chef)	Estelle (Soccer Player)
▪ Openness	0.8 , highly open	0.8, highly open
▪ Conscientiousness	0.95, highly conscientious	0.95, highly conscientious
▪ Extraversion	0.7, almost extraverted	0.37, slightly extroverted
▪ Agreeableness	0.13, slightly agreeable	0.83, highly agreeable
▪ Neuroticism	0.69, almost neurotic	0.19, slightly neurotic

The module of emotions and personality presented in this paper consists of four components which allowed the representation of the psychological component of the agents.

4.1 Perceptual Component

Its main function is the reception of events that occur in the world. In terms of the implementation, an event is a string describing the occurrence.

Each agent has a function, ***RecibeMensaje(evento)***, that is called by all event-emitter objects in the environment (radio, tv, other agents, etc.). This function uses message passing to transmit the event from the object to the agent.

A **message** is a tuple that consists of: the event as text *(tex)*, the id of the actor that initiate the event *(id)*, and the type of the event *(eT)*.

Based on the classification given in the OCC Model, events were classified in: events that affect a **goal**, events that affect an **attitude**, and events that affect a **standard.** These are the types *(eT)* of the event.

Then, the event is passed as message to the Emotion Generation Component and to the Historical Component.

4.2 Emotion Generation Component

This component is responsible for updating the emotional state of the agent according to occurred events. It takes three stages: event appraisal, intensity of emotions, and filtering of emotions.

4.2.1 Event Appraisal

For event appraisal the parameter in the message that is used is the type of event (*eT*).
If type is META (*GOAL*), affected emotions are *happiness* or *sadness*; and
satisfaction or *desilusion*. If type is ACTITUD (*ATTITUDE*), affected emotions are
liking and *happiness*; or *disliking*. If type is STANDARD, affected emotions of the
agent who did the action are *pride* or *shame*, and *admiration or reprobation*.
Furthermore, there is an extra value that is called **appreciation,** which is the
recognition on the part of an agent, of the quality or value of another agent.

4.2.2 Calculation of Intensities of Emotions

Each emotion has its own array that stores its intensities during the last *t* instants of
time. In our case, t = 5.

Intensities in *t* − 1 (previous instant) can be interpreted as *the emotional state of
the character. How he/she feels*. Intensities in *t* (current instant) can be interpreted as
what he/she is feeling. So, if position *i* of the array *e* contains a number zero (0), then
the event did not generate emotion *e* during instant of time *i*.

4.2.3 Filtering of Emotions

This stage allows to choose the final emotions that the character will exhibit.

At the beginning of the game a matrix *Po* was defined. It has the relations between
emotions and personality traits [6]. As was said, events according to their type, can
modified different emotions. Then, it might be said that personality traits affect, or are
characterized by those emotions related to goals, attitudes, and standards, to which
those traits are related.

Using this information the matrix *Po* was built in the following way: if the
personality trait is characterized by that emotion, then the value of the cell is 0.2. If
the personality trait does not intensify the emotion, the value in the table is -0.2. And
if the trait and the emotion are not related at all, then the value is 0.

Once that *Po* is filled, it is multiplied by the vector containing all the values for
each personality trait of the agent. The result of this product is another vector whose
values will modify each emotion, according to the personality of the agent. This
vector is called "modulation vector". Update of emotions is made by increasing the
intensity of the emotion felt in the last instant of time, $e_{i,t}$, in a percentage equal to the
corresponding modulator, m_i. This is shown in equation (**4**).

$$e_{i,t} = (e_{i,t} * m_i) + e_{i,t} \tag{4}$$

This module keeps a history of the emotions felt in the last *t* =5 instants. How the
character has felt lately, which is called mood, h_i, is calculated by adding all positive
emotions intensities registered in the last *t*-1 instants, and adding all negative
emotions intensities in the last *t*-1 instants. If the sum of positive emotions is greater
than the sum of negative emotions, then the mood at time t is positive. Otherwise, the
mood is negative.

Once mood is calculated, it is seen how it affects emotions. If the agent is in a good
mood, positive emotions in the current instant are incremented in a equal percentage
to the value of mood. If the agent is in a bad mood, negative emotions of the current
instant are increased. This is expressed by equation (**5**).

$$e_{i,t} = e_{i,t} + (e_{i,t} * h_i)$$

(5)

Then, it has to take into consideration that there cannot be two opposite emotions at the same time. For example, the agent cannot feel happiness and sadness at the same time. The one with the greater value will always be chosen. Also, if in the current instant (t) the agent felt an **opposite emotion with a lower intensity** than the emotion triggered at instant t-1, then the prevailing emotion is the one felt in t-1.

Finally, the four (4) emotions with higher intensities are chosen and fuzzified. The sets that are considered in this step are: HIGH_INTENSITY, MEDIUM_INTENSITY and LOW_INTENSITY, and the membership degree is calculated using the discrete value of intensity.

4.3 Historical and Actions Components

The historical component calculates the expectation of an event to occur using probability theory. It was explained in section 3.4.

The actions component evaluates these behaviors and generates animations or short dialogues that show the emotional state of the character.

4.4 Decay

In this module, the decay, or decreasing of intensities of emotions, takes place before the evaluation of a new event, and also every 60 seconds, just in case the agent does not appraise any event during that interval of time.

Each character has two fixed constants for decay, one is used with positive emotions (*delta*) and the other is used with negative emotions (*alpha*). The interval where *delta* is defined is greater than the interval for *alpha*, because positive emotions decay faster over time than negative emotions.

First, older emotions (t=0, if the current instant is t=5) are eliminated, leaving the last position of every array free, and ready to store the new intensities. After this, each emotion is subtracted with the corresponding decay constant. As far as motivational states, hunger, thirst, and fatigue are increased in a 1/8 part of *alpha*. On the other hand, surprise is decreased using *delta*.

5 Demo

The module of emotions and personality was implemented using the videogame engine *Unreal 2Runtime*. It was used to test the functionality of the module of emotions and personality. It included two characters (Melanie and Estelle) who feel and react to events triggered by the user, as well as by objects of the world that surrounds them.

The interface of the demonstrative version has a number of menus that activates using the keyboard. This was achieved using an Unreal component named **Interaction**.

Some screenshots of the menus are shown in figure 5.

Fig. 5. Events menu (left), Actions menu (middle), HUD showing the emotions of Estelle: happiness, surprise, fatigue, disliking; and Melanie: surprise, fatigue, disliking, remorse (right)

6   Results

In order to test the module, we "played" the videogame 20 times, with different sequences of events. Each game had duration of four to six minutes. During this time it was evaluated how consistent and believable were the emotional responses of the characters.

We tried making some changes in the personality values of Melanie and Estelle, but as most of events produced positive emotions, the differences in the results were seen more clearly when the changes were produced in the variables for event appraisal and filtering.

In each game, important differences were observed. But this is not only a consequence of the differences in the personality dimensions. Occurred events and previous instants of the game lead the character to different emotional states, which affect the final result. In the same way, expectations values have a great influence in these differences.

In this demo there are several events that trigger emotions with the same intensities, because their desirability is obtained from tables where these values are fixed. Although personality traits (or dimensions) are different, it can be seen that the modulator vector affect the emotions very little. The same thing happens with short dialogues to which we already know which emotions will trigger them.

Nevertheless, we tried to add non deterministic factors to increase uncertainty. These are: calculation of expectation using probabilities, increasing and decreasing of agent's appreciation based on the standards, and including motivational states that reaching some threshold (0.8) begin to decrease felt emotions. Motivational states are increased very slowly, so the user has to play for quite a long time to see changes.

Perhaps personality traits are the less considered factor with generation of behaviors, but their use during emotion modulation was indispensable to provide the corresponding modulator and thus, increased the believability of each agent.

The module of emotions and personality works with fuzzy values for emotions intensities, which could be used to generate facial expressions and body movements.

7   Conclusions and Future Work

Providing of psychological characteristics to synthetic characters was a very complex task, which required a lot of researching, and results obtained by trial and error.

Especially for the fact that the module had to be very general but at the same time, we had to keep the individuality of each character.

This module settles the basis for the AI, taking advantage of fuzzy logic and FSMs to create characters with emotions and personality.

In general, actors react to events in a very coherent manner, they interact with basis on their predefined standards, they learn how to expect non registered events, and they can move around a virtual world, designed according to each one's likings and preferences (that is the case with the chef and her kitchen). But, in order to see the module working with a 100% of its functionalities, there are needed many more game rules, more characters, and more events that allow exploring each one of the human aspects that have been simulated.

References

1. Bartneck, C: Integrating the OCC Model of Emotions in Embodied Characters. In: Proceedings of the Workshop on Workshop on Virtual Conversational Characters: Applications, Methods, and Research Challenges, Melbourne. (2002).
2. Bates J, Loyall A.B, Reilly W.S: An architecture for action, emotion, and social behavior. In: Artificial social systems: fourth european workshop on modeling autonomous agents in a multi-agent world. Berlin Springer (1992)
3. Bates, J., Loyall, A. B.: Hap. A Reactive, Adaptive Architecture for Agents. In: Technical Report CMU-CS- 91147, Carnegie Mellon University, Pittsburgh, Pennsylvania. (1991)
4. Boeree, C. G.: Teorías de la Personalidad. In: http://www.psicologia-online.com/ebooks/personalidad/eysenck.htm
5. Bui, T. D., Heylen, D., Poel, M., Nijholt, A.: ParleE: An Adaptive Plan Based Event Appraisal Model of Emotions. In: Parlevink Internal Report, University of Twente (2002).
6. Egges, A., Kshirsagar, S., Magnenat-Thalmann, N.: A Model for Personality and Emotion Simulation. In: Knowledge-Based Intelligent Information & Engineering Systems. (2003) 453-461
7. Johns, M., Silverman, B. G.: How Emotions and Personality Effect the Utility of Alternative Decisions: A Terrorist Target Selection Case Study. In: Tenth Conference On Computer Generated Forces and Behavioral Representation. (2001)
8. Ortony, A., Clore, G.L., Collins, A.: The Cognitive Structure of Emotions. In: Cambridge University Press, Cambridge. (1988)
9. Reilly, W. S., Bates, J.: Building Emotional Agents. In: Technical Report CMU-CS-92-143, Carnegie Mellon University, Pittsburgh, Pennsylvania. (1992)
10. Seif El-Nasr, M., Yen, J., Ioerger, T. R.: FLAME - Fuzzy Logic Adaptive Model of Emotions. In: Autonomous Agents and Multi-Agent Systems, Kluwer Academic Publishers Netherlands, 3, 219-257. (2000)
11. Zarozinski, M.: An Open-Source Fuzzy Logic Library. In: *AI Programming Wisdom*. Steve Rabin, compilation. United States, Charles River Media Inc. (2002) 90-121
12. Fuzzy Control System. In: http://www.fact-index.com/f/fu/fuzzy_control_system.html

Monocular Tracking with a Mixture of View-Dependent Learned Models

Tobias Jaeggli[1], Esther Koller-Meier[1], and Luc Van Gool[1,2]

[1] ETH Zurich, D-ITET/BIWI, CH-8092 Zurich
[2] Katholieke Universiteit Leuven, ESAT/VISICS, B-3001 Leuven
jaeggli@vision.ee.ethz.ch

Abstract. This paper considers the problem of monocular human body tracking using learned models. We propose to learn the joint probability distribution of appearance and body pose using a mixture of view-dependent models. In such a way the multimodal and nonlinear relationships can be captured reliably. We formulate inference algorithms that are based on generative models while exploiting the advantages of a learned model when compared to the traditionally used geometric body models. Given static images or sequences, body poses and bounding box locations are inferred using silhouette based image descriptors. Prior information about likely body poses and a motion model are taken into account. We consider analytical computations and Monte-Carlo techniques, as well as a combination of both. In a Rao-Blackwellised particle filter, the tracking problem is partitioned into a part that is solved analytically, and a part that is solved with particle filtering. Tracking results are reported for human locomotion.

1 Introduction

Bayesian approaches have been successfully applied to human body tracking. Typically, these approaches are generative and need a mechanism to predict a subject's appearance given hypotheses for the parameters that are to be estimated.

Previous tracking algorithms often work with hand-crafted geometric body models that are rendered and compared to input images in order to verify body pose hypotheses (*e.g.* [1,2,3,4,5]). These body models have many parameters such as limb lengths and widths that all have to be known or estimated, typically in an initialisation procedure or even on-the-fly.

As opposed to geometrical models, probabilistic Machine Learning methods naturally offer the possibility to learn the dependencies of body pose and its appearance while generalising over irrelevant variation of appearance and inter-person variance.

Core of the proposed approach is a model of the statistical dependencies between body poses and their appearance, which is learned from training data. We show how the learning problem itself can be alleviated by uncoupling global orientation and local body pose, and learn the joint distribution over pose and appearance as a mixture of view-dependent models. Within a view-dependent model, the distribution is captured by the means of Gaussian Mixture Models (GMMs).

The Recursive Bayesian Filter serves as an overall framework for inference. Appearance is encoded using image descriptors that are computed from the silhouette of

F.J. Perales and R.B. Fisher (Eds.): AMDO 2006, LNCS 4069, pp. 494–503, 2006.
© Springer-Verlag Berlin Heidelberg 2006

background segmented images. Silhouettes provide rich information about body pose, but leave certain aspects unobservable, *i.e.* are subject to ambiguities. This enforces the use of prior information on one hand, and will lead to multimodal posteriors on the other hand.

1.1 Related Work

There is a wide variety of literature about probabilistic body tracking. Most methods use geometric body models (*e.g.* [1,2,3,4]), sometimes in conjunction with learning techniques for dimensionality reduction or to estimate parameters of the prior or observation model. Example based approaches (*e.g.* [6]) are often based on nearest neighbour search and provide mechanisms for efficient lookup in large databases. Several authors have applied parametric machine learning methods to body pose estimation [7,8,9,10,11] and aim at learning the relationship between image observations and body pose, which is challenging because the mapping is nonlinear and multivalued. The further discussion will concentrate on these works.

In [7] the authors assume a functional relationship between silhouette descriptors and pose and propose relevance vector regression for learning. Grauman *et al.* [10] learn a density over multiple silhouettes and corresponding structure using a mixture of PPCA. Given a (static) set of silhouettes, the MAP estimate is obtained. Recently, inference algorithms that explicitly deal with multimodal posterior distributions have been applied to the body tracking problem. In the specialized mappings architecture [12], multiple functional mappings from visual features to articulated pose are learned. Inference yields a set of hypotheses, a problem specific method is then used to compute the likelihood of the different hypotheses. Most related to our work are [8] and [11] that both learn the conditional pdf of pose and appearance with a mixture of regressors (experts).

In [11] the temporal dependencies and image-pose dependencies are learned in a single discriminative model. The distributions are propagated analytically. In [8], a pdf over possible poses is inferred given an input silhouette. The analytical inference procedure does not include any temporal aspects. For tracking, a particle filter in high dimensions is used, where the inferred pdf is treated as the observation likelihood. The algorithms proposed in this paper follow well known generative formulations, however we propose solutions that are based both on sampling techniques and analytical inference where applicable, thereby avoiding the need to sample in high dimensions.

To summarise, this paper mainly contributes by explicitly addressing the issue of learning appearance from all view directions while allowing for multimodalities of the distribution. Analytic solutions to the generative formulation of the tracking problem are proposed, and a Rao-Blackwellised particle filter that combines the advantages of sample-based and analytic inference. Furthermore, since we learn the joint pdf of pose and appearance, rather than the conditional, we can use this model to estimate the 2d image position of the bounding box along with the body pose, an issue not addressed in [8,11].

The paper is organised as follows. Section 2 introduces the mixture of view-dependent models, and 3 formulates tracking algorithms based on the learned models. In 4 we describe our implementation and show experimental results and conclude in sect. 5.

2   Mixture of View-Dependent Models

We want to learn the dependencies of body pose and its appearance in images. The state space for the body pose is given by the variables α and $\mathbf{x}$, the global orientation of the body relative to the camera and its local pose, *i.e.* the configuration of its limbs. Under the assumption that the camera is in an approximatively horizontal position, at face or shoulder level, the global orientation can be described with a single parameter that determines the position on a circle around the object from which the latter is observed. We therefore face the problem of learning the joint pdf $p(\alpha, \mathbf{x}, \mathbf{y})$, where $\mathbf{y}$ is an observation, *i.e.* a descriptor that is computed the input image. In order to simplify the learning problem, we rewrite this pdf as a mixture of C view-dependent models p_c that each cover a section of possible view directions/global orientations.

$$p(\alpha, \mathbf{x}, \mathbf{y}) = \frac{1}{C} \sum_{c=1}^{C} p_c(\alpha, \mathbf{x}, \mathbf{y}) \tag{1}$$

Within the view-dependent models, there is little variation of view direction, so the view angle can be assumed independent from local pose and observation, which enables us to rewrite equation (1) as

$$p(\alpha, \mathbf{x}, \mathbf{y}) = \frac{1}{C} \sum_{c=1}^{C} p_c(\alpha) p_c(\mathbf{x}, \mathbf{y}), \tag{2}$$

where $p_c(\alpha)$ is a one-dimensional Gaussian $\mathcal{N}(\alpha; \alpha_c, \sigma)$[1] and $p_c(\mathbf{x}, \mathbf{y})$ is the joint pdf of pose and appearance for a certain view direction; this pdf will be learned from training data. Within a view-dependent model the view angles are normally distributed around the mean α_c, with α_c's uniformly spaced over the interval $[0, 2\pi[$, and variances chosen such that adjacent models overlap, and the whole domain of α is uniformly covered.

The view-dependent models $p_c(\mathbf{x}, \mathbf{y})$ themselves are approximated by a mixture of Gaussians (GMM), estimated using *e.g.* an EM algorithm. The joint distribution over orientation, pose and appearance is thus a mixture of mixtures of Gaussians.

$$p(\alpha, \mathbf{x}, \mathbf{y}) = \frac{1}{C} \sum_{c=1}^{C} \left[p_c(\alpha) \sum_{s=1}^{S} w_{c,s} \mathcal{N}(\mu_{c,s}, \Sigma_{c,s}) \right] \tag{3}$$

Here, S is the number of Gaussian components in each p_c, and $w_{c,s}$ are the weights estimated by the EM algorithm in the learning phase ($\sum_{s=1}^{S} w_{c,s} = 1$). $\mu_{c,s}$ and $\Sigma_{c,s}$ are the parameters of the Gaussian components.

Note that even though the omnidirectional model $p(\alpha, \mathbf{x}, \mathbf{y})$ consists of a discrete number of almost unidirectional models, we have defined a smooth and continuous overall model that covers the entire state space.

---

[1] We use the notation $\mathcal{N}(x; \mu, \sigma)$ for Gaussian distributions, where the first argument is omitted if clear from the context.

3   Tracking with Learned Models

According to Bayes' rule, the tracking problem can be formulated as

$$p(\mathbf{X}_t|\mathbf{y}_{1:t}) \propto p(\mathbf{y}_t|\mathbf{X}_t)p(\mathbf{X}_t|\mathbf{y}_{1:t-1}), \tag{4}$$

where $\mathbf{X}_t$ is the state variable we want to infer from aggregated observations $\mathbf{y}_{1:t}$ ($\mathbf{X}_t = [\mathbf{x}_t, \alpha_t]^T$ for the notation of Sect. 2). The image likelihood is obtained from our learned model of $p(\mathbf{X}, \mathbf{y})$ by

$$p(\mathbf{y}_t|\mathbf{X}_t) = p(\mathbf{X}_t, \mathbf{y}_t)/p(\mathbf{X}_t). \tag{5}$$

As we have not learned the temporal prior $p(\mathbf{X}_t|\mathbf{X}_{t-1})$ explicitly, we would like to include information about likely body poses as well as a motion model in its definition. We model the temporal behaviour as a Brownian motion around the expected new position multiplied by the time independent prior $p(\mathbf{X}_t)$. See Fig. 1a) for an illustration.

$$p(\mathbf{X}_t|\mathbf{X}_{t-1}) := k(\mathbf{X}_{t-1})p(\mathbf{X}_t)\mathcal{N}(A\mathbf{X}_{t-1}, \Sigma_T) \tag{6}$$

Here, A specifies the linear dependencies between subsequent states, and $k(\mathbf{X}_{t-1}) = \int_{X_t} p(\mathbf{X}_t)\mathcal{N}(A\mathbf{X}_{t-1}, \Sigma_T)$ is a normalisation factor. Using this definition, we obtain

$$p(\mathbf{X}_t|\mathbf{y}_{1:t-1}) = \int_{x_{t-1}} p(\mathbf{X}_t|\mathbf{X}_{t-1})p(\mathbf{X}_{t-1}|\mathbf{y}_{1:t-1})$$

$$= \int_{x_{t-1}} k(\mathbf{X}_{t-1})p(\mathbf{X}_t)\mathcal{N}(A\mathbf{X}_{t-1}, \Sigma_T)p(\mathbf{X}_{t-1}|\mathbf{y}_{1:t-1}). \tag{7}$$

The factor $k(\mathbf{X}_{t-1})$ depends on $\mathbf{X}_{t-1}$ which makes analytic integration intractable; it can however be computed explicitly in a sampling based approach. We propose a slightly different definition that is suitable for both analytic and Monte-Carlo integration.

$$p(\mathbf{X}_t|\mathbf{y}_{1:t-1}) := Kp(\mathbf{X}_t)\int_{x_{t-1}} \mathcal{N}(A\mathbf{X}_{t-1}, \Sigma_T)p(\mathbf{X}_{t-1}|\mathbf{y}_{1:t-1}) \tag{8}$$

This formulation corresponds to first propagating the old posterior according to the motion model, and then eliminating unlikely body poses. Both (7) and (8) define a pdf over $\mathbf{X}_t$ that takes into account temporal as well as static prior information.

By combining (4), (5) and prior (8), $\mathbf{X}_t$ can now be inferred analytically for any given sequence.

$$p(\mathbf{X}_t|\mathbf{y}_{1:t}) \propto p(\mathbf{y}_t|\mathbf{X}_t)p(\mathbf{X}_t)\int_{X_{t-1}} \mathcal{N}(\mathbf{X}_t; A\mathbf{X}_{t-1}, \Sigma_T)p(\mathbf{X}_{t-1}|\mathbf{y}_{1:t-1})$$

$$= p(\mathbf{X}_t, \mathbf{y}_t)\int_{X_{t-1}} \mathcal{N}(\mathbf{X}_t; A\mathbf{X}_{t-1}, \Sigma_T)p(\mathbf{X}_{t-1}|\mathbf{y}_{1:t-1}). \tag{9}$$

In order to account for noisy observations, the term $p(\mathbf{X}_t, \mathbf{y}_t)$ is computed by multiplying the learned model with a Gaussian pdf around the actual observation for $\mathbf{y}_t$, denoted $\mathbf{y}_{obs}$, and then marginalising over $\mathbf{y}_t$. This is illustrated in Fig. 1b). Marginalisation of a

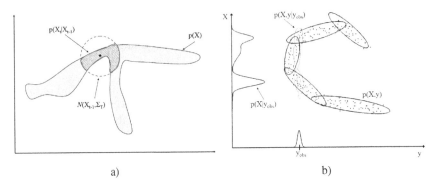

Fig. 1. a) The overall prior (red, hatched) is defined as the product of the motion model (blue, dashed, for this illustration a Gaussian pdf around the state of $t - 1$) and the static learned prior $p(\mathbf{X})$. b) Multiplication of the Gaussian distribution around the observation $\mathbf{y}_{obs}$ and the prior $p(\mathbf{X}, \mathbf{y})$ yields $p(\mathbf{X}, \mathbf{y}|\mathbf{y}_{obs})$. By marginalisation, the pdf $p(\mathbf{X}|\mathbf{y}_{obs})$ over unobserved variables is then obtained. Note the multimodality of $p(\mathbf{X}|\mathbf{y}_{obs})$.

GMM is straightforward; the marginal mixture has the same number of Gaussian components as the original joint mixture with the same weights. The means and covariances of the marginal mixture are simply the means and covariances of the original mixture with all elements corresponding to the variable $\mathbf{y}$ removed.

The integral in Eq. (9) can be calculated in closed form and will result in a Gaussian mixture, so the result of (9) is the product of two mixtures and thus a mixture itself. However, the number of mixture components will grow exponentially over time. Hence, at each timestep a mixture simplification step reduces the number of Gaussian components, by pruning components with very low weights and replacing clusters of components by their 'average' Gaussian.

3.1   Rao-Blackwellised Particle Filter

So far we assumed that an observation is available in the form of an image descriptor computed at a certain position in the image. This requires that the bounding box containing the person is either known on beforehand or estimated in some way. For the silhouette based image descriptor, one could imagine an ad-hoc algorithm for this 2d tracking problem. In general, however, we want to support multiple hypotheses for the 2d location variables l, so they have to be included in our state space and inferred by the overall tracking algorithm. A particle based approach can easily be extended accordingly by adding these location-variables to the state space. In the case of an analytic approach however, there is no straightforward extension since the posterior over this extended state space is unlikely to have parametric form. We therefore propose to partition our state space into a part that is solved using a particle filter and a part that is solved analytically using our learned models. By the chain rule of probability, the posterior over $\mathbf{x}$, α, and the location variable l can be written as

$$p(\mathbf{x}, \alpha, \mathbf{l}|\mathbf{y}) = p(\mathbf{x}|\alpha, \mathbf{l}, \mathbf{y})p(\alpha, \mathbf{l}|\mathbf{y}), \qquad (10)$$

where the temporal aspects of the problem are omitted for notational simplicity. Given our learned model, $p(\mathbf{x}|\alpha, \mathbf{l}, \mathbf{y})$ can be inferred analytically and described parametrically, whereas for $p(\alpha, \mathbf{l}|\mathbf{y})$ no analytic solution is obvious. However, due to its low dimensionality, it can be handled by a particle filter. The Rao-Blackwellised Particle Filter (RBPF, [13]) offers a framework for inference, when a part of the state space can be marginalised analytically. Figure 2 a) shows the graphical structure of this setting as a Bayesian network.

In RBPF, each particle will consist of a sample for $\mathbf{l}_t$ and α_t, a parametric pdf $p(\mathbf{x}_t|\mathbf{y}_{1:t}, \mathbf{l}_{1:t}^i, \alpha_{1:t}^i)$ and a weight w_t^i. The computation of $p(\mathbf{x}_t|\mathbf{y}_{1:t}, \mathbf{l}_{1:t}^i, \alpha_{1:t}^i)$ follows the general derivation for analytic density propagation (9), except that we only infer the variable $\mathbf{x}_t$, and that the expression is additionally conditioned on $\alpha_{1:t}^i$ and $\mathbf{l}_{1:t}^i$. We will denote as $\mathbf{y}_t^i$ the image descriptor computed at sampled location $\mathbf{l}_t^i$.

$$p(\mathbf{x}_t|\mathbf{y}_{1:t}^i, \alpha_{1:t}^i) = \frac{1}{L_i} p(\mathbf{y}_t^i|\mathbf{x}_t, \alpha_t^i) p(\mathbf{x}_t|\mathbf{y}_{1:t-1}^i, \alpha_{1:t-1}^i)$$

$$\propto \frac{K_i}{L_i} p(\mathbf{x}_t, \alpha_t^i, \mathbf{y}_t^i) \int_{x_{t-1}} \mathcal{N}(\mathbf{x}_t; A\mathbf{x}_{t-1}, \Sigma_T) p(\mathbf{x}_{t-1}|\mathbf{y}_{1:t-1}^i, \alpha_{1:t-1}^i)$$

$$(11)$$

Here we used the independence of $\mathbf{x}_t$ and α_t^i and the uniformity of $p(\alpha_t^i)$. K_i is the scaling factor from the prior (8), and the normalisation factor L_i is equal to the likelihood of the observation given the ith sample. Hence, if we choose the prior $p(\mathbf{l}_t, \alpha_t|\mathbf{l}_{t-1}, \alpha_{t-1})$ as a proposal function, the weights w_t^i are given by the normalisation factor L_i [13].

The RBPF harmonizes well with the mixture of view-dependent models; for the computation of $p(\mathbf{x}_t, \alpha_t^i, \mathbf{y}_t^i)$ in (11) we can exclude those mixture components that are not compatible with the hypothesis α_t^i, i.e that will have a very low weight in the posterior mixture. This decreases computation time per sample significantly.

4   Implementation and Experimentation

The previous sections are kept general with respect to the used image descriptors, the body pose parametrisation and the classes of motion for which the system is trained. In this section we present an implementation and experimental validation that serve as a proof of concept and aim at illustrating the potential of the overall approach. We chose human locomotion as a case in point, but expect that an extension to more general motions is feasible provided that such training data are available.

4.1   Image and Pose Descriptors

The chosen image descriptors are based on the silhouette of the tracked person. Using a stationary camera, the segmentation is obtained via background subtraction. To encode these segmented images using a descriptor of moderate size, we use signed distance functions, that assign to each pixel a signed value indicating the distance to the closest point on the silhouette [9]. These values are computed on a grid of equidistantly spaced sample points inside the bounding box of the segmented object. Several examples of such distance-transformed silhouettes are shown in Fig. 2 b).

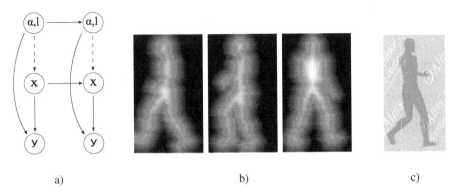

Fig. 2. a) Graphical structure obtained by partitioning the search space into two parts. This is the setting in which the Rao-Blackwellised particle filter operates. b) Signed distance functions as image descriptors. Positive values inside the silhouette, negative values outside, and 0 on the silhouette, rescaled here to the interval 0:255 for visualisation. c) Animated 3D body model (training data).

To compute this distance transform efficiently we use an algorithm similar to the chamfer image transform based on a hybrid distance measure that is an approximation to the real Euclidean distance. See [14] for an overview of algorithms.

Both image descriptors y and pose descriptors x are potentially high dimensional; this is a difficulty for the learning task. Furthermore we believe that the intrinsic dimensionality of the training data is much lower. A dimensionality reduction step is necessary. Here, we use PCA to bring down the dimensionality of both image and pose descriptor.

4.2   Experiments

To generate training data for this experiment, we rendered 11 MoCap[2] sequences from several subjects with different walking styles from 36 viewpoints using MotionBuilder PLE[3], a package that is designed for realistic human animation. On the silhouettes of these renderings, the image descriptors were computed, followed by a PCA dimensionality reduction that retained the first 15 principal components. The body pose was represented using 3d joint locations for a number of joints that constitute the overall body pose (foot, knee, hip, shoulder, elbow, hand and head). Only the first 15 principal components, capturing about 99 percent of the variation, were retained for the final pose representation. For each view dependent model, the joint distribution of appearance and pose descriptors was approximated by a GMM with 11 components using an EM algorithm.

Using a plain particle filter in combination with this pose representation would require a large number of particles. Here we report results that were obtained using the algorithm from sect. 3.1, where a part of the inference problem is solved analytically.

---

[2] Data obtained from http://mocap.cs.cmu.edu/

[3] www.alias.com

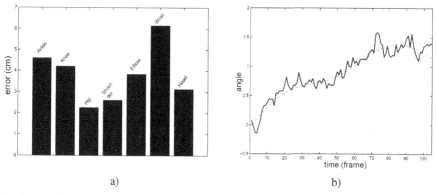

a)   b)

Fig. 3. a) Deviation from ground truth for a synthetic sequence. Euclidean distance (centimeters) between reconstructed joints and the ground truth, averaged over the sequence. The error is largest at the extremities (ankle, wrist). b) Estimated view directions α (radians) for a synthetic sequence with ground truth (dashed curve). The figure shows the angle encoded by the sample with the highest weight.

Samples for l and α are generated from a temporal prior that assumes constant velocity resp. Brownian motion. The temporal model for pose **x** assumed Brownian motion in PCA-reduced pose space, with a covariance matrix learned from the training data. For the initialisation of the 2d location variables l, an ad hoc proposal function at the center of gravity of the segmented image was used to sample from, **x** and α were initialised using the analytical inference equation (9), by assuming a uniform temporal prior.

Some quantitative results are shown in Fig. 3 a), for a sequence that was synthetically generated the same way as the training data, but using MoCap from a subject not contained in the training set.

Figure 4 shows tracking through a real office sequence. The images were recorded with a DV camera at a frame rate of 25 fps and segmentation was obtained using background subtraction. The reconstructed poses and motion look natural. Occasionally (*e.g.* frame c), the reconstruction of the arms is imprecise, especially when they are occluded by the torso, *i.e.* not visible in the silhouette images. In such cases the pose prior alone is responsible for the estimation of the arm pose. Figure 3 b) shows the estimated view direction for a synthetic sequence with varying viewpoint. The reconstruction follows the overall rotation of the person. Largest deviation from ground truth is about 15 degrees (frame 73), the average error is 5 degrees. However there seems to be no systematic misestimation since the mean difference from ground truth is only 1 degree, the negative and positive deviations basically sum to zero. These results are very convincing, when considering that it is very difficult, even for humans, to perceive the relative orientation of a body from the silhouette alone.

5   Summary and Conclusion

We presented a system for monocular tracking of people. From a MoCap training database distributions over body pose and corresponding image appearance descriptors

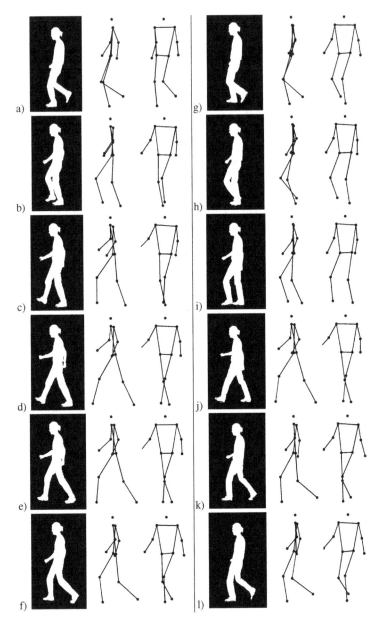

Fig. 4. Tracking through a real sequence. For each of the selected frames, the left column shows the tracked bounding box. The other columns show the estimated pose from side view resp. 45 degrees. To visualise a single pose per frame, we chose the mean of the component with the highest weight from the GMM that corresponds to the sample with the highest weight of the sample set. Note that between frame i) and j) the posterior mode that corresponds to stepping forward with the left leg suddenly becomes more likely, which can only be seen from the 45 degree view.

(silhouettes) are learned. Based on the learned model we were able to formulate generative tracking algorithms that either work with analytical inference or particle sets or a combination (Rao-Blackwellised particle filter). Compared to approaches with geometrical models, we do not have to sample in high dimensions, and in contrast to purely discriminative learning based approaches, we can solve to 2d bounding box tracking along with the pose estimation. The algorithms were evaluated on synthetic and real sequences of walking people.

Future research directions will include the investigation of different image descriptors that do not require a foreground segmentation. Further experimental evaluation will focus on the multimodality of the posteriors that reflects the inherent ambiguities of the body tracking problem. We will also try to include a wider range of motions and actions into our models. Finally we aim at designing more elaborate temporal priors, possibly learned from the training data.

Acknowledgements

This work was supported by the SNF project PICSEL, the EU Integrated Project DIRAC, and the SNF NCCR IM2.

References

1. Deutscher, J., Blake, A., Reid, I.: Articulated body motion capture by annealed particle filtering. In Proc. IEEE CVPR (2000)
2. Sidenbladh, H., Black, M., Fleet, D.: Stochastic tracking of 3d human figures using 2d image motion. In ECCV (2000) 702–718
3. Sigal, L., Bhatia, S., Roth, S., Black, M., Isard, M.: Tracking loose-limbed people. CVPR (2004)
4. Sminchisescu, C., Triggs, B.: Kinematic jump processes for monocular 3d human tracking. CVPR (2003)
5. Urtasun, R., Fua, P.: 3d human body tracking using deterministic temporal motion models. In ECCV (2004)
6. Shakhnarovich, G., Viola, P., Darrel, T.: Fast pose estimation with parameter sensitive hashing. ICCV (2003)
7. Agarwal, A., Triggs, B.: 3d human pose from silhouettes by relevance vector regression. In CVPR (2004)
8. Agarwal, A., Triggs, B.: Monocular human motion capture with a mixture of regressors. IEEE Workshop on Vision for Human-Computer Interaction at CVPR (2005)
9. Elgammal, A., Lee, C.S.: Inferring 3d body pose from silhouettes using activity manifold learning. CVPR (2004)
10. Grauman, K., Shakhnarovich, G., Darrel, T.: Inferring 3d structure with a statistical image-based shape model. In ICCV (2003)
11. Sminchisescu, C., Kanaujia, A., Li, Z., Metaxas, D.: Discriminative density propagation for 3d human motion estimation. CVPR (2005)
12. Rosales, R., Sclaroff, S.: Learning body pose via specialized maps. In Advances in Neural Information Processing Systems (2001)
13. Murphy, K., Russel, S.: Rao-blackwellized particle filtering for dynamic bayesian networks. In A. Doucet, N. de Freitas adn N. Gordon, editors, *Sequential Monte Carlo Methods in Practice*, pp 499-515, Springer (2001)
14. Bailey, D.G.: An efficient euclidean distance transform. IWCIA (2004)

Towards Hands-Free Interfaces Based on Real-Time Robust Facial Gesture Recognition

Cristina Manresa-Yee, Javier Varona, and Francisco J. Perales

Universitat de les Illes Balears
Departament de Matemàtiques i Informàtica
Ed. Anselm Turmeda. Crta. Valldemossa km. 7.5 07122 Palma
{cristina.manresa, xavi.varona, paco.perales}@uib.es

Abstract. Perceptual user interfaces are becoming important nowadays, because they offer a more natural interaction with the computer via speech recognition, haptics, computer vision techniques and so on. In this paper we present a
visual-based interface (VBI) that analyzes users' facial gestures and motion.
This interface works in real-time and gets the images from a conventional webcam. Due to this, it has to be robust recognizing gestures in webcam standard
quality images. The system automatically finds the user's face and tracks it
through time for recognizing the gestures within the face region. Then, a new
information fusion procedure has been proposed to acquire data from computer
vision algorithms and its results are used to carry out a robust recognition process. Finally, we show how the system is used to replace a conventional mouse
for human computer interaction. We use the head's motion for controlling the
mouse's motion and eyes winks detection to execute the mouse's events.

1 Introduction

The research of new human-computer interfaces has become a growing field in computer science, which aims to attain the development of more natural, intuitive, unob-
trusive and efficient interfaces. This objective has come up with the concept of
Perceptual User Interfaces (PUIs) that are turning out to be very popular as they seek to
make the user interface more natural and compelling by taking advantage of the ways in
which people naturally interact with each other and with the world. PUIs can use speech
and sound recognition (ARS) and generation (TTS), computer vision, graphical animation and visualization, language understanding, touch-based sensing and feedback (haptics), learning, user modeling and dialog management [18]. Of all the communication
channels through where interface information can travel, computer vision provides a lot
of information that can be used for detection and recognition of human's actions and
gestures, which can be analyzed and applied to interaction purposes.

When sitting in front of a computer and with the use of webcams, very common
devices nowadays, heads and faces can be assumed to be visible. Therefore, system's
based in head or face feature detection and tracking, and face gesture or expression
recognition can become very effective human-computer interfaces. Of course, difficulties can arise from in-plane (tilted head, upside down) and out-of-plane (frontal
view, side view) rotations of the head, facial hair, glasses, lighting variations and

F.J. Perales and R.B. Fisher (Eds.): AMDO 2006, LNCS 4069, pp. 504–513, 2006.
© Springer-Verlag Berlin Heidelberg 2006

cluttered background [14]. Besides, when using standard USB webcams, the provided CMOS image resolution has to be taken in account.

Different approaches have been used for non invasive face/head-based interfaces. For the control of the position some systems analyze facial cues such as color distributions, head geometry or motion [5, 17]. Other works track facial features [10, 3] or gaze including infrared lighting [13, 15]. To recognize the user's events it is possible to use facial gesture recognition. In this paper we consider as facial gestures the atomic facial feature motions such as eye blinking [9, 11, 12], winks or mouth opening. Other systems contemplate the head gesture recognition that implies overall head motions or facial expression recognition that combines changes of the mentioned facial features to express an emotion [8].

In this work, we present a visual-based interface (VBI) that uses face feature tracking and facial gesture recognition. In order to achieve this function, the system's feedback must be in real-time and it must be precise and robust. A standard USB webcam will provide the images to process; therefore it will allow the achievement of a low cost system. Finally, the last system's requirements is that the user's work environment conditions should be normal (office, house or indoor environments), that is, with no special lighting or static background.

The paper is organized as follows. In the next section we describe in general terms the system. Section 3 explains the learning process of the user's facial features. Then, in section 4, we explain how to estimate through time the facial features positions. The facial gesture recognition process for detecting eye winks is detailed in section 5. And finally in the last section, a system application is presented: a mouse replacement, and the overall work conclusions

2 System Overview

To achieve an easy and friendly-use perceptual user interface, the system is composed of two main modules: Initialization and Processing (see Fig. 1). The Initialization module is responsible of extracting the user's distinctive facial features. This process locates the user's face, learns his skin color and detects the initial facial feature locations and their properties such as appearance and color. Moreover, this process is completely automatic, and it can be considered as a learning process of the user's facial features. The chosen facial features are the nose for head tracking and the eyes for gesture recognition. We decided to use the nose as feature to track, because it is almost always visible in all positions of the head facing the screen and it is not occluded by beards, moustaches or glasses [10]. For the gesture recognition module, the main gestures to control were the eyes winks from the right or left eye.

The selected facial features' positions are robustly estimated through time by two tasks: nose tracking based on Lucas and Kanade's algorithm and eye tracking by means of color distributions. It is important to point out that the system is able to react when the features get lost, detecting when it occurs and restarting the system calling to the Initialization module.

Finally, there is the possibility of adding more gestures to the system if the head motions are taken in account [20] for building a higher level human-computer communication.

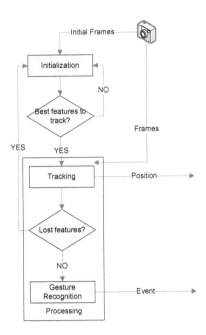

Fig. 1. The system is divided in two main modules: Initialization and processing

3 Learning the User's Facial Features

As it was remarked in the PUI's definition, it is very important for the interface to be natural; consequently, the system shouldn't require any calibration process where the user interferes. To accomplish this necessity, the system detects automatically the user's face by means of a real-time face detection algorithm [19].

When the system is first executed, the user must stay steady for a few frames for the process to be initialized. Face detection will be considered robust when during a few frames the face region is detected without changes (see Fig 2. (a)). Then, it is possible to define the initial user's face region to start the search of the user's facial features. Based on anthropometrical measurements, the face region can be divided in three sections: eyes and eyebrows, nose, and mouth region.

Over the nose region, we look for those points that can be easily tracked, that is, those whose derivative energy perpendicular to the prominent direction is above a threshold [16]. This algorithm theoretically selects the nose corners or the nostrils. However, the ambient lighting can cause the selection of points that are not placed over the desired positions; this fact is clearly visible in Fig. 2 (b). Ideally the desired selected points should be at both sides of the nose and with certain symmetrical conditions. Therefore, an enhancement and a re-selection of the found features must be carried out having in account symmetrical constraints. Fig. 2 (c) shows the selected features that we consider due to their symmetry respect to the vertical axis. This reselection process will achieve the best features to track and it will contribute to the tracking robustness. Fig. 2 (d) illustrates the final point considered, that is, the mean

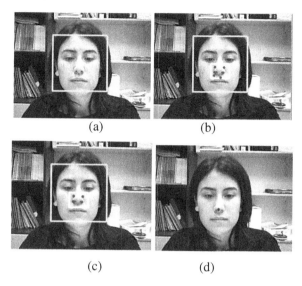

Fig. 2. (a) Automatic face detection. (b) Initial set of features. (c) Best feature selection using symmetrical constraints. (d) Mean of al features: nose point.

point of all the final selected features that due to the reselection of points will be centered on the nose.

The user's skin color is the next feature to be learnt. This feature will help the tracking and gesture recognition by constraining the processing to the pixels classified inside the skin mask. In order to learn the skin color, the pixels inside the face region are used as color samples for building the learning set. A Gaussian model in 3D RGB is chosen to represent the skin color probability density function due to its good results in practical applications [1]. The values of the Gaussian model parameters (mean and covariance matrix) are computed from the sample set using standard maximum likelihood methods [4]. Once calculated the model, the probability of a new pixel being skin can be computed for creating a "skin mask" of the user's face, see Fig. 3

Fig. 3. Skin masks for different users

The last step of the Initialization phase is to build the user's eyes models. Using the eyes and eyebrows region found in the face detection phase both eyes can be located. First, the region is binarized to find the dark zones, and then we keep the bounding boxes of the pair of blobs that are symmetrical and are located nearer to the nose region. This way, the eyebrows or the face borders should not be selected. In Fig. 4, an example of eyes' detection is shown. In the next section the eyes tracking based on their color distribution is explained. This fact is justified on the idea that eye color is different to the other facial features color (taking in account that the eye color distribution is composed by sclera and iris colors). Like this, our system could be used by users with clear (blue or green) or dark (black or brown) eyes. Eye models are obtained through histogramming techniques in the RGB color space of the pixels belonging to the detected eye regions.

Fig. 4. Example of eyes' detection: the blobs that are selected (in red color) are symmetrical and are nearer to the nose region.

The model histograms are produced with the function $b(\mathbf{x}_i)$, which assigns the color at location $\mathbf{x}_i$ to the corresponding bin. In our experiments, the histograms are calculated in the RGB space using 16 x 16 x 16 bins. We increase the reliability of the color distribution applying a weight function to each bin value depending of the distance between the pixel location and the eye center.

4   Facial Features Tracking

The facial feature tracking process consists in two tasks: eye and nose tracking. As we said before, eye tracking is based on its color distribution. By weighting the eye model by an isotropic kernel makes it possible to use a gradient optimization function, such as the mean-shift algorithm, to search each eye model in the new frame. Practical details and a discussion about the complete algorithm are in [6]. In our implementation this algorithm performs well and in real time. It is important to comment that small positional errors could occur. However, it is not important because the eye tracking results are only used to define the image regions where the gesture recognition process is performed. Besides, to add robustness to this process we only consider as search region those pixels belonging to the skin mask.

The important positional results for our system are reported by the nose tracking algorithm, where the selected features in the Initialization process are used. In this case, the spatial intensity gradient information of the images is used for finding the best image registration [2]. As it was before mentioned, for each frame the mean of all features is computed and it is defined as the nose position for that frame. The tracking algorithm is robust for handling rotation, scaling and shearing, so the user can move in a more unrestricted way. But again lighting or fast movements can cause the lost or displacement of the features to track. As only the features beneath the nose region are in the region of interest, a feature will be discarded when the length between this feature and the mean position, the nose position, is greater than a predefined value.

In theory, it would be possible to use Kalman filters for smoothing the positions. However, Kalman filters are not suited in our case because they don't achieve good results with erratic movements such as the face motion [7]. Therefore, our smoothing algorithm is based in the motion's tendency of the nose positions (head motion). A linear regression method is applied to a number of tracked nose positions through consecutive frames. The computed nose points of n consecutive frames are adjusted to a line, and therefore the nose motion can be carried out over that line direction. For avoiding discontinuities the regression line is adjusted with every new point that arrives. Several frames of the tracking sequences are shown in Fig 5.

5   Gesture Recognition

The gestures considered in this work are eye winks. The major part of the works use high quality images and good image resolution in the eyes zones. However, wink recognition with webcam quality images is difficult. Besides, this process depends on the user's head position. Therefore, our wink detection process is based on a search of the iris contours. That is, if the iris contours are detected in the image the eye will be considered as open, if not, the eye will be considered closed. It is important to point out that this process is robust because it is only carried out in the tracked eye regions by the mean-shift procedure described before.

Fig. 5. Facial feature tracking results

The process starts detecting the vertical contours in the image. For avoiding false positives in this process, the vertical contours are logically operated with a mask which was generated by thresholding the original image. Finally we keep the two longest vertical edges of each eye region if they appear to get the eye candidates. If these two vertical edges which correspond to the eye iris edges don't appear after the process for a number of consecutive frames, for gesture consistency, we will assume that the eye is closed. In Fig. 6 the process for gesture recognition is described.

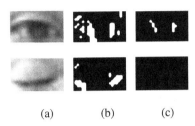

(a)   (b)   (c)

Fig. 6. Process for recognizing winks. The first row shows the process applied to open eyes. The second row represents the process over closed eyes. (a) Original image. (b) Vertical edges, (c) Iris contours.

5   HeadDev

Using the described techniques in previous sections, a functional perceptual interface has been implemented. This application consists in achieving a system that fulfills completely the functions of a standard mouse and replaces it by means of face feature tracking and face gesture recognition.

A highlight of this system is its potential users. Since the use of PUIs can help in e-Inclusion and e-Accessibility issues, the system can offer assistive technology for people with physical disabilities, which can help them to lead more independent lives and to any kind of audience, they contribute to new and more powerful interaction experiences. So, its use is focused on users with physical limitations in hands or arms or motion difficulties in upper limbs that can not use a traditional mouse. Other uses serve to entertainment and leisure purposes, such as computer games or exploring immersive 3D graphic worlds [5].

By means of the nose tracking process, *HeadDev* can simulate the mouse's motion. The precision required should be sufficient for controlling the mouse's cursor to the desired position. To reproduce the mouse motion it can be done through two different forms: absolute and relative. In the absolute type, the position would be mapped directly onto the screen, but this type would require a very accurate tracking, since a small tracking error in the image would be magnified on the screen. Therefore, we use relative motion for controlling the mouse's motion, which is not so sensitive to the tracking accuracy, since the cursor is controlled by the relative motion of the nose in the image. The relative type yields smoother movements of the cursor, due to the non-magnification of the tracking error. Then, if $n_t=(x_t,y_t)$ is the new nose tracked position for the frame t, to compute the new mouse screen coordinates, s_t, we apply

$$s_t = s_{t-1} + \alpha(n_t - n_{t-1}),$$

(1)

where α is a predefined constant that depends on the screen size and translates the image coordinates to screen coordinates. The computed mouse screen coordinates are sent to the system as real mouse inputs for placing the cursor in the desired position.

Finally, to represent the mouse's right or left click events, we control winks from the right or left eye respectively by means of the previously described gesture recognition process.

To evaluate the application's performance, *HeadDev* was tested by a set 22 users where half of them had never experienced with the application and the other half had previously trained for a short period with the interface. A 5 x 5 point grid was presented in the computer screen where the user had to try clicking on every point; each point had a radius of 15 pixels. While the user performed the test task, distance data between the mouse's position click and the nearest point in the grid was stored to study the accuracy. The error distance is the distance in pixels of the faulty clicked positions (clicks that weren't performed on the targets). In Table 1 the performance evaluation results are summarized.

Table 1. Summary of the performance evaluation

Users Group	Recognized clicks	Mean distance of errors
Trained	97,3 %	2 pixels
Novel	85,9 %	5 pixels

The experiments have confirmed that continuous training of the users results in higher skills and, thus, better performances and accuracy for controlling the mouse position. Besides, a fact to take in account is that this test can produce some neck fatigue over some users; therefore, some errors clicking the point grid could be caused due to this reason.

6   Conclusions and Future Work

In this paper we have proposed a new mixture of several computer vision techniques, where some of them have been improved and enhanced to reach more stability and robustness in tracking and gesture recognition. Numerical and visual results are given. In order to build reliable and robust perceptual user interfaces based on computer vision, certain practical constraints must be taken in account: the application must be robust to work in any environment and to use images from low cost devices. In this paper we present a VBI system that accomplishes these constraints. As a system application, we present an interface that is able to replace the standard mouse motions and events. Currently, the system has been tested by several disabled people (cerebral paralysis and physical disabilities) with encouraging results. Of course, more improvements have to be done, including more gestures (equivalents with BLISS commands or other kind of language for disabled persons), sound (TTS and ARS) and adaptive learning capabilities for specific disabilities. Enhancements have been planned as future work, such as including a bigger set of head and face gestures in order to support current computer interactions such as web surfing.

HeadDev for Microsoft Windows is available under a freeware license in the Web page http://www.tagrv.com. This will allow us to test the application by users around the world and we will able to improve the results by analyzing their reports. In near future, a linux version will be also available.

Acknowledgements

This work has been subsidized by the national project TIN2004-07926 from the MCYT Spanish Government and TAGrv S.L., Fundación Vodafone, Asociación de Integración de Discapacitados en Red. Javier Varona acknowledges the support of a Ramon y Cajal grant from the Spanish MEC.

References

1. Alexander, D.C., Buxton, B.F.: Statistical Modeling of Colour Data. International Journal of Computer Vision 44 (2001) 87–109
2. Baker, S., Matthews, I.: Lucas-Kanade 20 Years On: A Unifying Framework. International Journal of Computer Vision 56 (2004) 221–225
3. Betke, M., Gips J., Fleming, P.: The Camera Mouse: Visual Tracking of Body Features to Provide Computer Access for People with Severe Disabilities. IEEE Transactions on neural systems and Rehabilitation Engineering 10 (2002)
4. Bishop, C.M.: Neural Networks for Pattern Recognition. Clarendon Press (1995)
5. Bradski, G.R.: Computer Vision Face Tracking as a Component of a Perceptual User Interface. In: Proceedings of the IEEE Workshop on Applications of Computer Vision (1998) 214–219
6. Comaniciu, D., Ramesh, V., Meer, P.: Kernel-based Object Tracking. IEEE Transactions on Pattern Analysis and Machine Intelligence 25 (2003) 564–577
7. Fagiani, C., Betke, M., Gips, J.: Evaluation of Tracking Methods for Human-Computer Interaction. In: Proceedings of the IEEE Workshop on Applications in Computer Vision (2002) 121–126
8. Fasel, B., Luettin, J.: Automatic Facial Expression Analysis: A Survey. Pattern Recognition 36 (2003) 259–275
9. Gorodnichy, D.O.: Towards automatic retrieval of blink-based lexicon for persons suffered from brain-stem injury using video cameras. In: Proceedings of the IEEE Computer Vision and Pattern Recognition, Workshop on Face Processing in Video (2004)
10. Gorodnichy, D.O., Malik, S., Roth, G.: Nouse 'Use Your Nose as a Mouse' – a New Technology for Hands-free Games and Interfaces. Image and Vision Computing 22 (2004) 931–942
11. Grauman, K., Betke, M., Gips, J., Bradski, G.: Communication via Eye Blinks Detection and Duration Analysis in Real Time. In: Proceedings of the IEEE Conference on Computer Vision and Pattern Recognition (2001)
12. Grauman, K., Betke, M., Lombardi, J., Gips, J.,Bradski G.R.: Communication via eye blinks and eyebrow raises: video-based human-computer interfaces Video-Based Human-Computer Interfaces. Universal Access in the Information Society 2 (2003) 359–373
13. EyeTech Quick Glance, http://www.eyetechds.com/qglance2.htm (2006)

14. Kölsch, M., Turk, M.: Perceptual Interfaces. In Medioni, G., Kang S.B.(eds): Emerging Topics in Computer Vision, Prentice Hall (2005)
15. Morimoto, C., Mimica, M.: Eye gaze tracking techniques for interactive applications. Computer Vision and Image Understanding 98 (2005) 4–24
16. Shi, J., and Tomasi, C.: Good Features to Track. In: Processdings of the IEEE Conference on Computer Vision and Pattern Recognition (1994) 593–600
17. Toyama, K.: Look, Ma – No Hands!"Hands-Free Cursor Control with Real-Time 3D Face Tracking. In Proceedings of the Workshop on Perceptual User Interfaces (1998) 49–54
18. Turk, M., Robertson, G.: Perceptual User Interfaces. Communications of the ACM 43 (2000) 32–34
19. Viola, P., Jones, M.: Robust Real-Time Face Detection. International Journal of Computer Vision 57 (2004) 137–154
20. Zelinsky, A., Heinzmann, J.:   Real-Time Visual Recognition of Facial Gestures for Human-Computer Interaction. In: Proceedings of the IEEE Automatic Face and Gesture Recognition (1996) 351–356

Upper Body Tracking for Interactive Applications

José María Buades Rubio, Francisco J. Perales,
Manuel González Hidalgo, and Javier Varona

Universitat de les Illes Balears
Ed. Anselm Turmeda
Crta Valldemossa Km 7.4
Spain (E-07122) Palma de Mallorca
{josemaria.buades, paco.perales, manuel.gonzalez,
xavi.varona}@uib.es

Abstract. In this paper we describe a complete method for building a perceptual user interface in indoor uncontrolled environments. The overall system uses two calibrated cameras and does initialization: it detects user, takes his/her measurements, builds a 3D-Model. It performs matching/tracking for: trunk, head, left arm, right arm and hands. The system is waiting for a user in a predefined posture, once the user has been detected he/she is analysed to take measurements are taken and a 3D-Model is built. Tracking is carried out by a Particle Filter algorithm splited in three steps: tracking of head-trunk, tracking of left arm and tracking of right arm. This proposed divide and conquer solution improves computation time without getting better or similar results than sequential solution. The matching process uses two sub-matching functions, one to compute color and another to compute shape one. Finally the system provides numerical values for joints and end effectors to be used for interactive applications.

1 Introduction

In current computer systems the interaction is headed towards non-contact devices. This means that the user is allowed to interact without physical contact with the machine; this communication can be carried out by voice or user gesticulation capture, known as perceptual user interface. We are specially interested in visual information, that recognizes the human presence in color video images. Also we would like to define a general, robust and efficient system that can be used with non-expensive cameras and digitalizing cards.

The global process should detect a new user entering the system and analyse him/her to determine parameters such as hair color and clothes. Once the user who is going to interact with the machine has been detected, the system starts to track interesting regions such as the head, hands, trunk and joints, using information obtained in the user detection task. The input data for the gesture interpretation process are the position and orientation of these regions. This process will determine which gesture the user has carried out. Next, these gesture data are sent to the execution process, which ends the process by performing the action that has been specified, and so completing the feedback process.

F.J. Perales and R.B. Fisher (Eds.): AMDO 2006, LNCS 4069, pp. 514–523, 2006.
© Springer-Verlag Berlin Heidelberg 2006

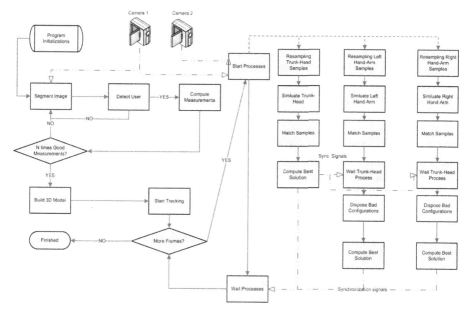

Fig. 1. Overall System. Also diagram shows synchronization signals between processes.

The initialization topic is a grouping field in research; some research obtains kinematical structures from monocular sequence [1]. In others, a generic humanoid model is used and adapted using 3D-scans, stereo or vision approaches [2, 3]. Finally, others carry out appearance initialization [4].

Many preceding projects have been developed in pose estimation; its main contribution using Particle Filter was [5] that developed a full body tracking. A hierarchical stochastic sampling scheme was introduced by [6], it initially estimates trunk pose, propagates samples to estimate the rest of body parts. Other projects refine the search process by introducing gradient descent for local pose refinement [3], getting more accurate results.

Our work involves user detection, taking measurements of the user, building a 3D model and finally tracking. The system detects the user, measures and builds a 3D model from one camera. The tracking process is performed by all cameras and splitting the problem in three Particle Filters, afterwards biomechanical restrictions dispose of bad configurations of Left Hand-Arm and Right Hand-Arm samples.

In the following section, we explain the main method that detects the user in front of the camera and carefully explains the analysis process. Section 3 explains how measurements are taken and the 3D reconstruction module from two calibrated color cameras. In section 4 the tracking system is presented, it uses Particle Filter search in three steps to reduce computation time. Finally, we conclude with some results including a set of color images, conclusions and references. Figure 1 shows the overall system.

2 User Detection

The inputs of the system are the images from two synchronized color cameras $\{\gamma_1, \gamma_2\}$ for tracking process, but for user detection and measurements only one camera is used $\{\gamma_1\}$. First, each image is segmented with the algorithm explained in [7] based on the Mumford-Shah segmentation functional, and is then analyzed to determine whether it is a user or not, as we can see below in a work related with this topic [8]. Once a user has been detected, the system studies him and obtains several parameters that will be useful in the tracking. By applying this process directly to the segmented images without using information from previous frames, the system is robust to background changes and variable illumination. The system obtains the upper torso configuration: shirt, hair, hands and face. The User detection process is waiting for a user located opposite the camera, with hands separated and at the same height that head, then it recognizes and later analyzes the user configuration.

This module receives a segmentation of the captured image, it analyzes each region O, and it is marked as skin region if its RGB mean value is in a characteristic color range of skin. To achieve more homogenous regions, neighbouring skin regions are merged. This merging is carried out to avoid detecting a hand or the face in two neighbouring regions, following the merging criteria:

$$\forall O_i, O_j / Neighbour(O_i, O_j) \wedge Skin(O_i) \wedge Skin(O_j) \Rightarrow O_i \cup O_j \qquad (1)$$

where $Neighbour(O_i, O_j)$ means that two regions are neighbours and $Skin(O_i)$ means that it is a skin region.

After of this merging process, we obtain a skin region set, called β, where any pair of skin regions is separated.

For all ordered set of three regions included in β, we identify each one as face Z, left hand Y_1 and right hand Y_2, then we evaluate a criteria to determine whether this configuration is correct.

$$\underset{i,j,k}{Max}\{\varphi(O_i, O_j, O_k) : \forall O_i, O_j, O_k \in \beta\} \qquad (2)$$

The user detection function is called φ. In this function we take into account the following:

- Central region, face, must be the biggest;
- Lateral regions, hands, have a similar area;
- Face region area $A(Z)$ must be between a minimum Z^- and a maximum Z^+;
- Hands area $A(Y_1)$ and $A(Y_2)$ must be between a minimum Y^- and a maximum Y^+;
- Vertical position Y_1 and Y_2 should be similar and nearest possible to Z.

The user detection function returns a value between zero and one that measures the likelihood that a user has been detected. From all possible combinations of Z, Y_1 and Y_2 the one with the greatest value is chosen as the best configuration. The Best configuration is discarded if it does not reach a minimum value.

In order to apply the above algorithm, we need to fix the following values: a color range of skin to detect hand and face regions. To avoid high differences of hands we include an area similarity criterion, a maximum size of hand area is also necessary. All these parameters are used in order to discriminate bad detections.

All values are established in relation with camera to user distance and image resolution. This distance is predefined by the initial application setup.

After a user has been detected, the same image is analyzed to determine hair and shirt color. The region proposed as hair, X is the upper neighbouring region of Z, if A(X) / A(Z) relation is greater than a ratio then the hair region is discarded and is considered that he/she is a bald user.

To analyze the shirt, the following algorithm is applied. Initially, the shirt region W is the greatest region whose upper boundary is included in the boundary of Z (see figure 2). Afterwards, neighbouring regions of W are joined until Z is connected with Y_1 and Y_2 through W. At every step a region T_i is chosen for joining it to W tanking into account: color space distance between mean color of T and W, and distance in pixels from T to Y_1 and Y_2. With this process, the system detects a user and obtains useful data for the tracking system.

Results of this step is a segmented image and a valid/invalid user detection.

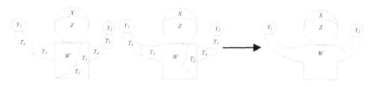

Fig. 2. Body Region Merging. Lower face region is considered as initial body region. Neighbors regions are merged until hands are connected by body region.

3 Measurement

Once the user has been detected, the systems continue building a 3D-Model that will be used later for the tracking process. The 3D-Model is a 3D representation of hands, arms, forearms, trunk, head and neck.

Hands are modeled as super-ellipsoids computed from its region, for user detection it is not necessary for user to wear long sleeves, but to build the 3D-Model it is necessary to split hands from arms. First, the elbow and shoulder 3D positions will be found to model the trunk, the upper arms and the forearms.

3.1 Elbow and Shoulder Finder

The localization of the elbow and shoulder joints is symmetrical for both sides, therefore we will only explain it for the right side.

The first point located is the elbow. Each point in the boundary of the trunk (c) is scored as elbow candidate, the conditions are the following:

– The straight line that joins point (c) with the upper point of the right hand in the image (m) must be inside the merged region of the right hand and trunk. In other words, this line can't be outside the person;
– The smoothed curvature of boundary in point (c) must be greater than 120°;

– If all conditions are true, point (c) is considered as a candidate and is scored with the distance from (c) to (m) multiplied by the cosine of its curvature.

The candidate with highest score is taken as the right elbow point. See figure 3 where (c) and (m) are drawn.

Now, we compute the shoulder joint. The shoulder position is not as accurate as elbow due to the fact that it is not a boundary point. The shoulder is taking into account the arms finishing points, the line where the trunk starts and the lowest face point.

We draw a straight line from the right elbow to the left elbow, to locate right shoulder; the algorithm covers this line's distance from right to left, searching for a high change in distance from this line to boundary in the normal direction (down-direction) to the line.

Once the point in this line where the change is higher is found, we take this point as the perpendicular point to the right shoulder point. The shoulder point is located in normal direction to the line (up-direction) to the face height (lowest face point).

3.2 Model of Segments

Once the elbow and the shoulder joints have been detected, we can build a 3D-Model of the arms and forearms. These segments are modeled with super-ellipsoids except for the trunk, to differentiate the hand from the arm it is necessary that the user wears long sleeves, in this way, the arm is in the body's region and not in hand's region. With this restriction the right arm is taken as the body's region part that is at the left side of the bisector of the lines that join elbow-hand and elbow-shoulder (left arm is symmetric); the bisector splits the arm and forearm.

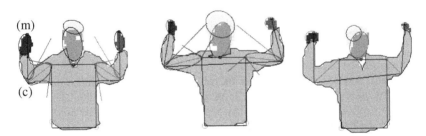

Fig. 3. 2D-Modelling from a single image (two good cases and a bad measurement detected case). 3D Reconstruction is carried out from one camera taking into account that user is located at same distance that calibrator object was.

To model the forearm two more restrictions are imposed. Two new lines are obtained: two perpendicular lines that form a 45 degree angle with the elbow-shoulder line. The forearm is the body region part that is inside these three lines: the bisector and these two lines.

The trunk is modelled as a 3D box, from the two elbows points to the distance of the two lower body boundaries. Two corners are elbow points, and the height is taken from the height obtained in the process that computes the elbow position as figure 3 shows. Finally, the neck joint is modelled as a distance, the minimum distance from the shoulder to shoulder line and the face ellipse. Figure 3 shows all geometrical operations used to find interesting points and split regions.

To solve scale factor problems we impose that the user must be at same distance as the calibrator object was.

4 Tracking Process

The tracking process starts in the first frame after user detection, and it is performed via Particle Filter using a matching function such as likelihood function, and using all cameras. The matching function takes into account the following visual cues: color and shape, also spatial constraints are applied to the human model. Pursuing real-time, the tracking process has been splited to reduce computation time. First, the search strategy is exposed, afterwards the matching function subsection explains how samples are measured, and finally the best solution is computed. See figure 1.

4.1 Search Strategy

The tracking problem is divided into minor problems to reduce computation time. Instead of an attempt to track all the body in one tracking process, three independent processes are carried out to track body-head, left hand-arm and right hand-arm. Also important concepts are used to guide this searching: biomechanical restrictions, time elapsed and collision detection.

Computation time is reduced due to the number of samples needed to achieve good results, with only one tracking process the system would try to track 14 degrees of freedom, dof from now on (6 for the trunk, 3 for the left forearm, 1 for the left arm, 3 for the right forearm and 1 for the right arm). With this division each process tracks a part of the body:

– Trunk and Head: 6 dof
– Left Arm: 6 dof
– Right Arm: 6 dof

Now, the overall system has 18 degrees of freedom, because we have introduced the possibility that the forearm separates from the body. Despite increasing the dof, dividing the problem in three tracking process reduces computation time because the number of samples needed is exponentially proportional to the dof (i.e. 2^{14} in contraposition to $2^6+2^6+2^6 < 2^8$). So, three particles filters are executed in parallel, one process for each object (Trunk-Head, Left Hand-Arm and Right Hand-Arm).

We define a pose Ψ as a vector with the root joint configurations (T, L, R), where T, L and R are the matrix transformations for Trunk-Head, Left Hand-Arm and Right Hand-Arm respectively.

Another benefit of increasing the dof is that shoulder is not fixed to the trunk; the shoulder is able to translate from trunk, this translation simulates the collar bone, so hands are able to reach more 3D space, and consequently is more realistic.

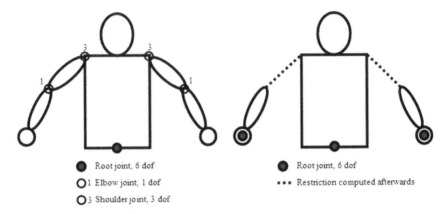

Fig. 4. Left structure is 14 dof, upper body is considered as only one hierarchical object. Right structure is the proposed solution, three independents objects (6 dof for object) with bio-mechanical restrictions computed afterwards.

The tracking process for arms is configured in a special way, since for applications hands have more information than arms. The root joint is the hand, and not the elbow as would be expected, with this approach we obtain better results when the hand is near the body. Due to this inverse configuration, the tracking process is more robust when arms and body colors are similar. Figure 4 shows upper body structure solution.

4.2 Matching Function

The matching function is composed of two parts: color comparison and shape comparison.

For each segment, the color model is computed from initialization process. The segment s (3D box or super-ellipsoid graphical primitive) is projected in the image to evaluate a color matching function; each pixel is compared with the color model and scored as good (1) or bad pixel (0). Segments are projected as a sample of pixels, getting so good results as projecting the entire segment. Thus, for each segment s we obtain a value of a color matching $m^{\gamma_i}_{colour}(s)$ where γ_i is the considered camera. For each segment color matching function returns the ratio of good pixels detected.

The shape matching function uses the contours. To detect contour in the captured image uses Sobel operand, as a result we get an image, called Sobel-image. In a first approximation, segment contours are projected in Sobel-image and pixels are scored as good (1) or bad (0) if it's coincident with a contour pixel in the Sobel-image. This function returns the percentage of pixels scored as good. This function has good results if the segment is just in the contour of the image, and it is very difficult because the real person shape is very deformable. Thus, if one pixel is scored as bad (0) we search in its normal direction (from near to far) the existence of a contour pixel in Sobel-image. (See figure 4). A pixel is evaluated with a value between 0 and 1, in relation to the distance to a contour in Sobel-image, more near to contour, greater value is assigned. So we obtain, for each segment s a shape matching function value $m^{\gamma_i}_{shape}(s)$ that define the shape matching function.

Matching function is the contribution of the color matching function and the shape matching function from all the cameras. For each segment s_j the matching value is defined as follows:

$$m(s_j) = \min_{\gamma_i \in H} \left\{ m_{colour}^{\gamma_i}(s_j) + m_{shape}^{\gamma_i}(s_j) \right\} \tag{3}$$

where H is a set of cameras, $\{\gamma_1, \gamma_2\}$ used in this work.

Finally, for the set of segments of a pose Ψ we define the matching value

$$m(\Psi) = \sum_{j=1}^{N} \delta_j \, m(s_j) \tag{4}$$

where δ_j is a value representing the importance of the segment in the body. To improve accuracy in end-effectors, head and hands are considered more important than others.

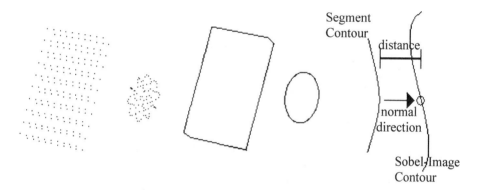

Fig. 5. Left: 3D Box and Super-Ellipsoid Segments projected by Color Matching Function. Center: Projection of segments for Shape Matching Function. Right: Distance computed to score a pixel by Shape Matching Function.

4.3 Compute Best Solution

For each frame, $\{\psi_i\}_{i=1}^{N}$ it's its poses set (that is the set of samples in the particle filter algorithm) and is ordered so that $p(\psi_j) = m(\psi_j) \Big/ \sum_{i=1}^{N} m(\psi_j)$ satisfies $p(\psi_j) \geq p(\psi_{j+1}) \forall j$, so $p(\psi_0) \geq p(\psi_j)$ and $\sum_{i=1}^{N} m(\psi_j) = 1$.

At each frame, the most probable sample Ψ_1 is a good result but very unstable. To avoid instability, we substitute the most probable sample by we called "best solution" $\tilde{\psi}$ that is computed obtaining the first k so that $\sum_{i=1}^{k} p(\psi_j) \geq \theta$ where $\theta \in [0,1]$ (and has been set 0.1 empirically, 0 would be most probable sample, and 1 would be mean value of all samples), then: $\tilde{\psi} = \dfrac{1}{q}\sum_{j=1}^{k} p\left(\psi_j\right)\psi_j$, $q = \sum_{j=1}^{k} p\left(\psi_j\right)$.

To avoid non possible configurations, samples of left and right particles filters are checked with trunk-head tracking solution. The checking of samples must be done after the best solution for trunk-head is computed. For each sample the distance from the elbow 3D point to shoulder 3D point in trunk is computed, and this distance must be in a valid range near the length of the forearm, else the sample is considered as impossible, $p(\Psi_j)=0$. Also samples where collision between hand and head has been detected are impossible. Figure 1 explains the processes, the communication among them and their dependencies.

5 Results

In this section we show the results obtained in a test sequence.

Fig. 6. The first and second columns are computed without biomechanical restrictions from camera γ_1, γ_2 respectively. The third and fourth columns correspond to camera γ_1, γ_2 and are computed with restrictions. From top to bottom are frames 51, 90, 150 and 250. Last row shows the improvement of biomechanical restrictions, right elbow joint position is right. Our best solution is displayed in green, red are mean solution, and blue are best particle solution.

Test sequence is ten seconds length and 30 frames/sec. User detection is carried out in frame 40, and user performs different movements, moving body, occluding one hand to other. The first and second columns are computed without biomechanical restrictions. The third and fourth columns are computed with restrictions. From top to bottom are different frames. Last row shows the improvement of biomechanical restrictions, right elbow joint position is right.

Green background has had to be used due to the original background is wood color and is very similar to skin color, and never is used as chroma key color.

6   Conclusions and Future Work

We have presented a good method for perceptual user interface applications. Process involves user detection, take measurement of the user, building a 3D model and the 3D tracking of interesting limbs: trunk, head, hands and arms. The matching function gives good results due to it using two matching criteria: shape and color matching functions. The divide and conquer technique improves performance, by splitting in three independent processes and later integrating information to dispose of bad configurations. However, it is necessary to improve yield to achieve real-time. Also we are planning to model segments with more accurate primitives and real texture obtained from initialization. More sophisticated searching criteria will be defined including more restrictions: time constraints, joint angles conditions. Over this work it is possible to build a gesture recognition system using provided data as 3D location and orientation of hands and head.

This work has been subsidized by the national project TIN2004-07926 from the MCYT Spanish Government. Javier Varona acknowledges the support of a Ramon y Cajal grant from the Spanish MEC.

References

1. N. Krahnstoever, M. Yeasin, and R. Sharme. "Automatic acquisition and initialization of articulated models", Machine Vision and Applications, 14(4), 2003.
2. B. Allen, B. Curless, and Z. Popovic. The space of human body shapes: reconstruction and parameterization from range images" In Proc. ACM SIGGRAPH, pages 587-594, 2003.
3. J. Carranza, C. Theobalt, M. Magnor and H.P.Seide. "Free-viewpoint of human actors". In Proc. ACM SIGRRAPH, pages 565-577, 2003
4. H. Sidenbladh and M.J. Black. "Learning the Statistics of People in Images and Video". Int. Journal of Computer Vision, 54(1/2/3):183-209, 2003
5. Deustcher, J., Blake, A., Reid, I.: Articulated body motion capture by annealed particle filtering. IEEE Conf. Computer Vision and Pattern Recognition, Vol. 2 (2000) 126-133
6. J. Mitchelson and A. Hilton. "Hierachical tracking of multiple people". British Machine Vision Conference, 2003.
7. J.M. Buades, M. Gonzalez, F.J. Perales. "A New Method for Detection and Initial Pose Estimation based on Mumford-Shah Segmentation Functional". IbPRIA 2003. Port d'Andratx. Spain. June 2003. pp 117-125
8. C. Ballester, V. Caselles and M. Gonzalez, "Affine invariant segmentation by variational methods", SIAM J. Appl. Math., Vol. 56, No 1, pp. 294-325, 1996

Author Index

Abásolo, María José   120
Alba-Castro, José Luis   356
Al-Zubi, Stephan   203
Arellano Távara, Diana   484
Ayache, Nicholas   346
Azkue, Iosu   474

Bénédet, Vincent   444
Black, Michael J.   185
Blanco, Francisco J.   165
Boesnach, Ingo   68
Boisvert, Jonathan   346
Bronstein, Alexander M.   38, 48
Bronstein, Michael M.   38, 48
Bruckstein, Alfred M.   48
Buades Rubio, José María   514

Carretero, María del Puy   234
Cerezo, Eva   405
Chellappa, Rama   78
Cheriet, Farida   346
Chihara, Kunihiro   305
Choraś, Michał   58
Costa Teixeira Orvalho, Verónica   223
Cristina, Federico   120
Curto, Belén   165

Dapoto, Sebastián H.   120
Davis, Larry S.   153
de Giusti, Armando   120
Di, Huijun   143
Dornaika, Fadi   110
Dugelay, Jean-Luc   326

Elgammal, Ahmed   315, 464

Faudot, Dominique   444
Fihl, P.   375
Fischer, Andreas   68
Frangi, Alejandro   356
Funatomi, Takuya   100

Gallego Sánchez, A.J.   213
Garay-Vitoria, Nestor   234
Gonzàlez, Jordi   110, 414, 424

González Hidalgo, Manuel   514
González-Jiménez, Daniel   356

Han, Dongfeng   196
He, Qing   244
Herrero, J. Elías   175
Holte, M.B.   375
Howe, Nicholas R.   271
Huang, Feiyue   143
Huerta, I.   424
Hupont, Isabelle   405
Huynh, Viet Quang Huy   366

Iiyama, Masaaki   100
Imura, Masataka   305

Jaeggli, Tobias   494

Kakusho, Koh   100
Kamada, Takahiro   366
Kang, Byung Jun   19
Kawashima, Hiroaki   453
Kellokumpu, Vili   153
Kimmel, Ron   38, 48
Koller-Meier, Esther   494

Labelle, Hubert   346
Lanquetin, Sandrine   132
Lee, Chan-Su   315, 464
Li, Wenhui   196
Liu, Yuncai   244
Lu, Xiaosuo   196

Maki, Atsuto   395
Manabe, Yoshitsugu   305
Manresa-Yee, Cristina   504
Marín-Jiménez, Manuel J.   336
Martínez, Jesús   175
Matsuyama, Takashi   395, 453
Matta, Federico   326
Meier, Andreas   484
Mezger, Johannes   434
Minoh, Michihiko   100
Moeslund, T.B.   375
Moldenhauer, Jörg   68

Molina Carmona, R.   213
Moreno, Vidal   165
Mukasa, Tomoyuki   395

Nam, Mi Young   252
Neff, Michael   262
Neveu, Marc   132
Nobuhara, Shohei   395

Orozco, Javier   110
Orrite, Carlos   175
Ortiz, Amalia   234
Oyarzun, David   234

Panagiotakis, Costas   385
Park, Jihun   281
Park, Kang Ryoung   1, 10, 19
Pellerin, Denis   385
Pennec, Xavier   346
Perales, Francisco J.   504, 514
Pérez de la Blanca, Nicolás   336
Pina, Alfredo   474
Pollefeys, Marc   90

Raffin, Romain   132
Ramasso, Emmanuel   385
Reng, L.   375
Rhee, Phill Kyu   252
Rius, Ignasi   414
Roca, Xavier   414
Rogez, Grégory   175
Rombaut, Michèle   385
Rowe, D.   424
Russo, Claudia   120

Sedai, Suman   252
Seidel, Hans-Peter   262
Shin, Young-suk   291, 300
Sigal, Leonid   185
Skala, Vaclav   29
Sommer, Gerald   203
Stein, Thorsten   68
Straßer, Wolfgang   434
Sukno, Federico   356
Sundaresan, Aravind   78
Susin, Antonio   223

Tanaka, Hiromi T.   366
Therón, Roberto   165
Tong, Minglei   244
Tsutsumi, Kimitaka   453
Tziritas, Georgios   385

Van Gool, Luc   494
Varona, Javier   414, 504, 514
Vasa, Libor   29
Vazirgiannis, Michalis   474
Villagrá Arnedo, C.   213
Villanueva, J.J.   424
Vitaladevuni, Shiv Naga Prasad   153

Wang, Yi   196

Xu, Guangyou   143

Yamazaki, Masayuki   305
Yan, Jingyu   90
Yasumuro, Yoshihiro   305

Zacur, Ernesto   223
Zou, Xiaoqiang   196

Lecture Notes in Computer Science

For information about Vols. 1–3978

please contact your bookseller or Springer

Vol. 4072: M. Harders, G. Székely (Eds.), Biomedical Simulation. XI, 216 pages. 2006.

Vol. 4069: F.J. Perales, R.B. Fisher (Eds.), Articulated Motion and Deformable Objects. XV, 526 pages. 2006.

Vol. 4068: H. Schärfe, P. Hitzler, P. Øhrstrøm (Eds.), Conceptual Structures: Inspiration and Application. XI, 455 pages. 2006. (Sublibrary LNAI).

Vol. 4067: D. Thomas (Ed.), ECOOP 2006 – Object-Oriented Programming. XIV, 527 pages. 2006.

Vol. 4066: A. Rensink, J. Warmer (Eds.), Model Driven Architecture – Foundations and Applications. XII, 392 pages. 2006.

Vol. 4063: I. Gorton, G.T. Heineman, I. Crnkovic, H.W. Schmidt, J.A. Stafford, C.A. Szyperski, K. Wallnau (Eds.), Component-Based Software Engineering. XI, 394 pages. 2006.

Vol. 4060: K. Futatsugi, J.-P. Jouannaud, J. Meseguer (Eds.), Algebra, Meaning and Computation. XXXVIII, 643 pages. 2006.

Vol. 4059: L. Arge, R. Freivalds (Eds.), Algorithm Theory – SWAT 2006. XII, 436 pages. 2006.

Vol. 4058: L.M. Batten, R. Safavi-Naini (Eds.), Information Security and Privacy. XII, 446 pages. 2006.

Vol. 4057: J.P.W. Pluim, B. Likar, F.A. Gerritsen (Eds.), Biomedical Image Registration. XII, 324 pages. 2006.

Vol. 4056: P. Flocchini, L. Gąsieniec (Eds.), Structural Information and Communication Complexity. X, 357 pages. 2006.

Vol. 4055: J. Lee, J. Shim, S.-g. Lee, C. Bussler, S. Shim (Eds.), Data Engineering Issues in E-Commerce and Services. IX, 290 pages. 2006.

Vol. 4054: A. Horváth, M. Telek (Eds.), Formal Methods and Stochastic Models for Performance Evaluation. VIII, 239 pages. 2006.

Vol. 4053: M. Ikeda, K.D. Ashley, T.-W. Chan (Eds.), Intelligent Tutoring Systems. XXVI, 821 pages. 2006.

Vol. 4052: M. Bugliesi, B. Preneel, V. Sassone, I. Wegener (Eds.), Automata, Languages and Programming, Part II. XXIV, 603 pages. 2006.

Vol. 4051: M. Bugliesi, B. Preneel, V. Sassone, I. Wegener (Eds.), Automata, Languages and Programming, Part I. XXIII, 729 pages. 2006.

Vol. 4048: L. Goble, J.-J.C.. Meyer (Eds.), Deontic Logic and Artificial Normative Systems. X, 273 pages. 2006. (Sublibrary LNAI).

Vol. 4046: S.M. Astley, M. Brady, C. Rose, R. Zwiggelaar (Eds.), Digital Mammography. XVI, 654 pages. 2006.

Vol. 4045: D. Barker-Plummer, R. Cox, N. Swoboda (Eds.), Diagrammatic Representation and Inference. XII, 301 pages. 2006. (Sublibrary LNAI).

Vol. 4044: P. Abrahamsson, M. Marchesi, G. Succi (Eds.), Extreme Programming and Agile Processes in Software Engineering. XII, 230 pages. 2006.

Vol. 4043: A.S. Atzeni, A. Lioy (Eds.), Public Key Infrastructure. XI, 261 pages. 2006.

Vol. 4042: D. Bell, J. Hong (Eds.), Flexible and Efficient Information Handling. XVI, 296 pages. 2006.

Vol. 4041: S.-W. Cheng, C.K. Poon (Eds.), Algorithmic Aspects in Information and Management. XI, 395 pages. 2006.

Vol. 4040: R. Reulke, U. Eckardt, B. Flach, U. Knauer, K. Polthier (Eds.), Combinatorial Image Analysis. XII, 482 pages. 2006.

Vol. 4039: M. Morisio (Ed.), Reuse of Off-the-Shelf Components. XIII, 444 pages. 2006.

Vol. 4038: P. Ciancarini, H. Wiklicky (Eds.), Coordination Models and Languages. VIII, 299 pages. 2006.

Vol. 4037: R. Gorrieri, H. Wehrheim (Eds.), Formal Methods for Open Object-Based Distributed Systems. XVII, 474 pages. 2006.

Vol. 4036: O.H. Ibarra, Z. Dang (Eds.), Developments in Language Theory. XII, 456 pages. 2006.

Vol. 4035: T. Nishita, Q. Peng, H.-P. Seidel (Eds.), Advances in Computer Graphics. XX, 771 pages. 2006.

Vol. 4034: J. Münch, M. Vierimaa (Eds.), Product-Focused Software Process Improvement. XVII, 474 pages. 2006.

Vol. 4033: B. Stiller, P. Reichl, B. Tuffin (Eds.), Performability Has its Price. X, 103 pages. 2006.

Vol. 4032: O. Etzion, T. Kuflik, A. Motro (Eds.), Next Generation Information Technologies and Systems. XIII, 365 pages. 2006.

Vol. 4031: M. Ali, R. Dapoigny (Eds.), Innovations in Applied Artificial Intelligence. XXIII, 1353 pages. 2006. (Sublibrary LNAI).

Vol. 4029: L. Rutkowski, R. Tadeusiewicz, L.A. Zadeh, J. Zurada (Eds.), Artificial Intelligence and Soft Computing – ICAISC 2006. XXI, 1235 pages. 2006. (Sublibrary LNAI).

Vol. 4027: H.L. Larsen, G. Pasi, D. Ortiz-Arroyo, T. Andreasen, H. Christiansen (Eds.), Flexible Query Answering Systems. XVIII, 714 pages. 2006. (Sublibrary LNAI).

Vol. 4026: P.B. Gibbons, T. Abdelzaher, J. Aspnes, R. Rao (Eds.), Distributed Computing in Sensor Systems. XIV, 566 pages. 2006.

Vol. 4025: F. Eliassen, A. Montresor (Eds.), Distributed Applications and Interoperable Systems. XI, 355 pages. 2006.

Vol. 4024: S. Donatelli, P. S. Thiagarajan (Eds.), Petri Nets and Other Models of Concurrency - ICATPN 2006. XI, 441 pages. 2006.

Vol. 4021: E. André, L. Dybkjær, W. Minker, H. Neumann, M. Weber (Eds.), Perception and Interactive Technologies. XI, 217 pages. 2006. (Sublibrary LNAI).

Vol. 4020: A. Bredenfeld, A. Jacoff, I. Noda, Y. Takahashi (Eds.), RoboCup 2005: Robot Soccer World Cup IX. XVII, 727 pages. 2006. (Sublibrary LNAI).

Vol. 4019: M. Johnson, V. Vene (Eds.), Algebraic Methodology and Software Technology. XI, 389 pages. 2006.

Vol. 4018: V. Wade, H. Ashman, B. Smyth (Eds.), Adaptive Hypermedia and Adaptive Web-Based Systems. XVI, 474 pages. 2006.

Vol. 4016: J.X. Yu, M. Kitsuregawa, H.V. Leong (Eds.), Advances in Web-Age Information Management. XVII, 606 pages. 2006.

Vol. 4014: T. Uustalu (Ed.), Mathematics of Program Construction. X, 455 pages. 2006.

Vol. 4013: L. Lamontagne, M. Marchand (Eds.), Advances in Artificial Intelligence. XIII, 564 pages. 2006. (Sublibrary LNAI).

Vol. 4012: T. Washio, A. Sakurai, K. Nakajima, H. Takeda, S. Tojo, M. Yokoo (Eds.), New Frontiers in Artificial Intelligence. XIII, 484 pages. 2006. (Sublibrary LNAI).

Vol. 4011: Y. Sure, J. Domingue (Eds.), The Semantic Web: Research and Applications. XIX, 726 pages. 2006.

Vol. 4010: S. Dunne, B. Stoddart (Eds.), Unifying Theories of Programming. VIII, 257 pages. 2006.

Vol. 4009: M. Lewenstein, G. Valiente (Eds.), Combinatorial Pattern Matching. XII, 414 pages. 2006.

Vol. 4008: J.C. Augusto, C.D. Nugent (Eds.), Designing Smart Homes. XI, 183 pages. 2006. (Sublibrary LNAI).

Vol. 4007: C. Àlvarez, M. Serna (Eds.), Experimental Algorithms. XI, 329 pages. 2006.

Vol. 4006: L.M. Pinho, M. González Harbour (Eds.), Reliable Software Technologies – Ada-Europe 2006. XII, 241 pages. 2006.

Vol. 4005: G. Lugosi, H.U. Simon (Eds.), Learning Theory. XI, 656 pages. 2006. (Sublibrary LNAI).

Vol. 4004: S. Vaudenay (Ed.), Advances in Cryptology - EUROCRYPT 2006. XIV, 613 pages. 2006.

Vol. 4003: Y. Koucheryavy, J. Harju, V.B. Iversen (Eds.), Next Generation Teletraffic and Wired/Wireless Advanced Networking. XVI, 582 pages. 2006.

Vol. 4001: E. Dubois, K. Pohl (Eds.), Advanced Information Systems Engineering. XVI, 560 pages. 2006.

Vol. 3999: C. Kop, G. Fliedl, H.C. Mayr, E. Métais (Eds.), Natural Language Processing and Information Systems. XIII, 227 pages. 2006.

Vol. 3998: T. Calamoneri, I. Finocchi, G.F. Italiano (Eds.), Algorithms and Complexity. XII, 394 pages. 2006.

Vol. 3997: W. Grieskamp, C. Weise (Eds.), Formal Approaches to Software Testing. XII, 219 pages. 2006.

Vol. 3996: A. Keller, J.-P. Martin-Flatin (Eds.), Self-Managed Networks, Systems, and Services. X, 185 pages. 2006.

Vol. 3995: G. Müller (Ed.), Emerging Trends in Information and Communication Security. XX, 524 pages. 2006.

Vol. 3994: V.N. Alexandrov, G.D. van Albada, P.M.A. Sloot, J. Dongarra, Computational Science – ICCS 2006, Part IV. XXXV, 1096 pages. 2006.

Vol. 3993: V.N. Alexandrov, G.D. van Albada, P.M.A. Sloot, J. Dongarra, Computational Science – ICCS 2006, Part III. XXXVI, 1136 pages. 2006.

Vol. 3992: V.N. Alexandrov, G.D. van Albada, P.M.A. Sloot, J. Dongarra, Computational Science – ICCS 2006, Part II. XXXV, 1122 pages. 2006.

Vol. 3991: V.N. Alexandrov, G.D. van Albada, P.M.A. Sloot, J. Dongarra, Computational Science – ICCS 2006, Part I. LXXXI, 1096 pages. 2006.

Vol. 3990: J. C. Beck, B.M. Smith (Eds.), Integration of AI and OR Techniques in Constraint Programming for Combinatorial Optimization Problems. X, 301 pages. 2006.

Vol. 3989: J. Zhou, M. Yung, F. Bao, Applied Cryptography and Network Security. XIV, 488 pages. 2006.

Vol. 3988: A. Beckmann, U. Berger, B. Löwe, J.V. Tucker (Eds.), Logical Approaches to Computational Barriers. XV, 608 pages. 2006.

Vol. 3987: M. Hazas, J. Krumm, T. Strang (Eds.), Location- and Context-Awareness. X, 289 pages. 2006.

Vol. 3986: K. Stølen, W.H. Winsborough, F. Martinelli, F. Massacci (Eds.), Trust Management. XIV, 474 pages. 2006.

Vol. 3984: M. Gavrilova, O. Gervasi, V. Kumar, C.J. K. Tan, D. Taniar, A. Laganà, Y. Mun, H. Choo (Eds.), Computational Science and Its Applications - ICCSA 2006, Part V. XXV, 1045 pages. 2006.

Vol. 3983: M. Gavrilova, O. Gervasi, V. Kumar, C.J. K. Tan, D. Taniar, A. Laganà, Y. Mun, H. Choo (Eds.), Computational Science and Its Applications - ICCSA 2006, Part IV. XXVI, 1191 pages. 2006.

Vol. 3982: M. Gavrilova, O. Gervasi, V. Kumar, C.J. K. Tan, D. Taniar, A. Laganà, Y. Mun, H. Choo (Eds.), Computational Science and Its Applications - ICCSA 2006, Part III. XXV, 1243 pages. 2006.

Vol. 3981: M. Gavrilova, O. Gervasi, V. Kumar, C.J. K. Tan, D. Taniar, A. Laganà, Y. Mun, H. Choo (Eds.), Computational Science and Its Applications - ICCSA 2006, Part II. XXVI, 1255 pages. 2006.

Vol. 3980: M. Gavrilova, O. Gervasi, V. Kumar, C.J. K. Tan, D. Taniar, A. Laganà, Y. Mun, H. Choo (Eds.), Computational Science and Its Applications - ICCSA 2006, Part I. LXXV, 1199 pages. 2006.

Vol. 3979: T.S. Huang, N. Sebe, M.S. Lew, V. Pavlović, M. Kölsch, A. Galata, B. Kisačanin (Eds.), Computer Vision in Human-Computer Interaction. XII, 121 pages. 2006.